Sociology

*

THE STUDY

OF HUMAN

RELATIONS

SOCIO

The Study of Human Relations

LOGY

Second Edition, Revised *Arnold M. Rose*

UNIVERSITY OF MINNESOTA

Alfred · A · Knopf · New York · 1965

L. C. catalog card number: 65-13707

THIS IS A BORZOI BOOK,
PUBLISHED BY ALFRED A. KNOPF, INC.

Published 1956, Reprinted 1957

Second Edition, Revised, 1965

THIS BOOK

IS DEDICATED TO

Ernest W. Burgess,

WHO PROVIDED

MUCH OF THE INSPIRATION FOR IT

PREFACE

This preface is a note to teachers which it might also profit students to read. Teaching an introductory course for college students is a difficult matter, and it is especially difficult when the students have so little background in the subject matter as is the case for sociology. The purpose of such a course, besides the formal one of adding to their "credits" so that they can get "through" with college, may be one or more of the following: (1) to introduce a new aspect of "meaning" to their perception of the world around them; (2) to help them to function more effectively as persons and as members of a society through an increase in relevant knowledge; (3) to stimulate them to delve further into the subject matter of sociology and related sciences, with a view to learning more and possibly to help extend the frontiers of knowledge themselves.

Knowledge must have a framework to be absorbed in large quantities. It might be possible for a student to drill a large number of unrelated facts into his head for purposes of passing an examination, but he surely will not retain most of those facts or be able to give those he retains much meaning in subsequent years. But once he grasps a framework into which large numbers of facts fit, he can do a better job of retaining many of the facts. Further, he will be able to use the framework to interpret new facts as he comes across relevant ones outside the classroom. It should be the essential task of an introductory course in any discipline to provide a framework for the understanding of that discipline, at least in rudimentary form. Yet, introductory college texts in sociology—in contrast with those in physics, biology or economics—often try to present the discipline as a mere collection of concepts and facts. It has been the main purpose of this textbook to offer a framework. Facts and studies are here in large profusion; concepts are made readily accessible through a glossary at the end of the book; but all are woven into a framework that interprets and gives relevance to them.

Our framework is not so rigorous as to deserve the name of theory, but it is broad enough to permit the student who is challenged to continue in sociology to fit into it the theories he will subsequently learn. It guides the student to *select* a certain kind of fact out of the unmarked continuity of reality, to *interpret* it for its varied significances, to *relate* it to other relevant facts, and to *give it perspective*.

The framework to use in an introductory sociology text must, I believe, be a *sociological* one, not a modified anthropological, psychological, or "general social science" framework—else the student properly wonders whether there is anything to be distinctively called sociology or whether another label is being put on the subject matter he knows to belong to another discipline so as to create more courses for him to take and more jobs for professors to live on. Our conception of sociology thus is that it is a *specialized* social science (whether *basic* or not is a moot question) rather than a *synthesis of* the social sciences.

If the distinctively sociological theory is going to make sense to the student and add to his perspective, it must be stated simply enough to be intelligible to the average college freshman. The subject matter of sociology is difficult enough without encumbering it with unnecessarily difficult language. Too many of our textbooks are written to impress the teachers rather than the students. Profundity is often confused with obscurity. On the other hand, sociology does have certain technical terms and certain specialized ways of using everyday terms, and not even an elementary book should avoid them. The introductory course should at least touch on all the fields sociologists are working on, and not give the student a false impression by limiting the subject matter only to those branches of sociology which the teacher believes beginning students will be interested in. It is the teacher's, and the textbook's, job to make the subject matter interesting, not to select only that which will intrinsically amuse or intrigue the student.

The above assumptions—or biases, if one prefers—suggest the general goals of this introductory textbook in sociology. The book is intended to hang together in a systematic framework, and not be merely a string of unrelated chapters. The theoretical framework for this volume is presented in Chapters 2, 3, and 5, and is used throughout the succeeding chapters. Still, the book attempts to cover, if only superficially and partially, all of the branches of sociology. It seeks to manifest a proper respect for facts and also to recognize that facts do not exist by themselves but only when interpreted into a framework. If our introductory framework is not deep enough or detailed enough to cover many kinds of sociological facts, then those facts are not brought into the introductory course but are reserved for more advanced courses. Thus this introductory textbook is not intended to be encyclopedic; it provides an *introduction to* sociology, not a *summary of* sociology.

Some sociologists might raise strong criticisms of the reliability of the findings of many of the studies reported in the book. This is scientifically healthy, and students should likewise be encouraged to raise such criticisms. Even if he sometimes believes that the "facts" reported may not be reliable, the student can still learn what sorts of questions the sociologist is raising. The first chapter includes a few indications of the techniques of research sociologists use in their empirical investigations. If the student learns nothing else he can learn the "sociological point of view"—that is, what slices of reality the sociologist wants to observe and to consider as problems for scientific study.

The book tries to be meaningful to students (1) by using simple language, and (2) by bringing in examples and allusions that are likely to have relationship to their previous experience, when this is possible. The details of the facts and examples are not intended for memorization, even up to the time of the term examination, since the emphasis of the book is on the sociological meaning or significance of huge bodies of data and experiences of which these facts and examples are only a small portion. If the student understands this sociological point of view he ought to be able to interpret much of the social world around him which is not directly referred to in the book, and through his interpretation understand much of causal development and future prospects of what he is interpreting. It is in this way that his knowledge should be extended, that he should get some personal use out of what he has learned, and that he should be intrigued to study further. Sociology should be a challenging field for any alert student, and it should be the function of an introductory sociology textbook to help create this challenge.

A major innovation of this book are the "boxes." In examining certain other textbooks in sociology, I have been appalled by the plethora of irrelevant materials they contain. They might be amusing and attractive, but most of them are "window dressing" to divert the student from the teachings of the text. In planning my own text, I decided to use only *pertinent* materials to divert the student. They should convey an important message even though slightly outside the continuity of the text. They could be photographs, but more often they would be cases, anecdotes, summaries of a specific research project, a pithy analysis by a wise sociologist, or any other materials which would contribute to the student's relevant knowledge of sociology. Otherwise, we shall end up with girlie magazines or coloring books as the "most attractive" of sociology texts. The boxes break the continuity of the text to some extent, but apparently teachers believe this helps to keep the student awake. I hope these boxes will break the continuity no more than a photograph or lengthy footnote. Above all, they find their excuse for existence in offering the students additional knowledge and not mere window dressing.

Such are the goals of this book; performance will unfortunately not be up to the level of the goals. Of some of the book's defects the author is already aware, but does not yet know how to remedy. Other defects will show up in using the book, and I invite all readers—teachers and students —to let me know about the book's deficiencies and how I may best reduce them.

Because the book has a theoretical framework, it would be best to have students read the chapters in the order in which they are presented, unless the teacher is willing to spend the time filling the gaps in framework when he assigns chapters in an order such that there are gaps between them. Exceptions are the chapters on population and ecology (Chapters 12 and 13), which cover subject matters so marginal to sociology (yet for historical reasons part of sociology) that they do not completely tie into the framework we use for the rest of the field. The book can readily be adapted for courses in Introductory Sociology on a quarter, semester or year basis. The footnotes are extensive enough to provide suggestions for additional reading for the student who wishes to, and has time to delve more deeply into the subject.

In a very real sense all of my teachers and colleagues, past and present, have helped me write this book. I wish especially to acknowledge the stimulation and encouragement of Herbert Blumer, Ernest W. Burgess, F. Stuart Chapin, Everett C. Hughes, Gunnar Myrdal, William F. Ogburn, Samuel A. Stouffer, George B. Vold, and Louis Wirth. Through their writings the following masters of the social sciences have influenced me greatly: Charles H. Cooley, Emile Durkheim, Sigmund Freud, George H. Mead, Robert E. Park, Georg Simmel, W. I. Thomas, Max Weber. My more immediate indebtedness is to those who have read many or all of the chapters of this book and have provided detailed criticisms: Charles H. Page, Caroline B. Rose, Sheldon Stryker. I am also grateful to those who have given clerical assistance on the book—Harvey Farberman, Janice Loge, and Leon Warshay—and to the copyright holders who have given permission to reproduce sections of their products.

ARNOLD M. ROSE

University of Minnesota
August, 1964

CONTENTS

12   *Population*   481

13   *The Human Community: Urban and Rural*   517

17   *Morale and Group Solidarity*   674

TABLES

FIGURES

ILLUSTRATIONS

Sociology

✻

THE STUDY

OF HUMAN

RELATIONS

1 * The Study of Sociology

A   What Sociology Is and What It Isn't

Sociology is the science of interaction among people and of the effects of this interaction on human behavior. There are a great many varieties of human interaction, ranging from the first physical contacts of the new-born baby with its mother to a philosophic discussion at an international conference, from a casual passing by on the street to the most intimate of human relationships, from the most informal greeting to the most formal meeting, from the most cordial cooperation to a conflict charged with hostility, from the physically close contacts of a crowded subway train to the reading of words hewn on rocks by ancient peoples living in the Mediterranean area. What processes lead to these interactions, what exactly occurs when they take place, and what are the short run and the long run consequences of them are subjects for study by sociologists.

Sociologists do not pretend that all human behavior is controlled by these interactions, because there are biological and psychological factors in human behavior as well. But the behavior of man, as distinct from the behavior of other animals, is predominantly influenced by these inter-actions, because man is distinctive among the animals in having a special means of interaction—namely language, or the communication of significant symbols. Men become human in their behavior through interaction with their fellows; thus sociology is the study of what is distinctively human in the behavior of man.

Yet this definition of sociology in terms of what takes place in inter-action gives a wrong impression because it seems to suggest that what is social is merely the relationship between two individuals at a time. Actually the important and most distinctive thing about human interaction most of the time is that the individuals involved are not merely representing themselves and their thoughts but rather the accumulated thoughts and ways of behaving of their whole society back through time, even before the beginnings of recorded history. That is, the human individual is not to be thought of solely as a representative of the biological species *Homo sapiens*, but as a member of a society with a culture. A society consists of all the groups and groupings of which the individuals within it are members. A culture consists of common understandings, most of which have been developed long before the birth of any existing individual, as to what is expected by way of behavior from members of a society.

There are, unfortunately, many erroneous ideas concerning what sociology is, even among some persons who call themselves sociologists. First, there is the conception of sociology as some kind of a reform movement. Sociologists may be individually interested in social reform and may have certain information which makes them effective reformers, but sociology as such is a science and not a movement. Second, sociology has been considered as a specific set of ideas, and a movement, otherwise known as "socialism," for changing the political and economic system. It is completely erroneous both in fact and in definition for sociologists to be considered socialists as such, although a few sociologists do happen to subscribe to socialistic philosophy. Third, sociology is also sometimes confused with social work, perhaps because both are interested in social problems. Where sociology is interested in securing facts and drawing generalizations about them, social work applies the information about society and the individual to the treatment of certain social ills. The difference between the two fields is comparable to the difference between the science of physiology and the practice of medicine, or between the science of physics and the practice of engineering. While it is understandable that sociology might be identified with social work, since both are taught in college, it is less excusable when sociology is confused with philanthropy, humanitarianism, or other applied efforts to improve the general welfare which have nothing to do with the acquisition of knowledge.

Fourth, there are some who have the misconception that sociology deals simply with people and define the field as "the study of man." Not only is this too broad a conception of sociology, but it places the focus of attention on man as an animal or as an individual. Such a definition would make sociology a branch of zoology, as in effect some aspects of psychology have become. Sociology is not this, but a study of social influences arising from the relationships among men. This definition recognizes that man is uniquely and primarily a social animal, never found apart from relationships with others, and that certain consequences flow from this fact which are the object of study for sociology.

Fifth, sociology is also sometimes confused with social science. In the nineteenth century, sociology was considered identical with social science, while today it is considered but one of a group of social sciences of which the others are economics, history, political science, parts of geography, anthropology, and psychology. "Social science" today is thus merely a category used to label all of these sciences considered collectively. While sociology does not include these other social sciences, it has important relationships with each of them.

Psychology is the science of individual behavior, and since sociology is concerned with the relations between individuals it must start with certain psychological facts, and it must overlap with that part of psychology which is interested in the social causes of individual behavior. *History* is the record of man's past, and sociology frequently finds its most important data in certain of men's past relationships with one another. *Anthropology*, in its social aspects, is the comparative description and science of culture, and sociology can learn much about human relationships under different cultures from anthropology. Anthropology seeks to determine the general or typical characteristics of cultures; sociology seeks to understand variations of human behavior and social structure within a culture. *Geography*, in its "human" aspect, studies man's adaptations to his physical environment, and the sociologist knows that some of man's relationships with his fellow men are conditioned by the physical environment. *Economics* and *political science* are specialized investigations of processes involved in the creation and distribution of material goods and services (for economics) and of power and influence (for political science). Some of the concrete facts of human relationships, which sociology must build upon, are turned up by the investigations of economists and political scientists. From this abbreviated set of distinctions one can see that sociology does not include all of the social sciences, but that it has significant relationships with all of them.

While sociology does not include the other social sciences, it may be considered as "basic" to them in some respects just as history and psychology are basic to them in other respects. Sociology studies relationships and processes, without the understanding of which one cannot explain certain phenomena of economics, politics, or history. Sociologists have developed certain methods of research which have proved useful for other social scientists. Thus, sociology is a basic, as well as a specialized, social science.

B   *Why Study Sociology?*

Those who take an introductory course in sociology or who read an introductory book in sociology, like this one, do so for a number of reasons. Some may have to pick up a couple of college credits and so are more or less forced by university rules to take the course. Can such students learn

> Sociology (in the sense in which this highly ambiguous word is used here) is the science which attempts the interpretive understanding of social action in order thereby to arrive at a causal explanation of its course and effects. In "action" is included all human behavior when and insofar as the acting individual attaches a subjective meaning to it. . . . Action is social insofar as, by virtue of the subjective meaning attached to it by the acting individual (or individuals), it takes account of the behavior of others and is thereby oriented in its course.
>
> Max Weber, *Theory of Social and Economic Organization* (New York: Oxford University Press, 1947), p. 88.

anything worthwhile in such a course? We shall try to answer this after considering what other types of students and readers there are, and the test of the answer will be the reader's own judgment after he finishes the book. Another type of reader or beginning student in sociology is one who feels that he ought to learn a little about all fields of knowledge, as part of his general education, even though he has no intention of going on to more advanced study. He, too, will make a judgment as to whether there is "anything in it." A third type of reader or student is one who has a highly specific interest in human behavior and who wants to find out why men behave as they do toward each other and toward themselves. He wants to find out what is already known about human behavior, and then perhaps to go on to make further studies that will increase knowledge. This third type has already accepted the challenge to study man's behavior, and while he will probably find defects in many of the studies that have already been completed, he will certainly find the questions and problems raised to be worthwhile.

Naturally, none of these types of students expects to learn all there is to be learned from the field in one introductory course or by reading one introductory textbook. At a more advanced level of sociology he can take courses or read books on such specialized institutions as the family or industry, on the characteristics of organizations that men form, on the behavior of children and the ways in which children learn, on the motives behind crime or suicide, on factors determining public opinion, on the number of births, deaths, and movements of people, on the bases of conflict and hatred among racial and nationality groups, on different patterns of living in the city and the country, on the ways in which major social changes take place, and so on. These matters can only be touched upon in an introductory text, sometimes serving simply to furnish examples for a more general point or principle. It is only the basic characteristics of human relations that will be the objects of our interest in an introductory course.

Relations among human beings seem like simple things to under-

stand, since each of us is having them all the time and we like to feel
we understand what we are doing. Some unkind person once said that
sociology is the science of saying what we all know in words that no one
can understand.[1] While some sociologists have undoubtedly been afflicted
with "word-itis," that is not a necessary consequence of their interests or
profession. One test, among several, of whether there is real knowledge to
be secured by a study of sociology is whether the knowledge is practical.

Probably the first question a person asks about a new field of study
is "What can I learn from it that will be useful to me?" Since relations
with other people contribute so much and so frequently to an individual's
immediate happiness or unhappiness, knowledge about human relations
ought at least to contribute to his understanding of some factors which
contribute to human happiness. Some sociological studies have been
specifically directed at determining factors associated with the achievement
of happiness, as, for example, Burgess and Cottrell's study of happiness in
marriage.[2] But even most of the others, which do not deal directly with
happiness, describe types of adjustment and maladjustment that could give
clues to means of attaining happiness. However, it would be a great mistake for a student to assume that simply by taking a course or reading a
book in sociology he would increase his happiness. Actually, there is a
great deal of difference between learning about something and putting it
into practice. Sociology is not a study of how to win friends and influence
people. Nevertheless, if we study the facts about important human relations, and understand them, we ought to acquire some of the knowledge
that could be put to practical use in daily living. The distinction between
theory and practice can be kept clear, and yet theoretical knowledge, if
it is correct theory, should also be practical when it is applied to a concrete problem.

There is a whole field of sociology, taken up in this book in Chapters
15 and 16, which analyzes "social problems"—that is, those maladjust-
ments which are faced by a large number of people and which are recognized to be a significant source of human unhappiness. These include

[1] Similar sentiments have been directed against other fields as well and reflect a
general anti-intellectualism. The following "joke," for example, is taken from the
Montreal Star, as reprinted in the *Minneapolis Tribune* (January 22, 1955, p. 4):
"A prominent businessman was asked to give his definition of an expert. His answer
was succinct and definite, 'An expert is one who can complicate simplicity.' " The
English statesman Disraeli is alleged to have remarked "The legal mind chiefly displayed
itself in illustrating the obvious, explaining the evident, and expatiating on the com-
monplace." Someone said that "A statistician is one who draws a mathematically precise
line from an unwarranted assumption to a foregone conclusion."

[2] Ernest W. Burgess and Leonard S. Cottrell, *Predicting Success or Failure in Marriage* (New York: Prentice-Hall, 1939). Also see Ernest W. Burgess and Paul Wallin,
Courtship, Engagement, and Marriage (Philadelphia: Lippincott, 1954).

crime, inadequate housing, alcoholism and drug addiction, suicide, mental disorder (popularly called "insanity"), neurosis, prostitution, relatively high rates of physical illness and death, unemployment, insecurity, marital discord, and family breakup. Some of these problems are faced mainly by individuals from certain classes in our society, while others are faced by individuals from all classes. Both types hurt the society as a whole, even if their immediate and direct effects are felt only by a small proportion of the people. An understanding of the causes and development of these problems should aid the student to combat them more intelligently as a citizen even if he does not have to face them directly as an individual.

There are social problems in a larger sense which seriously and directly affect every single person in our society: such are the problems of conflict among nations, the impact of rapid social change on the individual, the interdependence of peoples with greatly different social systems and cultural values, the decline of traditional values without new ones to take their place, the increasing dependence of individuals on others whom he does not know personally to satisfy his basic needs, and many others that have occurred to the thoughtful student. Sociology is not the only discipline that studies aspects of these problems but it does make a special contribution to their understanding and possible control. The more a person knows about these problems the better he should be able to cope with them personally and the more intelligent a contribution he should be able to make to the general discussion which leads to collective social action in regard to them.

For the student who decides to specialize in sociology, there are many vocational opportunities.[3] Sociologists, especially those trained in research procedures, are in increasing demand in business, government, city planning, social work supervision and practice, administration, race relations, and many other areas of community life. Teaching, both at the college and secondary school levels, continues to provide employment for many sociologists. But applied sociologists are increasingly employed in positions on local, state, national, and international levels. Professions in which sociology provides important auxiliary training include law, journalism, politics, medicine, nursing, architecture, business management, counseling, homemaking, and teaching in the related social sciences.

Whether or not the student sees any immediate utility in the specific subjects he covers in sociology, he is acquiring knowledge about human behavior. For well over a century universities have been teaching courses in the behavior of the stars, of rocks, of animals, and students have become used to such studies. It is still considered as something new and odd to study human behavior. Yet it would seem that the study of human behavior, and of how men relate themselves to each other in many ways to

[3] For a fuller discussion of job opportunities, see Appendix B.

form a complex society, would be just as much a natural part of general knowledge as any other kind of study. What we are suggesting is that the student should acquire an interest in the study of human behavior and social organization for its own sake, and not simply as something he expects to use in his daily life. It should be an intellectual adventure for the student to learn to be objective about the social world around him and to learn some of the principles, insights, and facts which sociologists have arrived at by painstaking efforts about that social world. It still remains true that accurate knowledge is useful knowledge, even though not everyone can use it all the time and much of it may not have practical utility for years after it is first discovered.

c   *The Nature of a Social Science*

Some of those who have thought of the possibilities of a social science have said that if we applied ourselves to the study of human relations as physical scientists have to the study of nature and relationships of atoms and molecules, we would be able to arrive at general laws of human behavior and thereby be able to solve most of the problems that confront mankind. At another extreme there are some who say that it is impossible to be scientific about human behavior because it is not subject to laws of nature and because it cannot be experimented with or observed from all angles. Neither of these extreme positions[4] seems to be supported by the actual experience of social scientists as they pursue their studies. Let us examine the characteristics of the well-established sciences and see to what extent sociology can have these characteristics and to what extent there have to be modifications.

1   CHARACTERISTICS OF SCIENCE

Probably the first essential of a science is that it be objective and unbiased. The scientist must get "the truth, the whole truth, and nothing but the truth," as the legal oath runs. When he studies something, he must get correct facts about it, not sugared to suit someone's taste, and he must get all the relevant facts about it, not just a selection of the facts. Can the social scientist meet this essential? Admittedly it is pretty hard, since he lives in the society he is trying to study, and he has interests, values, and prejudices as does every other member of that society. He is in favor of at least the greater part of the moral standards and other values of that society, and he is subject to the blindnesses created by a given cultural

---

[4] These two extreme positions are usually known in philosophy as "positivism" and "idealism." Classic statements of the two positions have been made by Auguste Comte and by Benedetto Croce. We do not believe that social science has been, or can be, based on either of them.

When we traverse the gallery of history, and observe its motley succession of fantastic paintings—when we examine in a cursory way the successive races of mankind, all different and constantly changing, our first impression is apt to be that the phenomena of social life are incapable of any general expression or scientific law, and that the attempt to found a system of sociology is wholly chimerical. But the first herdsmen who scanned the starry heavens, and the first tillers of the soil who essayed to discover the secrets of plant life, must have been impressed in much the same way by the sparkling disorder of the firmament, with its manifold meteors, as well as by the exuberant diversity of vegetable and animal forms. The idea of explaining sky or forest by a small number of logically concatenated notions, under the name of astronomy or biology, had it occurred to them, would have appeared in their eyes the height of extravagance. And there is no less complexity—no less real irregularity and apparent caprice—in the world of meteors and in the interior of the virgin forest, than in the recesses of human history.

Gabriel Tarde, from lectures delivered at the *Collège libre des sciences sociales*, 1897. Reprinted in Robert Bierstedt (ed.), *The Making of Society: An Outline of Sociology* (New York: Random House, 1959).

outlook. But the social scientist ought to be able to adjust for these things, at least to a large extent. He can realize that, even if he does not like something, he can learn the facts about it thoroughly so that he—and people who have the same tastes—will be in a better position to combat it. He can detect and examine his prejudices and his cultural blindnesses and say, "This is the way I feel about things; I must be careful not to let these feelings stop me from getting all the facts, and getting them accurately."

A second characteristic of science is that it is interested in arriving at generalizations, usually about cause-and-effect relations. It is not interested in individual facts alone. As Jevons put it, "The object of all science is the separation of what is common and general from what is accidental and different."[5] For example, science is not interested in the fact that an apple falls to the ground when it is released from a height nor in the fact that a man who has been unemployed for a while is not treated quite so much as the head of the family by his wife and children. Science is, however, interested in stating a relationship of attraction between the earth and other objects (including apples), and in the relationship between the coming of a depression and changing family roles. The relationships that science is interested in are usually cause-and-effect relationships, not in an ultimate sense of the cause being the underlying source or an "Unmoved Mover," but in a relative sense that, if certain conditions are present, a certain result may be expected to follow. The scientists must recognize that conditions are seldom the same in different real-life situations, and

[5] W. Stanley Jevons, *The Principles of Science* (New York: Macmillan, 1905), p. 13

that he must think of every concrete effect as having many causes. The scientist thus seeks generalization of two types: (1) *empirical generalizations,* or general summary statements about carefully observed facts of a certain class; (2) *theoretical generalizations,* or general statements about what takes place *if* certain conditions occur (when these conditions practically never occur in daily life unless the scientist creates them or looks into unusual places for them). To achieve theoretical generalizations, the scientist must first formulate *hypotheses,* or guesses as to what will occur under carefully controlled conditions (guesses based on logical and abstract thinking about observed phenomena and upon previously discovered empirical and theoretical generalizations). Then the scientist must seek to find or to create the controlled conditions specified in his hypothesis, and when he obtains these conditions to look for and measure the effects expected according to the hypothesis. One of the tools a scientist often uses to help him formulate hypotheses—a tool which will often be utilized in this book—is what Max Weber has referred to as *"ideal types."* An ideal type is a concept of a phenomenon which is exaggerated so that the implications of certain features of the phenomenon may be understood more clearly. The ideal type of the phenomenon is rarely, if ever, found in real life; thus it "exists" only in the minds and communications of scientists. But it aids materially in understanding the "impure" phenomenon of everyday life and in achieving generalizations.

If one has accurate knowledge about cause-and-effect relationships, one ought to be able to make accurate predictions, and many scientists have said that the aim of science is accurate prediction. Sociology is not able to make so many or such accurate predictions as physics or botany can, and for some aspects of human behavior highly accurate predictions will probably never be attained. But the aim is there, and the progress toward that aim has been considerable.

A third characteristic of science is that it constantly develops better and better methods for securing the facts that are deemed necessary to arrive at the generalizations it seeks. Facts do not simply lie around waiting to be picked up. Facts must be carved out of the continuous web of ongoing reality, must be observed within a specified frame of reference, must be measured with precision, must be observed where they can be related to other relevant facts. All this involves "methods." The older sciences have worked out the logic of experimental and other methods and have developed all sorts of machinery which help them utilize these methods. Some of the machines, like the cyclotron, are expensive and require great knowledge and skill to develop and use. Sociology is still in the process of working out the logic of its major methods. Some of these will be discussed in the next section.

In three major respects—an objective attitude, a set of methods for securing and analyzing facts, and a goal of seeking generalized conclusions about cause-and-effect relations—sociology has set out to be a science. In a fourth major respect it as yet lacks one of the characteristics of a developed science: it has not achieved a coherent body of theoretical generalizations into which all new research is integrated. Research is increasingly fruitful when it starts out with problems and hypotheses that are systematically interrelated and are based on previous research. This will obviously take time; some of the other sciences took more than a hundred years to build up a basic theoretic structure. Because sociology does not yet have this characteristic, some people refuse to call it a science. Others say that sociology could not be expected to have a trait that only mature sciences have, and that the possession of the other major characteristics is enough for the time being. The reader will have to choose his own side in this difference of opinion.

2   COMMON SENSE AND THE POSSIBILITIES OF SCIENCE

These four traits of science are what distinguish it from common sense. Everyone has common sense in a degree that depends on his native intelligence and the breadth of his experience. Common sense consists of generalizations drawn from personal experience, and is therefore partial and selective. But scientists also need specialized training and must acquire special habits of mind so that they will be objective, work toward generalizations not limited by personal experience, use methods and tools, and develop abstract theories. All these things can be learned just as any other habits and skills are learned. Scientists, like anyone else, are helped by common sense, since common sense usually helps them to learn the four types of habits and skills that scientists need, and it helps them to devise new tools for better observation. But scientists also have to be on their guard against common sense, since common sense is based on direct experience whereas science must be based on *controlled* experience.

For example, until the time of Galileo it was assumed, as a matter of common sense, that heavier objects fell faster than light ones. Galileo proved that when air and other sources of resistance were controlled, all objects fell with the same rate of speed. Similarly, common sense might tell you that when the income level is raised, people can afford to have more children and the reason why the population of the United States has gone up so rapidly is because it has been a relatively prosperous nation. By controlling observation in several ways, sociologists have shown that Americans have had until recently a steadily declining number of children and that the growth of population associated with the rise of income level has been accounted for mainly by a decreasing death rate (that is, people now live longer). Furthermore, systematic observation shows that, on the average, rich people bear and raise fewer children than poor people do. Common sense is like a wild horse in the service of science: it can provide a lot of valuable energy but it will often charge off in a wrong direction; it will serve best when it is tamed and its limitations are understood.

Some perhaps may feel that human relations cannot be studied objectively or generalized about because each social experience or event is personal and unique. The latter is, of course, true, but this does not preclude generalization. Generalization always involves abstracting out common elements from a selected series of unique events, and it inevitably loses that which is unique to each event. But it also involves a gain because it allows us to predict what may be expected of a future event, if it falls into the class and condition of events already generalized about. It is not certain yet whether our sociological knowledge has applicability beyond the given culture from which the knowledge has been derived, because comparable studies have not been made in a great variety of different cultures. But even culturally limited generalizations have great value. As far as objective study is concerned, it must be remembered that objectivity is a characteristic of the observer, not of the thing studied. We can be objective about the most personal and subjective things. It may be easier to be objective about an electric current or the alimentary tract of an insect than about family relationships in urban areas or about feelings of deprivation, but it certainly is not impossible to be objective about the latter things.

One of the reasons why students question whether sciences of human behavior are possible is that they believe that human behavior is not natural but is subject to "freedom of the will." This attitude misses two important truths: (1) Everything is natural, except that which is supernatural or "unnatural"; human behavior—even of the most extreme varieties—must therefore be considered as natural. If we distinguish "natural science" from "social science," this is an arbitrary and conventional distinction that does not imply that social behavior is not natural. (2) The assumption that there are causes which can be studied by science does not logically preclude an assumption that there is freedom of the will. The individual human being, under certain circumstances, may be free to make up his own mind as to what he should and will do, but there still are causes or reasons that lead him to make up his mind in this way.

Much of sociology must study what leads people to make the choices they do make. The more we learn concerning these causes or reasons the more freedom will the individual have to make his choice in a rational and informed way. Science never attempts to tell people what choices to make, but it can provide the information that will allow the choice to be more "moral"—according to the individual's own values. Thus social science can only enhance freedom of the will, not restrict it. There is a danger in all knowledge, however, in that knowledge is power. If only certain people learn the results of social-science studies they might use it to predict (and thereby control) the behavior of those who do not have this knowledge. To safeguard society from the possible abuse of knowledge, certain rules or laws can be set up, and every effort can be made to disseminate the basic knowledge as widely as possible.

The methods of science not only vary for each science, but they also change over time as new and better methods are developed. Science tests its results by seeing how well they work: a chemist *predicts* that if you add this chemical to that one, an explosion will result. If the explosion does occur every time it is tried over a large number of times, the chemist regards the information he has as "true"; if the explosion doesn't occur, he discards this information as "false." If the chemist finds that by raising the temperature of the chemicals, he can prevent the explosion from occurring, he has new, more complicated information which now becomes the "truth."

A criminologist may predict, on the basis of case histories, tests, and interviews, that a certain number of men who apply for parole will or will not succeed in staying out of prison. Unlike the chemist, he doesn't expect 100 percent success in his predictions because he doesn't know enough about human behavior yet and because he is dealing with many more factors than the chemist does. If he is able to predict accurately in 75 percent of the cases, he regards his information on parolees as "true" and, of course, tries to improve his prediction rate. (In actual fact, criminologists can predict about 75 percent accurately, which is considerably higher than common sense and experience can do.)

"Truth," then, in science, is a limited and changing thing. There is no such thing as absolute truth, but only the current and working "truth." More detailed or accurate information changes truth. Einstein's theories outmoded Newton's. New genetic information has outmoded Mendel. Not that Newton and Mendel were "wrong." Their theories simply explain less and predict less well than do the newer theories. They are, as scientists say, less "elegant" or less "sophisticated." The student can expect much of what he learns in any science to become outmoded. In a young science like sociology where even basic theories contradict each other, he may frequently have to reserve judgment on the "truth" or "correctness" of any theory until more evidence is in.

Since we have been using the word "truth," this is probably a good place to explain that the limited and changing "truth" of science is not the absolute and unchanging truth of religion. Much confusion results from using the same word to stand for different things. In the same vein we should point out that science is value-less or value-free. No science can tell you whether a given kind of behavior is good or bad. That is the task of religion or ethics. Criminology, for example, can predict with 75 percent accuracy which men will be successes on parole. It can say that parole will rehabilitate former prisoners faster than will confinement. But it cannot say that this is desirable. If one values rehabilitation, one would prefer parole. If one believes that a criminal should suffer for his sins, then one does not.

There is then no conflict between religion or values derived in other ways on the one hand and science on the other. Science can tell you only what will be the results of an action or series of actions with reasonable accuracy. The results one prefers depend on the values an individual or a society holds.

D   *Techniques of Social Research**

A sociologist uses a great variety of techniques to conduct research. Some of these he has adapted from the older sciences, making whatever adjustments are necessitated by the different character of his subject matter. Other techniques he has invented to meet the needs of a scientist for tools that will help him answer questions and test hypotheses. Whatever his technique, it must have *validity*—that is, measure what it is intended to measure; and *reliability*—that is, have the ability to give the same result each time it is used.

Validity is so hard to establish that most sociologists adopt the operationalist position because it solves or by-passes the question of validity. Instead of debating what sociability is, for example, the operationalist says "For the purposes of this study, I shall define sociability as the number of times the individuals being studied have visited the home of somebody other than close relatives during the three weeks we have been studying them." Each operation is specified in detail: who the individuals are; the length of time one must stay to be counted as a visitor; the purpose of the visit; what constitutes a "close relative"; and so on.

Some will argue that visiting is only a partial and inadequate definition of sociability. Because, however, a complete definition of sociability is in the end a value judgment and so complex we cannot measure it, most sociologists are content to solve the problem of validity this way. Operational definitions do have the advantage of being clear and repeatable. Those who do not like one definition of sociability will think up another, and eventually all the dimensions of sociability will get studied. The establishment of validity then depends upon the researcher's skill in finding suitable and practical operations.

There is no such short cut to establishing reliability. A test or scale

* This section is based on an unpublished manuscript prepared by Caroline B. Rose for *Project Social Studies*, Department of Education, University of Minnesota.

can be standardized so that it is reliable as long as it is given to the same kinds of people on which it was standardized. These may not be the people we want to study, nor do we always know if and how the group deviates from the original group; comparison is impossible. To make it worse, very few tests are ever standardized.

Any technique which enables us to understand social reality enough to predict events is to some extent valuable. A large number of ingenious techniques have been developed, and one would expect many more to be developed in the future. Unfortunately, one of the best known research techniques, the *questionnaire,* is also the technique which requires the most specialized training before one can use it effectively.

Questionnaires can be used to count with—as the Census does—or to explore attitudes, values, past and future behavior. Expected answers may be arranged in "yes," "no," or "don't know" fashion and may also be graded to show intensity: "strongly agree," "mildly agree," "agree," "mildly disagree," "strongly disagree." The respondent may be asked to choose from a list of possible answers or respond with a figure, or the question may be *open-ended,* allowing the respondent to contribute his own answer. *Projective* questionnaires probe for unconscious material and may consist of pictures, stories, or simpler verbal material. All these forms may be combined in a single questionnaire.

One would think that counting is a simple operation. The Census Bureau, however, found that babies under one year old were always underenumerated—not because people had any reason to hide the birth, but simply because they forgot about it. Census takers are now instructed to ask specifically about children under one in the families. A public school once sent out a questionnaire to the parents of the children in the school, asking among other things, "Do you have a television set?" The questionnaire had the name of the informants on them (not a very good practice), so that it was possible to check some of the answers. Two kinds of people gave wrong answers: intellectuals, who regarded TV as "degrading," but had succumbed; poor people, who did not want any one to know they did not have a TV. Today, we probably would not get this kind of misinformation because TV is more omnipresent and more taken for granted by both groups. One cannot, however, foresee all the things that will lead to concealment or boasting even when dealing with supposedly non-contro-versial questions. One needs an independent check.

It is much more difficult to measure *attitudes* than to count. Attitudes are defined as *tendencies to act*. Sociologists are interested in attitudes them-selves, but even more in the kind of social behavior that attitudes predict. People often say they will or will not do something or do or do not believe something, but this is no clue to what they will do when the time comes to act. Therefore, the researcher prefers to measure some action.

For example, he might ask people if they are going to vote for a particular candidate in the next election (rather than asking for the attitude toward the candidate). Sometimes one can actually check on how the informant voted, but usually all one can do is find out *if* he voted. In one case a post-election check showed that among those who indicated they would vote for a particular candidate many did not vote at all. They may not have been registered to vote; they may not have been willing to take the time and energy to get registered; they may have been sick or out of town or have changed their minds. They may never have voted in the past, but be unwilling to admit this to an interviewer. The frequency with which expressed attitudes do not lead to expected behavior makes researchers very skeptical about the measurement of attitudes. If one asks questions in "sensitive" areas, about marriage, sex, income, the discrepancy between expressed attitudes and actual behavior can be even greater. Careful theoretical background for the questionnaire; general knowledge about the behavior and attitudes being studied; and independent checks can control this to some extent.

Construction of a questionnaire must be painstakingly taught. It is probably obvious that a request for a "yes" or "no" answer may force the respondent into an unrealistic answer; it is less obvious until one begins to work with filled out questionnaires that five categories force people's answer in the same way as three do. It is assumed that people who hold intense attitudes on a subject are more likely to act in the direction of their at-titudes than are more neutral people. The measurement of intensity of re-sponse requires complicated techniques (Guttman, Thurstone, or Likert scaling techniques). Answers to open-ended questions must be categorized and coded, a process that requires both background knowledge and ex-perience.

Language must be simple and unambiguous to avoid loading questions —that is, stating the question in such a way that the answer is forced in a certain direction. The only way to test language is to pre-test the ques-tionnaire on a good sample of the population to be used in the larger, later, study.

Interviewer bias has been much studied. Although most researchers train their interviewers to some extent, it is not always easy to get non-professional interviewers to understand that they must do exactly as told. Unconscious and deep-seated bias can affect the results of any test or questionnaire. For example, it is known that Negro children will do much better on the second half of a test standardized to give the same results as the first half, if the person giving the second part of the test is a Negro and the one giving the first part is white. But it is hard to predict who has what bias or whether it will affect the results of a particular questionnaire.

Another major source of possible error in any sociological study lies in choosing a sample. The necessary size of a sample must be mathematically determined. This is not difficult, but it must be learned. It is both difficult and expensive to draw proper samples or to reach them afterwards, much less to find a suitable control group for comparative purposes. Almost without exception, sociological research uses too small and non-representative samples.

A substitute for the questionnaire technique is the use of the Census and similar government publications. Other Bureau of the Census publications, publications of the Department of Vital Statistics, and from the Women's Bureau, Children's Bureau, the Departments of Labor, Agriculture and Interior, to mention those most used by sociologists, are invaluable. In effect one has the kind of material one gets from a fact-collecting questionnaire, except that the sample is near-perfect and the work done and corrected by experts.

An example of how Census material can be used both to do independent studies and to establish an artificial control group follows: The studies done so far on single women have studied only the women in one locality, one profession, or one occupation. It is obvious that none of the studies can be generalized to all single women. If, however, all of the data on single women in the last five Censuses were collected and analyzed, one would have a good idea of the age distribution of single women, their education, housing, income, race, geographical and occupational distribution and also how the group has changed over the past fifty years. The smaller studies could then be compared with the Census Study to find out how representative of all single women the women in their samples were.

Still the most important method of sociology is direct observation and classification. Charles H. Cooley's concept of the development of the self came about through his systematic observation of his own two-year-old child. One subject only—but, of course, only one Cooley, too. This is an example of the case study method in which all possible details about an individual, a single institution or social movement are collected and interpreted. This is a very useful technique when one is interested in the development of the person or social structure over time: a famous sociological study, the *Jack Roller* by Clifford Shaw, consists of a detailed history of the development of a criminal career. By classifying case studies into groups showing similar characteristics or by comparing them, one can sometimes isolate causal factors. An example of the first technique can be found in Clark Vincent's *The Unmarried Mother* and of the second in Clifford Shaw's *Brothers in Crime.*

A special kind of observation and one of sociology's most seminal methods has been that of *introspection* or *understanding.* In one form, this method involves examining one's own behavior, attitudes, and values, and extrapolating them into tentative generalizations. *Empathy* is doing the same thing on another person. The experience, knowledge and wisdom of the researcher have much to do with the results.

The use of dream and other subconscious material falls into the category of introspection. The systematic study of autobiographies, diaries, letters, fiction and poetry, can be examined by sympathetic introspection. *The Polish Peasant in Europe and America* (1919), one of the most important of social psychological works, is based almost entirely on letters. There must be an explicit theory with a set of hypotheses to explore before one can call the analysis of such material research.

One technique of analysis of personal documents and other written material is called *content analysis.* In its dullest form it consists in counting how many times a certain word occurs. Counting ideas, situations, social types or characters is equally useful and more interesting. A good example of this is Dorothy Yost Deegan's *The Stereotype of the Single Woman in American Novels* (1951). Content analysis is indispensable training for categorizing the contents of open-end questionnaires. It is particularly useful in analyzing the products of the mass media.

A special kind of observation is called *participant observation,* in which the researcher either is, or pretends to be, a member of the group he is studying. Participant observation is the only tool we have for finding out about some social phenomena: one-time events like battles, riots, natural catastrophes, panics, or behavior in closed groups like criminal gangs.

Another useful kind of research is *historical.* Institutions and social movements exist in time; to understand them, we have to understand their pasts. This kind of research differs from history in that the sociologist starts with theory and hypotheses, and in that he is interested in the past only for the purpose of developing generalizations which are equally applicable to the present. Trend studies enable one to *compare* social structures, social situations, and different societies over time. By noticing the presence or absence of certain factors either over time or in different societies, one can do a kind of uncontrolled experiment. The quality of the sociological research one gets using the historical method usually depends on the quality of research historians do since most sociologists simply work with the material presented by historians rather than seeking out original sources themselves.

Sociologists have always tried to do true *experiments*. The small group theorists and group dynamicists take successive small groups into a laboratory situation, subject each group to the same experience and record what happens. How representative these groups are of non-laboratory groups is not known and there has been a tendency to over-generalize the laboratory findings. One sociologist tried to study what goes on during jury deliberation, but it was decided that the presence of recording equipment or observers might interfere with the objectivity of the jury. He then set up mock jury trials, using the material from actual trials and choosing the jury as it might actually be chosen.

F. Stuart Chapin proposed three ways of doing experiments with groups:[6]

1 The *Cross-sectional Experimental Design* in which two groups are matched for factors relevant to the results and then one of the groups receives some program or treatment which the other does not. Differences between the two groups after the treatment are attributed to the program or treatment.

2 The *Projected Experimental Design*. Groups, matched for factors relevant to the results, are pretested with respect to the behavior to be studied. One of the groups then receives some program or treatment which the other does not. Differences between the two groups after the treatment are attributed to the program or treatment. This differs from method 1 in that the groups are pretested and it is regarded as the most desirable method.

3 *Ex Post Facto Design*. In this type of experiment some present effect is traced backward on two groups, matched in all relevant ways except in the factor to be studied, to an assumed causal complex of factors or forces at a prior date using for this purpose such records as are available. This way is the least preferable, but is often the only way to do longitudinal studies and is resorted to usually when some systematic early data are suddenly made available.

A rare, but exceedingly fruitful type of research might be called *logico-deductive*. One example might be the discovery of covert elements in a culture. An underlying assumption is that everybody, except some mentally disturbed patients, thinks logically, that is, does not contradict himself. If an individual reaches conclusions that seem contradictory to openly stated premises, it can be deduced that he is operating from some unstated, covert

[6] The summary of Chapin's proposals is taken from Don Martindale and Elio D. Monachesi, *Elements of Sociology* (New York: Harper, 1951). Details can be found in F. Stuart Chapin, *Experimental Designs in Sociological Research* (New York: Harper, 1947).

premises. When a large number of people in a society do this, it can be deduced that the covert premises are contained in the culture and are thus shared by everybody.[7]

For example, Northerners are often baffled when a discussion with a Southerner about bus desegregation ends with the Southerner's question: "Would you want your daughter to marry a Negro?" (Note, it is never "your son.") The Northerners know that Negroes have used buses and all other public facilities in the North for generations, and that the Negro-white marriage rate has stayed at a very low level. Furthermore, the Southerners know it, too. Sociologists have postulated that in the Southern culture is a belief that the Negro male is so sexually attractive to white women that unless he is separated from her by all the devices of a segregated society, she will marry him in preference to white men. Such a hypothesis must find independent support in order to be accepted, and this one has a great deal. One learns after some experience with this technique to become sensitive to illogical conclusions or behavior and to seek out the real premises.

Another logico-deductive technique is to make a *theoretical model.* In *An American Dilemma,* Gunnar Myrdal[8] sets up a model of the upward or downward spiral of events concerning Negro-white relations in the United States. Each major event that occurs, such as the increasing level of education among both Negroes and whites, is assumed to affect all other factors being considered in such a way that other important trends move up or down a spiral. The improved education of Negroes increases the standard of living, political participation, and so on. Each other unit on the spiral in turn pushes other factors up; for example, increased standard of living increases education levels, which was the original unit considered. Events can move cumulatively up the spiral, cumulatively down, or both ways. One can intervene with laws or other public policies. This particular model has enabled people in the field of race relations to make remarkably accurate predictions.

A third type of logico-deductive method is the creation of an *ideal type.* Ideal types are complex models of social behavior or structure. They are not dreamed up but are constructed on the basis of empirical evidence, often the empirical generalizations mentioned above. Max Weber, who first used the term ideal types, "conceived them as hypothetically concrete individuals (personalities, social situations, changes, revolutions, institutions, classes, and so on), constructed out of their relevant components by the researcher for the purpose of instituting precise comparisons . . . Ideal types

[7] Arnold M. Rose, "A Deductive Ideal-Type Method," in *Theory and Method in the Social Sciences* (Minneapolis: University of Minnesota Press, 1954), pp. 327-42.

[8] Gunnar Myrdal, with the assistance of Richard Sterner and Arnold Rose, *An American Dilemma: The Negro Problem and Modern Democracy* (New York: Harper, 1944), Appendix 3.

are not general or abstract concepts, but hypothetical individuals consisting of a selection of items which could appear in reality . . . The ideal type is a strategy in empirical explanation. It is framed in terms of the scientific knowledge available to the researcher at the time of his study and in terms of the empirical situations he is trying to understand. There are two criteria for constructing an ideal type: objective possibility and adequate causation. . . ."[9] Examples of ideal types are: the acting crowd; the Bohemian personality type; the charismatic leader; the folk society.

The use of statistics opened up a whole new area for research for sociologists; it enabled them to deal empirically with large masses of data, as they had never done before. Two excellent examples of the large scale use of statistics can be found in *The American Soldier* and the Kinsey reports. Sociologists must, however, use statistical techniques developed for other fields with a great deal of caution.

First, one cannot deal with the raw data of social life—actual social behavior. The statistician must try to find a valid and reliable index of the behavior he wants to study, encountering all the difficulties already mentioned. This means that statistical manipulation of data is always at least one step removed from what we are trying to study, for example, an attitude is only an index of potential behavior. Every statistical manipulation we make—computing a mean, or a coefficient of correlation, or a test of significance—removes us another step from social reality.

For example: a correlation of .67 between I.Q. scores on the one hand (indices of expressions of intelligence, not intelligence itself) and the scores on a test indicating sociability (another index) does not mean that the more intelligent are more sociable, no matter how many cases one has or how high the statistical significance is. It means that there is a correlation between the two indices, which may arise because items in the indices are the same or related.

The various techniques of research we have been discussing are not all comparable. Some—like the questionnaire—are instruments for gathering information. Others—like statistical techniques—are tools for analyzing and summarizing information already gathered. We have not mentioned many techniques of the sociologist, and the opportunities and limitations for their use. The methodology and techniques of the sociologist form a highly complicated subject about which many books have been written, and in which issues are raised which are far from settled. At the introductory level, the student cannot be expected to learn much about research procedures. At best, he might sensitize himself to ask about each generalization or research finding that is presented to him "How did the researcher arrive at this?" After getting some basic subject matter orientation through

[9] Don Martindale, *The Nature and Types of Sociological Theory* (Boston: Houghton Mifflin, 1960), pp. 381-83 *passim*.

careful study of a book such as this, he may then be ready to take a course which explains to him how to advance knowledge in the field.

E   *Origins of Sociology*

Men have always been curious about how people get along with each other, or fail to get along with each other. In one sense, sociology began in pre-historical times when people first began to make observations about each other's behavior. In ancient and medieval civilizations, philosophers and religious leaders made some observations about human relations for the purpose of stating ethical principles. The observations were not systematic, in the sense of being complete, collected under controlled conditions, and checked for accuracy, but were simply made in the normal course of daily experiences, and the ultimate purpose was not generalization about cause-and-effect relations but was rather to express what the philosopher believed were proper rules of conduct. Philosophers and religious leaders have continued to do these things up to the present day, and they have a social function, but their work should not be confused with sociology. Still, in the course of their work, some penetrating questions were raised about the nature of man's behavior in groups, and some significant observations were made.

Several of the early philosophers predicted that there could and would be a science of human relations, and took the first steps to establish such a science without having any followers to build on their work. Included among such social philosophers were the Arabian Ibn Khaldun (1332–1406), the Italian Giovanni Battista Vico (1668–1747), and the Frenchman Charles Montesquieu (1689–1755). The development toward a general social science became more explicit in the seventeenth- and eighteenth-century political treatises on the "social contract" of Thomas Hobbes, John Locke, and Jean Jacques Rousseau, which sought to rationalize existing or projected theories of sovereignty and forms of government on the basis of different assumptions concerning the original or basic characteristics of human nature and the social bond between man and man, and between man and the state. The conception of a general social science owed a parallel impetus to develop-ments in the study of history. In trying to go beyond the establishment, description, and the interpretation of facts to the formulation of generaliza-tions or laws, the historians passed over the bridge of the philosophy of history to social science. More influential was Auguste Comte, a Frenchman who did most of his writing in the 1830's and the 1840's, and who coined the word "sociology" to apply to the proposed general social science of human behavior. Comte analyzed history as being divisible into three epochs. At first people gave theological explanations for everything by attributing all cause to the action of the gods; next society went through

> In the theological state, the human mind, seeking . . . final causes (the origin and purpose) of all effects,—in short, Absolute knowledge,—supposes all phenomena to be produced by the immediate action of supernatural beings.
>
> In the metaphysical state, which is only a modification of the first, the mind supposes, instead of supernatural beings, abstract forces, veritable entities (that is, personified abstractions) inherent in all beings, and capable of producing all phenomena. . . .
>
> In the final, the positive state, the mind has given over the vain search after Absolute notions, the origin and destination of the universe, the causes of phenomena, and applies itself to the study of their laws.
>
> Auguste Comte, *The Positive Philosophy* (New York: D. Appleton, 1853), Vol. I, p. 2.

a metaphysical phase in which people found causes in abstract principles such as Ideas or Goodness; he now observed society going into a "positive" or scientific phase in which causes were to be found in natural phenomena that are observable. Comte observed that the sciences of physical matter and of animal and plant life had already been founded, and he therefore felt that the time was ripe for a new science of social life, which he dubbed "sociology."

Comte's immediate successors—in France, Germany, England, Italy, Russia, and the United States—were either ethical philosophers who made unsystematic although shrewd observations on human behavior, metaphysicians who constructed elaborate but not well-grounded theories about the "basic nature" of society, or philosophers of history who collected observations on existing primitive tribes in order to jump immediately to the basic laws of human development. The late nineteenth century saw a ferment of "social thought" penned by men who were intelligent and broadly educated but not yet ready to submit their ideas to objective and systematic testing. We think, for example, of the wealthy, straitlaced Englishman, Herbert Spencer, who had a corps of secretaries collecting unrelated facts from all corners of the earth while he independently thought out what he believed were the laws of social evolution. Then there was the American civil servant, Lester Ward, who formulated theories of more flexible social change without putting up a pretense of having the factual resources of Spencer. In France, the pre-social science tradition was expressed by the eminent judge, Gabriel Tarde, who found the basic human relation, and the source of most human behavior, in "imitation." In Germany and Austria, some of the social philosophers (e.g., Gumplowicz and Ratzenhofer) used instead such concepts as "conflict" and "interests" as basic ones in the formulation of "grand theories" of society and human behavior. Throughout Europe, but especially in Germany, some philosophers of history (e.g., Albert Schaeffle, René Worms) likened society to a biological organism, and tried to deduce the characteristics of group behavior from this sociology.

Another type of presociologist of the late nineteenth century was the kind who collected facts in order to support a political system which he favored. In France there was the aristocrat, Gustav LeBon, who hated the masses of people so much that he wrote derogatory descriptions—but accurate descriptions nevertheless, and for the first time—of revolutionary crowds and criminal mobs. In the United States an outstanding pamphleteer against government or other organized interference in any sphere of life, William Graham Sumner, collected facts from primitive society to show how difficult it was to change social life by any group's deliberate efforts. Sumner formulated some major concepts of social organization and social control that have proved useful to this very day.

There was such a reaction to some of this philosophizing that certain conscientious sociologists resolved to collect facts only and let the facts speak for themselves. LePlay, in France, collected huge numbers of family budgets which he hoped would reveal the essential character of family life. In England, Charles Booth and a crew of careful interviewers put out volumes of facts about the daily lives and conditions of the poor people of London which they hoped would provide the explanation, and ultimately the cure, for poverty. The founders of sociology in the Netherlands—S. Rudolf Steinmetz and L. van Vuuren—believed that the extensive presentation of facts was sufficient for their new science. In the United States, Carroll D. Wright, through his position in the Census and Labor Bureaus of the federal government, organized nationwide surveys to get facts on a great variety of subjects. Also Professor Richmond Mayo-Smith of Columbia University collected statistical facts about all sorts of social phenomena in order to shift interest from social philosophy to the science of society. These people, however, left little mark on sociology because they did not seek to generalize, although they contributed to the tools of observation which later sociologists found useful.

The combination of careful and thorough fact gathering with a desire to arrive at coherent generalizations about significant social behavior marked the beginning of sociology as the science of human relations. First credit again goes to a Frenchman, Émile Durkheim, whose study of suicide (published in 1897) may be considered the first scientific sociological study. Durkheim had several ideas for research on other topics and some of his students carried on to build up not only sociology, but also anthropology and child psychology, in France and Switzerland. In Germany after the turn of the twentieth century most of the writers who called themselves sociologists followed the tradition of the ethical philosophers and the philosophers of history. But a few began a scientific sociology. These included Georg Simmel and Leopold von Wiese, who examined what they called the "forms" of social processes, and did studies of money, cultural contact, and small communities; Max Weber, who compared the great civilizations of mankind to determine what was basic among their differences, especially as revealed in such phenomena as religion and leadership; and Ferdinand Tönnies, who began to make more circumscribed and more detailed studies on such topics as crime, urbanism, and public opinion.

A great name in early American sociology was that of Charles Horton Cooley, who studied transportation, race relations, and the social growth of his own children. His influential contemporaries at the turn of the century included Albion Small, F. H. Giddings, and E. A. Ross, whose books on *Social Control* (1901) and *Social Psychology* (1908) began systematic study in those subfields of sociology. Another great pioneer was William I. Thomas, in his monumental study (with F. Znaniecki), *The Polish Peasant in Europe and America* (published in 1919–21). More important than the work of any one man, however, was the steady stream of monographic studies of specific communities, institutions, and social problems, based upon surveys and on the compilation and analysis of statistical data and case studies, which offered more realistic and reliable accounts of various aspects of the American social structure than had previously been available as guides to social action. More and more, reform movements came to see dispassionate, objective, sociological research as an indispensable prerequisite. Sociologists themselves, in turn, began to direct their interest increasingly to the discovery of a fundamental knowledge of social life, rather than to the promotion of practical policies.

Since sciences are more the product of unplanned development than of deliberate rational design, it is to be expected that sociology would not follow any preconceived pattern. Actually, being a latecomer in the ranks of intellectual disciplines to be recognized by institutions of higher learning, sociology had to gain academic status under various guises. It became something of a science of leftovers, and was preoccupied with subject matters which the established disciplines, such as economics or politics, considered irrelevant or too trivial to treat. Such obviously important phenomena as the state and the market being already preempted by political science and economics, respectively, sociology accordingly sought to treat such neglected subjects as the family, the community, crime, and the social pathologies generally.

Preoccupation with such a miscellaneous collection of subjects, however, was bound to prove unsatisfactory as an academic subject clamoring for recognition. At the same time, the pretension of some sociologists to represent a super-science subsuming under its banner such well-established academic subjects as history, economics, and political science inevitably aroused resentment.

Increasing numbers of scholars among historians, economists, and political scientists, however, came to see the importance of the hitherto neglected aspects of social phenomena; and as they began to turn their attention to these questions, a more or less common body of knowledge, and of interests, developed. This growth resulted in a series of secessionist movements from the older, scholarly, and scientific associations, in the establishment of separate sociological societies, and in the founding of independent sociological journals. In this respect, the United States was considerably in advance of other countries. Although isolated European scholars had taught and written on sociology under various titles, sociologists in the United States, from about 1880 on, found increasingly wide and rapid acceptance in academic institutions in their own right. The establishment of the Department of Sociology at the newly founded University of Chicago, in 1892, the initiation of the *American Journal of Sociology* in 1895, and the organization of the American Sociological Society in 1905 had a catalyzing influence upon the development of sociological teaching, research, and publication.

Sociology came gradually to assume the character of a systematic body of knowledge increasingly concerned with empirical investigations of human behavior and interrelations, primary attention being centered upon the group factor. Recognition of the fact that all of the social sciences are dealing with essentially the same subject matter, but raise differentiated questions concerning it, helped not merely to allay jurisdictional conflicts between academic disciplines, but also gave impetus to the efforts of sociologists to organize and systematize their own field of inquiry.

F   *The Development of Sociology*
     Outside the United States

It is an interesting question why sociology developed in some countries rather than others. Sociology, as a separate science, emerged simultaneously in Europe and America, but why it arose in Finland, France, Germany and Italy, rather than in England, Belgium, and Denmark, and why its later development was so irregular, are hard to explain.

In a small country, sociology may arise if, through some fortuitous circumstance, the country produces one distinguished sociologist. Finland and Poland are examples of this, although it must be pointed out that the presence of Jean Piaget, the famous student of child development, did little to develop sociology in Switzerland, nor did the presence of Theodor Geiger in Denmark directly lead to the expansion of the discipline there.

Sociology in Finland arose accidentally because E. A. Westermarck (1862–1939), starting out as an anthropologist studying Moroccan culture, came to specialize in the study of the family, which is also a subject of interest to sociologists, and he happened to be a Finn. There is no explanation of why Finland produced Westermarck, but once he was there, his presence helps explain the development of sociology. In a small country with few universities, his fame undoubtedly attracted students to the new field of sociology. Large numbers of students facilitated the establishment of professorial chairs in the field and so the subject became part of the university structure.

A similar occurrence probably explains why Poland, sometime later, alone among the eastern European countries, developed a broad, sociological tradition. Florian Znaniecki (1882–1958) was invited by W. I. Thomas, a leading American sociologist, to collaborate with him on a study of the immigrant, Polish peasant. Thomas wanted somebody to collect information on the background and experiences in the home country of the Polish immigrants to America. Znaniecki was thus introduced to the lively and flourishing sociology of the United States. The five-volume work that resulted from this collaboration, *The Polish Peasant in Europe and America* (1918–1920), had enormous influence and enhanced the fame of both its authors. When Znaniecki returned to Poland after World War I, the presence of such a distinguished sociologist in a country with few universities was enough to attract students and establish the discipline. Poland has managed to maintain its sociological traditions through war and dictatorship, which other countries have not been able to do. Polish intellectuals in all fields have resisted totalitarian control of thought to the limits of their ability to do so, and it may be that the detached point of view of sociology plus its predictive utility in a fast-changing society has been of use to Polish intellectuals in preserving their intellectual freedom in some measure.

Contrary to the Polish experience, the objective study of society has, in other countries, been incompatible with totalitarianism. German sociology was all but completely destroyed by Hitler. Many sociologists went into exile and continued their work; those who remained were silenced and not allowed to teach or publish. Today, more than thirty years after the advent of the Nazis, there is only a feeble development of sociology in Germany, although some of those returned from exile and some of the younger men—mostly trained in the United States—show considerable promise.

Sociology in Italy was less developed than in Germany and was strongest in criminology. It was, however, obliterated under Mussolini, although within the academic community, Benedette Croce, the distinguished philosopher-historian, did sociology as much damage as did the Fascist government. Sociology in Italy has begun to develop anew since 1955. A group of young men are redeveloping the discipline in a most promising way.

Sociology in Communist countries, other than Poland, is very new as a separate discipline and is severely handicapped by the limitations a Communist ideology imposes. Non-Communist sociologists regard Marxism as one of a number of nineteenth-century, Social Darwinist theories, parts of which are still useful. In Communist countries, Marxism is regarded as the only possible sociological theory, as well as the only possible economic, political, and even biological, theory; no competing ideologies are allowed. Such totalitarian monism is incompatible with the development of a modern science, although some Soviet writers have begun to use technical research methods of sociology to study non-controversial subjects, like the use of leisure time.

Nothing so far discussed explains why the development of sociology in Great Britain, Belgium, Holland, Norway or Sweden was so far behind their progress in other sciences, both natural and social, despite the great political freedom in these countries. One reason may be that the subject matter of sociology was investigated by other social sciences. This seems to have been the case in Sweden where economics, in particular, developed in a much broader fashion than it did in the United States. This may also have been true in England. English anthropologists have been numerous and among the world's leaders in the field. Much of the theory, elaborated in sociology in the United States, has been evolved in anthropology in England. The study of social problems and of urban sociology was carried on by the Fabian Socialists in the late nineteenth and early twentieth centuries, and by government agencies (such as the London County Council), special government commissions, through the settlement houses and by other social workers. In Holland sociology seems to have been done in the field of human geography, a field practically untouched in the United States.

A contributing reason for the slowness of the development of sociology as a separate science in the countries discussed above is the nature of their university systems. Most of these countries are small; the universities have limited funds and to divert part of university monies to establish a new chair requires considerable persuasion and acceptance on the part of already established disciplines. In some countries sociology has developed outside the universities in specially established research centers, sometimes financed by industry, as at the Solvay Institute at Brussels. In England, the dominant universities, Oxford and Cambridge, were for a long time extremely conservative in introducing any discipline not part of the medieval curriculum. Until about 1950, sociology in Britain was almost confined to the London School of Economics. After 1950, sociology began to grow with the growth of the "red brick" universities—new universities scattered around England usually in large industrial centers—which have been far more receptive to modern science. The four best known modern British sociologists, Morris Ginsberg, T. H. Marshall, Karl Mannheim (a German refugee) and David Glass have all taught at the London School of Economics. But by the 1960's, sociology was flourishing at most British universities, including Oxford and Cambridge. As in Great Britain, the Scandinavian countries and the Low countries have developed sociology considerably during the past decade or so, often building on American models. In all six of these countries, the level of sociological theory and research is on a par with that of the best today, even though most of the development came after World War II, and the names of the able sociologists are too numerous to mention.

Today, the situation is this: in only two countries—France and the United States—is there a full-fledged development of sociology with a long history; chairs in all the leading universities; departments granting advanced degrees in the science; separate, specialized institutes outside the universities; a long, continuous tradition which has produced a rich variety of sociological schools and theoretical approaches.

France has a brilliant roster of sociological names: Frederic Le Play; Emile Durkheim, Gabriel Tarde, and Gustav Le Bon; Durkheim's students, Marcel Mauss; Charles Blondel, Lucien Lévy-Bruhl, François Simiand, Maurice Halbwachs, Georges Davy. Today, Jean Stoetzel is the leader in public opinion research; Alfred Sauvy leads a group of demographers; Henri Lévy-Bruhl has headed the research in criminology. Georges Friedmann and his group of brilliant young students work in the field of industrial sociology. P. Chombart de Lauwe and L. Couvreur are young, urban sociologists. Gabriel Le Bras does empirical research in the field of religion. Raymond Aron, François Goguel, and Maurice Duverger work in political sociology, while Claude Lévi-Strauss does brilliant work on the border of sociology and anthropology. G. Balander, R. Bastide, and P. Mercier study colonial problems. Georges Gurvitch and Armand Cuvillier are the best-known theorists. The list could be extended, but it is long enough to show the richness and diversity of French sociology. It is in contrast with this elaborate development of the field and the similar one in the United States that other countries must be compared.

There is now sociology in all European countries, except, perhaps, Portugal and Albania. Japan, Israel, Egypt, Turkey, and India have a number of sociologists, and the work in the first two of those countries is often first-rate. South and Central American countries have sociology, and Brazil and Mexico—where the leading names are Gilberto Freyre and Lucio Mendieta y Nunez—may be said to have some strength in the field. The leading political opponent of Prime Minister Nkrumah in Ghana was

K. A. Busia, an English-trained sociologist, now in exile. New Zealand and Australia have begun to develop sociology. Sociology in Canada developed simultaneously and cooperatively with that in the United States. Students and professors have travelled back and forth between Canadian and American universities to study and teach.

In 1949 under the stimulation and with the financial support of UNESCO, a few sociologists met in Oslo to lay the foundations for an international sociological association. In 1950 the first full-fledged meeting of the *International Sociological Association* was held in Zurich, Switzerland, and was attended by 100 delegates from a score of countries. Since then meetings have been held at regular intervals, the last being in Washington, D.C., in 1962 and attended by over a thousand delegates. When one remembers that professors are not rich people, and that everybody but Americans had to come a long distance, this attendance was an indication of the great growth of sociology.

In addition to the help and stimulation scholars from countries with well-developed sociology can extend to those from countries where sociology is new, the *International Sociological Association* is important in a more direct way to the future of sociology. Sociologists, like other scientists, hope to find general or universal laws of human behavior. Some sociologists hold that this is impossible; that most human behavior is culture-bound. Until now there has been little opportunity for sociologists, unlike anthropologists, to do the kind of studies that would furnish proof on one side or the other. The programs of the ISA are always centered around a main subject and are announced three years ahead of time. This encourages sociologists from different countries to concentrate their research in the field which will be examined at the next international meeting. As a result the *Proceedings* provide a series of comparative studies about modern society never before available. The *Proceedings of the Second World Congress,* held in Liège, Belgium, in 1953, were mainly comparative studies of class and mobility. The Third World Congress, held in Amsterdam in 1956, was mainly on social change and the underdeveloped countries. The Fourth Congress, held in Stresa, Italy, in 1959 had the general theme of the sociology of knowledge. The Fifth Congress, held in Washington, D.C., in 1962, provides information on the applications of sociology.

G   *The Conditions of Social Life:*
Geographic and Biological

The social life which is the subject matter of the science of sociology takes place in a framework, and with a basic material, that is not itself entirely social. The framework is geography and the material is man's biology.

Human behavior cannot be explained or understood—even in its social aspects—without recourse to geographic and biological factors. It is the function of a branch of the science of geography—usually called human geography—to explain how features of the physical environment influence man's social behavior. It is the function of the science of psychology to explain how man's body, including his nervous system, affects his social behavior. While such considerations are thus outside the scope of sociology, it is desirable that the student of sociology be aware of them and to recognize both their importance and limitations for his own subject matter.

While sociology was emerging as a distinctive science in the late 19th and early 20th centuries, there were some human geographers and some psychologists who disputed the right of sociology to exist because they believed geographic or biological factors could explain most of social behavior. It would not be worthwhile here to examine the excessive claims of Ellen C. Semple[10] or Ellsworth Huntington,[11] on the one hand, or of William McDougall[12] and Wilfrid Trotter,[13] on the other. But it is useful to review a few of the geographic and biological factors they and others called attention to, and to recognize them as non-sociological conditions of social life.

Topography sets conditions of social contact and isolation, especially in pre-modern societies without access to mass communications. Communities in mountain valleys have generally been more ingrown than communities on the edge of a sea. Topography, along with soil and climate, largely control the possible economic land use, although the actual use of the land within the range of possibilities set by geography is determined mainly by purely social factors. Rivers, lakes, seas, mountain passes, and flat land surfaces facilitate transportation and often provide a major asset in the location of commercial or manufacturing cities. Mountains and large seas have in the past served as military barriers, to protect a society from attack or to prevent a society cut off by them from attacking others. Modern technology—including the wireless means of communication, the airplane, the guided intercontinental missile—has greatly diminished the limiting role of topographic features in man's life. But it would still be incorrect to say that the natural features of land and sea are unimportant for the social life of man.

Climate is another aspect of geography which has been of immeasurable influence on man. In prehistoric times, climate was a major factor in natural selection, and set the outcomes of raciation—the development of distinct races. For example, man could not survive in tropical climates

---

[10] *Influences of Geographic Environment* (New York: Holt, 1911).
[11] *Climate and Civilization* (New Haven: Yale University Press, 1915).
[12] *An Introduction to Social Psychology* (Boston: J. W. Luce, 1906).
[13] *Instincts of the Herd in Peace and War* (London: T. F. Unwin, 1916).

unless he had a dark skin, and could not survive in arctic climates unless he had small nostril openings. In some climates, man could not live at all, usually because no other form of life could exist there either. Some other climates were so harsh and extreme—as in deserts or arctic regions—that the whole human way of life had to be geared to adjusting to their demands. Still other climates offered a wider range of possibilities for economic activity and social organization, but nevertheless favored one social development rather than another. For example, dry climates formed a pastoral and nomadic way of life rather than a settled agricultural existence. While it is clear that climate was historically a major influence on economic activity, and through it on social organization, it has also been alleged that climate influenced the mentality and dispositions of a people. The evidence for this is not great. Climate continues to exert a considerable influence on man's way of life, but modern technology—in the form of heating and cooling systems, selective breeding of resistant plants and animals, artificial rain making, rapid transportation, and so on—has also reduced the controlling and limiting influence of climate on man's life. Still, it is incorrect to ignore climate when considering the conditions of modern social life.

Soil, in the broad sense of the term, is a third geographic factor of considerable consequence for man's behavior. Soil, coupled with climate determines the type of plants and animals that can exist in a given environment, and this in turn sets limits to the types of foods locally available to man. Diet differences—especially in amount and in the presence or absence of vitamins and minerals—affect the health and physical structure of man. The type of food locally available influences the food gathering or producing activities of man—determining whether he can engage in agriculture or pastoral activities for example. Soil also affects the technology of man: the availability of local clay limits the amount of pottery making; minerals locally available historically influenced man's use of these minerals as tools and building materials.

With the development of transportation, geographic influences became much less significant than they were when transportation was severely restricted. Transportation of foods, tools, and building materials allowed man to transcend his local environment. The range of man's activities in a given geographic environment became greatly extended when easy transportation brought materials to him not locally available. In recent centuries, man has also been learning how to modify his geography—transforming certain topographic features, initiating climate control, and growing crops in hothouses and even without soil. There has always been a considerable range of human activities in almost any geographic environment, especially in the less extreme environments. With modern technology, this range has become so greatly extended as to practically eliminate the limiting influences of the geographic factors (except for catastrophes such as hurricances and volcanic eruptions). These factors still influence man's activities by making certain among them uneconomic, rather than impossible.

In summary, a number of statements may be made about the relation of the geographic factors to social behavior:

(1) Before the Industrial Revolution for us, and for economically "underdeveloped societies" today, geographic influences have been extremely limiting.

(2) For the technologically and economically "developed" societies, geographic factors place no absolute limits on man's behavior if he is willing to pay for it in time and money. For example, it is possible to grow roses in the Antarctic settlements if one wishes to do so and can pay the huge costs.

(3) Many geographic settings around the world permit a great variety of economic, political and social activities without limitation or discouragement. In other words, in these many settings, one cannot at all predict human activities or social institutions from a knowledge of the geographic conditions. For example, California today supports a highly advanced civilization, but it was once the home of the most primitive Indian tribes to be found in the Americas. Similar geographic settings may be the home of the most diverse kinds of social and cultural developments.

(4) Even where geographic factors favor one type of economic activity over another, the less efficient economic activity is not impossible and man —because of his social history—may choose to follow it. For example, areas which will support efficient agriculture are sometimes used by man for less efficient grazing. Thus, diverse geographic settings may harbor similar social and cultural developments.

Man's biological equipment provides him with the capacities to engage in all of his behaviors. There is thus a biological component in all social behavior. While sociologists are generally not interested in studying this biological component, nothing they study can afford to fly in the face of it. Biology also sets limits to man's behavior; yet it can be said that any behavior which is within the physical and physiological range of man's capacities is, at some time or place, engaged in by man. Certain social behaviors that will be given close examination in this book—like the birth rate and adjustments to aging—have a special relationship to the biological nature of man, and this relationship will be noted when they are discussed. In Chapter 4, consideration is given to the various distinctive biological features of man which affect his behavior. Despite this frequent attention we find it necessary to give to man's biology in the analysis of his social behavior, it must be understood that sociology is not a branch of biology. It is a completely independent and co-equal science, which studies man's behavior on a level quite distinctive from that of biology. Yet, to fail to

> Taking man as a biological entity it is clear that certain minima of conditions can be laid down which are indispensable to the personal welfare of the individual and to the continuation of the group. All human beings have to be nourished, they have to reproduce, and they require the maintenance of certain physical conditions: ventilation, temperature within a definite range, a sheltered and dry place to rest, and safety from the hostile forces of nature, of animals, and of man. The physiological working of each individual organism implies the intake of food and of oxygen, occasional movement, and relaxation in sleep and recreation. The process of growth in man necessitates protection and guidance in its early stages and, later on, specific training.
>
> Bronislaw Malinowski, "The Group and the Individual in Functional Analysis," *American Journal of Sociology* (May, 1939), p. 939.

recognize biological influences as conditions of social life would be a gross mistake.

One line of evidence indicating the importance of man's biology for his behavior is that based on the biological variations within the species *Homo sapiens*. The differences between male and female in sexual function and average body build have considerable consequences for their life patterns. Woman's biological function of childbearing also make her, almost universally in all societies, chiefly responsible for child-rearing. This, coupled with the man's greater average height and large skeletal muscles, has resulted in most societies' allocating to him the large share of its military functions, both defensive and offensive. Practically all societies differentiate males and females in many other ways, ascribing a "feminine" character to the woman and a "masculine" character to the man. The content of this ascription varies considerably from society to society, indicating that the character differences are a matter of social definition, although one which each society finds it necessary or desirable to have for the maintenance of the functional division of labor between man and woman.[14] This does not mean, however, that all societies expect the same elements of character and personality in the two sexes—motherliness and sexual aggressiveness, for example; in fact, the expected sex characteristics may be quite different and even opposed from one society to the next.

Another important biological difference among men as a species is that along the continuum of age. The young of the species are not only biologically weak and dependent, but have not yet had the opportunity to

[14] For those students who are interested in sociological theory, it may be noted here that this grounding of social definitions on biological characteristics is the one scientifically legitimate use of the sociological theory known as functionalism. Advocates of this theory usually go well beyond this usage, and hence imply biological characteristics to man which have no basis in fact.

learn the culture, and thus are not capable of performing many of the society's activities. The non-appearance of the physiological capacity for sex relations until the age of puberty delays the association of males and females in marriage until that age at least, although most societies require a further postponement of an operational marriage until socialization is complete and the individuals are ready to assume adult life roles. The elderly of the species manifest certain physical debilities and a greater proneness to chronic disease. Retirement from certain adult life roles—such as that of child-rearing—are usually therefore required by most societies, although the elderly may acquire new roles such as that of wise consultant or baby-sitter. Further debility associated with extreme old age usually necessitates retirement from occupation and resumption of the infant's position of dependency.

Racial differences are made much of in a few societies, including our own, but biological racial differences are actually very minor in comparison with those of sex and age. No racial differences require social differentiation in the way that sex and age differences do. The gross differences of skin color, hair texture, and nose and lip form require no differential behaviors, and the slight differences in musculature result in only trivial differences in average performance, such as in speed of running. However, differential social values can be assigned to biological racial differences, and if they are so assigned, they have tremendous consequences for behavior.

Individual biological differences may also be important for behavior in the same ways that age, sex and racial differences are. Body size, strength, or physical debility may have a significant effect on the performance of life roles. Body shape and facial appearance may operate like racial differences in the attribution of values by others. Only some of these individual biological differences have their source in heredity, as sex, age, and racial differences do. Diet, disease, accident, and even learned habit (affecting posture, for example) may equally influence the physical structure and appearance of man.

None of the biological differences considered thus far—except for the obvious ones associated with youth—have any necessary psychological connections. Men and women are frequently assumed to have a different biological mentality, and the same is sometimes thought to be true of the elderly and the different races. There is absolutely no scientific basis for such an assumption, even though some scientists have been as guilty of this error as are laymen. However, because of this widespread assumption, and the different social roles imposed on persons with different biological characteristics, different psychological characteristics are learned and become characteristic of those in the biological category. As already noted, little girls learn how to become women, and boys men, as defined by the culture of a given society. In some societies with traditions of racism, such as the United States, members of the different biological races similarly learn how to behave and think and feel differently. While biological senility does occur in rare cases, for most older persons the psychological characteristics associated with advanced age are a result of learning and social definitions. Biology thus has a greater influence on behavior through social reactions to it than it does directly. Aspects of these assertions are taken up in different sections of this book.

H   *How to Study Sociology*

It is not the purpose of an introductory book to lead readers to develop a field themselves. Guides for experienced explorers in a field must be different than guides for first visitors, and this book cannot attempt the former. But it is certainly in order to offer the reader a few suggestions which may help him get more out of his introduction to sociology.

1   SOME SUGGESTIONS FOR THE READER

One peculiarity of studying sociology is that the student is studying certain aspects of his own behavior. In order for him to understand a general phenomenon of our society such as race prejudice or class he ought to be able to relate it to his own experience. If he cannot relate it to his own experience, and it is a widespread characteristic of our culture so that it has actually been part of his experience, he does not understand it. More specifically, if he feels it necessary to commit to rote memory the list of criteria of class—found in Chapter 8—he probably does not understand class. While this is true for an all-pervasive phenomenon in our culture such as class, it is not true for the many phenomena covered in this book which the average student cannot be expected to have past experience with. Take the "crowd," for example, which is described in Chapter 9. Most students may have experienced mild forms of crowd behavior at parties, football games, bull sessions, but few will have observed or participated in riots, lynching mobs, religious revival meetings, etc., which are fuller developments of the crowd. Case reports are needed there to supplement description. Even more valuable would be direct experience if it is not dangerous or immoral, and students should therefore attend, if possible, a religious revival meeting.

Seemingly, but not actually, opposed to this recommendation is another one: that the student should not regard his personal experience as the sole check on the truth of a statement. His experience may not be typical, and, in fact, is not likely to be typical because it was not selected in accord with all the rules of scientific sampling. The student's experience is not "controlled" in the sense that other influences probably entered to make his experience a mixture of many social phenomena, rather than only of the one that is under immediate consideration. The student might be biased when he had this experience, since he could not be expected to take all the precautions against bias which the objective scientist takes while conducting research. The student might not have derived all the implications out of his experience that were available, because he did not have at his command all the methods and tools which the scientist has developed.

The student should use his experiences as an aid to understanding and as a basis for asking questions, rather than as a sure means of contradicting what is being presented to him. The student must recognize that his common-sense *experience* is partial and selective, as distinguished from *knowledge* which is as complete and systematic as science and scholarship allow. Educated people have knowledge in the fields they have studied, and they can partially base some of their actions on this knowledge. But no one knows more than a tiny percentage of all the knowledge accumulated in Western culture, and so for everyday decisions—not important enough to consult specialists—we rely on common sense. Now, common sense may be in accord with knowledge or it may not, depending primarily on the degree to which knowledge is widely disseminated (especially in the public schools) and on the extent to which there is resistance to knowledge. Sociological knowledge is unfortunately not widely disseminated, being seldom found in the public schools or in popular magazines or books, and there is a good deal of resistance to it because it deals with matters concerning which there is a good deal of emotion and prejudice. Consequently, for matters studied by sociologists, common sense deviates considerably from knowledge.

Carrying on our argument one logical step further, we may say that the accumulation of knowledge, especially in sociology, involves an increasing recognition that common sense is often, or even usually, wrong. To put it in simpler but somewhat exaggerated language: the study of sociology will require us to unlearn much of what we learned in our childhood about human behavior and institutions. The great American psychiatrist, Dr. Adolph Meyer, has said that what ails most people is not that they are ignorant but that they know too much that isn't so. The student may (and should!) be somewhat unwilling to give up all he thought he knew because a college teacher and a textbook tell him he is wrong. But he has an obligation to himself to be open-minded, to be stimulated to think and study further when he feels the teacher or text is wrong, and to understand how his own "common sense" developed. It was a wise man who observed, "In my youth I regarded the universe as an open book . . . whereas now it appears to me as a text written in invisible ink, of which, in our rare moments of grace [substitute "deep study"], we are able to decipher a small fragment."[15]

A third thing the beginner in sociology should try to do is to be objective. He should try to think of himself, as far as possible, as the mythical visitor from Mars. Whereas the ordinary person, quite naturally, thinks of things as having intrinsic value, the sociologist must think of these things as having value *ascribed* to them by people. Whereas each person thinks of the social relationships he establishes to other persons around himself, the sociologist must look at the network of human interrelationships without taking the standpoint of any one individual more than temporarily. Whereas the participant in an association thinks of the purposes for which the association was founded and continues to seek, the sociologist must also search out the unplanned functions and effects of the association.

To do all these things the sociologist must emancipate himself from his culture, at least when he is thinking, observing, and writing as a sociologist. The beginning student cannot emancipate himself all at once from his culture and his personal relationships, but he should try to do so as much as possible while he is studying sociology. On the other hand, the student does not necessarily have to change his values on the basis of what he learns. What originally seemed to him to be all white or all black—all good or all bad—appears, after he studies the matter, to be a shade of gray. There is a proverb "To understand everything is to forgive everything." This can be a mistake: facts do not logically affect values. When one changes some of his values, he should logically consider all other relevant values. Above all, he should not fall into the error of being neutral because near-black and near-white are both shades of gray.

A fourth bit of advice relates to the understanding of abstract concepts. A concept is a generalized idea of a large number of similar observations or experiences. Its definition describes the scientific observations or experiences in a general way, but does not give a full or completely accurate description of them since it is concerned only with what is similar or common to all of them.

Take the concept of "status," for example, which is defined as a person's prestige or influence relative to that of other persons and which is given by the possession or achievement of certain values. It is evident from the definition that the status of a person, Mr. Jones, exists in the minds of other people who know him. These people do not all regard the same values in the same way and therefore would not agree as to what Mr. Jones's status is. And in another community a Mr. Smith might have the same possessions and achievements as does Jones, but since the community looks on these possessions and achievements differently, Smith might have a quite different status than Jones. Yet we can speak of Jones's status.

[15] Arthur Koestler, *The Invisible Writing* (New York: Macmillan, 1954), p. 15.

The situation is further complicated by the fact that people's reactions to Jones are not simply based on his status, but also on his "personality," his physical appearance, the specific experiences these people had with Jones, the specific experiences these people had with other persons who remind them of Jones, etc. Thus the scientific observer must abstract—that is, "pull out," figuratively speaking—Jones's status from the whole conglomeration of factors which determine Jones's behavior and the behavior of other people toward Jones. These are the complications in studying Jones's status, and if the sociologist wants to study status generally in that society he has to find out about the status of a lot of other people, his problems multiply. Yet he is justified in referring to status in a simplified way, ignoring these complications, when he uses the *concept* of status in formulating a general hypothesis or describing a certain culture. Concepts like these may bother the student until he realizes that they are abstract, oversimplified, and "unrealistic," but nevertheless useful and necessary as a shorthand way of summarizing a large number of similar, but not identical, observations.

A concept is a tool, a shorthand device for summarizing a large number of observations. The shorthand itself is the choice of a word to represent the summary, and the device is an arbitrary one. Instead of the word of direct Latin origin *status,* for example, he could just as well use the German word *zustand* or the French word *position sociale,* and many American scientists do use French, German, Latin, and Greek words to refer to concepts. There is also no reason why another English word, such as "social position," could not be used. As a matter of fact, there are some sociologists who refuse to use the term "status" but insist on using the term "rank" or some other term to refer to it.[16] There is no harm in that, because every other sociologist knows what they are talking about and they know what every other sociologist is talking about. To have different terms for the same concept on the same phenomenon is simply the mark of a young science. Gradually the differences disappear and everyone uses the same terms.

For example, until about 1950 even the term "sociology" was not used in course labels at Yale University, because some of the professors there preferred to speak of it as "the science of society," and at the University of California "social institutions" stood for the same set of academic courses as other institutions labeled "sociology." No harm done, but gradually the term "sociology" has become all but universally used in this country. Students sometimes become confused by this, for they ask if a "lake" is called a "lake," why is not "status" always called "status." They

---

[16] Those who follow the anthropologist Ralph Linton (*The Study of Man,* New York: Appleton-Century, 1936) use the terms *rank* or *class* to refer to what we have called *status.* They use the word *status* to refer to any type of position in the social structure.

have to realize that they are traveling in new country, and the experts have not yet got around to agreeing what all the signs should stand for. Therefore, we shall sometimes use two or three words to say the same thing, and even occasionally the same word to stand for two or three different things. Perhaps if the student reads carefully the contexts in which these words are used, and refers to the glossary of terms in the Appendix to this volume, he will have little difficulty with this weakness of sociology.

2 SOME DIFFICULTIES

There are other things the experts do not agree on. There are differences of opinion as to what is important, and there are differences of opinion as to whether the available evidence is sufficient to support a point. There are even differences of opinion as to the meaning of certain facts. Such differences of opinion are found in all sciences. They are found at the forefront of investigation, and they represent challenging problems for future discovery. Sociology differs from the older sciences chiefly in that it has not had time to build up a backlog of more-or-less settled findings: most of its investigations are still in the forefront of controversy. The student should go into the study of sociology with the realization that he is in frontier territory.

To some students this will be a challenge. They will quite frequently be traveling along rough footpaths instead of neatly paved highways. There are uncharted forests ahead of them. If they are thoughtful, they can raise significant questions which cannot yet be answered and which might lead them or someone else to seek the answer. If they are critical, they can detect the weaknesses in existing studies. If they are open-minded, they can see the challenges of the newer studies to older notions derived from tradition or from long-unchallenged expert opinion.

Another attitude which the student may find useful is to recognize that more than one point of view toward a given thing may be true. Beginners in sociology frequently feel that there is opposition between biology and sociology on a large number of questions. Actually there is no opposition, but there is a difference in the level of analysis or perspective, and both perspectives are correct and valuable. Man is an animal, and yet he is different from the other animals. A person is an individual organism, yet he is also part of a social group and cannot exist apart from all social contact. Man's intelligence is an hereditary, biological capacity, but for this capacity to receive development and operation the individual must have social contact and social stimulation. Similarly, man's physical capacities limit what he can do, and yet he has learned how to build extensions of himself in the form of machines and social organizations which allow him to achieve more than he can by his own unaided effort. If the student will avoid hasty judgment he will see that there is seldom if ever any real opposition between what he learns in biology, psychology, geography, or any other science, and what he learns in sociology.

There are basic differences in point of view, however, and these the student would be wise to understand early in his introduction to sociology. Sociology seeks an explanation of social phenomena in terms of other social phenomena—that is, in terms of the particular nature of human relations. It would no more do for sociology to seek explanations of social phenomena in individual psychology or biology than it would for the biologist to seek explanations of biological phenomena in physics and chemistry. Yet in one sense everything in the biological world can be thought of as analyzable ultimately into the terms of physics and chemistry. The movement of a man's arm can be analyzed into innumerable chemical transformations of sugars into simpler substances while releasing energy, which energy is employed to contract a muscle which straightens the arm in a certain way. Similarly, all mathematics can theoretically be reduced to certain primitive terms and primitive operations such as addition and subtraction.

But just as mathematicians find it useless, wasteful, and practically impossible to start every problem with primitive terms and operations, and biologists find it insufficient to study muscle contractions as so many chemical changes because this tells nothing about the function of the contraction or its relation to such other biological systems as the nerves, so sociologists find it meaningless, useless, wasteful, and impossible at present to turn to psychology, physiology, or physics to study the problems that concern them. Sociologists study the movement of a man's arm, for example, as a blow at another man. A physical blow is a kind of human relation, and sociology seeks an explanation of it on a social level. Was the blow intended as an expression of anger on the part of one man toward another or was it part of a competitive game or of a ritual ceremony, or was it simply an accident? Did other people approve or disapprove the blow, and if they did approve, did they take any steps to punish the man who gave the blow? If other people punished the offender, why did they do it?[17] If the man was punished, did that serve as a deterrent to future blows that he might give or did it create in him a desire for revenge?

Thus we see that a simple physical motion like that of a man's arm

[17] The social motives for legitimate punishment are a fascinating study. Some societies punish for retribution ("an eye for an eye"); others punish to deter other potential criminals; still others punish to "cure" the criminal or appease the gods. It is not always easy to ascertain why punishment is administered. The anthropologist G. P. Murdock reports that on Truk Island he saw an older boy punished after he had accidently struck a younger child. Murdock at first assumed that the punishment was for carelessness that might be dangerous, but he later found out that it was for creating a disturbance that annoyed the older men. (Reported in private conversation, February 28, 1953.)

has social antecedents and social consequences—they are caused by a man's previous relations with his fellow men and they affect the man's future relations with his fellow men. This is the "point of view" of sociology. It seems probable that every social action is accompanied by some chemical or physical change in the brains of those individuals involved in the action—although science is a long way from discovering what these chemical or physical changes are. But even if we did know what the chemical and physical accompaniments of social action were, why study them within the brain when they can more readily be observed in overt behavior and through careful questioning? Above all, why wait until some possible future time to study social behavior in terms of psychology and chemistry when it is feasible right now to study it in the terms of sociology?

FOR ADDITIONAL READING

GOODE, WILLIAM J., and PAUL K. HATT, *Methods in Social Research* (New York: McGraw-Hill, 1952). A survey and description of research methods used by the sociologist.

LIPSET, SEYMOUR MARTIN, and NEIL J. SMELSER, *Sociology: The Progress of a Decade* (Englewood Cliffs, N.J.: Prentice-Hall, 1961). A collection of articles reporting some of the recent studies and theoretical discussions in sociology.

LYND, ROBERT S., *Knowledge for What?* (Princeton, N.J.: Princeton University Press, 1939). An important, though not very systematic, statement about the need for social science to relate itself to the problems of human living.

ROSE, ARNOLD M., *Theory and Method in the Social Sciences* (Minneapolis: University of Minnesota Press, 1954). The adaptation of scientific theory and method to the study of the subject matter of the social sciences.

2 * The Relationship of the Individual to Society

A   Communication on a Non-Verbal Level

For people to have social relationships with one another they must communicate with one another. Communication thus becomes the basic process for sociology. Of course communication may not be direct between two persons but may involve a whole chain of persons, in which case the first and last links of that chain will still be in communication even if they have never seen each other and do not know each other's name. The person communicating may or may not be aware of the fact that he is communicating, and the person receiving the communication may or may not be conscious of the fact he is receiving a communication. Communication usually involves words, either spoken or written, but it does not have to. We shall first examine different means of communication.

On the non-verbal level—that is, when no words are used—communication takes place by means of movements of the whole body, gestures with hands or arms, movements of the eyes and of other parts of the face, touching, making noises that are not words, standing perfectly still or keeping perfectly quiet when movement or sound would be more "natural" in the sense of not having any meaning. Certain people use these non-verbal symbols as a means of communication much more than other people do, but all of us use them a good deal. You can walk toward a person threateningly; you can walk toward him and extend your hand for handshaking as a gesture of friendliness or politeness. You can smile to indicate pleasure, or scowl to indicate displeasure. Some women roll their eyes slightly to indicate sexual interest, or one can roll his eyes to indicate disdain. You can stand expectantly to suggest to someone else that he should move aside for you, or you can wave your arm at him to indicate that he should pass ahead of you. You can throw your arm across the shoulders of a friend to indicate friendliness or sympathy, or you can give someone a poke to indicate either friendliness or anger, depending on the way in which you do it. You can scream at a person to alarm or frighten him,[1] and you can laugh at a person to indicate sympathy for him or mild disdain at some of his actions. An indefinitely long list of non-verbal symbols, with each of their meanings, could be built up, but enough examples have been given to suggest the ways in which non-verbal symbols are used and the frequency of their use.

Many people believe that non-verbal symbols have universal meanings so that every person is born to understand them regardless of what culture he grows up in. This is not true. Different cultures assign quite different meanings to a specific gesture. What may be true is that an unanticipated body blow or a sudden loud noise is universally interpreted as an unfriendly act, since these seem always to provoke an immediate response which has been interpreted as fear or anger in infants who have not yet been trained in any culture patterns.[2] But even here, after the first momentary shock of the blow or noise is over, more mature individuals with different cultural backgrounds will give different interpretations to it, depending on the culture and on the situation. In one culture, the blow or noise might be given as part of a religious ceremonial, and the individual will feel honored to be the one chosen for the communication. Even in our society, a blow may sometimes signify a friendly greeting, and a sudden loud noise may occasionally be intended to frighten a person out of hiccoughs, rather than as any type of communication at all. Certain cultures make much more use of non-verbal symbols in communication than others do. The Italian and eastern European Jewish branches of our own culture make considerably more use of arm and body gestures than do the English or Swedish branches.[3]

Nevertheless, there are certain gestures which have substantially the same meaning in most branches of our Western culture (like shaking the head from side to side to indicate "no"). At least the culture area of similar meanings of most common gestures is broader than the culture area of any one verbal language. An English-speaking person may not understand a Frenchman's or a German's language, but he can understand a large number of his gestures. The understanding is not perfect or precise, but this is owing not so much to different meanings in the different countries as it is to the vagueness of the meaning of gestures in all countries. Perhaps it has been for that reason that no one has prepared a dictionary of gestures,

[1] It is to be noted that non-verbal symbols can include deliberately made *noises,* but they cannot include words, by definition.

[2] Experiments showing this have been carried on by the psychologist John B. Watson. See Chapter 4, Section A.

[3] For an interpretation of gestures among Jews and Italians, see David Efron, *Gesture and Environment* (New York: King's Crown Press, 1941).

comparable to the dictionary of a language, which would define precisely the meaning or meanings of each specific gesture. The lack of precise definition keeps the meaning of many gestures vague or indefinite, although this is true also, but to a lesser extent, of words. Nevertheless, gestures play a significant and definite enough role in communication for actors to consider it necessary to study them fairly thoroughly. Fully as important in acting as memory of lines and proper tones of voices are the use of appropriate gestures to communicate attitudes and sentiments. Many actors believe that the ability to communicate through subtle gestures, apparently to the other actors but actually to the audience, is what distinguishes a good actor from a poor one.

It is necessary to distinguish non-verbal symbols from physical gestures that carry meaning but are not deliberately intended as means of communication. The former are used deliberately to carry over certain meanings while the latter are made spontaneously and unintentionally in response to certain stimuli. George Herbert Mead,[4] the social psychologist who emphasized this distinction, called the former "significant symbols" and the latter "natural signs." Both of these kinds of behavior have meaning for those who see or hear them. The former are much like verbal language, in that the symbols are learned and their meanings are intended by the maker of the symbols and are understood in roughly the same way by the one who observes the symbol. The communication involved in puppet shows like Punch and Judy and in pantomime, like the older Charlie Chaplin movies, are almost completely of this deliberate non-verbal symbol type. We deliberately use non-verbal symbols frequently: We point to something to indicate it, we shrug our shoulders to indicate doubt or indecision, and so on. Natural signs—the second type—cannot be called symbols, since the person who makes them does not have the intention of communicating something to someone else, and therefore the gesture or noise does not "stand for" something. Natural signs are not learned, and are therefore not limited to any one culture or group of cultures, but are common to all mankind. However, they still involve communication between people, since the observer is influenced by them in his behavior.

The latter are quite common among the animals as well as among men, and provide a most important means of communication for them.[5] When one animal in a herd or flock sees (or hears or smells) a danger approaching, it sounds a note of fear, or it becomes tense to observe the situation, or it runs off precipitously. In Clarke's gazelle, whose native

[4] *Mind, Self and Society* (Chicago: University of Chicago Press, 1934) .

[5] There is a lengthy bibliography on this subject stretching back to Charles Darwin's *Expression of the Emotions* (New York: D. Appleton, 1897) .

habitat is Somaliland, the sign of alarm is simply an erect tail. Any one of these acts directly stimulates the other animals nearby to a similar state of fear or attention. Both the danger and the signal have served as stimuli which have called forth an immediate unthinking response. The first animal has not "intended" to warn his fellows, but his action has served as a signal to them nevertheless. A slightly more complicated form of natural sign is found among the social insects such as bees and ants. Like all natural signs it is an invariant and uncontrollable response to a given situation, but it seems to be a pure expression on the part of the insect and to have no other function for him. This natural sign apparently has evolved solely for the purpose of communication. An example is the "pollen dance" found among the bees. When a bee has discovered a great store of food and returns to deposit its mite in the hive, it invariably wiggles its rear end rapidly several times. Other bees jostle it and pick up the message through the pattern of the dance and the speed of its movements. The dances seem complex but they involve a series of simple movements stimulated by equally simple sense-receptors. The bees receiving the message go to the blossoms to help bring home the nectar.[6]

Human beings are not so reliant for their communication on such signals, which are themselves nothing more than direct responses, but they use them nevertheless. A loud yell, given by someone who has been hurt, commands our attention at least momentarily. When we watch a tightrope walker balancing himself precariously, we also usually find ourselves swaying a little from side to side to keep our balance, even though we are in a perfectly safe seat. A genuine smile or scowl of displeasure tends to provoke similar sentiments in the observers, unless the situation is specifically defined in a different direction. Psychologists call this "suggestion," although they use that term in other ways, too. Also much of what we call "sensing" belongs in this category of behavior: we can "sense" when another person is ill at ease, or angry, or something else, even when he is not trying to communicate that fact or may even be trying to hide it. What happens is that his body is making a number of responses to his mental state, and these responses serve as signs to those who observe him. Just how important to men are these various types of non-verbal communication no one yet knows. Man is, however, able to carry on a great deal of communication at the verbal level, which the other animals are scarcely able to do if at all. Since our subject is human relations rather than animal relations, we shall concentrate attention on verbal

[6] Martin Lindaver, *Communication Among Social Bees* (Cambridge: Harvard University Press, 1961). For a quite different form of natural sign communication, among birds, see Edward A. Armstrong, *A Study of Bird Song* (London: Oxford University Press, 1963).

communication because it is fairly distinctive to humans. We should not forget, however, that man is also an animal and all of his behavior is influenced by that fact.

While we have been emphasizing the distinction between non-verbal symbols and natural signs, in concrete behavior they often get mixed up. For example, in a Hawaiian hula dance the various motions of the body have a specific significance known to all adult Hawaiians but not to people unfamiliar with Hawaiian culture. At the same time these body movements are also apparently enjoyed by people who are completely unfamiliar with Hawaiian culture, possibly because they are natural signs conveying feelings of sexual stimulation. Similarly, it is quite possible that many of our significant symbols have natural sign accompaniments—to an extent of which we are usually not aware. For example, some of our angry words sound harsh to persons who know no English, while words expressing affection sound soft and liquid. Thus these words convey both meaning and feeling tone—which is another way of saying that they are both significant symbols and natural signs.

Sometimes what appear to the uninitiated as natural signs are actually prearranged symbolic signals: In bridge tournaments, for example, the slow pass has been used to signal to a partner "I almost have a bid"; the loud or confident double means "Don't take me out. I can beat them alone"; the hesitant play of a low card means "I have strength in this suit, but prefer to wait before using it." Sometimes "accidents" have been used to improvise signals to a partner: One player, wanting his partner to shift from leading hearts but having no heart lower than the eight, which would look like a signal to continue to lead hearts, dropped his entire hand on the floor. As he stooped to pick it up he said, "Don't wait for me. I'm playing a low heart."[7]

B   *The Use of Language as the Distinctive Characteristic of Human Relations*

1   WHAT LANGUAGE "DOES"

Man has several physical and psychological traits which distinguish him from the other animals (these are discussed in Chapter 4). But none is so important for his behavior as the ability to talk. The experts are not yet certain whether the relatively complex brain that man has or the greater range of sounds which he can voice is the more important biological basis of language. It is not too important to know the answer to that

[7] Albert H. Morehead, "Coffeehousing? Maybe — Cheating? No," *New York Times Magazine,* October 28, 1958, pp. 24–29.

question, since both brain and voice are essential. Man has a physiological capacity for making a much greater number of different sounds than any other animal, and he apparently has the kind of brain which can deal with a much wider range of behavior. The sociologist begins with the fact of language, and examines the consequences of its immeasurably great aid to communication. The following are the major ways in which language increases the possibilities of communication:

1 When words stand for things, man can communicate about these things even when they are not present. Even expected future events can be "brought into" the present when we have words to describe them.

2 Words can be used to stand for abstract or not observable concepts as well as for concrete things. As a matter of fact, it is probably impossible to have ideas or concepts—such as God, law, nation, justice, welfare, hope—unless one can designate them through words, since one cannot designate them by pointing to them or by hearing or smelling them.

3 Because words can designate things and concepts that are not present, they increase memory power immeasurably. It is easier for most people[8] to remember words than it is to remember sights or smells or tastes. It is part of folklore that an elephant has a powerful memory, that he can remember persons or places for fifty years. That may or may not be true, but the elephant cannot remember nearly so *many* things as even an absent-minded person can, and there are distinct limitations on the *kinds* of things the elephant can remember.

4 The use and knowledge of words aid reasoning power. Reasoning is really a process of communicating with oneself; it involves turning over in one's mind the advantages and disadvantages of various ways of doing something.[9] Reasoning requires other things—like a more complex brain than most animals have—but the ability to manipulate words which stand for objects and acts increases the power to reason to a tremendous extent. Many people say that the most important distinction between man and the other animals is that man has the power to reason. While apes and perhaps some other animals can reason to a certain extent, there can be no question that man's power to reason is many times greater and that this makes a great difference in man's way of life. Since man's reasoning powers depend so heavily on his ability to

[8] A possible exception exists for the few people who have "eidetic imagery"—who are alleged to be able to look at a scene once, for example, and then see a duplicate in their mind with every detail present.

[9] John Dewey, *Human Nature and Conduct* (New York: Holt, 1922) .

The question may be raised as to what would happen if an animal were raised in human society. This experiment was tried by Mr. and Mrs. W. N. Kellogg who reared a female chimpanzee along with their own son for nine months. The chimpanzee is perhaps most similar to man among all the animals. At the time of adoption, the chimp was already seven and a half months old while the boy was ten months old. They ate, slept, and played together, and both were treated in the same way. The chimp was physically more mature than the boy and hence could engage in more motor activities, such as climbing and acrobatics. The chimp learned to eat with a spoon, to drink out of a glass, to skip rope, and to open doors, and she learned these things better than the boy did. But in speech she lagged behind: she learned to act as if she understood many words, but of course she never learned to speak. She did emit at least four distinctive sounds, which the boy learned to imitate.

W. N. and L. A. Kellogg, *The Ape and the Child* (New York: McGraw-Hill, 1933).

use language, this statement is equivalent to saying that the difference between man and the other animals is that man can use language.

5   Words permit men to relate their behavior to each other to a much greater extent than do non-verbal symbols. Thus, the power to use language makes human relations quite different from animal relations. We shall examine the reasons for and implications of this statement in the remainder of this section.

6   Language permits men to learn from one another, both from other living men and from men who have lived in the past. Thus man can acquire the knowledge accumulated for many generations. As Linton points out, if it were possible to raise a child in complete isolation, he would be nearer to an ape in his behavior than to his own father.[10]

2   THE USE OF LANGUAGE IN ROLE TAKING

What is involved when one person speaks to another?[11] For the present, we may assume that the listener understands what is being said, and that is a correct assumption most of the time. The important matter in communication is that *each statement involves a prediction, or expectation.* The speaker expects that the listener will act in a certain way because of what is said. If the speaker says, "Would you please let me pass?" he expects that the listener will move a little to let him pass, unless the listener has some special reason for not wanting to do so. If the speaker says, "Let me tell you

[10] Ralph Linton, *The Study of Man* (New York: Appleton-Century, 1936), p. 68. See also Section F of this chapter.

[11] The following paragraphs are based largely on George H. Mead, *op. cit.*

what happened last night," he expects the listener to keep still so he can talk. If the speaker says, "Whom shall I see about this matter?" he expects the listener to answer with the name of a person whom the

---

Ideas, as distinct from acts, or as failing to issue in overt behavior, are simply what we do not do; they are possibilities of overt responses which we test out implicitly in the central nervous system and then reject in favor of those which we do in fact act upon or carry into effect. The process of intelligent conduct is essentially a process of selection from among various alternatives.

George H. Mead, in Charles W. Morris (ed.), *Mind, Self and Society* (Chicago: University of Chicago Press, 1934), p. 99.

---

speaker then can visit. Of course the expectation may not be so simple as that. The speaker may use words that say one thing but actually he expects to get a different response, and the listener understands the underlying purpose of the remark and may respond either to the underlying purpose or—if he is playing a game, too—to the words themselves. Sometimes the speaker may use certain words and not know if he means them or not, but is only interested in getting the listener's response. Sometimes the speaker does not care about the specific response of the listener, but merely wants any kind of friendly response.[12]

Of course the listener may not always respond in the way expected, still assuming that he understands what is being said. Instead of answering a question, he may turn and walk away, or play dumb, or slap the speaker in the face. None of these answers is one that the original speaker expected,

---

[12]Anthropologists call this a "joking conversation" and Simmel called it "talk for the sake of talking."

"In purely sociable conversation, the topic is merely the indispensable medium through which the lively exchange of speech itself unfolds its attractions. . . . For conversation to remain satisfied with mere form it cannot allow any content to become significant in its own right. . . . [Talk] thus is the fulfillment of a relation that wants to be nothing but relation—in which, that is, what usually is the mere form of interaction becomes its self-sufficient content. Hence, even the telling of stories, jokes, and anecdotes, though often only a pastime if not a testimonial of intellectual poverty, can show all the subtle tact that reflects the elements of sociability. It keeps the conversation away from individual intimacy and from all purely personal elements that cannot be adapted to sociable requirements. . . ." See *The Sociology of Georg Simmel*, trans. Kurt H. Wolff (Glencoe, Ill.: Free Press, 1950), pp. 52–53. Another translation of Simmel's essay, "*Die Soziologie der Geselligkeit*," that by Everett C. Hughes, appears in "The Sociology of Sociability," *American Journal of Sociology*, 55 (November, 1949), pp. 254–61. The paragraph referred to here is translated on p. 259. Also see Leo Bogart, "Adult Talk about Newspaper Comics," *American Journal of Sociology*, 61 (July, 1955), pp. 26–30. Bogart quotes Simmel and provides examples of "talk for the sake of talking."

but he can quickly change his expectations as to the future direction of the conversation. Whereas the original speaker at first intended to ask more questions along the same line, he may now drop the conversation entirely, or change the subject, or comply by changing the conversation into a fist fight. Each of these moves involves a new set of expectations, and the new expectations will either turn out to be correct or will have to be changed further. In this way, through communication, *people constantly adjust and readjust their behavior toward each other.*[13] The process has been appropriately called, by Mead, "taking the role of the other," or, more briefly, *role taking.*

In an important sense, the person with whom you are communicating is temporarily placed in your mind. You expect his reactions before he makes them, which necessarily means that you have some sort of picture of him reacting even before he actually reacts. You can have an imaginary conversation with him even when he is not around; you imagine yourself saying something to him, and you can imagine his response. In this sense, a person you know exists in your mind, and the better you know him or the more you are concerned about him, the more frequently he exists in your mind, and the more accurate can your expectations be about his behavior. Each of the people we know exists in our mind; at least that facet of him that we know exists in our mind. When he is called up from memory to the forefront of attention, even when he is not around, the mental image of him has certain expectations for our behavior and we have certain expectations as to his imaginary behavior. So we may adjust to someone's expectations even when he is not around, at least in so far as we can correctly judge what his expectations are.

We can do this not only for one person, but for a whole group of persons at one time. Suppose you are playing baseball, and your particular position at the moment is that of first baseman. Your attention is more or less fixed on the man at bat, but you have in mind a picture of the location of each man on your team, as well as the location of those on the opposing team who are on the bases, and you have an expectation of how each of these persons is going to act in the next few minutes. When the batter hits the ball on the ground toward third base, you expect the third baseman on your team to secure it and throw it to you as soon as possible. You need not see him, much less talk to him, and yet you know that he is there and you expect him to throw the ball to you. At the same time, the batter is running toward you at first base, expecting you to be trying to have the ball in your hands there before he arrives, and you expect his

---

[13] Throughout this book we shall use the words "adjust" and "adjustment" in the sense in which they are used above—involving fitting in one's behavior to the expected behavior of others. Thus, our use of the term is broader than the popular usage, in which only happy or successful accommodations to a situation are included.

coming even though you have now turned toward the third baseman fielding the ball. At the same time, another man from the opposing team is moving off of second base, and you expect him to try to run to third. You also know that the third baseman expects you to throw the ball back to him, after the put-out has been made at first, so that he can tag the man moving from second to third, or at least force him back to second base.

Then suppose the ball gets beyond the third baseman to the outfield, so that it cannot be thrown to you before the batter reaches first base. Everyone's expectations change. You expect the batter will go right on past you to second base. The third baseman redirects his attention from you to the outfielder chasing the ball, as he expects the outfielder will throw the ball to him directly. So there is a redirection of expectations all along the line. Two conclusions are obvious from this baseball case: (1) You can have in your mind a whole group of persons at once and have different expectations for each of them at the same time. (2) The expectations may not arise out of immediate communication, but out of past communication of the rules of baseball and out of past communications among members of the team and with the coach as to procedure under various circumstances. Whole sets of expectations may change rapidly, without much conscious effort, if one or more of the conditions change on the basis of which the original expectations are formed.

These points can be extended to more complicated but just as realistic situations. The group can be larger than a baseball team: it can be everyone in a school, in a club, in a city, in a nation, in a society, in the world. The nature of communication changes as the group considered gets larger. The communication changes from the direct, face-to-face kind to an indirect communication through one or more intermediaries or through a set of rules written down for all to read or to be taught by specialist teachers. The other whose role is being taken is not a single "other" or even a team of "others" but rather a "generalized other," as Mead called it.

Let us take the city as an example of a large group in which communication is indirect, and which becomes a generalized other for its inhabitants. When you—as a resident of a city—get up in the morning you expect the janitor to have heat in the house, the milkman to have delivered the milk, the workers at the gas company to be on the job so you can prepare your breakfast on a gas range, the workers at the electric company to be working the machinery that provides you electric light. If you take a streetcar or bus to work or school, you expect that someone swept out the car, that someone else got it going at a certain time, and that it will come by to pick you up at a certain corner within a few minutes after you arrive. If you buy anything, you expect that a whole factory of people have been meeting together daily to make it, that other people are organized into a distribution system to transport it from the factory to the store, and that the storekeeper will sell it to you for money because he expects that he can use the money to buy merchandise and other things. If you stop to think about the system a moment, you realize that thousands of people, perhaps millions, have had to do something to meet your expectations for only one day. You do not ordinarily think about it, of course, and the whole structure of past communications ordinarily works well enough so that you do not have to do any thinking until the system breaks down at one point or another.

Our conclusion is that, in one sense, a *social group* exists as a number of biological individuals who have a system of common expectations in their minds. This system of expectations arises out of communication, past or present, direct or indirect through other persons. Because there are these expectations, and because most of them prove to be accurate predictions most of the time, each individual is able to fit his behavior in fairly well with that of most other people. When individuals and groups of people can thus gear their behavior to each other fairly well, we have a relatively well-organized *society*. (A society consists of all the individuals and groups that have some significant number of common expectations.) There are times, however, in which the expectations are no longer valid, and the individual's behavior can no longer be fitted in with that of other people. Then we have a disorganized society, which will be considered in later chapters.

c   *Culture as a Set of Common Understandings*

1   THE NATURE OF CULTURE

How is it that people can have so many thousands of expectations regarding other people's behavior and have most of these expectations fulfilled in fact? Sometimes two or more people argue a matter out and come to some agreement as to how they will act toward each other in the future. But that happens relatively infrequently. For most people in most aspects of their behavior, formal agreement as to how they should act is unnecessary and indeed impossible. One could do very little if he had to think through and argue out each specific act that he performed. One can deviate on a few occasions only if he conforms most of the time. The individual *learns* most of his behavior patterns. Psychology studies *how* the individual learns; sociology is concerned (among other things) with *what* is learned and *who* the individual learns from.

The child learns from his parents, from other relatives, from friends of his parents, from teachers, from older siblings (both brothers and sisters), from playmates, and in fact from nearly everyone with whom he comes in contact. Social learning continues into adulthood and throughout life, although most of the usual social expectations are learned before one reaches the age of twenty. The content of the learning we are concerned with is called "culture." A summary definition of culture, formulated from the writings of many scholars, is: "Culture consists in patterned ways of thinking, feeling, and reacting, acquired and transmitted mainly by symbols, constituting the distinctive achievements of human groups, including their embodiments in artifacts; the essential core of culture consists of traditional (i.e., historically derived and selected) ideas and especially their attached values."[14]

The important idea in the concept of culture is that there are common understandings as to how individuals are to behave toward one another. These come down from the past, and are taught to us as the major part of the process in our becoming transformed from a baby human animal to an adult socialized member of society. They make it possible for us to adjust our behavior to each other without deliberately coming to specific agreements with everyone with whom we interact. Because a culture is thus socially "inherited," it may be thought of as a system of past communications[15] which have established common understandings. The people who have this culture, or common understandings, are a *society*, and they are a society because they have this culture, not because they live together or are of the same race, or anything else. Humans are thus unique in having a culture and a society, within our definitions of these terms.

In the broadest sense, our culture includes everything that all the people in our society know, believe, and expect, that is being transmitted —that is, communicated—to other members of the society, especially to the younger generation. There may be small, isolated societies, of the sort studied by anthropologists, where most of the members know practically all of their cultures. But obviously our culture is so detailed and so complicated that any one person can know only a small fraction of it. People who brag about our great Western culture—because of its high literary expression, its beautiful art, its engineering feats, its tremendous industrial output, its great thought and achievement in so many spheres of life— forget that any one of us can perform only a small fraction of these wonderful things. As a matter of fact the best informed among us can do scarcely any more things by himself than can the better informed members of a most backward, primitive tribe.

How can we then speak of culture as *common* understandings when the greater part of our culture is not known or understood by most mem-

[14] A. L. Kroeber and C. Kluckhohn, "The Concept of Culture: A Critical Review of Definitions," *Papers of the Peabody Museum* (Harvard University), Vol. XLI, 1950.

[15] In the previous section we considered the past communications operating in a baseball game. These "rules of the game" are the culture of the subsociety or "group" of baseball players and fans.

Koehler, Yerkes, and others have demonstrated that apes can solve certain kinds of problems and can learn from each other—by observation—how to solve these problems. Hoebel describes some of the findings of these psychologists and indicates how the apes' behavior differs from truly social behavior.

When one of a group of experimental apes accidentally jabbed the end of a pole into the ground and found to his immense delight he could hoist himself skyward, all the other members of the colony were soon searching for sticks; pole vaulting was the rage. Another discovered that by scattering bread outside the bars of his cage he could lure unwary chickens in close, while he lurked with a stick in his hand with which to jab them. Annoying the chickens then became the current sport of the group. The alarmed squawks of the hens provided rich simian diversion. These and other tricks were discovered by the apes without help from psychologists. When they spread among the group, they had for the time being all the qualities of customs. But, alas, when interest wore off and enthusiasm waned, as they always did after a few days or weeks, each practice was forgotten never to be done again. Their destiny was that of fads; they could not endure to become customs. The permanency of culture was lacking. Apes can spread a pattern of learned behavior through direct imitation, but they cannot talk about it, nor can an older ape tell a younger ape how things were done when he was young. Apes fall short of real culture, because although they can make rudimentary inventions and although their brains are essentially similar to men, they do not have brains enough to work out and retain complex interrelations between things and relationships in speech.

Culture exists in and through communication. Man still remains the sole producer of genuine culture.

E. Adamson Hoebel, *Man in the Primitive World* (New York: McGraw-Hill, 1949), p. 427.

bers of our society? The answer lies in the fact that there is a core of our culture which practically all people in it do know and understand. This core includes knowledge about behavior toward other people and about behavior toward certain commonly used objects. While very few of us can build a bridge or compose a song, most of us know that a chair is intended to be sat on. So there is a core of common understandings in our culture, and on the basis of these understandings we have correct expectations most of the time regarding the behavior of others.

But this distinction between common understandings and specialized knowledge does not fully describe the situation in our culture. We live in what is commonly called "Western culture," which geographically covers most of Europe, North America, South America, and Australia. When we consider the large number of different languages, different political systems, different ideals, different economic organizations, and so on, in this huge area, we realize that our culture is highly heterogeneous. Some would break it up into subcultures, also with a geographic base, such as the Slavic subculture, the Latin subculture, the American subculture, and so on. But this is hardly satisfactory either, when it is realized that, in some very important respects, there are more common understandings between Minnesota and Sweden than there are between Minnesota and Mississippi. A culture or subculture cannot be limited geographically: if they happen to be at present, they may not be in the future. In our culture, at least, specifying geographical location is a completely unsatisfactory way of describing the limits of a subculture. The limits of a culture have to be described in terms of the extent of common understandings regarding how people can be expected to behave toward one another.

This should not be taken to mean that there are common behavior patterns or common standards for all individuals within a culture. Even within a single city some radically different standards and behavior patterns will be found to exist. People act and think in different ways not only because of such obvious differences as those of age, occupation, and sex, but also because of differences in class, religious belief, and ideological orientation. People act in different ways because their position in the social structure is different; we call this their *role* difference. For example, a child is expected to go to school and to play while a man is expected to earn a living and to work; a bricklayer is expected to spend some time around an unfinished building and a teacher is supposed to spend some time in a classroom.

People also act in different ways because their beliefs as to how they should act are different. For example, a Seventh-Day Adventist believes

Society, then, in its immediate aspect, is a relation among personal ideas. . . . Society exists in my mind as the contact and reciprocal influence of certain ideas named "I," Thomas, Henry, Susan, Bridget, and so on. It exists in your mind as a similar group, and so in every mind. . . . I conclude, therefore, that the imaginations which people have of one another are the solid facts of society, and that to observe and interpret these must be a chief aim of sociology. . . .

In saying this I hope I do not seem to question the independent reality of persons or to confuse it with personal ideas. The man is one thing and the various ideas entertained about him are another; but the latter, the personal idea, is the immediate social reality.

Charles Horton Cooley, *Human Nature and the Social Order* (New York: Scribner's, 1902 ; rev. ed., 1922), pp. 84–85, 87, 89.

that he should not work on Saturday; a civic-minded citizen believes that he should devote part of his time to civic enterprises; a "bohemian" believes it is unnatural to limit his sexual expression to a legal wife. The divergent behavior patterns resulting from these different social positions and different beliefs are probably greater in our society than in any other, even within a small community. Nevertheless, people can have many common understandings in an area as large as a city or nation. Once they place each other as a bricklayer or a Seventh-Day Adventist, they have certain expectations with respect to each other's behavior and these expectations usually turn out to be right. This gives us a common culture despite the differences.

The anthropologists commonly distinguish between material and non-material culture, saying that objects which one can see and feel (such as chairs and buildings) are material culture, whereas traditional behavior patterns and beliefs (such as religious and political organizations) are non-material culture. The distinction has proved valuable to the anthropologist because he has sometimes been faced with the problem of having only material objects with which to describe a dead culture. But to the sociologist, who is interested only in the characteristics of relationships between human beings, a material object is a part of culture only in so far as one person can expect another person to act toward it in a certain way under certain circumstances. If a person makes something unique and no one sees him use it so that it has no meaning to other people, it is not a cultural object. Similarly, material objects which have a meaning and a use in other cultures but have absolutely no meaning to us cannot be given a definition in "material culture," even if we recognize that they are man-made.[16]

Look at the bottom picture facing page oo, for example, and see if you can guess what it is without looking at the printed description. It is simply a piece of intricately carved metal until you can express in words what people may be expected to do with it. Therefore, from the standpoint of the sociologist, there is not much difference between material and non-material culture.

Thus far we have spoken of culture as though everyone in the society were aware of it each time they communicated with anyone. Most of the expectations involved in culture become habitual, so that while they may once have been conscious, and can upon occasion be readily recalled to consciousness, they are ordinarily taken for granted and acted upon without conscious thought. Further, there is a section of culture that has been called *covert*, which people hide from themselves and which they

---

[16] If we recognize that an article is man-made, but have no idea as to how it was used, we can say that it was probably a piece of "material culture" but cannot otherwise give it a cultural meaning.

resist bringing to their consciousness. Elements in covert culture are difficult to study, because they are camouflaged and not discussed openly, and
therefore it is not known how numerous or important they are. Sociologists and anthropologists know that covert culture elements exist because
people show by their behavior that they have certain expectations for behavior of others which they deny having, and that they conform to the
same expectations in their responses to others but give an obvious rationalization when asked to explain why they did what they did.[17] We can
not here go into the intricacies of covert culture, but a few examples can
be given by way of illustration. There appears to be, in American culture,
a covert favorable value for certain "white-collar" crimes, such as tax
cheating, large-scale business fraud, and minor traffic violations. There
seems to be, on the part of white Americans, especially white Southerners,
a belief in and an attraction to a "strong sexual power" of Negroes.[18]
There seems to be, on the part of a significant number of Americans, an
attitude in favor of war.

2   VARIATIONS IN CULTURE

Culture consists of common understandings regarding proper ways of
behaving and its existence implies that there must be communication, in
the past and in the present, to arrive at these common understandings.
When people are out of contact with each other for a long time, and there
has not even been indirect contact through other persons, they have no
way of reaching common understandings and their cultures develop in
different directions. We know that all men belong to one species, *Homo
sapiens,* and since a species has certain common ancestors all men must
once have lived together in one limited geographic area.[19] The best scientific guess is that men's original home was in southern Asia and from there
they spread to every corner of the globe even before recorded history began.
For tens of thousands of years societies of men have been separated by
oceans and continents, and for most of this time transportation has been
slow and difficult. Once a group of men migrated to a hitherto-uninhabited
spot, a migration that might well have taken hundreds of years,[20] they

[17] For methods of studying covert culture, see Arnold M. Rose, *Theory and Method
in the Social Sciences* (Minneapolis: University of Minnesota Press, 1954), Chapter 21,
and sources cited therein.

[18] This has been observed by several keen but non-academic analysts, such as Margaret
Halsey, *Color Blind* (New York: Simon and Schuster, 1946); Helen V. McLean, "Psychodynamic Factors in Racial Relations," *Annals of the American Academy,* 244 (March,
1946), pp. 159–66; Lillian Smith, *Killers of the Dream* (New York: Norton, 1949).

[19] This is the majority opinion among scientists, although a few, like Carleton Coon,
dispute it.

[20] The Bible has it that the ancient Hebrews took forty years to migrate from Egypt
to Israel, a distance of around 400 miles. While historians have never been able to

may never have seen a person outside their society for ten thousand years —perhaps not until European explorers began to "discover" the world in the fifteenth century, A.D. Even if a stray individual should travel to a distant land—as Marco Polo went from Venice to China in the thirteenth century—the contact would usually be too limited and too brief for the establishment of a large number of significant common understandings. Significant exceptions occurred in ancient times when peoples with the earliest civilizations—in Africa and Asia Minor, and later in Greece and Rome—began to travel, have trade relations, and engage in military conquest and political domination of other peoples.

Thus hundreds of cultures have developed on the earth more or less independently of each other. Except for a few artifacts and practices which they have borrowed from one another in recent times, these cultures are different. There are also a few traits that are very similar because they have developed in a parallel fashion in response to similar needs. Each culture indicates what is proper behavior, but what is proper behavior in one is not proper behavior in another. All the members of one society have certain expectations as to how other members of that society will behave under certain circumstances, and these expectations will usually turn out to be correct. But for those respects in which the culture is different, there can be no correct expectations between members of two different societies unless they communicate with each other and come to a specific agreement for each aspect of their behavior. There is no body of past common understandings on the basis of which they can act toward each other, either as friends or as enemies or as chance acquaintances, so that each understands what the other is doing. Further, each person has his own idea of what is right and proper behavior, and it would be a rare chance if these ideas should happen to coincide if the two persons had no common culture. Differences in culture can be verp deep seated and can cover the most basic behaviors. If one surveys the cultures of the world he finds that human beings somewhere are behaving in every way that they can possibly behave. Physical biology sets the only limits. What is indecent in one culture is proper and expected in some other culture. What is humorous or ridiculous in one culture is serious and profound in some other culture. What is cruel in one culture is an act of charity in another culture. What is a religious act in one culture is a criminal act in another culture.

Let us illustrate cultural differences by comparing the structure of the immediate family in three different societies, of which our own is one. In our culture we consider that a family is formed when an adult male selects an adult female and she agrees to go through a ceremony—called marriage—which establishes her as his sole socially recognized and legal

---

verify the story, it is not incredible from what is known of the usual slowness of migration of primitive peoples.

spouse. They live together, have sex relations with each other, divide family functions along more or less customary lines, bear and rear children, and are not free to marry anyone else unless they go to court and get a divorce first. These two people are, respectively, father and mother to the children they bear.

In another society, that of the Nayar of India, sex relations are quite independent of the family institution.[21] Marriage for a girl at puberty is only a necessary ritual to be entered into with any obliging stranger of equal or higher caste,[22] the latter's relations and obligations beginning and ending here. Actual mating, on the other hand, occurs later by means of informal but socially recognized love affairs, which, however, establish no permanent bond between the man and his offspring.

The Nayars are matrilineal in descent, inheritance, and residence. A household, or taravad, consists of a group of related women with their brothers and children. The eldest woman is titular head but economic affairs are run by the eldest male for the benefit of the joint family as a whole. There is no place in the taravad for either the ceremonial husband or the informal lover.

If a woman and her lover are compatible, the relationship may continue for years but it can always be broken by either party without notice. Until recent times, women and men frequently each had several mates—that is, the Nayar were at the same time polygynous and polyandrous.[23] At the present, however, polyandry has virtually disappeared, while polygyny still persists to a limited degree.

Marquesan families, or households, when studied by Linton[24] during the 1930's, were polyandrous and, in the household of the chief or a wealthy family, involved a form approaching group marriage. The typical household would have two or three men to one woman, the well-to-do adding a wife, or even two, some years after the initial marriage. The household of the chief might have a dozen men and three or four women; only the poorest households were monogamous. Marriage as a formal ritual did not exist except where a ceremony for purposes of social elevation was desired.

---

[21] C. Daryll Forde, *Habitat, Economy, and Society* (London: Methuen, 1934), pp. 276–77; Ralph Linton, *The Study of Man* (New York: Appleton-Century, 1936), pp. 154–55. The Nayar, like most of the peoples of India, have been experiencing rapid social change, but their social structure in the 1930's serves to illustrate a point.

[22] For a description of caste in India, see Chapter 8, Section A.

[23] Polygyny is the customary practice of a man formally taking more than one wife. Polyandry is the practice of a woman taking more than one husband. The practice of having plural spouses—either polygynous of polyandrous or both—is called polygamy. The practice of having single spouses is called monogamy.

[24] Ralph Linton, "Marquesan Culture," in Abram Kardiner, *The Individual and His Society* (New York: Columbia University Press, 1939), pp. 152–59.

In attempting to understand a culture different from one's own, one must be careful not to take people's customs and words too literally. Just as we earlier noted for interpersonal relations, one must seek to find the meaning behind the words and not mistake the words for the expectation actually contained in the culture. A Japanese American provides examples from Japanese culture:

Japanese custom is such that when one asks a Japanese woman how her son is, she will reply, "Thank you for asking about my worthless son." She will then commence to tell of his recent doctorate, his $58,000 home, and his ten children. Faced with these accomplishments, you begin to wonder what her worthwhile sons are like.

Etiquette behooves one not to complain of a chilly house when visiting. One might even lie and say they enjoy cool rooms. Then the host, to comply with the guest's preference will lower the thermostat. The next time if the guest wears a bulky knit to ward off pneumonia, the host will lower the thermostat even more. The only thing to do in a case like this is to cut off the friendship.

Upon being complimented, a hostess will reply her cooking is unfit for pigs. (Then you wonder why you are eating it, but never, never say it.) After the twelfth course, she will say apologetically, "This was a simple meal." The hostess presses her guests to eat. One may be starved but it is politeness to refuse at least three times. A true Japanese hostess will play ball and continue to coax. When the hostess says: "I am a terrible cook, I can't cook," one must hastily say, "To the contrary." And the secret is never to stop contradicting the hostess and this takes care of any polite table conversation worries. Sometimes from sheer exhaustion and from a sense of being too argumentative, I have stopped. The result, of course, is disaster.

When I have been asked how my husband is, I have replied: "Oh, so-so." The next time around we hear that we are on the brink of divorce or some other calamitous conclusion.

Esther Suzuki, "Too-Politeness," *J. A. Journal, Minneapolis* (October, 1961) p. 7.

Families were constantly trying for status within a fairly fluid structure. The prestige of a household, dependent upon display of wealth at feasts and ceremonies and upon success in blood revenge and occasional feuds, required as large a number of active adult males as possible.[25] Each house was built on a stone foundation, and the size and weight of the stone used were also signs of prestige since they indicated roughly the number of able-bodied men in the household. A new house would often be built with each increment in wealth and/or man power, or with the birth of

[25] A chief or rich family head would sometimes marry a young woman because she had three or four lovers who would follow her and thus become members of the household.

the first son. Intermarriage and adoption were frequently entered into in order to stabilize status relations between competing households.

Within the family, top status was held by the eldest son, the woman, and the first husband, in that order. The first-born son (who may or may not be the biological offspring of the head of the house) became the official head of the household[26] at birth and the effective head at maturity. Few emotional ties with the parents existed and few parental claims to loyalty or assistance were made on the first son. Childless households usually would go to great expense to adopt a first-born son,[27] this practice fusing two households into one. This could not always be done, however, and, hence, some households were headed by first-born daughters.

Effective power lay with the woman who, by distributing sexual favors (she usually had no direct economic role), controlled not only the head husband but also subsidiary husbands, the more absolutely and openly if she was an eldest child as well. Sexually desirable women were thus sought as means of raising the prestige and power of the household.

The first husband, while subordinate in power to his head wife and to the first-born son, was superior to the other husbands in allocating household tasks and distributing favors. It was to his advantage, however, to see that the other husbands were satisfied lest they wander off with other women and attach themselves to other households.

Subsidiary husbands of one household were usually only the younger sons of others. There was no fraternal polyandry since brothers would always attach themselves to separate households. Occasionally subsidiary husbands might be first-born, too, for when a family was too poor to give its first-born son a start the latter might attach himself to a wealthy family as subsidiary husband.

This description of variation in family structure could be greatly extended. And any other institution could be used to illustrate cultural variation. But this is primarily the interest of anthropology rather than of sociology and is therefore left for other books. For our purposes it is important solely to note that within the great range of man's physical capacities a given society will set down certain behavior patterns as its culture and look upon other possible behavior patterns as peculiar, ridiculous, dangerous, immoral, or even impossible. One has really no conception of human possibilities until he has surveyed sympathetically a large number of cultures. Many people in our society believe it impossible to have a

[26] Linton describes an incident where the son of a local chief, following a quarrel with his father, kept his own family outside their house for several days. Until he lifted this taboo, the family had spent an uncomfortable time in the open while the boy sat in the house looking alternately glum and triumphant, (*op. cit.*, pp. 158-59.)

[27] The chief often avoided conflict with a rising household by adopting its first-born son to be his heir.

family system based on brother-sister marriages until they study the ancient Egyptian upper-class culture. Many people, including navigators and engineers, believe it impossible to sail regularly for hundreds of miles in open sea from one small island to another without a chart or compass or identifying speck of land until one learns about the Ifaluk people who live on a small island in the Southwest Pacific.[28] And there are many people in the world who regard it as impossible for man to build flying boats that can travel hundreds of miles an hour until one comes in contact with Western culture.

3   THE EVALUATION OF CULTURE

People can learn that the "impossible" is really possible when they see it demonstrated. But it is much more difficult to understand that what is "proper" and "good" is a matter of cultural definition.[29] Most people everywhere have a tendency to regard their own cultural practices as the best ones, or the only ones that are moral or virtuous. In so far as other cultures come close to their own, they are regarded as not being so bad. But in so far as other cultures diverge from their own culture, these cultures are regarded as immoral. This tendency, found everywhere in the world, although in especially high degree among certain people, is called *ethnocentrism*. Americans, along with the French, the Arabs, the ancient Greeks, and the ancient Hebrews, and a few other peoples, have cultures which are particularly characterized by ethnocentrism. Individuals who are most ethnocentric within any given culture are those whose experience has been narrow, whose ability to understand other people (even in their own group) is not great, or whose inner feelings of insecurity are so great that they are afraid of every deviation from the expected.[30]

When considering ethnocentrism, it is useful again to distinguish material from non-material culture. There are objects in material culture which achieve a given purpose with much greater efficiency and ease than other objects. For example, a buzz saw can do a better job of cutting wood than a handsaw, and a steel handsaw can do a better job of cutting wood

[28] Melford E. Spiro and Edwin G. Burrows, *An Atoll Culture: Ethnography of Ifaluk in the Central Carolines* (New Haven: Human Relations Area Files, 1957).

[29] Philosophers who are students of ethics set up certain criteria to judge a behavior pattern. Aristotle held that behavior that followed a "golden mean"—not too much toward either extreme—was truly virtuous behavior. Jeremy Bentham held that behavior which brought the greatest happiness to the greatest number was the best behavior. More recently, the psychoanalyst Erich Fromm (*Man for Himself,* New York: Rinehart, 1947) has set up the norm of psychic health as the best criterion of a good cultural pattern. These ethical philosophers try to divorce their criteria from their own cultural practices, and in so far as they do so they are acting as philosophers rather than as cultural apologists. The practice of setting ethical criteria is thus not the same thing as the "ethnocentrism" we describe in the text.

[30] T. W. Adorno *et al., The Authoritarian Personality* (New York: Harper, 1950).

The principle of cultural relativism has long been standard anthropological doctrine. It holds that any cultural phenomenon must be understood and evaluated in terms of the culture of which it forms part. The corresponding assumption in the organic field is so obvious that biologists have scarcely troubled to formulate it. The difference is that we, the students of culture, live in our culture, are attached to its values, and have a natural human inclination to become ethnocentric over it, with the result that, if unchecked, we would perceive, describe, and evaluate other cultures by the forms, standards, and values of our own, thus preventing fruitful comparison and classification. Realization of relativism can be shocking to the tender-minded, through taking away the affective security which seeming absolutes render. Basically, of course, relativism is no more than desire for inquiry coupled with readiness to undergo unrestricted comparison.

Beyond this, there is a real and profounder problem: that of fixed, panhuman, if not absolute, values. This problem is only beginning to come to the consciousness of anthropologists, who have perhaps done most to stress the relativistic principle. It is touched only by implication in the present book. My conviction is that value-judgments as between the values of different cultures are possible, though not by any majority poll or with absolute finality, and probably with a pluralistic outcome. It is not to be expected that any one culture will differ from all other imperfect ones in having developed perfect values.

Alfred L. Kroeber, *The Nature of Culture* (Chicago: University of Chicago Press, 1952), pp. 8–9.

than a sliver of stone. It could easily be agreed that a buzz saw was a superior element in material culture as compared to a stone sliver. In this sense, many material culture objects in our culture are superior to the corresponding objects in other cultures. Other cultures have borrowed many items from our material culture, and we have borrowed a few items from other cultures. A qualification to this identification of certain aspects of material culture as superior must be recognized when non-material values adhere to the use of primitive techniques and tools.

When it comes to non-material culture there is no way of describing one culture as superior to another. If we use the criterion of complexity, we find that many cultures have more complex institutions than our own, and yet there is no reason to say that these other cultures are superior to our culture or vice versa. If we use the criterion of satisfaction of basic biological and psychic needs, we find that different cultures accomplish this end in different degrees for different needs, that all pass a minimum standard, and no one culture is superior to any other in all respects. Then the question can be raised: Why judge a culture in terms of its complexity or its basic satisfactions? Might not a simple culture or a culture that placed continual challenges before the individual be just as "good" a culture as a complex or completely "satisfying" one? When it comes to such things as art forms, dances, tabooed and preferred foods, and even family structure, one would indeed be narrow-minded if he believed in an inherent superiority of one culture over another. It is true that we tend to have tastes for things in our own culture, and we have to live in another society for a while before we can develop a taste for some things in its culture. But to set up our culture as superior in these respects is to set up one's own tastes as the rule and the ideal for all men.

The recognition that the non-material culture of one society cannot be judged superior to that of another society is called "cultural relativity." It took a long while for students of human society to reach this point of view. Up through the nineteenth century and even into the twentieth century anthropologists and sociologists tended to rank all societies from high to low, and of course place their own—whether that happened to be German, English, French, or American—on top, while they placed the so-called "primitive societies" at the bottom. In the nineteenth century, when a biological justification was given to this ranking, the dominant point of view assumed a "societal evolution," in which the lower societies were expected to evolve into more advanced ones. For some decades now we have known that this point of view is nonsense, and that all societies and cultures have developed as long as every other one, and in their own way each is as advanced as every other one.[31]

This does not mean that we cannot evaluate cultures if we set up certain explicit criteria of evaluation. As Kluckhohn puts it, a recognition of cultural relativity does not prevent one from setting up moral absolutes: "Cultural relativity means, on the contrary, that the appropriateness of any positive or negative custom must be evaluated with regard to how this habit fits in with other group habits."[32] If one chooses this criterion of "adequacy of fit," he will find that in some respects our own culture is pretty good and in other respects pretty bad. And so it will be with every other criterion of cultural superiority if one does not arbitrarily choose our own culture as the standard. It is quite possible that there are common standards in all cultures, which arise out of universal experiences, common psychic mechanisms, and certain common human needs. These may

[31] But see Chapter 11 for a contemporary evolutionist viewpoint.
[32] Clyde Kluckhohn, *Mirror for Man* (New York: McGraw-Hill, 1949), p. 41.

be designated as universal values on the basis of which we can judge every culture.[33]

Some have tried to evaluate culture in terms of the rationality of the origins of specific customs. This is a hopeless task, for social origins are lost in unrecorded prehistory and in far-from-complete history. Sociologists have learned that it is only a pastime to speculate on most social origins:

> Englishmen, always fascinated by the foreign ways of foreigners, got a new question to mull over when a reader raised in the *Times*'s letters column the question why Americans cut their food with knife held in right hand, put down the knife, shift the fork from the left hand, and then eat with fork held in right hand. Some answers supplied by other readers: Because in early days each American family had only one knife and had to share it . . . or knives were put down to assure strangers no one planned to attack them . . . or the process slows the rate of eating and thus improves digestion.[34]

Further, customs often change drastically, and what may be justified in one way at one time may have to be justified in quite another way later. The Irish custom of wearing something green is often attributed

[33] An informed discussion of the contemporary social scientist's attitude toward ethical and cultural relativity is Clyde Kluckhohn's "Ethical Relativity: Sic et non," *The Journal of Philosophy*, 52 (November, 1955), pp. 663–77.

[34] *New York Times*, August 4, 1963, p. E2.

Ethnocentrism is found even in language, as is amusingly illustrated in a story by Harry N. Young:

> While visiting England, Mr. Randler, a man of firm and noisy convictions, was constantly irritated by British terms. So, as an English friend drove him around the countryside, he kept up a steady fire of criticism. He snorted at the name "bobby" for policeman. He explained at length to his patient host just how ridiculous it was to call a drugstore a chemist's shop or a trolley car a tram. And when his driver-host happened to mention that the windscreen of his car was dirty, Mr. Randler practically sizzled.
>
> "Windshield," he snapped. "Not windscreen."
>
> "But we call it windscreen," his host said mildly.
>
> "Well, you're wrong. After all, I'm an American, and we invented the automobile."
>
> "Ah, old boy," the Englishman said quietly, "and who, if I may ask, invented the language?"

Saturday Evening Post, May 7, 1955, p. 99, as cited in the *Minneapolis Morning Tribune*, May 14, 1955, p. 4.

RELATIVITY VS. UNIVERSALITY OF VALUES
The Case of Trousers

The trousers, for instance, that are now considered by some the most obvious symbol of Westernization—and also of Western moral behavior, so far as men are concerned—have almost always met in the tropics, or among tropical peoples, a contrast varying from nakedness to a cloth wrap. Not only this: as Professor Ralph Linton recently pointed out, in an essay on "The Problem of Universal Values,"* nearly all societies "have a conceptual value for modesty which is reflected in specific patterns of coverage for various parts of the body under various circumstances," with "the custom of wearing a garment of a particular type" constituting in itself a value of what Professor Linton calls "the instrumental type," as distinct from a value of conceptual type. To illustrate the distinction between the two classes of values the well-known social anthropologist mentions a very interesting example: "Thus some years ago the head of a great Christian denomination refused to receive the late Mahatma Gandhi because the latter insisted on wearing a loin-cloth instead of trousers. Both the parties involved would certainly have agreed on the conceptual value of modesty; yet for each the behavior pattern by which this was instrumental in his own culture had acquired meanings and attitudes which made it a value in its own right. . . . Trousers, as the garb of the politically dominant European, had acquired negative associations. He (Gandhi) no doubt felt that to don them for his reception would be an act of obedience to the British Raj."

Gilberto Freyre, "Morals and Social Change," *Transactions of the Third World Congress of Sociology* (London: International Sociological Association, 1956), Vol. I, pp. 22–23.
    * In Robert F. Spencer (ed.), *Method and Perspective in Anthropology* (Minneapolis: University of Minnesota Press, 1954), p. 151.

to the greenness of Irish fields and moors. Originally, however, the Irish had a superstition against wearing anything green, for fear that fairies or leprechauns would seize them. The only safe day to flaunt the fairies was St. Patrick's Day.[35]

4 · WRITING

The communications that build culture are written as well as oral. The invention of *writing* had crucial effects on culture and society because it involved an extension of communication both in space and time. People who are able to read and write can communicate without being in hearing distance of each other. This permits a radical expansion of the limits of the society. It also permits an individual to be influenced without ever seeing or knowing the one who is influencing him.[36] The extension of com-

[35] *New York Times*, June 22, 1958, p. 27.
[36] Some of the consequences of this fact will be examined in Chapter 9, Section C.

munciation through time had even more drastic effects on society. The cultural heritage could now be written down; hence less of it was lost. It could become more rigid and precise—as in the case of law—permitting change only through a deliberate act. The art forms of poetry and story-telling could be greatly expanded, and science—which demands precision and detail—was made possible.

Several ancient peoples independently discovered writing in one form or another—the Egyptians, the peoples of Asia Minor, the Chinese, the Hindus, the Aegeans, the Mayans, and perhaps others. From them it spread to other peoples: the ancestors of the white people who now in-habit Europe (outside of Italy and Greece) and the Americas picked it up sometime in the period we know as the "Dark Ages" (A.D. 400–1000). When writing was invented or borrowed, it did not mean that all people in the society could read and write. In fact, no more than a tiny fraction (perhaps 5 per cent) of the white people of Europe and North America could read by the year 1800. Even today there are "civilized countries" in which only a minority of the population is literate, even in the minimal sense that they can read a newspaper. In Turkey, for example, only about 35 per cent of the population is literate, and the proportions are lower in Spain and in most civilized countries of South America, Asia (outside of Japan), and Africa. Still, the society is greatly affected even when only a small proportion of its population can read and write. During the period of world exploration from Europe that began at the end of the fifteenth century and lasted through the nineteenth century, many societies were discovered that did not possess writing. They seemed so different from the civilized societies, not only in the content of culture but in the basic forms of culture, that they were called "primitive." We know now that these differences were basically a function of the absence of a written language, rather than a result of being less "evolved," and that therefore societies should more correctly be called "preliterate."[37] Today, practically every used language has been set down in writing, and at least a minority of persons in nearly every society can read and write. Hence, preliterate so-cieties are disappearing, and basic differences in cultural forms are to be traced to differences in technology and political organization rather than to the knowledge or lack of knowledge of writing.

D   *Obstacles to Communication*

The adjustment of an individual to his group, and of one group to another, requires communication, as we have seen. On the other hand,

[37] Ellsworth Faris, *The Nature of Human Nature* (New York: McGraw-Hill, 1937), pp. 251–53. More recently, Melville J. Herskovits has argued for the term "nonliterate." See *Man and His Works* (New York: Alfred A. Knopf, 1948), p. 75.

individuals and groups may not adjust, may not conform, after learning what the society's expectations are, and either creative or criminal behavior follows. But this is not an immediate concern. The question for this section is: What are the barriers to communication, and what happens when communication does not work, when an individual or a group has no way of knowing what the society's expectations really are?

Barriers to communication may conveniently be classified as geographic, biological, psychological, and social. Geographic barriers used to be far more important than they are today in causing isolation. Sheer physical distance, mountains, and large bodies of water may be more easily overcome by the railroad, the airplane, the telegraph, the telephone, the modern postal system, and other inventions of the last century, than by the motor power of a man with a horse or sailing vessel. But there are still geographic barriers to communication: it is expensive to communicate long distances, and often we do not know people who live beyond the confines of our community so that we have little desire to communicate with them. Biological barriers prevent us from communicating back to the dead and to other species of animals. Psychological differences often make us dislike other people so that we have no desire to communicate with them. The mentally disturbed person also has a psychological difficulty in communicating. But by far the most important barriers to communication are the social ones. We have extreme difficulty in communicating with peoples of foreign countries because they speak other languages. More than 2,800 different languages are spoken throughout the world; usually many languages are spoken within a given country. We cannot communicate with an infant because it has not yet learned a language. Social class (based on differences of wealth, prestige, etc.) is an effective barrier to communication. On the near north side of Chicago some of the richest people and some of the poorest people in the city live within a few blocks of each other and often pass each other on the street. Yet they are as completely isolated as though they were a thousand miles apart.[38] Any difference in social conditions or interests may serve as an important barrier to communication.

As an example of the implications of barriers to communication, let us examine what happens when two people come together who speak different languages. There is no meeting of minds: One might insult the other, and the latter believes he is describing the weather. They may have a common culture—whole sets of common understandings—but no terms understandable to both in which they can call upon each other's understandings in order to make successful predictions of each other's behavior. When a translator—a person who knows both languages—comes along

[38] Harvey W. Zorbaugh, *The Gold Coast and the Slum* (Chicago: University of Chicago Press, 1929).

they can communicate quite adequately. Translators exist in abundance, and it is relatively not hard to learn a language, so that language differences today are only a minor obstacle to communication. On the other hand, it should be recognized that translation is not mechanical. There are many words in each language for which there are no exact equivalents in other languages, and the only proper way to translate such a word is with a long sentence. For example, the French word *syndicat* is regularly translated as "trade union." This is quite misleading; it should be translated as "organization of workers according to political philosophy, having as its purpose the reform or revolution of society to bring it in line with the political philosophy." Cognate words that sound alike but have different meanings often cause difficulties in translation. The French verb *demander* (meaning "to ask") has almost led to several international crises when careless reporters translated it as "to demand" (as in "The French Premier demanded that the American President give more funds for French economic development.")

Idioms are especially difficult to translate. The German saying "Morgenstunde hat Gold im Munde" can be literally translated into English as "Morning hour has gold in its mouth." But this grammatically correct sentence has no real meaning. An adapted translation that would convey the correct meaning would be Franklin's aphorism, "Early to bed and early to rise maketh a man healthy, wealthy and wise." Since much of everyday language involves idiom, simile, metaphor, analogy, aphorism, or slang, it is necessary to make drastic adaptations in translation in order to avoid misunderstandings and ambiguities. This is even true in "translating" gestures: the nod, expressing confirmation in the United States and Western Europe, accompanies a negative reply in Greece and Middle Eastern countries. When a Greek wants to motion you to go away, it looks to an American as if he wished you to come to him.[39]

Culture differences create an even greater obstacle to communication, as we have seen. What seems to us to be a simple concept—such as "father" —has such different meanings in different societies that even if a translation is made there may be no understanding. Such conceptual differences become major obstacles in an international assembly such as the United Nations. An American makes a complete misinterpretation if he assumes that the hatred between the Arabs and the Jews in the Near East is anything like the hatred between whites and Negroes in the United States. To use an expression like "black as sin" will insult a large number of one's colleagues. "Democracy" means something entirely different to a Russian than it does to an American, and frequently international talks bog down for hours, literally hours, while the gentlemen who determine

[39] Ralph J. Kaplan, "Breaking Through the Language Barrier," *Journal of Educational Sociology* (February, 1954) pp. 278–79.

the world's fate search for a single word which they can agree will fit a certain sentence. The representatives of several nations will be fresh after a session lasting until 2 A.M. while the American representative is ready to collapse: he does not follow the custom of siesta, or sleeping for three hours every afternoon. Ambassador John Kenneth Galbraith became the center of a furor in the Pakistani National Assembly when it was claimed that he deliberately insulted Moslems by naming his cat "Ahmed," one of the forms of the name Mohammed. There were also public meetings in several Pakistani cities to protest this insult to the founder of the Moslem religion.[40] The reader who is interested in the challenges to understanding created by differences in basic cultural meanings will find it instructive to read F. S. C. Northrop's *The Meeting of East and West.*[41]

If one is willing, one can make a great effort and learn another culture's meanings and expectations. But there is another obstacle to communication, much more difficult to overcome, when one is unwilling. The deliberate closing of one's mind to communications and experiences, which —if accepted—would change one's mind is called *prejudice*. Prejudices are always maintained for a reason. The consequence of prejudice is that the person who is the object of prejudice is seen in terms of preconceived patterns. Instead of the expectations regarding his behavior resulting from communication, they result from the preconceptions. The individual is thus not seen for what he really is, or what he is really saying, but is seen simply as this preconception or stereotype. DuBois has provided an excellent description of one relation between prejudice against Negroes and the barriers to communication involved by envisioning a "plate glass" separating American whites and Negroes which allows each group to see each other all the time, but does not allow them to hear—that is, communicate with—each other.

> It is difficult to let others see the full psychological meaning of caste segregation. It is as though one looking out from a dark cave in a side of an impending mountain sees the world passing and speaks to it; speaks courteously and persuasively, showing them how these entombed souls are hindered in their natural movement, expression, and development; and how their loosening from prison would be a matter not simply of courtesy, sympathy, and help to them, but aid to all the world. One talks on evenly and logically in this way, but notices that the passing throng does not even turn its head, or if it does, glances curiously and walks on. It gradually penetrates the minds of the prisoners that the people do not hear; that some thick sheets of invisible but horribly tangible plate glass is between them and the

---

[40] *New York Times,* April 20, 1963, p. 2.
[41] New York: Macmillan, 1946.

world. They get excited; they talk louder; they gesticulate. Some of the passing world stop in curiosity; these gesticulations seem so pointless; they laugh and pass on. They still either do not hear at all, or hear but dimly, and even what they hear, they do not understand. Then the people within may become hysterical. They may scream and hurl themselves against the barriers, hardly realizing in their bewilderment that they are screaming in a vacuum unheard, and that their antics may actually seem funny to those outside looking in. They may even, here and there, break through in blood and disfigurement, and find themselves faced by a horrified, implacable, and quite overwhelming mob of people frightened for their very own existence.[42]

The "plate glass" as here described exists in the minds of the white man.

Although one may be unwilling to do so, one *can* break through his plate glass of cultural difference or prejudice. An even more serious barrier to communication exists when one cannot communicate even though there are no language or cultural barriers. Such a person has a mental disorder—or, in legal terminology—he is insane. He cannot understand what another person tells him since he changes the words around to fit another meaning in his mind. Thus he cannot conform to the expectations of others. His own statements to others are similarly not expressions of what he expects from others in accordance with customary behavior in his society. They are rather verbal expressions of what is going on in his disordered mind, and are no more communications to other people than are the singing of songs by a normal person when he is in the privacy of his own shower bath. The inability to communicate or to understand communication is the most distinctive characteristic of the mentally disordered person, and this characteristic seems to be related to the cause and cure of many mental disorders.

The psychiatrists—those who study mental disorders and try to cure them—have demonstrated that mentally disordered people differ only in degree, and not in kind, from so-called "normal" people. The inability to communicate is characteristic of everyone to a certain extent. The extent is probably greater than most people imagine. People who hear someone else say something pay attention not only to what is said but also interpret what is said in terms of their own mental sets. In a surprising number of cases the interpretation bears no relation to what is actually said. The reader may experiment with himself by rereading a paragraph of this book —say the paragraph from DuBois on the preceding page—and asking a number of friends to read it also, each person writing down his interpretation of what is said. Then the interpretations can be compared; from past experiments we may expect that the interpretations will differ widely. It is not that one person is necessarily more intelligent than the other, or that

[42] W. F. B. DuBois. *Dusk of Dawn* (New York: Harcourt, 1940), pp. 130–31.

one person has a better memory than the other, or that some do not "want" to give a correct interpretation. It is simply that an individual's mind distorts, to a greater or lesser degree, depending on the individual, what is communicated to him.

A similar thing happens when the individual tries to communicate with someone else. He wants to say something, but the words that come out of his mouth seldom express exactly what he wants to say. The words also express the distortions in his mind. If there is very little relation between what the individual wants to say to another person and what he does say, the individual is regarded as having a mental disorder. But the lack of relationship is true for everyone in our society to a slight extent, at least, and there is another obstacle to communication.

This difficulty can be illustrated by the teaching situation. Quite frequently even the best teacher cannot get across to the students what he is trying to say. The skilled teacher realizes when he is not communicating adequately to the students and tries another approach, another line of communication, or perhaps two or three other lines. One teacher made a careful study of how much of his lectures his students understand. He calculated that the average student understood only 64 per cent of the ideas he was trying to get across in an average lecture (when the students were trying to pay attention because they knew they were being studied). No matter how clear the teacher's statement, there will always be a few students who do not understand what is being communicated to them. This is most evident on examinations: even where the teacher has taken great pains to state the questions clearly and unambiguously, there will always be a few students who "misread" the questions. It is not that the students cannot read perfectly well; it is simply that the words bring up certain ideas to their minds which are not contained in the words themselves. Of course this is not the only difficulty in examinations, but it is one of the problems to be reckoned with.

A final barrier to communication that may be mentioned is that of selective inattention due to specialized interest. Veblen called our attention to the "trained incapacity" of the specialist, and in a humorous vein Ed Zern provided an example in his spoofing review of *Lady Chatterley's Lover* in the magazine for sportsmen, *Field and Stream*.

> This fictional account of the day-by-day life of an English gamekeeper is still of considerable interest to the out-door-minded readers, as it contains many passages on pheasant raising, the apprehending of poachers, ways to control vermin and other chores and duties of the professional gamekeeper. Unfortunately, one is obliged to wade through many pages of extraneous material in order to discover and

The following story, illustrating the difficulties of precise communication in daily life, is taken from the *Montreal Star*. It is entitled "Taken Literally." " 'Now,' said the village blacksmith to the apprentice, "I'll take this iron out of the fire, lay it on the anvil, and when I nod my head, you hit it.' The apprentice did so, and now he's the village blacksmith."

savor these sidelights on the management of a Midland shooting estate, and . . . this book cannot take the place of J. R. Miller's *Practical Gamekeeping*.[43]

E *"Self" as a Product of Communication and as a Means of Social Adjustment*

1   THE SOCIOLOGIST'S CONCEPTION OF "SELF"

We shall have to reserve to later chapters the discussion of the *causes* of this obstacle to communication. Just one special aspect of it needs to be considered at this point, however. Starting with William James, psychologists and sociologists have developed the realization that the individual's conception of himself is very much a function of what other people think of him. "Other people" means here not only those he communicates with directly or indirectly through face-to-face conversation, but also all those who communicate with the individual through letters, books, movies, etc. Charles H. Cooley expressed this idea of the self most explicitly in his concept of the "looking-glass self." This idea of self has three elements: (1) the imagination of our appearance to the other person; (2) the imagination of his judgment of the appearance; (3) our reaction to that imagined judgment, such as a feeling of pride or of mortification.

> As we see our face, figure, and dress in the glass, and are interested in them because they are ours, and pleased or otherwise with them according as they do or do not answer to what we should like them to be; so in imagination we perceive in another's mind some thought of our appearance, manners, aims, deeds, character, friends, and so on, and are variously affected by it. . . . The thing that moves us to pride or shame is not the mere mechanical reflections of ourselves, but an imputed sentiment, the imagined effect of this reflection upon another's mind. . . . We are ashamed to seem evasive in the presence of a straightforward man, cowardly in the presence of a brave one, gross in the eyes of a refined one, and so on. We always imagine and

[43] *Minneapolis Morning Tribune*, December 24, 1959, p. 4.

in imagining share the judgments of the other mind. A man will boast to one person of an action—say some sharp transaction in trade —which he would be ashamed to own to another.[44]

From this point of view, our "self" consists of an integration of the communications we get relating to ourselves as individuals. We select the communications toward which we decide to pay most attention, and occasionally one may decide to pay most attention to only a few other people's evaluation of him. But most people are more or less influenced by all those with whom they are in contact.

However, mental distortion comes in to affect this sense of self. The individual may not receive the communications in the same way that other people expect him to receive them. His own conception of himself begins to vary from other people's conception of him. This probably happens to most of us to a certain extent for short periods. For example, one person may strive to build up in others the opinion that she has attractive features: she powders heavily over her skin blemishes, she holds her mouth in a pert fashion, she never lets anyone see her without make-up and carefully combed hair, she is outspokenly pitying of others who are "not attractive," she exaggerates compliments about her appearance and ignores the absence of compliments. This is a harmless little pose which most people see through; they do not act toward her as though she were particularly attractive unless they are trying to "kid her along." But they are all aware that their conception of her physical appearance does not coincide with her own.

Our example has used physical appearance as the trait which is distorted in communication. The trait could just as well be a personality or character trait. Each of us probably has some trait which he values so highly that he thinks he has it to a greater extent than other people think he has it. It might be intelligence, honesty, generosity, affectionateness, sense of "good taste," or anything else. Sometimes the distortion reaches a point where the individual has no ability to judge what other people really think of him. One young man was pleased to think that he had good "business sense" and wanted everyone to believe it. Actually he had little business experience and what little he had did not turn out too successfully. He rationalized this by saying that uncontrollable circumstances never gave him a fair chance and that if he had done one little thing differently he would actually have been the great business success he thought he should be. It so happened that this young man inherited some money with which he felt he could successfully pretend that he had made a good deal of money in a business venture. He therefore invented a story of his

---

[44] *Human Nature and the Social Order* (New York: Scribner's, 1902; rev. ed., 1922), pp. 183–85.

In the same socio-physiological way that the human individual becomes conscious of himself he also becomes conscious of other individuals; and his consciousness both of himself and of other individuals is equally important for his own self-development and for the development of the organized society or social group to which he belongs.

The principle which I have suggested as basic to human social organization is that of communication involving participation in the other. This requires the appearance of the other in the self, the identification of the other with the self, the reaching of self-consciousness through the other. This participation is made possible through the type of communication which the human animal is able to carry out—a type of communication distinguished from that which takes place among other forms which have not this principle in their societies.

George H. Mead, in Charles W. Morris (ed.), *Mind, Self and Society* (Chicago: University of Chicago Press, 1934), p. 253.

business success which he repeated at every likely occasion. Some believed him and their communications of admiration and praise pleased him very much. Others seemed skeptical and a few even laughed at him because they felt his story did not jibe with other facts they knew, and he defended himself warmly against them. The admiration from some and the need to defend himself against others gradually led him to believe the story himself. He knew the "details" were made up, but he felt that the main part of the story was true, "because if only one thing had happened," which had not happened, the story would have been completely true.

This young man's whole life happened to be tied up with this story because he valued business success so highly, and because an independent income allowed him to spend a good deal of his time in telling his story and elaborating it to himself and to others. But probably each one of us has his little poses of this sort which are not so important to us. It is interesting that the Latin root word for "personality"[45] is *"persona,"* which means mask. Our personalities are, in one important sense, masks which we put on to communicate to other people what we think we are. Other people may either accept the mask, or see it in distorted form, or try to see beneath it, so that their evaluation of ourselves does not always agree with our own evaluation of ourselves. But these evaluations of other people are communicated back to us and normally bring our own conception of ourselves into adjustment with the conceptions of others.

This is "normally" true: A normal person's conception of himself is not too far out of line—out of "adjustment"—with that held by other people. But if the individual does not get the communications of other

[45] We shall consider "personality" more systematically in Chapter 4.

> We are more or less unconsciously seeing ourselves as others see us. We are unconsciously addressing ourselves as others address us; in the same way as the sparrow takes up the note of the canary we pick up the dialects about us. Of course, there must be these particular responses in our own mechanism. We are calling out in the other person something we are calling out in ourselves, so that unconsciously we take over these attitudes. We are unconsciously putting ourselves in the place of others and acting as others act. I want simply to isolate the general mechanism here, because it is of very fundamental importance in the development of what we call self-consciousness and the appearance of the self. We are, especially through the use of the vocal gestures, continually arousing in ourselves those responses which we call out in other persons, so that we are taking the attitudes of the other persons into our own conduct. The critical importance of language in the development of human experience lies in this fact that the stimulus is one that can react upon the speaking individual as it reacts upon the other.
>
> George H. Mead, in Charles W. Morris (ed.), *Mind, Self and Society* (Chicago: University of Chicago Press, 1934), p. 68.

people's conception of himself—because of a mental disorder, the causes of which are outside the scope of our present discussion—his own conception of himself will be out of adjustment with that of other persons. This is one of the most identifying characteristics of mental disorders—ranging from the case who has delusions of grandeur and thinks he is Napoleon, for example, to the case who imagines himself the chosen victim of terrifying and malevolent forces. The mentally disordered person not only behaves contrary to the expectations of others, but his very "self" is out of adjustment to others' conception of him. In both matters the individual is not communicating with his fellow men: his "human relations" are out of joint.

There are other types of situations in which the individual is perfectly capable of communicating adequately with his fellows, but nevertheless his conception of himself and others' conception of him do not jibe. In this situation a struggle between the individual and the group takes place. Ordinarily the group wins and the individual changes his conception of himself, for the simple reason that his "self" is a reflection of all his past and present communications. But occasionally an individual lives in one group physically but most of his important communications are with another group that has different standards of behavior. There are a relatively few individuals whose selves are determined largely by standards communicated by books written in New York, Paris, London, and Moscow, even though they live in Grand Forks, North Dakota. They might manage to get along all right if they do not neglect completely the communications coming to them from their local community, and adjust outwardly to these communications to a considerable extent. Then they might be regarded simply as slightly queer or unusual, at worst an independent "character."

A group seldom understands the behavior of another group—which we noted in discussing ethnocentrism—and much less does it understand the behavior of one of its own members who conforms to the standards of another group. If the individual does not adjust in some major way to group standards he will be an outcast, even though he understands perfectly what the group expects him to do. Depending on how he deviates from group standards, he may even be regarded as a criminal, for what is proper behavior in one group may be regarded as criminal behavior in another group. These are, then, the kinds of situations in which the individual regards himself as a good and normal man, while the group regards him as an eccentric, a "character," an undesirable or a criminal. There is no mental disorder here, nor any impossibility of effective communication, but simply a lack of desire for communication with, and adjustment to, one's immediate group—because one is communicating with and adjusting to a more distant group.

In this case there is no serenity for the non-conforming individual, even though he thinks he is doing what is right and may be able to persuade himself that he is suffering as a martyr. No one likes to be in the bad graces of his fellows. The communications that come to the non-conformist are derogatory to his self and are therefore not pleasant. They usually result ultimately in a decreased self-esteem, unless the individual has an unusually strong character.

An example, with a slightly humorous twist, can be taken from a college class experiment. The subject of the experiment was a student who was absent from class—because of a minor cold—the day the instructor planned the experiment. Under the instructor's guidance, all other members of the class were to comment unfavorably on the subject's physical appearance and health when he returned to class the next day. The subject's roommate, who was a member of the class, was to report the effects. The next morning the unsuspecting subject showed up bright and cheerful after his day's rest. The person in the adjoining seat started off by asking what was wrong with him, as he did not look good. Another nearby person observed that the subject looked rather pale. The instructor interrupted the class to ask the poor young man if there was anything wrong. After class the roommate solicitously offered the guess that the subject should probably have stayed in bed longer. The class was large, and every hour three or four classmates had occasion to remark sympathetically about the subject's poor appearance. By the end of the day the subject was back in bed, feeling poorly—as he told his roommate—in several vague places, and resolving to visit the clinic the next morning for a thorough physical

> If the given human individual is to develop a self in the fullest sense, it is
> not sufficient for him merely to take the attitudes of other human individuals
> toward himself and toward one another within the human social process, and
> to bring that social process as a whole into his individual experience merely
> in these terms; he must also, in the same way that he takes the attitudes of
> other individuals toward himself and toward one another, take their attitudes
> toward the various phases or aspects of the common social activity or set of
> social undertakings in which, as members of an organized society or social
> group, they are all engaged; and he must then, by generalizing these individual
> attitudes of that organized society or social group itself, as a whole, act to-
> ward different social projects which at any given time it is carrying out, or
> toward the various larger phases of the general social process which constitutes
> its life and of which these projects are specific manifestations.
>
> George H. Mead, in Charles W. Morris (ed.), *Mind, Self and Society* (Chicago: Uni-
> versity of Chicago Press, 1934), pp. 154-5.

checkup. This fellow's conception of even his physical self was a reflection
of the communications he had received from others. Much more determined by the views of others are those aspects of our behavior, character
traits, and personality which have much less of a physical basis.

A few non-literate societies form single closely knit groups. In fact,
some of them are organized on a two-family basis: every person in the
society is a member of one's own family or of the family of one's in-laws.
In such a society a normal individual gets a more or less unified picture
of himself from the communications of all the people who make up his
society. The expectations for each person's behavior are based on tradition, which is communicated to all members of the society. Thus all members of the society have more or less a common understanding about how
every person in the society should behave. This common understanding
they communicate to each individual involved, and so his looking-glass
self is practically a single reflection. This kind of society has the form of
what we shall call an "integrated group."

In our society, however, there are a multiplicity of groups, and any
one individual is likely to belong to several dozen at one time. He must
adjust to all of them: several distinct groups of friends, a church group,
an occupational group, probably two family groups, several recreational
groups, some special-interest groups, some groups that he keeps up with
only casually, several groups that communicate with him only through the
printed word, etc. Quite often he may be the only link among all these
groups, and certainly few people in our society have exactly the same set
of group contacts that another person has. The people who communicate
with any one person are *not* in communication with each other, and so

they cannot come to any common understanding regarding him and his behavior. Therefore the reflection of himself which each individual gets from his communications is different for each group of which he is a member. He is as many selves as there are groups to which he belongs, and he must make an integration of them himself.

2 THE FREEDOM OF THE INDIVIDUAL

Thus far we have given a rather static picture of the relation of the individual to society. We have exaggerated the facts and made it appear that an individual's behavior is a result of the group's expectations for him and that an individual's self ("personality") is a creation of others' conceptions of him. This is not quite a correct picture as it gives the individual no scope for initiative or intelligence, nor does it allow for social change. Much less does it take into account the biological and physical factors underlying human behavior.

These topics will be more fully dealt with in later parts of the book, but it is necessary to make a first qualification in this discussion of the plurality of groups. For it is the plurality of groups of which each individual is a member in our society which gives him a degree of freedom from social determination. Being "determined" by a large number of diverse groups, the individual is "determined" by no one of them. Each group expects different behavior of him, and if he is obliged to conform in one group—say his family—he is not obliged to conform in the same way in another group—his recreational associates. Also, the individual has a certain choice over the distribution of his time, and if the expectations of one group appeal to him more than do the expectations of another group, he can decide to spend more time in the former group. While he cannot completely escape the obligations to his family, he can spend more time with his recreational groups. Even if there is social group determination—which there is not in any complete sense—the individual's behavior and personality will change in accord with the shifting group affiliations. The process of growing up in a society is just such a process of expanding and changing group affiliations.

The plurality of groups works in still another way to create individual freedom from social bonds and social determination. The individual who belongs to several groups is confronted with several possible patterns of behavior. Especially as these are divergent from one another, he realizes the possibilities of still greater divergence. Such a realization obliges him to raise a question with himself as to which is the best way for him to behave and which self-reflection is most satisfactory. Every time he moves from one group to another and is forced to change his pattern of behavior accordingly, he is offered the opportunity to wonder and to think. Not infrequently the result of this wondering and thinking is a questioning as to whether *any* of the groups or behavior patterns he is associated with are the best ones. And so modern man, who lives in a plurality of groups, quite frequently becomes an idealist. He imagines a better society than now exists and sometimes gears some of his behavior to working toward that better society. Thus the modern individual reads romances and imagines himself a hero in them, thus he changes his vote perhaps as frequently as every election or two, thus he joins new groups and new movements, thus he keeps his mind open to new ideas. The individual is not one determined by a single organized group or a homogeneous culture. On the other hand, only the criminal and insane person is seriously out of adjustment to the society. The great majority conforms most of the time.

Not all groups are equally important in determining the individual's personality and behavior patterns. Some groups are made up of persons whom the individual knows intimately, with whom he comes in contact frequently, and toward whom he has strong attitudes of love, respect, fear, or hate. Other groups are made up of persons whom the individual knows but slightly, with whom he only occasionally comes in contact, and toward whom he holds no strong attitudes. The former are called primary groups; the latter are called secondary groups.[46] Primary groups are intimate groups, nearly always based on face-to-face relations. Secondary groups are characterized by impersonal and often casual social relationships. The individual's conception of himself and his major behavior patterns are determined to a much greater extent by his primary groups than by his secondary groups. The family is the most important of the primary groups for most individuals, and that is why the sociologists spend so much time on this group. However, as our society grows more diverse and more complicated, other groups increase their importance for the individual. He may come to evaluate very highly certain groups, regardless of whether they are his primary or his secondary groups, and to choose their standards and expectations for behavior as his own. Groups which are thus evaluated very highly and whose standards are followed in actual behavior are said to be the individual's "reference groups."[47]

The individual is only as free as his society is structured to allow him to be. If the society has many groups with which the individual may affiliate, he has greater freedom of choice than in a society with relatively few groups. On the other hand, if he is *expected* to affiliate with these many groups, his freedom is restricted. Secondary groups generally demand less of an individual than do primary groups, since they usually involve

[46] These are terms first systematically used by C. H. Cooley and Robert E. Park. See Chapter 14.

[47] Herbert Hyman, *The Psychology of Status*, Archives of Psychology No. 269 (New York: Columbia University, 1942).

only a segment of his time, interest, and personality. On the other hand, some modern societies have secondary groups which sometimes demand practically the whole life of its members—the State in the Soviet Union, or the competitive Business Enterprise on Madison Avenue or Main Street. In speaking of the freedom of the individual, we must ask "In terms of what values?" and the values are culturally specified in each different society. Thus, while society limits the freedom of the individual, there is no freedom for an individual outside of society (if there even be such).

Society should not be thought of as a mere agglomeration of groups. Just as individuals adjust their behavior and personalities to society, so do groups—which, after all, are made up of nothing but individuals—adjust to each other in such a way as to form an integrated society. Groups mesh in a society just as the numerous gears of a most complicated machine. The individual also integrates into his mind all the groups of which he is a member—they adjust to one another in each individual's mind. If his self (or social personality) is a reflection of each group with whom he associates, it is also true that the multiple selves—one for each group— are geared together in the individual's mind. It is thus that the individual has an integrated self, a self that is adjusted to society, and a society that integrates its component groups.[48]

F   *Social Isolation*

Since communication is so important, the question may be raised as to what happens when the individual is socially isolated. This question may be considered in two parts: (1) What are the consequences if a newborn infant is reared apart from other people; (2) what changes take place in a fully socialized adult when he is completely isolated from other people. Cases in which these things occur are very rare, and even when they occur they are seldom fully described and studied. So information for answering our questions is very meager and unsatisfactory.

There are no instances in which a newborn infant is known to have been separated from all human companionship immediately after birth. It is highly doubtful whether such an infant could live. Cases of extreme isolation that are known to have occurred are of two types: (1) Infants of a few months or years of age are lost or abandoned and are alleged to have been found and nourished by hermits or wild animals; when later found as older children or youths they are the so-called "feral men." (2) Children have been raised by their mothers in hidden rooms without contact with others until the police or other outsiders discover them. There

[48] These points are expanded in Chapter 4, Sections F and H.

have been no recently discovered cases of feral men and only about a dozen or so cases that seem to have been more than fictitious legend in past centuries,[49] although it is by no means certain that any human beings have been reared by animals. There definitely have been cases of children reared in near-isolation. One of the best described cases is that of Casper Hauser, a boy who appeared in Nürnberg, Germany, in 1828, bearing a letter saying that he had been born in 1812, left on the doorstep of a Hungarian peasant's hut, and reared by him in strict seclusion. When first found, he could barely walk, had no idea of visual distance, suffered pain from the light (but could see well at night). He burned his hand in the first flame that he saw, had no fear of being struck by a brandished sword, but the noise of a drum made him very apprehensive. He acted as though pictures, statues, and physical objects that chanced to be in motion were alive. He seemed to lack sexual urges. Like all children reared in isolation, Casper was described as stupid, but an autopsy (he died about five years after being found) revealed that his brain had no abnormalities, although it was small.

Other children alleged to have been raised by animals carried on animal habits long after they were discovered. For example, a boy said to have been found with bears in Lithuania in 1647 learned to talk a little but his voice was like a growl; he ate only what bears eat, and he had a habit of rolling up in secluded places and taking long naps. Descriptions of all these children would suggest they were feeble-minded, but it is of course not known whether they were born feeble-minded, or whether the absence of human contact prevented them from developing more than a small child's intelligence.

Children who were born deaf, dumb, and blind in the days before techniques were developed for communicating with them were quite like animals that were similarly afflicted. The famous Helen Keller was such a case until the age of seven when a teacher was brought to her.[50] After a dismally slow beginning, she was educated to be a brilliant, educated, and socially poised woman. A thirteen-year-old boy discovered by the police in Boston in 1949 had been kept in a secret room for over eleven years by his mother because he was illegitimate.[51] He had been boarded out with a family for thirteen months after he was born, but after that was kept in seclusion. He had learned to talk by listening through a keyhole to other

[49] Description of feral men is taken from Maurice H. Small, "On Some Psychical Relations of Society and Solitude," *Pedagogical Seminary*, 7 (No. 2, 1900), pp. 32–36. See also D. G. Mandelbaum, "Wolfchild Histories from India," *Journal of Social Psychology*, 17 (1943), pp. 25–44; J. A. L. Singh and K. M. Zingg, *Wolf-Children and Feral Men* (New York: Harper & Brothers, 1942).

[50] Helen Keller, *The Story of My Life* (New York: Doubleday, Page, 1917).

[51] *St. Louis Post-Dispatch*, March 15, 1949, p. 3A.

members of his family, and he had regular contact with his mother and occasional contact with an older brother. He did not know whether he was a boy or a girl, and it did not seem to make much difference to him when he was told. He took a "childish" delight in simple things like a cat. Another case is that of a six-year-old girl discovered in an atticlike room on the second floor of a farmhouse in Pennsylvania.[52] She also had been illegitimate and had been badly neglected. She could not talk, walk, feed, or clothe herself. The humane society placed her in a private home for retarded children where she received kindly care and attention. At the time of her death, at the age of ten and a half, she had learned to walk well, to feed herself, and to attend to her clothing and bodily care. But she was still backward, especially in speech. The general description of children found after being raised in isolation is one of mental retardation and inability to act in a manner expected of children of their age.

In describing the "Wolf Boy of Agra," found in India in the early 1950's, Ogburn[53] points out there is no real evidence that the child was actually raised by wolves, but merely that he had been reared in social isolation. In commenting on this and similar cases, the psychiatrist Bruno Bettleheim[54] concludes:

> Study of the so-called feral children, and comparison of them with known and well-observed autistic (that is, schizophrenic) children, suggests strongly that their behavior is due in large part, if not entirely, to extreme emotional isolation combined with experiences which they interpreted as threatening them with utter destruction. It seems to be the result of some persons'—usually their parents'—inhumanity, and not the result, as was assumed, of animals'—particularly, wolves'—humanity. To put it differently, feral children seem to be produced not when wolves behave like mothers but when mothers behave like non-humans. The conclusion tentatively forced on us is that, while there are no feral children, there are some very rare examples of feral mothers, of human beings who become feral to one of their children.

Sometimes, after patient psychotherapy, these schizophrenic—allegedly "feral"—children can be made normal again.[55]

Already socialized adults have sometimes been cut off from human

[52] Kingsley Davis, "Extreme Social Isolation of a Child," *American Journal of Sociology,* 45 (1940), pp. 554–64; "Final Note on a Case of Extreme Isolation," *American Journal of Sociology,* 50 (1947), pp. 432–37.

[53] William F. Ogburn, "The Wolf Boy of Agra," *American Journal of Sociology,* 64 (March, 1959), pp. 449–54.

[54] Bruno Bettleheim, "Feral Children and Autistic Children," *American Journal of Sociology,* 64 (March, 1959), pp. 455–67, at 467.

[55] Such an instance is reported by Mira Rothenberg, "The Rebirth of Jonny," *Harper's,* 220 (February, 1960), pp. 57–66.

contact for significant periods of time, either as a result of solitary confinement in prison or as a result of being lost in an isolated area (as during
a shipwreck). A military physician described cases of captured soldiers kept
in "solitary" by the Chinese and North Koreans during the Korean War
of 1951–53.[56] There is great variation in their ability to retain their sanity.
In all cases memory begins to fade, and they lose track of time; they become greatly interested in the trivial things around them but think less
and less of what is going on in the outside world. Ability to think logically
declines, and "social manners" disappear. A Canadian prisoner reported,
following his release, his feelings after 465 days in solitary confinement,
with only minimal contact with his captors:

> I felt frustrated, defeated and helpless, as though I were in a
> fight with my arms held, and I was not allowed to fight back while
> someone beat me to the ground. There seemed to be a continual
> feeling of oppression hanging over me, pressing down on my chest
> like a heavy weight. Try as I might, I could not push it off. It finally
> reached the point where I had to burst my bonds or suffocate.[57]

In this man's case it is not clear whether his mental state was due to his
captivity and oppression or to his isolation. A non-prisoner, W. H. Hudson, reported his own state of mind after spending the "greater part of one
winter" more or less isolated in Patagonia.[58] He would spend more and
more time doing nothing but "listen" to the silence. His feeling was one
of suspense and watchfulness, yet without apprehension. He did less and
less thinking, his mind became more of a blank, he acted without thinking,
yet he had a feeling of elation.

Isolation of this sort is to be sharply distinguished from *privacy*, which
is a brief absence from social contact, with ready access to it whenever
the individual wishes. Writers and scientists often report that they feel
that privacy is necessary for creative work.[59] They find their work easier
if they can be cut off from outside stimulations and distractions. All of
their thought can then be concentrated on the work at hand. But they
spend a part of each day in the company of others, and draw new ideas
from their own social experiences and from what they read. While other
people often think their habits of solitude queer, and call their absorp-

---

[56] Major G. B. Kirkland, RAMC, in the *London Daily Mail*, September 4, 1953, p. 4.
[57] *New York Times*, February 16, 1955, p. 8.
[58] W. H. Hudson, "The Plains of Patagonia," *Universal Review*, 7(1890), pp. 551–57;
quoted in Robert E. Park and Ernest W. Burgess, *Introduction to the Science of
Sociology* (Chicago: University of Chicago Press, 1924), pp. 245–47.
[59] See, for example, the revealing statement by J. B. Priestley in the *New York Times
Book Review* section, May 30, 1954, p. 5. Also see Paul Halmos, *Solitude and Privacy:
A Study of Social Isolation, Its Causes and Therapy* (London: Routledge and Kegan
Paul, 1952).

tion "absent-mindedness," they do not lose the minimum requirements of social adjustment so long as they have frequent and periodic access to social contact.

FOR ADDITIONAL READING

COOLEY, CHARLES H., *Human Nature and the Social Order* (New York: Scribner's, 1902; rev. ed., 1922). A classic sociological essay, based largely on observations of the social growth of the author's own children. Still invaluable for its analysis of the social nature of the "self" and of its development out of social relationships.

DEWEY, JOHN, *Human Nature and Conduct* (New York: Holt, 1922). One of the greatest of American philosophers and social scientists.

ROSE, ARNOLD M., *Human Behavior and Social Processes* (Minneapolis: University of Minnesota Press, 1954). A presentation of the systematic theory of symbolic interaction which underlies this book.

SHIBUTANI, TAMOTSU, Society and Personality (Englewood Cliffs, N.J.: Prentice-Hall, 1961). A textbook in social psychology using the symbolic-interactionist approach modified by psychoanalysis.

3 * Social Control

A central interest for sociologists in the study of human relations is to examine the ways in which people, as members of a society, influence one another. The collectivity of these ways is called "social control." We have already examined the basic process of social control when we considered how, through communication, people expect certain things of each other. Mutual expectation is the way in which people control each other's behavior in their day-to-day relationships. In this chapter we shall examine only the specific forms of social control which arise out of mutual expectation, reserving for later chapters institutional ways in which people's behavior is controlled (through government, for example). In this chapter we shall also examine the *degree* of control found in various areas of life and the *sanctions,* or means of enforcement, supporting the control.

A   Customs: Commonly Understood Values and Meanings

1   COMMONLY UNDERSTOOD VALUES

People everywhere are aware that most of their behavior patterns have come down to them from past generations. Probably every language in the world has a word meaning "customs" or "traditions." On the other hand, many people are not aware of the extent to which their social past influences the present. This is partly due to a popular but erroneous assumption—especially strong in our society—that the things which people have always done are rooted in man's biology and are therefore inevitable and "natural." By a study of behavior patterns in other societies, and by an examination of social change throughout history in our society, social scientists have become aware that much of what people think is rooted in biological instinct is simply rooted in custom. Custom may, of course, become so stable and so unquestioning that it seems as natural as instinct. Indeed, custom is truly as natural as instinct, if we but recognize that social facts, as well as biological facts, are part of nature.

Another reason why people are not aware of the great influence of tradition is that people like to feel free, to feel that they are thinking things out for themselves and making their own decisions. Actually people do think many things out for themselves to a considerable extent, but many of the decisions are still determined by custom because the social pressures or influences are so strong that they force the decision along certain lines. We know that in our daily lives we do not respond like automatons to social forces coming out of the past. Yet this obscures the fact that the expectations of other people encourage us to do our thinking in traditional terms. The very language in which we do our communicating and thinking is just one factor which forces us to follow tradition. Finally, it should be emphasized, we follow tradition often because no alternative is apparent to us.

Following the lead of William Graham Sumner,[1] sociologists have called the traditional ways of doing things in a society the "folkways." Sumner classified folkways into two types: (1) the *usages,* which were simply customary ways of behaving that had no great compelling force behind them; (2) the *mores,* which were usages that people had come to believe were essential to the welfare of the society. The mores had much more powerful sanctions behind them than did the usages, and allowed for much less deviation and individual choice. The mores are so powerful, said Sumner, that people cannot even discuss whether they are right or wrong. The mores are regarded as inevitably right and all the power in the society is set to back them up. Sumner developed these concepts out of a study of primitive societies, in which, it is generally believed, the mores have more applicability than in our own society.

In our society probably most of those values that Sumner considered to be mores are more properly called *pseudomores.* These are values which were formerly in the mores but at the present are considered to be in the mores by only a minority of the group. The prohibition against public discussion carries over, however, so that most people believe that almost everyone but themselves regard these values as mores. Some individuals, of course, actually do regard these values as mores, and they are usually the ones who punish violation or who most vociferously demand punishment. Since most people regard these values merely as usages, they will occasionally discuss the values with their close friends, and some even deviate from them in their behavior if they believe they will not be observed. This seems to be true of most taboos against the so-called sex

[1] *Folkways* (Boston: Ginn, 1906).

SOCIOLOGY MUST STUDY VALUES

Positive sociology has been accused of having a fetish for fact and a systematic indifference to the ideal. We can see now the injustice of such an accusation. The principal social phenomena, religion, morality, law, economics and aesthetics, are nothing more than systems of values and hence of ideals. Sociology moves from the beginning in the field of ideals—that is its starting-point and not the gradually attained end of its researches. The ideal is in fact its peculiar field of study. But (and here the qualification "positive" is perhaps justified if such an adjective were not otiose before the word "science") sociology cannot deal with the ideal except as a science. It does not set out to construct ideals, but on the contrary accepts them as given facts, as objects of study, and it tries to analyse and explain them. In the faculty of ideation (*faculté d'idéal*), sociology sees a natural faculty for which conditions and causes can be found for the purpose, if possible, of giving man a greater control of it. The aim is to bring the ideal, in its various forms, into the sphere of nature, with its distinctive attributes unimpaired. If to us, as sociologists, the task does not seem impossible, it is because society itself fulfils all the necessary conditions for presenting an account of these opposing characteristics. Society is also of nature and yet dominates it. Not only do all the forces of the universe converge in society, but they also form a new synthesis which surpasses in richness, complexity and power of action all that went to form it. In a word, society is nature arrived at a higher point in its development, concentrating all its energies to surpass, as it were, itself.

Émile Durkheim, *Sociology and Philosophy*, trans. D. F. Pocock and J. G. Peristiany (Glencoe, Ill.: Free Press, 1953), pp. 96–97.

The folkways: Ways of doing things were selected which were expedient . . . there was concurrence towards that which proved to be expedient . . . hence the ways turned into customs and became mass phenomena. . . . The mores are the folkways, including the philosophical and ethical generalizations as to societal welfare which are suggested by them, and inherent in them, as they grow.

William Graham Sumner, *Folkways* (Boston: Ginn, 1906), p. 2.

---

perversions[2] and the taboos against intimate equal-status relations between whites and Negroes in the Southern states. Because of the existence of pseudomores, there is such a thing as overconformity. There are people who demand of others that they do not drink, smoke, or dance, or engage

[2] Alfred C. Kinsey, W. B. Pomeroy, and C. E. Martin, *Sexual Behavior in the Human Male* (Philadelphia: W. B. Saunders, 1948).

in any secondary sexual behavior other than that which leads to marital sex relations.

Despite the occasional distinction between what people say and what they really believe, it is useful to think of customs in terms of the degree of deviation which people tolerate in them. Instead of grouping all folkways into two classes—the usages and the mores—it is more realistic to think of them as forming a sort of continuum, with complete freedom of individual choice at one extreme end and with no deviation ever tolerated at the other extreme end. To emphasize the fact that cultural elements pressuring individuals into conformity form a continuum, we shall call these cultural elements *common values* rather than folkways, since the latter term of Sumner has always implied strong pressure toward conformity. Figure 1 attempts this description, although even a casual examination of it reveals serious weaknesses in the scheme: (1) our society is not so well knit that what is permissible behavior in one group is also permissible to the same degree in another group; (2) some of the common values govern behavior only for certain roles and for certain situations, but not for other roles or situations; (3) people engage in many practices secretly which they would not dare to do openly (the pseudomores); (4) several sociologists and anthropologists find it necessary to distinguish between the *"ideal" values*—which people verbally express as their values —and the *"actual" values or norms*—which the observer finds are used in average, everyday behavior, and some people are more likely than others in the same society to act more in conformity with the ideals;[3] (5) some behavior may deviate from the norm in one direction and other behavior may deviate in an entirely different direction. On the other hand, the diagram is very useful, since it allows us to state the following observations and hypotheses:

1   There is only a gradual difference in degree, and not a sharp difference in kind, between behavior in which there is a large amount of permitted deviation and behavior in which there is only a small amount of permitted deviation.

2   As we move down the graph from A to F, social control not only becomes stronger but it utilizes different means to exert pressure (that is, different *sanctions*). Where a mere glance serves as a sanction around B, gossip is more frequently used around D, and physical violence or complete ostracism around F.

---

[3] A famous historical example is provided by the British General Napier, who—when he was ordered by his government to capture the city of Sind in the nineteenth-century British takeover of India—objected strongly on moral grounds but nevertheless believed he had to obey orders. He was successful militarily, but, in order to express his moral objections, he informed the British Foreign Office of his subjugation of Sind with a one-word telegram in Latin: *Peccavi* (I have sinned).

3   As we move down the graph from A to F, social control increases as
    pressure from the outside in two ways: (a) other individuals who ob-
    serve the deviant feel an increasing sense of concern or uneasiness and
    an increasing desire to push the deviant back toward the norm of ex-
    pected behavior; (b) more and more people get this feeling. When there
    is deviation from an F pattern of behavior—that is, a violation of the
    mores—practically everyone in the society becomes excited and emo-
    tional. In more homogeneous and smaller societies than our own people
    get the feeling of concern about the deviant at about the same time and
    in the same degree. But in our society people have different attitudes
    toward behavior deviation, and so it is not likely that they will feel the
    need to repress the deviant all at the same time or in the same degree.

4   As we move down the graph from A to F, social control increases within
    each individual in the society, since it is ultimately based on mutual
    expectations and the looking-glass self. When a member of the society
    deviates, therefore, he is likely to develop guilt feelings and a sense of
    estrangement from his fellows. These serve as internal pressures to push
    him back into line.

2   COMMON MEANINGS

When the values permit almost complete deviation and individual choice—
in the A sector of our diagram—this does not imply the absence of culture or of social expectations. For besides the values there are also what
we call *meanings* included among the common understandings.[4] These
are a different type of cultural element, and while they may be seen in a
relatively pure form—practically uncomplicated by the values—in the A
sector of the diagram, they must have something to do with all social behavior. The meanings simply define what things are, and if they are cultural meanings they of course define them in traditional or customary
ways. The object defined may be material or non-material, concrete or
abstract, "real" or "imagined." The meaning indicates how an individual
may act toward the object; that is, it usually indicates the "purpose" of the
object and how it will respond to action toward it.[5] For example, the meaning of "pillow" is a soft, elliptical, pad-like object for resting the head,

[4] It was apparently Thomas and Znaniecki who first introduced the distinction between values and meanings. (W. I. Thomas and F. Znaniecki, *The Polish Peasant in
Europe and America* [New York: Alfred A. Knopf, 1927], II, pp. 21–22). The func-
tionalists make a similar distinction in drawing a contrast between the "cultural" and
the "societal" (for example, Robert K. Merton, *Social Theory and Social Structure*, rev.
ed. [Glencoe, Ill.: Free Press, 1957], pp. 131–60). This is misleading, since the usual
meaning of "cultural" includes the social structure and its many meanings. We use the
word "society" to refer to people in interaction and "culture" to refer to the means
and products of their interactions.

[5] What we call a "meaning" is somewhat comparable to, although probably broader

The mores come down to us from the past. Each individual is born into them as he is born into the atmosphere, and he does not reflect on them, or criticise them any more than a baby analyzes the atmosphere before he begins to breathe it. Each one is subjected to the influence of the mores, and formed by them, before he is capable of reasoning about them. It may be objected that nowadays, at least, we criticise all traditions, and accept none just because they are handed down to us. If we take up cases of things which are still entirely or almost entirely in the mores, we shall see that this is not so.

William Graham Sumner, *Folkways* (Boston: Ginn, 1906), p. 78.

It is sometimes difficult to convey the notion that a meaning is an arbitrary social custom rather than something inherent in the nature of a physical object (it is even more difficult to convey the notion that this arbitrary social custom is subject to social change). This difficulty is the point of the following folk story: "Once, someone asked Motke Chabad, the wag, 'Tell me, Motke, you're a smart fellow—why do they call noodles "noodles"?'

"Motke answered without hesitation, 'What a question to ask! They're long like noodles, aren't they? They're soft like noodles, aren't they? And they taste like noodles, don't they? So why shouldn't they be called noodles?' "

Nathan Ausubel, *A Treasury of Jewish Folklore* (New York: Crown Publishers, 1948), p. 303.

but it does not coerce one into using it in the way indicated, as a cultural value would prescribe a pattern of behavior. A meaning is quite like a definition that can be looked up in a dictionary; it differs in some cases when the dictionary differs from common usage. The meanings and values may be considered to be scientifically useful *units* for sociology, just as dollars or francs are scientifically useful units for the economist.

Meanings change. With much greater rapidity than most of us are aware, words shift their referents, and new words and referents enter the language while old ones sometimes disappear. According to the lexicographers of the Oxford English Dictionary, the first recorded use of the verb *canvass* in the English language was in 1508. Shortly after its birth it had a meaning approximate to the sense in which we now use it: to solicit, as

than, what Thomas had in mind when he spoke of "definition of the situation" and enunciated his famous sociological principle, "If men define situations as real, they are real in their consequences." Thomas wrote about this first in his chapter "The Persistence of Primary-Group Norms in Present-Day Society." (Herbert S. Jennings *et al.*, *Suggestions of Modern Science Concerning Education* [New York: Macmillan, 1917], pp. 159–97). Thomas dealt with this concept more extensively in *The Child in America* (New York: Alfred A. Knopf, 1928), p. 572.

FIGURE 1 • AMOUNT OF INDIVIDUAL DEVIATION FROM EXPECTED
BEHAVIOR TOLERATED IN A GIVEN SOCIETY.

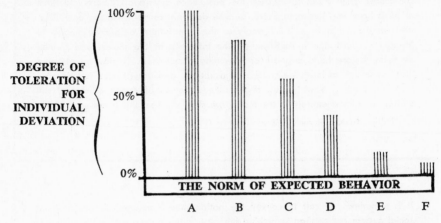

A is a pattern of behavior for which any degree of individual deviation is permitted,
and therefore it could not be said to be a folkway or tradition at all. This is the
sector in which the meanings alone are the cultural elements' guiding behavior.
For example, the expected action toward one's table is to place things on it, but
society does not prevent an individual from doing other physically possible things
with it.

B is a pattern of behavior in which a great deal of individual variation is permitted,
but there is a limit beyond which a "respectable" person should not properly go. B
is quite common in our loosely knit, individualistic, democratic society. An example
is keeping one's teeth clean so that one does not have bad breath.

C is a pattern of behavior in which a proper standard is quite clear but in which
individual deviation is nevertheless allowed. An example would be following table
manners or wearing neat, clean, customary clothing.

D is a pattern of behavior which allows for only a small amount of deviation, but
nevertheless enough deviation so that it is not unusual. An example would be getting
divorced.

E is a pattern of behavior which allows for only the smallest amount of deviation.
When deviations occur, they are likely to be punished, but not always and not
with the greatest severity. An example would be robbing another person. At E also
belong what we have called the pseudomores.

F is a pattern of behavior which conforms strictly to Sumner's concept of the mores.
No deviation is permitted in the sense that if it occurs people are shocked and
promptly punish the offender in an extreme fashion. The pattern is assumed to be
right, and no discussion as to its possible wrongness is permitted. An example is
following the incest taboo—that is, not having sex relations with a person of one's
immediate family.

support, votes, contributions, etc. But not many years later it could mean,
to toss in a canvas sheet, or to knock about, to beat or to batter. About
the same time it was used figuratively to mean, to buffet in writing or to
criticize destructively, and a little later, to bargain with. In the eighteenth
century it came to mean, to sue for a thing. In 1812 occurs the first recorded use of its contemporary sense, to solicit the support of a constituency, or to ascertain the number of one's supporters.

Slang changes even more rapidly than the "approved" language.

Whereas the approved "goodbye" has long been with us, the slang "so long" and "I'll be seeing you" is apparently only a generation old, and "goodbye now" grew up with the post-World War II generation. "Hi" as a corruption of "hello" seems actually to have been started by the small fry and has been rapidly spreading among their elders.

The introduction of new referents brought along their terms from alien cultures. "Paprika" came both materially and linguistically from the Hungarians, and "curry" from the East Indians. "Radio" and "X-rays" were popularized from the technological and scientific subculture, just as "getting hep" and "playing it cool" were popularized from the "jive" set. A considerable number of meanings are yet limited to regional, ethnic, class, and other subcultures, and are scarcely understood outside them, but may become so if those subcultures should become less segregated and isolated. The musical terms of Negro subculture, "jive talk," for example, are much better known today among American whites than they were before 1920 because of the greater welcoming of musical forms and themes developed by Negroes among the whites.

The distinction between cultural elements at the two ends of our continuum is a most important one, for a failure to recognize the distinction has led to many futile arguments. Many laymen and some social scientists have falsely assumed that all culture consists of the folkways, and is thus coercive in the sense of telling the individual that he should or must behave in certain ways. These people fail to recognize that much of culture consists of simple meanings, which merely tell individuals that they may act in such and such ways under given conditions or toward certain objects, so that the individual does not have to puzzle out his behavior for himself in that situation or toward that object by a trial-and-error process. Persons who fail to recognize this fact tend to assume that there is a large realm of *individual* behavior which is outside of, independent of, and, by implication, opposed to social influences (which they think of as entirely coercive).

The psychoanalysts, for example, have developed a theory that the natural relation between the individual and society is one of conflict, in which the society seeks constantly to coerce the individual, and the individual seeks to avoid that coercion and is discontented when he is forced to conform.[6] Many psychologists assume that there is a large realm of purely individual behavior, as distinct from social behavior—which is usually defined by them as behavior of individuals as a result of the immediate presence of other individuals. This leads them, for example, to consider intelligence as a fixed, biological tendency, uninfluenced by cultural or other social factors—defined, as the sociologist would define them, as any influences coming or having come from other people. Some political

[6] Sigmund Freud, *Civilization and Its Discontents* (New York: Cape and Smith, 1930).

> We must voice our grave skepticism toward the simple explanatory scheme concerning the role of valuations in social life typified by William Graham Sumner's concepts, "folkways" and "mores." Since his time these concepts— or one of their several synonyms—have been widely used by social scientists and have, in particular, determined the approach to the Negro problem. The formula will be found to be invoked with some regularity whenever an author expresses his attitude that changes will be slow, or, more particularly, that nothing practical can be done about a matter. It is closely related to a bias in social science against induced changes, and especially against all attempts to intervene in the social process by legislation. The concept of mores actually implies a whole social theory and an entire *laissez-faire* ("do-nothing") metaphysics, and is so utilized.
>
> Gunnar Myrdal, with the assistance of Richard Sterner and Arnold Rose, *An American Dilemma* (New York: Harper, 1944), p. 1031.

philosophers have accepted Rousseau's conception of "the noble savage" as a free individual, untrammeled by the narrowing influences of society, and have come to regard social influences as distorters of man's natural goodness. The ordinary person has taken over these misconceptions, and has a similarly narrow conception of "social" influences and mistakenly does not believe they influence him very much.

Actually there are very few observable human behaviors which are purely individual, and man in a "state of nature" is an animal, neither better nor worse. Where "individualism" is a mode of behavior or a philosophy of life, this is because the culture itself encourages deviation from an average of all people's behavior, and because the culture offers many diverse meanings so that the individual may deviate. "Individualism" cannot occur where society and the culture have little variation in behaviors to offer the individual—there would then be the most narrow conformity to what little the society does offer, or merely random, goalless activity. Some of the really primitive societies (by no means including all preliterate societies, some of which—like the African tribes—have a most complicated and diversified culture) offer such a narrow range of meanings to their members that much individualism is inconceivable.

An example of a most vigorous current controversy, which can be shown to have no point if the contestants recognized that much of culture consists of non-coercive meanings, is over whether Soviet communism offers the Russians more opportunities for individual self-expression than did the government of Tsar Nicholas II. The pro-Communists point to the fact that only about 20 per cent of the adult Russian population could read and write in 1917 when the Communists took over and that at least 80 per cent are literate today. They point to the tremendous increase in political participation, to the much greater number of people now able to enjoy—and even produce in an amateur way—music and art, even to the gradual distribution of modern conveniences to the masses. The anti-Communists, while often not considering the tsarist government a good one by any means, claim that things have gotten worse since the Communists took over. They point to the banning of numerous books, the restriction of writers and artists to an unvarying pedestrian style, to the harsher punishment of slighter deviations, to the complete absence of any political opposition. It should be quite clear that these two camps are talking about different orders of things. The pro-Communists are referring to the greater range of cultural phenomena available to the hitherto-submerged part of the population. The anti-Communists are referring to the forced movement of cultural elements from the permissive meanings end of the continuum to the obligatory end of the continuum.[7] Russia was not a liberal country before 1917, but it has become less liberal and more puritanical since then, even for the workers and peasants.

B   *The Relation of the Past to the Present*

1   PARENTS AND OLDER CHILDREN
AS TRANSMITTERS OF CULTURE

The passing down of customs is not a mechanical process. It is not simply because people have always done things in a certain way that they must continue to do them that way in the present or the future. The small child has to learn from his parents and other adults, and from older children, how he shall do all sorts of things. He is well-nigh helpless and has no fund of innate behavior patterns which allow him, at birth, to walk off, find his own food, provide his own shelter, etc. All the thousands of expected behavior patterns must be learned. The fact that all this learning takes place and the varying manner in which it occurs is called *socialization*. Since the child wants to learn how to be like an adult, at least usually and to a large extent, he deliberately tries to copy the older folks. Since the parents feel that the child must grow up properly and eventually be-

[7] The question may be raised as to whether the Russian people's own values have moved toward the obligatory end, or whether the government is trying to create new values at the obligatory end. This is an empirical question for which we do not have sufficient data to answer systematically. Newspaper accounts suggest that both are happening, and that the government is partially successful in making the Russian people more "puritanical." For example, an article in the *New York Times* (December 16, 1952, p. 31) reports that Soviet newspapers have been warning citizens that they ought to keep a closer watch on the spending habits of their relatives and tell the government if any start living beyond their means. *Pravda,* the leading Moscow newspaper, said: "It is the direct duty of close relatives to protect every member of the family from a serious sin against society." In the Soviet Union a certain number of people actually do inform on their close relatives when they believe they are engaged in graft or fraud against the government.

come independent of them, they deliberately teach him how to behave. Other adults play a similar role toward the child, although usually of lesser importance. Older children teach younger children how to behave, partly because they want to exploit the younger as aides or to join them as playmates, and partly because they feel the need to see everybody follow the proper social-behavior patterns. Also much, perhaps most, of learning is not deliberate. Elders act toward children in the only ways they know how, and this behavior serves to teach children how to act in socially acceptable ways. It is because of these relationships of children to their elders that customs can exist. People have a tendency to think of customs as having an existence in themselves, but actually we should think of them as behavior patterns which children learn from their parents and other older (i.e., more socialized) folk.

This implies two things. One is that children in the early years of life do not follow any of the usages or mores, and make no distinction between them. The other is that they feel no emotion or guilt about violating the mores, and they do not feel the need to repress others who violate the mores. Young children do not mind running around naked; they think nothing of hitting each other casually on the head with a hammer. They make sexual advances toward their mother, and they make little distinction between males and females as sexual objects. Through the process of learning social customs, which we call socialization, it is deeply impressed on them that such behavior is strictly taboo (that is, against the mores). They also learn such things as table manners and how to dress properly, but here the demands are not so stringent (that is, these are only usages, and in the C or D portion of our diagram). After the age at which they can be expected to have learned these things, they are also expected to know that violations of usages may be regarded simply as childish behavior, but that violations of the mores are inherently evil and dangerous. More studies have to be made of the transformation of the amoral infant into a moral youth and of the psychological effects of the transformation of the child and of observing the infant's amorality on the adult.

The conditions under which children learn the customs of their society have a good deal to do with how those customs will be acted out when the children become adults. According to studies made by anthropologists and psychiatrists, if rigid demands are made on the child at a fairly early age and if a good deal of punishment accompanies the learning process, when that child becomes an adult he is likely to be very compulsive about the customs. That is, he will be exceptionally intolerant of violations of customs and will feel exceptionally guilty when he has any tendency to violate them. Some students of Japanese culture[8] say that this is typical

[8] See, for example, Ruth Benedict, *The Chrysanthemum and the Sword* (Boston: Houghton Mifflin, 1946).

in Japan, and accounts for the extreme devotion to duty and the readiness to commit suicide when duty cannot be performed. In our society we occasionally come across the more compulsive type of person, who cannot stand any violation of customary behavior. If anyone spits on the street, it fills him with disgust. If someone is not clothed properly, he expresses a strong sense of shame. At one time during the career of President Truman there was a good deal of newspaper and street-corner discussion about whether it was wrong or of no consequence that he referred to a well-known radio commentator as an S.O.B. for attacking one of his appointments. All sorts of opinions came out: some said that Truman was immoral or too undignified for his office; others treated it as a joke; still others said that the matter was too inconsequential to debate. We would hypothesize that those who were most vocally critical of the president because of this incident were not simply the Republicans as a political group opposed to the president, but rather people who were taught their customs rigorously and early, and who did not have their childhood training rubbed away by contact with variant patterns of behavior.

Certain customs are taught to children by older children, seldom by parents or other adults. This is obvious in the case of certain children's games, sayings, and rhymes but it is also true of certain attitudes. Loyalty to one's group, while highly valued by adults, is seldom taught by them to children because it often conflicts with obedience to parents. Children teach other children loyalty to one's group of equals, frequently—in our society—when it conflicts with demands of parents or even demands created by other customs. The transmission of values and behavior patterns from older child to younger child is one of the ways in which family patterns change. Most of the studies of immigrants from Europe to the United States show that young children learn American ways of doing things more rapidly than do their parents.[9] They pick them up from other children, at school or in play groups. This learning process often creates conflicts between parents and children, partly because the parents frown upon certain American customs and partly because both parents and children see the latter getting ahead of the former. But despite this opposition, the rapid Americanization process goes on, and the third generation learns relatively few of the customs of its immigrant grandparents.

Social change can come to the society as a whole through the transmission of values and behavior patterns from older child to younger child rather than from parents to children. Much of the greater flexibility with respect to sex behavior and swear words, to take one example, has come about through transmission of new attitudes through several generations

[9] See, for example, Robert E. Park and Herbert A. Miller, *Old World Traits Transplanted* (New York: Harper, 1925); W. I. Thomas and F. Znaniecki, *The Polish Peasant in Europe and America* (Chicago: University of Chicago Press, 1918), 5 vols.

of adolescents. Many public-opinion polls have shown that younger adults and adolescents have certain more "liberal" attitudes regarding public issues than do the older generations. What is "liberal," of course, is always decided by each generation anew, somewhat regardless of what was thought liberal in past generations or of what various social scientists might consider to be liberal. But there is no doubt that attitudes toward these public issues—like social-security legislation, public housing, trade-union organization—change from generation to generation. Some of these attitudes are part of "college culture" rather than of American culture as a whole. They are passed down by older students to younger ones during the process of living, studying, and playing together.[10]

While the process of transferring culture from one generation to the next opens these possibilities for cultural change, it should not be thought that children are naturally radical and that age inevitably brings conservatism. That this frequently happens in contemporary society is in itself a peculiar characteristic of our culture. As far as young children are concerned—say those between the ages of two and ten, the evidence suggests that they tend to be strongly conservative. Students of Western culture, for which we have a long historical record, are frequently startled by the fact that children's games and the mottoes accompanying games are practically unchanged over two thousand years.[11] One factor in this conservatism is that the child learns a custom without qualification and he has little opportunity to observe deviation from it; thus he comes to consider it as natural and invariable. Another factor is that children are not sufficiently developed mentally and socially to organize social change deliberately. Their little rebellions develop no positive new direction, and so they almost invariably end up on the same path from which they deviated. Still another factor seems to operate around the ages of two to four, when a child seems to manifest a compulsive desire for uniformity and repetition; this is a factor as yet little understood even though very adequately described.[12]

2   OTHER TRANSMITTERS OF CULTURE

In addition to parents and older children, the functionaries of certain institutions serve as transmitters of culture to the young. Most important of these is the schoolteacher, whose function it is to transmit basic general skills, specific vocational skills, or the broader aspects of culture.[13] The basic general skills are those which all citizens are expected to be able to

[10] Theodore M. Newcomb, *Personality and Social Change* (New York: Dryden, 1943).
[11] Unpublished paper by Ronald Johnson, University of Minnesota.
[12] Arnold Gesell *et al., The First Five Years* (New York: Harper & Brothers, 1940).
[13] See Chapter 7, Section E.

manipulate: reading, writing, proper speaking, arithmetic, elementary repairing and woodworking or elementary sewing and cooking, participation in games. The specific vocational skills are those taught in the technical schools and colleges that prepare students for their life vocation. The broader aspects of culture include literature, the arts and music, history and government, the sciences, the social studies, especially sociology, psychology, and economics. The teacher thus seeks to transmit an enormous range of our culture, usually a considerable part of that which is organized into formal knowledge. In addition to this, the teacher—consciously or unconsciously—instills character traits and attitudes into students, since the manipulation of skills and the understanding of the broader aspects of culture carry along with them certain expected character traits and attitudes. For example, when studying history, every student learns certain standards for what is good or bad in history, as well as the facts of history themselves. Studies have been made which also show that certain interests and personality traits are associated with certain occupations and not with others, even among the liberal professions.[14]

Functionaries of other institutions play other roles in transmitting the past culture to the newer generations. We need not go into the details of what is taught by the minister, rabbi, or priest, by the policeman, the social worker, the doctor, the scoutmaster, the storekeeper, or the host of others who regularly come in contact with children and youth. Each has a role in the socializing process. These "secondary" socializers—to distinguish them from parents and older playmates—transmit culture in a manner which is at once more partial and more rational. Each is concerned with only a small part of the individual's behavior, not with his total personality. Each impresses on the child only a narrow section of the culture which his society has built up in the past. Their relations with him are neither so intimate nor of such long duration that he loses awareness of their specific influences. He is thus in a better position to consider the influences one at a time and to decide with some measure of rationality how and in what measure he will incorporate them into his life. The culture of the past is not then forcefully imposed, but is voluntarily accepted. Of course certain rewards accompany acceptance, and certain punishments attend non-acceptance, but the individual has the feeling that he is making a choice and to a certain extent he does make a choice where the culture permits variations. We thus maintain a sense of individual freedom while society controls us through the inculcation of its culture.

We may now turn to a consideration of the system of rewards and punishments which society uses to help us make up our minds that we

[14] See, for example, the studies made in connection with the development of the Strong Interest Test and its modifications.

will follow the culture. Radcliffe-Brown refers to these as social sanctions, and classifies them into positive and negative sanctions, and diffuse and organized sanctions.

> All social usages have behind them the authority of the society, but among them some are sanctioned and others are not. A sanction is a reaction on the part of a society or of a considerable number of its members to a mode of behavior which is thereby approved (positive sanctions) or disapproved (negative sanctions). Sanctions may further be distinguished according to whether they are diffuse or organized; the former are spontaneous expressions of approval or disapproval by members of the community acting as individuals, while the latter are social actions carried out according to some traditional and recognized procedure.[15]

c   *The Rewards for Obedience*

We have already observed that the strongest sanction to conformity is manifested through the constant expectations that meet us on all sides. Practically every contact each of us has with every other human being involves a whole set of mutual expectations. Constant exposure to expectations—which are more or less consistent because of a common past and a common language—operates as a powerful force on us. But the force is not only on us; it is also on each of the others. This provides the first of the "rewards" that we have to consider: if we conform to the expectations of others, they will probably conform to our expectations. If we do not conform to others, they will shortly cease to conform to our expectations and then we are in trouble.[16] Conformity to the expectations of our associates brings their approval, their continuing companionship, their help when it is desired, and so on. And we give the same to those who generally conform to our expectations. Social control is a two-way process, in which we influence others as they influence us.

Part of every culture is a set of values which specify what is "the good life." These are somewhat differentiated, depending on age and sex, as well as the social class and social group to which one belongs, but they nevertheless take a fairly consistent form throughout the society. The values of our society specify that a child shall attend school, help with certain chores around the house, participate in games and follow their rules "like a good sport," and so on. If he conforms, he usually receives the respect of his fellows and approbation of his parents. Similarly an adult male is expected to hold a steady job, manifest affection toward his

[15] A. R. Radcliffe-Brown, "Social Sanction," *Encyclopedia of the Social Sciences* (New York: Macmillan, 1933), Vol. XIII, pp. 531–34.

[16] See Chapter 2, Section B.

wife and children, entertain his friends, and so on. Values specifying the
good life for an adult woman are not so clear or consistent with respect to
getting a job or maintaining a home, and they change more drastically as
her children reach various stages of independence. This flexibility in the
values for women creates a special problem to which we shall have to turn
our attention later.[17] But conformity to those values which are generally
specified gain for the adult woman and man the respect and approbation
of their associates also.

At least two major qualifications must be recognized: (1) Going
outside the general values to secure special ones which only a few can
achieve will sometimes provide greater rewards than those given for mere
conformity to the general values. (2) When external circumstances forcibly
prevent conformity, there need be no lessening of the usual reward of
respect and approbation. An example of the first situation is that of the
life of a writer or scientist who does not follow the nine-to-five working
routine of other white-collar workers and whose leisure-time pursuits are
also different. Yet the life of a writer or scientist is so much in accord
with certain special values of our culture that he is permitted to deviate
to some extent from certain general values (even though he may be regarded as queer or a little immoral at the same time). An example of the
second situation occurs when a catastrophe prevents one from pursuing the
usual daily routine expected in the culture but one deviates by helping
people who are in trouble. Under these circumstances the deviator gains
more approbation through deviation than he could through conformity
to the usual everyday rules.

Reward is involved in many social sanctions; in fact, all social sanctions are based on either reward or punishment. Most psychologists now
hold that all learning requires reward or punishment to fix (or "reinforce")
a behavior into a habit or to maintain a habit once formed. It needs to be
pointed out, however, that the culture determines, in large part, what are
considered to be rewards, so that the social factor operates along with the
psychological factor in the learning and continuation of culture. For example, a blow on the shoulder with the flat of a sword may hurt, but it
will still be regarded as a great reward if done by a king in a ceremony
of creating knights.

It would be pointless to enumerate the many kinds of rewards which
society offers the conforming individual. Instead, we shall content ourselves with a few general observations about the character of these rewards: (1) They are very numerous, and range from very formal rewards
presented in a ceremonial manner to very informal rewards which are
almost imperceptible except to a well-trained social scientist (and perhaps

[17] See also Arnold M. Rose, "The Adequacy of Women's Expectations for Adult Roles,"
Social Forces, 30 (October, 1951), pp. 69–77.

to those who do not receive them—if such persons are capable of observing, abstracting, and articulating the subtle social influences in their own milieu). (2) Social rewards differ in content, form, and number from one culture or subculture to the next. (3) Social rewards may not be distributed or received by all individuals in the society to the same extent or in the same manner. In fact, nearly every society has certain specialists in the distribution of the more formal rewards (such persons are said to have power, and are sometimes given special attention by political scientists). Also, some individuals are more responsive than others to social rewards (which furnishes a problem for the psychologist). But in every society, every individual—if he is to be called "socialized"—must participate to some degree in the distribution, and especially in the reception, of social rewards. (4) Rewards are much more frequent and more effective in creating conformity than most of us are aware of. In fact, the researches of the "learning theory" psychologists lead us to believe that no society could maintain itself (because individuals would not learn sufficiently to be socialized) unless there is an extensive system of rewards for conformity. Punishments are more obvious, but it is likely that rewards are more numerous, more pervasive, and in the long run more effective.

D   *The Punishments for Disobedience*

Punishments, like rewards, range from the very formal to the very informal, and it is likely that for punishments, too, the informal ones are more numerous, more frequently applied in any given society, and perhaps are more effective ultimately than the formal ones. It is very difficult to prove such a hypothesis because informal sanctions, either of reward or of punishment, are quite difficult to observe and to count. The function of social punishments, of course, is to prevent the individual from deviating from expected patterns of behavior more than the culture tolerates. Since different members of the society usually have somewhat different conceptions of how much deviation is permissible, and since each individual has a different circle of acquaintances and friends from any other individual, punishments are applied somewhat differentially for different individuals deviating in the same manner and for different deviations on the part of the same individual.

The informal punishments for non-conformity, at least in our culture, are the cold stare, the "raising of eyebrows," the deprivation of association, the refusal to grant favors and privileges and kindnesses which can otherwise be generally expected. The formal punishments usually include those inflicted by the formal punishing agents of the society (including formal warning, fine, imprisonment, exile, forced labor, torture—in some societies—and capital punishment) or by self-appointed punishing agents who have been variously called vigilantes, minute men, or mobsters (depending on the point of view of those who name them). Somewhere between the formal, conscious punishments and the informal, unconscious ones are those which are conscious but are not planned or structured in advance, such as gossip, informal but deliberate ostracism, verbal advice, and so on. It may be hypothesized that the punishments for non-conformity are the more conscious and the more formal when the deviation is greater and the society or group more used to deviation (that is, more cosmopolitan). Of course, some of our contemporary subcultures or groups are so impersonal or disorganized that they rely almost exclusively on the formal sanctions to provide punishment for non-conformity because the members of the society are not enough aware of each other's behavior or do not know each other well enough to employ the informal sanctions of punishment. Since the formal punishments are administered by specialized agencies of society, and then only on a limited number and on specified kinds of occasions, it seems obvious that punishments are less frequent and less pervasive than are rewards, which must be administered and received by every socialized person in the society fairly frequently for the society to continue to function.

Punishments, like rewards, are distributed according to the specific circumstances of the deviation which evokes the punishment, the status and power of the deviator, the seriousness of the deviation according to the values of the society. Further, punishments and rewards are distributed for reasons other than to promote conformity to the expected behavior or standards of the society. Punishment may be meted out to the weak simply because they are weak and cannot strike back, and rewards are given to the strong and powerful in order to gain favors from them. Certain individuals—who can sometimes make up a whole group or society—may have a psychological urge to administer punishments to other people regardless of who these other people are (except that they should be weak so they cannot strike back) or what degree of conformity they maintain.

Psychiatrists tell us that such "free-floating aggression" exists, and psychologists have demonstrated that an individual who is frustrated in some activity has an impulse to be aggressive. If he cannot, for some reason, be aggressive toward the frustrating force, he will be aggressive toward any convenient substitute object or person.[18] Further, psychiatrists inform us that there is a certain personality type—the "sadist"—who has a more or less incessant desire to inflict punishment on others, regardless of the behavior of others and even regardless of the specific frustrations of his daily life. On the other hand, there are certain ideologies—or philosophies of life—favoring non-punishment under any circumstances.

[18] John Dollard, Leonard Doob *et al.*, *Frustration and Aggression* (New Haven: Yale University Press, 1939).

Many of the religious philosophies, for example, favor the exaction of conformity through reward ("love") and try to discourage the employment of punishments, especially of the more violent type. Finally, there are personality types, and whole groups or societies composed of these types, that seem to have a distaste for the employment of punishment. Considering all these factors, it is obvious that reward and punishment, especially the latter, do not always serve as teaching devices for socialization. Yet a society must use a considerable number of rewards, and at least a few punishments (if only of an informal or mild type), to socialize its members and to keep them from deviating too far from expectation based on conformity to standards.

E   *The Positive Formal Social Controls*

Most of the sociological researches conducted on concrete aspects of social control have been directed to one or another type of punishment and have almost completely neglected the study of social rewards.[19] This is unfortunate, as we have given some reason to believe that the positive social sanctions are more powerful and more pervasive than the negative ones. But we shall have to present what material is available, and simply point to the serious gaps in our information. The following discussion is organized in terms of the degree of formality of the sanction, rather than in terms of its positive or negative ("reward or punishment") character. We take up first the formal social sanctions, of which the sanctions of the law are by far the most studied.

Before passing to these negative sanctions, let us merely mention the formal positive sanctions that remain to be investigated, from the standpoint of social psychology as well as sociology. A high income, legitimately secured and publicly approved, is one of the most important rewards in Western culture. Not only does such an income bring many material comforts but it is one of society's most powerful ways of expressing approval for skillful or unusual service or for generally desired investment of funds. In speaking of approval here, we are not referring to the expressed ideology of the members of the society but to their effective demand. Monetary rewards, of course, are not solely a result of effective public demand for certain services but are also a function of the existing distribution of wealth, the relative supplies available of these services and of competing ones, and the freedom of the public to distribute its wealth as

[19] A noteworthy exception, who influenced several later sociologists, and whose classification is adopted with some modifications in this book is Paul Fauconnet (*La ré-sponsibilité, étude de sociologie*, Paris, 1920, p. 12). Fauconnet recognized both "retributive" and "restitutive" sanctions and within the former class "organized" and "diffuse" sanctions (the latter including public opinion).

it wishes. Thus monetary rewards are not to be considered simply and directly as social sanctions. The achievement of powerful positions or offices in a society has much the same character as that we have described for the acquiring of money.

The public presentation of rewards other than money and power (including token monetary rewards) also needs to be studied for its influence as a social control. That this influence is a powerful one is suggested by the fact that authors of autobiographies not infrequently mention the great effect the witnessing of such an event had on them. The presentation of medals, trophies, scholarships, high-prestige offices (especially honorary ones), and so on, is frequently done in some sort of ceremonial fashion. The function of the ceremonial is ostensibly to express the gratitude or good wishes of a large number of people toward the recipient, since the reward itself often has little material value, but the ceremonial also serves—more importantly—as a means of reminding the public that conduct highly in accord with the values of the society brings rewards. The ceremonial affects not only those who are physically present at it, of course, but all those who hear or read about it.

The according of highly prestigious rewards may not be done in a ceremonial fashion, or only partially in such a manner. Praise, or simply mention without value terms, in the newspaper, or over the radio, frequently reflects public sentiment. Public sentiment, favorable or unfavorable, may be expressed in innumerable indirect ways (one could almost "feel" the public emotion in the streets when Lindbergh first flew the Atlantic in 1927), but here we are edging over in the semi-informal social sanctions. Before turning to these it is necessary to consider the negative formal sanctions.

F   *The Law and the Penal Sanctions*

Law consists of formally specified rules governing behavior, formulated by those authorities having political power in the state and ultimately enforced by them (although intermediary enforcement is usually determined by judges, who, when a specific case in controversy over which their court has jurisdiction, is brought before them, decide what law applies and therefore what is to be enforced against whom). Law is usually classified according to the type of behavior controlled: for our purposes only criminal law and civil law are important because they are the only types that directly affect all individuals at all times. Criminal law governs the behavior of individuals in so far as that behavior is believed to affect directly the welfare of the whole society. Civil law governs the behavior of individuals in their direct relations with each other, where society is not formally affected except in so far as the fulfillment of an agreement between any two (or more) private persons is believed to be necessary for the maintenance of good order and good relations between any other two private persons.

In societies that possess the written form of their language, practically all law is in writing. Laws are of several types according to their source: (1) constitutions approved by the people or by conventions elected by the people, (2) statutes passed by legislatures, (3) court decisions, (4) rules or resolutions passed by administrative bodies under a general statute, (5) executive orders. All these are written in various forms. Even where one person has the political power to declare laws by himself, the fiction is maintained that his command is not legal until it is set forth in writing and signed by him. This illustrates the impersonal character of law, which has the function of making law a real or pretended expression of the society as a whole. In societies that do not possess writing, often certain individuals (usually those who act as judges, who may be the same persons as the statute writers) are charged with memorizing the law and with transmitting it to other persons so that it will not be lost when they die. To facilitate the memorizing of law, some preliterate societies put it in the form of poems, stories, or proverbs. In some preliterate societies a decision to punish a criminal may be reached through a process akin to public opinion formation,[20] which also designates the individual who is to carry out the punishment in the name of the whole society. In general, the process of formal punishment in preliterate societies is much less systematic and regularized than in our own society.[21]

In the United Kingdom and the United States, a distinction is made between statutory law (written by legislators) and common law (written by numberless generations of judges in deciding cases where there was no specific statute). In all literate countries, general statutes have to be interpreted by judges in specific cases, and these interpretations serve as "precedents" to aid judges in deciding future cases. Since practically all new court cases involve slightly different circumstances from previous cases, especially those in civil law where the commencement of a suit is more voluntary than in criminal cases, new precedents are constantly being made. Significantly new precedents are more likely to be made by the "higher" or appellate courts, rather than the "lower" or trial courts, since the latter's decisions can always be overruled by the former. Suggested new precedents can be offered in the decisions of the trial courts, but unless the appellate courts accept them, they do not stand. On the other hand, the appellate court can overturn a precedent and make it stand. Thus the highest appellate court in the United States, the Supreme

[20] See Chapter 9, Section D.

[21] E. Adamson Hoebel, *The Law of Primitive Man* (Cambridge: Harvard University Press, 1954).

Court, becomes an important instrument of social change, and a regular creator of new law.

Law was originally and basically the formal expression of the folkways. However, as some heterogeneous societies developed which had little unified agreement on the folkways, and as political authorities developed which had no intimate relation with the society as a whole, laws were formulated that had little relation to the folkways and mores. Most laws formulated today, either by legislators, judges or administrators, have little to do with the folkways, but the basic body of criminal law, and much of civil law, is still generally in harmony with the folkways. There are some major types of exceptions to this general observation:

1   The folkways change while some laws remain stationary. The deliberate murder of a person suffering from an incurable and painful ailment ("mercy killing") is now fairly generally sanctioned by the folkways, but not by the law, which still reflects the older folkways that the taking of life in any form is just as great a religious sin as any form of murder for selfish reasons. In this case the violation of the older folkways has acquired a new moral sanction as reflected in the term "mercy killing." Many of the pseudomores are in the laws, since they were once in the mores themselves, but have lost their emotional and moral support and are given only public lip service. Sometimes the value behind the law disappears completely, and the law is no longer used even though it remains on the books. In 1952 it was discovered that a 1787 law—giving New York sheriffs the power to call out the militia—was still in the statute books, even though no sheriff knew that anyone but the governor could exercise this power.[22] In 1953 the United States Supreme Court for the first time applied a principle of old English common law that a convicted offender could not be sentenced for a second time when his first trial had been nullified on technical grounds—that is, his second sentence would have to be regarded as his first one and must therefore be shorter. This principle had not been used for hundreds of years.[23] A different example of the lack of close association between law and folkways, in which the folkways are stronger than the law, relates to child beating.[24] The law reflects the folkway of past centuries, when it was believed that parents had absolute rights over their children, and provides for low penalties for this crime. In recent years children have become evaluated more highly and most people think they have rights independent of their parents. Under these circumstances it seems likely

[22] *New York Times,* December 10, 1952, p. 33.

[23] *New York Times,* May 20, 1955, p. 27.

[24] Arnold M. Rose and Arthur E. Prell, "Does the Punishment Fit the Crime: A Study in Social Valuation," *American Journal of Sociology,* 61 (November, 1955), pp. 247–59.

that some well-publicized cases of brutal child beating will promote
a movement to raise the legal penalties for this crime.

2 The laws express public policy as well as folkways, and while the
behavior demanded by such laws may eventually enter into the folkways, in the meantime there may even be an indefinitely long period in
which there is a conflict between law and mores. An example of the
latter is bringing valuable goods into the country for one's own use
without paying tariff duty on them (technically a kind of smuggling).
Government policy is to erect a trade barrier and to prohibit the
importation of certain foreign goods altogether or charge a high duty
for their importation; this conflicts with an older folkway that a person
should have the right to move his personal property at will. There is
probably more conformity to the law against smuggling by individual
citizens than there used to be, but still no strong stigma is attached
to a person caught smuggling goods into the United States for his own
personal use. The enforced payment of direct taxes on income would
have been considered somewhat immoral a hundred years ago, and
was prohibited originally by the American Constitution. But in 1913
an amendment to the Constitution was passed, and there was gradually
increasing public support for this form of taxation. Today nearly
everyone in the United States thinks this is a good ("moral") form
of taxation, and, even though most people complain about the high
rates and many cheat on their payments, the revelation of such cheating
now carries a mild stigma—which suggests that paying income taxes
is now part of our folkways. This development has not occurred yet
in such countries as France and Italy, where the collection of income
taxes is very difficult and most people do not feel hampered by possible
publicity when they try to get away with non-payment.

3 The mores are theoretically so powerful that they cannot be discussed.
Hence it is often difficult to get a lawmaking body, especially when
it is culturally homogeneous and unsophisticated, to discuss the passage
of a law governing a behavior that is fairly strongly in the mores. An
approximate example is the nervous unwillingness of several state
legislatures to accept expert advice in the formulation of laws concerning sex crimes against children. Similarly it is difficult to get
such a law written down, except by the use of circumlocutory or non-
popular language. Of course there is considered to be little need for
such a law, as few would think of challenging the mores, and the community itself punishes the rare violator of the mores when the law does
not. For these reasons some of the strongest mores of a society are
never written into law. This does not mean that the violation of such
mores would necessarily go unpunished by law-enforcement officials,
but they would have to find some law originally intended for another

purpose under which they could arrest and punish a violator of the mores. An example would be a case where a person who deliberately desecrates a sacred object or interrupts a church service is arrested and punished for disturbing the peace (if he is fortunate enough to be apprehended by the police before a mob of the faithful administers punishment on its own).

4   The amount of deviation tolerated in the folkways varies from one generation to the next, while the laws tend to be more stable (although not all laws governing criminal behavior are more stable than their corresponding folkways). The folkways may strongly prohibit a type of behavior (that is, the prohibitions have become mores), but the laws remain from an earlier period and punish the deviation only slightly. The law and mores prohibiting incest seem to provide an example.

5   The laws contain meanings as well as values, and meanings may vary even where values do not. For example, every state in the United States has a law prohibiting incest, and there is a strong negative value for incest throughout the country. Yet the law *defines* incest differently in the different states, so that one may readily marry one's first cousin in some states but be subjected to penal sanctions and public disapproval if one does the same thing in other states.

While the above five major types of exceptions exist, in general there is a fairly obvious relationship between the laws and mores of a society. In general, the relationship would probably be strongest in a preliterate society (ignoring the third type of exception mentioned above) and least strong in an unpopular dictatorship or in a highly heterogeneous society. The relationship is illustrated in Great Britain and the United States by the existence of "common law"—that is, law that has its expression in innumerable and often ancient judicial precedents rather than in statutes legally enacted. In all countries the formal laws fail to be explicit enough or broad enough to cover all cases that come before the courts, and the latter decide—within the framework of formal law—in terms of the judges' opinions. In such cases, which are much more numerous than the average citizen realizes,[25] the judges' opinions generally reflect the current folkways—sometimes confused with "public opinion"—on the matter, if relevant folkways exist. (Of course judges may also decide such cases in terms of personal ideology, personal interest, or political developments— as Mr. Dooley said, "The Supreme Court follows the election returns.")[26]

[25] Jerome Frank, *Courts on Trial* (Princeton: Princeton University Press, 1949).

[26] For a study and discussion of variations among judges in sentencing behavior, see F. J. Gaudet, G. S. Harris, and C. W. St. John, "Individual Differences in the Sentencing Tendencies of Judges," *Journal of Criminal Law and Criminology*, 23 (January–February, 1933), pp. 811–18; F. J. Gaudet, "The Sentencing Behavior of the Judge," *Encyclopedia of Criminology* (New York: Philosophical Library, 1949), pp. 449–61.

The judges' decisions provide precedents for future judicial decisions, and thus the folkways are further codified into the informal law of judicial precedent.

Because of the relation between folkways and law, the expectations which people have in regard to the behavior of others—based in large part on the folkways—have a better chance of being fulfilled in practice than if there were no such relationship or no law. The law-enforcement officials stand ready, with penal sanctions, to see to it that those expectations for the behavior of others that have been codified into law are fulfilled.[27]

If law differs too greatly from the common values, and if this discrepancy seems important enough to people, they will either seek to change the law,[28] or—if this is impossible—they react with apathy or self-deception. In speaking about the Soviet Russian people under these conditions, Koestler observes that they "know that rebellion against the largest and most perfect police machinery in history amounts to suicide. So the majority lives in a state of outward apathy and inner cynicism, while the minority live by self-deception."[29]

The laws are the most important type of broader category of social expectations which we call "rules." This category also includes codes of ethics, religious commandments, and other explicit regulations which have provisions for sanctions. All rules are either *prescriptive*—specifying positive regulations for behavior—or *proscriptive*—specifying what shall *not* be done. The proscriptive rules are usually more specific than the prescriptive rules. The sanctions for proscriptive rules are also usually more definite. Most of criminal law appears to be proscriptive, whereas much of civil law and administrative law appears to be prescriptive. Both types of rules include those which the individual internalizes and does not perceive to be specified by the society and those which he regards as external to himself and perhaps restrictive or even oppressive. Proscriptive rules are usually closer to the "mores" or high-conforming—demanding end of the social expectations, while the prescriptive rules are often more permissive. Some rules of specific organizations—like a business or voluntary association—are more useful than others to an individual who occupies a role in that organization as they help to sustain and give sanction to his role. Rules of *etiquette* are devoted primarily to the maintenance of *social distance* between individuals and castes.[30] Etiquette places individuals in different categories and prescribes the manner in

[27] Georges Gurvitch, *Sociology of Law* (New York: Philosophical Library, 1942); Nicholas Timasheff, *An Introduction to the Sociology of Law* (Cambridge: Harvard University Committee on Research in the Social Sciences, 1939).

[28] See Chapter 11, Sections D and E.

[29] Arthur Koestler, *The Invisible Writing* (New York: Macmillan, 1954), p. 53.

[30] See Chapter 8, Section A.

which persons must interact with one another according to the category to which they belong.[31]

G   *The Deliberate Informal Sanctions: Public Esteem, Gossip, Ostracism, and Public Opinion*

The most important of the positive deliberate informal sanctions is *public esteem,* but like all positive sanctions it has been little studied. A society may have no facilities and no laws providing for the awarding of formal positive sanctions, or it may be that public officials are opposed to a popular leader or hero, and thus no formal reward is offered. Or public esteem may accompany and/or follow the application of a formal reward. In any case, public esteem is a very powerful social sanction.

A society must have a significant degree of integration before it is capable of giving public esteem. That is, the members of the society must be able to communicate about the individual toward whom the sanction is applied and they must have some common values so that their communication turns into a form of public esteem. That public esteem is apparently at least as frequent in Western societies as it is in preliterate societies, and just as frequent in modern societies as in medieval or ancient societies, suggests that a society organized on the basis of many strong traditions is not necessary for the development of informal as well as formal sanctions. We shall return to this point, and help clarify it, when we come to a discussion of the "public."[32] It is probable, however, that a society like ours has more deliberate sanctions, whether formal or informal, than it has unconscious, non-deliberate sanctions, relative to the more traditionally organized societies. This hypothesis is, of course, very difficult to prove, since it requires detection of unconscious, non-deliberate sanctions.[33]

Public esteem accords *influence* and/or *authority* to an individual, which in turn are means of social control emanating from this individual onto others. Influence is the ability (socially accorded) to affect the behavior of others when the latter are willing to be thus affected and generally when the one who wields the influence does not have the power to enforce his influence. When he has the *power,* he is already using a formal social sanction and there is no necessary implication that those affected are willing. Authority is quite like influence except that there is the added implication that the reason why people are willing to have their behavior affected is that the person in authority has special knowledge or status which makes the following of his suggestions desirable. We need not go

[31] Portions of the above paragraph are drawn from an unpublished paper by Ramon Oldenburg, "Some Thoughts on the Sociological Significance of Rules," 1963.
[32] See Chapter 9, Section D.
[33] See the discussion of covert culture in Chapter 2, Section C.

into details concerning influence, authority, and power,[34] but simply note
the differences between them and recognize them as means of social control.
Public esteem can be negative, and be expressed through ridicule or pity
as a direct and deliberate control tending to restrict the individual from
continuing to do what he has been doing. The individual who receives the
messages of ridicule and pity from others is not only cut off from the
rewards others can grant through positive esteem, but he tends to accept
these negative attitudes toward himself. In both ways he is punished
psychologically and is generally moved to change his behavior.

Gossip—simply defined as conversation about an individual in his
absence—might theoretically be favorable as well as unfavorable. Since the
term is generally used, however, in the negative sense, we have distinguished the formation of public esteem as the positive sanction to which
gossip corresponds as a negative sanction; both are deliberate but informal. Gossip is to be sharply distinguished from rumor: the major function of gossip is social control, whereas the major function of rumor is to
carry information (or misinformation) when no more satisfactory form of
information dissemination is available or is believed.[35] Gossip is typically
about people—since only people can be controlled—whereas rumor is
about events. Of course a personage may be so important that his acts
affect the whole group or society. In such a case a rumor may develop about
him, his acts, or his health. This can be called rumor and not gossip because people's motives in transmitting the information is to inform themselves on a matter which affects themselves and no more reliable information
is available or is credited; it is not to be considered as gossip unless
people's motives in transmitting the information are to express their emotions and attitudes toward the person gossiped about and so exert social
pressure on him and/or on others.[36] Gossip generally directly reflects
the folkways of a group or subgroup and is directed against someone who
has violated the folkways. As such its content is one of the best indices
of the folkways, at least in so far as they affect personal behavior, available
to the outside observer. The violation of the folkways that elicits gossip is
not always a specific act which is tabooed; it may also be a failure to perform

[34] Important writings on the subject include Herbert Goldhamer and E. A. Shils,
"Types of Power and Status," *American Journal of Sociology*, 45 (September, 1939), pp.
171–82; Lord William H. Beveridge, *Power and Influence* (London: Hodder and
Stoughton, 1953); Robert Bierstedt, "The Problem of Authority," in M. Berger, T. Abel,
and C. H. Page (eds.), *Freedom and Control in Modern Society* (Princeton, N.J.: Van
Nostrand, 1954), Chapter 3.

[35] Some such distinction is made by almost all writers on rumor. For a summary of
definitions, see Arnold M. Rose, "A Study of Rumor," unpublished master's thesis, University of Chicago, 1940. See also Gordon Allport and Leo Postman, *The Psychology of
Rumor* (New York: Holt, 1947).

[36] Albert Blumenthal, *Small Town Stuff* (Chicago: University of Chicago Press, 1932).

an expected act, such as getting married when the age of marriage has arrived.[37]

Gossip varies considerably in terms of the proportion of the effective group participating in it, and in the intensity of negativeness toward the individual against whom it is directed. Most everyday gossip is of the minor sort, not very intense and not involving many people. All gossip cuts off, to a certain extent at least, the person against whom it is directed from those who gossip about him. This is its "punishment," the negative sanction involved in it. When gossip is intense, and many are involved in it, the individual against whom the gossip is directed may be said to be ostracized.

Ostracism is, of course, a very powerful social sanction, partly because it cuts the individual off from most social rewards, partly because it lets the individual know explicitly that his behavior or personality is negatively regarded by others, partly because it isolates the individual from social contact. We have already seen how important social rewards are, and we can easily understand that no one likes to be looked down on by his fellows.[38] When these three effects are added together, the force which creates them—ostracism—can be understood to be a most powerful negative sanction. As we have already considered when discussing gossip, ostracism can be partial or complete, and be effectuated against an individual by all the other members of a society or by only some of them. In any case, the ostracism created by gossip is probably the mildest form because it still allows the ostracized individual to move freely in his physical environment. Stronger forms of ostracism occur when the individual is forcibly excluded from his society either by exile or imprisonment. These latter forms are usually effectuated by formal laws and law-enforcement officials, although exile occasionally occurs outside the instruments of law through the use of physical force mobilized by ordinary members of the community. Further, even without the use of physical force or its threat, an individual can be so isolated by deliberate snubs and gossip that he "voluntarily" exiles himself.

The deliberate informal sanctions in our society are largely exercised by "public opinion," as distinct from the formal sanctions which are largely exercised by the government. While we shall reserve for a later chapter a consideration of how public opinion develops, it is necessary to consider it here as an instrument of social control. There is no formal sanction to enforce the demands of public opinion *per se,* but in a democracy strong

[37] For an example of how this occurs in a minority community in the United States, see J. Mayone Stycos, "The Spartan Greeks of Bridgetown: The Second Generation," *Common Ground,* 8 (Summer, 1948), pp. 72–86.

[38] In Chapter 2 we considered how powerful a force social isolation is.

public opinion on an issue is likely to be enacted into law. Legislators do not really have to listen very hard to hear the voice of the people; "having one's ear to the ground" really refers to individual responsiveness to public opinion. The ballot is a sanction on the elected official in this sense, but since it controls with respect to so many issues over so long a time, it cannot be very effective by itself in any specific issue. In so far as public opinion on a specific issue can get expression through the activities of pressure groups, through the formation of local protest or action groups, through petitions, or even occasionally through public-opinion polls conducted by disinterested organizations, it can have greater force.

Media of mass communication—newspapers, books, the radio, movies, etc.—are thus media of social control in so far as they express public opinion. Under dictatorial governments, however, they are arms of the state, and under free-enterprise systems they are sometimes little more than mouthpieces of private interests. Nevertheless, under both systems public opinion—in so far as it can form—does set limits of the activities of the propagandist. Further, the propagandist must take account of the less rational attitudes, the basic needs, the frames of reference, the degree of knowledge, of the people he is seeking to influence. Society sets at least the forms and the limits to the activities of the propagandist. Media of mass communication should not only be thought of as tools of propagandists to influence the people. They are also facilitators in the formation of a real public opinion over a wide area, since they aid in the exchange of ideas. They also reflect standards, values, fashions, tastes, current in a society, and through their mere repetition, with the added implication that they are proper and normal and expected, they serve as important tools of social control in a heterogeneous and geographically spread-out society.

In certain areas control by public opinion may take the form of physical coercion even when law does not provide a sanction. Vigilantism was common on the Western frontier of America before legal agencies were strong enough to take control. It was commonly exercised by whites against Negroes until very recently in the South, because most whites are strongly against the laws in so far as they apply impartially to Negroes.[39] Vigilantism (or "terror," as it is more commonly known when applied to a whole group of people not engaged in criminal activities) occurs when the persons practicing it feel very strongly about the matter, feel they have the support of a broader public opinion, and have little respect for the law or for law-enforcement agencies. In its extreme form, vigilantism inflicts torture and death on its victims, and thereby exerts social control on other persons, of the same social group as the victim, as a warning against

[39] Gunnar Myrdal, with the assistance of Richard Sterner and Arnold Rose, *An American Dilemma* (New York: Harper, 1944), especially Part VI.

doing the thing the victim was alleged to have done. Much more frequently vigilantism inflicts bodily punishment without killing, and the control is thus exerted on the victim as well as on other members of his group. Still more frequently, vigilantism works through threat and intimidation, so that there is only a promise of harm rather than actual harm. Occasionally the punishments are economic or social rather than physical.

Social ostracism, economic boycott, and the employment of such religious sanctions as excommunication and promise of damnation represent another level of social control. These are even less complexly and deliberately organized than propaganda and vigilantism, but sometimes indicate a higher degree of group consensus. They frequently come into play when the mores or the pseudomores are violated. Upon violation, the group reaction is spontaneous and immediate and practically unanimous. In our society, probably everything in the mores is also enacted into law, so the punishment for violating the mores is regular criminal punishment. But occasionally the group will take matters into its own hands, either before the law gets a chance to operate or after the law is through with the punishment, and either will do bodily harm to the violator or will ostracize, boycott, or excommunicate him. These sanctions are also frequently the formal ones used by primitive societies that have no formal law.[40] Ceremonies and rituals are continuing and organized non-specific controls on this level, for violation of them calls forth the sanctions.

The reprimand, or the "man-to-man talk," is a form of social control when the person administering it is a person in authority or one designated by the group to represent it. Thus a judge or a clergyman exercises social control over adults, and any adult—especially a parent—exercises social control over a child. The effort is to get the individual to conform to group demands, not to the judge's or parent's individual demands. Occasionally one not in authority administers the reprimand, but this is not effective (assuming no threat of bodily harm is involved) unless the reprimander uses many words to indicate that the group attitude would be identical with his own if the group were apprised of the circumstances.

H   *Informal Non-Deliberate Sanctions*

We have already paid considerable attention to the positive non-deliberate sanctions involved in the fulfillment of everyday expectations based on conformity to the folkways.[41] In this brief section we wish to pay closer attention to both positive and negative sanctions involved in spontaneous gestures. When we speak of "non-deliberate" or "spontaneous" we do not intend to convey the impression that the gestures or the sanctions they

[40] Hoebel, *op. cit.*
[41] See Section A of this chapter.

imply are instinctive or biological in character. These are still social ("learned"), but they are evoked so immediately and without conscious thought and effort that they are of a character somewhat different from the deliberate sanctions. One difference is that they are usually so effortless that they may very well be applied much more frequently than the deliberate sanctions, although this is quite difficult to verify for any behavior that is unconscious. Another major difference from the deliberate sanctions is that the non-deliberate sanctions are applied by individual members of the society acting separately rather than in collaboration. They are still social, nevertheless, in that they are learned and in that they express the purposes of the whole group or society in exacting conformity to the folkways.

Non-deliberate sanctions may be expressed either verbally or through body gestures. Every language contains numerous words, expressions, exclamations, and commands that contain negative sanctions toward the listener's behavior and that may be employed quite spontaneously and non-deliberately. Merely to illustrate with some negative sanctions of this type, we may cite the following from the English language: "Stop it!" "Get hep, man," "Disgusting!" "Oh, for God's sake!" "Can't you behave yourself?" Comparable positive sanctions would be "That's right!" "You're O.K., fellah!" "Good for you!" "Bravo!" "Hooray!" "Gosh!" "Good try!" Each culture, similarly, has body gestures which spontaneously express approval or disapproval in a quite spontaneous way. The smile and the frown, the nodding of the head (in either direction), the shrug of the shoulders, the sneering glance, rejecting and accepting movements of the hands, are such gestures that are most familiar to us. It is likely, however, that there are gestures involving other parts of our body which communicate positive and negative sanctions almost as effectively but of which we are much less aware. Novelists or poets sometimes write about, and artists paint portraits, revealing some of these: "welcoming faces," "disgusted expressions," "easy postures," "rigid and rejecting stances." These are all social controls when the individual on whom the control is being exerted thinks of them as being expressed by representatives of the group. The individual may be mistaken, of course; he may merely be the recipient of the expressions of a single person expressing his own private tastes.

I   The Appropriateness of Social Controls

While the common meanings and values provide social controls that function in practically every aspect of human life, the other social controls discussed in this and other chapters are appropriate only to certain aspects of life and are not highly effective in other aspects. The study of the effectiveness of various kinds of social controls in different life situations is a major continuing interest of sociologists. Only one aspect of this analysis and research will be considered here.

One of the earliest, and greatest, of American sociologists, Charles Horton Cooley, developed the concept of the "primary group" as a small group in which the relations among the members are intimate and which provides the basic socialization and humanization of the human animal.[42] The family and the friendship group are the most important examples of the primary group. Some years after Cooley described the primary group, Robert E. Park[43] delineated the "secondary group" in contrast to it. The secondary group was the impersonal "acquaintanceship" group in which relations were segmental for any one member of it. Obviously, these two categories of groups are ideal types, and for an understanding of ongoing social life it must be recognized that they represent merely the poles of a continuum, with a range of mixtures between them.

Nevertheless, it is important to recognize also that different social controls are appropriate and effective in the two kinds of groups. In the family and other primary groups, the mutual expectations, customs, and the interpersonal rewards and punishments are the most effective social controls. In the market place, the university, the legislative halls, and other secondary groups, the law, other rules, public esteem, and public opinion are the most effective social controls. For in-between groups, like the voluntary association, the occasional bridge club, and the research institute, perhaps gossip and ostracism provide the most effective social controls.

Groups run into problems when they try to use inappropriate sanctions. Efforts to run a family or a friendship group on the basis of rules will destroy them. Not so well recognized is the fact that trying to run a voluntary association, a research institute, or a business like a primary group will result in unhealable conflicts. When there are differences of opinion, as there are bound to be, one cannot be completely frank, fight, and then "kiss and make up," as one can in a family. There must be rules in a secondary group, to govern the extent and conditions of dissension. If there are none—that is, someone has tried to restructure the group as a primary group—there are no procedures available for restoring harmony in the group, and the group will disintegrate.

Each different type of group or organization has different sanctions considered appropriate for the enforcement of its rules or "codes," as MacIver and Page call them.[44] Whereas the state uses imprisonment, execu-

[42] Charles H. Cooley, *Social Organization* (New York: Scribner's, 1909), p. 15.

[43] Robert E. Park, "The City: Suggestions for the Investigation of Human Behavior in the Urban Environment," *American Journal of Sociology* (March, 1915). Reprinted in R. E. Park *et al.*, *The City* (Chicago: University of Chicago Press, 1925), pp. 1–46, at 23.

[44] Robert M. MacIver and Charles H. Page, *Society: An Introductory Analysis* (New York: Rinehart, 1949), Chapters 7–9. This source provides one of the most systematic analyses of social control in the literature.

tion, fines, damages or restitution to enforce its laws, the church uses excommunication, penance, loss of privileges, and fear of the displeasure of the deity to enforce its religious code. Professional organizations and voluntary associations use loss of other privileges and denial of membership as their chief sanctions. The family can deny still other privileges, and uses parental punishment frequently and disinheritance occasionally. The community uses ostracism, ridicule, loss of status and the other informal sanctions we have considered. Organizations working outside the framework of law use various forms of violence to enforce their codes. Each different kind of group—depending on the character of its interpersonal relations, its purposes, its longevity, and other characteristics—thus has different social controls that will function to keep the group alive.

J   Conclusions

The social controls briefly described and illustrated in this chapter have been regarded from the standpoint of their effectiveness, their side effects on both controllers and controlled, the variations in their use, the areas of behavior for which they are likely to be employed, the extent of their use, and the degree of formality and deliberateness in their employment. The behavior to which individuals are expected to conform was labeled as customs or folkways, and the means of exacting conformity were called sanctions. The basic classification of sanctions was into positive and negative, according to whether the behavior of the individual toward whom the sanctions were directed was approved or disapproved.

In any discussion of culture, especially of the non-material culture with which the sociologist is mainly concerned, or of sanctions supporting culture, an impression is almost unavoidably but incorrectly given of a tremendous social pressure and individual conformity. That is true of no culture, and less of ours than of some others. To correct this false impression we have pointed out that there are different degrees of demand for conformity in the various cultural values, and that the individual can be a member of different groups, each with somewhat different values, and that he can isolate himself to a certain extent. In the next chapter we shall consider the variety of influences impinging on the individual, of which the culture is only one. The present chapter on social control is basic, however, to an understanding of how a society can maintain itself at all, how individuals can usually expect what other individuals' behavior will be and have those expectations fulfilled in actual behavior. Our culture surrounds us and envelops us; in fact, we—most of our behaviors—*are* our culture. In most respects, the social controls are "internalized"—are part of our own acquired mentality and attitudes.[45] It is thus important for objectivity to examine culture and social control as outsiders, as "men from Mars," and see what they consist of and how they operate on the biological creatures called *Homo sapiens*.

[45] Gardner Murphy, "The Internalization of Social Controls" in Berger, Abel, and Page, *op. cit.*, Chapter 1.

FOR ADDITIONAL READING

DAVIS, F. JAMES, *et al.*, *Society and the Law* (New York: Free Press of Glencoe, 1962). The only book to date which offers a summary of the sociology of law.

HOEBEL, E. ADAMSON, *The Law of Primitive Man* (Cambridge: Harvard University Press, 1954). The outstanding work on law and its implementation in primitive society.

LA PIERE, RICHARD T., *A Theory of Social Control* (New York: McGraw-Hill, 1954). A textbook.

MAC IVER, ROBERT M., and CHARLES H. PAGE, *Society: An Introductory Analysis* (New York: Rinehart, 1949), Chapters 7–9. A leading theoretical analysis of social control, based on MacIver's 1937 work, *Society*.

SUMNER, WILLIAM GRAHAM, *Folkways* (Boston: Ginn, 1906). A classic statement, in its first chapter, of the nature of tradition in controlling behavior. The rest of the volume is hardly worth reading, as it is based on out-of-date anthropology.

4 * The Individual Personality and Its Social Setting

Having considered how people relate themselves to one another and the ways in which they control each other, within a social framework, it is appropriate to consider what an individual person is. While it is absolutely certain that society is made up of individuals, it is more important for the sociologist, and indeed for all those who observe life as it is lived, to recognize that society and its culture exist before any one living individual. That is, each individual is born into an ongoing society with a ready-made culture, and the first thing to note about an individual's behavior is that he adjusts to, and becomes a member of, that society. It is therefore proper to consider the social bond before analyzing the individual participating in this bond. But it is essential also to examine the individual as a unique entity, else the sociologist gives the false impression that society forces all people into the same mold, so that all are alike. We have already made numerous observations to show that this is not so, but special attention needs to be given to all the separate forces which make up the unique individual so that he can be seen as an entity in his own right.

Following the lead of many psychologists, we shall use the word "personality" to designate the combined reactive tendencies of an individual as products of all the forces playing on him. The forces influencing personality will be considered in three categories—biogenic, psychogenic, and sociogenic—depending on whether their origin lies in the inherited gene structure and other aspects of the constitution of the body, in experiences with the environment as physical objects, or in the social relationship.[1]

[1] Perhaps the best-known definition of personality is that of Gordon Allport. His definition is not antithetical to the one proposed in the text, but it seems to limit the forces affecting personality to the biogenic and psychogenic ones, and to place the sociogenic forces in an external environment. In this book we consider social influences as at

Since the sociologist is not primarily concerned with the first two sets of facts except as elements prerequisite to and influenced by social behavior, we shall deal with them in much shorter space than they would properly deserve in a completely rounded presentation, and even then emphasize their relationships to social phenomena rather than their intrinsic character.[2]

A   *The Biogenic Personality: Instincts and Reflexes*

Not many decades ago most people thought that the entire personality was biologically inherited and that the other components we shall later consider did not exist. Today we feel that even some of those elements of the personality which we suspect to be inherited are so only by hypothesis— that is, they have not been sufficiently studied to be certain of their origin even though the weight of present evidence is that they are biological in origin. The great difference between the past and the present attitude is that in the earlier days most people believed that men have instincts. Today no reputable scientist holds that man has instincts, in the strict zoological sense of the term. The era of belief in human instincts (lasting from about 1860 to about 1920) arose out of the study of animal behavior. It was then observed—and the observations are still valid—that each species of animal has its own unique configuration of behavior patterns.

These behavior patterns were observed to be common to all members of the species, manifested by each and every member of the species when a certain condition existed, not taught; and an animal reared in isolation could exhibit the behavior pattern as well as one enjoying the continual presence of full-grown members of the species. Further, they are invariant —that is, no amount of training could change the expression of the behavior pattern—although they might maturate—that is, an animal might not be able to manifest the behavior pattern at birth but show increasing ability to do so as he grew older. Familiar examples can be given from the nest-building instinct among birds, the web-building instinct among spiders, the care-of-young instinct among mammals.

The invariant character of instincts is sometimes not understood by persons not trained in zoology. It may be illustrated by the instinct of birds to hatch the eggs in their nest and to feed the young. The cowbird has no

---

least partly incorporated within the individual personality. Allport's definition is: "Personality is the dynamic organization within the individual of those psychophysical systems that determine his unique adjustments to his environment." *(Personality* [New York: Holt, 1937], p. 48.)

[2] For some of the best modern research in the psychology of personality, see M. T. Mednick and S. A. Mednick, *Research in Personality* (New York: Holt, Rinehart and Winston, 1963).

such instinct, and always lays its egg in the nest of another bird that has already deposited some of its own eggs in its nest. The foster mother hatches the cowbird egg along with its own eggs and then proceeds to feed all of the young birds. The baby cowbird grows rapidly to a larger size than the host bird and therefore takes more food than the other babies. Eventually the baby cowbird pushes the other babies out of the nest and they are killed, but the foster parents continue to feed the cowbird. Thus the care-of-young instinct is a series of mechanical responses to the stimulus of eggs and young, and does not vary even though the adult bird has to work much harder to feed the young and even though its own young are killed. It appears to the human observer as a tender expression of mother love, but it is in fact a mechanical process that bears little relation to human affection.

Yet, as the zoologists were demonstrating the presence of these instincts among most species of animals it was easy to assume that comparable instincts would exist among humans. Each psychologist made up his own list of human instincts out of his general experience, instead of following the zoologist's procedure of careful observation and experimentation.[3] Some psychologists said there were just two instincts—sex and self-preservation; others added two more—hunger and fear of ghosts; still others made lists of up to 250 instincts. The procedure was ludicrous, not to speak of its unscientific character. Voices of scientists began to be raised in protest: Charles H. Cooley[4] made observations of children, and he found that there were no fixed behavior patterns such as instincts. Franz Boas[5] examined all the known various ways in which people lived in primitive societies and found no universal behavior patterns such as instincts.

The psychologist John B. Watson[6] convinced many people that humans could not be considered to have many instincts. He experimented on babies only a few weeks old—before they were old enough to have learned much—and subjected them to all sorts of stimuli and situations. He found only three behavior patterns common to all the babies, and these were expressed under such varying circumstances that he preferred to call them emotions rather than instincts. The only three innate "emotions" discoverable were labeled by Watson as:

    a   Anger—a behavior syndrome composed of flushing, wriggling, and a cry starting out with a whimper and ending with a sustained

---

[3] The history of thinking in terms of instincts is reviewed by Ellsworth Faris, *The Nature of Human Nature* (New York: McGraw-Hill, 1937), Chapters VI and XV.

[4] *Human Nature and the Social Order* (New York: Scribner's, 1902; rev. ed., 1922).

[5] *The Mind of Primitive Man* (New York: Macmillan, 1911).

[6] *Psychology from the Standpoint of a Behaviorist* (Philadelphia: Lippincott, 1919), pp. 199–202.

yell. This was evoked in the infants when the experimenter held their limbs and head tightly so that they could not move.

b Fear—a behavior syndrome composed of blanching, throwing the arms and legs outward, and a sharp cry like a scream. This was evoked in the infants when the experimenter dropped them from a height into a net or when he produced a sudden loud noise behind their heads.

c Love—a behavior syndrome composed of cooing, wriggling, and —in older infants—smiling. This was evoked in the infants when the experimenter stroked their skin softly or tickled them.

While Watson considered himself to be an opponent of the instinct theory, his "emotions," while only three in number, were not much different from instincts. Later research failed to get the same invariant pattern of response that Watson reported, and motion pictures of the infants' responses —without showing the stimuli that provoked them—could not be consistently identified as Watson's three emotions.[7] Observations of Hopi and Navaho Indian children showed that they seldom cried when strapped to the cradle board, and yet they flex their muscles as do other children when released from the board.[8] Thus, while Watson's work seems to us today to give erroneous support to a modified instinct approach, during the 1920's it was considered to be an effective attack on the notion that human behavior was compounded of instincts. Watson's work had the important effects of showing the limited number of presumably innate responses, the fact that they could be evoked by a number of stimuli, and that they were not exactly invariant.

After 1924, when the sociologist L. L. Bernard[9] summarized the evidence against the existence of instincts in human beings, no reputable scientist has maintained that any significant behavior was based on instincts.[10]

[7] K. C. Pratt, "The Neonate" in L. Carmichael (ed.), *Manual of Child Psychology* (New York: Wiley, 1946).

[8] Wayne Dennis, "Does Culture Appreciably Affect Patterns of Infant Behavior?" *Journal of Social Psychology*, 30 (1940), pp. 305–17.

[9] *Instinct: A Study in Social Psychology* (New York: Holt, 1924).

[10] There has been some serious questioning as to whether sucking might not be called an instinct, since it is a universal, invariant, and complicated behavior pattern present at birth. While critics point out that many infants have to be "taught" to suck by pushing their lips out and in, a good case can be made that sucking exhibits all the other characteristics of an instinct. It might very well be called an instinct, and yet its scope is so limited that we may still say that human behavior is for all practical purposes not to be thought of as instinctive. Some would also put "grasping," sneezing, coughing, and the "startle reflex" into the instinct category, but these are simple enough to be regarded as reflexes. We need not take a stand on the question as to whether these behaviors are or are not instincts, since they cannot be regarded as important when considered in relation to the rest of human behavior.

The psychologist William McDougall, in his *Outline of Psychology* (New York:

When social psychologists found that the concept of instinct was either inapplicable to human behavior or useless for purposes of explanation, they did not mean that there was nothing in human behavior that was inherited. They recognized several kinds of biological influences in human behavior. The first that we shall consider are the *reflexes*, which are defined as simple, unitary, spontaneous, and immediate responses to stimuli. They are universal to all mankind, present at birth (except when they maturate as the organism develops), and are inherited. They differ from the instincts in being simple—consisting of a single muscular motion —and in expressing themselves immediately after the stimulus evokes them. Man probably has hundreds of reflexes, many of which have been carefully observed and labeled, ranging from the jerk of the knee when it is tapped to the contracting of the muscle around the pupil of the eye when light is focused on it. The Russian physiologist, Ivan Pavlov, demonstrated that human behavior could build on these reflexes by a learning process which he called *conditioning*. Pavlov's basic experiment involved the reflex of salivation among dogs. He attached a tube to a dog's mouth so that he could count the number of drops of saliva dripping when a steak was presented to a hungry dog. Then he would ring a bell each time the steak was presented. After a while Pavlov found that the salivation would appear in the same degree when the bell was rung alone, with the original stimulus of the steak not present. The bell had become a *conditioned* stimulus that evoked the original inherited reflex.

That the same conditioning process applies to human as well as dog behavior has been demonstrated in hundreds of experiments. In one of them, for example, a group of people were seated in armchairs and told to place their arms on the metal sides of the chairs. The chairs were

Scribner's, 1923), tried to save the instinct point of view by redefining an instinct as "an innate disposition which determines the organism to perceive any object of a certain class, and to experience in its presence a certain emotional excitement and an impulse to action which find expression in a specific mode of behavior in relation to that object." Using this later definition of "instinct" in terms of an impulse and an emotion, which is quite different from the original definition employed by the zoologists, there has never been a refutation of McDougall's viewpoint that human behavior is "instinctive." But there is not much value in McDougall's use of the term since it simply says that there are innate needs behind human behavior, without telling us exactly how innate needs are related to observable behavior. Since the sociologist and psychologist wishes to understand why human behavior takes the form it does, McDougall's concept offers simply another complication without explaining anything. McDougall's viewpoint has therefore been ignored by psychologists rather than disproved. A few contemporary psychologists still think of human behavior in terms of instincts, although they seldom use that term. See, for example, Raymond B. Cattell, *Description and Measurement of Personality* (Yonkers, N.Y.: World Book, 1946). The history and present status of the argument over the relative importance of biological inheritance in the psychological behavior of man is related in Nicholas Pastore, *The Nature-Nurture Controversy* (New York: King's Crown Press, 1949).

wired so that a small electric shock could be administered to the subjects' arms when they touched the sides of the chairs. The shocks caused the reflex of jerking the arms away. Each time the experimenter sent the electric discharge to the arms of the patients, he flashed a blue light on a screen in front of the room. After a number of times the light was flashed by itself without the electric charge being sent to the sides of the chairs, and each person flopped his arms as though he had had an electric shock.

It is easy to imagine numerous circumstances under which the conditioning process operates in everyday life and in which the conditioned stimulus is a social object. Suppose a young man, who does not care for classical music, is induced to attend a concert by a young lady of whom he is very fond. He spends the evening gazing at her and even when his eyes are fixed elsewhere he is daydreaming of her. The music "drifts in one ear and out the other," but it has nevertheless been a conspicuous stimulus in an evening full of sexual charm. The young man probably could not remember the name of the music he heard, but it nevertheless remains as a conditioned stimulus for him which evokes mildly pleasurable sensations whenever he hears it.

There are undoubtedly many minor facets of our everyday behavior and experience, the origin of which we are not aware, but which come to us immediately and spontaneously. We meet someone whom we "instinctively" do not like, even if we know next to nothing about him. This might be simply due to the shape of his nose that is a conditioned stimulus for a long-forgotten unpleasant experience. Or we visit a home we have never been in before and we feel spontaneously fearful. This may simply be due to something like the position of its windows, that has become a conditioned stimulus for an earlier frightening experience.

B   *The Biogenic Personality: The Influence of Man's Anatomy and Physiology*

1   THE LIMITATIONS OF THE BODY

In the past few decades the science of physiology has been adding greatly to our knowledge of human behavior by its studies of the action of the endocrine glands.[11] These are small organs located at various points in our body which secrete small amounts of chemical substances into our blood stream. These substances contain active agents called hormones, a certain amount of which is essential to the normal functioning of our bodies. Some hormones, such as insulin or pituitrin, are catalysts essential for digestion and growth and so are basic to a general sense of well-being. Others are

---

[11] A summary work on the effects of glandular activity on behavior is Frank A. Beach, *Hormones and Behavior* (New York: Hoeber, 1948).

more directly related to overt behavior: adrenalin, for example, primes our bodies for greater effort. An insufficient amount of adrenalin in the blood stream may make us act sluggishly; and too much at times when it is not necessary will make us act "nervous" or "overaggressive." The thyroid gland's secretion is the main determinant of the "basic metabolic rate" (BMR), or the rate at which energy is used by the body in a state of quiescence. If this rate is too high, body reactions will tend to be rapid and "excited," while if it is too low body reactions will tend to be sluggish. We say "tend to," for it is sometimes found that a person with a low BMR will compensate psychologically by driving himself to great and rapid activity, while a person with a high BMR will calm himself down to a slow pace. Quite a number of people have minor malfunctioning of one gland or another at different times of their lives, and their behavior is accordingly influenced.

Most of what we know about the behavioral effects of endocrine secretions comes from studies of those with malfunctioning glands. Thus most of our knowledge about the relation of normal gland functioning to behavior is inference. This is somewhat dangerous when human behavior is such a complex resultant of many factors. Even the various glandular secretions interact in their effects on behavior. What seems to be needed is more research of the experimental type on normal subjects. The more that is learned about the influence of glandular secretions on behavior and personality, the more it is realized that the influence is never a one-to-one relationship and—except in extreme cases of glandular malfunctioning— it is seldom an important cause of variations in behavior. Other factors— physiological, psychological, and sociological—tend to "compensate" for small deviations in glandular functioning so that the effect of the glandular factor alone cannot be observed in overt behavior. The importance of the glands for human behavior is as a limiting influence; they help to set the extreme limits of energy, speed, etc., beyond which an individual cannot go. And except for individuals who have serious glandular disturbances, the range between the limits is very broad so that almost any "normal" behavior is compatible with any "normal" degree of functioning of the various glands.

Glands and heredity are important determinants of the size and shape of the body, and these in turn have direct influences on personality. A tall person is physically able to do certain things a short person cannot do. A slim person is physically able to do certain things that an obese person cannot do. Most obvious is the ability to participate in certain sports: the successful basketball player is usually of at least medium height. But body build is also important in other activities; a successful burglar cannot be too heavy; a heavy person has to cut down on more activities in old age than does a slim person; a physically handicapped person frequently finds it more difficult to perform many kinds of tasks than a person who is physically whole.

This list could be greatly extended. Each activity one engages in has some relationship to the kind of personality one has. While we shall consider this statement in greater detail in a subsequent section, an example here may suffice to stimulate the reader's imagination to consider the nature of the relationship. A burglar—one of whose requirements is that he be not too heavy-set—is a different kind of a person than, say, a swindler. The burglar must develop mechanical ingenuity and skills; his major relationship to strange people is to avoid them. A swindler, on the other hand, is most successful when he can develop insight into the habits and weaknesses of people. The burglar can be quite tenderhearted when he has dealings with other people on a face-to-face basis; the swindler must be coldly calculating. The burglar must learn how to avoid attracting attention to himself; the swindler must learn how to attract people and to create confidence in himself. There are probably other personality differences developed by the burglar and the swindler which have not been studied. Yet, in a *given social situation* which is conducive to the development of criminals, one youth *may* be led into a career of burglary, rather than swindling, largely because of his slim body build. This example may be a little farfetched, but it illustrates the point that biological influences cannot be ignored when one is attempting to explain some concrete human behavior.

There have been various claims made that body build—especially the thinness-stoutness and shortness-tallness aspects of body build—is closely related to temperament, which in turn is said to determine one's entire personality. Especially well known are the theories of Kretschmer and Sheldon.[12] We need not go into these rather extreme claims, as they have been effectively disproved by analysis and research.[13] Nevertheless, there may be indirect ways in which body build and temperament are related, although we now know that there are many other factors influencing personality and behavior besides the biological forces which also influence body build. It is probable, although evidence is not conclusive on the matter, that certain glandular secretions affect both temperament and body build, so that correlations between the latter two are to be expected.

We must be careful, however, to think of temperament as a very

[12] Ernst Kretschmer, *Physique and Character* (New York: Harcourt, 1926); William H. Sheldon, *Varieties of Delinquent Youth: An Introduction to Constitutional Psychiatry* (New York: Harper, 1949).

[13] See, for example, Edwin H. Sutherland, "Critique of Sheldon's *Varieties of Delinquent Youth*," *American Sociological Review*, 16 (February, 1951), pp. 1–14.

generalized tendency referring to such things as speed of reaction time and spontaneity—within which specific behavior can take place. Temperament can be defined as the biogenic element in the affective or emotional side of personality. It is not specific behavior itself, nor is it a direct determinant of specific behavior. It is only a small part of the whole range of behavior forms and modes we call personality. If we think of temperament, or the influence of glandular secretion, as being anything more than this we fall into the ludicrous error made first by Cesare Lombroso,[14] a nineteenth-century Italian criminologist, or more recently by the anthropologist, E. A. Hooton.[15] Proceeding on the theory that criminals are born rather than developed, these investigators measured various parts and proportions of the body, especially the head, of criminals. They came out with the conclusion that criminals had certain "stigmata" or characteristic physical features, and consequently inferred that "the primary cause of crime is biological inferiority."[16] But when studies are made of non-criminal populations they are also found to have the "stigmata" discovered by Lombroso and Hooton. There is no evidence, therefore, that criminals have any different physical features than anyone else, on the average.[17] Participation in crime is, as we shall see in a later chapter,[18] a specific type of social behavior, and general body build or temperament could not possibly be more than one of many contributing factors to it.

We have seen that reflexes are one kind of inherited human behavior, and that, especially when attached to new stimuli by the learning process called conditioning, they play a regular role in everyday life. We have also seen that glandular secretions influence human behavior by providing a general emotional set, especially with regard to speed of movement, spontaneity, and perhaps other similar matters. There is a third general way in which biological inheritance influences our behavior: this is indirectly through our physical appearance. People who are tall are often regarded as more "impressive" than people who are short. Handsome people are often considered to be more desirable associates than are ugly people. One study, based on evaluation of photos of actual criminals, shows that robbers, forgers, and other criminals whose "work" brings them into face-to-face relations with their victims are judged to be better looking than burglars

---

[14] *L'uomo delinquente* (Torino: Bocca, 1896–97). For a summary and critique of Lombroso, see Edwin H. Sutherland and Donald R. Cressey, *Principles of Criminology,* fifth ed. (Philadelphia: Lippincott, 1955), pp. 54–55.

[15] *Crime and the Man* (Cambridge: Harvard University Press, 1939); *The American Criminal: An Anthropological Study* (Cambridge: Harvard University Press, 1939). Probably the most careful critique of Hooton's work is that by Robert K. Merton and M. F. Ashley-Montague, "Crime and the Anthropologist," *American Anthropologist,* 42 (August, 1940), pp. 384–408.

[16] Hooton, *Crime and the Man,* p. 130.

[17] Sutherland and Cressey, *op. cit.,* pp. 54–55, 103–06, summarize the evidence.

[18] See Chapter 15, Section B.

and other criminals who are not seen by their victims.[19] Of course, "handsomeness" and "ugliness" in physical appearance are culturally defined, so to say that handsome people are considered to be more desirable associates is almost a tautology. A person who is clubfooted is usually handicapped socially as well as physically. Short people sometimes seek to compensate for the lack of attention they get by being overaggressive, and ugly people sometimes develop "a heart of gold beneath their rough exterior" as a compensation.

It would seem, then, that our physical appearance—which is largely determined by heredity—influences the perceptions and actions of other people in relation to us. In accord with the familiar mechanism of the "looking-glass self," the behavior of other people toward us helps to determine what we think we are and how we are going to react to other people. Thus our physical appearance, through a social mechanism, is part of our personality. This indirect influence from our biological inheritance is probably more significant for personality than the direct "body-build" influence of Kretschmer and Sheldon. Each individual (except for identical twins) has a unique physical appearance, and we may expect that the reactions of various others to the variant physical appearances would be somewhat different. So what we have illustrated with tallness and ugliness could be applied to countless other characteristics of physical appearance.

There are other physiological influences on personality and behavior that work in much the same way as glandular secretions. Diet and digestion, for example, have noteworthy relationships to behavior. Deficiencies in calorie intake, vitamin intake, roughage intake, or defects in the gastrointestinal system can have noticeable temporary or permanent effects on personality and behavior. The English writer, Thomas Carlyle, was said to be constantly grouchy, and his writings reflected a pessimistic outlook, at least partly because he was a chronic dyspeptic. Some sort of peculiarity of personality and behavior might be expected to accompany malfunctioning of any organ of the body.

But what we have said about glandular variations also holds for other physiologic variations. There can be psychological compensations for them, they set only the broad limits of behavior, and their influence is apparent only when they are malfunctioning. It is noteworthy, for example, that a vitamin deficiency can cause behavioral peculiarities, but no increase in vitamin intake beyond what is normal for the body to use makes any difference to behavior. It was rumored during 1940 that the German soldiers were given large quantities of Vitamin B, and this was why they were able to overrun France and the northern countries in so short a time. This was nonsense; the rumor had no basis in fact but was probably started to

[19] Raymond J. Corsini, "Appearance and Criminality," *American Journal of Sociology*, 65 (July, 1959), pp. 49–51.

rationalize the defeat. So great, however, is the popular misunderstanding of the relation between physiology and behavior that the rumor was widely believed, even in Great Britain and the United States.

2   POSSIBILITIES OF THE BODY

Thus far we have been considering the limiting influences of the anatomy and physiology of man on his behavior and personality. We have been forced to point out how minor these influences are, because extravagant claims were made for them by past generations of biological scientists and because these fallacious ideas are still prevalent in popular thought. Still, there are some anatomical and physiological characteristics of man that play a generally ignored role in his behavior, and these will be the subject of the present section. We can best bring out the nature of these human traits by comparing them with comparable traits of the lower animals.[20] All of them contribute to or are associated with man's development of social behavior and culture and will be considered in other contexts after being enumerated at this point. It should be understood that none of these traits were developed for the "purpose" of making man what he is, but have developed according to the usual evolutionary processes.

1 *Erect posture*, which is partially found only among a few mammals (apes, bears, kangaroos) as well as among men. This anatomical trait: (a) enables man to get a broader overview of his surroundings for his size than if he were obliged to walk on all fours; (b) frees man's forelimbs to manipulate and create (manufacture, in the literal sense of "making by hand") objects instead of requiring them for locomotion.

2 *Prehensile hands*, involving movable fingers and opposable thumbs, which are found only among the apes in addition to man. This anatomical trait: (a) greatly increases man's ability to examine objects, even to the extent of pulling them carefully apart to see "how they work"; (b) permits him to manipulate and manufacture.

3 *Forward vision*, involving eyes that look in the same direction and are coordinated, which is found only among certain of the mammals. This anatomical trait permits man to see objects in three dimensions, and to get perspective on his surroundings, so that he can manipulate his environment better.

4 *Large and complex brain* (especially the cerebrum) which, relatively speaking, is unique to man. This anatomical trait permits man a greater variety and complexity of mental functions.

5 *A complex voice mechanism*, including a different structure of the larynx and fleshy lips, which is unique to man. This permits man to utter a great variety of different sounds, and so allows him to develop a language.

[20] Much of the following discussion rests on Alfred S. Romer, *Man and the Vertebrates* (Chicago: University of Chicago Press, 1937).

6 *Relatively greater dependence in infancy and slower rate of maturation* force a newborn man to have a closer relationship to mature members of his species and permit him to learn more from them than is possible among the other animals.

7 *Flexibility of innate drives and needs,* including the practical absence of instincts, the relative unimportance of reflexes, the adaptability of needs to a variety of different satisfactions, permit man to learn much, to develop a great variety of behaviors, and to adjust to a great variety of environments.

8 *Constant sex drive,* which man and several other species have, encourages him to develop relatively permanent sexual partnerships, which become the basis of the institution of the family, rather than to separate from his mate at the end of each childbearing period (as most species of animals do).

9 *Longevity,* which man shares with several other species, enables man to develop a more complex culture and social organization than would be possible if he were shorter-lived. It should be recognized that the actual *length of life* seldom reaches the potential *span of life,* and that man himself can control the former within the limits set by the latter.

Some of the above anatomical and physiological traits are obviously more important than others for his social development. They will be considered again in other contexts in this book when they have a special relevance to the subject under discussion. At this point we merely wish to consider them as a biological contribution to man's unique behavior. While we have emphasized the anatomical and physiological uniqueness of man, the fact remains that man is an animal, and his body is similar to that of other animals, especially to that of the anthropoid apes, in most respects. Still, one must be careful not to confuse man's behavior with similar-appearing behavior among animals: the anthropoligist Leslie A. White provides an example.

> Tool-using among men is a different kind of activity, fundamentally and qualitatively different in a psychological sense, from tool-using among apes. Among apes the use of tools is a conceptual process as well as a neuro-sensory-muscular one. By conceptual we mean the formation by the ape of a configuration of behavior in which he, a tool, and the thing upon which the tool is to be used are functionally related to one another. The ape is able to solve his problem by means of insight and understanding, and to effect the solution implicitly before he executes it overtly. This is what we mean by conceptual. In the human species, the tool process is also conceptual and neuro-sensory-muscular in character. But it is more than this; it is symbolic as well. Human beings express their concepts in symbolic form. Thus they not only have tools and concepts of tools,

but they have and use words of tools—axe, knife, hammer, etc. It was the introduction of symbols, word-formed symbols, into the tool process that transformed anthropoid tool-behavior into human tool-behavior.[21]

Another concept that we shall consider is that of "drives," which has had increasing recognition as an important biogenic component in man's personality and behavior. After it was learned that man has no fixed instincts, many psychologists felt a need to postulate some inherited basis of behavior and so spoke of "drives" (or "impulses" as equivalent to drives), which are inherited *tendencies* to act in a certain general way. It is questionable whether this new concept is simply a pragmatic tool, or whether it is intended to refer to some real independent element in the heredity of man. Some of the endocrine secretions—like those associated with sex—quite obviously push toward a certain general type of behavior. There are also "needs," the physiological basis of which is almost mechanical—for example, hunger is felt when the stomach has been empty for a while and has a muscular contraction.

These not very well-defined, from a physiological standpoint, "pushes" and "needs" are called "drives" by the contemporary psychologists who have done the most careful research on learning.[22] For these neo-behaviorist psychologists the biological drives are basic to all learning, although after a certain amount of learning takes places "learned drives" can take the place of innate ones. Drives from within the individual combine with "cues" from the environment (that appear to offer satisfaction of the drives) to stimulate the individual to respond. Trial and error, success and failure with these responses are found to build a learned habit. Success serves to "reinforce" the response which leads to the most satisfactory reduction of drives, and failure tends to "inhibit" the responses which fail to reduce the drives. The products of learning, or learned responses, are in the realm of the psychogenic component of personality and behavior—which is the subject of a following section—but the basis of learning in drives and the fixed process itself are rooted in the biology of the individual organism. This neo-behaviorist theory of learning is not the only effort

[21] Leslie A. White, *The Science of Culture, A Study of Man and Civilization* (New York: Farrar, Straus, 1949), pp. 44–45.

[22] We refer to the "learning theory" developed by Clark Hull and his students; see his *Principles of Behavior* (New York: Appleton-Century-Crofts, 1943). Our very brief statement of the heart of his theory is taken from John Dollard and Neal Miller, *Personality and Psychotherapy* (New York: McGraw-Hill, 1950). For a general consideration of contemporary psychological theories of learning, see Ernest Hilgard, *Theories of Learning* (New York: Appleton-Century-Crofts, 1948). Hull's system is undergoing revision within the behaviorist framework—see, for example, William K. Estes *et al.*, *Modern Learning Theory* (New York: Appleton-Century-Crofts, 1954).

to explain learning, but it is the one which is held by most American psychologists today. Sociologists need not subscribe to any one theory of learning, but they have to be aware of the sources of what are considered to be important components in man's behavior and personality.

c   *The Biogenic Personality: Intelligence*

A third component of hereditary and other congenital influences very important for the individual's behavior and personality is "intelligence." Despite man's long preoccupation with intelligence and the many excellent researches on it, we are still far from certain what its exact biological basis is. It has long been known that intelligence was a function of the brain, particularly of the large frontal lobes of the brain known as the cerebrum, and used to be thought that different sections of the cerebrum controlled the various intellectual "faculties," such as perceiving, cogitating, etc. (this early, but now discarded, "faculty psychology" gave rise to the popular pseudoscience called phrenology). Studies of persons who had lost various parts of their brains proved that the cerebrum functions in a generalized way, and that there were no faculties localized in the different parts of the brain that could not be transferred to other parts. But what exactly makes for efficient functioning of the brain—which we call intelligence—is still not known. It may be a function of the chemical composition of the cells of the brain, which permits impulses to travel with different rates of speed through the brain. Or it may be some other physiological or anatomical characteristics of the brain not yet known.

Our ignorance of the nature of intelligence extends not only to its physiological base but also to its psychological function. There has been a great debate among psychologists, as yet unresolved, as to whether intelligence is a general psychological ability or a number of specific abilities for different types of behavior (for example, verbal ability, number ability, etc.). The researches led by Spearman[23] have tended to emphasize the former conception, while those of Thurstone and his followers have supported the latter contention.[24] Sociological studies do not depend on the resolution of this controversy, since the sociologist needs only the knowledge that intelligence is a mental characteristic with some biological basis, in which individuals vary.

The sociologist is concerned, however, with the influence of social factors on biological intelligence and with the social manifestations of intelligence. If intelligence be defined in behavioral terms, rather than strictly

[23] Charles E. Spearman, *The Abilities of Man* (London: Macmillan, 1927).

[24] Louis L. Thurstone, *Factorial Studies of Intelligence* (Chicago: University of Chicago Press, 1941).

physiological and anatomical terms, intelligence is a social as well as a biological phenomenon. That is, there is no intelligent behavior on the part of a socialized person which does not have a number of social components thoroughly intertwined (and inseparable except in theoretical terms) with the biological component. We can think of the biological component of intelligence merely as a *capacity* for intelligent behavior, with the social components activating and depressing this capacity. In an earlier chapter we have considered the essential role of language in all intelligent human behavior. Here we may consider only some specific social influences that expand or contract the capacity for intelligence in its concrete manifestations.

1   EXPERIENCE

To a considerable extent, our capacity to learn, and otherwise to behave in intelligent ways, is a function of what we already know. This can be illustrated on a crude level by observing that obviously one must know how to manipulate simple values before one can engage in higher mathematics. But the principle has a most extensive application. For example, our ability to understand a political decision is a function of our comprehension of the political forces operating in the situation. Our ability to understand another culture is a function of our experience with cultural variation.

This principle suggests the important role of education, both formal and informal, for intelligence. To the extent that school systems are not equal, and to the extent that the educational ladder is not equally open to all, intelligent behavior—including performance on an intelligence test—has little relationship to biological capacity for intelligence. While there is a certain amount of selection of intelligent people for higher education in our fairly open educational ladder in the United States, there are still so many social blocks to getting a higher education that the observed high relationship between educational status and I.Q. scores does not necessarily indicate that college graduates have the highest biological potential capacity for intelligent behavior. Negroes in American society, for example, are so held down by inferior schools in the South, the distracting effects of poverty and slum life, their fear of performing too well in front of whites (a result of past terrorism), and their lack of tradition of seeking a good education that their low scores on such general intelligence tests as those given by the Army tell us nothing about their average biological capacity for intelligent behavior as a group. Some of the same factors operate to hold down the intelligence levels of lower-class whites.[25]

[25] Allison Davis, *Social Class Influences Upon Learning* (Cambridge: Harvard University Press, 1948).

2   EMOTIONAL ADJUSTMENT

In recent years, as a result of the investigations of psychiatrists and child psychologists, we have become increasingly aware of the tremendous potency of the so-called emotional "blocks" in inhibiting the manifestation of intelligent behavior. Compulsions are "unintelligent" by definition, since they make people do things which have no relation to their conscious purposes and goals. Anxieties can be highly distracting to intelligent behavior, since they involve worry which does nothing to resolve the source of the worry. All psychopathology wastes time and efficiency which are essential components of intelligent behavior. Recent studies suggest that some children who appear feeble-minded—for example, who cannot talk or engage in organized play up to the age of eight or ten years—can by special psychiatric treatment be brought up to the intelligence of a normal child, and that children of "low normal" intelligence can have their I.Q. raised to the "high normal" level.[26]

3   IDEOLOGY AND CULTURE

It may seem odd to consider ideology—which is a highly specific cultural trait consisting of the organized and intellectualized beliefs as to why a society functions as it does—as a factor in intelligent behavior, when intelligence has for so long been considered purely as a biological function. But one has only to observe a person whose whole way of life and thought is dominated by a single ideology try to solve a problem that his ideology defines as non-existent or drastically limited. The problem appears meaningless to him, even though he may appear to be very intelligent otherwise. Or one can observe one's own confusion and lack of comprehension about a matter which seems so simple to a group of people whose ideology is drastically different from one's own. Much of what we call intelligent behavior is culturally limited, especially in those value aspects of culture that we call ideology. There is such a thing as "learned incapacity."

Let us consider some concrete illustrations. A Frenchwoman once told me of her difficulties in getting her boy of seven to school every morn-

[26] See, for example: Bernadine G. Schmidt, "The Rehabilitation of Feeble-Minded Adolescents," *School and Society*, 62 (December 29, 1945), pp. 409–12; *New York Times*, May 23, 1947, p. 29; Benjamin Fine, "More and More, the IQ Idea Is Questioned," *New York Times Magazine*, September 18, 1949, pp. 7 ff.; Don Charles, "Ability and Accomplishment of Persons Earlier Judged Mentally Deficient," *Genetic Psychology Monographs*, 47 (February, 1953), pp. 3–71; S. E. Perry, "Mental Deficiency; Program Planning and Development," mimeographed report of the National Institute of Mental Health (July, 1953); Lewis Dexter, "Naming as Social Process and the Classification of the Mentally Deficient," unpublished paper read to the American Association on Mental Deficiency (May 27, 1955). In opposition, see: Joseph Jastak, "A Rigorous Criterion of Feebleminded," *Journal of Abnormal and Social Psychology*, 44 (July, 1949), pp. 367–78.

ing; she had to get two younger children dressed and fed and take them along because she had no one to leave them with while she was taking the older boy to school and she could not afford to hire someone to take the older boy to school. I suggested that there must be other mothers in the neighborhood with a like problem, and if she found out their names from the teacher, they could take turns in bringing the six- and seven-year-olds to school every morning (or, better still, they could organize a patrol system among the older boys). A great light dawned on her face and she exclaimed, "How intelligent you are!"[27] Actually it is doubtful whether there was any difference in the biological capacity for learning between this woman and myself; it was simply that her culture had little or no value for voluntary group organization and thus she could not solve unaided a problem which required that cultural value. Another example. I remember the amazement of a group of us Americans when an Austrian first presented to us certain techniques of determining how certain commercial products could be made to attract consumers. He seemed to be extremely clever because his whole way of thinking *assumed* unconscious motivations in people, whereas we accepted the existence of these unconscious motivations intellectually, but did not assume them in our ordinary thinking.[28]

4   PHYSICAL WELL-BEING AND THE AVAILABILITY OF TIME
     TO THINK

It has long been a popular axiom that a healthy (and intelligent) mind requires—among other things—a healthy body. The truth of this becomes most apparent when we see the many evidences of stupidity in a starving people. But the principle has much broader application. A person who is physically ill for a long time often begins to show impairment of his mental functions (depending on the traits of the disease: the extent to which the germs attack the nervous system, the poisons given off into the blood stream, etc.). The physical impairment of the mind can—and often

[27] It is questionable whether she ever followed up my suggestion, although I did not check to find out. The ideology and social structure of France are not conducive to the private organization of voluntary activity. My suggestion was almost "unthinkable" to the Frenchwoman, both in the sense that she was not likely to think of it herself in trying to solve her problem and in the sense that she and the other mothers would regard it as bizarre and unworkable. See "Voluntary Associations in France," in my *Theory and Method in the Social Sciences* (Minneapolis: University of Minnesota Press, 1954), pp. 72-115.

[28] A survey of the cross-cultural studies of test intelligence and of critiques of such tests is to be found in Anne Anastasi and J. P. Foley, *Differential Psychology*, third ed. (New York: Macmillan, 1958). An excellent single study, which attempts to measure abstract behavior among Gold Coast Africans, is that of Gustav Jahoda, "Assessment of Abstract Behavior in a Non-Western Culture," *Journal of Abnormal and Social Psychology*, 53 (September, 1956), pp. 237-43.

does—begin before birth; physical trauma, starvation, certain poisons, that can affect directly the infant *in utero,* can often impair his mental functioning for life. Also, a person who is physically maimed may be cut off from certain activities and certain social contacts that extend intelligent behavior.

Allied to this is the requirement of time for certain types of problem solving. While intelligence tests try to avoid this factor in their measuring devices by asking only questions that take little time to answer, it must also be recognized that the intelligent solution of many problems in everyday life (as in science and other intellectual pursuits) requires time. The person whose time is absorbed solely in earning enough to maintain his physical existence, or is "wasted" in trivial pursuits, does not have enough time even to try to solve intelligently these kinds of problems.

5   THE MEASUREMENT OF INTELLIGENCE

From what we have said about the powerful sociogenic and psychogenic influences on intelligence we can see that the biogenic basis of intelligence—while one can never doubt that it exists and is important—cannot be measured directly by tests that measure only its behavioral manifestations. Until physiologists and psychologists learn what the exact biogenic basis of intelligence consists of and devise techniques for measuring it directly, the biogenic component in intelligence must remain a hypothetical construct and non-measurable. Some psychologists have recognized this and have sought to get around the problem by studying biogenic intelligence only under limited, controlled conditions.

The most important of these studies is that on identical twins reared under variant social conditions.[29] Knowing the practical impossibility of controlling the numerous psychogenic and sociogenic influences operating on any individual, these investigators have limited themselves to controlling the biogenic influence and measuring the effects of environmental influences. Nature has provided them their control in the form of identical twins; genetic study has demonstrated that certain twins, those developing from a single sperm and a single ovum, have identical heredity. Thus any differences between them in intelligence and other aspects of physical and mental make-up must be due to psychogenic and sociogenic factors. About twenty cases have been discovered of such twins who have been reared apart, and among them a few cases where one twin has been reared under exceptionally favorable social circumstances, and the other under poor circumstances. Intelligence and basic ability tests, as well as physical

[29] Frank N. Freeman and H. H. Newman, *Twins: A Study of Heredity and Environment* (Chicago: University of Chicago Press, 1937); Robert S. Woodworth, "Heredity and Environment: A Critical Survey of Recently Published Material on Twins and Foster Children," *Social Science Research Council Bulletin* 47 (New York, 1941).

measurements, of these twins show small differences between any two twins with the same biogenic background. The differences can be ascribed to psychogenic and sociogenic influences (or to lack of reliability in the measuring instruments) but what similarity between any two twins remains still cannot be ascribed completely to the biogenic factor.[30]

The reason should be easy to understand. The twins remain in the same culture and are treated as members of the same race, in practically all cases they spent their early infancy together (and of course their intrauterine period together) so that their psychogenic influences must be fairly similar. In terms of what we know of cultural and other environmental variations, any two twins studied can be said to have grown up in fairly similar environments even in cases where one twin was raised by a well-to-do and educated family and the other twin by a poor, ill-educated family. Nevertheless, the extraordinary similarity between identical twins on certain specific traits is impressive. Thus, the studies are valuable in suggesting the dimensions of psychological difference due to sociogenic and psychogenic influences on the one hand and biogenic differences on the other.

D *Psychogenic Personality*

The psychogenic personality can be defined as those elements in the mental make-up of an individual which arise out of certain experiences not involving other persons as social beings bearing a culture. It is generally held that the important psychogenic characteristics which become deep seated in the individual's personality are those which arise out of experiences occurring in the formative period of early infancy, although it is possible that there has been insufficient recognition of psychogenic traits developing in later life. These experiences are direct and involve no cognitive factor, and most of them express themselves in the individual's behavior beyond his control and usually outside of his awareness. Since the psychogenic influences have been very inadequately studied, and are apparently so difficult to detect and measure, it is often very difficult to distinguish them from the sociogenic influences (except in theory). Everything to be said about them, therefore, is very tentative and hypothetical.

Let us first consider psychogenic traits that tend to be universal to all mankind. While Charles H. Cooley[31] independently identified what we

---

[30] The biogenic factor seems to be very important, however, in view of the fact that the scholastic achievement and certain personality test scores are sometimes very different for twins reared under different conditions, while their basic ability and intelligence test scores are close together. See Horatio H. Newman, *Multiple Human Births* (Garden City, N.Y.: Doubleday, 1940), pp. 189–99.

[31] *Op. cit.*

call the universal psychogenic elements in personality (his name for them was "the sentiments that constitute human nature"), he did not follow up his ideas with concrete research, nor did his followers extend his thinking. Most of the credit for developing the concept of the psychogenic personality and for stimulating others to do research on that concept goes to Sigmund Freud.[32] Thus we shall have merely to mention Cooley's thought and then pass on to the specific theories and researches under a Freudian or neo-Freudian framework.

There is a curious similarity between some of the thinking of Cooley and that of Freud, even though they had little or no influence on each other, and their backgrounds and terminologies were quite different. Cooley was the more cautious of the two in framing his hypotheses in a fairly simple form and in never neglecting the fact that there were biogenic and sociogenic elements in the human personality as well as the psychogenic. Freud, on the contrary, developed his theories into rather extreme and complicated forms, which—when sometimes later proven wrong in detail—have unfortunately led some modern social psychologists to reject his ideas completely. He also tended to give a feeble and often inaccurate picture of the sociological determinants of behavior, and, indeed, often gave the impression that all of the human personality was biogenic and psychogenic. Notwithstanding, it has been largely Freud's influence that has developed and extended our knowledge of those elements in personality which have their origin in purely psychological functions, although some of the more recent clinical researchers have deviated markedly from Freud.

1   COOLEY'S ANALYSIS

Cooley started from the problems raised by two important observations on human behavior: 1. Despite drastic differences in social influences on the individual in different cultures, a person from one culture could usually gain a sympathetic insight into the motives and emotions of persons from another culture. 2. Yet these motives and emotions were not fixed and unchanging, like biological instincts should be, and could be called into play by the most diverse and changing social situations.

Cooley's solution for this apparent paradox was to postulate certain universal experiences that practically all human beings had, although in different degree, and that gave to their behavior a certain similarity—a certain universal "humanness"—no matter what the cultural expression of this behavior happened to be. He called these universal motives and emotions the "sentiments" and proceeded to suggest that they included such things as fear, envy, love, hate, and so on, without being at all explicit as to how the sentiments could be detected and identified. He recog-

[32] *The Basic Writings of Sigmund Freud* (New York: Modern Library, 1938).

nized that one culture might develop and encourage the expression of a certain sentiment much more than another culture would. Yet he believed that no sentiment could be completely unknown in any given culture because the experiences which gave rise to the sentiments could not be avoided completely by any culture.

Cooley was not very explicit in indicating how the experiences gave rise to the sentiments, since he felt that this was a question for empirical research, but he spoke in general terms of how the touching and fondling of an infant stimulated the sentiment of love, how the deprivation of an infant gave rise to the sentiment of envy, and so on. It is a pity that these early speculations of Cooley, so undogmatic and well balanced, did not encourage the empirical research which he hoped for and which they deserved. They led right to the investigation of the developing infant, research on which had hardly begun when Cooley first wrote on these matters but which has since then proved to be the very heart of sociopsychological research.

2   FREUD'S ANALYSIS

Freud developed his ideas about the psychogenic personality soon after his discovery of the profound influence of the "unconscious" mind on behavior. While he rather vaguely held that certain hereditary (biogenic) "instincts" formed part of the unconscious motivations to behavior, he regarded certain developmental experiences of early childhood as having the more important role.[33] It is interesting to note that while Cooley formulated his theories by making observations (albeit casual ones) on children, as well as by reading anthropological literature on behavior in different societies, Freud deduced his theories of childhood development from intensive observations of neurotic adults. Practically none of Freud's many theories have been scientifically proved—in fact, some of them are discredited—but there has been a considerable amount of support adduced for a few of the theories (such as infantile sexuality, the unconscious influencing of behavior, some sort of relationship between childhood experiences and adult personality). Freud's work is sufficiently influential, however, that we must consider relevant parts of it even if we retain some skepticism regarding it.

[33] The biogenic personality Freud called the *Id*, and the psychogenic the *Ego*. His narrow conception of the sociogenic personality—as limited to a repressive, limiting influence on behavior—was given the name of *Superego* or Censor. It is highly questionable whether Freud intended to use the concept of instinct. Writing in German, he used the word *triebe* which his English translators—working mainly in the period when instinctivism was dominant—translated as "instinct." Actually the word "drive" or "impulse" would be just as accurate.

Freud's basic theory states a fairly uniform pattern of "normal" childhood development arising out of certain interpersonal experiences and reactions. The pattern is somewhat different for boys than it is for girls, and since Freud gave greater attention to the boys, and since we can devote but little space to the theory, we shall present it in cursory fashion for boys only. The primary element is the biogenic instinct of the libido, or the sexual impulse in the broadest sense of the term. This impulse the newborn boy first directs toward himself, in what Freud called the narcistic stage of development. Then, as relations of feeding, fondling, petting, etc., develop with the mother, the libido becomes directed toward her, under normal conditions of development. The next step occurs when the child becomes "aware" that he is not allowed to be the sexual partner of his mother, that rather this role belongs to his father. This period of primary love for the mother and rivalry with the father is the so-called Oedipal stage, and lasts normally until the age of three or four. Then the child learns, from outsiders as well as from older family members, that it is not proper to hate his father and have sexual desires for his mother, and so he represses these early desires into the unconscious, and transfers his affections first to other little boys, in the homosexual "latency period," and then to other girls (from among whom he eventually selects a mate, in one advanced stage of the process of transference of the libido).

Several experiences during this developmental process form the ego of the child and give it a universal character with only minor features unique to the individual: (1) The transference of the libidinal impulse to other persons (which permits love toward others); (2) the recognition of a rival for the affection of the libidinal object (which permits hate toward others); (3) the unconscious recognition of the necessity of repressing certain impulses (which permits frustration and socialized impulses); (4) the experiences which are repressed. These elements form the core of the psychogenic personality; the repression agent itself and what it selects for repression are determined by society and thus it constitutes the sociogenic personality (the "superego" in Freud's terminology).

Freud and his disciple, Karl Abraham, also developed a theory of the "erogenous zones" which permitted a further development of the theory of the psychogenic personality. This theory was based on the observation that there are three apertures into the body where the skin is very sensitive and where stimulation or use permits sexual feeling: the mouth (or oral opening), the anus, and the genital opening. These receive differing amounts of attention and different degrees of satisfying or frustrating stimulation at different stages of infancy. The sucking of the newborn baby is associated at one extreme with complete ease and satisfaction in obtaining nourishment (fixation at this stage gives rise to the easily satisfied, expansive, optimistic elements in personality which Freud called the "oral personality type"). At the other extreme, when food is not readily forthcoming, there is an experience of frustration and struggle for the barest necessities of existence.

Around the age of one or two years, toilet training begins in our society, and the child may get the experience that giving out (generosity) is pleasant or that it is associated with pain, frustration, and punishment. If the latter, certain traits like penuriousness, overcleanliness, and overprecision may become developed in the infant's psychogenetic personality (which Freud called the "anal personality type"). At a still later age the child becomes interested in his sexual organs and either receives direct satisfaction by stimulating them or is punished in some way for stimulating them. These experiences determine the individual's attitudes toward sex in adult life and form another important component in his psychogenic personality (if the individual gets his sexual satisfaction primarily from genital stimulation, Freud called him the "genital personality type").

In his many writings Freud developed and presented voluminous case evidence for these and other hypotheses about elements of the psychogenic personality. Our brief presentation, of course, does not approach an adequate picture of his work along these lines, but it does indicate that Freud attributed central importance to the psychogenic personality, and that he thought it had the following characteristics: (1) its elements were universal to all mankind, since it was based on a natural history of development; (2) its formulation developed out of interpersonal relations, usually quite physical and mechanical in character (rather than socialized and sympathetic); (3) individual variations were a function of the degree of ease or frustration in the natural development. At the extremes of frustration, which prevented movement toward the next stage of development, the neurotic or psychotic personality was produced.

Large numbers of case studies have been published by Freud's disciples to support the general outline of his theories regarding psychogenic personality and to explain how certain individual variations fit into the general framework of the theories. Certain anthropologists have applied the theories to preliterate societies and have come out with some modifications and extensions. For example, Bronislaw Malinowski[34] showed that among the Trobriand Islanders the father was usually permissive toward his child, whereas it was the maternal uncle who repressed and socialized it, so that in this society the Oedipal hatred developed toward the uncle rather than toward the father. The implication of this modification is that it is not the sexual rivalry with the father which develops repression and socialization but rather the repressive role of the older man.

[34] *The Sexual Life of Savages* (London: G. Routledge, 1929).

The psychoanalyst, Abram Kardiner,[35] along with several anthropologists, has extended Freud's theories to other societies with the concept of the "basic personality." This involves the observation that certain specific psychogenic personality traits are typical of practically all members of one society but are scarcely to be found in another society. This is attributed to certain typical practices, characteristic of a given society, in child rearing. For example, in societies where toilet training is strongly emphasized for infants at an early age, adult personalities typically take the form of being unyielding, penurious, overprecise, and otherwise have the characteristics of "anal personalities."

Finally, a large number of psychologists and sociologists have sought to test, by scientific methods of statistics or experiment, the specific hypotheses emanating from Freud's general theory of the development of the psychogenic personality. For example, one implication of his theory of transference is that the mate a man finally chooses must have some of the traits that unconsciously remind him of his mother, who was his original love. While this and other of the hypotheses are not specific enough to test adequately, the many careful studies made show many hypotheses verified and many disproved.[36] There has been no evidence, however, which discredits the general postulate of a psychogenic personality.

There are close interrelationships between psychogenic and sociogenic influences. Psychogenic traits are changeable when the individual holding them is subjected to certain kinds of experience. Social conditions and sociogenic aspects of the personality are major factors in determining whether the individual is to have these experiences. On the other hand, the psychogenic traits help to limit the kinds of communication an individual has and his sociogenic personality is built on communication. Newcomb[37] illustrates the interrelations of psychogenic and sociogenic factors in his discussion of psychogenic hostility. He observes first that psychogenic "fixations of any kind may owe their persistence to the fact that they are safely barricaded against interpersonal communication . . . person-

[35] Abram Kardiner *et al., The Psychological Frontiers of Society* (New York: Columbia University Press, 1945). For a recent survey of the work of the anthropologists using psychoanalytic concepts and tests, see Victor Barnouw, *Culture and Personality* (Homewood, Ill.: Dorsey Press, 1962).

[36] For a summary of all researches testing Freudian hypotheses to 1943, see Robert R. Sears, *Survey of Studies of Psychoanalytic Concepts* (New York: Social Science Research Council, 1943). For an interesting, more recent study, see William H. Sewell, "Infant Training and the Personality of the Child," *American Journal of Sociology*, 58 (September, 1952), pp. 150–59. Also see Harold Orlansky, "Infant Care and Personality," *Psychological Bulletin*, 46 (January, 1949), pp. 1–48; A. R. Lindesmith and A. L. Strauss, "Critique of Culture—Personality Writings," *American Sociological Review*, 15 (October, 1950), pp. 587–600.

[37] Theodore M. Newcomb, "Autistic Hostility and Social Reality," *Human Relations,* I (1st issue, 1947), pp. 69–84.

alities are more likely to become distorted when barriers to communication encourage autistic frames of reference for perceiving interpersonal relations." Freud found so much repression in the sexual area possibly because, in his culture, there were so many barriers to communication regarding sexual matters between parents and children. Concerning the psychogenic traits of hostility Newcomb hypothesizes:

> Hostile impulses commonly arise, then, when status relationship is so perceived that another is viewed as threat. Such a perception arises through interaction, and it is likely to persist until modified by further interaction. If, as a result of a hostile attitude emerging from the newly perceived status relationship, communication with the other person is avoided, the conditions necessary for eliminating the hostile attitude are not likely to occur.[38]

Psychotherapy helps reduce psychogenic distortions because the individual can lower his defenses with the psychiatrist and establish two-way communication; he can "take the role of the other" such as he cannot do when he is interacting with a person with whom he is in conflict. The psychiatrist's behavior is perceived by the patient as response to his own behavior, as determined by a set of conditions rather than as arbitrary or willful antagonism. "The interpersonal conflict becomes a situation in which he is involved rather than a hostile force with which he is confronted."[39] Thus the psychogenic trait and social interaction are mutually dependent for this individual. Of course, many other social relationships besides the doctor-patient one have the same effect of reducing psychogenic deviation.

E   *The Sociogenic Personality: Cultural Features*

In an earlier chapter we defined a culture as the sum of meanings and values found among people in a given society.[40] The *meanings* of a culture define the "experiences" of the individuals who participate in that culture. Experiences do not simply impinge themselves on the individual from the outside. A stimulus from the outside becomes an experience when the individual gives it a meaning (and responds to it in some way, muscularly, emotionally, or intellectually). Indeed, as Dewey first pointed out,[41] the individual *selects,* out of the innumerable stimuli that physically impinge on the individual from the outside world, those stimuli to which

[38] *Ibid.,* p. 72.

[39] *Ibid.,* p. 77.

[40] See Chapter 2, Section C, and Chapter 3, Section A.

[41] John Dewey, "The Reflex-Arc Concept in Psychology," *Psychological Review,* 3 (July, 1896), pp. 357–70.

he will respond. The stimuli thus selected are those that can be given meaning. Meaning can be attributed to a stimulus by an individual when his culture includes a meaning for it.[42] Thus culture, directly or indirectly, makes possible an individual's experience and gives form to an individual's reactions. And, to a certain extent, the individual's personality consists of his past experience and his recurrent reactions to stimuli (that is, his consistent behavior).

A very simple example would be the perception by an individual of a banana. The stimuli coming from the banana are simply longness, firmness, and a wave length that we learn to associate with yellow color. It becomes a "banana"—that is, a fruit that can be eaten when peeled, that tastes good, that provides nourishment, etc.—when the individual can ascribe the meaning of banana to it. This meaning in mind, the individual reacts to the stimuli (by reaching to grasp the banana, by noting it mentally for future action, by ignoring it, etc.) and he has had the experience of seeing a banana. The experience has become part of his personality (although a small part in the case of a mere banana) and his reaction to it is an expression of his personality.

Among the *values* of a culture are those specifying what a desirable personality should be like.[43] Such values tend to mold the personalities of the members of a society, so that a typical personality is often characteristic of a given culture. This "culture-ideal personality" molded by values is to be sharply distinguished from the psychogenic "basic personality" —referred to by Kardiner and the anthropologists. Whereas the "basic personality" is fairly well completed in infancy, the "culture-ideal personality" cannot begin to take shape until the child is old enough to internalize the values of his culture, and receives its most striking development when the child comes in contact with institutions and older persons other than his family members (in our society, the school, Sunday school, scouts, "gang" of older children, etc.). Some psychiatrists and anthropologists fail to make the distinction between psychogenic and sociogenic personality elements, and attribute traits that are products of cultural values to such psychogenic influences as toilet training, excessive fondling of infants, etc. When we speak of the "culture-ideal personality" (as part of the sociogenic personality) we do not mean it as necessarily ideal in an

[42] There are also certain ways for an individual to develop new meanings, but this happens relatively infrequently and the process is a difficult one which we cannot go into here. Piaget has devoted considerable research to the development of meanings— both individual and cultural—in the mind of the child. See Jean Piaget, *The Child's Conception of His World* (New York: Harcourt, 1929).

[43] An interesting study of the molding of a personality by culture is provided by Camara Laye, *The Dark Child: The Autobiography of an African Boy* (New York: Noonday, 1954).

ethical sense; we mean simply that it reflects the values of the culture, and might include aggressiveness, dishonesty, or cynicism as well as their opposites. Nor does the culture-ideal personality have to be uniform for all members of the society holding a given culture. Sapir pointed out that an individual's personality "embodies countless cultural patterns in a unique configuration."[44]

Some societies do not have clear values specifying what a person should be like in certain areas of behavior. Some societies have conflicting values, each of which pretends to specify the culture-ideal personality governing certain areas of behavior. In some societies, where the values exist and are consistent, although not very strong, individuals may still not incorporate the values into their personalities for all sorts of reasons. Thus it is not to be expected that the culture-ideal personality would be uniform for all persons in a given society.

Let us offer a few simple illustrations; these illustrations are based on general descriptive reports rather than careful measurement of cultural values, so that the illustrations may be inaccurate in detail but the underlying principle correct. In Chinese culture there appears to be a strong value against boastfulness, whereas in American culture such a value does not exist or is not very strong. Consequently, in China practically no one is boastful, whereas in the United States one can find a great range between persons who are "naturally modest" to persons who are unabashedly and spontaneously boastful. A different example: In the United States equalitarianism is a fairly strong value. But so also is racism (a system of beliefs that different categories of people have different innate abilities for cultural achievement and that any mixture of these people will result in cultural degeneration). The incompatibility between these two values results in a great variation among Americans in their treatment of strangers, and even in inconsistency in the behavior of any one single American from one occasion to another. In France, on the other hand, where equalitarianism has also had a long development but racism has hardly developed at all, a spontaneous equalitarianism toward strangers seems to be fairly characteristic of the French personality.

The culture values governing personality may be fairly clear and consistent in a society and yet not be uniform for all persons in the society. This is especially true for persons of different age and sex, and in some societies is also true for persons of different socioeconomic classes and other categories.[45] In many societies, to a certain extent including the United States, one culture value for a child's behavior is dependency: a

[44] Edward Sapir, "Personality," *Encyclopedia of the Social Sciences* (New York: Macmillan, 1934), Vol. 12, pp. 85–88.

[45] The most thoroughgoing analysis of the differential effect on personality of the different structures and institutions of a society is Hans H. Gerth and C. Wright Mills, *Character and Social Structure* (New York: Harcourt, 1953).

child is supposed to come to older people to do all sorts of things for him, even when he is quite old enough mentally and physically to do them himself. Then, as the child reaches late adolescence, he is supposed fairly rapidly to become independent—to avoid asking other people to do things for him even at great personal inconvenience. To some foreigners American children appear overdependent and American adults exaggeratedly independent, but of course such an observation merely reflects the fact that their own culture does not contain these differing values for personalities at different age levels.

American culture is now changing in its values governing the personality differences of men and women, so it would be difficult to be specific about illustrations in this domain. Descriptions of many other societies, however, leave little doubt that, in them, the culture-ideal personality for men includes dominance toward women, and for women includes submissiveness toward men. Especially within the last thirty years or so American culture has not specified a culture-ideal personality greatly different for the upper classes than for the lower classes. But several European cultures do so: for example, the peasants and other lower-class people are expected to have "thrifty natures" whereas upper-class people are expected to be personally extravagant.

The fact that an individual may change, and is expected to change, from one culture-ideal personality to another is important to the understanding of the nature of sociogenic personality. Through the simple process of growing up, or through mobility from one social class to another, the individual changes his culture-ideal personality. The transition may not be easy, of course, and there are always a good number of stories in American and European society about "men who have never grown up" or the middle-class traits of the "newly rich." Yet the change in personality does occur for most of those who change from one position to another. The roles that one plays, which is part of the sociogenic element in his personality and behavior, is a function of that person's position in his society.

Many of the elements in the culture-ideal personality are quite similar, at least superficially, to those in the psychogenic personality; we have spoken, for example, of dominance-submissiveness, thriftiness, dependence-independence, under both rubrics, and the list could be greatly extended. Yet the psychogenic personality, formed largely in early childhood, is relatively unchangeable. The confusion between psychogenic and sociogenic elements in personality is so easy to make that it has not been avoided by the experts. Much research has yet to be carried out clearly delimiting the two sources of personality traits and determining how they interact in concrete behavior.[46]

[46] E. W. Burgess, Karen Horney, and Erich Fromm have investigated along this line.

F   *The Sociogenic Personality: The Influence of Several Cultures on the Single Personality*

The sociogenic personality is, by definition, a function of the meanings and values which make up the culture of a society. But by no means does it consist only of traits which reflect the specific cultural values directly. Among the other influences involved are the degree of complexity of the cultural values influencing personality, the diversity of cultures with which the individual comes in contact, the amount of conflict inherent in the relations between the cultures with which the individual comes in contact, the degree of opposition of certain cultural values to the biogenic and psychogenic aspects of the individual's personality, the number and complexity of the roles the personality is called on to play.

It would seem that cultures differ considerably in the complexity of demands they make on the individual (we are not considering at this point the strength of the demands, but the number and diversity of the demands for different behavior manifestations). American culture seems to be relatively simple in this respect. Any given trait in the culture-ideal personality is supposed to be manifested in behavior in a wide variety of situations. But let us compare this with the culture of the Italian Renaissance. That culture made many more differing demands on the personality depending on the situation in which it found itself. Moderns are amazed to read of the richness and versatility of such personalities as Leonardo da Vinci, Niccolò Machiavelli, and Benvenuto Cellini, to mention merely some extreme cases. These men were geniuses, it is true, but they also reflected their cultures, and we have men of equal biological genius today who have the same abilities as those gentlemen but whose personalities do not contain as many facets.

While the contemporary American culture's demands on the personality are relatively simple, this is by no means true in all spheres of behavior. Many Frenchmen have told me that there is one thing (at least) they do not understand about the American businessman: how is it that he drives such a hard, exacting bargain in a business deal and later gives away a large share of his profits in a burst of generosity? The answer is quite simple for an American but difficult for an intelligent, friendly Frenchman to understand. American culture contains several divergent values concerning wealth and its use in different situations, and thus a typical American personality can be grasping and penurious in some situations and generous or extravagant with his money in other situations. Since the situations are explicitly different, there is no necessary conflict or inconsistency within the culture or the personality. Whereas the Frenchman will quite regularly and "logically" regard money as something to be acquired as one can and utilized to purchase the necessities and luxuries of life, the American typically sees money in at least two different relations: (1) Money is the prize of a competitive game in which one uses his skills and wits to the utmost (as in a game of chess or tennis); (2) money is something with which to make other people happier or better, and American culture also contains the value of reform, or the desire to make other people happier or better. Thus the typical American's personality, in the area of behavior having to do with money, is more complex and versatile than the average Frenchman's. The Frenchman, consequently, finds great difficulty in understanding why the American wants to put so much effort into the acquisition of money that he does not need and does not intend to use, and why he is so foolish as to give it away while he is working so hard to get more.

The complexity of personality we have described above comes from the complexity within a given culture; another kind of complexity of personality may arise from the individual's contact with several cultures. Whereas the former kind does not involve any inconsistencies or internal conflicts—as each facet of the personality comes into play in a different situation—the latter kind may involve inconsistency and internal conflict, since two different cultures are more likely to have different values for one given situation than one culture is. The individual may act on the basis of one value at a time and the other for the same kind of situation at another time, and not know why he made such a choice; or he may have quite an internal struggle in deciding which of the two values to act on. In either case, his personality can be said to be more complex than that of a person who has one value to act on in a variety of comparable situations.

A person who incorporates two (or more) sets of cultural values, by virtue of having been part of two (or more) different societies during his life, is spoken of in the sociological literature as a *"marginal man."*[47] Immigrants and other persons who have made drastic moves during their lifetime, from membership in one society to membership in another society, are marginal men, since no one can forget his past completely, or is likely to think his former culture completely wrong and inadequate, when one is acquiring a new culture. Marginal men thus have a complexity of personality, an inconsistency of behavior, and often what might be called a "divided conscience" as to what is right and wrong in any given behavior or situation.

This does not necessarily make all marginal men unhappy and maladjusted: they may work out a satisfactory resolution of their two sets of values, especially if the society in which they dwell permits deviation in behavior. The new resolution can permit a greater degree of adjustment to a variety of social situations, because it is more rational, than would a

[47] See Everett V. Stonequist, *The Marginal Man* (New York: Scribner's, 1937).

> The marginal man is a personality type that arises at a time and a place where, out of the conflict of races and cultures, new societies, new peoples and cultures are coming into existence. The fate which condemns him to live, at the same time, in two worlds is the same which compels him to assume, in relation to the worlds in which he lives, the rôle of a cosmopolitan and a stranger. Inevitably he becomes, relatively to his cultural milieu, the individual with the wider horizon, the keener intelligence, the more detached and rational viewpoint. The marginal man is always relatively the more civilized human being. He occupies the position which has been, historically, that of the Jew in the Diaspora. The Jew, particularly the Jew who has emerged from the provincialism of the ghetto, has everywhere and always been the most civilized of human creatures.
>
> From what has been said one may infer that the marginal man is an incidental product of a process of acculturation, such as inevitably ensues when peoples of different cultures and different races come together to carry on a common life. He is, as I have suggested, an effect of imperialism, economic, political and cultural; an incident of the process by which civilization, as Spengler has said, grows up at the expense of earlier and simpler cultures.
>
> Robert E. Park, "Introduction" to Everett V. Stonequist, *The Marginal Man* (New York: Scribner's, 1937), pp. xvii–xviii.

simple response based on one set of cultural values. Contact with more than one set of cultural values can thus result either in confusion of mental conflict, on the one hand, or a higher degree of choice and rationality on the other hand, depending on the permissiveness of the situation, the flexibility of the individual's psychogenic personality, and the content of the cultural values he incorporates.

The person who has been part of two (or more) cultures incorporates in his personality not only the two sets of values, and the resolution or choice he makes between them, but also the new element of relativism. The knowledge that an alternative is possible to one set of cultural values allows one to comprehend that many other alternatives are possible. With such a perception that cultural values are relative, the personality is usually no longer bound by any single set of cultural values. This does not mean that such a personality makes a rational choice in his behavior under all circumstances, since no one has the time or the inclination to examine all possibilities for action in every situation he confronts. But when the situation is important for such a personality, he can make the effort of running his mind over a great range of logical possibilities and decide on the basis of which one seems most advantageous in terms of his personal values, rather than reacting more or less mechanically in terms of a single set of culturally imposed values. Rationality in this sense, as well as complexity of personality, seems to be a function of a personality exposed to more than one set of cultural values.

Rationality based on relativism permits a high degree of adjustment to a diversity of situations, although it may also permit mental conflict which is maladjustive. It permits opportunism, or behavior which is in accord with purely self-aggrandizing values, but it also permits a broader kind of voluntary loyalty to a "higher" set of values than is common in any one single culture. Much more research is needed on the personality who incorporates two or more sets of cultural values to learn the conditions under which he becomes more rationally adjusted or more neurotically maladjusted, more selfish or more altruistic, than the personality who reflects only one set of cultural values. Presumably his specific experiences, his biogenic personality, and his psychogenic personality are the forces which turn him in one direction or another.

The relations between the sociogenic and the psychogenic and biogenic traits, within one personality, also need further investigation. Any one culture can make difficult, and even intolerable, demands on the biogenic and psychogenic personality (for example, by demanding too much intelligence and quickness of reaction, or too much repression of emotions and of manifestation of psychogenic traits such as love or hate). It seems likely that incorporation of two or more sets of cultural values would permit a better adjustment of the sociogenic to the psychogenic and biogenic elements in personality because the more difficult cultural values would be abandoned for the less difficult ones. Some students of the social psychology of children have begun to look into these questions but their researches have not yet reached the stage where reliable answers can be given.[48]

G   *The Sociogenic Personality: Role Playing*

As Mead first observed and Coutu clarified,[49] there is an important distinction between role taking and role playing. *Role taking* is the universal process through which one man adjusts his behavior to another so that an organized social life can exist.[50] It involves imagining how other people will respond to one's own actions and how one is expected by

[48] The first one to have raised questions like these seems to have been Lawrence K. Frank. See, for example, his "Cultural Control and Physiological Autonomy," *American Journal of Orthopsychiatry*, 8 (1938), pp. 622–25. Also see his *Society as the Patient* (New Brunswick, N.J.: Rutgers University Press, 1948).

[49] George H. Mead, *Mind, Self, and Society* (Chicago: University of Chicago Press, 1934); Walter Coutu, "Role-Playing vs. Role-Taking," *American Sociological Review*, 16 (April, 1951), pp. 180–87.

[50] See Chapter 2, Section E.

others to respond to their actions, largely in terms of the meanings and values of the culture. Role taking is what permits the existence of the sociogenic personality, but it is too general a process to give it its specific content. The specific content of the sociogenic personality is given, first by culture in a general way (as we have noted in the two preceding sections), second, by the playing of specific roles within a society.

Role playing sounds a bit as though it belongs to the terminology of the stage, and this is very natural, for the specialized part one plays in society is very much like the specialized part one would play on the stage.[51] As we have already pointed out, the word "personality" itself has its root in the Latin word *persona,* which means the mask that ancient performers wore when performing their role in a tragedy or comedy. One has several roles in life, some being played alternately at one period during life and some appearing only when others have been abandoned. Park went so far as to define the personality (in its sociogenic aspects) as the "sum and organization of those traits which determine the role of the individual in the group."[52] The notion is much older than the sociologists, of course: Shakespeare, for example, likened man's personality to all the roles an actor might play in a dramatic performance:

> *All the world's a stage,*
> *And all the men and women merely players:*
> *They have their exits and their entrances;*
> *And one man in his time plays many parts,*[53]. . .

A role is a fairly stable complex of behavior patterns, more or less consistent among themselves, which either society requires or the individual chooses the performance of in his relation to a certain individual or group. The analogy to acting and the notion of "playing" a role should not be taken to mean that role aspects of personality are superficial. Actually, roles are usually thoroughly incorporated into self, and there is no "real" social self underlying the roles.

There are a huge number of roles an individual is expected to play during the course of his life, and he usually has a large choice of characters within each. Society requires usually that he (if a male) play the role of son, brother, pupil, suitor, husband, father, in-law, coworker, employee, perhaps employer, new acquaintance, organized group member, informal group member, old friend, and so on. The great psychologist of the late

[51] For an elaboration of this notion, see Erving Goffman, *The Presentation of Self in Everyday Life* (Edinburgh, Scotland: Social Sciences Research Centre, University of Edinburgh, 1956; reprinted as a Doubleday Anchor Book, New York, 1959).

[52] Robert E. Park and Ernest W. Burgess, *Introduction to the Science of Sociology* (Chicago: University of Chicago Press, 1924), p. 70.

[53] *As You Like It,* Act II, Scene VII.

nineteenth century, William James, expressed this idea in his statement
that a person "has as many social selves as there are groups to which he
belongs."[54] There are a large number of behavior patterns involved in
each role, and some are more or less required or expected in the culture.
In some societies all the behavior patterns in a given role may be fixed by
the culture, so that the individual has no leeway at all in the performance
of his role. This is true, for example, of the mother-in-law and son-in-law
roles in relation to each other among the Andaman Islanders where the
occasions of contact and the content of what is said between them are
specified very precisely by the culture.[55]

For most roles in most societies, however, the culture specifies only
the bare outlines of expected behavior, and the individual fills in the rest.
How he fills it in depends in large measure, of course, on the psychogenic
traits in his personality. But sometimes, in a manner we know very little
about as yet, the culture requirements of the role interact with the psychogenic personality of the individual to produce a role which is not completely in accord with the psychogenic personality of the individual.

As an example let us take the case of a man who has a psychogenic
trait of submissiveness and non-aggressiveness and who occupies the role
of manager in a small business concern. The social demands of his role
are that he be present at the plant at the appropriate time, dressed in a
business suit rather than overalls, that he formulate the work allocation
and keep records of production and distribution, that he point out to those
responsible when the quality of production is not up to standard, that he
delegate responsibility for various specialized activities within the plant to
the personnel director, the foremen, the bookkeeper, and the secretary.
These activities require a certain level of intelligence, but they seldom
require a consistent element of dominance. When the few occasions occur
in which he must demonstrate authority, he is unhappy, but steels himself
to carry out the demands of the role. Most of the time he is regarded as an
easygoing boss, pleasant to work for.

Nevertheless, the fact that he is "the boss" causes the workers and
other functionaries of the plant to put him in a dominant position. He is
shown deference as he moves about the plant, and his opinion is sought on
all sorts of matters and is taken as a rule of action in the plant. There is
nothing in his psychogenic personality that seeks this dominance, and
there is nothing in the social requirements of his position that demands
that he be dominant in all these little ways. Yet he plays a dominant role
in the plant often in ways unknown to himself. Thus, in his relations to
other people, this man has a dominant personality. The dominance lies in

[54] William James, *The Principles of Psychology* (New York: Holt, 1890), Vol. I, p. 294.
[55] Alfred R. Radcliffe-Brown, *The Andaman Islanders* (Cambridge: The University
Press, 1922).

his sociogenic role rather than in any psychogenic element of his personality.

Of course we might wonder what would happen if one of the foremen should be a psychogenically dominant personality and discern his superior's "weakness," or if a crisis occurred in which our manager was called upon to exercise more dominance, over a longer period of time, than his psychogenic personality was capable of. Under these circumstances he might lose his sociogenic role of dominance. But things might go along indefinitely without much demand on the manager to be aggressively dominant over a long period of time. Even a psychogenically dominant foreman would be hesitant about attempting to dominate his superior; he might be aware of the manager's "weakness" and still not want to take a chance at dominating because he is not sure but that occasionally "the worm turneth." And in a well-ordered plant, where the manager is intelligent and efficient, very seldom would a crisis occur where prolonged dominance rather than easygoingness would be necessary for a solution. Thus we see that a person can play a sociogenic role of dominance in his relations to other people, and that this role can be regarded as an important part of his personality by these people without his having the slightest element of dominance in his psychogenic personality.

Less extreme cases would probably be much more common. Within the broad limits set by the cultural requirements for a role the individual has a large measure of "choice" as to the specific content of his sociogenic role. This "choice" is made by the individual largely in terms of his psychogenic and biogenic characteristics, but there is also in it the sociogenic element of the expectations of other people toward whom he plays this role. Their expectations, in turn, may be a function of their own psychogenic and biogenic traits, as well as their conception as to what his sociogenic role should consist of. A husband can be attentive and demonstrative in his relations with his wife, for example, or he may be casual, and this difference may be due to such sociogenic factors as the role their friends expect them to play toward each other, as well as to the cultural demands on husband-wife relationships, to the degree of intensity of their love for each other, and to the psychogenic and biogenic elements in the personalities of the two. Even though it is such a sociogenic factor which makes a man attentive and demonstrative, rather than casual, it can still be said that this is what "he is"—that is, what his personality is.

Different sociogenic roles are characteristic of personalities in certain types of relations in different groups having the same general culture. Class groups are very important in determining sociogenic roles. We may take an example from the many descriptions of class differences among Negroes in the southern states in regard to husband-wife roles relative to each

... each of us has as many conscious sociocultural egos as there are organized groups with which we are in contact. The totality of these egos occupy almost the whole field of our conscious mentality, and the totality of these roles and activities fill a major part of our time, activities, and life. . . . If the groups to which a given individual belongs are in a solidary relationship with one another, if they all urge the individual to think, feel, and act in the same or concordant way, push him towards the same or concordant goals and prescribe to him the same or concordant duties, rights, then the different egos of the individual which reflect these groups will also be in harmony with one another, unified into a single, large harmonious ego. (On this socio-cultural level) he will be blessed with peace of mind and consistency in his conduct. . . . If on the other hand the groups to which an individual belongs are in conflict; if they urge him to contradictory ideas, values, convictions, duties and actions, then the individual's respective egos will be mutually antagonistic. The individual will be a house divided against himself and split by inner conflicts. His conduct will be irresolute, inconsistent, and contradictory, as will also be his thoughts and utterances.

Pitirim A. Sorokin, "Comments," in George K. Zollschan and Walter Hirsch (eds.), *Explorations in Social Change* (Boston: Houghton Mifflin, 1964), p. 418.

other.[56] In the lower-income groups, the greater difficulty for a man than for a woman to find steady employment in the period between the Civil War and World War II, and the tradition from slavery days of not-too-stable marital ties, gave the wife a dominant and independent role vis-à-vis her husband. The husband was often dependent economically on the wife, and this tended to give him a "dependent personality." He was influenced, however, by the larger society's conception of the dominant role of the man, and one of his reactions under the circumstances often was to assume a certain fickleness. He turned his attention away from family responsibility toward the pursuit of individual pleasure; he frequently even deserted his family and sought to establish a relation with a different woman. Dependency and fickleness thus easily tended to become characteristic of the lower-class southern Negro male's personality, although there were many individual exceptions.

The middle classes among southern Negroes, before World War II could be defined as families in which the husband had steady employment at a wage level which did not require that the wife also work. These fami-

[56] E. Franklin Frazier, *The Negro Family in the United States* (Chicago: University of Chicago Press, 1939); John Dollard, *Caste and Class in a Southern Town* (New Haven: Yale University Press, 1937); Allison Davis, Burleigh B. Gardner, and Mary R. Gardner, *Deep South* (Chicago: University of Chicago Press, 1941); Gunnar Myrdal, with the assistance of Richard Sterner and Arnold Rose, *An American Dilemma* (New York: Harper, 1944).

lies, which struggled hard to gain their higher status and which were concerned about future mobility, quite consciously rejected the lower-class pattern of female independence and male fickleness. They often sought the other extreme of strict monogamy, a stable family throughout life, male dominance, and other cultural patterns that Frazier identifies as "puritan." It is possible that these middle-class Negroes deliberately adopted a way of life that they believed to prevail among whites of middle- and upper-class status. Actually the latter have broken away from the puritan ideal to a considerable extent during the last fifty years, but there has been such social isolation between castes in the South[57] that middle-class Negroes do not know that they have been emulating an ideal now relatively discarded among whites. Whether it is simply in rejection of the Negro lower class, or also in emulation of an out-of-date conception of the white society, middle-class Negroes in the South tend to have a "puritan" element in their sociogenic personalities.

All sorts of groups and groupings of persons within a society tend to impart different sociogenic elements to an individual's personality. A child may be quite average at home and in his neighborhood play group, but when he starts in at a new school level, such as high school or college, he may have the ability to perform remarkably in a specialized field that hitherto was unknown to him. This gives him a prestige and a sense of satisfaction in a new group that may radically transform his personality. Or a man, hitherto fairly successful in most aspects of life, may fail in a community project for which he was chosen as leader. While this does not alter his role in his family or his business, it does alter his role in the community and his conception of himself. His sociogenic personality thus takes on a new aspect.

Examples of this sort could be multiplied, but enough have been given to illustrate how an individual's relations to various groups or groupings affect his sociogenic personality. As we describe various types of groups and groupings in later chapters of this book we shall have occasion again to refer to their characteristic influence on their members' sociogenic personalities. Some are quite special—like the audience[58]—and their particular impact on the personality can be quite important, but we are not ready to consider these special influences yet.

H   *The Sociogenic Personality:*
     The Conscious Private Self

Thus far we have been considering the sociogenic personality as a reflection of the groups to which he belongs and as a product of the expectations

[57] See Chapter 8, Section A.
[58] See Chapter 9, Section B.

of these groups. Consciously we also have the feeling that we have a self which is not merely the sum of the roles we play. Mead called this the subjective "I" and distinguished it from the objective "me" which reflects the group expectations. The poets have celebrated the conscious private self as the true self. Clearly there is a subjective feeling that there is a conscious, private self which is an initiator of action and not a mere responder. It includes an ideal element—an "ideal-personal self" comparable to the "ideal-cultural personality" discussed earlier—that represents the "I" which the individual would like to have and which he may be striving toward rather than what he realistically knows he now is.

While the subjective aspect of the personality has been thought about and written about a great deal, it cannot be said to be well studied or understood. Our tentative interpretation of it will be based on the observations of Cooley and Mead. They held that the conscious private self is sociogenic, even though it is not determined directly by our experiences with other persons. They considered it sociogenic because it arises out of symbolic communication, and hence requires language before it can develop. It arises out of two kinds of communication: (1) The individual talks to himself—usually silently, but small children do it out loud—and sets expectations for his own behavior just as he does for anyone else's; (2) others communicate to the individual in such a way as to imply that he has an independent, conscious, private self.

While some people believe that their private selves always existed, or sprang up full-blown when they were born, observations of children indicate that they not only had to learn to communicate symbolically first but also had to have some rudiments of looking-glass selves first. It is probably not until the child realizes that he can react in different ways that he can play more than one role, that he requires a conscious feeling that he has an independent, private self as distinct from the various roles he plays. It is quite possible that biogenic and psychogenic influences within him that resist social expectations for his behavior encourage him to develop his private self.

One of the important early behaviors and experiences which strengthens a child's conception of his private self is the discovery that he can play-act or "play at roles" (which must be distinguished from role taking and role playing, which were discussed earlier). The child plays at being a soldier, a storekeeper, a fairy, or at some other role he has either observed, heard about, or imagined. While he does this he is well aware that he is still himself and that his overt behavior is merely a played role. Thus this acting gives him a sense of self as distinguished from role. As he gets older and sees other people play-acting he acquires a keener sense of the distinction between self and role. Somewhere along the line he realizes that this regular, non-acting life consists of role playing in which he is boy, son, friend, pupil, etc., and he distinguishes his private self from the roles he is expected to play and does play. In some such manner the subjective self is separated conceptually from the self as object (or looking-glass self). When, as in our pluralistic society, he is obliged to play different roles in several distinct groups which have little contact with each other except through him, his conscious private self becomes the means whereby he integrates these various roles. In Chapter 2, these matters were discussed in terms of the adjustment of the individual to society; here we have considered them as aspects or components of personality.

I   *Personal Definitions, or the Self-Concept*

The constituent elements of the conscious private self—or the "self-concept," as some social psychologists call it—are the "personal definitions." Just as glandular activity and traumatic experiences in early childhood may set individual personality throughout life, so may personal definitions. A definition of one's career in terms of a profession or a definition of a member of the opposite sex as a loved one may mold one's whole personality and determine one's reactions to a great variety of experiences. Anything which our society happens to place a high value upon, or charges with high emotion, or makes intriguingly mysterious, is likely to become invested with a set of strong personal meanings that may well influence in large degree the lives of a large proportion of the population.

Sex may be taken as an example of something that is frequently invested with strong personal meanings. Biologically, sexual behavior is simple to understand: glandular activity and the pressures of liquids create muscular and nervous tensions which can be released in a variety of ways. Social psychologically, sex is most complicated and far from understood. The complication is due to a huge number of social and personal definitions centered on it. While modern sophistication and Freud have done much to make sex more understandable, they have also spread knowledge about the possibilities in sex and thus may be said to have "romanticized" sex. There is so much in sex, and sex is so important in our lives, they have taught us, that it deserves a great deal of our time, thought and energy. For people in many other societies, such as the Japanese, and indeed for most persons of the middle and lower classes in our own Western society prior to the Renaissance, sex was considered a more casual aspect of life. They considered it essential, of course, and it may be guessed that they enjoyed it, but they avoided a strong preoccupation with sex. It was not until the Renaissance in Western society that any large proportion of the population began to concern themselves with sex in their daily thoughts, although at first this was simply the extension of an upper class pattern downward through the social structure.[59] The Puritans, in their reaction to the Cavalier glorification of sex, sought to repress it in various ways, and in so doing became equally preoccupied with it. This strain between the emphasizers and detractors of sex, both contributing to the attention paid it, continued down through and past the nineteenth century. It was thus natural that Freud should find that false attitudes toward sex would be a common cause of neurosis. But his solution to the problem also encouraged a large proportion of the population to build their personal definitions around sex; in denouncing one set of personal definitions, he simply substituted another set.

The typical "modern" youth will engage in stereotyped courting behavior whether or not he feels a biological urge for sexual expression. This courting behavior becomes more and more frequent as the youth reaches his 20's, until it tends to dominate his life. He invests sexual expression with a very high value, and creates a great variety of personal definitions to aspects of his relations with potential sex partners. Little details of personal appearance, of gesture, of language, are given special personal definitions by the couple "in love." Of course, any two people who interact frequently will have something of a private language, but when sex is involved in that relationship in our society, the definitions are charged with high value and great emotion. These carry on into marriage but generally their emotional intensity then gradually diminishes. Marriage thus may become a "letdown" for many moderns, since it does not permit the continuous exemplification of the cultural and personal definitions set up for sexual expression.

Money-making in our society may also be taken as an example of something that is frequently invested with strong personal meanings. One need not be as extreme as a miser to be fascinated by money-making and to orient a large part of one's life around it. Many other values—

[59] Ernest W. Burgess, "The Romantic Impulse and Family Disorganization," *Survey*, 57 (1926), pp. 290–94; William L. Kolb, "Family Sociology, Marriage Education, and the Romantic Complex: A Critique," *Social Forces*, 29 (October, 1950), pp. 65–72.

such as social prestige, agreeable appearance, good health, large amount of leisure time—are much more available to those who have money than those who do not. Childhood, for a boy, is pointed toward selecting a vocation and, for a girl, toward selecting a mate who will have a worthwhile vocation. The youth are taught to value money, and their own experience soons reveals to them its value. The average adult spends a large part of his day in money-making, and in his leisure time he is concerned about making a wise expenditure of his earnings.

Thus it happens in our society that money and money-making are invested with strong personal meanings. Some individuals will state their life's goal in terms of a desired income; nearly everyone has defined to himself what he considers to be the minimum income he needs to be "happy." Other values and activities are usually translated into money terms; alternatives are weighed by translating them into units of money. Friction between individuals—including quarrels between husband and wife and between parents and children—may be about money. The accepted ethics of the society are violated—in such forms as crime, prostitution and treason—frequently for the sake of money. In a similar manner, money considerations enter into many other spheres of life.

The influence of "concern with money" on a great variety of activities —the "economic motive," as it is sometimes abstractly named—gives an individual's life a certain stability. Not stability in the sense that it keeps the individual on an even keel (because concern over money may be a personally disorganizing matter), but stability in the sense that it allows for prediction regarding an individual's behavior in certain situations. Knowledge of what personal definition an individual has given to money will permit one to predict with a fair degree of accuracy how that individual is likely to act in those situations which he has defined as connected to money. In this sense, a strong personal definition—and money tends to be the object of strong personal definitions in our society—has a stable (or static) influence on behavior in the same manner as does a glandular secretion, a psychogenic trait, a Freudian "complex," or any of the other mechanisms usually believed to "mold" behavior.

Such is the static aspect of a personal definition. It also has a dynamic aspect: an individual can redefine any object to himself. A person who has placed money or sex, or anything else, as the apex in his hierarchy of values can lower the relative value of this thing. Or he can raise a formerly insignificant value to the position of main life goal. It may be extremely difficult to do as one may have to change his whole conception of himself and of his relation to other people. A redefinition of an object with strong personal meanings involves changing lifelong habits.

No matter how difficult, however, the redefinition can be accomplished, and it is in this way that a major reorganization of an individual's life can take place. The redefinition of self may come about in a form of conversion, often occurring in a crowd setting,[60] in which the individual suddenly sees himself in a new light, as with a startling flash of insight. Conversions of this sort traditionally took place in connection with religious experiences,[61] but today they probably occur more frequently in other crowd settings, or in connection with the use of drugs or alcohol which affect body feelings and physiological processes. In some instances, personal redefinition of a drastic sort takes place after a period of rational thought. The individual "sits down with himself," so to speak, and attempts a conscious specification of who he "is" and where he is "going." After evaluating his findings in this conversation with himself, he resolves with a great deal of emotion and conviction to make of himself a "new man." Sometimes this personal redefinition sticks, although little is yet known as to the factors affecting the success or failure of such a process of self-redefinition.

A full understanding and prediction of an individual's behavior thus requires a knowledge of his personal definitions, both in terms of what they have been and in terms of what they are changing to. Some of the best studies in sociology have been of the relation between individual behavior and personal definitions. Alfred Lindesmith's study[62] shows how the process of becoming a drug addict involves—among other things—the redefinition of oneself as a drug addict. Donald R. Cressey's study[63] of the embezzler shows how a person in a position of trust, with a definition of himself as an honest and socially responsible person, can become an embezzler.

J   The Internal Integration of the Personality

The biogenic elements of personality (reflexes, body build, glandular activity, and intelligence) and the psychogenic elements of personality (the sentiments, emotion, and "basic personality traits," such as affection, hatred, envy, tendency toward dominance or submission, etc.) have been described in a cursory fashion, not only for their own contribution to human behavior, but also to show how social factors interact with them in their manifestations in behavior.

Similarly, in describing the sociogenic influences in personality (social experience, "culture ideal," the degree of complexity and integration of cultures, group roles) they were presented not only in their direct relation

[60] See Chapter 9, Section A.

[61] William James, *Varieties of Religious Experience* (New York: Modern Library, 1902).

[62] Alfred R. Lindesmith, *Opiate Addiction* (Bloomington, Ind.: Principia Press, 1947).

[63] Donald R. Cressey, *Other People's Money: A Study in the Social Psychology of Embezzlement* (Glencoe, Ill.: Free Press, 1953).

to behavior, but also with an indication of some of their relations to psycho-genic and biogenic elements. There is a danger in any analytic description, such as was undertaken in this chapter, that the reader will get the impression that the "elements" exist as independent units. Actually, there is a high degree of integration and mutual adjustment between these abstracted elements, and nearly every human act is based on something from all three levels. Certainly there is nothing in human behavior that is purely sociogenic or psychogenic which does not have a biogenic element in it, and there is very little that is purely biogenic without a sociogenic and/or psychogenic element in it.

It is basically important to understand that no human personality can exist or function in a human way for any length of time, without a high degree of integration among the biogenic, psychogenic, and sociogenic elements of his personality. In thus using the word "integration" we mean something more than the simultaneous functioning of the three levels of personality. Integration implies mutual adjustment and lack of conflict between the elements. We have already pointed out that the individual's culture ideal and the group role must not make demands on his psychogenic and biogenic personality which the latter cannot meet. It could similarly be said that a biogenic or psychogenic trait in an individual completely out of harmony with a cultural demand will result in some pathology of his personality: the individual's conscience and conception of himself could not tolerate his own drives.

Thus, for all functioning personalities, each of the three sets of influences tend to *select* elements of the other two which are compatible with it. The fact of this mutual selection, as well as of mutual influence, should warn us of the difficulties in any attempt to speak of, or measure, the influence of one factor alone. While we cannot devote the space required to prove the statement here, we would hold that no scientific study has yet measured a "pure" biogenic, psychogenic, or sociogenic behavior or personality trait, save for the reflexes which are unmodifiable. Behavior is generally a resultant of interlocked elements from all three levels.

Yet it would not be correct to say that behavior is an expression of always completely integrated elements. There is, first, a large measure of tolerance within one trait for variation in another trait. The gears can mesh even though they do not fit each other exactly, because many are so made that they can accommodate quite a range of other elements. Second, to continue with our mechanical analogy, the personality can be compared to a machine with a great deal of "give" or flexibility in it. A certain amount of grinding and scraping, pulling and twisting, will not hurt it and will not prevent it from operating. For these two reasons the personality should not be thought of as completely integrated, or behavior at any one moment a resultant of fully-integrated elements.

FOR ADDITIONAL READING

GOFFMAN, ERVING, *The Presentation of Self in Everyday Life,* rev. ed. (Garden City, N.Y.: Doubleday, 1959). A challenging interpretation of personality in interaction with others.

KATZ, ELIHU, and PAUL F. LAZARSFELD, *Personal Influence* (Glencoe, Ill.: Free Press, 1955). A study of how some people influence others.

KLUCKHOHN, C., H. A. MURRAY, and D. M. SCHNEIDER (eds.), *Personality in Nature, Society and Culture* (New York: Alfred A. Knopf, 1953). A wide-ranging series of articles on the social influences of personality.

LINDESMITH, A. R., and A. L. STRAUSS, *Social Psychology* (New York: Dryden, 1949). A textbook that stresses the role of symbolic communication in human behavior.

STONEQUIST, EVERETT V., *The Marginal Man* (New York: Scribner's, 1937). The effect of a marginal social position—that is, membership in two discrete cultures or groups—upon the personality.

5 * The Social Structure: Institutions and Integrated Groups

A *Institutions: Definition and Characteristics*

1 DEFINITION AND CLASSIFICATIONS

The common meanings and values making up the culture of a society do not exist in the minds of the members of the society independent of one another, but rather often form interrelated clusters, where one element has a high degree of dependency on the others in the same cluster.[1] Since each meaning or value indicates what members of the society may or should do, each cluster may be thought of as an interrelated group of guides and directions for complex-behavior patterns. Such clusters, or groups of complex-behavior patterns within the culture, and the interrelations among them, make up a large part of the social structure of the society. If one of these clusters has a high degree of specificity and internal cohesiveness, it is generally spoken of by social scientists as an *institution,* although the popular meaning of "institution" is usually not quite so broad.

Not all of social structure is made up of the institutions of a society because deliberately excluded from institutions are structures of common meanings and values governing the behavior of such groupings of persons as socioeconomic categories or ethnic groups. Socioeconomic categories may be organized into classes, and minority groups may be organized into castes,

---

[1] Many meanings and values—especially those relating to material objects—are more or less independent and are not related to a cluster. We shall not be concerned with these independent elements of a culture in this chapter. We shall also not concern ourselves with a simple sequence of behaviors, specified by a small number of meanings and values, which the anthropologists have called a "culture complex." This chapter considers only the large clusters of meanings and values, which in this text are called "institutions."

and both classes and castes are a part of social structure that are not so internally cohesive and specific as institutions. They will be given separate attention in Chapter 8.

Sociologists have been divided in their use of the term "institution." Some have used it to refer to interrelated clusters of meanings and values, as we have defined it above, while others have used it to refer to a number of people in organized interaction. The French sociologist, Maurice Hauriou,[2] distinguished between the "institution as object" and the "institution as group" to refer to these two definitions.[3] This distinction need not bother us if we recognize the limited sense in which the concept of "group" is used when considered to be an institution. It is not merely a number of people, or a category of people, or such a special mode of relationship linking a number of people as the crowd or audience.[4] In the context of social structure, a group is to be narrowly considered as an "integrated group," a mode of relationship which we have already considered.[5] An "integrated group" is a number of *socialized* persons who have already had some history of interaction with each other. They have learned to predict each other's behavior fairly accurately so that they can adjust to each other. This is made possible by means of common meanings and values, occasionally devised out of the communication between the members of the group, but much more often transmitted to them from long-past communications through the process of socialization.

Considered in this limited sense, an "institution as group" *is* an "institution as object" when attention is focused on the interacting members rather than on the meanings and values on the basis of which the members interact. Keeping in mind that we shall use the word group in this limited "integrated group" sense of the term in this chapter, we can thus use the terms "group" and "institution" interchangeably. We can now also understand why the institution continues when a unit of its individual members leave or die out. The interrelated cluster of common meanings and values

[2] *La science sociale traditionelle* (Paris: La Larose, 1896); *L'Institution et le droit statutaire* (Paris: La Larose, 1906). See also Florian Znaniecki, "Social Organization and Institutions," in G. Gurvitch and W. E. Moore, *Twentieth Century Sociology* (New York: Philosophical Library, 1945), pp. 187 ff.

[3] MacIver and Page are most explicit in expressing the need to distinguish between an organized group, which they call an association, and a social "procedure," which they call an institution. We shall not follow the terminology of these authors. See Robert M. MacIver and Charles H. Page, *Society: An Introductory Analysis* (New York: Rinehart, 1949), p. 16. Another author, besides Hauriou, who considers the distinction simply as one between two different kinds or aspects of institutions—which is the position we take in this book—is F. Stuart Chapin. Chapin distinguishes between diffused-symbolic institutions and nucleated institutions. See F. Stuart Chapin, *Contemporary Social Institutions* (New York: Harper, 1935), p. 13.

[4] These will be considered in Chapter 9.

[5] See Chapter 2, Sections C and E.

Institutions are: (1) "apparatus of social life," "modes or organs," "mechanisms," "instruments," "forms of order," and in turn (2) "part of the social structure," "units in the total social oganizations," "component part of the total structure of a plurality pattern"; they are also, from another angle (3) "human achievements," "forms of culture," "culture complexes," "configurations," "accumulations of social capital" (with the elements or "traits" composing them occasionally set forth), and they have "considerable permanence, universality"; (4) they meet "some persistent need or want," "supply the fundamental needs of human beings," "are necessary to the satisfaction of basic needs," "center around the achievement of some human end or purpose," "do collectively the things that are right and proper with respect to some particular aspect of life," guide "the individual into modes of behavior which assist in one way or another in the maintenance of group life"; (5) they take the form of "usages," "forms of social activity," "forms or conditions of procedure," "systems of activities," "systems of controls," "patterns of behavior," "collective action," "collective behavior," "patterns of social organization," or, if social psychologically expressed, "phase of the public mind," "states of mind," "configurations of segments of the behavior of individuals," "patterns of attitudes," "conceptualizations of behavior and attitudinal relationships"; (6) these are "established and recognized," "incorporated within the social framework," "systematized," "instituted," "sanctioned," "have attained some measure of formalization and hence of permanence," (7) "by the authority of communities," or "by some common will," and, finally, (8) they are concretely expressed in "social habits," "overt conduct," "similar and reciprocal habits of individual behavior."

J. O. Hertzler, *Social Institutions* (Lincoln: University of Nebraska Press, 1946), pp. 4–5.

which constitute the family continues even when the father and mother die and the children are dispersed, for the children form almost identical family units based upon most of the same common meanings and values.

Thus far in this book, when we have been speaking of society or the social relationship, we have been assuming a certain stability and a certain uniformity. We have neglected to consider changes and variations within the "integrated group" mode of relationships. Changes in institutions will be considered later in this chapter and in a special chapter on social change. Variations in organized groups had best be recognized before we proceed further. Groups can be classified in a very large number of different ways; the merit of a classification depends on the use one has for it. Since our purpose at this point is to note variation, we shall adopt the lengthy classification of groups proposed by Georges Gurvitch.[6] The list of types of groups should not be thought to be complete, but merely as helpful in social research and in understanding social variation.

[6] "Groupement social et classe sociale," *Cahiers Internationaux de Sociologie,* VII (1949), pp. 1–33.

Groups can be thought of in terms of the number of functions they serve. Some groups exist entirely for one purpose, many have one dominant purpose and several lesser ones, others have several coordinate purposes. Functions can be classified in many different ways; one of the simplest is into child rearing, friendship, economic, educational, scientific, political, social welfare, military, religious, occupational, recreational, esthetic, communicative, and so on. A group can carry on its activities with a great deal of vigor and fervor, or it can operate slowly and lackadaisically. A group can be composed of only two persons or it can be as large as a nation. The number of members helps to determine the nature of the contacts between them: intimate and frequent (primary contacts) or segmentalized and occasional and often based on intermediaries (secondary contacts). Individuals are born into certain types of groups (families, nations, religious denominations), membership in other groups is imposed on them later (schools, armies), while still other groups they join more or less voluntarily. Groups that one joins voluntarily may be open to everyone, may be limited to certain specified categories of the population, or may be open to everyone who will go through certain ceremonies. Groups may be deliberately organized or they may take form slowly and without intention (these are Sumner's *enacted* and *crescive* types of institutions).[7] Groups may be formal or informal, highly structured or practically unstructured, related to other groups or unattached, open to outside influences or highly resistant to outside influences, unified or composed of subgroups, highly directive of the

---

[7] William Graham Sumner, *Folkways* (Boston: Ginn, 1906), p. 54.

Social action, like other forms of action, may be classified in the following four types according to its mode of orientation (1) in terms of rational orientation to a system of discrete individual ends (*zweckrational*), that is, through expectations as to the behaviour of objects in the external situation and of other human individuals, making use of these expectations as "conditions" or "means" for the successful attainment of the actor's own rationally chosen ends; (2) in terms of rational orientation to an absolute value (*wertrational*); involving a conscious belief in the absolute value of some ethical, aesthetic, religious, or other form of behaviour, entirely for its own sake and independently of any prospects of external success; (3) in terms of affectual orientation, especially emotional, determined by the specific affects and states of feeling of the actor; (4) traditionally oriented, through the habituation of long practice.

Max Weber, *The Theory of Social and Economic Organization*, trans. A. M. Henderson and Talcott Parsons (Glencoe, Ill.: Free Press, 1947), p. 115. Copyright 1947 by Oxford University Press.

behavior of its members or permissive toward them, in conflict with the outside society or accommodated to it. In other words, the common meanings
and values that govern the integrated group can vary in many respects.

The general sociologist is not interested in the workings of any specific
institution as such. He studies institutions for the light they throw on the
broader problems of social organization and social control. Some of the
specific interests of a sociologist making a study of an institution would be:
the social situation out of which the institution arose, the process of growth
of the institution, the external structure of the institution, the means by
which the institution is perpetuated, the means by which the institution will meet an unexpected crisis, the manner in which new members
or functionaries are brought into the institution, the relation of the institution to other institutions and to the general community, the spheres
of life in which the institution operates, the extent and manner of control
over the members, the expansion of function or structure of the institution,
the functions of the institution and the relation of function to location,
and the career of an individual in the institution. In short, an institution
is studied as a means whereby a number of people act collectively on the
basis of common understandings that have a high degree of persistency.

2   FUNCTIONS

While each institution contains within itself many values, it can be itself
regarded as a *means* whereby individuals who perform the behaviors it
prescribes can attain certain more inclusive, or "higher," values. This instrumental character of the institution is often spoken of as its "function."[8]
An institution typically has more than one function:

> The real component units of culture which have a considerable
> degree of permanence, universality, and independence are the organ-
> ized systems of human activities called institutions. Every institution
> centers around a fundamental need, permanently unites a group of
> people in a cooperative task, and has its particular body of doctrine
> and its technique or craft. Institutions are not correlated simply and
> directly to their functions; one need does not receive one satisfaction
> in one institution. But institutions show a pronounced amalgamation
> of functions and have a synthetic character.[9]

[8] Sumner defined an institution as consisting of a concept and a structure. In our
terminology, the "concept" of an institution is its function; its structure is the cluster
of meanings and values which specify behavior within it and in relation to it. (Sumner,
op. cit., p. 53.) Another possible term for "function" here would be "purpose" or "goal"
if we do not take this to be always deliberate and conscious.

[9] B. Malinowski, "Culture," *Encyclopedia of the Social Sciences* (New York: Macmillan,
1931), Vol. 4, pp. 621–46; p. 626 quoted.

Durkheim originally, and more recently Chapin[10] and Merton,[11] have distinguished the "latent functions" from the "manifest functions" of institutions.[12] The latter are what appear to be, and are deliberately intended to be, the functions of institutions. The former are the regular but unanticipated consequences of the activities of institutions. The latent functions are often not perceived by those who participate in an institution, but are discernible only to objective outsiders who look at the recurring effects of group activity and not only at the expressed intentions. Even when participants understand the latent functions of their institution, they usually do not discuss them. Thus latent functions can be considered to be among the covert elements of culture.[13] In studying an institution it is important to discover its latent as well as its manifest functions.

It is also important to recognize that an institution can change its functions and that the same function can be performed by several institutions.

> Certain functions are performed by elaborate systems of interconnected institutions. The traditional doctor's office, which once served as clinic, medical school, surgery, and laboratory, is today but one among many institutions concerned with healing. In addition to those already named there are hospitals for various kinds of people and various ailments, the schools and professional associations of various auxiliary occupations, the associations and examining boards of special branches of medicine, as well as the governmental, philanthropic, and private institutions for distributing medical care and protecting the health of the public. To say that the function of any one of these institutions is healing, without specifying its particular function in the whole healing system, would be a truism without meaning.[14]

Let us now get down to cases. Institutions in our culture include the family, the church, the government, the schools, business enterprises, trade unions, the public-relief system, recreational facilities, voluntary associations of all types, libraries, museums, courts, jails, and dozens of others. Each consists of a large complex of meanings and values which specify how its members may act, or should act, under certain circumstances.

[10] F. Stuart Chapin, "Latent Culture Patterns of the Unseen World of Social Reality," *American Journal of Sociology*, 40 (July, 1934), pp. 61–68; *Contemporary Social Institutions, op. cit.*, pp. 31 ff.

[11] Robert K. Merton, *Social Theory and Social Structure* (Glencoe, Ill.: Free Press, 1949), pp. 21–81.

[12] Sumner considered institutions to be consciously utilitarian; hence by implication he would not have considered them to have latent functions.

[13] See Chapter 2, Section C.

[14] Everett Cherrington Hughes, "Institutions" in Alfred McClung Lee (ed.), *New Outline of the Principles of Sociology* (New York: Barnes and Noble, 1946), p. 231.

The meanings involved in a school, for example, define a textbook, a blackboard, an examination, a grade, etc., while the values suggest that a student should do enough studying at least to pass from one grade to the next, should be at least outwardly respectful toward the teachers, should participate in some extracurricular activity, and so on. The institution as a whole is an instrument for the achievement of certain higher or broader values which indicate its functions. The manifest functions of schools are, of course, to provide certain basic skills for all persons, to provide children with the breadth of knowledge that will make them intelligent citizens when they become adults, to assist in vocational training, to stimulate at least a few youngsters to have the curiosity that will make them future scholars and scientists.

The latent functions are more difficult to discern, to prove, and to talk about, since they are by their very nature somewhat hidden. One latent function of a school might be to develop in children certain loyalties, to a trade for example, or to a nation. Another—at the university level—is to provide monetary compensation for scientists and scholars, who are seldom recompensed in their capacities directly in our society. Still another would be to provide certain outlets for the ambitions of some teachers or school administrators—a certain avenue of ascent in social prestige. The public school might be said to have the latent function of putting into contact with one another children of different socioeconomic and ethnic groupings. We would find it very difficult to prove any of these latent functions; we observe them by noting what the regular consequences of the school are, and by imagining what effects would occur if schools were to disappear completely.[15] Of course, if we could perform the experiment of eliminating the schools from a community and observing the consequences, we would have a more scientific answer to the question of what the latent as well as the manifest functions of schools are. It is also obvious from these examples of latent functions of the school that other institutions can and do perform them, and that the school formerly did not perform them and may not in the future perform them.

3   STRUCTURE

The meanings and values which constitute an institution do not, of course, exist in themselves.[16] They are the rules or prescriptions for behavior of individuals and they manifest themselves in the regularity and

[15] It is beyond the scope of this book to analyze the special methodology needed to ascertain the functions of an institution. This difficult topic is discussed by Harry C. Bredemeier, "The Methodology of Functionalism," *American Sociological Review,* 20 (April, 1955), pp. 173–79.

[16] A number of thoughtful essays and studies on the institution as an organized group are contained in the collection of readings edited by Joseph A. Litterer, *Organizations* (New York: Wiley, 1963).

consistency of that behavior. One observes only the behavior; the meanings and values can only be inferred from the consistency of the behavior. Institutions tend to use organized sanctions, in Radcliffe-Brown's sense of the term[17]; its rules are explicit and generally recognized. Only the proper officers may perform the various procedures expected in an institution.

Thus, one way of thinking of the structure of an institution is as a set of rules, both formal and informal, with not all of them necessarily completely understood by all members. The rules govern most aspects of behavior possible within the group: manner of entrance and replacement, division of labor among members, expected and proscribed behavior among members in the various roles, expected behavior toward outsiders, time schedules, procedures for accomplishing the functions of the institution, and almost any other behavior within the institution which can be anticipated in advance. The rules give regularity and predictability to the behavior within institutions.

Reference to the regularity and consistency of behavior does not mean that every person who is a member of an institution is expected to have the same behavior. In the first place, he has much of his life outside the institution, and few people in society have exactly the same rounds of institutions and activities. Second, within the institution he plays a role which is never the same for all members of the institution. Each institution has a *division of labor* among its participants: there are several roles and each fits into the other to make the institution operate.

In the school, for example, the roles are those of teachers at different levels, students at different levels, a principal or director, a supervisor, one or more secretaries, clerks, maintenance persons, often specialized teachers for the blind or feeble-minded, a visiting doctor and nurse, and others, depending on the level and size of the school. The roles of each of these persons are different, and they must gear into each other to allow the institution to operate. Of course there is a good deal of leeway where the gears meet, and the roles change over time, but there must be mutual adjustment of roles within certain limits for the institution to operate. The principal is the head of a school, but he can do nothing if the other persons working and studying at the school do not understand what they are supposed to do, are not capable, or do not have the willingness or morale to carry out their roles in relationship to the other people at the school.

The behavior expected for each role differs in relation to each other role. The teacher behaves differently toward the student, the parent, the principal, the clerk, the janitor, and toward another teacher. The full range of these expected behaviors is what constitutes the role of a teacher in a school institution. They do not exhaust by far the behavior of the

[17] See Chapter 3, Section B.

person who holds a teacher's role, since he or she is also likely to be a spouse, a parent, a friend, a church member, a member of a community, a member of a voluntary association, etc.—and in each role has different relationships to other persons occupying related roles in other institutions. Behavior in social roles must always be understood as mutual interactions defined by common meanings and values with some tradition behind them. Some roles can exist only because other roles exist: There cannot be a husband without a wife, a doctor without a patient, a foreman without a workman.

Some of the roles are especially important in the institution and are filled by a small number of the members of the group. These are called the *offices* of the institution, and those who fill them are called the *officers* or *functionaries*. They derive a certain *authority* by virtue of their office and thus have influence over the behavior of other members. Since their roles are generally fairly well prescribed by the meanings and values relevant to their offices, their behavior is largely sociogenic in the institutional setting. Still, each officer is also a person with a complete personality, and thus his behavior is also individualized and never completely in accord with his institutional role.[18] Thus, no two school principals are exactly alike. Different offices permit different degrees of individual initiative, just as different individuals are ready to assume different degrees of initiative. Thus there are often special qualifications for offices.

Institutions vary in the degree of specialization expected of persons, and this is often related to the degree of control the institution has over the life of its members. The more specialized and segmentalized the relation of a given member to an institution, the less is its control over him. The teacher is associated with the school only in his occupational life, whereas the nun is associated with the church in most aspects of her life. Even within the same institution this holds true: the religious leader (rabbi, priest, minister) has a less specialized relation to his church than does the average member, and his life is much more controlled by the institution. To the extent that an individual's life is controlled by one institution, he must have fewer relationships to other institutions. A priest, for example, must even withdraw from family life.

Much has been written about the minimal performance necessary for the maintenance of an organized group. Caplow offers three criteria without which "no organization can continue to exist:"[19] (1) a minimal effectiveness in the performance of its objective functions; (2) limitation on spontaneous conflict within the group; (3) provision of sufficient satisfaction to mem-

[18] Everett C. Hughes, "Institutional Office and the Person," *American Journal of Sociology*, 152 (1937), pp. 404–13.
[19] Theodore Caplow, "The Criteria of Organizational Success," *Social Forces*, 32 (October, 1953), pp. 1–9.

bers of the group so that membership will be continued. Of course, these are all modified by the extent to which sanctions—of force or tradition—are used in the group, and are also functions one of the other. But the structure of any organized group must somehow provide for them.

Durkheim[20] distinguished two types of societies which should be thought of as end points of a continuum rather than as merely two distinctive categories. He was interested in what holds the society together, on what basis there is a mutual adjustment of roles. The first type is a society in which there are not many different roles, and most individuals have therefore to play only one or two of a limited number of roles; this he called a society with *mechanical solidarity*. The second type is a society with many different roles, and each individual plays several different roles which are not likely to be the same for all individuals; this he called a society with *organic solidarity*. In a society with mechanical solidarity it is similarity of role of individuals that holds the society together. In a society with organic solidarity it is mutual dependence of roles that holds the society together. From our knowledge that mutual dependence of roles is characteristic of institutions, we can deduce that a society with many institutions and complicated institutions is a society held together in organic solidarity.

Durkheim implied, somewhat incorrectly, that the preliterate societies have mechanical solidarity and that the literate societies have organic solidarity. Actually our better knowledge of anthropology today shows us that some preliterate societies have a huge number of complicated institutions with a great deal of dependence of role. In fact, some of these preliterate societies have more organic solidarity than many societies possessing knowledge of writing. What is valuable in Durkheim's analysis, however, is his recognition that contemporary Western society is held together largely by mutual interdependency of roles, that the existence of many institutions and the high division of labor within and between institutions makes us highly dependent on one another. The cohesiveness or solidarity of our society is thus based on our "awareness" of the many diverse roles played in the many diverse institutions of our society and our "willingness" to adjust our role to the others in a division of labor.

An institution usually has characteristics other than the roles of the people who carry on its activity. Some of these are meanings and values that specify or clarify the manifest functions of the institution; others are meanings and values attributed to the tools or instruments which aid the members in performing the functions (both manifest and latent) of the institution. Chapin has classified the constituent elements of an institution into four "type parts":

[20] Émile Durkheim, *The Division of Labor in Society* (Glencoe, Ill.: Free Press, 1947; 1st edition, 1893).

The four main type parts that combine to produce the configuration or cultural concretion known as the social institution are:

First, common reciprocating attitudes of individuals and their conventionalized behavior patterns.

Second, cultural objects of symbolic value; that is, objects charged with sentimental meaning to which human behavior has been conditioned.

Third, cultural objects possessing utilitarian value; that is, material objects that satisfy creature wants and through conditioned response and habit attach the other parts of the pattern to a specific location; objects called property.

Fourth, oral or written language symbols that preserve the descriptions and specifications of the patterns of interrelationship among the other three parts—attitudes, symbolic culture traits, and utilitarian culture traits or real property. When the formulation is compactly organized it is called a code.[21]

The extent to which the manifest functions of an institution and of the techniques for performing them are overtly specified, to that extent it may be called a *formal* institution. "A statement of purpose" or preamble to the constitution of a voluntary association would be a most obvious example of meanings and values specifying the manifest functions of a formal institution. The remainder of the constitution of a voluntary association, or the administrative regulations set by a school board to govern a school, would be obvious examples of the "code" specifying the expected attitudes, symbols, and tools used in accomplishing the manifest functions of a formal institution (the tools or utilitarian objects themselves are, of course, to be distinguished from the written specifications for them). In the case of the family, the manifest functions, and some of the means for achieving them, are specified in law in our society, and also in the words with which a marriage ceremony is performed. In France, where the law is modeled after ancient Roman law, the manifest function, expected attitudes, and tools of nearly all institutions are specified in law or the administrative regulations of the state, so that in France practically all institutions are formal.

4   CEREMONY AND RITUAL

Ceremonies are rules of behavior that govern the members of an institution on special occasions, usually when they come together and celebrate some recurring event important for the functioning of the institution. Ceremonies often accompany the change of role or assumption of a new role by a member of the group. In the family, for example, ceremonies accompany the christening or circumcision (for Christians and Jews, respectively)

[21] F. Stuart Chapin, *Contemporary American Institutions* (New York: Harper, 1935), p. 15.

of new members. Transition from childhood to adulthood is marked by puberty rites in many societies, by confirmation in our own society.[22] The ceremony of marriage accompanies the creation of a new family unit.[23] In many organized groups ceremonies accompany the inauguration of a leader. Initiation ceremonies are performed when new members enter some voluntary association, and graduation ceremonies are performed when qualified members leave the institution of a school. Sometimes ceremonies accompany the entrance of a new tool into the institution, if the tool is important enough, such as a building (such a ceremony is spoken of as a "dedication").

Another category of ceremonies is that involved in the commemoration of events in the past which have been crucially important to the group. Holiday ceremonies are used principally by nations and religious denominations, but families celebrate anniversaries and birthdays in similar manner. The important functions of ceremonies, if there are any, must be latent, since overtly they merely call attention to what every member should know anyway. Sociologists have generally hypothesized that the function of ceremonies is to re-cement the group by recalling attention to its fundamental values. Since the values are always old ones, ceremony is a conservative force that discourages change. The conservatism of ceremonies suggests another latent function. Since ceremonies so often occur at critical stages in the lives of members of the institution, it may be that a function of ceremonies is to help the members over these crises and so keep them attached to the institution.

A crisis in the life of an individual is not necessarily a crisis for an institution in which he participates. Indeed, one of the most common of institutional functions is provision for crises in the lives of individuals. To the individual, his marriage, illnesses, sins, and fear of death are unique and critical. To the church these crises are recurrent, and there is a way of dealing with each. Institutions, so long as they can meet the crises of the individual, are not themselves in a critical state. When, however, some new type of situation, not provided for by the existing institutions, becomes chronic and widespread, the institutions themselves are in a parlous state.[24]

[22] A term by Arnold van Gennep has come to be used to refer to these ceremonies of transition from childhood to adulthood—*rites de passage*. (See his *Les rites de passage* [Paris, 1909]).

[23] The universal need for a marriage ceremony is suggested by the negative reaction among the Russian people when the Soviet government tried to dispose of it. Tremendous efforts were made to find new secular rites to replace the old religious ones. See Alex Inkeles and Kent Geiger (eds.), *Soviet Society: A Book of Readings* (Boston: Houghton Mifflin, 1961).

[24] Everett Cherrington Hughes, "Institutions" in Alfred McClung Lee (ed.), *New Outline of the Principles of Sociology* (New York: Barnes and Noble, 1946), p. 236.

Perhaps this much can be agreed upon, however: Ritual is a society-building force which should be used as a *tool* of organization but not become an end in itself. Nor should solidarity become an end in itself in the institutions of the great society. Always prior to ritual should be the critical work of reason: what institutions do we want and how attain them; what is a good society? Having decided this, we can justifiably use ritual to build up desired institutions and values, increase the sense of solidarity and security, and provide amusement. But, particularly in the following fields, a progressive civilization cannot replace reason with ritual: determination and ranking of ends, criticism of institutions, and solution of social problems. It is true that ritual can function as a sop to make people passably contented with inferior institutions. It is also true that emergencies occur where much ritual is needed, and also where there is not enough time for desirable ceremony. But neither of these exigencies can provide a rule for a good society improved by the work of reason, which recognizes the necessary place of ritual in the scheme of things— a good servant but a bad master.

Orrin E. Klapp, *Ritual and Cult: A Sociological Interpretation* (Washington, D.C.: Public Affairs, 1956), p. 39.

Rituals are often parts of ceremonies, but may be used more frequently in non-ceremonial settings. A ritual is a prescribed set of words and acts, used practically without variation, that is believed to have symbolic powers to produce certain desired results. Ritual sometimes loses its meaning, but is repeated merely out of respect for tradition. If its meaning, that it produces a certain result, is believed, it is a form of magic.[25]

It used to be thought by some anthropologists that ritual and magic were the equivalent of science among primitive man—that it was their way of attempting to control nature. "But now anthropologists incline more to the idea that natives know the difference between ritual and sheer practical techniques; that they do not confuse a charm with a tool, or fertility-rites with the hard work of agriculture."[26] Modern, scientific man also uses ritual and magic: "A curse may be futilely uttered by a person who has no means of physical retaliation against an enemy; but he may curse also when equipped with the best weapons and beating his enemy; indicating that the ritual and practical are two kinds of behavior, with different functions, occurring in the same act or separately."[27] Ritual serves to please or appease the emotions, not the need for practicality.

[25] For a discussion of how magic underlies ritual, see Ruth Benedict, *Patterns of Culture* (Boston: Houghton Mifflin, 1934). We shall discuss magic further in Chapter 7, Section D.

[26] Orrin E. Klapp, *Ritual and Cult: A Sociological Interpretation* (Washington, D.C.: Public Affairs, 1956), p. 10. The remainder of our discussion of ritual relies heavily on Klapp.

[27] *Idem.*

A ritual has regularity, in the sense that its elements must be presented in the proper way and order, according to some pattern or formula. It also has periodicity, in the sense that it is usually repeated at certain times. Rituals are practiced in connection with certain holidays, anniversaries, and festivals. Rituals are meaningful to a number of people; the gestures which make it up are meaningful. What is conveyed is mnemonic —rituals symbolically stand for things that people do not wish to forget. Thus rituals are often presented in a dramatic way; even those who do not participate actively get a vicarious sense of participation out of their observation of the ritual. In sum, ritual builds up a consensus of the feelings and imaginations of people in a vicarious, participative, dramatic experience. Rituals sometimes fail to build consensus when they are overly formal, do not occur with enough frequency, are insufficiently dramatic or meaningful, or are in conflict with other aspects of the integrated society.

5   PHYSICAL APPURTENANCES

Some institutions have *formal symbols* which are simple physical objects that are intended to convey the meaning of the major manifest function

---

In a given community it is appropriate that an expectant father should feel concern or at least should make an appearance of doing so. Some suitable symbolic expression of his concern is found in terms of the general ritual or symbolic idiom of the society, and it is felt generally that a man in that situation ought to carry out the symbolic or ritual actions or abstentions. For every rule that *ought* to be observed there must be some sort of sanction or reason. For acts that patently affect other persons the moral and legal sanctions provide a generally sufficient controlling force upon the individual. For ritual obligations conformity and rationalisation are provided by the ritual sanctions. The simplest form of ritual sanction is an accepted belief that if rules of ritual are not observed some undefined misfortune is likely to occur. In many societies the expected danger is somewhat more definitely conceived as a danger of sickness or, in extreme cases, death. In the more specialised forms of ritual sanction the good results to be hoped for or the bad results to be feared are more specifically defined in reference to the occasion or meaning of the ritual.

The theory is not concerned with the historical origin of ritual, nor is it another attempt to explain ritual in terms of human psychology; it is a hypothesis as to the relation of ritual and ritual values to the essential constitution of human society, i.e. to those invariant general characters which belong to all human societies, past, present and future.

A. R. Radcliffe-Brown, *Structure and Function in Primitive Society* (Glencoe, Ill.: Free Press, 1952), p. 149.

of the institution as a whole. A common example of a formal symbol is a flag. The flag of the United States not only symbolizes the nation, but also its function of uniting all the separate states. The flag of the Union of Soviet Socialist Republics not only symbolizes that nation as a whole, but also the collaboration of manual workers and peasants (hammer and sickle) in "red" revolution. The flag of the Red Cross symbolizes not only that voluntary association, but also its major manifest function of bringing aid to those in distress. Religious institutions usually have symbols also representing what is conceived to be the major manifest function of the religion. The Christian cross, for example, symbolizes the death of Jesus, which is believed to have made possible the salvation of sinful man. The latter is intended to be the major manifest function of the Christian church. The statue of Buddha, seated cross-legged, symbolizes the aim of Buddhism to encourage the contemplative life as a means of achieving what is good. Some sports groups or youth groups may use a live animal as a symbol ("mascot") of what are conceived to be the desirable virtues for members of the group. All such formal symbols represent the unity of the institution as a whole. When they also obviously represent the major manifest function of the group, it is understood that this function is an ideal, not always achieved in practice.

Other physical appurtenances of an institution usually belong to its "tool" side. There are physical objects which aid the members in the performance of their various roles in the institution. A school has a building with rooms of a certain type, books, blackboards, desks, laboratories, pay checks, etc., which are physical implements aiding the members to perform their roles, not only in relation to each other, but also in furtherance of the functions described earlier. Quite often the building that implements the functioning of the institution is taken to stand for the institution as a whole and thus it becomes the symbol of the institution.

While it is quite likely that an institution will acquire physical appurtenances to aid its functioning, just as a person does, the absence of these does not mean that there is no institution. Among the ancient Greeks there were some schools—on what we today would call the "university level"—which apparently had no physical appurtenances whatsoever; a teacher would meet his students at prearranged times and places, and they would sit or walk together while he gave them instruction. This arrangement was still an institution, and deserves the name of school, because of its functions and the specialized roles which the persons played toward each other. It is to be considered, however, as a very informal institution. Not only were there no physical appurtenances, but there were no symbols, no written specification of the functions, no written specification as to how a person acquired or lost a certain role.

We have considered in a general manner all of the characteristics associated with institutions. Not all institutions have all of these characteristics. The minimum essentials of an institution are that a number of persons play certain roles toward each other, in a regularized division of labor, for the purpose of accomplishing certain functions.

B   *Formal and Informal Organization: Bureaucracy and Its "Other Face"*

The various defining characteristics and type-parts of an institution will differ somewhat in their character depending on whether an institution is formal or informal. For instance, the symbol of identification that gives a group continuity will be a dignified name, a charter or constitution, and a written, prescribed ritual if the group is formally organized (e.g., school, corporation, fraternal organization). But the same function will be performed in an informal group (e.g., clique, friendship group, gang) by secret understandings, private jokes, and in informal routine of activity. All societies have both formal and informal institutions, sometimes running parallel to each other and carrying on the same social activities.

In its fully developed form, a formal institution in any sphere of life takes the form of a bureaucracy. Max Weber[28] specifies that a bureaucracy has the following characteristics:

1 A bureau consists of a series of integrated offices, each with its fixed and official duties.

2 Positions within the offices are strictly graded as to status and authority, and the holders of the lower positions are supervised by higher officials. Because of this, there is always the possibility that a client may appeal a decision made by a lesser official to higher ones, following the "chain of command."

3 In principle, the business of the bureau is always carried on in the same way regardless of the personality of the office holder and regardless of the prestige of the client. All transactions are reported in writing, and these reports are carefully checked and filed, according to "a consistent system of abstract rules."

4 Ideally, the officials are fully trained and experienced to the degree required by the office. They fulfill their duties impersonally, and make a career of their work.

5 The officials follow relatively general, stable, and exhaustive rules in accomplishing their work. Knowledge of these rules constitutes a special technical learning which the office holders must possess.

[28] H. H. Gerth and C. Wright Mills (eds.), *From Max Weber: Essays in Sociology* (New York: Oxford University Press, 1946), Chapter VIII. Also see Max Weber, *The Theory of Social and Economic Organization,* trans. A. M. Henderson and T. Parsons (New York: Oxford University Press, 1947), pp. 330–40.

The rules and the structure make the bureaucracy, "from a purely technical point of view, capable of attaining the highest degree of efficiency."

For Weber, bureaucracy is the most effective way of organizing the behavior of many individuals for the purpose of promoting a social goal.[29] This is so because the necessary elements of organization are made specific and public, behavior is seen as a rational means to the social product, and the flow of communication takes place within a set of publicly defined channels. Sanctions are appropriate for the behavior they are expected to control, and are supposed to be publicly known and understood by superior and inferior, thus it is in Blau's terms, that the "basic characteristics of bureaucratic organization" are: specialization, a hierarchy of authority, a system of rules, and impersonality.[30]

Bureaucracies can develop in any society, but they are most frequently associated with societies that develop large-scale institutions that have to depend on impersonal relationships among people. When organizations service many people and handle large sums of money they have to develop more or less rigid, impersonal rules for carrying on their operations. Chaos would develop if each citizen demanded that the department store gave him individualized service and assigned a personal clerk to follow him about the store while he decided on his purchases, or if the amount of postage required for a letter or a parcel were to be determined on each occasion by means of bargaining between the customer and the postal clerk. Large-scale organizations need not only impersonal rules, but also lines of communication and chains of command that are understood by all. Promotions and other rewards must be distributed rationally, and not on chance or whim, if the morale of the staff is to be preserved. Everyone must perform his specialized task in a predictable manner, so that each can gear his work to that of others. This type of bureaucracy will occur in any large-scale organization—even those organized for recreation, sport and science, and not merely in those organized for government and business.

But even in a large-scale organization there are not only formal role expectations based on an explicit division of labor. There is also a recognition of the other as an individual with a unique personality. As a foreman and workman come together for the first time, there is a "feeling out" and a "working out" process between them. Workmen ask

[29] Among the best contemporary discussions of bureaucracy are Peter Blau, *Dynamics of Bureaucracy* (Chicago: University of Chicago Press, 1955); Philip Selznick, "Foundations of the Theory of Organization," *American Sociological Review*, 13 (February, 1948), pp. 25–35; Reinhard Bendix, "Bureaucracy: The Problem and Its Setting," *American Sociological Review*, 12 (October, 1947), pp. 502–07.

[30] Peter M. Blau, *Bureaucracy in Modern Society* (New York: Random House, 1956), p. 19.

If every worker manufactured a complete car, each would have to be a graduate of an engineering college, and even then he could not do a very good job, since it would be impossible for him to be at once an expert mechanical engineer, electrical engineer, and industrial designer. Besides, there would not be enough people with engineering degrees in the country to fill all the positions. Specialization permits the employment of many less-trained workers, which lowers production costs. Moreover, whereas the jack-of-all-trades is necessarily master of none, each employee can become a highly skilled expert in his particular field of specialization.

What has been taken apart must be put together again. A high degree of specialization creates a need for a complex system of coordination. No such need exists in the small shop, where the work is less specialized, all workers have direct contact with one another, and the boss can supervise the performance of all of them. The president of a large company cannot possibly discharge his managerial responsibility for coordination through direct consultation with each one of several thousand workers. Managerial responsibility, therefore, is exercised through a hierarchy of authority, which furnishes lines of communication between top management and every employee for obtaining information on operations and transmitting operating directives. . . .

Peter M. Blau, *Bureaucracy in Modern Society* (New York: Random House, 1956), p. 17.

*

Bureaucracy, as the foremost theoretician on the subject points out, "is a power instrument of the first order—for the one who controls the bureaucratic apparatus."

Under normal conditions, the power position of a fully developed bureaucracy is always overtowering. The "political master" finds himself in the position of the "dilettante" who stands opposite the "expert," facing the trained official who stands within the management of administration. This holds whether the "master" whom the bureaucracy serves is a "people," equipped with the weapons of "legislative initiative," the "referendum," and the right to remove officials, or a parliament, elected on a . . . "democratic" basis and equipped with the right to vote a lack of confidence, or with the actual authority to vote it.

From Max Weber: Essays in Sociology, trans. H. H. Gerth and C. Wright Mills (New York: Oxford University Press, 1946), pp. 228, 232.

themselves and each other, "What is he like?" How does he compare with other bosses we have known? What does he specially expect of us? How demanding will he be in assigning tasks?" They quickly come to know in what respects the foreman is demanding, and in what respects he is lax. The foreman will learn the strengths and weaknesses of his various subordinates as individuals. Thus, their expectations of each other are unique and particular as well as general and in conformity with the formal role. This fact becomes part of the informal organization of the institution. Page has described the informal side of a bureaucracy:[31]

> . . . Like the formal, it consists of rules, groupings, and sanctioned systems of procedure. They are informal because they are never recorded in the codes or official blueprints and because they are generated and maintained with a degree of spontaneity always lacking in the activities which make up the formal structure. These rules, groupings, and procedures do, nevertheless, form a structure, for, though not *officially* recognized, they are clearly and semipermanently established, they are just as "real" and just as compelling on the membership as the elements of the official structure, and they maintain their existence and social significance throughout many changes of personnel.

Page goes on to point out the ways in which efficient solutions to bureaucratic problems are developed outside of the framework of the formal structure, to detail the relevant occupational culture and the enforcement of informal rules, and to examine the consequences of the impact of the informal organization on various types of units and on various types of personalities.

For a better understanding of informal organization we shall concentrate for a moment on the informal structure and processes of a single institution, that of business management. Paralleling each formal structure and process of management is at least one informal one. The informal structure is not planned, and does not appear on any organization chart, but grows up spontaneously. It develops for several reasons: (1) the personalities of those on the various levels of work may not be suited to the jobs they are expected to perform; (2) the personnel of the organization do not always fit together as they are planned to in the formal organization, and "naturally" work out new relationships with each other; (3) the structure may not be suited to the performance of the task, so that a given person in the organization cannot actually perform all that is expected of him; (4) unexpected contingencies are always arising which sometimes makes the planned structure inoperative. Under these circumstances an informal structure arises, temporarily or more-or-less permanently, to modify the formal organization in fact. To be effective, the manager must recognize the existence of informal structure and processes, not be disturbed by them except when they interfere with the performance of the organization's task, and seek to turn them to the more effective performance of the task. Structure and processes are only means to the performance of an

---

[31] Charles H. Page, "Bureaucracy's Other Face," *Social Forces,* 25 (October, 1946), pp. 88–94, at p. 89.

organization's goal or task, and if the formal, planned ones do not seem adequate or sufficient to meet all the needs of the personnel, they will be supplemented by informal ones. The manager's concern should not be to defend the formal structure and processes, but rather to see that the organization's tasks are accomplished: If informal structure and processes seem to accomplish the tasks satisfactorily, the wise manager will let them alone.

People want to work in "their own way," according to their unique individual "rhythms" of work. If not allowed to, they will often become less efficient and will engage in activities damaging to the performance of the organization's tasks and to the higher managers themselves. Workers on every level make their own friends and enemies; the resulting pushes and pulls in the organization are not necessarily destructive to the accomplishment of the organization's goals. The task of a manager is not to suppress these things, but to detect them and seek ways of turning them to the better performance of the organization's goals.

One informal development that happens in practically all organizations is that resentments against the restraints and frustrations that occur during work are directed at the next higher level of management by those experiencing the restraints and frustrations. The top manager can seek to minimize the restraints and frustrations, but some are bound to occur nevertheless. The top manager would be thus wise not to interfere too much or too openly with his subordinate managers, else the "heat" from below be redirected against him. If this heat gets too strong, he may want to shift the middle managers to different positions so they will not be associated with the same subordinates. But he should never attempt to take over a portion of their jobs himself; if he does so, the resentments may be redirected onto him and he will have a much more difficult time avoiding their consequences. Informal "leaders" of the lower echelon of workers who express resentments against the management are not solely to be regarded as "troublemakers" (unless it can be shown that they directly sabotage the attainment of the organization's goals); they can often be the means by which natural resentments of all the workers are released harmlesssly. Sometimes the middle managers have only a technical competence, rather than also a competence in human relations, and the informal leaders of the lowest echelon perform some of the necessary human tasks. The wise manager learns about the informal structure and processes of his organization, and seeks to modify them only to enchance the achievement of the organization's goals.

In a business organization, the formal division of labor is written up in the form of an organizational chart and of job specifications.[32] But there are also implicitly agreed upon rules for on-the-job behavior, not specified in

[32] Delbert C. Miller and William H. Form, *Industrial Sociology: The Sociology of Work Organizations* (New York: Harper and Row, 1964), pp. 107–222.

any written document, and a system of interaction patterns based on the unique personalities of the participants. If the top manager is not able to turn this informal organization to the ultimate purposes of the company, it might become "subversive"—that is, it may result in restriction of output, the protection of workers who violate management rules flagrantly, and the systematic ignoring of certain orders.[33] Often the "subversive" character of the informal organization can be avoided by perceptive and flexible behavior of the higher management. Violation of orders and restrictions of output should be strictly observed but not always punished; the manager can make it clear that he understands the worker may have some reason to act in this way and seek to correct the grievance, or grant a special privilege with the understanding ("bargain") that the subversive activity will not occur again. Opening clogged channels of communication, creating more explicit mutual understandings, and clarifying authority and goals, are devices useful for managers to minimize the "subversion" that tends to take place in large-scale organizations. Informal organization can exist alongside formal organization without being subversive. Formal organization develops because of the necessities of goal-oriented behavior in large-scale structures; informal organization develops alongside it because of the uniqueness of individuals and situations as well as because of other structural pressures.

Parallel formal and informal organization can also develop in small-scale groups, although certain friendship and acquaintance groups will characteristically have only an informal organization. A traditional and socially-recognized division of labor will tend to impose a formal organization even on a primary group. In a family, for example, the father must take on certain formal responsibilities as head of the family—for example, he must sign certain papers and be responsible for the economic maintenance of the family. In a gang, the position of "leader" tends to get formally recognized, and no member will challenge the leader's rights and obligations unless he is ready for combat. There is a "strain toward formal organization" that arises out of all recurring interactions because they tend to take on the character of tradition and mutual agreement, regardless of the unique personalities and situations involved in each new encounter. Yet the informal organization is likely to assert itself in constantly new ways in the small group. The teacher who expects class participation and oral reports may relieve the shy student of this obligation. Friends are continually making unique adjustments to one another. Still, if there is a formal organization, the informal tends to adjust to it: At a Christmas party

[33] Many students of work relationships seem to suggest the inevitability of conflict between the formal and informal organization. See Scott A. Greer, *Social Organization* (Garden City, N.Y.: Doubleday, 1955), pp. 1–4, 63; Theodore Caplow, *The Sociology of Work* (Minneapolis: University of Minnesota Press, 1954), p. 116.

at the office, no matter how free the liquor flows and no matter how expansive the boss feels, no one forgets who the boss is and how different his behavior will be on the morrow.

c   *The Effective Operation of Institutions*

As we now turn to the question of *how* institutions operate we will see that the roles do not always neatly and precisely gear into one another, and that the functions are seldom performed completely. To inquire concerning the effective operation of institutions raises a very difficult question. In part it can never be answered to everyone's satisfaction, since what is effective is partly a matter of values that differ from culture to culture and from individual to individual. The value premises we shall adopt here are: (1) An institution may be said to function effectively to the extent that it achieves its stated purposes; (2) without pressing too strongly on the biogenic, psychogenic, and sociogenic limitations of the individual personalities it affects. Among the sources of ineffective operation of institutions are the following:

1 Individuals do not have the same conception of their own role and of the role of others in the institution.
2 Outside pressures on the institution prevent it from functioning as its members and others intended that it should function, and outside interests distract the members from their role within the institution.
3 The roles of the members are not geared to perform the functions which the members consciously or unconsciously want performed.
4 Every institution is always in the process of changing the role prescriptions for its members and its functions. Hence it is almost inconceivable that a changing mechanism should be able to work smoothly or toward a consistent goal at any time.

As observed earlier,[34] persons in interaction tend to have correct expectations concerning one another's behavior. When the interaction is regular, and the behavior is in accord with a set of traditional meanings and values, the persons in interaction easily develop a common set of expectations for each other's behavior in that situation. This is what occurs in an institution ideally. But certain influences may prevent the expectations for all the roles in the institution from being conceived in an identical way, and this of course reduces the effectiveness of the institution. Among such influences are: (a) Psychogenic and biogenic elements in the personality of one (or more) of the persons involved which happen to be incompatible with the sociogenic role required for that person by the insti-

[34] See Chapter 2.

tution. (b) Other sociogenic roles of one (or more) of the persons involved which happen to conflict with the sociogenic role required for that person by the particular institution under consideration.[35] (c) Some failure in communication between the various persons in the institution; this is much more likely in an incidental situation than in an institutional one but it can happen when a member is a newcomer to an institutional role or when the role is changing and not all members have kept up with the changes.

Besides these internal reasons for the malfunctioning of institutions there are external ones. While some institutions grow up in harmony with the rest of the social environment, others are organized in protest or in reaction against it. The resistance of the opposed social environment may dishearten the members of the opposing institution and so pull them out of their roles. This not infrequently happens to voluntary associations of the "social influence" type.[36] When they fail to secure quickly the reforms they seek, their members often lose interest and the organization gradually declines. On the other hand, a reform movement may succeed in changing another social institution by making its earlier form unpopular. This has apparently happened in the case of the boss-dominated form of the city government that was prevalent before World War I. Where the political "boss" insisted on remaining behind the scenes, he gradually lost influence; where he openly entered the political arena as the champion of some large group in the population, he often succeeded in maintaining himself in this new role. That is, the institution either weakened or took on a new function.

The external pressures on an institution are more likely to be changes in the composition or status of the population, or changes in the technical environment, than the influence of another institution. For example, other factors in the decline of the hidden political boss as an institution were the reduction in the number of recent immigrants (who, because of their ignorance of regular legal channels for satisfying their needs, often played an important supporting role in this institution), the invention and adoption of the voting machine which made it more difficult to manipulate elections, the general rise in the level of living of workers which made them less dependent on the covert, illegal activities of the boss. Other examples will be considered in a later chapter on social change.

Perhaps the most important outside presssure on an institution is that which consists of distracting influences on its members. No person lives his entire life in performing a role within one single institution, and each institution permits variation in the amount of time and activity which a member may spend within it. Thus there is competition between institu-

[35] This is known in the sociological literature as "role conflict." Pioneer researches on this problem have been carried on by Samuel A. Stouffer, "An Analysis of Conflicting Social Norms," *American Sociological Review,* 14 (December, 1949), pp. 707–17.
[36] See Chapter 10.

tions for the time and interest of their members. Sometimes the competition is keen, as often between the family and recreational institutions. Sometimes the competition occurs only during one stage of a person's life, as in the case of the school and an occupational institution during the late adolescence or early adulthood of a young man. In a society based on organic solidarity, where the individual plays different roles in a variety of different institutions, there tend to be many distracting influences for the individual with respect to his role in any one single institution.

Since an institution is usually spoken of as having one or more functions, it might be expected to satisfy some need, either hereditary or acquired, on the part of the people who play a role in it. This is probably usually true, but it is certainly not always true, and the fact that it is not always true illustrates the danger of speaking of the consequences of an institution as its function. For the fact is that probably every society contains some cultural elements which do not satisfy any individual needs, nor serve to buttress any other part of the social structure, but exist merely because of traditional expectations.

The simplest but perhaps the most important case of this is what Professor W. F. Ogburn has popularized under the name of "cultural lag." When a segment of the culture changes, not all of its elements change at the same rate, so that some elements which may once have satisfied a need now no longer do so. The analogy of the appendix in the human body comes at once to mind, but we must be careful not to take this analogy too literally, as a biological organism has much more interdependence of parts than does a society. At this point we shall present only a most simple example. Before 1933 in the United States the election for president and congressmen occurred on the first Tuesday in November of certain years, but they did not assume office until March 4 on the following year. This delay was created to permit the slow process, when the country was young, of collecting ballots, notifying winning candidates, and permitting them to organize the slow trip to Washington. After a few decades new inventions in transportation and communication made this delay completely unnecessary. The only effect of the delay was to create a "lame-duck" president and Congress, an institution in which the chief executive, if not re-elected, could not plan a long-term policy, and defeated congressmen were sometimes more concerned with obtaining new positions for themselves than they were with passing laws for the benefit of the country. This cultural lag institution lasted about a hundred years before the Twentieth Amendment (1933) moved the date at which a new Congress would assume office back from March 4 to January 3, and a new president back from March 4 to January 20.[37] Another example of a century-long lag in a

[37] When the Twentieth Amendment was formulated, it was not expected to eliminate the "lame-duck" president from November to January, but it was expected to eliminate

political institution is the failure of Congress to provide clearly for the exercise of the presidential powers when the President is incapacitated.[38]

Sometimes a cultural-lag institution comes to serve a new need, and with only a few new meanings and values, and with only a minor modification of roles, it is no longer manifesting cultural lag. A case in point is that of the National American Woman Suffrage Association, a voluntary association the major aim of which was to secure the vote for women in the United States. With the passage of the Nineteenth Amendment to the Constitution in 1920, which gave women the same voting rights as men had, the Association became a cultural-lag institution. It might have been expected to disband immediately or gradually decline through loss of membership as it continued with some very minor functions. Some of its latent functions may be said to have transformed it. The desire of the members to meet together and to work together in a "good cause," and the desire of the leaders to do the same and keep their leadership status, resulted in the transformation of most of the organization into the League of Women Voters. The latter has been a lively and growing institution ever since, with its new major manifest function being to educate its members and other women on major political problems of the day.

Cultural lag is not the only source of institutions that do not satisfy human needs. An institution can be deliberately created for a purpose, and yet be known not to satisfy that purpose. In this situation, people's biogenic, psychogenic, and sociogenic personality may be quite adequate, but some of their needs do not get satisfied because the social structure does not permit the satisfaction. An example can be taken from the executive branch of the French government. France has had a history of difficulty with governmental executives. Its kings were among the most absolute of monarchs, and several of its elected executives—especially Napoleon I and Napoleon III—seized absolute power illegally. Thus, when the constitutions of the Third and Fourth republics were approved by the people in 1875 and 1946, they set up an executive institution which basically had practically no executive powers.

Symbolic executive authority was given to the President of the Republic, but his only real function was to find among the legislators a man who was acceptable to the legislature as head minister. The latter— officially called President of the Council and popularly called Premier—was often mistakenly thought of as equivalent to the British Prime Minister.

---

the "lame-duck" Congress, since Congress had practically never been in session between November and January. The greatly increased needs for legislation have quite frequently kept Congress in session during these months after 1933, so that the "lame-duck" institution has only been shortened, not eliminated.

[38] Richard H. Hansen, *The Year We Had No President* (Lincoln: University of Nebraska Press, 1963).

But his powers were considerably more limited than those of the British Prime Minister. He was expected to submit bills and perhaps a whole program to the legislature for approval, but so could any other legislator. If the legislature would not approve any one bill, and the President of the Council refused to withdraw it, he was obliged to resign. When a bill was passed, he and the other ministers did not administer it as law; they simply set up a structure of civil servants to administer it. Civil servants had complete control over the administration of all laws. At any time the legislature might overthrow the President of the Council and his ministers by a majority vote of no confidence. Only four times in French history from 1875 to 1959 was the legislature not in session, prepared to overthrow any President of the Council within a few days. No party was strong enough to keep its leaders in office, partly because small parties and political factions did not find control of the executive of sufficient value to justify their fusing, through compromise, into a larger party which might occasionally command a majority in the legislature. Thus we see that France had no independent functioning executive for over three-quarters of a century; a few executive powers were distributed among the President of the Republic, the President of the Council and his ministers, and the permanent civil service, but the fundamental executive powers were retained by the legislature.

Thus France has set up a governmental executive institution superficially similar to that of the United Kingdom, but it had no important executive function. A legislature composed of over six hundred deputies is an unwieldy executive, especially when the majority coalition was composed of at least four different parties. This means that the functions of an independent executive—as they exist in other countries—did not get performed, or were performed only irregularly and "accidentally." For example, there was no person or group of persons responsible for instituting a program of new legislation and carrying through its administration until it had been shown to work or not work. There was no person or group of persons responsible to the electorate and to the pressures of public opinion who supervised those who administer the laws. There was no person or group of persons to whom the temporary powers of a dictator could be entrusted during a time of national crisis. Without an independent executive, France had to resort to such extremes as revolutions to institute major new policies, to the entire legislature trying to supervise the civil service, to would-be-permanent dictators, and so on. These expedients either fell outside the democratic framework which most Frenchmen prefer or they did not operate effectively at all, and they resulted from one of the major weaknesses of the French political system—the inadequate operation of the institution of the executive branch of the government.

Yet most Frenchmen could not see the cause of the extreme weakness of their governmental system until Charles de Gaulle assumed the premiership during the Algerian crisis and persuaded the French electorate to vote for a new constitution. The Fifth Republic—operating since the adoption of this Constitution in 1958—does have an independent executive, combining features of both the British and American systems. Some would raise the question whether the new Constitution did not go too far in creating a strong executive, because today the legislature in France is extremely weak. France will probably have to wait until after the political demise of de Gaulle to find out whether it has a governmental system that will work without the presence of a unique leader like de Gaulle.

A third type of malfunctioning of institutions occurs when they take on certain activities that satisfy the needs of certain persons but hurt the society as a whole and are not "essential" to even the persons benefited. Many organized criminal activities are of this type. For example, in late 1951 it was discovered that certain offices of income-tax collection—a governmental institution—were accepting bribes from certain private individuals in return for overlooking irregularities in the income-tax declarations of the latter. This activity was satisfying the "needs" of both the bribers and the tax collectors, of course, and therefore the office of income-tax collection could be said to have this illegal function. But also both groups of persons involved did not require the activity for their existence, and probably not even for their happiness (since the risk of being detected for violating the law must have counterbalanced whatever gains in happiness the bribes brought to the tax collectors). And of course the activity hurt the pocketbooks and the respect for law of the people as a whole.

Another type of malfunctioning of institutions—excessive bureaucracy —has received a good deal of public attention, and its importance has probably been exaggerated. Bureaucracy is inevitable in any institution —especially as it becomes large, complex, and impersonal—for bureaucracy means the setting up of formal rules and roles for accomplishing the functions of the institution. The problem arises when the rules become so numerous and rigid, and the offices become so numerous and specialized, that each obstructs the functioning of the other. To a certain extent this is inevitable, and provides an argument in favor of keeping an institution small or decentralized. For example, when a business corporation expands, middle-level supervisors must be added to supervise the lower-level foremen because the task becomes greater than the top-level managers can handle.

Another example can be taken from the armed services, which is often the butt of popular criticisms against bureaucracy. When two lower-level officers under different commands have to work together, the rules require that they communicate by each sending his message upward in his chain of command until it reaches an officer who is in charge of both commands, from whom it may filter downward through the other chain of command until it reaches the other lower-level officer. The reason for this is obvious. Military activity must be coordinated and top-level officers must take responsibility for the subordinates who take their orders; therefore the top-level officers must know what is going on among their subordinates and must approve or disapprove what the latter do. But certain difficulties inevitably arise under the system. The communication process takes so long that it often seriously hampers the work of the various military units; the top commander is harassed by having to make more decisions than he has time for; middle-level officers may be afraid of annoying their superiors with a communication or request the purpose of which may not be immediately apparent to them. Military "channels" are notoriously inadequate for quick, effective communication, but seldom can they be dispensed with without losing the coordination without which an army would be doomed.[39]

Another defect of bureaucracy is that it tends to expand because of processes inherent within it rather than because the carrying out of its functions require expansion.[40] To a considerable extent the status of the functionaries depends on how many subordinates and tasks they have, and so they try to increase their number. As the daily operation of an institution becomes routine, little ceremonies and rituals tend to develop and add themselves to the regularly expected activity of the institution. An obvious example is the parties that organizations give for their members on all sorts of occasions. Opportunities for new activities often become available to existing organizations, and they thus often expand into new lines of activity for which they were not originally set up. These expansions frequently get in the way of effective carrying out of the main purpose of the institution. Sometimes the ceremonial and expanded activities that tend to accrete to a bureaucracy are so numerous that it is scarcely able to function in its main capacity at all. Then people served by the bureaucracy suffer until higher political authorities "overhaul" it.

We have considered four major types of institutional malfunctioning

[39] The defects of bureaucratization in military organization have been described in Page, *op. cit.;* Ralph H. Turner, "The Navy Disbursing Officer as a Bureaucrat," *American Sociological Review,* 12 (June, 1947), pp. 342–48; Arthur K. Davis, "Bureaucratic Patterns in the Navy Officer Corps," *Social Forces,* 27 (December, 1948), pp. 143–53; Morris Janowitz, *The Professional Soldier* (Glencoe, Ill.: Free Press, 1960).

[40] F. Stuart Chapin, "The Growth of Bureaucracy: An Hypothesis," *American Sociological Review,* 16 (December, 1951), pp. 835–36. A satirical, though serious, description of the process of bureaucratic expansion is the famous *Parkinson's Law: And Other Studies in Administration* by C. Northcote Parkinson (Boston: Houghton Mifflin, 1957). Also see Wilbert E. Moore, *The Conduct of the Corporation* (New York: Random House, 1962).

that fail to satisfy the needs of the persons involved: that involving cultural lag, that involving deliberate avoidance of the function, that involving activity for the benefit of the few at the expense of the many, and that involving excessive bureaucracy. Lesser kinds of malfunctioning of institutions are those characteristic of weaknesses in carrying out any kind of activity—such as using a poor strategy or plan of action, not using the proper techniques in carrying out plans, not taking intelligent advantage of opportunities, and so on.

D The Interrelations Among Institutions and Changing Functions

Just as meanings and values are patterned into institutions, so certain institutions may have interdependent relations with one another.[41] Some institutions, such as a government, include within themselves several sub-institutions, and the dividing line among them shifts from time to time. In this situation the function of any one sub-institution has no value in itself, but has value only in relation to the functions of the other sub-institutions. Other institutions have a true measure of independence, in the sense that the function of each has value in itself for members of the society, but nevertheless have important relations with and make important adjustments to certain other institutions. Within government, for example, the legislative, executive, and judicial institutions have a certain degree of independence in their operation and in their value for the citizen, but they also have a significant relationship to each other at several points. Certain other governmental institutions—such as the electoral college to elect the president of the United States—have no meaning or value in themselves but can only be understood in relation to the operation of certain other political institutions.

Some institutions are in the process of losing some of their functions to other institutions so that their mutual relationships have an ever-shifting character. Immigrant institutions in the United States have generally been gradually dying as fewer new immigrants are allowed into the country and as the older immigrants are assimilated. The immigrant press, for example, changes its character radically as its readers become used to the daily American newspaper, and the prognosis for it—based upon a good deal of experience already—is disappearance.[42] More characteristic is a mere shift in functions to other institutions and the development of the remaining functions.

[41] An important study of the interrelations of institutions in American society is Robert C. Angell, *Integration of American Society* (New York: McGraw-Hill, 1941).

[42] Robert E. Park, *The Immigrant Press and Its Control* (New York: Harper, 1922).

A more important example of the changing functions of an institution in the United States in the past century has been that relating to the family. Prior to the Industrial Revolution, the family had economic, protective, educational, recreational, status-conferring functions which have been largely taken over by other institutions today.[43] At the same time, the family has retained fully its affectional, sexual, and personality-forming functions. The economic function of the family in pre-industrial society was well expressed in the name of the then-dominant system of production—the "domestic system." The economic unit in most lines of production was the family, or the slight extension of it to include journeymen and apprentices. In the crafts, for example, wife and children aided the man of the house in the manufacturing and sale of his products, and these activities took place in a section of the home. Many of the necessary products and services for the home were provided by the family, whereas now they are provided by outsiders. Clothes making and even cloth-weaving, food preserving, house improvement, for example, were then carried on almost entirely by members of the family, so that the family was much more an economically self-sufficient unit than it is today. The farm family follows the older pattern to a much greater extent than does the city family, but it also has been losing economic functions. The factory system, the highly specialized system of production, the modern inventions were the causes of the decline of the family's economic function, for they outcompeted the family for these functions and won because they are economically more efficient.

The family of the pre-industrial era—especially in the frontier conditions of the United States—had two important protective functions. The first one was to secure itself against marauders and thieves (and, on the frontier, against wild animals). The need for this activity has somewhat declined, and the police have taken over what remains of the function, so that practically no family in the United States provides for its own defense.

The other protective function was the care of weak or dependent members. The family still takes care of children, of course, but it has sharply reduced its obligation to aged parents, unmarried aunts, and incapacitated collateral relatives. This loss of family function took place largely without other institutions competing to assume the function, and it was only after years in which no institution performed the function that the government set up such institutions as old-age-security programs and extended facilities for the care of certain kinds of incapacities. The function is still not being

---

[43] This description of the shifting functions of the family has been borrowed and condensed from W. F. Ogburn, "The Family and Its Functions," in *Recent Social Trends in the United States,* Report of the President's Research Committee on Social Trends (New York: McGraw-Hill, 1933), pp. 661–708.

performed to the extent that it was by the family in the pre-industrial era and thus constitutes one of the problems of our society. The aged, the chronically ill, and certain other categories of dependent persons are not adequately taken care of in our otherwise affluent society, whereas they are taken care of adequately in many poorer societies. Unlike the loss of the economic function, where a changing technology more or less forced the family to give up the function, the loss of this second protective function was sloughed off more gradually and the forces of change were permissive rather than compelling. The increased geographical mobility caused by the Industrial Revolution seems to have been the major influence in decreasing the family's sense of responsibility for aged, incapacitated, or lonely relatives. The increasing cost of housing, the decline of minor tasks around the household, and the increased possibilities of carrying on an unattached existence are among the other causes.

The basic education of the child—teaching him how to speak, to behave in acceptable ways, to manipulate material objects to satisfy his needs—has always been one of the functions of the family in our culture. Prior to the Industrial Revolution, the family also taught children a large number of vocational and household skills, and in so far as reading was taught at all to children, the family usually taught it, too. With some minor exceptions, elementary and vocational schools are a product of the past century and a half. They grew up in response to two influences: (1) an ideology calling for progress and equality of opportunity; (2) an economic need for people trained in specialized skills. The family was not equipped to provide the increasingly complex education called for, and so the school developed and took away part of the educational function of the family. Family and school retain a close relation, however. They deliberately try to complement each other's activity, and—within legal limits—the family maintains a certain control over the school through its power to withdraw its children from one school and place them in another, private school, and through its influence on elected boards of education through the vote and other avenues of public opinion.

The school has also taken over a few of the recreational functions of the family, but the major development in recreation in the past century and a half is that of greatly increased facilities and opportunities. Some of the new recreation is in the family but much is provided by outside institutions, public and private. What the family has lost to these other institutions is its near-monopoly over recreation. To a considerable extent the family or its individual members still exercise a good deal of control over the recreational institutions, either because the latter are democratically operated or because the individual chooses which recreational facilities he wants to use.

The status-conferring function of the family in the pre-industrial period arose out of the caste system then prevalent. We shall examine the characteristics of this system in Chapter 8, but we may here note its basic principle that everyone is born into a given stratum of a social hierarchy and that his position in this hierarchy cannot be altered. Under this system the family one was born into determined irrevocably one's status in the hierarchy. When the caste system disappeared, the family was no longer completely determinant of one's social status, although it still remains one important factor among several, such as the acquisition of wealth, achievement, education, and some others. This statement applies to the United States; for a nation such as France the partial disappearance of the caste system did not sharply reduce the status-conferring function of the family but simply altered it.[44] When it became possible to change one's position in the social hierarchy, the family took on the new function of providing this opportunity. One might marry a person of different status and so change his own status and especially that of his children. Or when a collateral relative rose in status through achievement or marriage, one could assimilate some of that rise in status for oneself if one developed a close association with the relative. Thus the French family took on new status-conferring functions when the breakup of the caste system weakened its original monopoly on status conferring.

The above analysis of the shifting functions of the family has illustrated several of the types of relations between institutions. These relations are pointed up by a contrast with another society where the family has been the central institution and the other institutions more or less non-existent. The contrast was philosophically stated by an elderly Pomo Indian of California:

> What is a man? A man is nothing. Without his family he is of less importance than that bug crossing the trail, of less importance than the sputum or exuvial. At least *they* can be used to help poison a man. A man must be with his family to amount to anything with us. If he had nobody else to help him, the first trouble he got into he would be killed by his enemies, because there would be no relatives to help him fight the poison of the other group. No woman would marry him. . . . He would be poorer than a newborn child, he would be poorer than a worm. . . . The family is important. If a man has a large family, . . . and upbringing by a family that is known to produce good children, then he is somebody and every family is willing to have him marry a woman of their group. In the White way of doing things the family is not so important. The police and soldiers take care of protecting you, the courts give you justice,

[44] Unpublished Ph.D. thesis by Jesse Pitts, Harvard University, 1955.

the post office carries messages for you, the school teaches you. Everything is taken care of, even your children, if you die; but with us the family must do all of that.

Without the family we are nothing, and in the old days before the White people came, the family was given first consideration by anyone who was about to do anything at all. That is why we got along. . . .

With us the family was everything. Now it is nothing. We are getting like the White people and it is bad for the old people. We had no old people's home like you. The old people were important. They were wise. Your old people must be fools.[45]

One of the important types of relations among institutions yet to be discussed is that of social conflict.[46] By conflict between institutions the sociologist means a utilization of whatever force an institution may have to prevent or change the functioning of some other institution. The force employed is by no means limited to the physical, and institutions within a society may use all the forces that we earlier considered under "social control" when they are in conflict with each other. While conflict can occur for all sorts of reasons, conflict between two institutions usually involves some opposition between their aims or functions. Since the opposition is seldom complete, the conflict is usually also limited.

An illustration of such limited conflict between institutions in our society would be between the Catholic Church and the public school. The Church would prefer to see its youth trained in its prescribed morals and beliefs under all possible circumstances. The public school permits no religious or sectarian moral teaching within its doors. Unable to change the public school because of the law and majority opinion, the Church concentrates on getting Catholic children into parochial schools, getting public support for parochial schools so that more children can afford to go to them, getting "released time" for public-school children to go to religious training courses during school hours. To acccomplish these ends, the Church uses a strong set of rational arguments, moral pressures on Catholic parents, political pressures on the rest of the society. Advocates of the public school oppose efforts for religious control or for the substitution of a series of parochial schools for public ones. They also use a strong set of rational arguments, moral appeals to non-sectarianism in education, and court cases to oppose every extension of religious influence within the public schools. The conflict is a continuing one, and will not necessarily result in the victory or strengthening of either side. The conflict is a limited one, and is run along fairly gentlemanly lines.

[45] B. W. Aginsky, "An Indian's Soliloquy," *American Journal of Sociology*, 46 (July, 1940), pp. 43–44. Published by The University of Chicago Press.

[46] This topic is taken up in a more general way in Chapter 16.

Certain institutions are formed deliberately for conflict purposes. These will be considered more fully in a later chapter. Our interest in them at this point is merely to observe that their relations with one or more other institutions or culture patterns are directed primarily toward modifying or destroying the latter.

E   *The Unifying Theme of a Culture*

Many sociologists and anthropologists have pointed out that a culture forms an interrelated whole and has a character that permeates all its institutions and distinguishes one society sharply from another. When one crosses a national boundary and makes his first superficial observations of another culture, one usually gets a definite impression of this difference in *"national character"* that is reflected in all the institutions of the society. In the nineteenth century writers attributed these differences in national character to differences in the racial composition of the people making up the various societies. Today we are aware that cultural differences have to be explained in terms of historical and social forces and not in biological terms. But it is quite possible for the distinctive history and unique concatenation of social forces of a society to give a characteristic quality to all its institutions. Certain meanings and values central to the culture permeate all its institutions and give them a coherence which justifies the use of the term "national character."[47]

A related observation about a society is that its various institutions mesh as do the numerous gears of a complicated machine or as do the organs of a living body. Taking his cue from Durkheim, the anthropologist Radcliffe-Brown[48] has held that each institution in a given culture tends to have characteristics which make it uniquely fitted to function in that society. For example, the family and legal institutions that develop in a democratic, decentralized, free-enterprise society will be sharply different from those that grow up in an autocratic, centralized, planned society. Talcott Parsons[49] is a contemporary American sociologist who has carried this "functional" point of view one step further. He holds that a given form of an institution that develops in a certain society is the only possible one that could exist in that society because it is the only one that satisfies cer-

---

[47] Some sociologists have used other terms to refer to national character. Sumner, for example, spoke of the *ethos* of a society. For a summary of the thinking and research on national character, see Otto Klineberg, *Tensions Affecting International Understanding* (New York: Social Science Research Council, 1950); Alex Inkeles, "National Characters," in Gardner Lindzey (ed.), *Handbook of Social Psychology* (Cambridge, Mass.: Addison-Wesley, 1954).

[48] Alfred R. Radcliffe-Brown, *Structure and Function in Primitive Society* (London: Cohen and West, 1952).

[49] *The Social System* (Glencoe, Ill.: Free Press, 1951).

tain needs that develop as pressures from all the other institutions. For example, he says that the hospital has developed in our society as an institution to take care of the seriously sick partly because the ties of family relationship are loosening and no longer provide the solicitous and continual care that is needed when one becomes ill.[50] Parsons also holds that when there is a change in one institution there follow changes in other institutions to adjust to the first change.

This functional point of view is an important corrective for a point of view in anthropology and sociology that regards a culture as a mere bundle of accidentally associated traits. It makes a few exaggerations, however, which ought to be guarded against.[51] First, the institutions of a culture are not so mutually interdependent as the organs of a body. Not only can a society exist indefinitely with many of its institutions out of adjustment to each other, but even in conflict with each other. Social processes are much more flexible than biological processes, and there can frequently be failures in one or several institutions without the society dying in the way a biological organism will die if one of its organs should fail to function. Second, a social function of an institution is more in the nature of an effect than a necessity. Sociologists have learned much about social effects; they have not yet discovered a single absolute social need or necessity. Third, even more so than the organs in the biological organism, in a society many institutions can serve the same function so that one can readily substitute for another. Fourth, change and "disorganization" are as natural to societies as are stability and mutual adjustment of parts.

Some students of culture have become so interested in the internal harmony of the parts of a given culture that they have sought to account for it in the common elements of the psychogenic personalities of the members of the society. Independently, the anthropologists Ralph Linton[52] and Ruth Benedict[53] and their followers have held that each society has a typical pattern of child rearing which in significant ways is distinctive from the child-rearing pattern characteristics of other societies. This child-rearing cultural pattern produces a certain kind of "basic personality,"[54] which in turn gives a distinctive character to all the institutions of the society. This approach has provided a promising relationship between the

[50] Talcott Parsons and Renée Fox, "Illness, Therapy, and the Modern Urban American Family," *Journal of Social Issues,* 10 (4th issue, 1954), pp. 31–44.

[51] One neo-functionalist who has dealt with the inadequacies of orthodox functionalism is Robert K. Merton in his *Social Theory and Social Structure,* rev. ed. (Glencoe, Ill.: Free Press, 1957), Chapter 1.

[52] Abram Kardiner and Ralph Linton, *The Individual and His Society* (New York: Columbia University Press, 1939); *The Psychological Frontiers of Society* (New York: Columbia University Press, 1945).

[53] *The Chrysanthemum and the Sword: Patterns of Japanese Culture* (Boston: Houghton Mifflin, 1946).

[54] See Chapter 4, Section D.

study of personality and the study of culture, but it has at least two serious defects: (1) it ignores the great variations in personality and cultural practices within any society, (2) it neglects historical influences as the culture and sociogenic influences on the individual. These defects may help to explain why Benedict and her students failed to use the same classification of culture types in their studies after 1940 as she used in her book published in 1934, *Patterns of Culture*.

The defects in the theory and researches in the "national character," "functionalist," and "basic personality" traditions should not blind us to the important truth that underlies them. There is an important interrelationship between the parts of a culture which gives it a distinctive quality. It is obvious that the problem needs much more study and much more refinement of concepts and theories. It is as important to account for the many exceptions as it is to account for the unifying theme.

FOR ADDITIONAL READING

BLAU, PETER M., *Bureaucracy in Modern Society* (New York: Random House, 1956). A short summary of the theory of bureaucracy.

GOULDNER, ALVIN W., *Patterns of Industrial Bureaucracy* (Glencoe, Ill.: Free Press, 1954). A study of bureaucracy in industry.

GREER, SCOTT A., *Social Organization* (New York: Random House, 1955). A short summary of factors involved in social structure.

HUGHES, EVERETT C., "Institutions," in A. M. Lee (ed.), *An Outline of the Principles of Sociology* (New York: Barnes and Noble, 1946). One of the most complete of brief descriptions of the nature of institutions.

WILLIAMS, ROBIN, *American Society* (New York: Alfred A. Knopf, 1952). A penetrating sociological analysis of American society, from a modified functionalist point of view.

6 * The Intimate Human Association

It was one of the major sociological discoveries when, in 1909, Cooley pointed out that the "primary group"—the intimate, face-to-face association of humans—was the "cradle of personality."[1] As we had occasion to observe in Chapter 4, knowledge of the fact that human beings differed from the other animals in not having their behavior patterns and personality traits pre-formed in their genetic constitutions led sociologists to recognize the central importance of association and interaction. It was natural that a distinction should grow up between primary and secondary relationships, between relationships that were intimate and involved the emotions and the whole personality, on the one hand, and those that were casual, superficial, and segmentalized on the other hand. The former were most important, not only in shaping the personality of the infant and transmitting to him the meanings and values of his general culture, but in providing a sense of security and emotional satisfaction throughout life. The purpose of the present chapter is to examine a few of the groups and institutions providing these primary, intimate human relationships, not only from the standpoint of their relationship to the individual, but also from the point of view of their internal structure, the characteristic processes within them, and the fundamental changes now going on in regard to their role in the general social structure.

The most important primary group in our culture and in most other cultures is the family, and it is to this institution that we shall give our first attention in this chapter. Other important primary groups are the friendship group, the recreational group, and the expressive group. There are still some parts of our society in which the community, the church, and the work group follow the pre-Industrial Revolution pattern of pro-

[1] Charles H. Cooley, *Social Organizations* (New York: Scribner's, 1909). Chapter 3.

viding regular primary relationships. Those who live in convents and monasteries are living in primary groups, but we shall pay no further attention to these as they affect such a small segment of the population.

It should be recognized at the outset that families and friendship groups are not primary groups all the time for most people. Our culture is segmentalized. We play different roles in different groups, and our friends and family members are often not aware of all our activities that take place outside their presence. We often tell them about our behavior in other settings, but sometimes we do not, and sometimes they are not capable of understanding our behavior in other settings even when we do tell them. Every culture probably encourages some barriers between family members and friends, but our segmentalized culture probably provides more of these barriers than most. Thus a primary group is intimate in *degree:* it is a group in which *relatively* we express our whole personality.

A   *The Family as an Institution*

It is difficult to find a definition of "family" that is sufficiently broad to cover the groups described as families in all known societies. The nearest we can come to an adequate definition is that a family is a group of interacting persons who recognize a relationship with each other based on common parentage, marriage, and/or adoption. Some authors attempt to define "family" in terms of function, but the functions of families vary in different societies, and there is no one central function that all societies grant to the family. It is sometimes said that a childbearing and child-rearing function is what defines a family, but in our own society that would not include a childless married couple having one or both sets of parents in their home. If the regular satisfaction of sexual urges be considered as the central function of the family, an exception would have to be made for certain preliterate societies in India and Oceania where sexual activities are regularly and properly carried on only outside the household where one lives and raises one's children. If the satisfaction of needs for affection and intimate response are considered to be the central function of the family, it must be recognized that the family shares this function with other primary groups. Still, one can say that the functions of sex, provision of affection and intimate response, childbearing, and child rearing are almost universally found in connection with families. MacIver states that there are certain other characteristics of families that are almost universally found, even though they are manifested in many different ways:

> (1) a mating relationship, (2) a form of marriage or other institutional arrangement in accordance with which the mating relation is established and maintained, (3) a system of nomenclature, involving also

> By primary groups I mean those characterized by intimate face-to-face associa-
> tion and cooperation. They are primary in several senses, but chiefly in that
> they are fundamental in forming the social nature and ideals of the individual.
> The result of intimate association, psychologically, is a certain fusion of in-
> dividualities in a common whole, so that one's very self, for many purposes
> at least, is the common life and purpose of the group. Perhaps the simplest
> way of describing this wholeness is by saying that it is a "we"; it involves the
> sort of sympathy and mutual identification for which "we" is the natural ex-
> pression. One lives in the feeling of the whole and finds the chief aims of his
> will in that feeling.
>
> C. H. Cooley, *Social Organization* (New York: Scribner's, 1909), p. 25.

a mode of reckoning descent, (4) some economic needs associated with childbearing and child rearing, and generally (5) a common habitation, home, or household, which, however, may not be exclusive to the family group.[2]

If these are the stable features of the family, there have also been some important changes affecting the family as we know it in our culture.[3]

First, as to size, there has been a marked decline, for two reasons. There are now fewer children born into the family, and the persons considered members of the family have decreased—that is, the family much less typically includes aged parents of the married couple, their unmarried sisters or brothers, aunts or uncles. The average completed American family consists of a married couple and three to four children. In 1960 the average size of all American families, not only completed ones, was 3.5 persons. In 1910, to contrast, the average American family had five children, while in 1800 it had eight children.[4]

Second, as to basis of construction, the family is now usually formed by the voluntary[5] and mutual choice of a young man and a young woman whereas formerly it was arranged by the respective parents of the young people, or by the young man and the parents of his chosen bride.

Third, as to internal government, there is now much more democracy,

[2] Robert M. MacIver, *Society: A Textbook of Sociology* (New York: Farrar and Rinehart, 1937), p. 197.

[3] Perhaps the most systematic sociological study of the modernization of the family, in several societies, is that of W. J. Goode, *World Revolution and Family Patterns* (New York: Free Press of Glencoe, 1963).

[4] In 1800, the birth rate in the U.S. was about 55 births per 1,000 population; by 1910, the rate had fallen to about 30. It reached a low point in 1933 at 18.4 per 1,000 population, but rose slowly after that and reached stability after a peak of 26.6 in 1947.

[5] In using the word "voluntary" we of course do not mean that there are no pressures on the young people influencing their mutual selection. The word is used here to indicate that the selection is not made for them by some other person or persons.

whereas in the nineteenth century the husband had at least most of the formal authority. The wife today, both in law and in practice, has as much control over family matters as does the husband.[6] In some families there is a trend toward self-determination of children at a very young age, whereas formerly children were under the control of their parents at least until they set up a household of their own.

Fourth, as to stability, the family which has not yet completed its "normal" cycle is now less likely to be broken by death but more likely to be broken by divorce. Divorces reached a peak of one for every 2.5 marriages in 1946 and now has dropped to one in five. The children, the teen-age couples, veterans, the low income and poorly educated groups, have the highest divorce rates. More of those who get divorced remarry.

Fifth, as to function, the family has sloughed off most of its economic, protective, medical, educational, and some of its recreational functions, and now concentrates more on its affectional, sexual, and personality formation functions.[7]

These changes, as well as an increase in rational discussion about the family, have given rise to a common impression that the family is on the decline. This is far from the truth: actually there has been a steady increase in the proportion of the American population married—from 55 per cent of those fourteen years of age and over in 1890 to over 69 per cent in 1962.[8] Fewer persons spend their lives as single persons (now only about 10 per cent), remarriage is more frequent for widowed and divorced females, and people now tend to get married at a younger age (the median age at first marriage dropped from 26.1 years in 1890 to 22.7 years in 1962 for men, and from 22.0 years in 1890 to 20.3 years in 1962 for women). Table 1 summarizes some of the changes in the family as indicated in the average ages of the married couple: the age of marriage, the age when the last child is born, and the age at which the last child is married are all decreasing. On the other hand, the age of death of the spouse is going up, so that the length of the marriage after all children have left home is also increasing.

What has been happening is that the family is taking on a new form; it has new meanings and new values. Burgess and Locke have summarized the change, with some exaggeration, in the following way:

> The family in historical times has been, and at present is, in transition from an institution to a companionship. In the past the important factors unifying the family have been external, formal, and

---

[6] Other changes in the status of women are discussed in Chapter 11.

[7] The causes of these changes in family functions were discussed in Chapter 5, Section C.

[8] U.S. Bureau of the Census, *Current Population Reports, Population Characteristics,* Series P. 20, No. 122, March 22, 1963.

TABLE 1 • MEDIAN AGE OF HUSBAND AND WIFE AT SELECTED STAGES OF THE LIFE CYCLE OF THE FAMILY, FOR THE UNITED STATES: 1890–1980

Stage	1890	1940	1950	1960	1980
MEDIAN AGE OF WIFE AT					
First marriage	22.0	21.5	20.1	20.2	19.5–20.4
Birth of last child	31.9	27.1	26.1	25.8	27–28
Marriage of last child	55.3	50.0	47.6	47.1	48–49
Death of one spouse	53.3	60.9	61.4	63.6	65–66
MEDIAN AGE OF HUSBAND AT					
First marriage	26.1	24.3	22.8	22.3	22–23
Birth of last child	36.0	29.9	28.8	27.9	29–30
Marriage of last child	59.4	52.8	50.3	49.2	51–52
Death of one spouse	57.4	63.6	64.1	65.7	68–69

Source: P. C. Glick, D. M. Heer, and J. C. Beresford, "Social Change and Family Structure: Trends and Prospects," unpublished paper presented to AAAS, December 29, 1959. The figures in this table for 1890, 1940, and 1950 were previously published in Paul C. Glick, "The Life Cycle of the Family," *Marriage and Family Living*, Vol. XVII, No. 1, February, 1955, Table 1. Those for 1960 and 1980 have not been previously published; they were estimated by methods similar to those used for earlier dates.

authoritarian, as the law, the mores, public opinion, tradition, the authority of the family head, rigid discipline, and elaborate ritual. At present, in the new emerging form of the companionship family, its unity inheres less and less in community pressures and more and more in such interpersonal relations as the mutual affection, the sympathetic understanding, and the comradeship of its members.[9]

One of the major long-run changes has been the weakening of the *extended family* (consisting of all the relatives, as distinguished from the *nuclear family*, which consists solely of husband, wife and children). By comparison with pre-industrial periods, there has certainly been a relative decline of the extended family. But perhaps earlier sociologists exaggerated the decline, because recent studies suggest that extended family relations are still significantly to be found in contemporary cities. Studies among middle-class residents of Buffalo,[10] Detroit,[11] and Los Angeles[12] indicate that almost 50 per cent of the respondents saw relatives at least once a week or more often. In San Francisco, another study[13] reported that almost

[9] Ernest W. Burgess and Harvey J. Locke, *The Family* (New York: American Book, 1945), p. vii.

[10] Eugene Litwak, "The Use of Extended Family Groups in the Achievement of Social Goals," *Social Problems*, 7 (Winter, 1959–60), p. 179. (Reference to own unpublished Ph.D. thesis, 1958, pp. 79–81.)

[11] Morris Axelrod, "Urban Structure and Social Participation," *American Sociological Review*, 21 (February, 1956), pp. 13–18.

[12] Scott Greer, "Urbanism Reconsidered," *American Sociological Review*, 21 (February, 1956), p. 22.

[13] Wendell Bell and Marion D. Boat, "Urban Neighborhoods and Informal Social Relations," *American Journal of Sociology*, 42 (January, 1957), p. 396.

90 per cent said that some extended family member was one of their closest friends. In New Haven[14] close to 70 per cent of a sample of middle-class interviewees said that they received a significant amount of aid from some person or persons in their extended family. In Cleveland,[15] these help and service exchanges approached 100 per cent in the middle classes and 92.5 per cent in the working class. In a study of a working-class community in London, England,[16] the extended family relations were close enough to result in pressures toward living nearby and toward obligations to find jobs for relatives. The authors of all of this research implicitly assume that their findings prove that extended family relationships have not declined as much as earlier sociologists thought. However, in the absence of earlier or longitudinal studies, the alternative hypothesis can reasonably be entertained that the extended family did deteriorate badly in Western cities toward the end of the 19th century and has been reviving somewhat within the last few decades. No direct evidence is known to support this alternative hypothesis, but it is generally known that overt rebellion against parents by young adults has declined somewhat since the 1930's, that there is less rejection of ethnic identification than there was before 1930, and that shirking family obligations is less likely in periods of extended prosperity than in periods of frequent unemployment. Thus, it is possible that both the older and the newer sociologists are correct, and that the extended family is becoming somewhat stronger lately, after reaching a low point in the early decades of the twentieth century.

Burgess and Locke have pointed to the several historical traditions shaping the American family as an institution: (1) The puritanical tradition has contributed a basic patriarchal control,[17] a community control superior to the father's, and a negative attitude toward sex. (2) The Renaissance tradition has contributed the secular marriage and the individualism of family members. (3) The Romantic tradition has fostered the idealization of sex, the small family as distinguished from the extended family, and freedom to select one's own mate and to get a divorce. (4) The frontier tradition encouraged the practice of equalitarian relations between husband and wife and the training of children for family self-sufficiency. (5) Urbanization has reduced community controls, created a cynical attitude

[14] Marvin B. Sussman, "The Help Pattern in the Middle Class Family," *American Sociological Review*, 18 (February, 1953), p. 27.

[15] Marvin B. Sussman, "The Isolated Nuclear Family: Fact or Fiction," *Social Problems*, 6 (Spring, 1959), p. 335. Also see reference to other studies on p. 334.

[16] Michael Young and Peter Willmott, *Family and Kinship in East London* (London: Routledge and Kegan Paul, 1957).

[17] Even as the husband and wife become more equal in their control of the family, no one thinks of changing the children's inheritance of their father's name, and the usual location of the family near the husband's place of work.

toward courtship, discouraged having many children, and made other changes that we have noted in Chapter 5.

There have been many classifications of modern families depending on differential family structure and the nature of interpersonal relationships within the family. The classification used by Murray Straus[18] in one research may be taken as illustrative. He finds there are four types of families depending on their internal power structure: (1) husband dominant, (2) wife dominant, (3) autonomic, or equalitarian spousal relationship with close family integration, (4) conflict, or equalitarian spousal relationship with weak family integration. Some types of families have been singled out for special study—for example, the integrated family characterized by high "familism," which is "the ascendance of family interests over the interests of the individual members as expressed in the maintenance of family tradition, property, social contacts, and occupational pursuits."[19]

The first White House Conference on Family Life prepared a succinct statement for studying the internal growth and development of families which provides a useful introduction to the following sections:

> The family may be viewed as an arena of interacting personalities each striving to obtain the satisfaction of his basic desires. Parents who themselves have urgent needs make most of the adjustments in the building of complementary roles between themselves and their children. If we hold the entire family in focus in dealing with this drama, we see that many of the normal tangles of members during the family's life cycle are due to fundamental incompatibilities of the diverse developmental strivings of siblings and parents at critical points of growth. There can be identified, using these concepts, seven well-defined stages of the family life cycle each with its own peculiar sources of conflict and solidarity. . . . Each of these stages may be seen in three dimensions of increasing complexity: (1) the changing developmental tasks and role expectations of the children; (2) the changing developmental tasks and role expectations of the parents, both mother and father, in their capacities as providers, homemakers, spouses, and persons; (3) the family developmental tasks of the family *as a family* which may be obtained by integrating the functional prerequisites of survival and growth . . . and implications for the family of the personal development patterns of children and parents.[20]

[18] Murray A. Straus, "Conjugal Power Structure and Adolescent Personality," *Marriage and Family Living*, 24 (February, 1962), pp. 17–25.

[19] Burgess and Locke, *op. cit.*, p. 64.

[20] Quoted by Reuben Hill, "A Critique of Contemporary Marriage and Family Research," *Social Forces*, 33 (March, 1955), p. 276.

B   *The Selection of a Mate*

In this new "companionship" the process of mate selection is an intimate one. A young man or a young woman looks for someone he or she can be most intimate with. Each is attracted by the potential mate's personality, beauty or handsomeness, social standing, the economic advantages he or she can provide, or one or more of many other features. Seldom does a person succeed in selecting what seems to be a completely ideal mate, but one does select what seems to him to be a person with mostly desirable characteristics. The process of courtship is one of achieving greater intimacy so that one can know better the qualities of the potential mate. On the other hand, there are a number of features of the courtship process which keep the intimacy from being a real one. Romance, for example, tends to result in idealization of the potential mate and prevents true communication. A large number of studies have been made of the basis of mate selection and the process of courtship, and a few of these will be mentioned here.

1   SOME STUDIES OF MATE SELECTION

There is a tendency for an individual to select as a mate a person who has traits similar to his own; this is called *assortative mating*.[21] Like attracts like more than opposites. The traits of similarity may be physical, psychological, or social. Burgess and Wallin, studying 1,000 engaged couples, found a correlation of .31 between the heights of the male and the female, .21 on weight, .20 on health, and .20 on physical appearance or "good looks," and up to .27 on various personality traits.[22] Since the coefficient of correlation is a measure of association ranging from .00 to 1.00, these are not high relationships. Similarity between husband and wife is greater in respect to intelligence. In seven different studies the correlation ranged between .44 and .74 on I.Q. scores.[23] In regard to social characteristics, there is also a moderate amount of assortative mating. The coefficient of correlation was .54 for church membership and attendance, .38 for a combined measure of family background (including nativity, rural or urban childhood, social and economic status of parents, etc.), .24 for social participation, .31 for

[21] Ernest W. Burgess and Paul Wallin, "Homogamy in Personality Characteristics," *Journal of Abnormal and Social Psychology*, 39 (October, 1944), pp. 475–81.

[22] Hill has thoroughly covered the literature on this topic and reports that there are 150 studies, most of them showing that—for the different characteristics studied—people tend to marry people like themselves rather than opposites. See Reuben Hill, *op. cit.*, p. 268.

[23] Mapheus Smith, "Similarities of Marriage Partners in Intelligence," *American Sociological Review*, 6 (October, 1941), pp. 697–701.

conceptions of marriage.[24] Several studies show a strong tendency for young people to marry someone of their own educational level.[25]

By comparing the addresses listed for the man and the woman on applications for marriage licenses in Philadelphia, Bossard found that 21 per cent lived within five blocks of each other, and 51 per cent lived within twenty blocks of each other.[26] Other studies have confirmed the influence of residential propinquity in mate selection for other cities and for rural areas.[27] It is not only because it is easier to get to meet people who live close by that there is this influence of residential propinquity on choice of mate; it is also that neighborhoods tend to include people of the same socioeconomic status, religious affiliation, and other social characteristics so that assortative mating operates.

Race and nationality background are very strong bases of assortative mating. Most of this operates as a matter of voluntary choice, but in addition there are laws in twenty-six states[28] which prohibit racial intermarriage in some way. Some of these laws are directed at preventing intermarriage of whites with Negroes; others are directed at preventing intermarriage of whites with orientals, American Indians, or "colored races" in general. Wirth and Goldhamer[29] have shown statistically how little intermarriage there is between whites and Negroes in those states where such marriage is legal, and how intermarriage has been decreasing, at least until very recently.

Marriage across nationality lines occurs more frequently than marriage across racial lines. It is becoming increasingly common, especially in areas where the different nationalities have a significant amount of social contact with each other. In rural Minnesota, where each ethnic group represented tends to occupy a separate area, two thirds of the husbands and wives had the same nationality background.[30] In New York City at about the same time nearly half of the marriages crossed either a nativity or a nationality

[24] Ernest W. Burgess and Paul Wallin, "Homogamy in Social Characteristics," *American Journal of Sociology*, 49 (September, 1943), pp. 109–24.

[25] Paul H. Landis and Katherine H. Day, "Education as a Factor in Mate Selection," *American Sociological Review*, 10 (August, 1945), pp. 558–60. Metropolitan Life Insurance Company, *Statistical Bulletin*, 26 (September, 1945), pp. 3–5.

[26] James H. S. Bossard, "Residential Propinquity as a Factor in Marriage Selection," *American Journal of Sociology*, 38 (September, 1932), pp. 219–24.

[27] Alvin M. Katz and Reuben Hill, "Residential Propinquity and Marital Selection: A Review of Theory, Method, and Fact," *Marriage and Family Living*, 20 (February, 1958), pp. 27–35.

[28] These include all of the southern states and all but eight of the states west of the Mississippi River. In the northern states east of the Mississippi River, only Indiana has a law forbidding racial intermarriage.

[29] Louis Wirth and Herbert Goldhamer, in Otto Klineberg (ed.), *Characteristics of the American Negro* (New York: Harper, 1944), pp. 276–300.

[30] Lowry Nelson, "Intermarriage among Nationality Groups in a Rural Area of Minnesota," *American Journal of Sociology*, 48 (March, 1943), pp. 585–92.

line, or both.[31] Much of the crossing of nationality lines occurs within the same religious faith, so that Catholic Poles and Italians are more likely to marry each other than either is to marry Protestant Scandinavians.

For this reason Kennedy raises the question whether the trend toward amalgamation in the United States is occurring in three melting pots— Catholic, Protestant, and Jewish—rather than one general melting pot for all whites.[32] Many of the churches deliberately encourage their members to marry within the faith, and this keeps assortative mating stronger along religious lines than along nationality lines. Cultural differences along lines of nationality background break down very rapidly in the United States, so that for third-generation Americans they have become largely fused with class and locality characteristics. Associated with religion, on the other hand, are some basic cultural values that go much beyond the purely theological. These cultural differences as well as the deliberate teachings of the churches do much to keep young people apart and unwilling to marry across religious lines.

In the preceding paragraphs we have discussed the *facts* of assortative mating, not whether it is good or bad. There are many criteria of whether a marriage is good, but one criterion often used by sociologists is the happiness of the couple. Certainly any given marriage might turn out to be happy regardless of the physical, psychological, or social differences between the husband and wife. But for many of the traits we have considered the studies made by sociologists show that, to a certain extent, similarity of traits makes for happiness in marriage.[33] Apparently most people like themselves best and find their own attitudes, traits, and backgrounds most congenial, so that a mate who is most like unto oneself has the best chance of being suitable. Similar social traits have been found to be most important for successful marriage, apparently because they reflect similarity of cultural meanings and values. People can be most intimate with those with whom they can communicate most easily and with whom they share common basic attitudes. This is probably also how the process of assortative mating works. One does not check to see that the potential mate has the same traits as oneself; rather one finds that one likes someone better than others—finds him or her more congenial, finds him or her easier to communicate with—and this, in effect, means that one picks a person like himself.

We have been emphasizing the social similarity factor in mate selec-

[31] James H. S. Bossard, "Nationality and Nativity as Factors in Marriage," *American Sociological Review*, 4 (December, 1939), pp. 792–98.

[32] Ruby J. R. Kennedy, "Single or Triple Melting Pot? Intermarriage Trends in New Haven, 1870–1940," *American Journal of Sociology*, 49 (January, 1944), pp. 331–39.

[33] On the other hand, some unpublished data on cross-religion marriages in Iowa, collected by Lee Burchinal, shows that only a slightly greater number of Protestant-Catholic marriages than of Protestant-Protestant marriages are likely to end in divorce.

tion, which is popularly known as congeniality or compatibility. Marriage partners are selected for a host of reasons, although the reasons that are given verbally are not always the real reasons. In addition to congeniality, people marry for money, social prestige, sense of obligation, lack of satisfactory alternatives, "pure" sex attraction (although sex attraction plays a role in most mate selections, it tends to become associated with other desired traits), and so on. These traits or "reasons" reflect the values of our culture, so that the specific choice of marriage partner as well as the practice of monogamous marriage itself is intimately associated with the most valued elements in the culture. Another factor in mate selection has been that emphasized by the psychoanalysts—namely, that a person seeks a mate who unconsciously reminds him of his parent of the opposite sex. Studies by Robert F. Winch and Anselm Strauss show that most people do have conscious "ideals" regarding future mates and that the traits, especially the physical traits, of these ideals have a slight, but significant relationship to the corresponding traits of their parents.[34]

Winch has also recently suggested that individuals choose each other as mates on the basis of complementary psychological needs—for example, a husband who feels the need to be deferred to generally seeks a wife who feels a need to be dominated.[35] Winch presents strong evidence in support of this theory, but of course his findings are contradictory to some of the evidence we presented on similarity of personality traits as a basis of mate selection. Young people are generally not aware that they are acting in accord with cultural and psychogenic imperatives and influences, but these gradually express themselves in individual behavior through the periods of initial social contact, dating, courtship and engagement.

2   DATING AND COURTSHIP

Casual dating, without marriage as its immediate goal, seems to have developed only in fairly recent times. It is still not uniformly accepted throughout our society. A study of 2,000 naval inductees[36] showed that

---

[34] Robert F. Winch, "Further Data and Observation on the Oedipus Hypothesis: The Consequence of an Inadequate Hypothesis," *American Sociological Review,* 16 (December, 1951), pp. 784–95; Anselm Strauss, "The Influence of Parent-Images upon Marital Choice," *American Sociological Review,* 11 (October, 1946), pp. 554–59; "The Ideal and Chosen Mate," *American Journal of Sociology,* 52 (November, 1946), pp. 204–08.

[35] Robert F. Winch and Thomas and Virginia Ktsanes, "The Theory of Complementary Needs: An Analytic and Descriptive Study," *American Sociological Review,* 19 (June, 1954), pp. 241–49; Robert F. Winch, "The Theory of Complementary Needs in Mate Selection: A Test of One Kind of Complementariness," *American Sociological Review,* 20 (February, 1955), pp. 52–56; also see James A. Schellenberg and Lawrence S. Bee, "A Re-examination of the Theory of Complementary Needs in Mate Selection," *Marriage and Family Living,* 22 (August, 1960), pp. 227–232; Robert F. Winch, *Modern Family,* rev. ed. (New York: Holt, Rinehart and Winston, 1963).

[36] *Family Life,* 6 (October, 1946), pp. 1 ff.

twenty-five-year-olds claimed an average of only 6.7 dates. In this age group 7 per cent had dated only one girl, and an additional 10 per cent had dated only two. For those who date frequently, Baber suggests that dating has the functions of permitting youths to "(1) learn to be at ease with members of the opposite sex, (2) have close companionship with selected persons, and (3) discover which qualities wear well and would therefore be desirable in a partner when the courtship stage is reached."[37]

In a fairly closed group of young people—as on a college campus or in a small town—dating is also used as a means of gaining social prestige. Dating often arises out of the childhood friendship group, but it soon takes on a pattern of its own. It permits social intimacy, fellowship, and fun, and at least some physical stimulation, without commitment to further association on the part of either party. While dating generally provides pleasant social contact desired for its own sake, it also permits young people to look each other over and eventually decide whom they are going to pursue seriously as a marriage partner. When dating becomes "steady" and has marriage as its goal, it is quite like the courtship found in earlier times, even though its specific manifestations are different. Dating involves both the extension of the scope of those who might be selected as marriage partners and the narrowing down to a limited number of likely prospects. When the latter process has reached a certain point, and the young people consider themselves about ready to marry, dating gives way to courtship.

Courtship implies that a selection has been made, even if it has been made by only one party and even if it does not always result in marriage. Since our culture gives the male the formal initiative, it is usually said that the male does the courting. But the female has indirect techniques of taking the initiative. Either party, then, is interested in attracting the other party into marriage. Both parties size each other up as potential marriage partners much more seriously than they do during the dating period—seriously not in the sense of rationally but in the sense of having marriage in mind.

There is no sharp distinction today between courtship and engagement, since the public announcement that marriage is intended and the formal giving of a ring are often dispensed with.[38] In past generations engagement was almost as binding as marriage itself and was considered a necessary prerequisite to marriage. Even though formal engagements are not so frequently engaged in today, there is some feeling of mutual obligation during the period when an "understanding" is reached that the couple will sometime get married. If today there are fewer "fiancés" and "fian-

---

[37] Ray E. Baber, *Marriage and the Family* (New York: McGraw-Hill, 1953), p. 116.

[38] James H. S. Bossard, "The Engagement Ring—A Changing Symbol," *New York Times Magazine*, September 14, 1958, pp. 32, 73–74.

cées," the "steady boy friends" and "steady girl friends" have taken their place. It is easier to break off the latter relationships than the former ones.

Kirkpatrick and Caplow[39] studied 399 university students, whose average age was twenty-two, and found that they had had 896 "serious love affairs," or an average of two and a fourth per person. Almost three fourths of these relationships had already broken up at the time of the survey. The most frequent reason given for the breakup was that one or the other party had become "interested in another person," 45 per cent of the men and 47 per cent of the women reporting this reason. The second most frequent reason given (by 47 per cent of the men and 38 per cent of the women) was "mutual loss of interest." In one research study covering 1,000 engaged couples, Ernest Burgess and Paul Wallin found that, at the time of their participation in the study, 24 per cent of men and 36 per cent of the women reported earlier engagements that had been broken. In addition, 15 per cent of these couples subsequently broke their engagements, so that by the close of the study, almost two-fifths of the men and more than half of the women reported broken engagements.[40]

If the period of courtship and "understanding" does not always end in marriage for the specific couple, this does not mean that there is less marriage today. As we have already seen, there is a larger proportion of the population getting married, and at a younger age, than in previous generations. Young people generally recuperate rapidly from a breakup. In the Kirkpatrick-Caplow study, half the university students who reported a breakup said that adjustment took no time at all, and an additional 34 per cent of the men and 20 per cent of the women said that adjustment required only a few weeks. About one in fourteen of the men and one in nine of the women said the adjustment took several years. With respect to their feelings at the time of breakup only 5 per cent said they felt "bitter," 12 per cent said they felt "hurt," 3 per cent felt "crushed," 7 per cent felt "remorseful," 3 per cent felt "angry." The most frequently reported feelings were "mixed regret and relief" (16 per cent), "satisfaction" or "happiness" (14 per cent). Thus young people at present are likely to experience several periods of "going steady" before they finally marry. However, some recent observers claim that there is a tendency today for some young people to have only one "steady" before getting married.[41]

[39] Clifford Kirkpatrick and Theodore Caplow, "Courtship in a Group of Minnesota Students," *American Journal of Sociology*, 51 (September, 1945), pp. 114–25.

[40] Ernest W. Burgess and Paul Wallin, *Courtship, Engagement, and Marriage* (Philadelphia: Lippincott, 1954).

[41] Charles W. Cole, "American Youth Goes Monogamous," *Harper's*, 214 (March, 1957), pp. 29–33. Also see Alfred C. Kinsey, W. B. Pomeroy, and C. E. Martin, *Sexual Behavior in the Human Male* (Philadelphia: W. B. Saunders, 1948), A. C. Kinsey, W. B. Pomeroy, C. E. Martin, and P. H. Gebhard, *Sexual Behavior in the Human Female* (Philadelphia: W. B. Saunders, 1953).

Dating especially, and even the period of "going steady," does not provide opportunities for the greatest ease and frankness of communication. Modern young people think of themselves as very frank and informal in their communication, and indeed they are, in a superficial sense. They are often willing to talk about each other's personalities and interests, but they are often not willing to analyze the future situations they are likely to face and to see if they agree on how to meet them. They tend to avoid subjects of conversation on which they have differences of opinion, as they do not like to "bicker."

Dating is characterized by what sociologists call a "joking" type of conversation: people are given to making witty and amusing remarks and to express points of view which they do not really hold. This is not done with the intent to deceive but because it is expected on dates and at parties. Nevertheless, it prevents serious and frank conversation. Those who are adept at making joking conversation, or who are otherwise the "life of the party," may be most attractive or congenial to the opposite sex during dating and courtship. But these are not necessarily qualities which will make for success in marriage.

There are also some false beliefs held by young people about what makes for happiness in marriage that serve as barriers to effective communication during courtship. Two of these beliefs go together, and constitute what some sociologists call "the romantic complex": (1) the notion that a certain person is preordained to be the proper mate of another specific person (in past generations, there was conceived to be only one ideal "soul mate"; today this is modified to a category of persons as in the expression "he's my type"); (2) the notion that this ideal mate can be detected immediately ("love at first sight")

Actually, successful marriage requires a good deal of adjustment for almost any two persons, and flexibility is often just as important as any particular combination of personality traits. Young people are often not aware of what characteristics in a potential mate are most suitable for themselves, but if they believe that they can identify their "type" of girl or man immediately this reduces the testing-out process. The fact that there are so many breakups during courtship should be taken as evidence that increasing acquaintance often reveals incompatibilities. Two important studies[42] show a significant association between length of engagement and happiness in marriage. Apparently the longer the couple has an opportunity to test each other out, and to see if they really have the traits and attitudes which will make for long-run compatibility, the better the marriage will work out.

[42] Lewis M. Terman, *Psychological Factors in Marital Happiness* (New York: McGraw-Hill, 1938); Ernest W. Burgess and Leonard S. Cottrell, *Predicting Success or Failure in Marriage* (Englewood Cliffs, N.J.: Prentice-Hall, 1939) .

Most college graduates are married and employed full time two years after they graduate.

A survey of about 41,000 who graduated in 1958 showed that most of them were already married, most of the marriages having taken place shortly before or after graduation.

More than a third had done some graduate work, although only one-third of these had earned an advanced degree.

Three-fourths were full-time employees, the remainder being in the military, in school or doing housework.

Of those employed, the greatest number were teachers—a quarter of the men and two-thirds of the women—while business, engineering and sales also took large percentages of the men.

From a report of the National Science Foundation.

c *The Marriage Relationship*

1 MARRIAGE AS A CHANGE IN ROLE

Marriage involves one of the major role changes that one faces in life. It typically means that there will be several important and rapid changes in a person's pattern of living. In the first place, it often involves leaving the parental home and setting up a living arrangement for which one is primarily responsible himself. Even if a young man or woman leaves the parental home before marriage, and lives for a while as an unattached person, he typically does not take on the responsibility of seeking a residence that will serve his needs for a long while and of buying furniture, establishing neighborly relations, starting a collection of valuable family possessions (such as a set of silver, a set of good china), and so on. This kind of "settling down" usually comes with marriage and changes a person's relationships and sense of responsibility toward his material surroundings. Soon after marriage one is likely to become the "head" or mistress of a household, and this is different from living in a household where someone else has primary responsibility.

A more important change is involved in *sharing* responsibility and making *joint* decisions. From childhood on one learns to participate in making cooperative decisions in all sorts of settings. But marriage requires something more than this. It requires making practically all decisions as joint decisions, and these with the same person. Especially if one has been living a fairly independent existence as a single person, or if one was rather dominated in the parental home, the new role of taking responsibility jointly may be a difficult one to learn. Quite unconsciously one may try to continue his previous role, and adopt the behavior required in his new role only with deliberate effort. To a certain extent many newly wedded husbands unconsciously act toward their wives as they have been accustomed to act toward their mothers and many newly wedded wives act toward their husbands as they have been accustomed to act toward their fathers. This obviously involves some difficulties if both partners in the marriage try to do this simultaneously. Thus there is a tendency to carry over into one's newly established family the role one has been playing in the parental family (sociologists call these, respectively, the *family of procreation* and the *family of orientation*). There are obvious possibilities for role conflict, especially if the young couple maintains close relations with either or both sets of parents.

There are other adjustments to be made from the very outset in marriage. One's sex life is expected to assume regularity, both in the sense of having periodic sex experience and having it with the same person. Whether the newly wedded persons have had premarital sex experience, as most young people today have had, or whether one or both of them enters marriage as a virgin, this is a new relationship which they must adjust to. Both husband and wife only gradually learn what is most satisfying both for themselves and for their marriage partners. One's sociosexual life also changes with marriage: at parties, dances, and other sociable affairs one is no longer the eligible young man or woman, one is no longer accessible for dating, one assumes a new role even with respect to old friends and acquaintances of the opposite sex. This, too, requires learning and adjustment.

Still another necessary change in basic life patterns involved in marriage is that concerning one's attitudes toward privacy and possession. Individuals vary in the extent to which they have personal privacy and private possession in their family of orientation, and the persons they marry are not necessarily likely to have the same habits and standards in these respects. Marriage also inevitably involves a decrease in both of these: for example, another person now does his sleeping and dressing in the same bedroom, one's bank account may now be a joint account, one's letters and other personal papers may now be accessible to another person. These adjustments may not be difficult or unpleasant, but they require learning new nuances of interpersonal relationships and new expectations for one's behavior.

2   HAVING CHILDREN AS A CHANGE IN ROLE

If marriage requires an important role change, having the first child requires an equally important and difficult one. Assuming the responsibility of a household is not nearly so serious as assuming the responsibility of raising a child. A household can always be broken up, a child cannot be discarded. The relationship of a husband and wife changes when there is a third person in the family with whom they must interact. A child makes strong demands one one's time, freedom, mobility, and sense of privacy and possession. There are countless new techniques and skills one must learn as a new parent, and one cannot avoid the responsibility of learning them and learning them rapidly. A helpless infant, who must make all sorts of demands on his parents in order to survive and to develop physically, emotionally and socially, probably forces many more changes in the lives of his parents than their marriage does.

As young people approach the age of marriage, they usually gradually learn the roles appropriate to married life, even if they do not practice these roles until they are actually married. This is called *anticipatory learning*. They observe, and observe more consciously, the differences between their own roles and those of married persons, such as slightly older friends and relatives and even those of their parents, although the age discrepancy between themselves and their parents prevents the latter from being a completely satisfactory model. The more aware they are of the role changes required by marriage, the more easily and successfully will they make the transition. Some things they cannot learn in advance, not only because certain things can be learned only from experience and not from observation, but also because they have to adjust in marriage to a unique individual who does not have exactly the same characteristics and background as other married individuals they have known. Thus, intelligence, experience (mostly of the indirect sort), and flexibility are all very important in helping to make this most drastic role change known as marriage.

Drastic role change between the ages of approximately eighteen and thirty is inevitable for members of our society. We have been considering that which is involved in marriage, but some kind of drastic role change is not to be avoided by not getting married. One can put off the transition for a couple of years—somewhat longer for a man than for a woman— but one cannot permanently remain the eligible single person. If one does not get married by a certain age—say thirty-five or forty—one is inevitably forced to change his or her role to that of old bachelor or spinster. This is usually a less sudden role shift than that involved in marriage, but in the long run it is no less drastic or difficult. In fact, it is often a good deal harder because it does not meet with the social approval that marriage does and does not involve the special satisfactions provided by even a moderately successful marriage.

3   THE NATURAL HISTORY OF LOVE

Love inevitably changes its quality from the premarriage situation through the early days of marriage to the more settled marriage state. As we have noted earlier, it is likely that, before marriage, the two parties know more of the "good" congenial qualities of the other than they do of the "bad" qualities. Young people also tend to have relatively strong sex drives, and this is especially true when they are not having regular and frequent sex experiences.[43] Thus the young couple usually have a stronger sexual component in their love for each other before marriage than after marriage.

The honeymoon is a custom which the culture provides to aid the transition from the premarital state to the marital one. It permits a period of almost complete direction of attention toward the loved one. During this period there is typically a high degree of sexual activity which allows the young couple to satisfy their sexual drives almost freely so that they can eventually be reduced, and there is a rapid learning about the other which also changes the love relationship to a more realistic and probably more permanent one. Still, the typical honeymoon is a highly atypical experience in the life history of any person, and a new and different adjustment process must take place when the newlyweds settle down after their honeymoon.

The intense and sexually charged relationship of the courtship and honeymoon period does not effectively permit either party to carry on their life roles other than as lovers. Their roles as responsible members of their community and society, their occupations and careers, eventually their roles as parents, reduce their preoccupation with each other and with their roles as lovers. Thus, love inevitably changes its character as the honeymoon period is left behind.

With increasing age other changes occur: the sex drive gradually lessens, especially for the husband; illusions and misunderstandings of one kind regarding the marriage partner are dispelled; new erroneous images of the other sometimes get built up in the imagination; new interests, obligations, and affections—toward children, for example—are gradually developed; mutual habituation and new kinds of interdependence are formed. All of these influence the relationship of the couple. The love of a middle-aged or elderly couple is not any the less deserving the name of love than that of a newly wedded couple, but it certainly has a very different quality. The mature married couple have built their relationship into their achievements, their common experiences, their common possessions, their aspirations for themselves and their children, rather than solely into romance.

Marriage is not something that is adjusted to all at once, even though the most drastic role change takes place early in its history. Any two people no matter how much in love or how compatible their personalities, are likely to have continuing friction in their personal relationships. At first they are surprised and at least a little shocked by the limitations of the other, in respect to knowledge, abilities, and attitudes. Time will cushion the initial shock, but it does not overcome the continuing annoyance. While the basis for communication—in common meanings and common experiences—may be improved over time, even a long-married couple

[43] Kinsey, Pomeroy, and Martin, *op. cit.*

will fail to understand each other on certain issues. Two people are bound to have differing, and even opposing, values and interests, and time and common experience do not necessarily eliminate these differences. There are restrictions on what the couple get out of their life together, and these frustrations require that both partners to the marriage readjust constantly to each other in order to keep the marriage going.

In addition to these hurdles arising out of the marriage relationship itself, outside factors create problems for married couples in their relations to each other. In the first place, one's role as a partner in marriage is never the only role that one plays. Obligations and frustrations from the outside—from work, friends, relatives, and so on—can and do create problems within the marriage. An employed husband or wife, for example, has to adjust to the demands and expectations of employers, customers, and coworkers, even when these go contrary to the demands and expectations of the spouse. The spouse may grit his or her teeth and put up with the employers or coworkers, but not feel like doing so for "mere" friends.

4   CRISES IN MARRIED LIFE

Events are likely to occur at any point in an individual's life history which can create a crisis for his marriage. The average couple lives together for forty years,[44] and the opportunities for family crisis must therefore be many. One critical event, the effects of which have been extensively studied, and which can be cited to illustrate the problem, is the loss of a job by the husband without immediate opportunity to get another.[45] This happens to a large number of men during depressions and recessions, when heads of families are unemployed for months or years. The standard of living goes down, and with it disappear many of the economic satisfactions which the family considered to be permanent, such as its home, its automobile, its regular recreations. Perhaps more important than these are the loss of self-confidence on the part of the unemployed husband, his uncertainty as to how to spend his forced leisure time, the difficulties involved in his taking over tasks that were formerly performed by his wife or children (who now may have to supplement the family's meager income). These problems may cause the breakdown of the family. In the extreme instance, the father or mother may desert the family, or the older children will leave without making much effort to keep in contact with the family. Milder changes

[44] P. C. Glick, D. M. Heer, and J. C. Beresford, "Social Change and Family Structure: Trends and Prospects," unpublished paper presented to AAAS, December 29, 1959.

[45] S. A. Stouffer and P. F. Lazarsfeld, *Research Memordandum on Family in the Depression* (New York: Social Science Research Council, 1937); Robert C. Angell, *The Family Encounters the Depression* (New York: Scribner's, 1936); R. S. Cavan and K. H. Ranck, *The Family and the Depression* (New York: Scribner's, 1938); Mirra Komarovsky, *The Unemployed Man and His Family* (New York: Dryden, 1940); Earl L. Koos, *Families in Trouble* (New York: King's Crown Press, 1946).

are a reduction in the sense of family solidarity and in mutual confidence among family members. Angell found that a crisis like the depression and unemployment would have the least adverse effect on a family if it had a strong integration before the crisis began and if the family members were flexible in their relationships with each other (so that, for example, the unemployed father did not mind taking care of the house when the mother was able to find a job).

Another type of crisis for some families is created by a disaster, such as fire, flood, tornado, bombing, etc.[46] The immediate impact of the disaster is usually to draw the family together; the members usually provide as much aid and comfort for each other as possible. But the long-run effects may be to separate the family members, especially if there was little sense of family unity before the disaster struck. The disaster may have destroyed much of the family property, thus putting an added economic burden on the members. Irritability and even neurosis may be precipitated by the shock and damage caused by the disaster. The slackness or failure of any family member during the period of extreme emergency will often cause a permanent estrangement between him and the others. If the family leader showed any weakness in his role during the emergency, there may be a permanent shift in family roles that could lead to eventual dissolution of the family. Some family members may have been killed in the disaster, and it takes a long time for the family to readjust. On the other hand, if the family is well-integrated before the crisis, and has what R. C. Angell called "adaptability," it is likely to come out of the disaster more strongly integrated than ever.[47] Much of what happens to the typical family depends on what the experience of the whole community has been, during the emergency and its aftermath. After a survey of the literature, Hill and Hansen conclude that communities where nuclear families are dominant are more adaptive in short-term recovery to disaster, but that communities where the extended families are strong provide the more effective long-run aid to its members.

One problem that every family faces is the forced role changes that come with age. Elsewhere in this book is discussed the crisis that some women meet when their children grow up and leave home and they find themselves with very little to do around the home.[48] This is not only diffi-cult for them but may also cause a crisis in husband-wife relationships. If the wife reacts to her problem of role change by becoming increasingly

[46] Material for this paragraph is summarized from Reuben Hill and Donald A. Han-sen, "Families in Disaster," in George W. Baker and Dwight W. Chapman (eds.), *Man and Society in Disaster* (New York: Basic Books, 1962), pp. 185–221.

[47] See, especially, Helmut Schelsky's study of German families that went through the bombings of World War II: *Wandlungen in der deutschen Familien in der Gegenwart* (Stuttgart: Enke Verlag, 1954).

[48] See Chapter 11.

withdrawn into herself, her husband may find it difficult to communicate with her. If she reacts by becoming restless, she may want to travel or to go out frequently in the evenings while he sees no reason to change from the old, relatively placid routine of life. If she adjusts to her forced role change by getting a job, or by becoming very active in community affairs, he may resent the loss of comforts which the wife formerly provided when she was in the home regularly. The home the family lived in for many years is now usually too large for their needs so either the husband and wife "rattle around in it" or they move to a small home or apartment—with what may seem to them to be a decline in certain kinds of comforts.

Still another kind of family crisis may come when the husband retires from his job and is consequently forced to undergo a role change. He is suddenly faced with an even more drastic decrease in things to do, he is more dependent on his wife for social relations, he may no longer have the physical strength to engage in the sports or hobbies that please him. The loss of the job also usually means a decline in income, unless the savings accumulated over the years are very large, so that the elderly couple cannot afford to do many of the expensive things they always looked forward to doing when they would have the free time (such as traveling). If the couple go to live with one of their married children (or the married children come to live with the old folks) there is another kind of adjustment necessary. The role changes and frustrations consequent to retirement and old age may make for strain in marital relationships. Thus the family is not a static entity but requires constant readjustment of relationships among the persons who are its members.

There are many sources of problems in husband-wife relationship other than those we have given primary attention to. There are different degrees of incompatibility of personality and temperament, and they cause differing amounts of friction. People hope to achieve certain values and satisfactions in life, and when they achieve these only to a limited extent, whether for reasons related or not related to their marriage, they are often likely to blame their marriage partners for their frustrations. Patience, flexibility, and self-insight are, of course, most important in overcoming these difficulties and in keeping the marriage relationship reasonably happy. We have already noted the finding of several studies that similarity of interests, attitudes, and personality traits between husband and wife is a significant factor in happiness in marriage, presumably because it is what makes for easy relationships and for the elusive factor of "compatibility."

Terman's study[49] also emphasized the husband's and wife's childhood experiences with happy family life as a major factor in their own marital success, presumably because their parents' happy relationship provide them

[49] *Op. cit.*, p. 372.

with a good model and because their happy childhood helped to give them flexible and "pleasant" personalities. More specifically, Terman found that the following ten background factors (in order) were most predictive of marital happiness, and all of these, but possibly the last, were a function of relationships in the family of orientation.

1 Superior happiness of parents
2 Childhood happiness
3 Lack of conflict with mother
4 Home discipline that was firm, not harsh
5 Strong attachment to mother
6 Strong attachment to father
7 Lack of conflict with father
8 Parental frankness about sex
9 Infrequency and mildness of childhood punishment
10 Premarital attitude toward sex that was free from disgust or aversion

Happiness in marriage is a subjective state, and it is relative to the expectations and previous experience of the marriage partners. A relatively high degree of unhappiness may result in separation and divorce, but not always so. Nor is overt quarreling an infallible measure of unhappiness in marriage, since some kinds of quarrels reduce tensions that are a source of unhappiness, and since there are kinds of relationships worse than that which involve occasional verbal conflict. A relationship of constant but repressed antagonism or of the complete domination of one marriage partner by the other can be productive of much unhappiness even if it does not show to the superficial observer. Difference of opinion, and its display, is a natural consequence of individual personality and differences in values. It, like everything else in marriage, is a matter for continual adjustment.[50]

D   *The Child in the Family*

1   THE CHILD'S RELATIONSHIP TO HIS PARENTS

The family is the chief socializer of the child, who is born into the world as a helpless animal and is expected, after a number of years, to function as

[50] There are many reliable textbooks on applied family sociology (sometimes called "functional") advising young people how to become happily married. Among them are Henry A. Bowman, *Marriage for Moderns*, fourth ed. (New York: McGraw-Hill, 1960); Robert O. Blood, *Marriage* (Glencoe, Ill.: Free Press, 1962); Ruth S. Cavan, *American Marriage* (New York: T. Y. Crowell, 1959); Evelyn M. Duvall and Reuben Hill, *Being Married* (Boston: Heath, 1960); J. T. and M. G. Landis, *Building a Successful Marriage* (New York: Prentice-Hall, 1963), Harold T. Christensen, *Marriage Analysis* (New York: Ronald, 1957); E. E. LeMasters, *Modern Courtship and Marriage* (New York: Macmillan, 1957); J. A. Peterson, *Education for Marriage* (New York: Scribner's, 1956); Floyd Martinson, *Marriage and the American Ideal* (New York: Dodd, 1960).

a responsible member of a very complex society.[51] At least this is true in our society, where the immediate family is given the responsibility for the child until it reaches the legal age of independence. The family provides for the physical maintenance of the child, offers him his first and most continuing social contacts, gives him affection and other emotional satisfactions, teaches him most of the social requirements of his behavior (although no longer provides what is now called "formal education"), often puts him in contact with other socializing institutions such as the school, the play group, the church, the recreational facilities.

On the other hand, the family also provides most of the early frustrations in life (some of which may cause unhappiness and even mental unbalance in later life), teaches the child bad habits ("bad" from the standpoint of psychiatry or of the traditional expectations in the society), sometimes fails to provide him with a sufficient sense of security and emotional maturity, sometimes fails to do an adequate job on his socialization. All this is to say that the family is the main influence in the psychogenic and sociogenic development of the individual. For these reasons above, despite the decline in many of its functions,[52] the family may still be said to be the most important institution in our society.

The individual is born with certain impulses, many of them random in character but others that are fairly specific (such as the ones involved in sucking, defecating, and urinating). He learns many habits, and consciously or unconsciously formulates desires or imitates the expression of others' wishes. Only some of the behaviors based on these things are acceptable to or favored by his parents, and the others are generally discouraged sooner or later, directly or indirectly. The parents thus not only offer new meanings and values to the child; they serve as censors to what he picks up from others (mainly other children) and to his biological impulses. Not all of this censoring involves complete repression, as some psychoanalysts assume, but much is better described as "channeling." The child's elimination, for example, is seldom repressed; rather, it is channeled according to time and place, and if this channeling process does not occur at too young an age the child may never be repressed in any psychologically harmful sense.

The parents generally reflect the larger society—or at least the community, the class, the ethnic group to which they belong—in their teaching and channeling of the child. But this is true only in a general sense, for each adult in our society is unique in many significant ways and the

[51] For a survey of the recent research literature on the socialization of the child, see William H. Sewell, "Some Recent Developments in Socialization Theory and Research," *The Annals of the American Academy of Political and Social Science*, 349 (September, 1963), pp. 163–81; Frederick Elkin, *The Child and Society: The Process of Socialization* (New York: Random House, 1960).

[52] See Chapter 5, Section C.

society itself is so heterogeneous that no parent could reflect it even if he tried desperately. One aspect of this heterogeneity arises out of social change. Often what the parent thinks proper to teach his child is what was proper when the parent himself was growing up but which is no longer the correct standard for young people. Thus in a rapidly changing society such as ours parents prepare their children for adult living in their (the parents') generation rather than the child's own generation.

This is complicated if the parents are rising in social status or if the parents come from a culture different from that in which their children are growing up (from one country to another, from the South to the North in the United States, from a farm to a big city). In such instances the parents are not so likely, as less mobile parents, to know enough about the expectations of the local culture to teach them to their children, while they—out of conscious preference and unconscious habit—continue to behave according to the value system of their former society and so provide an incorrect model for the children. When the children get old enough to be strongly influenced by the expectations of the local culture or of the culture of the "peer group" of friends, there is often conflict with the parents over what is proper or decent behavior.[53] From the standard of the social circles in which the children are now moving they see their parents as "greenhorns," "hicks," or "lower class," and if the conflict becomes overt, the children sometimes call their parents that.

In the Soviet Union, where the ruling Communist party has always claimed to represent youth as over against the "old-fashioned" ways of their parents, the youth of today is apparently rebelling just as strongly against the restrictions imposed by the Communist Party as ever it did against the earlier Tsarist government.[54] Youth apparently tends to rebel against the dominant ideas of their parental generation, no matter what the content of those ideas. The form and duration of that rebellion varies, however, from country to country and from generation to generation, depending on the culture and social structure of the society.

There are many sources of opposition between parents and children besides that which is a function of culture change. Each child rapidly acquires an infinitude of wants as he discovers more and more of the world around him. The parents have to deny most of his requests and demands. As the child develops muscularity and agility, he usually wants to experiment with all his new-found "abilities." Since these include throwing stones, pulling the cat's tail, climbing out on the roof, and so on, the parents have to restrain the child. It is true that the restraint may not be

[53] Bernard C. Rosen, "Conflicting Group Membership: A Study of Parent-Peer Group Cross-Pressures," *American Sociological Review*, 20 (April, 1955), pp. 155–61.

[54] Congress for Cultural Freedom, "The Ferment Among Soviet Youth," *Soviet Survey*, No. 12 (February, 1957), pp. 1–16.

made in a completely "authoritarian" way; the parents, with well-chosen words, may fool the child into believing that he made the decision himself or that he was naturally diverted into some other activity.

It is doubtful, however, whether any parents are so successful with their children that they can fool them all the time in this way. Because of the frustrations which the parents must bring to a child there is likely to develop a certain degree of feeling of hostility on the part of the child toward his parents. This parallels and does not necessarily supersede the love and admiration a child has for his parents as the source of his physical and emotional satisfactions and as the model for his developing behavior.

In our society grandparents are not so likely to be heads of household in the same household as their grandchildren and hence have little to do with their development. In recent decades, especially, it has become a convention that grandparents should not "interfere" with the parents in the raising of children. Grandparents are more likely than parents to be regarded by children as "old-fashioned," "hicks," "immigrants," and otherwise representative of a different culture, and hence children may feel a little ashamed of their grandparents. But since the grandparents seldom repress the children—seldom attempt to impose their meanings and values on them—the children are seldom antagonistic toward their grandparents. On the contrary, the modern role of grandparents is to indulge children, to give them luxuries which parents cannot afford, and to entertain them in ways that parents have no time for. Hence modern American grandparents tend to be somewhat "unrepressive" and we have the phenomenon of "alternation of generations" in which grandparents and grandchildren find mutual satisfactions in each other and a common antagonism against the parents. Because in many cultures grandparents are less frustrating to children than parents are, this relationship of indulgence and camaraderie between grandparents and children is found in those cultures. This is much less true in the Soviet societies, where the mothers are usually employed, and the children are raised almost entirely by the grandparents.

2   THE CHILD'S RELATIONSHIP TO HIS SIBLINGS

Perhaps more important a family relationship than that between children and grandparents is that between siblings—brothers and sisters. In emphasizing the socializing role of parents in relation to children, sociologists and child psychologists have tended to neglect the socializing role of the older sibling, especially when the older and younger are of the same sex. Older siblings cannot be considered by younger ones as "old-fashioned," which parents sometimes are, and older siblings have less of a problem in translating their knowledge, wishes, and attitudes to younger children than adults do. The older sibling may not always socialize the younger toward an adult role, however, since they may have little conception of such a role and they may also be in rebellion against parents. Siblings seldom combine in their antagonism toward parents, except in trivial ways, apparently because competition between them for the favor of parents is stronger than the similarity of their antagonisms.

"Sibling rivalry" is one of the oldest social psychological phenomena to be noted in history, and it is apparently found in many diverse cultures.[55] It arises when second and subsequent children are born into a family.[56] Up to that time the older child has been getting the lion's share of his parents' attention and affection, and now the parents are naturally obliged to give greater attention to the baby and to divide their manifestations of affection. As the baby grows up and becomes self-conscious, he begins to compete with the older child for parental attention and praise, and the rivalry becomes reciprocal. A child may feel that his parents are partial to his sibling when this is not true at all. Sometimes parents stimulate sibling rivalry without intending to, by comparing the abilities and achievements of their children, or by promising something for one without promising something for the other. But parents must pay differential attention to children, on the basis of their different needs, and this also often provokes sibling rivalry.

As children get older they tend to compare themselves with each other, as to abilities, possessions, achievements, and so the rivalry between siblings is extended much beyond their relationship to their parents. The rivalry may continue even into young adulthood when two sisters or two brothers will compare their respective attractiveness to the opposite sex. Rivalry between siblings seems to be greatest where the children are close together in age—that is, when they are more comparable and when the older is not sufficiently developed at the time of the younger's birth to shift his interest somewhat away from his parents. Sibling rivalry seems to diminish when children are separated from each other. Socially speaking, this tends to happen between siblings of the opposite sex around the time of adolescence, and there often develops a strong fondness between siblings of the opposite sex after this time, while siblings of the same sex —who are more comparable and tend to interact more frequently—often continue their rivalry into adult years. Rational discussions with older siblings by parents, showing them that differential attention is not a sign

[55] For an example of sibling rivalry among the Pilaga Indians of Argentina, see Jules and Zunia Henry, "Symmetrical and Reciprocal Hostility in Sibling Rivalry," *American Journal of Orthopsychiatry*, 12 (April, 1942), pp. 256–61. For an earlier general summary, see David M. Levy, "Sibling Rivalry Studies in Children of Primitive Groups," *American Journal of Orthopsychiatry*, 9 (January, 1939), pp. 205–14.

[56] Some of the following observations about sibling rivalry are drawn from a study by Mabel Sewall, "Some Causes of Jealousy in Young Children," *Smith College Studies in Social Work*, I (September, 1930), pp. 15–22.

of differential affection but merely differential response to obvious differences of need based on age, sex, and interests; an effort to separate siblings in their activities and companions; and an absolute refusal to compare their children in their presence (even through the giving of material satisfactions) have been known to diminish sibling rivalry.

3   THE MUTUAL RESPONSIBILITIES OF PARENTS AND CHILDREN

The "giving" in parent-child relationships is not all in one direction. The parent gets satisfactions out of the child, most obviously affection and sense of achievement out of raising a helpless little animal into an independent, creative member of the society. Some parents also "project" their own ambitions onto their child, in one of two senses: Most parents want their children to be a credit to themselves, to contribute to their own prestige, to manifest their own abilities as responsible members of the society. They thus want their children to be "good," creative, skillful, and so on. If the parents are frustrated in their ambitions, they may try to get for the children what they failed to achieve for themselves. Both of these tendencies may result in "pushing" the child too much. The end result may be good from the child's own standpoint, but the process of arriving there may be too rapid in terms of the child's abilities and it may not allow for the child's learning things for himself. On the other hand, the ambition which the parent has for the child may be completely inappropriate for the child's abilities and personality.

Some psychiatrists attribute much of the emotional maladjustment of people to overdominance by their parents, usually involving one or both of these forms of projection. The psychiatrist Edward A. Strecker, for example, asserts that the chief source of the high rate of neuropsychiatric difficulties in the armed services during World War II was overdominance by mothers.[57] This phenomenon, which is now attributed almost exclusively to mothers and rarely to fathers, has been popularized under the name of "momism" by Philip Wylie[58] and is considered by some to be the chief source of personal unhappiness and maladjustment in our generation. On the other hand, at least one empirical study shows that the closer the relationship between college-age youth and their parents, the more responsible are the youth in their college roles and the more willing are they to assume responsible roles in adult life.[59] Another study showed that, while a sample of psychotic teen-age children had oversolicitous,

---

[57] *Their Mother's Sons* (Philadelphia: Lippincott, 1946).

[58] *Generation of Vipers* (New York: Farrar and Rinehart, 1942).

[59] Arnold M. Rose, "Acceptance of Adult Roles and Separation from Family," *Marriage and Family Relations*, 21 (May, 1959), pp. 120–26. This article includes references to many of the earlier studies on child responsibility and child-parent relationships. For a survey of studies, and a further test, of the relationship between child personality and family power structure, see Murray A. Straus, *op. cit.*, pp. 17–25.

domineering, and hyper-emotional parents, a sample of delinquent children had negative, cold, and rejecting parents, and a third group of normally adjusted youth had parents who scored between the other two groups in dominance and warmth.[60]

The assumption of responsibility by growing children is a complicated matter which has not been sufficiently studied. Child psychologists, educators, and psychiatrists have given a good deal of attention to the acquisition of skills and of a balanced personality. They have apparently assumed that a sense of responsibility grows "naturally" along with these things, and that responsibility is taught through the gradual and cumulative assignment of household tasks and family roles.[61] The one empirical study in the field shows that there is no relationship between the number of household tasks a child regularly carries on (at any given age) and the rating of him as responsible by his parents, teachers, and classmates or the number of "responsible attitudes" he holds.[62] Apparently a sense of responsibility in relation to other people, even other family members, is based on family experiences far more complicated than the carrying on of household tasks.

We know both from civilian and military experience that a significant proportion of young adults "graduate from their families," so to speak, and yet are quite unable to carry on adult roles as responsible members of society. Often they acquire this ability after a number of painful experiences, but some never do acquire it and go through life dependent on other people for the satisfaction of even their most elemental desires. They are unable to hold a job and thus support themselves (even though they have learned an occupation); they are too immature socially to act as husband and father (even though they have no difficulty in sex relations); they are too self-centered to participate in any community activity or to bother about voting intelligently. Nature may have endowed them with all the abilities it takes to function effectively in society, but their family relationships have failed to bring them to social maturity. For some this is a problem of emotional maladjustment arising from some highly disturbing childhood experience. Others may not have had adequate opportunity, in their families of orientation, to learn adult social roles, or they are not

[60] M. P. Wittman and A. V. Huffman, "A Comparative Study of Developmental, Adjustment, and Personality Characteristics of Psychotic, Psychoneurotic, Delinquent, and Normally Adjusted Teen-Aged Youths," *Journal of Genetic Psychology*, 66 (1945), pp. 167–82.

[61] For a review of the literature, see Betty L. Mitton and Dale B. Harris, "The Development of Responsibility in Children," *The Elementary School Journal*, 54 (January, 1954), pp. 268–77.

[62] Dale B. Harris, Kenneth E. Clark, Arnold M. Rose, and Frances Valasek, "The Relationship of Children's Home Duties to an Attitude of Responsibility," *Child Development*, 25 (March, 1954), pp. 29–33.

provided with adequate models in their parents so that they do not acquire the proper attitudes toward assuming responsible adult roles. Writing with special reference to the learning of adult sex roles, Fleming states:

> The best initiation is obtained by those boys and girls who are reared in the presence of happy married relationships within their own homes, and receive their schooling in places where wholesome relations are observable among members of a coeducational staff. Even for such boys and girls there may, however, be questions which still need deliberate answering—especially under the conditions of life in a city where information as to the processes of life, birth, and death is withheld by accident or design. Most boys and girls desire to be "virtuous" in the sense that they are prepared to conform to the code of their group. They often wish, for example, for guidance through intimate talk or through illuminating reading as to the normal consequences of varying types of personal caressing.[63]

The process of "growing up" is a continuous one throughout childhood and adolescence,[64] and the child must be continually oriented toward more and more responsible behavior rather than expected to assume responsibility all at one time. This does not mean that the child will not have periods when he rejects greater responsibility and seems to revert to more childish behavior,[65] and it does not mean that the parent has continually to indoctrinate deliberately toward more responsible behavior patterns. The general culture patterns—in so far as the parents are unconsciously influenced by them—and the child's associations outside the family will normally bring him to social maturity by the time he reaches the age of adulthood. What is meant by the statement that a child must be continually oriented toward adulthood is that the general cultural processes must be allowed to work. If the parents continue to treat their child as an infant and shelter him from the normal social experiences to which a child is exposed, their child will reach physical maturity without having social maturity.

This involves letting a child experiment with independence of behavior and judgment even if he is awkward at first, provided the experiment is not completely beyond his capacity and does not expose him to physical danger or emotional shock. It involves answering a child's ques-

[63] C. M. Fleming, *Adolescence: Its Social Psychology* (London: Routledge and Kegan Paul, 1948), p. 218.

[64] For some sociological and social psychological studies on adolescence, see Robert E. Grinder (ed.), *Studies in Adolescence* (New York: Macmillan, 1963); James S. Coleman et al., *The Adolescent Society* (Glencoe, Ill.: Free Press, 1961); Charlotte M. Fleming, *Adolescence: Its Social Psychology* (New York: Grove, 1962).

[65] Gesell has shown that occasional reversion to younger behavior patterns is characteristic of child development. See Arnold L. Gesell and Frances L. Ilg, *The Child from Five to Ten* (New York: Harper, 1946).

tions seriously and generally treating him as mature as he takes himself to be. It involves giving him praise for achieving new levels of responsibility and helping to soothe over the discouragement of failure. In general, social responsibility is probably developed in much the same way that physical and mental skills are developed, except that the parents have to play a much more important role in the former as the schools do not and cannot develop social responsibility to the extent in which they teach physical and mental skills.

4   THE INFLUENCE OF THE FAMILY ON THE CHILD'S RELATIONSHIP WITH THE OUTSIDE WORLD

The family is not the sole influence in the socialization of the child, of course. But the family is not only a prime influence in itself but also helps to determine the relationship of the child toward other socializing influences. Parents determine who visits the home, and guests can be significant socializing influences.[66] The parents can make it easy or difficult for the child to adjust to play groups and school, can get their child into Cub Scouts or the Brownies or not, enlist their child in the "Y," craft classes, dancing classes, or not. Thus, while these organized groups assume an increasing role in the average child's life, the parents are still the main influence in establishing the child's relationship with these groups. The child can make his own friends in school and the neighborhood, even when his parents inhibit him during out-of-school hours. But with an increasing number of children going into the organized activities, the parents must play an active role in getting their child into the organized activities else he finds that he is isolated while his school and neighborhood friends spend their time in the organized groups. The parents have an influence even on the relationship between the child and his informally selected friends from school and the neighborhood by the amount of free time they leave the child to cultivate his own friendships, by the opportunities they give their child to join in the activities (usually costing money) that the other children engage in, by the permission they give their child to bring his friends into the house for play, and by the general encouragement or discouragement of his choice of friends.[67]

A circumstance in which parents are especially important for the child's relationships to other children occurs when the family moves its home to another area. Then the child is forced abruptly to break off all his social relationships, except that with his family, and establish entirely new

[66] James H. S. Bossard and Eleanor S. Boll, *Ritual in Family Living* (Philadelphia: University of Pennsylvania Press, 1950).

[67] For a consideration of some of the ways the modern middle-class family controls youth activities, see E. Gartly Jaco and Ivan Belknap, "Is a New Family Form Emerging in the Urban Fringe?" *American Sociological Review*, 18 (October, 1953), pp. 551–57.

sets of relationships. This can be quite a disruptive experience, the full significance of which we can realize only by understanding that the child's conception of the world and of himself is based on his previous social contacts, limited by his low ability to move about and to communicate by letter. In the new setting an entirely new set of relationships must be established, and new rules for these relationships learned, and these involve a new status for himself and a new outlook on the nature of the social world. The importance of the parents in making this transition is obvious since they are the only stable element in an otherwise unstable social world. They can aid the transition by preparing the child for what will happen by helping him maintain some continuity with the old social world by means of letters or arranged visits, and by facilitating his acceptance into new social surroundings.

E *The Friendship Group*

1 STUDIES OF THE SELECTION OF FRIENDS

As has already been indicated, the friendship group is second in importance only to the family as a primary group. Friendship groups may take an organized form and become a kind of voluntary association,[68] but much more often it is a self-selected group with no formal organization.[69] Sumner[70] distinguished between "crescive" and "enacted" groups, the former being the kind that develop spontaneously as a result of congeniality or common interest on the part of a number of people and the latter being formed by some elective or appointive process to accomplish certain specific purposes. The friendship group is a good example of a crescive group, and has its characteristic of having its members informally selecting each other on the basis of social and psychological characteristics that are found to be compatible and convenient. While Bühler[71] found that social behavior begins in the infant at the age of three months, young children do not seem capable of forming what would usually be considered friendships until they are two to three years of age. From then until puberty there is a steady increase in the average number of friends and the stability of the friendships.[72] The "depth" of friendships and social participation and

[68] See Chapter 10.

[69] See, for example, M. B. Seidler and M. J. Ravitz, "A Jewish Peer Group," *American Journal of Sociology*, 61 (July, 1955), pp. 11-15.

[70] William G. Sumner, *Folkways* (Boston: Ginn, 1906), p. 54.

[71] Charlotte Bühler, "The Social Behavior of the Child," in C. Murchison (ed.), *Handbook of Child Psychology* (Worcester: Clark University Press, 1931), pp. 392-431.

[72] J. E. Horrocks and G. G. Thompson, "A Study of the Friendship Fluctuations of Rural Boys and Girls," *Journal of Genetic Psychology*, 69 (December, 1946), pp. 189-98.

leadership behavior in general increase during the nursery-school years.[73] Boll suggests convincingly that childhood experience in preschool play groups, though it has been neglected as a field of study, is of real significance in the development of the personality and the behavior patterns.[74]

Proximity—that is, closeness of residence or being in the same class in school—is a highly dominating influence in the choice of friends,[75] and it is closely followed by sameness of chronological age.[76] With residential proximity there tends to be a similarity in social class as a basis for children's friendships.[77] Children also seem to pick their friends in terms of certain physical and psychological similarities to themselves, although the various studies do not agree in regard to their friendships in this regard. For example, some studies find a close relationship between the intelligence test scores of friends among the children of given neighborhoods, while other studies fail completely to find such a relationship in other neighborhoods.[78] Children tend to pick friends of the same sex, even at preschool ages,[79] although school-age children tend to be increasingly selective along the lines of sex until adolescence.[80] Other factors which have

[73] E. H. Green, "Friendships and Quarrels among Pre-school Children," *Child Development*, 4 (1933), pp. 237–52; Mildred B. Parten, "An Analysis of Social Participation, Leadership, and Other Factors in Preschool Play Groups," unpublished Ph.D. thesis, University of Minnesota (December, 1929); A. P. Beaver, *The Initiation of Social Contacts by Preschool Children* (New York: Columbia University, 1932); A. S. Salusky, "Collective Behavior of Children at a Preschool Age," *Journal of Social Psychology*, 1 (1932), pp. 367–78.

[74] Eleanor Stoker Boll, "The Role of Preschool Playmates—A Situational Approach," *Child Development*, 28 (September, 1957), pp. 327–42.

[75] P. H. Furfey, "Some Factors Influencing the Selection of Boys' Chums," *Journal of Applied Psychology*, 11 (1927), pp. 47–51; M. V. Seagoe, "Factors Influencing the Selection of Associates," *Journal of Educational Research*, 27 (September, 1933), pp. 32–40.

[76] Green, *op. cit.*; R. C. Challman, "Factors Influencing Friendships among Preschool Children," *Child Development*, 3 (June, 1932), pp. 146–58; E. P. Hagman, "The Companionships of Preschool Children," *University of Iowa Studies in Child Welfare*, 7, 4 (1933).

[77] Furfey, *op. cit.*

[78] Showing correlation of mental age: Seagoe, *op. cit.*; J. C. Almack, "The Influence of Intelligence on the Selection of Associates," *School and Society*, 16 (November, 1922), pp. 529–30; L. M. Warner, "Influence of Mental Level in the Formation of Boys' Gangs," *Journal of Applied Psychology*, 7 (September, 1923), pp. 224–36; P. E. Williams, "A Study of Adolescent Friendships," *Pedagogical Seminary*, 30 (December, 1924), pp. 342–46; R. Pintner, G. Forlano, and H. Freedman, "Personality and Attitudinal Similarity Among Classroom Friends," *Journal of Applied Psychology*, 21 (February, 1937), pp. 48–65. Showing little or no correlation of mental age: Challman, *op. cit.*; Hagman, *op. cit.*; G. G. Jenkins, "Factors Involved in Children's Friendships," *Journal of Educational Psychology*, 22 (September, 1931), pp. 440–48; F. M. Vreeland and S. M. Corey, "A Study of College Friendships," *Journal of Abnormal and Social Psychology*, 30 (July–September, 1935), pp. 229–36.

[79] Challman, *op. cit.*

[80] Green, *op. cit.*

. . . The general fact is that children, especially boys after about their twelfth year, live in fellowships in which their sympathy, ambition, and honor are engaged even more, often, than they are in the family. Most of us can recall examples of the endurance by boys of injustice and even cruelty, rather than appeal from their fellows to parents or teachers—as, for instance, in the hazing so prevalent at schools, and so difficult, for this very reason, to repress. And how elaborate the discussion, how cogent the public opinion, how hot the ambitions in these fellowships.

Nor is this facility of juvenile association, as is sometimes supposed, a trait peculiar to English and American boys; since experience among our immigrant population seems to show that the offspring of the more restrictive civilizations of the continent of Europe form self-governing play-groups with almost equal readiness. Thus Miss Jane Addams, after pointing out that the "gang" is almost universal, speaks of the interminable discussion which every detail of the gang's activity receives, remarking that "in these social folk-motes, so to speak, the young citizen learns to act upon his own determination."*

C. H. Cooley, *Social Organization* (New York: Scribner's, 1909), pp. 24–25.
* *Newer Ideals of Peace*, p. 177.

been shown, in at least one study, to be a basis of selection for friends are: height,[81] maturity,[81] "sociality,"[82] physical activity,[82] extraversion,[83] similar moral standards,[84] neuroticism,[85] cleanliness,[86] and courtesy.

There are no comparably systematic studies of similarity of characteristics among adult friends. But our general sociological knowledge indicates that similarities of class, age, residence, and personality are characteristic of adult friends also. In rural areas and in homogeneous urban areas, people who live nearby are a major source of friends.[87] In heterogeneous urban areas, common employment and occupation are more important as a basis of friendship than is residential proximity.

[81] Furfey, *op. cit.*; Seagoe, *op. cit.*

[82] Challman, *op. cit.*; Seagoe, *op. cit.*

[83] B. Wellman, "The School Child's Choice of Companions," *The Journal of Educational Research*, 14 (September, 1926), pp. 126–32.

[84] H. Hartshorne and M. A. May, *Studies in Deceit* (New York: Macmillan, 1928).

[85] Vreeland and Corey, *op. cit.*

[86] Seagoe, *op. cit.*

[87] A number of studies show that in student housing projects at large universities and other communities built rapidly with unselected people in a certain population category, friendships are developed primarily on the basis of the closeness of front and back doors. L. Festinger, S. Schachter, and K. Back, *Social Pressures in Informal Groups.* (New York: Harper, 1950); T. Caplow and R. Forman, "Neighborhood Interaction," *American Sociological Review*, 15 (June, 1950), pp. 357–66; also theses done at the University of Minnesota replicating the Caplow-Forman study.

2   PATTERNS OF FRIENDSHIP

In addition to studies of the characteristics of friends there have been studies of the patterns of friendship. By asking children or adults such questions as whom their best friends are, whom they would like to sit next to in school, and so on, diagrams can be made showing the patterns of preferences. These have been given the name of "sociometric studies."[88] They show that groups of children or adults are made up of highly popular individuals (sometimes called "informal leaders," who are often not the same individuals as those formally elected as leaders in the group), those who are popular with a few but not popular with others, and persons who are not chosen by any others as friends (sometimes called "isolates"). The studies also show that some groups are divided into cliques, with only the weakest of ties between them, whereas other groups have strong internal cohesiveness.[89]

Where cliques exist they can be very important in determining the lives of their members. Warner and Lunt consider them to be "next in importance to the family in placing people socially."

As we define it, the clique is an intimate non-kin group, membership in which may vary in numbers from two to thirty or more people. As such it is a phenomenon characteristic of our own society. When it approaches the latter figure in size, it ordinarily breaks up into several smaller cliques. The clique is an informal association because it has no explicit rules of entrance, of membership, or of exit. It ordinarily possesses no regular place or time of meeting. It has no elected officers nor any formally recognized hierarchy of leaders. It lacks specifically stated purposes, and its functions are less explicit than those of the family, the association, or the institution. The clique may or may not include biologically related persons; but all its members know each other intimately and participate in frequent face-to-face relations.

Despite the lack of explicit rules of entrance, exit, and membership behavior, the clique does have very exacting rules of custom which govern the relations of its members. In-group feelings are highly charged, and members speak of others in the community as outsiders. Feelings of unity may even reach such a pitch of intensity that a clique member can and does act in ways contrary to the best interests of his own family.

[88] The technique of asking such questions, making such diagrams and calling them "sociometric" seems to have originated with J. L. Moreno. See his *Who Shall Survive? A New Approach to the Problem of Human Interrelations* (Nervous and Mental Disease Publication, 1934).

[89] See, for example, Raymond E. Bassett, "Cliques in a Student Body of Stable Membership," *Sociometry*, 7 (August, 1944), pp. 290–302.

A person may belong to several cliques at the same time. The clique may or may not be age graded, although the smaller ones ordinarily are. It may also be unisexual or bisexual, depending on its general character. Its activities vary according to the social position and relative wealth of its members. It may be composed of employees of a factory, or of the members of a fraternity, political organization, or church.

The life span of a clique tends to be short in comparison with that of other social structures because, unlike a formal association, it does not provide for continuity over long periods of time. Cliques, it is true, do accept new members and older ones drop out, but the changes which take place under such circumstances frequently disrupt the structure. The span of existence of a clique, therefore, is highly contingent on the longevity of its members or the continuation of their common interests.[90]

Questions have been raised as to the bases of friendship, and some studies have been done on these questions. Man is a social animal, and it is natural for him to have associates, friends, and acquaintances, and un-natural for him to be isolated. The general process of socialization relates a person to a host of different groups. The general tendency to relate one-self to other people is, of course, abetted by special motives and purposes under varying circumstances. There may be a specific and deliberate pur-pose for which people associate, or they may come together because they want to be sociable and find each other congenial. Love, in both its sexual and non-sexual senses, is a basis of friendship. An English study has dealt with love in the friendship of adolescents:

> This love between two adolescent friends is a complex phenom-enon which involves their whole personality—their likes and dislikes, their emotional and intellectual characteristics and the degree of attraction and affection existing between them. Beneath the obvious unisexual friendships revealed at about the age of eleven to twelve, the beginnings of heterosexual interest are clearly evident. . . . It is difficult to decide how far this idea of love was identical with a grow-ing sexual urge. One thing that came out clearly from their statements was that they were aware of an intense desire to love and be loved.[91]

3   THE GANG AS A FRIENDSHIP GROUP

Adolescent and preadolescent children tend not only to pair but also to form "gangs" of three to a dozen or so members. In a study of Australian

[90] W. Lloyd Warner and Paul S. Lunt, *The Social Life of a Modern Community* (New Haven: Yale University Press, 1941), pp. 110–11.

[91] J. E. Richardson, J. F. Forrester, J. K. Shukla, and P. J. Higginbotham, *Studies in the Social Psychology of Adolescence* (London: Routledge and Kegan Paul, 1951), pp. 198–99.

college students, four-fifths of the men and two-thirds of the women reported that they had been gang members between the ages of nine and thirteen years.[92] Most of there were single-sex gangs and were at least verbally antagonistic to the opposite sex. Preadolescent gangs typically have a gang name, secret signals, badges, initiation ceremonies, secret meeting places, and other characteristics of secret societies. They engage in mildly predatory and criminal activities, sociable activities, sports, gang warfare, and occasionally social-service activities.

While probably most gangs—and at least most boys—engage in what the law defines as criminal activities, only a small proportion are caught by the police, brought into court and punished in some way.[93] Those that go through this process, and often become confirmed in a career of delinquency and crime, are those that live in poor environments such as city slums.[94] They are apprehended and punished because the law-enforcement authorities expect them to be delinquents, whereas children who live in better environments are seldom apprehended and practically never punished by the courts when their gangs engage in the typical occasional crimes. The socially disapproved character of the activities of children's friendship groups seems to be part of our culture and to play some role in the transition to adulthood. On the other hand, it is also one of the major bases of organized crime and political racketeering.[95]

The general truth seems to be that the child relates himself to friendship groups that are most accessible, and if these happen to engage primarily in criminal activities, he is likely to be a criminal. If, on the other hand, the friendship group engages mainly in what the larger society defines as expressive or constructive play, the child will grow up to be a relatively law-abiding citizen. As the child approaches adulthood he gains more freedom of movement, and his interests become more specialized, so that he makes more of a deliberate choice in selecting his friendship groups. Adult friendship groups have been little studied, but they are undoubtedly of great influence as molders of behavior and as providers of many of the satisfactions of life that the individual can find only in intimate association with his fellows.

[92] A. R. Crane, "Pre-Adolescent Gangs: A Topological Interpretation," *Journal of Genetic Psychology*, 81 (September, 1952), pp. 113-23.

[93] See Chapter 15, Section B.

[94] There are three excellent studies of adolescent and young adult gangs: Frederic M. Thrasher, *The Gang: A Study of 1,313 Gangs in Chicago* (Chicago: University of Chicago Press, 1927); William F. Whyte, *Street-Corner Society* (Chicago: University of Chicago Press, 1943); Lewis Yablonsky, *The Violent Gang* (New York: Macmillan, 1962).

[95] See Chapter 15, Section B, for further material on the delinquent gang, and Chapter 17, Section E, for a summary of research on the "small group."

FOR ADDITIONAL READING

BOSSARD, JAMES H. S., *The Sociology of Child Development* (New York: Harper, 1953). The most complete sociological survey of child development available.

BURGESS, ERNEST W., and PAUL WALLIN, *Courtship, Engagement and Marriage* (Philadelphia: Lippincott, 1954). One of the most systematic studies of pre-marital relationships and how they affect marriage.

GOODE, W. J., *World Revolution and Family Patterns* (New York: Free Press of Glencoe, 1963). A study of the modernization of family structure in several societies.

KIRKPATRICK, CLIFFORD K., *The Family as Process and Institution* (New York: Ronald, 1955). A textbook on the family.

WHYTE, WILLIAM F., *Street-Corner Society* (Chicago: University of Chicago, 1943). A study of a group of young men in a lower-class neighborhood of Boston.

7 * Specific Social Institutions

The purpose of this chapter is to consider a few selected characteristics of certain social institutions to indicate what it is regarding these institutions that the sociologist is interested in. We shall take up economic, political, military, religious, educational, and scientific institutions, but overlap very little with the interests that economists and political scientists, for example, have in them. The distinctions between these types of institutions are somewhat arbitrary. Economic institutions certainly have political influence and even religious institutions have economic functions. The chapter will deal with more concrete facts than Chapter 5 did, but will not pretend to give a comprehensive survey of the information regarding the institutions.

A   Economic Institutions

1   THE NATURE OF AN ECONOMIC INSTITUTION

Economic institutions are those which are engaged in the production and distribution of scarce[1] goods and services. Farms and factories produce goods, transportation facilities and merchandising companies distribute them, banks and other credit institutions facilitate their exchange, advertising agencies encourage their exchange. There are parallel organizations for the production and distribution of services, such as entertaining, educating, giving spiritual guidance, repairing, cleaning, financial advising,

---

[1] By "scarce" we mean not so available that people can have all they want whenever they want it. By this definition, even drinking water is scarce since it is not always available where it is wanted, but air is not scarce except for the few individuals who occasionally become entombed in caves.

and so on. These are subject to "economic laws," which are studied by economic theorists, but they are also subject to a number of political and sociological influences—which will be our focus of attention here.

One of the most important economic institutions is that surrounding the use of money. While money existed in ancient society, especially in the Roman Empire, ordinary people relied mostly on barter for exchange until modern times. Georg Simmel, who made the most extensive sociological study of money,[2] holds that its universal introduction into the economic life of our society had far-reaching effects. (1) It created greater freedom for both buyers and sellers of goods and services, since payment in money makes for a depersonalized relationship between the two parties to a transaction and eliminates all obligation not connected with the deal. By allowing one to sell to a person from whom one does not at the same time buy, individuals are much freer in their economic behavior. (2) Money creates a common denominator of economic value, so that everything can be assigned a monetary worth. This tends to give a pecuniary coloration to all scarce values. (3) As economic contacts become depersonalized because of money, they lose much of their social overlay—that is, they become purely economic and do not imply any continuing social relationship or integration. (4) Money makes possible certain other institutions: banks, with savings and credit facilities; foreign-trade facilities; risk-insurance agencies; the stock exchange; and so on.

On the other hand, every economic enterprise is also a social institution, an established and changing relationship of persons who gear their behavior to each other, in part, on the basis of certain expectations they have for the others' behavior. The general principles of human interaction as well as the special principles governing institutions apply to economic enterprises. People are motivated to engage in economic activity primarily for economic gain (that is, to be able to take care of their physical needs and to satisfy other desires which require money), but they also work to gain prestige, power, fellowship, a sense of usefulness or achievement, a sense of fulfilling social expectations that they be suitably employed, and probably other motives. While the latter are probably not *primary* motives for most people, they are for some, and they enter into practically every entrepreneur's and every worker's motivation to a certain extent.

Occasionally these non-economic motives will become uppermost in the minds of even those who are obliged to work steadily to earn their living. There are certain conflicts between the economic and non-economic motives, although for some people—especially those in managerial, professional, political, and entertainment positions—their non-economic motives as well as their economic ones are satisfied by their occupations.

[2] *Philosophie des Geldes* (Leipzig, 1900).

Where the motives conflict and people follow their non-economic motives, economic institutions are run partially contrary to economic principles.

Most of the non-economic motives are sociological in character. Able-bodied adult males, at least up to sixty years of age, are expected to pursue a gainful economic activity in American culture, no matter how wealthy they may be, although this is not true in Europe or many other parts of the world. For adult women in Western cultures, gainful employment is optional except when they are not married or are otherwise obliged to support themselves or help to support their families. In Soviet cultures, as a contrast, there is increasing political and social pressure to oblige all able-bodied adult women to work.

Different types of occupations carry different prestige ratings,[3] and prestige, of course, is a function of social evaluation. Different occupations have associated with them different opportunities for the exercise of power, which may be defined as control over the values that other people want. It is probably true that few people choose an occupation or a certain specific employment for the congenial fellowship it offers; nevertheless, once they are in a job they often develop loyalties to their coworkers which transcend almost any other motive. A sense of usefulness or achievement in a job is given partly by the psychogenic satisfactions one acquires by engaging in the work, but also partly by the cultural definitions that the work is useful or constitutes an achievement. Thus an economic position is a means of satisfying or not satisfying a whole series of sociological needs and pressures as well as economic ones.

People with these motives typically come together into an economic enterprise. Whereas in pre-industrial days economic organization was based on community cooperatives, forced labor, or individual enterprise, today in Western culture it is most common for a number of individuals to join voluntarily in an ongoing large-scale enterprise. There is a division of labor within the enterprise and most individuals have a fairly specialized function in producing or distributing the goods or services.

The workers' relationship to the management of the enterprise is usually contractual, often informal, but increasingly formal, so that wages, hours of work, conditions of promotion and firing, "working conditions" such as those relating to overtime work, rest and lunch periods, "fringe benefits" such as vacations and medical care, and so on, are part of a written agreement between management and representatives of employees. In addition, there are government regulations controlling minimum wages, maximum hours, conditions to protect safety and health, unemployment

[3] For a summary of studies of the prestige rating of occupations, see Theodore Caplow, *The Sociology of Work* (Minneapolis: University of Minnesota Press, 1954), pp. 39–41, 52–57.

and old-age insurance, compensation in case of accident while on the job, employment of women and children, and sometimes conditions for striking.

2   SOME TRENDS IN ECONOMIC ORGANIZATION

There have been several important trends in economic organization over the past few centuries which have changed considerably the mutual expectations of participants in an economic enterprise. In the first place, there has been a tremendous development of industrial technology, so that the need for skilled labor and for heavy labor has gone down greatly. Up to about the time of World War I, there was a trend in the United States to specialize work in great detail, so that an increasing number of workers were given very simple, mechanical, repetitive tasks. In the name of efficiency, Frederick Taylor and other industrial engineers calculated ways of reducing the number of physical motions performed by factory laborers in carrying out their job. The result was a strong trend toward tedious, unskilled labor, a trend which is still going on in countries less industrialized than the United States.

Sometime during the 1920's a new trend began in American labor, from unskilled to semiskilled labor. This had several causes: (1) New developments in machine design and use of electric power (substituted for steam and water power) permitted the use of more complicated machinery, which could perform combinations of several of the simple and tedious tasks formerly performed by many unskilled laborers. Men were now needed to tend these complicated machines, move parts from one machine to another, and do some of the more intricate tooling and assembling. This required some training and development of skill—taking perhaps several weeks or a few months—although not nearly so much as was required for pre-industrial production, which was almost art. (2) A series of studies—led by Elton Mayo and his colleagues—began to emphasize the human side of labor as compared to the physical or mechanical aspects. They showed that "fatigue" could come from boredom as well as from muscular exertion, and that workers wanted to be treated as human beings rather than as mechanized robots. In recent years writers like Peter Drucker and Georges Friedmann have emphasized the value for morale and efficiency of getting the worker acquainted with the whole productive process and not simply a tiny specialized aspect of it. (3) Increasing unionization of workers after 1933 and shortage of labor after 1940 made it increasingly profitable and necessary for management to substitute machines for workers wherever possible. The result of all these influences is that an increasing proportion of workers are semiskilled rather than unskilled and are being spread over a rapidly growing national productive plant.

A second major trend is for economic enterprise to be larger and to involve a hierarchy of managers rather than a single boss. There are now

The representative social phenomena of the industrial system of our time are the mass-production plant and the corporation. The assembly line is the representative material environment; the corporation is the representative social institution. The large-scale plant has taken the place of the rural village or of the trading town of the eighteenth and early nineteenth centuries. The corporation has replaced the manor and the market as the basic institution in and through which the material reality is organized socially. And corporation management has become the decisive and representative power in the industrial system.

Peter F. Drucker, *The Future of Industrial Man* (New York: John Day, 1942), p. 74.

thousands of firms in the United States whose size was unheard of a century ago. A single top manager—or, as he is usually called, the president of the corporation—can manage a whole mammoth company because he has several echelons of managers under him (as well as staff to advise him on special matters, such as law, scientific research, personal selection, labor relations, and so on). Not only workers are employed at specialized tasks, but managers as well. This is alleged to make for productive efficiency,[4] although economists are not all agreed as to whether large-sized or middle-sized firms are more efficient. There is probably a point at which the cost of an increasingly spread-out hierarchy of managers overbalances the savings gained from coordinated marketing, specialized staff, and other obvious advantages of "big" business.

For the ordinary workers, for the foremen (as the lowest-level managers are called), and even for most of the managers, the trend has meant that they have no direct contact with the top management which directs the course of the company.[5] Except for retail stores, small farms, and a few other kinds of economic units that have kept their pre-industrial organizational form, there really is no contact any more between workers and bosses. An economic enterprise today is structured like an army, in which ranks up through captain practically never see a general while engaged in their work.

A third major trend in economic institutions is a separation of ownership and management.[6] Increasingly, business has become legally organized in the form of corporations, so as to accumulate larger amounts of

[4] Peter Drucker, *The Concept of the Corporation* (New York: John Day, 1946).

[5] A description of how this trend developed in one factory is contained in W. L. Warner and J. O. Low, *The Social System of the Modern Factory* (New Haven: Yale University Press, 1947).

[6] This was early suggested by Thorstein Veblen (*The Theory of Business Enterprise* [New York: Scribner's, 1904]), more specifically noted by William Z. Ripley (*Main Street and Wall Street* [Boston: Little, Brown, 1927]) and has been documented by A. A. Berle and G. C. Means (*The Modern Corporation and Private Property* [New York: Macmillan, 1936]).

In a survey of the executives of 500 of the largest industrial firms in the United States in 1962, the typical company president was found to be 56 years old, graduated from college, has worked for no other company and rose through the ranks via manufacturing or merchandising.

Twenty-two per cent of the presidents of the 500 industrials are under 50 years of age, 43 per cent are between 50 and 59 and 35 per cent over 60. The range of ages at which they assumed the presidency was 24 to 73, but the average president had held his job for only five years at the time of the survey.

Ten per cent did not attend college, 16 per cent attended, but received no degree, 49 per cent received a bachelor's degree and an additional 25 per cent have graduate degrees.

Harvard, Yale and Princeton were the most-attended colleges.

Forty-one per cent had worked for only one firm, 23 per cent for two and 16 per cent for three. Four per cent had been employed by seven or more companies during their careers.

The list of industrials was one compiled annually by *Fortune* magazine.

Survey of business executives undertaken by Heidrick and Struggles, executive recruiting firm of Chicago.

capital than individuals are able to or want to pay out, and so as to limit the liability of owners to the amount of money they invest. The relationship between the stockholders and the corporation they own is generally remote. Not only are they not legally responsible for anything the corporation does, but their interest is mainly focused on the change of prices of shares at the stock exchange, which is only partly related to the profits made by the corporation. Stockholders may vote for or against the management, but seldom do more than a small minority of them appear at stockholders' meetings. The majority turn in their voting proxy to the management, whose election or proposals for changes in the corporation's structure are practically never contested.

The reason for this apathy is not only the stockholders' lack of interest in the corporation, but also the extreme difficulty of overturning the incumbent management. The management generally controls a block of voting shares, which, while only a small proportion of the total stock, is larger than that controlled by any other individual. The bylaws of corporations are often so drawn up that the time and place of meetings are fixed for the advantage of management and not for stockholders. Often only a small number of directors may be elected each year, so that to get a majority of directors on their side, dissident stockholders would have to fight for several years. The year 1954 was notable in the economic history of the United States in that, for the first time in about half a century, there were major struggles for the control of three large corporations. This was possible only because the dissident stockholders got leaders who were willing to take over management of these companies, obtained the financial backing of some of the wealthiest men and banks in the United States, and carefully organized over several years their campaign to take over the incumbent management. The corporation battles of 1954 were not repeated in the following decade, nor are they likely to be in the future because of the tight control by management.

3   THE STRUCTURE OF BUSINESS ENTERPRISES AND TRADE UNIONS

As a result of the long-run trends we have been considering, the modern business enterprise is organized in a fairly impersonal way: owners are separated from managers, top owners are separated from lower managers and workers, workers are separated from the to..al process and the integration of the enterprise. Nevertheless, the worker and the manager who are hired by a corporation are human beings, and they relate themselves socially to the other participants in the enterprise. They become interested in each other as people, and often develop loyalties to each other and/or to the enterprise. They compete with each other in terms of the values of the group. Managers try to get ahead by attracting the favorable attention of their superiors; workers often do the same, but sometimes the values of the working group are such that individual workers are urged not to work so hard as to set difficult standards for their less able fellow workers.

Several studies show that contemporary workers are aware that they as individuals cannot rise out of the workers' level to the management

---

Washington, D.C.—*(UPI)*—Americans by the thousands are now turning to "moonlighting" to supplement their incomes, the government reported Wednesday.

A special Labor Department survey showed that the number of people holding two or more jobs stood at 3.9 million last May—600,000 higher than a year earlier.

This was the first "significant increase" in multiple job-holding since the Labor Department started keeping track of the practice in 1956.

But government economists declared that only a "very small proportion" of the nation's 4 million unemployed could or would fill the extra jobs if moonlighting were abolished.

They said that nearly all dual job holders work relatively few hours on their second job—averaging about 13 hours a week.

Minneapolis Morning Tribune, April 2, 1964, p. 17.

1 The number of people owning shares in publicly-held corporations totalled 8,630,000 at the end of 1955—an increase of 2,140,000, or 33 per cent, since early 1952.

2 One out of 12 adults now owns shares compared with one in 16 in 1952.

3 Approximately 1,400,000 individuals owned shares *only* in privately-held corporations, bringing total shareownership to over 10,000,000 people.

4 For the first time, women outnumbered men as shareowners in public corporations—by a margin of 51.6 per cent to 48.4 per cent.

5 In the past four years shareownership has increased among all income groups. Almost two-thirds of America's adult shareowners have household incomes of under $7,500.

6 America's typical shareowner is 48 years old, three years younger than his 1952 counterpart. The estimated median age of the 2,140,000 net new shareowners added since 1952 was 35 at the time of the *Census*. Overall, the typical shareowner is a high school graduate, and lives in a community of about 25,000.

7 The average shareholder owns 4.24 issues compared with 4.1 issues four years ago.

8 The greatest increase in shareownership—125 per cent—has occurred in communities ranging from 2,500 to 25,000.

Who Owns American Business? 1956 Census of Shareowners. By the New York Stock Exchange (New York, 1956).

level, since management is recruited from among those specially trained for it.[7] The result is that the values of workers do not always include making themselves appreciated by managers at the expense of fellow workers. Nevertheless, workers look for status and prestige also, but they seek them by such behavior as outwitting the management, displaying skills which win the respect or admiration of their fellow workers, or getting favored positions in the shop or union.

Approximately sixteen and a half million workers belong to unions in the United States.[8] While this figure is less than a fourth of the total labor force of about 71 millions, it includes practically all non-Southern workers in factories and a large proportion of other workers not on farms or in white-collar jobs. In Scandinavia, Great Britain, and a few other countries the proportion unionized is considerably higher.

Unions developed shortly after the beginning of the Industrial Revo-

[7] See, for example, *Fortune* magazine's polls for January, 1937 (pp. 86–87) and May, 1947 (pp. 10 ff.); Caroline B. Rose, "Morale in a Trade Union," *American Journal of Sociology*, 56 (September, 1950), pp. 167–74; Ely Chinoy, "The Tradition of Opportunity and the Aspirations of Automobile Workers," *American Journal of Sociology*, 57 (March, 1952), pp. 453–59.

[8] *New York Times*, May 25, 1964, p. 1.

lution in practically every industrial country to protest against the conditions of work and to try to gain some security of employment for workers. They had a very slow and checkered growth in the United States until about 1935,[9] when the great depression, the New Deal administration, and the internal politics of the established unions combined to create conditions favorable to the rapid growth of unions. They reached a plateau in membership in 1945, and have not grown much since. American unions take some part in politics, but they have not been the chief sponsors of a labor party as unions have been in Scandinavia and Great Britain, and certainly American unions do not have essentially political aims as do the French *syndicats*. American union activity is directed primarily at getting more out of management for the benefit of workers and of the union itself.

Some unions are democratically run; others are not. Like many another voluntary association, some unions are completely controlled from the top, and the leadership puts its own interests above that of the rank-and-file members. A few unions have fallen into the hands of racketeers who have seen the possibilities for gaining wealth and power out of such an organization. But most unions, even some of the undemocratic ones, are engaged primarily in improving conditions for workers.[10]

Unions have many different patterns of organization, but they recruit members in two general ways. The "craft" unions try to organize all workers who practice certain skills, no matter in what industry these workers are employed; the "industrial" unions try to organize all workers who help to produce a certain kind of product, no matter what kind of specialty these workers engage in. Originally, the Congress of Industrial Organizations (C.I.O.) was organized in 1935 to unionize workers (especially unskilled and semiskilled ones) along industrial lines, in contradistinction to the older American Federation of Labor (A.F. of L.) unions which were predominantly of the craft type. Since then, however, the A.F. of L. has also organized industrial unions, and by 1955—when the two labor groups voted to merge—it was twice as large as the C.I.O.

Membership participation in unions is quite low, although this makes them no different from most other voluntary associations. Some members, especially when they have been forced into the union as a requirement for getting a certain job or when the unions are racketeer-dominated, are actually opposed to unions. But where votes have been conducted by the impartial government agency, the National Labor Relations Board, most

[9] For a history and description of the American labor movement, see Philip Taft, *Organized Labor in American History* (New York: Harper and Row, 1964). For an excellent comparative study of unions, which helps to explain the nature of American unions, see S. M. Lipset, "Trade Unions and Social Structure," *Industrial Relations* 1 (October, 1961), pp. 75–89, and 1 (February, 1962), pp. 89–110.

[10] For a discussion of union techniques and effects, see Chapter 16, Section A.

memberships have voted by large majorities to maintain their unions.[11] Unionzied workers vote more in accord with the recommendations of union leaders than non-unionized workers do, and there are other evidences of union influence on worker behavior. One study shows that union solidarity and participation are greatest among those workers who believe (1) that the unions are successful in accomplishing what the workers think their functions are, and (2) that the unions are democratically run.[12] A number of studies show that, for the United States at least, loyalty to the union is not opposed to loyalty to the company but rather tends to go along with it.[13]

4   THE IMPORTANCE OF ECONOMIC INSTITUTIONS

Economic institutions are extremely important in any society since every individual has to relate himself to them in a number of ways, while he might be able to keep his contacts with the political and religious institutions down to an insignificant minimum. In our highly mechanized society we are especially dependent on economic institutions, since we have become used to having so many services provided for us rather than providing them for ourselves or getting along without them. On the other hand, work may be less satisfying than it used to be, as many writers claim, because it is now so specialized for most workers that it is no longer creative and there are more distracting leisure-time activities to compete with work for one's time and enjoyment. Still, most people are more concerned with their economic functions as producers than they are with their economic functions as consumers.

Economic institutions are related to other institutions in intimate ways. Before the Industrial Revolution, the family was the economic unit of production; it is still the economic unit of consumption. Religious insti-

[11] In a study of local unions in Buffalo, New York, for example, employers and outside observers alike were surprised by the conclusions. "In only two of the 127 elections studied did a majority of the eligible votes fail to authorize a union shop. Over ninety-six per cent of the workers who voted in the elections cast 'yes' ballots. More than ninety-one per cent of those who were eligible to participate did vote." Horace E. Sheldon, *Union Security and the Taft Hartley Act in the Buffalo Area* [Ithaca: New York State School of Industrial and Labor Relations, 1949], p. 37.) In Teamsters Local 688, in St. Louis, the proportions in favor of the union in the NLRB elections ranged from 94 to 98 per cent for the various shops. (*Midwest Labor World*, September 27, 1950, p. 1.)

[12] Arnold M. Rose, *Union Solidarity: Internal Cohesion in a Labor Union* (Minneapolis: University of Minnesota Press, 1952).

[13] Benjamin Willerman, "Group Identification in Industry," unpublished Ph.D. thesis, Massachusetts Institute of Technology, 1949; Arnold M. Rose, *op. cit.*, pp. 65–69; Leonard R. Sayles and George Strauss, *The Local Union* (New York: Harper, 1953); T. V. Purcell, *The Worker Speaks His Mind on Company and Union* (Cambridge: Harvard University Press, 1954); Hjalmer Rosen and R. A. H. Rosen, *The Union Member Speaks* (New York: Prentice-Hall, 1955).

tutions have economic functions, but a more important relationship is that the basic economic institution of property is invested with various kinds of moral significance. We have noted that nowadays unions concern themselves with politics, and businessmen have always tried to influence politics. Government is increasingly regulating economic activity, and in some ways it is absorbing economic institutions. In the United States postal service and now the furnishing of electric power are examples of wholly or partly government-run economic enterprises. In France, about 40 per cent of all industry is government owned and operated, including the railroads and most automobile production. In totalitarian dictatorships, practically all economic activities are completely controlled by the government. Thus we see that the singling out of economic institutions is partly arbitrary and partly a function of the fact that we happen to have a free-enterprise economy at this stage of our history.

B   *Political Institutions*

1   FORMAL AND INFORMAL POLITICAL INSTITUTIONS

The political sphere of social life is that of formally organized power, which is exercised by the institutions of government, the law, the army, the hierarchies of business enterprises, labor unions, professional associations, churches, etc.; voluntary associations concerned with some aspect of social change; large-scale criminal gangs. It is obvious from this broad listing that the political function of an institution, which is its use of organized power to achieve certain goals, is but an aspect of it. Consequently, we shall consider at this point only the institutions that are primarily political in purpose and function—that is, those that are part of the government.

Every society—no matter how "primitive"—has some kind of government, some ultimate power in the society which is generally recognized as legitimate. Governments assume many different forms, and political scientists have proposed to classify them in many different ways. Since our purpose is not to duplicate the work of the political scientists, but to indicate how the institutions of government are related to the rest of the society, we shall mention only a few classifications relevant to the interests of sociologists.

An important distinction is that between formal and informal government. Formal government is an expression of the legitimized authority in the society. If there is a constitution, formal government has its structure and functions outlined in the constitution. The informal government is the actual exercise of political power; if the informal ruler operates in a formal monarchy he is literally "the man behind the throne." Formal and informal government coincide in a nation to the extent that the formal government has the effective power. There are many types of situations, however, in which the informal government is distinct from and more power-ful than the formal government. (See Figure 2.)

One kind of example is provided by the Japanese government until the end of World War II. For centuries the formal government was cen-tered in the emperor, but informally all political power was held by a group of upper-class men. Until 1867 the latter were the traditional war leaders known as "samurai," but in that year the Emperor Meiji restored some power to himself, expanded the political aristocracy to include more than the military leaders, and even established some semi-democratic po-litical authorities. The military leadership was thoroughly reformed and modernized, but after World War I it again moved into the ascendancy. By 1931 the military chiefs were once more in political control, and used the formal government composed of emperor and parliament as a front. After the Japanese military defeat in 1945, the theoretically absolute powers of the emperor were removed and he was formally made a constitutional monarch like the British king, and the formal and informal powers of gov-ernment were combined into an elected parliament.

Another example of the separation of formal and informal govern-ment is that found in the so-called "boss system" which characterized many American city governments, and some state governments, in the period between the Civil War and World War II. There are some remnants of the boss system in a few American cities today, but in no place (with the possible exception of Chicago) is the "boss" so completely in control of the city government as his counterpart was until about 1945. Today no one man could correctly say, as did former boss Frank Hague of Jersey City, "I am the law." Occasionally the boss got himself elected as formal head of the city government (mayor), but often he found this an additional chore that was completely unnecessary.

Lincoln Steffens's[14] classic analysis of the boss system is that the boss came into existence to meet the needs of businessmen and racketeers who wanted special privileges from government. Steffens thus blamed the sys-tem of private enterprise, since it was concerned only with the advancement of the individual businessman, legitimate and illegitimate, and did not concern itself with law, justice, and the rights of the community.

Looking at the boss system with hindsight, and with a sociological rather than an economic determinist orientation, it seems to have resulted from an ignorant electorate and the absence of diverse pressure groups all seeking to influence public opinion in opposing directions. The boss was able to remain in power and to deliver privileges to those who would pay for them, because he was able to get people to vote for his puppet candi-dates. He gave a few dollars to, or did small favors for, citizens too ig-

[14] *The Autobiography of Lincoln Steffens* (New York: Harcourt, 1931). See also Steffens' *Shame of the Cities* (New York: McClure, Phillips, 1904).

norant to realize what they gave up in civic benefits for these paltry values.
He picked as subordinates men who could deliver votes on the basis of
their wide "friendship"—the "friends" being fools enough to sacrifice their

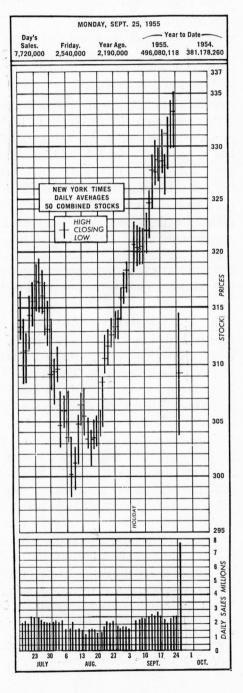

**FIGURE 2 • PANIC IN STOCK
MARKET FOLLOWING
THE HEART ATTACK OF
PRESIDENT EISENHOWER**

The upper chart shows the *New
York Times* daily average of prices
of stocks on the New York Stock
Exchange (note the sudden drop).
The lower chart shows the daily sales
(in millions) of shares traded on the
New York Stock Exchange (note the
sudden increase).
Source: *New York Times,*
September 27, 1955, p. 50.

community's welfare for the smiles and handshakes of the petty politicians. By controlling election officials, the boss used various techniques of rigging the elections and obtaining fraudulent votes.[15] The boss also traded on people's beliefs that politics was inevitably a kind of racket, in which no fundamental improvements could possibly be made. By believing that government is evil, the people helped to maintain it as evil. Perhaps most important of all, the boss seldom had any rivals besides other would-be bosses and practically no opposition from private organizations.

Gradually the educational level of the population rose, immigrants were acculturated, voluntary associations of all sorts began to put legitimate pressure on city governments, both government and private groups provided more services for citizens so they did not have to rely on the boss's organization for help and information, and reform movements were organized to "clean up" local politics. As a consequence, the period between the two world wars saw great changes in city government,[16] even though petty graft continues and racketeers can often "buy protection" from the police. On the whole, there has been a uniting of formal and informal governments; most of the old-time bosses have disappeared or they play a much reduced role. There are exceptions, but even Richard Daley of Chicago and Carmine DeSapio of New York never had the same powers and functions that their equivalents had a few generations ago.[17]

2   CONSTITUTIONAL AND FUNCTIONAL LOCATION OF POWER

Closely related to the distinction between formal and informal government is the distinction between the constitutional and the functional location of powers in government. The largely unwritten British Constitution accords sovereign power to the monarch, but functionally the monarch's powers are wielded by the prime minister and his cabinet. The latter formally state that they do everything in the name of the monarch, the various officers of the government are labeled His Majesty's (or Her Majesty's when the monarch is a woman), and the prime minister's speech at the opening of Parliament is delivered by the monarch. In fact, practically the only power exercised by the monarch is the choice of a new prime minister when Parliament overthrows the former one, but even this choice is rather strictly governed by traditional rules. In the United Kingdom the prime minister and his cabinet have some of the king's former powers and retain them independent of Parliament's powers. For example, the cabinet does not have to accept a parliamentary vote of "no confidence"

[15] For example, Joseph P. Harris, *Registration of Voters in the United States* (Washington: The Brookings Institution, 1929), pp. 356 ff.

[16] Edward C. Banfield and James Q. Wilson, *City Politics* (Cambridge: Harvard University Press, 1963).

[17] Robert L. Heilbroner, "Carmine G. DeSapio: The Smile on the Face of the Tiger," *Harper's*, 209 (July, 1954), pp. 23–33.

but can choose to dismiss Parliament and call for a new election, and the cabinet may name new "lords" who have a great deal of prestige and accessory legislative functions. In France, as we have seen,[18] the Constitution accords executive power to the president and the premier, but actually the main executive powers are held by the Chamber of Deputies and the top civil servants.

We have thus far been considering "the government" as the controlling power in an area. Actually, many countries have several levels of government, sometimes having overlapping jurisdictions. Among democratic nations the United States is extreme with its large number of strong local governments; France, on the other hand, has relatively few and relatively weak local governments. For 1930–1933, Anderson[19] estimated that there were 175,418 independent units of local government in the United States— including counties (or parishes in Louisiana), incorporated places (cities, villages, etc.), towns and townships, school districts, and certain others— and most of these types, along with the federal and state governments, have jurisdiction over the same areas and people. Since each of these units of government has elective as well as appointive officials, the United States has probably one of the largest proportions of government officials in the world, and certainly the largest proportion of elective officials.

Because few citizens can inform themselves about more than a dozen or so candidates for public office, most of the minor officials get elected on the basis of chance, partisan advice, or the sound of their names.

> The number of public offices filled by popular election, besides the mayor and members of the council, varies from city to city; but except for the comparatively few municipalities under the commission plan or the city-manager plan, the number of elected officials is too large for the voters to know. This being the case, it falls to the professional small-town politician and to very partisan political interests to frame the slate, to control the primary, and to organize vigorously to win the election rather than to get the most competent persons in office. What with too many offices to fill by election, highly complex socioeconomic problems to solve, and most people intent upon their own personal interests and immediate economic welfare, elections go by default to the political machine.[20]

Since the areas controlled by these local government units are usually fairly small and correspond to no sociologically relevant divisions of the population, their activities are hampered by each other, and combinations

[18] See Chapter 5, Section B.

[19] William Anderson, "The Units of Government in the United States," *Public Administration Service*, No. 42 (Chicago, 1934), p. 1.

[20] F. Stuart Chapin, *Contemporary American Institutions* (New York: Harper, 1935), pp. 31–33.

would greatly enhance government efficiency without sacrificing the principle of local government.

A study of metropolitan Chicago[21] showed that it had more than 1,600 separate units of administration and finance, including parts of 4 states and embracing 200 cities and villages, 15 counties, 165 townships, almost 1,000 school districts, 190 drainage districts, 70 part districts, 11 sanitary districts, 4 forest preserve districts, 4 mosquito abatement districts. The area had 350 different police forces and over 550 independent units. Chicago is only a little more extreme than other cities in its plethora of disjointed governmental units. In no metropolitan area can the diverse units get together for an efficient performance of their functions. Among the more obvious examples of the inefficiency of the present system are the fact the criminals can cross governmental lines freely while the police cannot, and the fact that communicable diseases cannot be controlled when artificial boundaries restrict health officers.

Queen and Thomas attribute "this confusing and expensive structure" to "the expansion of great cities, their economic and social absorption of suburbs and satellites, and the creation of special authorities to meet new needs . . . the vested interest of officeholders, the inertia of voters, and the struggles of property owners to secure or preserve advantageous tax rates."[22] Some communities have tried to solve the problem by annexation of suburbs by cities, consolidation of city and county governments, restriction of county governments to rural areas, intermunicipal agreements, forming of new special authorities to combine a specific function of several geographically distinct governments.[23] In the late 1950's, Miami, Nashville, and Toronto reorganized themselves on a metropolitan government basis. But these efforts have only begun to touch on what is still one of America's greatest internal problems because they meet resistance and inertia, and because they do not go far enough to meet the needs for effective functioning.

3   POLICY-MAKING AND ADMINISTRATION

A distinction in government personnel in which sociologists are interested is that between policy makers and administrators. The theoretical distinction between them is that policy makers have the power and make the laws or orders while the administrators are employees whose job it is to enforce these rules. The administrators, who should technically be called bureaucrats if that word were not used so often in a derogatory manner,

---

[21] Charles E. Merriam, S. D. Perratt, and A. Lepawsky, *The Government of the Metropolitan Region of Chicago* (Chicago: University of Chicago Press, 1933), pp. xv–xx; Harvey M. Karlen, *The Governments of Chicago* (Chicago: Courier, 1958).

[22] S. A. Queen and L. F. Thomas, *The City* (New York: McGraw-Hill, 1939), p. 218.

[23] *Ibid.*, pp. 219–21.

range from generals and government bureau chiefs to postmen and government clerks. While the administrators are not supposed to have power in their own right, in effect they do since the laws are never specific or detailed enough to control all their official actions and since administrators often exceed their powers.

Some governments officially accord great powers to top administrators: in the United Kingdom and Sweden, for example, the permanent undersecretaries in each ministry are civil servants with great power and prestige. In France, the top administrators officially form a body known as the Council of State, which more or less decides how existing laws are to be enforced, and these men carry on the processes of government in a stable manner despite the frequent changes of cabinet.[24] In northwest Europe lower civil servants have a tradition of rigorously adhering to rules, but there are many other countries—both democracies and dictatorships— where even the minor civil servants are somewhat arbitrary in serving the public. In the United States this arbitrariness is associated primarily with a tradition of casualness and informality in local government as well as with the tradition of petty graft and bribery. The casualness takes the form of the officials' acting on the basis of their personal likes and dislikes rather than exclusively on the basis of law. The southern states especially have had casual and arbitrary minor government officials.[25]

Top military leaders are a special kind of government administrator, since they are entrusted with control over the instruments of violence and they have special skills and usually high prestige. In most stable governments the military is subordinated to the civilian political leaders, but in a few—as in Japan between 1931 and 1945—the military leaders have taken over effective control of the country. Even where civilians are normally in control in stable governments, military leaders occasionally take powers which they are not granted in law. For example, in 1944 some of the German generals and colonels tried to assassinate Hitler; and in the United States in 1951 General MacArthur briefly violated the orders of President Truman in his conduct of the Korean War. In non-stable governments military leaders periodically seize top political power, although seldom do they seem to want to hold the formal government for long. In several South American countries, for example, the generals frequently change the head of state, and sometimes they form factions whose shifting fortunes mark frequent changes in governments. This pattern is very rare in Europe and North America—Napoleon in 1797 being the notable exception—but the French have experienced at least one unsuccessful try in the late nineteenth century and are worried that it might occur again.

[24] Herbert Luethy, *France Against Herself* (New York: Praeger, 1955).
[25] Gunnar Myrdal, with the assistance of Richard Sterner and Arnold Rose, *An American Dilemma* (New York: Harper, 1944), pp. 523–38.

4   TYPES OF LEADERSHIP

Top political leadership may be classified in many sorts of ways, but sociologists have found Max Weber's classification[26]—into traditional, bureaucratic, and charismatic types of leadership—most useful. This classification is based on hypotheses about the relationship between the nature of the social order, the relationships between leaders and followers, and the personality of the leaders. Traditional leadership can occur in a society to the extent that it is organized in terms of traditional meanings and values (what we have earlier called an "integrated group" form of society).[27] The leader assumes power by right of certain traditional rules of succession, and his powers are fairly specific and limited (even though he be an "absolute monarch") to what the meanings and values of the culture grant him. Monarchies, aristocracies, or democracies may have the traditional type of leadership, but the modern dictatorships do not. The traditional leader himself acts in a rational fashion in terms of the existing values of the culture; thus he is a consistent conservative.

Bureaucratic leadership occurs when the "public" form of social structure has, to a considerable extent at least, supplanted the "integrated group" form of social structure. The public debates "rationally" as to what rules and procedures will best achieve its purposes, and then designates leaders or functionaries to carry out these rules and procedures. The leaders are conceived of as "servants of the people"[28] even though high prestige may be accorded their offices. Their loyalty is to the laws or regulations, and their main observable trait is efficiency in carrying out these laws. The laws are not sacred, however, as they are not traditional, and so the bureaucratic leaders may advocate changes in them if they think the public's purposes can be more effectively served by new laws. In their sense, bureaucratic top leadership is "dynamic" and "liberal." The Western democracies have been tending toward a bureaucratic type of top leadership for several centuries, although they still have certain elements of traditional leadership and some of them have occasionally been punctured by brief periods of charismatic leadership.

Charismatic leadership can exist only to the extent that the society is organized in the form of an audience or mass. The charismatic leader is nearest to being all-powerful, as he is not bound either by laws or by

[26] Max Weber, *The Theory of Social and Economic Organization* (New York: Oxford University Press, 1947).

[27] See Chapter 5, Section A.

[28] The "people" need not include all the adults in the society, but simply the effective public which makes the laws. This public may range from all adults down through all adult males to a small body of "citizens" as in the free Dutch cities of the sixteenth century or in ancient Athens.

traditional values. He has to figure out the most expedient ways of getting his will accomplished, but his will is usually the ultimate arbiter of the goals of the government. He controls the population absolutely by the force of his personality. Nothing is sacred to the charismatic leader, except perhaps some of his inner urges, but he himself soon becomes sacred to his followers. In this sense, the decisions of the charismatic leaders are "emotional" rather than "rational" and his relationship to his followers is emotional. Because the past means nothing to the charismatic leader, he is essentially a radical and his government may do all sorts of things undreamed of before.

Whereas a traditional leader often, and a bureaucratic leader sometimes, lets his subordinates carry on the functions of government, the charismatic leader functions in a highly personal manner, and his subordinates derive all their power and prestige from him. In traditional and bureaucratic governments leadership may be vested in more than one individual; in governments based on charismatic leadership there is effectively only one individual who is really the leader (although he, of course, designates many subordinates to carry out the administration of his broad policies and even to advise him). Many of the modern dictators are charismatic leaders—Lenin, Stalin, Mussolini, Hitler, and Peron—but this could not be said to be true of most of the South American dictators, who rule by the rational decision of a small group of military or civilian leaders rather than through any personal hold they have on their followers. Because Stalin was a charismatic leader, and he died leaving a stable government without a charismatic successor, there was much speculation upon his death as to whether the Russian government would change drastically in form or a new charismatic leader emerge. The successors were not charismatic and the government did change significantly.

While we have pointed to examples of Weber's three types of leadership it should be recognized that they are "ideal types" which are found only in some mixed form in actual life. Weber applied his classification to groups smaller than the nation. He described Jesus and Savonarola, for example, as charismatic leaders to their relatively small groups of followers. We find charismatic leaders occasionally in small groups in our society; usually they are of the informally organized type, such as gangs. Most voluntary associations and economic institutions have the bureaucratic type of leadership, and churches alone in our society have a large amount of the traditional type of leadership.[29]

[29] For references to sociological studies on leadership, see Philip J. Allen, "The Leadership Pattern," *American Sociological Review,* 17 (February, 1952), pp. 93–96; Alvin W. Gouldner (ed.), *Studies in Leadership* (New York: Harper, 1950).

C   *Bureaucracy and the Army*

1   THE NATURE OF BUREAUCRACY

Much has been written about bureaucracy, although little of this could be said to be in the form of systematic studies.[30] A brief addition to the analytic commentary will be offered here, based largely on observation of a government institution, the United States Army.[31] In the strict Weberian sense, bureaucratic rules are to be distinguished from traditional rules. The former are not necessarily internalized, and taken as unquestioned rules for the guidance of behavior, by the political leaders of a government, a business enterprise, or voluntary associations. Rather, they are used by the leaders as guides for the behavior of their subordinates, as a means to keep the latter acting in conformity with policy. The leaders themselves do not feel bound by the bureaucratic rules of their organization, although in a democratic society they are bound by the duly-enacted statutory law governing the whole society.

To a certain extent the bureaucracy functions according to sociological principles independent of the policies they are supposed to serve, although it is probably true that they have to effectuate these policies in the long run or be shaken up and some of the bureaucrats dismissed. In general, bureaucracies are more conservative—that is, adhering more to the traditional rules of the society—than the policies they are set up to serve. Top army staff officers have observed that they can obtain only a small proportion of observance of orders when the latter conflict with the time-honored "traditions of the service." There are several reasons for this. (1) A policy is set by those at the top of the hierarchy, but it is put into actual operation by those at the bottom. In being transmitted through the hierarchy, a new rule or order cannot be liberalized at any point but it can always be made more restrictive (that is, in the direction of not affecting the *status quo*). Thus the more levels there are in the hierarchy, the more conservative does it tend to be. (2) Questions about the actual operation of the new rule are raised by those at the bottom, active level of the hierarchy to their superiors. Communication is always somewhat faulty —the superior does not always understand all the problems and needs of his subordinates. To be on the safe side, the superior tends to make a conservative decision or interpretation. (3) There seems to be a tendency in bureaucracies to assume that if the rules say nothing about a given behavior, it is forbidden. Since no statement of a new rule can foresee

---

[30] See Chapter 5, Section B. A representative series of statements and studies on bureaucracy are presented in R. K. Merton, A. P. Grey, B. Hockey, and H. C. Selvin (eds.), *Reader in Bureaucracy* (Glencoe, Ill.: Free Press, 1953).

[31] The most comprehensive sociological study of the army is Morris Janowitz, *The Professional Soldier* (Glencoe, Ill.: Free Press, 1960).

COMMENT ON CUSTOM IN THE ARMY

I was in the Army only two days before the commanding officer of my induction center told a group that all passengers would be punished if someone broke a window on the train carrying us to a camp. At the training camp the company commander said the whole company would be denied passes for ten days unless the one who broke a toilet bowl confessed.

I asked the officer for his authority for such punishment, and he said it was an old Army custom. I told him it was not wise to follow old customs. "It once was a custom in this country to burn grandmothers as witches and sell human beings like cattle," I related. He replied that customs have the "force of law" in the Army.

I said that I never had read any such statement in the Articles of War passed by Congress. My superior read from the *Soldiers Handbook,* which says: "Customs have come into existence which are recognized as our unwritten law of conduct."

He also quoted from the *Officers Guide,* page 343: "Customs which live and endure tend to take on the force of law, as indeed they are—the Common Law."

According to Colonel Thomas R. Phillips: "Army regulations on discipline remain unchanged, in all essential respects, from those of 1821, and those were copied from the regulations of the noble and peasant army of royal France of 1788" (*Infantry Journal Reader* [1943], p. 291).

Thomas H. Hall, "Comment on Custom in the Army," *American Journal of Sociology,* 51 (March, 1946), p. 364. Published by the University of Chicago Press.

all the contingencies that can possibly arise under its application, this tendency inevitably leads to conservative application. (4) Those at the bottom of the hierarchy, who apply the rules, seek to simplify their work; therefore they apply a rule to all cases in exactly the same manner, even when the policy makers at the top do not intend to have such uniformity independent of the individual differences among the cases that arise.

Bureaucracies thus slow down the momentum of drives or pushes applied at the top. One of the reasons the charismatic leader is more effective than the bureaucratic leader in accomplishing change is that he ignores the hierarchy and goes directly to the action level where the lowest-level bureaucrat is meeting the public. He thus keeps the action people acting more closely in accord with what he considers to be proper behavior. In comparison with the morality or immorality of the policy makers, the bureaucracy tends to be amoral, as it is bound by orders from above and by its own internal security.

There are ways of circumventing the rules as applied by the lowest echelon of the bureaucracy, although they are not always successful. (1) Claiming a personal contact with a higher official is a time-honored way of getting a "break" from a low-echelon official. (2) An appeal to a "higher cause"—especially to tradition—when the bureaucratic rule is somewhat at odds with tradition is sometimes an effective way of utilizing the inherent conservatism of bureaucracy. (3) An informal approach, using humor and grace, will sometimes get the bureaucrat to distinguish between his role as an ordinary person and his role as a bureaucrat, and the former may do the deciding. (4) Whatever the approach, the apparent innocence of the deviation must be effectively communicated to the official. He must be able to "take the role" of the offender in order to tolerate the offense.

2   THE UNITED STATES ARMY AS A SOCIAL INSTITUTION

We shall now go on to consider the Army as a specific institution. The social structure of the United States Army is determined by three traditions: (1) the modern American tradition of business efficiency, self-interest, individualism, democracy, and equalitarianism; (2) the medieval tradition of rigid separation of castes, of hierarchical control, of absence of moral accountability for the upper social strata, of regarding the privileges of the lower strata as a matter of the whim of the upper strata; and (3) the changing body of military doctrine that goes into the formal body of rules known as Army Regulations. While the Army Regulations (and subsequent orders, circulars, letters, etc.) theoretically govern the Army, the basic structure of the Army's organization is set by the medieval tradition. As far as social organization is concerned, Army Regulations serve to define proper behavior in situations not envisaged by the other two traditions and to bring to awareness of military leaders the existence of the modern American tradition.

There exists in the minds of most military leaders—that is, the officers —a theoretical picture of what the Army's social organization should be. This "theory of the Army" is largely common to all armies in Western societies. The reason for this similarity is simply that modern armies have developed out of the feudal system of the Middle Ages, and no civil government has been strong enough or interested enough to change them drastically.

While the medieval one is the strongest of the three traditions in the United States armed services, it has been weakened over the course of years by the infusion of men with modern civilian attitudes and by the growth of new military organizations—the Air Corps, for example. But whenever there is a clash between any two of the traditions, the medieval one will still win out, as shown by unpublished studies conducted during the Second World War, and to the response—or lack of response—to the postwar Doolittle report which aimed to change officer-enlisted men relationships. An example of this is given by the War Department's first "Readjustment Regulations" (RR 1-1, 1945). This states, as part of a plan to maintain soldier morale in a period following the end of a war, that "particular emphasis must be given to living conditions and the elimination of instructions which tend properly to be regarded as harassing instead of necessary." It is safe to state that very few military installations reduced, much less eliminated, such instructions. Some installations, operating on the theory that enlisted men should never be allowed to forget that they were in the Army, increased their harassing instructions: ties will be worn, reveille will be held at 6:00 a.m., beds will be made with the "U. S." facing the head, there will be an additional period of drill every day, and failure to wear a hat out-of-doors will result in disciplinary action. These are simply "customs of the service," strengthened for fear that enlisted men would let down because the war was over, in direct violation of an Army regulation.

When civilians are incorporated into the Army, they usually unwittingly give up their civilian standards of efficiency—developed in a business office, on a construction job, or in college—for the traditional means of getting things accomplished in the "Army way." Go-getting American businessmen, when transformed into officers, often wait until their superiors place detailed instructions on their desks before they proceed to accomplish a job. They often refuse to take responsibility for the simplest decision but will pass it to their already overburdened commanding officer. They forward information to other responsible Army officers only through hierarchical channels, even when they know that the information will arrive at its destination too late to be of any use. They promote their subordinates according to their length of service and responsiveness to orders rather than according to their initiative or efficiency. The reason subordinate officers do these things is that the Army system of rewards and punishments forces them into this mold, and they gradually come to accept it.

While the medieval tradition is pre-eminent among the three traditions, the others have a role. Each one operates under the conditions set by the other two. The "American tradition" leads to recognition—more in regulations than in practice—that each soldier is an individual, with individual interests and rights. Most of the information and education activities —new to World War II and still meagerly practiced—are based on this assumption. So are many of the personnel activities of the adjutant general's office, such as classification based on civilian skills and education. There is a certain confusion between this concern for the individual, based on the American tradition, and the medieval tradition. For example, a colonel in a Special Service Section was heard to state that the purpose of providing movies for soldiers was not to entertain them but to keep them off the streets so they would not get venereal diseases.

While the American tradition operates through the medium of the

Discipline can be effective only if the ideal patterns are buttressed by strong sentiments which entail devotion to one's duties, a keen sense of the limitation of one's authority and competence, and methodical performance of routine activities. The efficacy of social structure depends ultimately upon infusing group participants with appropriate attitudes and sentiments. . . . These sentiments are often more intense than is technically necessary. There is a margin of safety, so to speak, in the pressure exerted by these sentiments upon the bureaucrat to conform to his patterned obligations, in much the same sense that added allowances (precautionary overestimations) are made by the engineer in designing the supports for a bridge. But this very emphasis leads to a transference of the sentiments from the *aims* of the organization onto the particular details of behavior required by the rules. Adherence to the rules, originally conceived as a means, becomes transformed into an end-in-itself; there occurs the familiar process of *displacement of goals* whereby "an instrumental value becomes a terminal value." Discipline, readily interpreted as conformance with regulations, whatever the situation, is seen not as a measure designed for specific purposes but becomes an immediate value in the life-organization of the bureaucrat.

Robert K. Merton, *Social Theory and Social Structure* (Glencoe, Ill.: Free Press, 1949), pp. 154–55.

Army Regulations and tends to work against the medieval tradition, it also works *against* Army Regulations and for the medieval tradition, because it stresses individualism and "looking out for number one." From the day a man enters the Army he learns—sometimes painfully—that he must look out for himself. Officers, of course, are in a much better position to do this than are enlisted men. Practically every officer knows that he can "get around" almost any Army rule if he can see the right people. He also comes to regard Army property as for his own use. Seldom did officers hesitate, when overseas, to use Army vehicles and gasoline for taking out "dates" or going sight-seeing, and officers in small units regularly took clothing out of enlisted men's supply rooms when they were supposed to purchase it at reduced rates at the P-X. If done on a small scale, this practice was not likely to get officers in trouble.

This spirit of "looking out for number one" does violate the medieval tradition of "responsibility" for the welfare of subordinates. While Army Regulations try to preserve the paternalism of the medieval tradition, the American tradition has all but discarded it. Rare is the officer who will make himself available to enlisted men for consultation on personal affairs. It is of interest to observe that the German Army made this paternalism the very heart of good officer-enlisted-men relations, which in turn was a keystone of German military morale. The United States Army has emerged from paternalism, but it has no satisfactory substitute. The inspector general and the chaplain—who could be substitutes—have little influence in the United States Army. Thus the enlisted man, without enforceable rights and practically without recourse to authority outside his command- ing officer, is left to the good heart or carelessness of his immediate officers or to their fear of occasional inspection.

It is "natural," under these circumstances, for enlisted men to have developed an informal "underground" for self-protection. This is another manifestation of the American tradition of "looking out for number one." This did not exist in the early stages of the draft in 1940 and 1941, and it never existed under the rigid discipline of the training camp. But it developed with all sorts of ramifications when the American armies went overseas. To understand how this informal organization could develop when enlisted men had so few enforceable rights, it is necessary to realize that every staff officer has at least one enlisted man to do "menial tasks," such as accumulating information, typing, and keeping files. An officer may get otherwise occupied or lazy when he finds that there is no pressure to keep him at routine work. Then his enlisted man will do all the work of the office, leaving the officer the sole task of signing his name to papers. At any rate, this system permits at least one enlisted man to know every piece of information there is to know in the Army overseas. It also permits most staff officers to be subject to the influence of the enlisted man who does most of their work. While "latrine rumors" circulating in an isolated company may be largely wrong, the very best place in the Army to get information of what the latest and highest decisions and plans are is the enlisted mess hall or barracks of a headquarters company. And the best and surest way for an enlisted man to get the Army to do something for him is to talk personally to the enlisted men who "run" the staff sections at headquarters. These "underground" channels can more than make up for official callousness and unconcern. Sometimes the solidarity of enlisted men is so strong that an enlisted man can get a privilege which his officer cannot get even for himself.

Needless to say, some enlisted men are more adept at using under- ground channels than others. Such men are known to other enlisted men as "big time operators" (BTO's) or "wheels" (because they get around?). A BTO will make it a special task to cultivate a friend in each of the various headquarters staff sections. He will assiduously do favors for these friends and in return expect them to do favors for him. The BTO is an enlisted man who, by his own efforts and by means of the amorphous solidarity of enlisted men, can get most of the irregular privileges which most officers take by themselves.

Rules and orders contrary to tradition are badly enforced in the United States Army outside of the actual combat situation. This is largely because traditional discipline is regarded as something for the enlisted men and not for officers, while it is the officers who must see that the rules and

orders are carried out. Thus the medieval tradition of weak accountability
for the upper caste and the American tradition of being concerned only
for one's personal interests combine to make Army rules and orders the
weakest influence of the three in the running of the daily business of the
Army.[32] This is not true of combat operations, probably because the situation is not structured there, and the great danger makes everyone willing
to follow whatever structuring of the situation becomes available. Orders
do define the situation and give direction to behavior.

There are examples too numerous to mention of orders being repeated over and over again without effect and of repeated letters from
commanding generals calling subordinate commanders' attention to the
fact that a certain Army regulation is not being followed. An overseas
Army newspaper reports one example: After repeated orders of the Commanding General of the Mediterranean Theater in 1945 to ship back to
the States men who had a certain point score, and there still remained
thousands of men with this point score in units throughout the Theater,
Major General White (G-1 of the Theater) expostulated that these men
"are being held in direct contradiction to specific orders from the Theater
Commander."[33] The Commanding General of the air base at Santa Ana,
California, designated a "gripe day" when enlisted men in his command
could speak to him personally. Five hundred and fifty men showed up, and
the general conducted a group conference in which he learned of some
of the violations of his orders. He concluded the session with the following
remark: "If you don't see any improvement in the next couple of days
come back and give me the facts of your case and I'll either do something
about it or wring someone's neck.[34]

Army rules and orders, while they are as dated as one would expect
the regulations of a highly bureaucratic structure to be, nevertheless exert
a modernizing influence on the Army. The social structure of the Army
is gradually changing under the constant repetition of Army regulations.

[32] The tradition of weak accountability for officers is reinforced by differential punishments for the two castes for the same violation. Whereas an enlisted man will be punished
for violation of a rule or order by fine, "breaking" in rank, and imprisonment, an officer
will be punished by removal from command and reprimand. When twenty American
soldiers stationed in Turkey in 1960 were caught in a black market scandal, the officers
were punished solely by oral reprimand and removal from command. A U.S. Senate committee investigated, and its chairman—Senator J. W. Fulbright of Arkansas—complained
to the Army about the light punishment. "General Lyman L. Lemnitzer, Army Chief
of Staff, testifying on behalf of the Chairman of the Joint Chiefs, insisted with considerable vigor that such punishment was quite severe for an officer.' (*New York Times*,
March 24, 1960, p. 13). The General was correct in terms of the traditional norms, but
he probably failed to understand the civilian-oriented attitudes of the guilty lieutenants
and enlisted personnel.

[33] *Stars and Stripes* (Mediterranean), October 8, 1945, p. 8.

[34] *Ibid.*, October 11, 1945, p. 3.

The regulations themselves change as public opinion, the practices of business, and the findings of social science gradually penetrate to the chiefs. But for the fact that they presuppose a rigid caste system, Army regulations today are fairly modern and almost radical in the eyes of many Regular Army officers who are expected to enforce them.

D   *Religious Institutions*

1   THE NATURE AND ORIGIN OF RELIGION

There is no agreed-upon definition of religion which seems to fit all its forms. Webster's New International Dictionary defines religion as:

> The outward act or form by which men indicate their recognition of the existence of a god or of gods having power over their destiny, to whom obedience, service, and honor are due; the feeling or expression of human love, fear, or awe of some superhuman and overruling power, whether by profession of belief, by observance of rites and ceremonies, or by the conduct of life; a system of faith and worship; a manifestation of piety.

Probably most religions have the following elements: (1) beliefs regarding the nature and ultimate power of the universe, or metaphysics; (2) beliefs regarding the ideal or proper mode of behavior, or ethics; (3) ceremonial ways of expressing these beliefs. A religion must also be a social tradition rather than a purely personal philosophy. Religious institutions are built around the ceremonial ways of expressing religious beliefs, and they include churches, shrines, convents and monasteries, pilgrimages, and many others. In our brief consideration of religious institutions we shall be obliged to restrict ourselves to the church as the central religious institution. The word "church" is used in two ways: (1) the religious body, or the active organization of persons who adhere to a particular religion (there were 258 of these in the continental United States in 1962);[35] (2) the local community's material apparatus for manifesting religious ceremonials (there were over 400,000 of these in the continental United States in 1953).[36]

There are many theories of the origin of religion. Most churches hold that they result from a revelation of truth (both metaphysical and ethical truth) by someone inspired by the ultimate source of power in the universe. Anthropologists who have studied the religious practices of preliterate and dead civilizations have proposed a number of theories, such

---

[35] National Council of Churches, *Yearbook of American Churches* (New York, 1964), pp. 273–75.

[36] *Ibid.*, p. 252. The figure is an estimate. The larger religious bodies, claiming 98.2 per cent of all church members, reported having 319,240 churches.

. . . the scientific analysis of religion is possible for there are common elements in all religious systems as regards substance, form, and function. Every organized faith must carry its specific apparatus, by which it expresses its substance. There must be a dogmatic system backed by mythology or sacred tradition; a developed ritual in which man acts on his belief and communes with the powers of the unseen world; there must also be an ethical code of rules which binds the faithful and determines their behaviour towards each other and towards the things they worship. This structure or form of religion can be traced in Totemism and Animism, in ancestor-worship as well as in the most developed monotheistic system. . . .

The substance of all religion is thus deeply rooted in human life; it grows out of the necessities of life. In other words, religion fulfils a definite cultural function in every human society. This is not a platitude. It contains a scientific refutation of the repeated attacks on religion by the less enlightened rationalists. If religion is indispensable to the integration of the community, just because it satisfies spiritual needs by giving man certain truths and teaching him how to use these truths, then it is impossible to regard religion as a trickery, as an "opiate for the masses," as an invention of priests, capitalists, or any other servants of vested interests.

Bronislaw Malinowski, *Foundations of Faith and Morals* (London: Humphrey Milford, 1936), pp. 58–9.

as the ghost theory which holds that religion arose out of speculation concerning what happens to people after death, or the naturistic theory which holds that religion arose out of attributing souls to non-human objects such as trees, mountains, the heavenly bodies, and so on.

Theories of social origins are usually fruitless since no one can go back in time to test such theories by controlled observation, and records of what took place at the origin of some major social institution are usually quite inadequate if the event took place a long time ago or in an obscure corner of the world. Our best information comes from observation of the origin of institutions which are currently being formed. Anthropologists are studying the peyote cult which is developing among some of the southwest Indian tribes, and sociologists have studied certain modern religious movements such as Moral Rearmament, Christian Science, Mormonism, Neomonism, and so on. The quest for social origins is not always relevant to the matter which concerns sociologists more: why do social institutions and other aspects of culture continue in the form they now take? Social practices do not generally continue for the reasons for which they originally began.[37]

The theory that seems to explain the largest number of observable facts about religion, although it is far from proved, is Durkheim's "col-

[37] This observation was frequently made by the late Professor Louis Wirth.

lective experience" theory.[38] The chief defect of the theory is that it goes into the fruitless quest for social origins and uses data from anthropologists' and travelers' reports; its chief strength is that it conforms to observations about contemporary religion. Durkheim's theory is that religions begin where there is a common experience which gives a sense of unity to a group of people, and they continue by means of a repeated reminder of this strong sense of group unity. Would-be prophets and philosophers are constantly writing down systems of metaphysics and ethics; these become religions only when a group of people have this deep emotional experience of group unity with which the system of metaphysics and ethics becomes associated. In other words, the church, in its broad sense, is what makes a philosophy into a religion.

Originally, Durkheim held, there is some collective experience with all the characteristics of what sociologists call crowd behavior,[39] in which participants feel their individual selves superseded by something greater than themselves. This feeling of "possession" they later feel a need to explain as a powerful supernatural and spiritual force, but students of collective psychology recognize it to be a characteristic of collective experience and excitement under crowd conditions. It always involves a mystic quality of "communion" with the powerful force, which anthropologists call "mana" and which Durkheim interprets as communion with society. Physical objects which for some reason are prominently displayed during the period of collective experience become identified as the material symbols of the supernatural power. In certain Indian tribes this is often an animal or statue of an animal; in Christianity it is the cross; in some forms of Buddhism it is the familiar statue of Buddha.

As we know, there is a powerful feeling of goodness, greatness, and emotional well-being associated with the crowd experience, and consequently there is a desire to repeat the experience. Some religions call for repeating the experience literally, as some Indian tribes do in their dances and as the orgiastic Christian sects do with their revival meetings. Most religions, however, repeat the collective experience only symbolically. Communion with the supernatural power—which the people call their God or gods and which Durkheim identifies as the feeling of group unity—is achieved by such ceremonies as circumcision, confirmation, and the periodic revealing of the usually hidden Torah (Bible) in Judaism; by sprinkling water on people's heads and by eating wafers and drinking wine (a symbolic transubstantiation of the body and blood of God) in the dominant Christian denominations.

In all religions there is a periodical coming together of the faithful

---

[38] Émile Durkheim, *The Elementary Forms of the Religious Life,* trans. J. W. Swain (Glencoe, Ill.: Free Press, 1947).

[39] See Chapter 9, Section A.

to celebrate these ceremonies. According to Durkheim, this coming together and the performance of a collective ritual are essential requirements for a continuation of the feeling of group unity, and hence necessities for the continuation of the religion. Religion cannot be long practiced by individuals in isolation, although religious symbols help an isolated individual to recapture for a time the feeling of group unity when he is not with other people.

Marcel Mauss, a disciple of Durkheim, in his study of the Eskimos, discovered an interesting bit of evidence to support Durkheim's theory. He found that the Eskimo people have little interest in religion and very little religious behavior in wintertime, but have a high degree of religious interest and behavior during the summer. He traced this to the different modes of life imposed by climate and limited natural resources on the behavior of the Eskimo. During the winter people are dispersed in small family groups with very little contact with each other. In summer they come together in large groups and can therefore have collective experiences. Totems and other physical symbols of religion are more or less ignored during the winter but in summer they become objects of high veneration. In summer people get together in religious meetings, but in winter all religious ceremonials are more or less ignored. Thus religion and community experience are found to be associated for the Eskimos. Another study of religion in the Durkheim tradition is that by Jane Harrison[40] who attempted to show how ancient Greek religion developed out of crowd rituals accompanying major life crises.

The system of ethics and metaphysics, as well as the ceremonials, accretes gradually around the central religious experience and its symbols, in order to explain them, justify them, and round them out. These peripheral aspects of religion are constantly changing but the central experience and its symbols do not change unless the church dies or is reorganized on the basis of a new group experience. The meanings and values of the central experience and symbols—which Durkheim called "collective representations"—are partly in the overt culture and partly in the covert culture and are usually transmitted with great care to children by functionaries of the church and by adults generally.

2   RELATION OF RELIGION TO OTHER PARTS OF CULTURE

Religions take many different forms, since their specific details are built up as independent traditions, although a religion such as Mohammedanism borrowed extensively from the older paganism, Judaism, and Christianity. The specific characteristics of a religion are intimately related to the central values of the culture as a whole. The sociologist Max Weber attempted

[40] *Themis; A Study of the Social Origins of Greek Religion* (Cambridge: The University Press, 1912).

to show how major elements in the metaphysics and ethics of several world religions are related to dominant themes in the cultures where they have developed. His analysis of the "Protestant ethic" has become best known.[41] His thesis is that Protestantism differed from the older Catholicism by emphasizing individual responsibility as compared to group responsibility, activism as compared to quietism (the latter being not quite passive, but rather adjustive to things as they are), direct relationship to God rather than through the intermediation of priests, and generally favored saving, interest-taking, self-help, hard work and competition. These Protestant values were conducive to free-enterprise capitalism which was just beginning in those parts of Europe where Protestantism was developing in the fifteenth century. The values of Protestantism mentioned above became the dominant themes of modern capitalist society, and capitalism never became fully accepted in the Catholic and Orthodox Christian countries even when they became industrialized.

There is undoubtedly an element of truth in Weber's thesis, but actual events seem to be much more complicated, since capitalism had its roots among the Jews and among the Catholic Lombards and Flemish long before Protestantism was dreamed of, because religions have had their rise and fall in popularity in various modern countries regardless of the steady trend toward capitalism through the eighteenth and nineteenth centuries.[42] For example, in the United States at the time of its founding, and especially in the following decades up until about 1830, only a small portion of the population professed to have any organized religion or to attend church. The educated people tended to be deists, which meant that they believed in a God who, having once set the world in motion, did not interfere with it thereafter—a belief which none of the established churches accepted. The people on the rapidly expanding frontier had no opportunity to become members of churches. Many of the small businessmen in the cities did not concern themselves with religion even though churches were readily available. During the 1830's and 1840's there was a great religious revival, which brought many new sects into existence and strengthened the older ones.

Guy Swanson has undertaken a systematic study correlating cross-culturally seven religious belief systems with aspects of social structure in fifty societies (of which forty-six are preliterate).[43] Each of the seven was found to be distinctive and not derivative from another: (1) monotheism,

[41] Max Weber, *The Protestant Ethic and the Spirit of Capitalism,* trans. Talcott Parsons, from *Gesammelte Aufsätze zur Religionssoziologie* (New York: Scribner's, 1930), Vol, I, Ch. 1.

[42] Richard H. Tawney, *Religion and the Rise of Capitalism* (New York: Harcourt, 1926).

[43] Guy E. Swanson, *The Birth of the Gods: The Origin of Primitive Beliefs* (Ann Arbor: University of Michigan Press, 1960).

(2) polytheism, (3) active ancestral spirits, (4) reincarnation, (5) witchcraft, (6) belief in the soul as immanent in the body, and (7) belief in the supernatural as a source of morality. He found that each of these beliefs was associated with some distinctive type of social order. For example, the belief in witchcraft usually occurs in societies in which "people must interact with one another on important matters in the absence of legitimated social controls and arrangements." A few other authors have sought to show a relation between some aspect of religion and political forces.[44]

3   CHURCH AFFILIATION AND RELIGIOUS ORGANIZATON[45]

There were rises and falls in church affiliation after that, but the long-run trend has been steadily upward,[46] although even as recently as 1936, the date of the most recent U.S. Census of Religious Bodies, only about half the population were claimed as members by the churches. In 1962 the churches themselves reported[47] a total membership of 117,946,002, or about 65.78 per cent of the total population, but it is likely that this number is slightly inflated. A public opinion poll in 1962 asked a cross-section of civilian adults whether they went to church or religious services during the previous week: 46 per cent said that they had.[48] While these answers cannot be taken as accurate, they do suggest a high degree of church attendance. The rise in church attendance does not necessarily mean that there has been a tendency toward stronger religious belief. Several studies suggest that the trend has been toward increasing skepticism about the metaphysical beliefs contained in organized religion.[49] Will Herberg suggests that Americans are becoming more secularized at the same time as they are attending churches more.[50] The trend toward church affiliation thus

[44] Ralph B. Perry, *Puritanism and Democracy* (New York: Vanguard, 1944); J. Milton Yinger, *Religion in the Struggle for Power* (Durham, N.C.: Duke University Press, 1946); Arnold M. Rose, "The Mormon Church and Utah Politics," *American Sociological Review*, 7 (December, 1942), pp. 853–54; B. B. Ringer and C. Y. Glock, "The Political Role of the Church as Defined by Its Parishioners," *Public Opinion Quarterly*, 18 (Winter, 1954–55), pp. 337–47.

[45] Perhaps the best book on this subject in the United States is David O. Moberg, *The Church as a Social Institution* (Englewood Cliffs, N.J.: Prentice-Hall, 1962).

[46] It is estimated that only about 20 per cent of the American people were Church members in 1850. By 1900 the figure rose to 36 per cent. (National Council of Churches, *Yearbook of American Churches for 1956* [New York, 1955].)

[47] National Council of Churches, *Yearbook of American Churches for 1964* (New York, 1963). For detailed figures, see Chapter 12, Table 13.

[48] Gallup poll, as reported in *Minneapolis Sunday Tribune*, December 30, 1962, p. 2a.

[49] Sarah Stone, "A Comparative Study of the Religious Attitudes of Parents and Their Children," unpublished M.A. thesis, University of Minnesota, 1933; Hornell Hart in President's Research Committee on Social Trends, *Recent Social Trends in the United States* (New York: McGraw-Hill, 1933), pp. 397–414; J. H. Leuba, "Religious Beliefs of American Scientists," *Harper's* (August, 1934), pp. 291–300.

[50] Will Herberg, *Protestant-Catholic-Jew: An Essay in American Religious Sociology* (New York: Doubleday, 1955). For a comment on this by a Roman Catholic, see Rudolph

It is this secularism of a religious people, this religiousness in a secularist framework, that constitutes the problem posed by the contemporary religious situation in America . . .

The outstanding feature of the religious situation in America today is the pervasiveness of religious self-identification along the tripartite scheme of Protestant, Catholic, Jew. From the "land of immigrants," America has, as we have seen, become the "triple melting pot," restructured in three great communities with religious labels, defining three great communions or faiths. This transformation has been greatly furthered by what may be called the dialectic of "third generation interest": the third generation, coming into its own with the cessation of mass immigration, tries to recover its "heritage," so as to give itself some sort of "name," or context of self-identification and social location, in the larger society. "What the son wishes to forget"—so runs "Hansen's law"*—"the grandson wishes to remember." But what he can "remember" is obviously not his grandfather's foreign culture; it is rather his grandfather's religion— America does not demand of him the abandonment of the ancestral religion as it does of the ancestral language and culture. This religion he now "remembers" in a form suitably "Americanized," and yet in a curious way also "retraditionalized."

Will Herberg, *Protestant-Catholic-Jew: An Essay in American Religious Sociology* (New York: Doubleday, 1955), pp. 15, 272–73.

* Marcus L. Hansen, *The Problem of the Third Generation Immigrant* (Rock Island, Ill.: Augustana Historical Society, 1938), p. 9.

probably reflects, in part, a growing interest in the non-religious functions of the church, which we shall consider shortly.

Many studies have shown that women attend Christian worship services more faithfully than do men, and otherwise express greater interest in religion.[51] Among Jews, by contrast, men appear to attend services more regularly than do women. Lenski attempts to explain this by stating that the ideal role of the Christian is more compatible with the modern role of the woman in Christian society, while for Orthodox Jewish values it is the other way around.[52] "Whereas males are trained from an early age to view the world in competitive terms to prepare them for the highly competitive job world, women are oriented to cooperative (or love) relations

E. Morris, "Problems Concerning the Institutionalization of Religion," paper delivered at the 17th Annual Convention of the American Catholic Sociological Society, 1955.

[51] Bernard Lazerwitz, "Some Factors Associated with Variations in Church Attendance," *Social Forces*, 39 (1961), pp. 301–09; Joseph Fichter, S.J., *Social Relations in the Urban Parish* (Chicago: University of Chicago Press, 1954); Joseph Schuyler, S.J., *Northern Parish* (Chicago: Loyola University Press, 1960); Louis Bultena, "Church Membership and Church Attendance in Madison, Wisconsin," *American Sociological Review*, 14 (1949), pp. 384–89; Gerhard Lenski, "Social Correlates of Religious Interest," *American Sociological Review*, 18 (1953), pp. 533–44; *Catholic Digest*, 17 (November, 1952) and subsequent issues.

[52] Lenski, *op. cit.*

In his monumental work, *The Social Teaching of the Christian Churches,* Ernst Troeltsch formulated a distinction, which has become classic, between the Church type and the sect type of religious institution. He defined the Church as being, in essence, an objective institution into which an individual is born, and by which, under the direction of duly constituted ecclesiastical officials, he is trained and disciplined for life in the religious community. Desiring to cover the whole life of humanity and to be coextensive with society, the Church accepts the secular order and becomes an integral part of existing social structures; it correspondingly becomes especially dependent on the upper classes and overwhelmingly conservative in outlook. It vests authority in religious matters in an established ecclesiastical hierarchy, in the precedents of tradition, and in the sacraments, while it seeks to dominate and to use political institutions for authority in secular matters. The sect, on the other hand, was defined by Troeltsch as a small, voluntary community, aiming at the inward perfection and fellowship of its own members, who have joined it by conscious choice. Rather than seeking to penetrate or dominate other social spheres, the sect is indifferent, tolerant, or antagonistic toward secular matters, and attempts to be a moral community separate and sufficient unto itself. Rather than locating religious authority in the religious institution or its officers, it appeals directly to the Scriptures and to Christ, practicing within itself the priesthood of all believers and criticizing the Church for apostasy from the original charter of Christianity. It is especially connected with the lower classes, working "upwards from below, and not downwards from above."*

Liston Pope, *Millhands and Preachers* (New Haven: Yale University Press, 1942), pp. 117–18.

* Ernst Troeltsch, *The Social Teaching of the Christian Churches,* trans. Olive Wyon (New York: Macmillan, 1931), Vol. I, pp. 331–36.

to prepare them for the normally non-competitive world of family activities." Thus, the Christian ethic of cooperation and love attracts women more than men; Judaism, however, stresses that religion is primarily a male responsibility.

There are no significant age differences in church attendance among Americans, except among Jews where older people are more participant than younger men.[53] However, among the very old, church attendance drops, apparently because of physical debilities.

The people of most European countries are less church affiliated than Americans. In France, the best estimate is that less than half the population practices any religion,[54] and in Scandinavia, while there is a government-

[53] Lazerwitz, *op. cit.;* Harold Orbach, "Aging and Religion," *Geriatrics,* 16 (1961), pp. 530–40; *Catholic Digest* Survey, *op. cit.*

[54] For a summary of the evidence, see Arnold M. Rose, *Theory and Method in the Social Sciences* (Minneapolis: University of Minnesota Press, 1954), pp. 106–07. In 1947 a public-opinion poll of a representative cross-section of Frenchmen found only 66 per cent saying they believed in God, 20 per cent stated that they did not believe in God, and the remaining 14 per cent did not answer. In the United States in 1952,

established church to which everyone nominally belongs if he is not a member of some other denomination, only a small minority of the people attend church. The Communist countries discourage all of the traditional religions, and only a very small minority apparently keep up with traditional religious practices in the Soviet Union, with the proportion somewhat larger in the satellite countries and Yugoslavia. Communism itself has taken on all the characteristics of a religion, with its ultimate supernatural power being History and Karl Marx as the prophet of its basic Truth, and with a new ethics, ceremonials, symbols, and sense of group unity based on collective experiences. The effort to establish a new religion to avoid rival loyalties seems to be characteristic of modern totalitarian governments, since Hitler tried to do the same in Nazi Germany, although Mussolini and Franco came to terms with established Catholicism.

Building on a distinction between church and sect made by Max Weber and Ernst Troeltsch,[55] H. Richard Niebuhr[56] studied the American history of religious organization to show that the lower classes rather than the middle classes supported dissident sects. But he also concluded that sects must evolve into churches if they are to survive. The class basis of sectarianism has been corroborated for recent decades in several studies.[57] But it does not seem to be that economic deprivation *per se* causes sectarianism, but rather the general alienation and social disorganization relatively frequently found among certain lower class groups.[58]

Niebuhr's other thesis—that sects naturally evolve into churches if they survive—has also been supported by several studies.[59] However, Harold Pfautz, on the basis of a study of the Christian Science movement, concludes that this group evolved into an "institutionalized sect" rather

---

99 per cent said they believed in God, and 87 per cent said they were absolutely certain (10 per cent said "fairly sure" and 2 per cent "not quite sure"). (The French data were taken from the files of the *Institut Français d'Opinion Publique,* and the American poll was taken for the *Catholic Digest* magazine, as reported in *Presbyterian Life,* 5 [November 15, 1952], pp. 18–20.).

[55] *The Social Teachings of the Christian Churches,* trans. Olive Wyon (New York: Macmillan, 1931).

[56] *The Social Sources of Denominationalism* (New York: Holt, 1929).

[57] Walter Goldschmidt, "Class Denominationalism in Rural California Churches," *American Journal of Sociology,* 49 (1944), pp. 348–55; Russell Dynes, "Church-Sect Typology and Socio-Economic Status," *American Sociological Review,* 20 (1955), pp. 555–60; Jay Demerath, "Religious Orientations and Social Class," unpublished Ph.D. thesis, University of California at Berkeley, 1961.

[58] Renato Poblete, S.J., and Thomas O'Dea, "Anomie and the Quest for Community," *American Catholic Sociological Review,* 21 (1960), pp. 29–37; John Holt, "Holiness Religion," *American Sociological Review,* 5 (1940), pp. 740–47.

[59] Earl Brewer, "Sect and Church in Methodism," *Social Forces,* 30 (1952), pp. 400–08; Liston Pope, *Millhands and Preachers* (New Haven: Yale University Press, 1942); Paul Harrison, *Authority and Power in the Free Church Tradition* (Princeton: Princeton University Press, 1959).

than a church.[60] By the former, Pfautz means a group which retains certain of the characteristics of sects (e.g. conflict with the prevailing culture) but has many of the characteristics of churches (e.g. formal organization, "respectability"). Pfautz believes that the Christian Science movement will retain these sectarian characteristics indefinitely. In a study of the behavior of ministers during the racial crisis at Little Rock, Arkansas, in 1957, Campbell and Pettigrew found that the established church leaders were unable to take a moral stand, but compromised or rationalized instead.[61] A minority of the younger ministers did take a stand in favor of racial justice, but they usually received severe reprimands from their parishioners. The ministers of the small fundamentalist sects took a stand in favor of the traditional folkways.

4   THE NON-RELIGIOUS FUNCTIONS OF CHURCHES

Churches in Western countries have always carried on non-religious functions as well as religious ones. The Catholic Church has an extended parochial school system, providing education from kindergarten through the university levels, and several of the Protestant denominations, as well as Jewish groups, have less extensive parochial school systems in the United States. The churches usually run various social-welfare programs which are extensions of their traditional function of providing charity for the poor. A large proportion of the private hospitals and colleges in the United States have been organized under religious auspices although they are often not under the complete control of the clergy.

The church has also traditionally been a center of community activities. In Latin countries the square of land that is frequently left open in front of the Catholic church building is a favorite meeting place, especially after mass on Sunday. In the United States many Protestant and Jewish church buildings contain meeting rooms where all sorts of neighborhood groups—including persons not members of the church—meet and where church-sponsored groups for recreation or community welfare are organized. Among Catholics, the parochial schools furnish equivalent facilities. A major exception to the extension of functions on the part of the churches is the long-run trend away from politics and government. Especially since the Protestant Reformation and the American Revolution there has been a tendency to separate church and state.

The development of church-sponsored non-religious activities has been a strong trend of the past several decades in the United States, especially among the Protestant denominations.[62] Ministers have been devoting an

[60] "The Sociology of Secularization," *American Journal of Sociology*, 61 (September, 1955), pp. 121–28.

[61] Ernest Campbell and Thomas Pettigrew, *Christians in Racial Crisis* (Washington, D.C.: Public Affairs, 1959).

[62] Unpublished study by Samuel W. Blizzard.

increasing proportion of their time to such activities, which have probably been one of the reasons why there has been an increase in church membership. Thus the minister has been becoming a community leader, not only because of his religious function and his professional training, but also because of his community activities. This is an individual matter, and ministers vary considerably in the extent to which they have participated in the activities and the extent to which they have been successful at them. A large proportion of the community activities are of the sort that attract women rather than men, and an increasing proportion of church offices are being held by women[63] although the clergy itself is overwhelmingly male. In many other ways organized religion has been more attractive to women than to men.

Both the religious and non-religious functions of a church depend on the ethical principles contained in its religious doctrine and on the character of the community in which the church is located and from which it draws its members. Some religious denominations are favorable to the non-religious functions of the church, while others are less so. The relevant character of the community is not only the culture of the people who attend church but also their demographic, economic, and ecological characteristics.

Some years ago Ross Sanderson found, from a study of 1,950 urban churches, that "the ratio between Sunday-school enrollment and church membership varies directly as the distance of a church from the center of the city, and inversely as the age of the church."[64] This may appear to be a very profound law of religious behavior, but it is actually nothing more than the consequences of certain cultural, ecological, and demographic facts that we shall examine in Chapter 13. The larger middle-class families move out to the new neighborhoods at the edge of the city and in the suburbs, leaving single people and couples without children near the older city center. Thus children, and consequently Sunday-school attenders, are relatively numerous away from the city center where the churches are relatively new. The children who do live near the city center tend to have immigrant parents, and the "culture conflict" between them results in the children rebelling against what their parents want them to do, including attending Sunday school.

Religion is studied by the sociologist[65] not only for its societal func-

[63] Marvin J. Taves, *Factors Influencing Personal Religion of Adults,* Washington Agricultural Experiment Stations Bulletin 544 (Pullman: State College of Washington, 1953). The National Opinion Research Center poll referred to earlier shows that women attend church more frequently than do men.

[64] Ross W. Sanderson, *The Strategy of City Church Planning* (New York: Harper, 1932).

[65] For an excellent survey of studies of the sociology of religion in the United States, see Gerhard Lenski, "The Sociology of Religion in the United States," *Social Compass,*

tions but also for its influence on the individual. The individual as well as the group is integrated with the help of religion (although for both individual and group there are usually other sources of integration). The individual's faith in the ultimate power of a good force gives him faith that ultimate justice will be done and perhaps that his own minor sins will be forgiven. Perhaps more important than this ethical function of the supernatural power is the metaphysical one. Human beings have a need to understand what takes place around them—to attribute cause to everything that exists and to every change. Since no one has a satisfactory naturalistic explanation for everything, and some people have fewer naturalistic explanations than others, the concept of supernatural powers can be used to fill the gap.

The normal course of life brings frustrations, and the individual can tolerate only so much frustration. Faith, which is more subjectively controllable than the external frustrating world, can ease frustration by providing such rewards as subjective conviction that one "understands," that "good" will ultimately triumph, and that there is future happiness in the after life. Religion thus can work against fear, guilt, and misery in the individual. In times of great personal stress some individuals intensify their religious beliefs and increase their performance of religious ceremonies. This often helps them objectively as well as subjectively: soldiers in combat who prayed when the external danger became extremely distressing were somewhat less likely to be overcome by psychoneurotic disturbance.[66] Of course, certain other thoughts and activities can serve the same function, and there is the danger that prayer or other religious behaviors will distract one from taking the action necessary to help oneself objectively. Those who rely too strongly on religion to overcome physical disease are likely to succumb, although religion can be of great help when the illness has a mental source.

5   RELIGION AND MAGIC

Magic is closely related to religion, although many of the organized religions frown on certain magical practices. Magic may be defined as behaviors which seek to control the observable world by invoking supernatural power. Magic can thus range from throwing salt over one's shoulder in order to avoid evil to mumbling formal prayers for the same purpose. Magic can and does exist independent of religion, and many people who have no systematic religious beliefs and who participate in no organized

9, *4* (1962), pp. 307–37. For an even broader context, see the UNESCO publication *Current Sociology*, "Sociology of Religions: A Trend Report and Bibliography," 10, *1* (1956).

[66] Arnold M. Rose, "Conscious Reactions Associated with Neuropsychiatric Breakdown in Combat," *Psychiatry*, 19 (February, 1956), pp. 87–95.

religion practice magic. To practice magic all one needs to believe is that some supernatural force, perhaps never clearly defined, will act automatically in a desired fashion when the magic user engages in some act. Magic usually is employed for some private, often antisocial purpose, although it may also be used for the intended benefit of the whole society as when witch doctors seek to bring needed rain by certain incantations. Religion is always thought of as necessary for the welfare of the society.

Durkheim[67] has provided a criterion for the differentiation of magic and religion on the basis of the kinds of cults they form and of values involved. Religion unites people into a moral or sacred community, called a church; whereas magic typically creates only a clientele of individual followers or practitioners, who have little in common. The followers of a religion often think of themselves as "brothers" and have strong solidarity, whereas it cannot be said that those who purchase the services of a fortune-teller, for example, usually feel this way. Moreover, the rites of religion have an obligatory, moral character, nonperformance of which leads to feelings such as impiety or guilt; whereas an individual is free to practice magic or not, though neglect of the latter may cause him some anxiety. Yet, the exact distinction between magic and religion is still much in doubt, at least according to Radcliffe-Brown.[68]

Certain kinds of magic may be employed by anyone, usually with the purpose of seeking his own personal advantage. Such, in American society, are the practices of knocking on wood, avoiding walking under ladders, and preventing black cats from crossing one's path. Individuals devise their own private rituals for similar magical purposes. Some persons hang their clothes in a certain way at night, others carry a "charm" which has a purely private meaning and history, and so forth. Magic may also be employed for the benefit of other individuals and groups by specialists in the use of magic. In our society such specialists include faith healers, certain kinds of fortunetellers and spiritualist "readers" (those who petition the supernatural powers as well as communicate with them), and those religious leaders—mostly those serving poorly educated congregations—who use prayer and ritual in an effort to gain various specific benefits for their flock. We may be amused at the following description of the efforts of a magic specialist to influence the outcome of a football game among the natives of South Africa, but comparable behavior occurs in the United States. The Africans are simply a little more systematic than the Americans.

> Durban, South Africa (Canadian Press)—The most important member of Durban's twelve-man African football team never kicks

[67] Émile Durkheim, *Elementary Forms of the Religious Life* (Glencoe, Ill.: Free Press, 1947).

[68] A. R. Radcliffe-Brown, *Taboo* (Cambridge: The University Press, 1939).

the ball. He is a witch doctor or "unyanga," upon whose "mtakati" (magic) the outcome of every match depends.

The witch doctor gets a retaining fee of £10 to £12 ($28 to $33.60) a month, and if you watch a football field on a dark night before an important league match you will see him earning his keep with the surreptitious making of the mtakati.

From a cow's horn, carried on his belt, he smears the goal posts and crossbar with "umuti" (medicine). He has smeared also the boots and uniforms of the players with umuti, and on the day of the match he will treat the legs of each member of the team. On the day of the match supporters of the opposing teams take their seats keeping clear of rival supporters for fear of a spell being cast on them to make their team lose.

The opposing teams enter the playing area from separate points, taking care not to tread on the ground over which their rivals have walked. They fear that they may be contaminated by witchcraft, which will cause their skill to deteriorate.

If the star player of the home team makes a valiant sally to the visitors' goal but misses by a bare inch, the home supporters howl despondently, "Mtakati!"

When the game is lost, it is not the skill of the team that is at fault. It is the mtakati of the visitors' unyanga that won the game for them.[69]

6   RELIGION AND SCIENCE

There is commonly thought to be an inevitable opposition between science and religion, and some scientists and religious leaders have shared this belief. It is true that certain scientific discoveries have proven false certain religious beliefs—for example, the discovery of organic evolution disproved the Christian and Jewish conception of the origin of the plants and animals, including man. But science cannot by its very nature ascertain what is ultimately real or true, and it cannot say what is ultimately good, so that some metaphysics and ethics are needed if one wishes to have any beliefs in these matters. Metaphysics and ethics can come from several sources—the great philosophers, one's own ingenuity, or from organized religion. Thus, if organized religions would be willing to allow science to ascertain the nature of the observable world, they would have no conflict with science. In fact, one study suggests that it was the Puritan religion of 17th century England which encouraged the rise of modern science.[70] This author held that "the deep-rooted religious interests of the day

[69] New York Times, February 25, 1951, p. 42.

[70] Robert K. Merton, "Science, Technology, and Society in Seventeenth-Century England" in George Sarton (ed.), Osiris, Vol. 4, Part 2 (Bruges, 1937). For a criticism, see Lewis S. Feuer, The Scientific Intellectual: The Psychological and Sociological Origins of Modern Science (New York: Basic Books, 1963).

A man desires his child to grow, therefore he chews the sprouts of the salmon berry and spits it over the child's body that it may grow as rapidly as the salmon berry. He smears the dust of mussel shells on the child's temples that it may endure as long as mussel shells. A man ties the dried navel string of his baby boy and a woman that of her baby girl to their wrists while they are busy at highly trained occupations, so that the child will have the same proficiency in these techniques. Fish hawk eyes are rubbed over a sleeping baby's lids to give him the fish hawk's sight; and because the raven is supposed never to be sick, the raven's beak is laid by the child that it too may be free of illness. One desires the death of his enemy, therefore he stuffs a bit of the enemy's clothing down a dead snake's throat and ties it with the sinews of a corpse; he puts it in an exposed tree top and the venom of the snake and the contact with the corpse will bring about the death of the enemy.

Ruth Benedict, "Magic," in *Encyclopedia of the Social Sciences* (New York: Macmillan, 1933), Vol. X, p. 39.

demanded in their forceful implications the systematic, rational, and empirical study of Nature for the glorification of God in His works and for the control of the corrupt world."

We have seen that religion can perform certain valuable functions for society and for the individual, although other means may also be used to achieve these effects, and although religion has sometimes been used to avoid making improvements in or adjustments to the material and social world around us. Religion will probably continue because it performs these valuable functions, and because most individuals do not know how to or do not want to look for substitutes. On the other hand, specific religions may die or be killed, or change drastically, and new religious forms take their place, as happened in northern Europe when Protestantism supplanted Catholicism, and as is now happening in the Soviet Union.

The trend of the past two centuries toward a non-religious condition of society is a function of the growing mobility and heterogeneity of society and of the relative role of secondary social contacts as compared to primary ones. In another sense it is also a function of the failure of organized religion to meet the changed needs of individuals as a consequence of the shift toward a mobile and segmentalized society and of the rigidity of organized religion in the face of the advancement of science and education. Since relatively few individuals are informed enough and understanding enough to adopt personal philosophies, the great bulk of the people are seeking an already developed philosophy—which could be organized religion.[71]

[71] The growing interest in the sociological study of religion has led to the development of several journals to report research and theory in this sub-discipline. At least two of these journals are published in the English language: *Social Compass* and

E   *Educational and Scientific Institutions*

1   KINDS OF EDUCATIONAL INSTITUTIONS

Educational institutions are those which seek to socialize people—especially children and youth—into the specialized aspects of culture. By specialized aspects of culture we mean literature, science, technology, vocational skills, the arts, and all the other knowledge accumulated in the society except that concerning the basically proper way of living in the society and the dominant values and metaphysics of the culture. The latter are quite generally left for the family and the church to transmit, although we shall see later in this section that the school also plays a role in teaching values to children.

Not every society has educational institutions that transmit the aspects of culture listed above. In fact, most societies have the family transmit the technology and vocational skills, and the church or the community as a whole transmits literature and the arts. While schools have existed in Western culture since ancient times, attendance at them has been restricted to an intellectual or religious élite, and it has not been until very recent times that they have been made available to everyone. Among the first schools open to the masses, without restrictive fees, were the ones established by the New England colonies, although even they did not make elementary education compulsory for all able-minded children until some years after they became states. The southern states did not have public-school systems until the federal government established them after the Civil War.

Most of the western European countries established compulsory elementary public-school systems after the middle of the nineteenth century. Western countries generally have free secondary schools but these are not compulsory except up to some age such as fourteen or sixteen. These countries also have higher institutions of learning available at small or even nominal cost. Outside the West public education is only occasionally found. Japan has had compulsory elementary education for many years, and has one of the lowest illiteracy rates in the world. The Soviet Union has established a school system much like that of the West in its coverage. Some of the Balkan countries have only very recently begun free compulsory elementary schools. In Greece, for example, there is a nominal fee for matriculation into the elementary schools, which are otherwise free and compulsory, but many of the rural areas still do not have easily accessible schools and make no effort to require attendance at the schools that do exist. Secondary schools in Greece charge for attendance, and are

Journal for the Scientific Study of Religion. Also see a special issue of the *Annals of the American Academy of Political and Social Science* on "Religion in American Society" (November, 1960).

little used except by those who are economically well off. In the Near East public education is rudimentary, except for Israel, which has a Western-type educational system. In Africa formal education is largely reserved for descendants of Europeans, although public-school systems are being established for native Africans in a few countries. India and China have long had complete educational systems, but only a small proportion of the children attend school.

Besides elementary and secondary schools and colleges, both public and private educational institutions in the United States include specialized technical, professional, and trade schools; adult-education courses; workers' education courses; art and music appreciation classes for the general public; craft, dancing, and foreign-language classes for the general public; institutes for learning the latest developments in specialized fields; courses to aid the naturalization of immigrants; public lecture and forum series; exhibitions put on by certain industries; museums of various types; libraries; fairs with educational exhibits. Economic institutions often have educational branches to train workers to carry on the industry and sometimes to inform the public of their functions. The medieval guilds included an apprenticeship system, which has continued in simpler form in the skilled crafts up to the present day. Probably most of the factories that rely heavily on semiskilled labor train such workers themselves. Many other economic institutions provide "in-service training" to raise the skill level of their employees. In listing the types of educational institutions we must not overlook the educational activities of the mass media—radio, television, the press, and even the movies with their "documentaries" and training films. Our discussion of educational institutions will be practically limited to the schools at the three basic levels.

2   SOME STATISTICS ON EDUCATION

There are highly reliable figures available on the participants in the educational process in the United States. Table 2 shows the degree of current participation by age level. It shows that most children begin school at five years and end it at eighteen. Today a majority attend kindergarten, almost 16 per cent of the youth sixteen and seventeen years of age are no longer in school, beginning with this age girls drop out of school more frequently than do boys.

International studies of educational activity, prepared by the United Nations Educational, Social and Cultural Organization,[72] reveal the following interesting facts:

[72] UNESCO, *Basic Facts and Figures* (Paris: 1954 and 1961); UNESCO, *World Illiteracy at Mid-Century* (Paris: 1957); UNESCO, *World Survey of Education: Organizations and Statistics* (Paris: 1955); UNESCO, *World Communications* (Paris: 1964); Wood Gray, "Higher Education in the Nations of the World," *AAUP Bulletin,* 43 (December, 1957), pp. 594–97.

TABLE 2 · SCHOOL ENROLLMENT OF THE UNITED
STATES POPULATION 5 TO 34 YEARS OF AGE,
OCTOBER, 1962

Age	Total	Male	Female
5 years	66.8	67.1	66.5
6 years	97.9	98.5	97.3
7–9 years	99.2	99.1	99.3
10–13 years	99.3	99.2	99.4
14–15 years	98.0	98.8	97.3
16–17 years	84.3	87.1	81.6
18–19 years	41.8	51.2	33.7
20–24 years	15.6	23.4	9.1
25–29 years	5.0	8.6	1.8
30–34 years	2.6	3.9	1.4

Source: U.S. Bureau of the Census, *Current Population Reports, Population Characteristics*, Series P-20, No. 126 (September 24, 1963), pp. 1, 3.

1 Three per cent of the population aged 15 years and over of the United States, the Soviet Union, and France can neither read nor write at all. The nation with the lowest illiteracy rate is Sweden, with less than one-tenth of 1 per cent in this category. Countries with the highest illiteracy rates are Afghanistan, Saudi Arabia, and Yemen with 95–99 per cent illiteracy, Indonesia with 92 per cent, and Haiti with 90 per cent. India's proportion of illiterates was between 80 and 85 per cent. For the world as a whole, about 44 per cent of those 15 years old and over are illiterate.

2 The United States has the largest number of students attending colleges and universities. While this is partly a result of the fact that what are considered the first two years of college in the United States are considered part of secondary education in Europe, it nevertheless remains true that the United States is the country with the largest proportion of children of its lower income ("worker") population attending college. The Soviet Union has the second largest number of college students, 775,000 as compared to the United States' 2,659,000. European rates of college attendance are high, especially for Italy and France, but total numbers are greater in such Asiatic countries as India, Japan, and the Philippines. For the year of estimation (usually 1951), there were a total of 6,591,000 students attending institutions of higher education in the world, and about 480,000 faculty members.

3 Many countries have more book titles published every year than does the United States. Britain led in 1952 with 13,150 new titles, as compared to 9,399 in the United States. West Germany, France, and Japan also led the United States. The Soviet Union had

752,604,000 public library books available in 1958, compared with 200,000,000 in the United States, and 71,000,000 in Great Britain.

4 A number of European countries and Australia have more newspapers per person than does the United States. There are an estimated 573 copies of daily papers for each 1,000 persons in Great Britain every year, as compared to 327 published in the United States and a like number published in Japan. During the decade 1953–1963, daily newspaper circulation in the world rose by 20 per cent.

5 The U.S. leads in number of radios and television sets. By the end of 1959, the U.S. had 290 TV receivers for every 1,000 persons; the second country was Britain with 195 TV sets. During the 1953–1963 decade, the number of radio receivers in the world increased by 60 per cent, and the number of television sets tripled.

6 Japan leads the world in production of movie films, 516 full-length feature films in 1958, as compared to 288 produced by the United States, and several countries have a higher movie attendance than does the United States. The Austrians lead by attending an average of 17.4 films a year, while in the United States the average is 12.5 (for 1958).

3   THE SOCIAL STRUCTURE OF EDUCATIONAL INSTITUTIONS[73]
We shall now turn to a consideration of the social structure of schools. Educational institutions seldom control themselves. While a distinction is often made in law between financial control and control over educational policy, and the latter is not infrequently in the hands of the teaching faculty, the former is often so powerful as to minimize the independence of the latter. Financial control of public educational institutions is usually in the hands of the government, although a special elected board may be set up by the constitution to raise public funds for schools as well as to set their general policies. Some American state constitutions provide a special source of funds for public schools, such as the income from exploitation of certain natural resources or exclusive use of certain taxes, and since these funds cannot be diverted to other purposes, they give the educational policy board an independence of the government. A few state universities —notably the University of California—are significantly endowed with private donations.

Financial control of private institutions is, of course, in the hands of

[73] Sociological studies of the structure and problems of institutions of higher education have greatly increased in recent years. Among them are: Theodore Caplow and Reece J. McGee, *The Academic Marketplace* (New York: Wiley, 1958); Paul F. Lazarsfeld and Wagner Thielens, *The Academic Mind* (Glencoe, Ill.: Free Press, 1958); Burton R. Clark, *Open Door College* (New York: McGraw-Hill, 1960); R. Nevitt Sanford, *The American College* (New York: Wiley, 1962).

those who raise the funds, such as churches, boards of trustees, and so on. A small proportion of schools charge such high tuition fees that they are able to support themselves entirely from this source, and in such cases financial control takes the form of a market relationship between buyers and sellers of the educational service. Private endowed schools had an important development in Great Britain in earlier centuries, but their main recent development at the college level has been in the United States. There are private schools that support themselves by tuition fees all over the world, but they serve only a small proportion of the population. Outside the British dominions and the United States, private schools and colleges that charge fees within the range of the middle-class family's budget are largely church controlled.

Control over educational policy is sometimes directly in the hands of those who wield financial control. But there is a strong and ancient tradition in Western culture of academic freedom, which means that teachers are best qualified to determine what to teach, and the only checks on them are the judgments of their colleagues and of the general public and the elective choices of the students. At the elementary and secondary levels of education, academic freedom is largely a fiction, since the curriculum is largely determined by school administrators, and school boards watch the "morals" and expressions of opinion of teachers outside of school. In self-protection some teachers in American city schools have joined unions which serve to bring collective pressure on school administrators to maintain the security and advance the status of teachers. Public-school teachers in most western European countries are unionized. College teachers hold fast to the tradition of academic freedom, and by retaining some degree of cohesiveness in its defense as well as by having organized themselves into a professional association—the American Association of University Professors —to protect it, they have thus far succeeded in avoiding many serious violations of it.

Academic freedom, however, is a personal right, and has little to do with the over-all guiding policy of an educational institution. In most European universities, following another ancient tradition, this policy control is also in the hands of the faculty taken collectively. The professors meet periodically and through their joint decisions, or those of elected committees and officers, decide how their institution is to be run, within the limits of the funds made available to it. American university faculties have lost a significant amount of this power, although there may be a fiction that it is maintained in full.

Control over educational policy in the colleges—as in American elementary and secondary schools—is effectively in the hands of administrators, who are specialized functionaries comparable to top management and their staffs in industry. The administrators can be controlled by the financial controllers, by the legislature, and by the boards of trustees elected by the legislature or directly by the public. But in practice the latter generally do not interfere except on major matters that may affect public relations. The elaborate administrations of some American universities—who with their staffs are sometimes now larger than the teaching faculty—have grown out of the office of the president. The president of a university was originally—and still is in some European countries—an elected representative of the faculty to deal with the financial authority and the general public. In American universities the president is appointed by the board of trustees, and he in turn can appoint all of the other administrators. He is conceived of as equivalent to the president of a corporation with the board of trustees being the board elected by the stockholders. His power over educational policy is great, not only because the board and the public behind them are divided and uninterested in the details of educational policy, but also because of the unused tradition of faculty control over policy. He represents the faculty to the board, and the board to the faculty, and can thus exercise great power in relation to both. At the elementary and secondary school levels the administrators do not exercise so much power, as the tradition of faculty control is gone and the ultimate power is undivided in the hands of the board.

The students at the elementary and secondary levels have practically no influence over educational policy, except in so far as they inform and influence their parents who contribute to the public opinion that elects the school board. In recent years American secondary schools have introduced a certain proportion of elective subjects, through the choice of which the students indirectly influence educational policy. At the college level, European students exercise no more control than American secondary-school students. But American college students sometimes are as influential as their teachers. If active and cohesive, students get representation on administrative faculty committees, and their collective voice may carry more weight than that of the faculty, since students have no jobs to lose at the college. Most American colleges have extensive course-elective programs, and by deciding what courses they wish to take, students have a major influence in determining the direction of educational policy.

4   THE FUNCTIONS OF EDUCATION

We have pointed out that the function of educational institutions has generally been considered that of transmitting the specialized aspects of culture. But since they have contact with children in the latter's formative years, and since their contact with children is exclusive for a good part of their working day, they are bound also to have an effect on the transmission of the general values and basic pattern of living in the culture. General morality, personal habits of cleanliness, conceptions of "modern" life, have always been taught unwittingly by teachers even when these values conflict with those of family and neighborhood.

The schoolteacher is generally "middle class," even if his wages may be below those of many lower-class working parents, and he may be serving in a lower-class district.[74] The teacher, like the minister, is supposed to be "better"—in terms of the ideal standards of the general culture—than the general run of people who live in the district where he teaches. Thus he offers to children something closer to the valued model of their general culture than they are likely to find among their parents or neighbors. The influence of teachers thus is constantly toward "improving" the behavior of the community in terms of its ideals. The specialized knowledge of the teacher also tends to be more compatible with the higher, more general, standards of the culture than with the everyday values of the local culture: for example, the English teacher knows the intricacies of grammar and style and so serves as a model and a force for "better" verbal expression; the vocational-arts teacher knows the latest scientific findings about agriculture and so becomes a stimulant to "more efficient" farming.

In addition to this unintended imparting of values there is a deliberate transmission of values by teachers. In France, the influence of the teacher in transmitting the highly valued general culture of the society, as opposed to provincial and local variations, has long been recognized by the political and intellectual leaders of the society. The French government maintains a strict and deliberate centralized control over what is taught in the public schools. In the United States, education is locally controlled, but teachers find no difficulty in speaking, and in fact are encouraged to speak, in favor of the dominant and almost official creed of our culture and of its leading class. Such values would include patriotism, religion in general, ambitiousness, capitalism, and so on.

But teachers do not follow only the general culture, but also the subcultures with which their special characteristics have brought them into contact, and some of these subcultures are in opposition to general culture. There is one subculture a good number of teachers share—that which they pick up as a consequence of their professional training and association as teachers. This subculture is somewhat in opposition to the general American culture in its "liberalism," its emphasis on non-material rewards, and so on. From the teachers' standpoint, the values of their subculture would lead to a better society if more widely adopted. Since they are in a position to indoctrinate the young, they have from time to time debated among themselves whether they should not use this means to "build

[74] The varied influences of class on education are considered in A. H. Halsey, Jean Floud, and C. Arnold Anderson (eds.), *Education, Economy and Society* (New York: Free Press of Glencoe, 1961).

a new social order."[75] Many teachers favor the idea, but many oppose it. Nevertheless, while the schools are to be thought of as following the parents in socializing their children, they are also to be thought of as somewhat emancipating the children from their parents, and hence serving as instruments of social change.

The voting public, or merely their economic or political leaders, is in a position to strike back hard at teachers who teach values opposing theirs, and it often does. The result has been that few teachers—and these mainly at the relatively few private schools that have achieved a large measure of financial independence—emphasize the teaching of values strongly opposed to the general culture. But a good many teachers give mild support to such values as permissiveness (as distinguished from authoritarianism), non-material rewards, and others which are not very common in the society at large and thus exert, through the flexible minds of children, a slow, steady pressure toward social change. The Englishman A. V. Dicey[76] held that the teachers of one generation created the moral and intellectual climate of opinion in the next generation, and there is at least a measure of truth in his remark.

5   THE UNIVERSITY AS A SCIENTIFIC
      AND PROFESSION-CREATING INSTITUTION

It is often overlooked that a university is a scientific and profession-creating institution as well as an educational institution. American culture evaluates science very highly, but until recently there were very few specialized institutions for the promotion of science. Some economic enterprises and government agencies hire scientists to develop new knowledge that will be an asset to their operations. The philanthropic foundations—created by very wealthy individuals—help to support specific research operations of a scientific character. Museums subsidize a small amount of scientific effort of certain types. It was not until after World War II that the federal government established the National Science Foundation and other agencies to aid the natural sciences, and it was not until the late 1950's that it provided significant support for the social sciences.

Most scientific work, however, is supported by the scientists themselves and by the universities. There are no well-defined allocations of scientists' time between teaching and research, and it is usually only the prestige of scientific achievement that motivates teaching scientists to

---

[75] This was part of the title of a very widely discussed pamphlet by George S. Counts, written during the 1930's: *Dare the School Build a New Social Order?* (New York: John Day, 1932).

[76] A. V. Dicey, *Law and Public Opinion in England* (New York: Macmillan, 1905), pp. 19–41.

turn from academic duties to scientific activities. Universities give differing amounts of recognition to scientists' need for time to do research, but even where there is a most cooperative attitude it is considered that teaching duties generally have priority over the scientists' research activities. Thus, for all practical purposes, science is an adjunct of higher education in America.[77] France some decades ago established a government-subsidized research organization which employs a large proportion of the younger scientists to do research in subjects their senior colleagues believe worthwhile. Norway has a comparable organization which, by law, gets its funds from the sale of tickets in a national lottery (in which guesses are made as to the outcome of sports events). The communist and fascist dictatorships have government-supported and government-controlled research organizations, which hire significant numbers of scientists to engage in pure research. In countries where neither universities nor philanthropic foundations nor the government support research, it is done by individual scholars or not done at all.

Institutions of higher learning are also profession-creating bodies. Not only do the professional schools train the new members of the professions, but they are among the main sources of the standards of the professions, the new knowledge that advances the professions, the journals which are the main channel of professional communication. Often the intellectual leaders of the professions are professors. The fact that this important function is performed by the universities is usually not realized by the general public and sometimes not fully understood even by those who run the universities. One of the results is that teachers in the professional schools at the universities face a dilemma. They get the highest prestige by teaching at the university, but they would earn more money by going into practice. After much internal debate, some choose the prestige, some choose the money, and still others try to get a bit of both by dividing their time between the university and private practice.

A final educational institution to be given brief consideration is the teachers' convention. Only a small proportion of elementary and secondary-school teachers attend these conventions, but since the profession is so large, the number attending is quite significant. They hear papers by leaders of their profession, discuss educational issues at formal round tables, and exchange observations and ideas in the corridors. The convention is thus an educational institution for teachers, as comparable organizations are for other professionals and businessmen. The convention, of course, is the chief activity of a permanent organization, which carries

[77] To an increasing extent this is also true of literary work. An increasing number of poets and novelists are earning their primary living by teaching at a university. Their teaching, like that of the scientist, is relevant to their creative work. See Paul Engle, "A Writer Is a Teacher Is a Writer," *New York Times Book Review,* July 17, 1955, pp. 1 ff.

on activities all during the year, such as publishing a professional journal, studying professional problems, publicizing views on matters of professional interest.

At the college level most of the teachers' organizations and conventions are organized rather sharply by subject matter and have more of the character of scientific societies rather than of professional associations. A very large proportion of college teachers are members of their societies and attend the annual conventions; in fact, a college teacher loses status even in his home college unless he attends the convention for his special subject once in a while. The conventions of the college-level teachers are seldom concerned with purely educational issues and seldom even with professional issues. They emphasize the latest increments to knowledge and aid in spreading the use of techniques for acquiring new knowledge. Thus they become the highest level of educational institution. They teach the (college) teachers who teach the (secondary and elementary school) teachers as well as other leaders in the society. The knowledge they impart, however, is rather strictly limited to the level of new meanings, seldom to the level of values.

FOR ADDITIONAL READING

DURKHEIM, ÉMILE, *The Elementary Forms of the Religious Life,* translated from the French by J. W. Swain (Glencoe, Ill.: Free Press, 1947). A classic study of primitive religion. Presents a cogent theory of the nature of religious institutions.

HALSEY, A. H., JEAN FLOUD, and C. ARNOLD ANDERSON (eds.), *Education, Economy, and Society* (New York: Free Press of Glencoe, 1961). A series of independent analyses of the influences of stratification on various aspects of education.

JANOWITZ, MORRIS, *The Professional Soldier* (Glencoe, Ill.: Free Press, 1960). A systematic study of the mind and behavior of the military.

MERTON, R. K., A. P. GRAY, B. HOCKEY, and H. C. SELVIN (eds.), *Reader in Bureaucracy* (Glencoe, Ill.: Free Press, 1952). A collection of readings on bureaucracy.

WARNER, W. LLOYD, and J. O. LOW, *The Social System of the Modern Factory: The Strike: A Social Analysis* (New Haven: Yale University Press, 1947). A study of the development of a strike in a small New England city.

8 * Social Stratification: Castes and Classes

This chapter considers a part of social structure that is not so internally cohesive and specific as institutions. Castes and classes are too diffuse to be said to have functions as institutions do. They are not groups in the sense that the members are in frequent interaction with each other. Yet they also have common meanings and values which prescribe what behavior may be, should be, or must be. Their behavior prescriptions are always relevant to "status," a word of Latin origin meaning "standing." Thus we are concerned in this chapter with the behavior and characteristics of people relevant to how they "stand"—higher, lower, or at the same level—in relation to other people.[1]

A given society may or may not be divided into castes or classes—this depends on the specific historical circumstances through which a society has developed. But if a culture includes a caste division or a class division this implies that people are expected to act differently toward people of their own status than toward people of different status, and that people of a lower status must act differently toward people in a higher status than people in the higher status would act toward people in the lower status. The terms class and caste are used both to designate a number of people of similar status and a group of common meanings and values specifying the expected behavior of these people. It is the same kind of

[1] In using this definition of "status," we follow an old tradition in sociology. In 1936, the anthropologist Ralph Linton used the term in a broader meaning, which has become popular with some sociologists and anthropologists. Linton used the term to refer to position in any social structure, not solely in the stratification system; thus he spoke of the status of "father" or "foreman" for which we use the term "role," while Linton and his followers have another meaning for the word "role." The student should not become confused between Linton's and our use of the concept "status." See Ralph Linton, *The Study of Man* (New York: Appleton-Century, 1936).

double meaning that was noted for the concept of institution. The distinction is between "caste" and "a caste," "class" and "a class," where the first term of each pair refers to the set of behaviors prescribed by the meanings and values and the second term refers to the group of people for whom this behavior is prescribed.

Caste always involves a much sharper prescription of behavior and of the people for whom it is prescribed than does class. In ideal type terms, a caste is a group of persons whose membership in it has been determined by birth—that is, whose parents were known to be of that caste —and who are prohibited from marrying outside of the caste,[2] so that their offspring must also be members. The castes of a given society are usually ranked from higher to lower in status, but it is conceivable that two castes might in some societies occupy the same status position. A class is a somewhat less rigid grouping of people. One is born into a certain class but one may change one's class and one may marry outside of one's class, although usually one does not do so. By definition classes always occupy different positions on the status hierarchy since a class includes all persons of roughly the same status. Using Linton's distinction between *ascribed status* and *achieved status*[3]—the former being the position accorded to one by virtue of one's inherited social position, and the latter being the position accorded to one by virtue of one's own individual efforts—a caste is always ascribed while class is partly achieved and partly ascribed. That is, while one cannot, by any individual merit or achievement, change one's caste, one can—through one's own individual behavior —go up or down in class position even though one is born into a given class. Warner provides good summary definitions of caste and class:[4]

> Caste as here used describes a theoretical arrangement of the people of the given group in an order in which the privileges, duties, obligations, opportunities, etc., are unequally distributed between the groups which are considered to be higher and lower. There are social sanctions which tend to maintain this unequal distribution. Such a definition also describes class. A caste organization, however, can be further defined as one where marriage between two or more groups is not sanctioned and where there is no opportunity for members of the lower groups to rise into the upper groups or of the members of the upper to fall into the lower ones. In class, on the other hand,

[2] Marriage within the group is technically known as *endogamy*. The opposite—a customary requirement that marriage be outside the group—is technically known as *exogamy*. We consider here endogamy and exogamy only as applied to caste, but the terms may also be applied to other groups.

[3] Ralph Linton, *op. cit.*, Chapter 8, esp. p. 115.

[4] W. Lloyd Warner, "American Caste and Class," *American Journal of Sociology*, 42 (September, 1936), pp. 234–37; p. 234 quoted. Published by the University of Chicago Press.

there is a certain proportion of interclass marriage between lower and higher groups, and there are, in the very nature of the class organization, mechanisms established by which people move up and down the vertical extensions of the society.

A *Caste*

1 THE CASTE SYSTEM OF INDIA

The term caste was first used to describe a certain characteristic of the Hindu population of India. There are some writers, such as Oliver Cox,[5] who use the term caste to apply only to the social system of India and to that of no other society. If the distinguishing features of what is called caste in India are specified, however, it will be found that these social characteristics apply in certain other societies as well, although certainly not in a great number of other societies. Whichever point of view is adopted, it is of course necessary to get a clear idea of what is meant by caste in India. We shall describe here the major outlines of the caste system of India as it existed before 1920[6]—that is, before Gandhi led the increasingly successful movement to break down the caste system.

There are hundreds of castes in India. New ones occasionally formed and old ones occasionally disappeared even before the system itself began to break down. Each caste in India performs a given occupation and has a near monopoly over that occupation. New castes arise when new occupations are in demand or when old ones no longer have a function in the economic process. One is born into a certain caste and one cannot change one's caste. Thus a baker's son must himself become a baker and marry the daughter of a baker, and his children will be bakers. It is considered to be illegal, undesirable, and even unspeakable for anyone to attempt to change his caste.

Perhaps more important than the lines dividing the specific castes are lines dividing five major caste categories. All of the castes are in either the Brahman or priestly caste category, the Kshatrya or warrior caste category, the Vaisa or merchant caste category, the Sudra or peasant and worker caste category, and the Harijan,[7] or "untouchable" caste category. There is no mobility across these caste lines. When new occupations are

---

[5] *Caste, Class and Race* (New York: Doubleday, 1948).

[6] For descriptions of the caste system of India, see: John H. Hutton, *Caste in India: Its Nature, Function and Origins* (Cambridge: The University Press, 1946); Radhakamal Mukerjee *et al., Inter-Caste Tensions,* a survey under the auspices of UNESCO (India: University of Lucknow, 1951); G. S. Ghurye, *Caste, Class and Occupation* (Bombay: Popular Book Depot, 1961); Noel P. Gist, "Caste Differentials in South India," *American Sociological Review,* 19 (April, 1954), pp. 126–37.

[7] The word "Harijan" is not a traditional one. It was coined by Gandhi as a term favorable to the caste.

formed, they are formed within one of the caste groups so that an individual might change his specific occupation and his specific caste but never his caste category.

These caste categories have different prestige, in the order listed above, but this is not generally matched by wealth or power. The top caste group, the Brahmans, for example, which consisted originally only of priests, now includes a large number of persons whose occupations are professional, clerical, and scholarly. Some Brahmans are even beggars. Their only support comes from begging, even though they have very high status. They are holy beggars and must be treated with a great deal of deference. The Kshatrya castes consisted originally only of soldiers and government leaders, but now they have expanded into most of the governmental occupations. The Vaisa castes, including the merchants, include some of the wealthiest men of India. Much of their wealth is of relatively recent origin, developing within the past few centuries, because their caste monopoly over commerce and industry made them the only ones to have access to new wealth created by the Commercial and Industrial revolutions. The Sudra is by far the largest of the caste groups. It includes most of the people who work for other people: farm workers, employed craftsmen, industrial workers, and servants. Finally, at the bottom of the heap are the Untouchables, whose status is so low that they cannot even be approached by people of the higher castes. Their occupations are primarily those connected with scavenging. They are the garbage collectors, the street sweepers, the junk collectors. Many of them cannot find remunerative work, and either die off or live on a bare margin of existence by begging and scavenging.

The principle underlying the Hindu caste system is a religious one. One's status has been given one on the basis of behavior in one's previous life. One should accept one's lot in life, because if one is good and accepting, whatever the disagreeable characteristics of one's occupation or others' behavior toward one's caste may be, one has a good chance of rising to a higher caste in the next life. It is also proper to segregate and scorn an Untouchable, as this gives him an opportunity to rise in status in the next life, as well as to avoid contamination oneself. This religious theory may be a rationalization having arisen to explain caste, after caste itself had developed for other historical reasons. A good number of Hindus practicing caste do not believe this religious theory. It is, however, the traditional explanation of the caste system, which has existed as far back in Hindu history as historians can trace. And it gives religious sanction to caste behavior, so that religious people who follow caste rules unpleasant or costly to themselves believe they are getting religious benefits therefrom. That the Hindu religious theory should not be taken too seriously as an explanation of the popular support of caste is demonstrated by the fact that when Indians have become Christians, and presumably have abandoned Hindu religious beliefs, most of them have retained caste practices.[8]

Some of the characteristics of the Hindu caste system affecting personal behavior have already been suggested. One is the deference pattern. The lower castes must show deference to the higher ones, and the higher castes must accept deference but not reciprocate. There is an obligation to give money and food to a begging Brahman. Second is the behavior associated with occupation. In India, as in any Western country, one's occupation determines a good part of one's daily life. It specifies what one has to learn, what hours one keeps, with whom one tends to associate, and even what "face" one presents to the world. Occupation also determines the income one has to provide one's self with a home, food, clothing, and recreation. Historically the Kshatryas were the wealthiest caste group, but in recent years some of the Vaisa have outstripped many of them. Since one cannot change one's occupation, one can grow significantly wealthier only when new economic opportunities are presented to one's whole caste, such as through a sharp increase in the demand for the occupation's product or service.

A third behavioral element in caste is the restriction on personal association. While people in all societies have a certain limitation on whom they associate with, resulting from common interests and economic contacts among persons within given occupations, the caste system sets it as a formal requirement that one have sociable relations only with members of one's own caste category. The requirement has different degrees of rigidity as it affects different kinds of personal association. For purposes of sex relations or of seeking a potential mate one is strictly limited to one's own caste and cannot even have a tentative relationship with a person outside one's caste.

Various symbolic acts must be performed in the relations between members of two different castes (depending on which castes are involved). Mukerjee describes these as "a variety of distance-creating gestures and expressions which are invested with socially derived meanings and values for the participants."[9] These include the use of distinctive titles and epithets in addressing people or referring to them, the mode of greeting (for example, touching feet as distinguished from saying "prosperity to you"), the offer of cooked or uncooked food, the offer of water or tobacco from a common receptacle, limits on touching household pots and utensils, the manner of seating (for example, not sitting, sitting on floor, sitting at head or at foot of cot), restriction on use of certain articles of clothing and adornment, and avoidance on certain occasions.

[8] *New York Times*, February 4, 1943, p. 10. According to the author of this report, Herbert L. Matthews, the Protestant churches have attempted to combat the caste system, while the Catholic Church considers it to be a social and not a religious matter.

[9] *Op. cit.*, pp. 6–7.

There is a set of explicit laws to enforce conformity to the caste system. The laws are specified in holy books that have existed for thousands of years. They prescribe in great detail the exact punishments which must follow for violation of each of the caste rules, and differentiate punishments according to the degree of violation involved. For example, a mild punishment is prescribed for sex relations between a Brahman man or woman and a Kshatrya man or woman. When the intercaste sex relation is between a Brahman and a Vaisa the punishment is somewhat stronger, and considerably graver still is an intercaste relation between a Brahman and a Sudra. In the case of cross-caste sexual relations with an Untouchable, the penalty is usually death. For some accidental violations of the caste taboos, the violator is expected to purify himself by a mild ritual which serves in lieu of punishment.

People who are not members of this society frequently ask why Hindus conform to the caste system, why the Harijans are willing to be scorned and deprecated, why people do not seek economic advancement by changing their occupation, why they do not marry for love if lovers are in different castes, and so forth. The most important answer, of course, is that caste is the traditional and expected system. Seldom does any person ever think of wishing to change the system or even his own position in it. Caste is as "natural" as eating and sleeping in the Hindu's thoughts. Mukerjee gives other reasons for acceptance of lower caste status:[10]

> There are certain social mechanisms that contribute to make the rigid and cramped life of the lower castes tolerable. (a) There is complete autonomy within the caste or occupation. The caste panchayat [religious lawyers and judges] not only maintains discipline and morale within the boundaries of the caste or sub-caste and punishes infringement of caste regulations in respect of marriage, food and incidents and customs of caste, but also offers hope and ambition for the individual. Panchayats show a great keenness in maintaining their clientele and . . . show an equal readiness to strike . . . when their grievances cannot obtain redress otherwise. [Often one does better economically in one's own caste than in a higher caste.] (b) The occupation hardly comprehends the entire values and interests in life of the caste people. Each caste has its own code of etiquette and social manners, worship and observances. Village festivals, panchayat meetings and caste codes of etiquette and social manners constantly remind men of the inferior castes of values and interests which over-reach their role or vocation as offering the road to status. Certain duties . . . demand participation in civic life and elicit the enthusiasm of all caste men, however low in the social scale. Thus in some measure even the water-tight caste compartments leave the door open for par-

[10] *Op. cit.,* pp. 12–13.

ticipation in the more comprehensive goals and interests of the society. (c) Indian society accepts the doctrine of "karma" according to which man reaps the cumulative fruit of his good and evil deeds through a long succession of births and rebirths. He thus becomes in some measure reconciled to his caste, occupation or status in life and even finds joy and reward in his peculiar role in the social regime.

Finally, it should be recognized that a caste monopoly of a given occupation often gives a basic economic security which people are loath to give up in a poor country. Even the Harijans have a monopoly over scavenging jobs; hence many of them are assured of a very low, but steady, income.

2   VIOLATIONS OF CASTE PRINCIPLES

The question can be raised as to how much resistance there was to the caste system even before it began to break down in the twentieth century. There were probably always a certain small proportion of persons who failed to conform and whose deviations often went undetected. Because this was in the past and therefore cannot be checked, and because earlier scholars made contradictory statements regarding the amount of deviation, it is difficult to know what actually did occur. But from our general knowledge of social behavior we know that much occurs that is secret or, even if known, unacknowledged.

It is even likely that there was a certain amount of "passing" under the old Hindu caste system, although it probably was a very minimal amount. By "passing" is meant the secret moving of a person from one caste to another. India is a large country and one can disappear one day, move into another area, and identify oneself as a member of another caste. To do this one has to be sociologically "dead" and "reborn." One can never retain one's old identity and move into another caste. In order to pass, one has to abandon all one's friends, one's family, and one's former way of life, and if one should ever be identified by former acquaintances who would be willing to reveal one's original caste the penalties are rather severe. Nevertheless, some scholars report that a certain amount of passing did occur under the old Hindu caste system, mostly in the cities. The extent of passing cannot be known, not only because of the usual defects in historical records, but also because passing is by its very nature a secret.

In addition to individual passing there have always been ways in which a whole caste might improve its status. Taking on a new occupation often meant improvement in caste status. When there was an increasing demand for the caste's economic product, the caste was regarded as of higher value. Adoption of high-caste religious customs could raise the status of a caste—for example, refusing to eat pork or other animal foods, prohibiting widow remarriage, secluding women, using Brahmans instead of caste priests. Castes have always been rising and falling in status. In fact, there has always been a good deal of competition among castes for status, even though individuals do not compete across caste lines as individuals.

There was a curious kind of violation of the caste system in certain sections of India. This was not a violation in the common sense of the term, but a ritualistic deviation as occurs on some holidays everywhere. The ritualized caste violations—called *sakti-puja*—occurred on a holiday that was not regular, but could be called whenever enough people (especially Brahmans) felt like having it. On the announced day all the caste rules were deliberately violated; in fact, people went to the opposite extremes of behavior from that required under the caste rules. It was the upper-caste people who would serve and defer to the lower-caste people. There was deliberate touching of the Untouchables and the passing of food containers for use among members of all castes. Sometimes the holiday would include a sex orgy, with sex partners always being members of different caste groups. On this day people seemed to get all the frustrations created by caste out of their systems, and when a new day dawned they went back to behaviors demanded by a most rigid and unyielding caste system. This ceremonial means of reducing the interpersonal tensions created by the inequalities of caste seems to occur where the caste system is not accompanied by intercaste hatred.

3   THE GENERAL CHARACTERISTICS OF CASTE SYSTEMS

There is no doubt that some of the above-mentioned features of the Hindu caste system are peculiar to the social structure of India. The religious explanation, for example, is strictly part of the Hindu religion and its doctrine of reincarnation. The particular occupational hierarchy is also fairly unique to the Hindu caste system. But if we select our certain basic elements, we will find that the caste system has occurred in other societies in different parts of the world. Individual deviations occasionally occur from the demands of caste systems everywhere, depending on the local strength of the caste system, the power or prestige of the deviator, the presence of institutions that oppose a certain demand of the caste system,[11] and so on.

The central demands of the caste system are: no individual social mobility ("passing" being an unrecognized exception), endogamy or marriage only within the caste, deference and associational patterns indicating a certain hierarchy of prestige of the different castes. All these features, for example, existed in western Europe during the Middle Ages, where

[11] For example, the Catholic Church has always insisted on recognition of marriages performed with the proper sacrament, even when the parties were of different castes.

An interesting ritual violation of the caste mores occurs in the Greek village of Monoclissia. Once a year in this town, men and women exchange social roles. The men do the household work and stay at home all day. The women circulate on the streets, drink and smoke in the cafes, play cards and backgammon, exchange opinions on all subjects, and end up the evening with a big spree at the tavern. The next day, and for the rest of the year, they revert to their usual social roles. The women seem to appreciate the day, and the men express their relief when the day is over. The traditional sex division of labor has been ritually broken for one day, but this seems to strengthen it for the rest of the year.

New York Times, January 23, 1962, p. 55.

the castes were the nobility, yeomen and burghers, and serfs.[12] All of these features prevailed in the relations between Negroes and whites in the southern states of the United States during the period between 1820 and 1940. The same features characterize the relations between the Eta and other Japanese in Japan, even at the present time, although discriminating laws were abolished in 1871.[13]

A feature which the caste systems of Japan and medieval Europe had in common is that their castes were of the same race, whereas the castes of the United States, of South Africa, and possibly even of India in ancient times[14] (although not today), are of different races. This indicates that caste is not necessarily based on race differences, although it may be that the presence of two or more races in a society can make more likely the formation of a caste system under certain circumstances.

4   THE CASTE SYSTEM OF THE UNITED STATES:
NEGRO-WHITE RELATIONS

We shall extend our analysis of caste by describing Negro-white relations in the United States.[15] This caste system of the United States is breaking down to a considerable extent today, as is the caste system of India. Thus for purposes of noting its similarities to the caste system of India we must

[12] Certain features of the medieval caste system have lingered on in Western culture, especially in the military services. See John J. Leuny, *Caste System in the American Army* (New York: Greenberg, 1949).

[13] Hugh H. Smythe, "The Eta: A Marginal Japanese Caste," *American Journal of Sociology,* 58 (September, 1952), pp. 194–96. There are about 3 million Eta today. Although they have always had a low social status, the Eta were wealthy in the fifteenth and sixteenth centuries because of the heavy demand for leather, on the preparation of which they have a monopoly.

[14] The best historical evidence is that the light-skinned Aryans had caste even before they had any contact with the darker-skinned Dravidians in India.

[15] The fullest description is contained in Gunnar Myrdal, with the assistance of Richard Sterner and Arnold Rose, *An American Dilemma* (New York: Harper, 1944).

describe the situation that existed around the year 1900. Nevertheless, we shall use the present tense, since we are describing the caste pattern or "ideal," even if it is not followed in all localities or by all people today. The system in its full form prevailed only in the southern states, athough many of the features carried over into the northern states.

The caste system of the southern states has its keystone in endogamy, that is, the most rigorously enforced control in relations between whites and Negroes is the prohibition against interracial sex relations. This has a peculiar form. The prohibition is directed solely against sex relations between white women and Negro men, not between white men and Negro women (provided there is no formal marriage), since the offspring of sex relations between white men and Negro women are always considered to be Negroes and since it is the general custom for mothers rather than fathers to assume primary responsibility for the care of children. Thus, the caste principle of endogamy is still preserved in public eyes even when there are—as there used to be in the South—extensive sex relations between white men and Negro women.

The principle of no mobility between the castes is rigorously enforced in all cases. Most Negroes, of course, cannot cross the caste line because of their skin color and other physical features, but because of the extensive sex relations between white men and Negro women during the 300-year period in which Negroes and whites have been living together in America, the so-called Negro population includes a large amount of white ancestry. During the 1920's a study by Melville Herskovits[16] indicated that almost three-fourths of all American Negroes had some white ancestry. Today there is probably hardly an American Negro left who does not have some white ancestry. For most American Negroes, white ancestry is such a small proportion of their total ancestry that their physical appearance is more Negroid than Caucasoid. But for some, white ancestry forms a predominant element in their heredity. Such Negroes are really more Caucasoid than Negroid, and their appearance shows it; nevertheless, they are identified as Negroes in the United States, because anyone who has *any* known Negro ancestry is defined as a Negro. Many of these Negroes can "pass" as white people where they are not known.

Especially in the large cities, where everyone does not know everyone else, and especially in the North, where penalties for passing are not severe, some Negroes engage in what is called "temporary passing," that is, they pretend to be whites part of the day in order to take and hold a certain job or to get into certain places where Negroes are barred, but they retain their family and friendship ties in the Negro world. Permanent passing, which occurs much less frequently now than it used to, requires

[16] Melville J. Herskovits, *The Anthropometry of the American Negro* (New York: Columbia University Press, 1930).

that the passer give up his family, his friends, his identity, references to his background, and sometimes even his name. He changes his location and lives an entirely new life with new people. Sociologically speaking, the passer is a new person. If he is ever identified with his old self, he must go back to his former caste, often being punished as well. Thus, no matter how extensive passing may be—and it was done by many thousands of "Negroes" every year in the United States before 1910—it involves no violation of the caste principle of no mobility from one caste to another.

Occupations were also caste-defined in the South until about the year 1940. Negroes were rigorously prohibited from practicing most occupations, except where their clients were other Negroes. They were limited to the service, agricultural, and unskilled manual occupations, with exceptions being made in other occupations where they were serving the Negro community only. Many of the service and manual occupations were strictly Negro; that is, whites could not enter them without "losing caste." Agriculture, on the other hand, remained equally open to both whites and Negroes. Exceptions to the caste limitation on occupations were made here and there in the South, but they always involved some unusual circumstances so that the caste separation of occupations remained as a principle.

In the American South, until World War II, the caste system has meant the denial of most political and legal rights to Negroes. Few Negroes were allowed to vote, and none were allowed to run for political office. The courts and police discriminated against Negroes in the following ways: (1) when whites committed crimes against Negroes, they were seldom arrested and practically never convicted; (2) when Negroes committed crimes against whites, they were often treated brutally by the police and given harsh punishments by the courts; (3) when Negroes committed crimes against other Negroes, they were often ignored by the police and treated leniently by the courts; (4) Negroes, whether alleged to be criminals or not, were subjected to extralegal violence by whites, including the police, without the police taking action to stop it; (5) certain state and local laws were designed to discriminate against Negroes, and although these were later declared unconstitutional in the federal courts, they were in operation for many years; (6) restrictive and repressive laws were generally much more rigorously enforced against Negroes than against whites.

The castes have a superordinate-subordinate relation to each other. While some Negroes have higher income, higher educational achievement, higher recognition for their achievement or for their personal qualities than do some whites, nevertheless there is a sense in which all Negroes are regarded as being inferior to all whites. This status difference is manifested in certain behavior patterns required in the relations between members of the two castes. Literally hundreds of rules govern these behavior differences, and while there is some variation in them for different parts of the South, they form a sufficiently consistent pattern for anyone to observe their general features.

The Negro is always expected to act as a subordinate toward a white person in public situations in the South, and a white person is always expected to act as a superior to a Negro. This requires, for example, that Negroes speak in a deferential tone to whites, that they frequently use "sir" when talking to a white man or "ma'am" when talking to a white woman, that they address their white interlocutors as Mr., Mrs., or Miss, or by some prestigious title, that they guard themselves against insulting a white person, or using angry tones, that their physical behavior when talking to white persons includes a humble demeanor, formerly taking the pattern of the Negro shifting his feet and keeping his eyes on the ground. Formerly, a Negro was always expected to stand up when talking to a white person. On the other side, the white person could take an easy posture, and either stand or sit, according to his convenience. He would never address the Negro by his last name with the title Mr., Mrs., or Miss, but always by his first name or by such semi-derogatory terms as "auntie," "boy," "darky," or the most derogatory of all, "nigger."[17] The white person's tone of voice in addressing Negroes could range from ordinary, everyday casual to supercilious or derogatory, depending upon his state of mind at the moment and on his degree of antagonism toward Negroes.

The caste rules require as much separation as possible between Negroes and whites as well as superordinate-subordinate relationships. Separation not only means an almost complete absence of sociable relations but also the adoption of almost completely separate facilities for Negroes and whites, including separate schools, separate libraries, in some cases separate public parks, separate toilets, separate drinking fountains, separate entrances to the railroad station, separate trains, separate sections on streetcars and buses, and so on. The rules requiring separation govern conversation as well. Conversation is expected to be limited to the casual exchange of pleasantries and whatever is needed to carry on the necessary business of the community. In general, Negroes are not expected to start a conversation unless there is some definite economic need for it. Certain topics of conversation are supposed to be taboo, although there is no doubt that the taboo has often been violated under circumstances of privacy. Whites and Negroes are expected not to gossip about other white people. Whites and Negroes are not supposed to discuss the important aspects of community life, such as politics, or the state of business in general, or the social prestige hierarchy in the communty, and so on.

[17] Occasionally, as a device for showing personal respect without violating the caste rule, whites would address Negroes as "professor" or "doctor."

We have presented thus far only the caste rules governing the conversational area of behavior. There are hundreds of other caste rules governing nearly every other area of behavior in which whites and Negroes come in contact with each other.[18] For example, there are rules governing the behavior of Negroes using streetcars and other public conveyances, which provide that Negroes allow whites to enter the cars first if there is a common entrance and that they move to the rear of the car. There are similar caste rules governing the behavior of Negroes in the courts, in railroad stations, and other public places. Despite the variations that occur between different sections of the South there seem to be two underlying rules governing caste behavior. These are: (1) That Negroes avoid contact as much as possible and set up behavioral barriers to intimacy when they have contact. (2) That when contact is necessary, the Negroes manifest subordination, if only symbolically, and whites manifest superordination.

B   Changes in Caste

Caste is so complex and rigid a part of social structure that it gives the impression of unchangeability. Where caste systems have existed, the whole culture is intimately tied up with it so that there is a functional resistance of the whole society to change in caste. When caste is in full strength, its rules are in the mores (whereas the rules governing class are much weaker), so that it is very difficult to begin to change caste deliberately.[19] Nevertheless, caste does change like any other aspect of society or culture. Frequently the changes are minor modifications within the framework of the caste system as, for example, when a new occupation rises to meet new needs, one caste or the other expands to take it over. Other changes in the caste system strike at the heart of the structure itself and sometimes cause its complete destruction, or at least drastic modification. Since the beginning of the twentieth century the caste systems of both India and the United States have declined sharply,[20] although caste systems prevailing in other parts of the world—especially South Africa, Japan, Guatemala[21]— have not changed materially or have become stronger.

[18] For a fuller description of the caste rules, see Charles S. Johnson, *Patterns of Negro Segregation* (New York: Harper, 1943); and Bertram W. Doyle, *Etiquette of Race Relations in the South* (Chicago: University of Chicago Press, 1937).

[19] See Chapter 3, Section A.

[20] Another caste system that is breaking down is that of Ceylon. For a description of this, see Bryce Ryan, *Caste in Modern Ceylon: The Sinhalese System in Transition* (New Brunswick: Rutgers University Press, 1953).

[21] For a description of the caste system of Guatemala, see Melvin M. Tumin, *Caste in a Peasant Society* (Princeton, N.J.: Princeton University Press, 1952).

1   THE SOURCES OF CHANGE IN CASTE

The sources of change in caste seem to be general social changes in other aspects of the culture. Caste is so rigid a system and is generally so intimately tied up with other aspects of culture that when other aspects of culture change significantly, the caste system is materially damaged. Industrialization, with its concomitant geographic mobility and shift in power distribution, seems to have been an important cause of the recent changes of caste systems of India and the United States. Industrialism, especially under the free-enterprise system of economic organization, affects the caste system through the relatively rapid movement of people to take new jobs (people thereby lose their fixed relationship to each other and have to establish new relationships to strangers) and through an emphasis upon competition for jobs (in competition, individual abilities tend to become more important than traditional caste characteristics).

Certain ideological factors also enter into the breakdown of the caste system. In the United States, for example, there was a sharp increase in the rate of breakdown of the caste system during World War II when there was a great revival of attention to the ideals of equality and liberty in American democracy as reasons for fighting the war. For many people it became a matter of conscience to try to eliminate some aspects of the caste system, no matter what their personal prejudices had previously been. In India, perhaps the strongest single force working for the destruction of the caste system has been the Gandhi religious philosophy which emphasizes equalitarianism and brotherliness,[22] although the impersonal forces of urbanization and modernization have been of paramount importance in India as well as in the United States. Gandhi was able to exercise great influence on the Indian population by virtue of his political and religious leadership. The rational element in his appeal was made in terms of the desire of most Indians to create a strong independent nation. He employed the propaganda of the deed, as well as of the word, by taking every possible occasion to demonstrate in his own behavior that rules—both those of the British and those of caste—could be safely violated. He always insisted, for example, upon having Untouchables in his immediate entourage.

The struggle against external enemies—the British and, to a lesser extent, the Moslems—also tended to unite the various categories of Hindus. The breakdown of the caste system was thus associated in India with a national movement, and when the peaceful revolution took place by means of which India became independent of Great Britain, it was natural

[22] B. R. Ambedkar, *What Congress and Gandhi Have Done to the Untouchables,* second ed. (Bombay: Thacker, 1946).

for the caste system to be legally abolished. The new constitution of India provides for the abolition of all caste rules and the equality of all Indian people, although it permits a temporary period of adjustment before certain rules are abolished. For example, during the first ten years after the adoption of the constitution, the Untouchables and the "backward tribes" are to be represented in India's parliament and state legislative assemblies by reserved seats in proportion to their relative numbers and in government services by a similar precentage of posts. These privileges were accorded to permit the uneducated members of the lowest caste to learn how to exercise their prerogatives as citizens, but are to be abolished in ten years after the adoption of the constitution. In 1955 the Indian parliament passed an enabling law making discrimination against Untouchables a punishable offense.[23]

The recent changes within the social structure of India have been profound, but this does not mean that the caste system has completely disappeared.[24] Many Indians still retain caste habits out of inertia, through sheer force of habit. Others have an emotional attachment to the age-old customs which were deeply imbedded in India's religion and general culture. Many persons of the higher castes who have abandoned caste practices in their behavior toward the lower castes still would not think of taking on some of the occupations which the lower castes traditionally performed, even when they are unemployed and impoverished. Some Untouchables have become well educated and have adapted themselves into the economic and political life of a nation which has democratic and equalitarian ideals. But a great number of others continue on with subordinate caste behaviors, again through inertia and passive acceptance of a lot which they have inherited.

A report presented to the Indian parliament by L. M. Shrikant, Commissioner for Scheduled Castes and Scheduled Tribes, presented the situation in 1952, four years after the adoption of the independent Indian constitution. In extensive tours of India, Mr. Shrikant reported that he had found no instances of Untouchables being forbidden public schools or roads, as once was almost universally the case, and they are now usually permitted to enter formerly forbidden Hindu temples. Generally there is little discrimination in giving them access to shops, public restaurants, places of entertainment, wells, tanks, and bathing ghats. However, the Untouchables isolate themselves to a certain extent, and have generally not left their so-called dirty jobs, such as tanning and skinning of hides, manufacture of leather goods, sweeping streets, scavenging, etc. Their lack of training for better jobs, as well as the extensive unemploy-

[23] *New York Times*, April 29, 1955, p. 3.
[24] Noel P. Gist, "Caste Differentials in South India," *American Sociological Review*, 19 (April, 1954), pp. 126–37.

ment in India, has helped ignorance and orthodoxy to maintain this feature of the caste system. The law abolishes castes, and the principles underlying the Indian caste system seem to have been broken, but there is little doubt that certain aspects of the caste system will remain in India for decades as a matter of personal habit.

2   CHANGES IN THE AMERICAN CASTE SYSTEM

Changes in the American caste system of the southern states were slow from 1900 to 1940, but since 1940 they have been at least as spectacular as those in the Hindu caste system. The improvement in the educational status of Negroes—involving both a larger proportion of Negroes reaching the level of literacy and an increasing number of Negroes having achieved a high degree of education—was the first factor to dent the caste system. The fact that Negroes could read put them in contact with each other throughout the country by means of newspapers and letters, so that they could protest collectively. The rise of an educated class among Negroes provided a leadership for the protest and a group that was obviously not inferior according to the demands of the caste system. Although there had been Negro newspapers throughout the nineteenth century, they had reached only a small group of intelligentsia and their circulation was so limited that they usually had short lives. In 1905, however, the first of a number of modern Negro newspapers was started —*The Chicago Defender*—which directed themselves toward the masses of Negroes and which built their circulation partly by voicing an opposition to the caste system. A further step in the attack on the caste system occurred when Negro leaders began organizations to oppose caste through publicity, legal cases, and pressure activities of various sorts. The most important of these organizations has been the National Association for the Advancement of Colored People (NAACP), founded in 1909.

World War I—by stopping immigration of European workers to the United States and by creating new demands for labor in the northern industrial cities—inspired an extensive migration of Negroes to the North where the caste system was considerably weaker. Because their vote was unrestricted in the northern cities, Negroes gradually became a political force that bartered votes for support in opposition to the caste system. When, during the 1930's, Negroes abandoned their century-old loyalty to the Republican Party and became a flexible, independent group in the body politic, they were a much-sought-after group at elections. Candidates getting their support had to put themselves on record in support of "civil rights," which became the popular legal term for the abolition of the caste system.

The 1920's saw numerous distinctive achievements by Negroes in art, literature, science, and athletics. The interest and enthusiasm which these achievements stimulated among whites were further blows to the caste system. The 1920's also saw the first successful mass educational campaign to abolish lynching. This was accomplished by a moral appeal on the part of southern liberals, especially women, and publicity on the part of the NAACP to get a federal law against lynching. While the moral appeal of the white Southerners did not eliminate violence from the South and the anti-lynching law has never been passed, the educational effects of both of these activities reduced the lynching rate from several hundred in the 1890's to one or two a year in the post-World War II period.

The 1930's saw a great expansion of government services to citizens generally, and most of these services were distributed on the basis of need without discrimination on the basis of race. Since Negroes had relatively great need, because of their caste restriction to marginal occupations and because their jobs often were taken over by whites during times of business depression, they benefited in larger proportion than did whites from the extension of government services. Moreover, the federal government under President Franklin D. Roosevelt and his successors abandoned its passive acceptance of the caste system and sought generally to follow the constitutional provisions for equality in government services. The 1930's, however, were not a period of consistent advance for Negroes because the competition for scarce jobs put them to a competitive disadvantage, and many of the service and unskilled jobs which they formerly held almost unchallenged were now sought by whites, who sometimes took over entire occupations. In several northern cities more than half of the able-bodied Negro males were unable to secure employment during the 1930's, and in the South some of the jobs that Negro males were able to secure paid less than a minimum necessary to maintain life, and they were often forced to work on them rather than allowed to accept government relief.

The 1940's saw a very rapid change in the caste system in the United States. The great shortage of manpower for war production encouraged employers to try Negroes on various jobs from which they had hitherto been excluded. The political and moral pressure of Negro organizations obliged President Roosevelt to set up a Fair Employment Practices Commission with authority to investigate and stop cases of discrimination in employment where the employers had war contracts with the federal government. By 1945 there was probably not a single occupation left in the United States which did not have at least a few Negroes employed at it. As we have already noted, there was also an ideological factor in the change in the caste system during the 1940's. Because the war brought home to many Americans the character of racism in Germany and made them aware of other people's reactions against American racism, many

Americans began to think of the relation between their democratic heritage and race relations in the United States. This awareness, of course, was most characteristic of the more educated and internationally minded people, but it reached down into all educational levels of the population. The first major effect was to reduce sharply certain discriminatory practices, especially in the applications of laws. Beginning in 1944 the United States Supreme Court started a series of major case decisions which stopped the use of the law to restrict Negroes from voting and from having full rights. In 1948 the Supreme Court went so far as to refuse the use of courts of law to enforce residential segregation, although that could always be maintained on a personal basis, of course. As a minority of Negroes began to vote in the South and to have some legal protection in courts of law, they had a slight but significant rise in status[25] which changed the interpersonal relationships across caste lines in an equalitarian direction.

The shift in American ideology also had a direct effect on the behavior of some white people in that they became more interested in Negroes and made efforts to get acquainted with Negroes on an equalitarian basis. For example, when the Supreme Court in 1950 insisted that several southern state universities open their doors to Negro students where the state-supported segregated Negro colleges did not provide certain courses for them, quite a number of white students welcomed the Negro students to their campuses, and there were no unpleasant incidents at any of the universities where the Negroes started school. Negro members were also welcomed into certain professional associations from which they had hitherto been barred.

Outside of the universities and some professional associations, however, the southern caste barrier against social contact has remained at almost full strength. In the North, many voluntary associations have eliminated caste restrictions for membership, but in the more personal spheres of life a great deal of caste separation remains. In so far as the Supreme Court's decision of May 1954—ordering the abolition of segregation in the public schools—is followed, there will be a significant breakdown in caste segregation in social relations. But thus far it is largely in the occupational, political, and legal spheres that one perceives a breakdown of the caste system in the United States. The changes have been increasing in rapidity with the passage of each year. While new developments—such as an international or economic crisis—could reverse the trend, if the present trend continues at the pace at which it has been moving since 1945, the caste system will have been practically eliminated in the United

[25] B. A. Jones, "New Legal Requirements of Race Relations in the South," *Phylon,* 13 (2nd quarter, 1952), pp. 97–106.

States within a few decades. During this period sociologists will have many unusual opportunities for observation and experimentation on rapid social change in a basic social structure.

C *Class*[26]

1 CHARACTERISTICS ASSOCIATED WITH CLASS

Class systems are much more common than caste systems throughout the world. In fact, only a few of the smaller and simpler societies do not have a class system. Class systems vary a good deal around the world, depending upon the different factors conferring status which each society happens to emphasize. While in many societies, including our own, the *possession* of wealth is an important factor in giving status to a person, in a society such as that of the Kwakiutl Indians, on the west coast of Canada, the *distribution* of one's worldly possessions to other people—so that one is constantly poor while he is accumulating wealth—is a major factor in determining one's status. We shall see that there are many "factors" contributing to class in this sense, but the essential character of class is a feeling of social distance,[27] without the rigidity that caste involves. MacIver has phrased this succinctly:

> Wherever social intercourse is limited by considerations of status, by distinctions between "higher" and "lower," there the class principle is at work. We shall then mean by a social class any portion of a community which is marked off from the rest, not by limitations arising out of language, locality, function, or specialization, but primarily by a sense of social distance. Such a subjective character involves also as a rule objective differences, income levels, occupational distinctions and so forth, within the society. But these differences, apart from a recognized order of superiority and of inferiority, would not establish cohesive groups. It is the sense of status, sustained by

[26] For surveys of the literature on class, see Harold W. Pfautz, "The Current Literature on Social Stratification: Critique and Bibliography," *American Journal of Sociology*, 58 (January, 1953), pp. 391–418; D. G. MacRae, "Social Stratification: A Trend Report and Bibliography," *Current Sociology*, 2 (No. 1, 1953–54). Leading textbooks in the field include: Reinhard Bendix and S. M. Lipset (eds.), *Class, Status, and Power* (Glencoe, Ill.: Free Press, 1953); John F. Cuber and William F. Kenkel, *Social Stratification in the United States* (New York: Harcourt, 1957); Joseph A. Kahl, *The American Class Structure* (New York: Rinehart, 1957); Kurt B. Mayer, *Class and Society* (New York: Random House, 1955); Egon E. Bergel, *Social Stratification* (New York: McGraw-Hill, 1962); Leonard Reissman, *Class in American Society* (Glencoe, Ill.: Free Press, 1959).

[27] While Gabriel Tarde and Georg Simmel first used the concept of "social distance," the term was developed mainly by Robert E. Park and first used in a measuring scale by Emory S. Bogardus. (Personal communication from E. S. Bogardus, February 16, 1960).

economic, political, or ecclesiastical power and by the distinctive modes of life and cultural expressions corresponding to them, which draws class apart from class, gives cohesion to each, and stratifies a whole society.[28]

A variable which differentiates class systems in different societies is the degree of sharpness between classes. In some societies one can properly speak only of an unbroken status hierarchy with no distinct class divisions; in other societies one can find fairly sharp divisions between the classes, so that it is perfectly clear whether a person belongs to one class rather than another. As we shall later attempt to show, American society is somewhere in between the two extremes. Many European countries have a much sharper class distinction than that which occurs within the United States, probably as a result of a carry-over from the medieval caste system dividing nobility from commoners. Norway, which never had much of a nobility, seems to have the least sharp class lines among European nations, and the Scandinavians generally in recent years have made more effort than any other group of people to reduce class differences. Because of the many different forms which class takes in different societies, we shall restrict our discussion to the class system of the United States after a few introductory remarks.

Certain concepts have proved to be valuable in the analysis of class. One that we have already used a good deal is that of *class differences*, by which is meant simply differences in status among people on the basis of their degree of possession of certain valued traits, such as wealth, prominent family background, education, etc. Whereas class differences are based on degrees of possession of the sources of status, *class correlates* are the effects of status, on life and behavior, even though differences and correlates cannot be distinguished in all circumstances. Status, or at least one of the sources of status, is an important factor in determining where one lives within a community; the quality of one's house and other possessions; the selection of newspapers and magazines one reads and of radio programs one hears;[29] the way one treats his children;[30] the number and kind of diseases one gets and the quality of treatment one re-

[28] Robert M. MacIver, *Society: A Textbook of Sociology* (New York: Farrar and Rinehart, 1937), pp. 78–79. Permission granted by Rinehart and Company, Inc., copyright holders.

[29] W. Lloyd Warner, *The Status System of a Modern Community* (New Haven: Yale University Press, 1942), Vol. II of the Yankee City Series.

[30] Eleanor E. Maccoby and Patricia K. Gibbs, "Social Class Differences in Child Rearing," *American Psychologist,* 8 (August, 1953), p. 395. The study involved standardized interviews with 379 mothers of kindergarten children. "In contrast with some previously published research, we find that the upper-middle class mothers are consistently more permissive, less punitive, and less demanding than upper-lower class mothers."

ceives to combat them;[31] the length of one's life;[32] the political party one votes for.[33] The treatment one is accorded by storekeepers, classmates, teachers, public officials, and so on—even the sex behavior patterns one follows[34] and the ease or difficulty of childbirth[35] are related to class. These are among the many characteristic correlates of class in the United States[36] and other Western countries. As Ralph Turner and Louis Kriesberg[37] point out, there are two different kinds of explanation for these behavioral differences associated with class differences. One is that the sources of status create different objective opportunities—for example, if one is wealthy he can afford better medical care than if he is poor. The other explanation is in terms of the subcultural differences associated with the different classes as social groups—for example, the upper classes have different traditional values concerning the amount of permissiveness to be used in rearing children than the lower classes do. Both of these types of explanations—situational and subcultural—undoubtedly operate in the many factual behavioral differences between the classes, but sociologists have often disagreed as to which of the two types is more important in Western society.

Class correlates are not only to be thought of as static, but also as reflecting the dynamic pattern of change in a society. Many cultural traits are adopted first by the upper class and then—with a speed depending on the flexibility of the social structure—filter down through the lower classes. This is true of clothing styles, food fads, automobile designs, and

[31] Research Council for Economic Security unpublished study of the nonindustrial illness experiences of 400,000 working Americans; A. B. Hollingshead and F. C. Redlich, *Social Class and Mental Illness* (New York: Wiley, 1958).

[32] Albert J. Mayer and Philip M. Hauser, "Class Differentials in Expectation of Life at Birth," *Revue de l'institut international de statistiques* (Nos. 3–4, 1950), pp. 197–200.

[33] H. D. Anderson and P. E. Davidson, *Ballots and the Democratic Class Struggle* (Stanford: Stanford University Press, 1943); P. F. Lazarsfeld, B. Berelson, and H. Gaudet, *The People's Choice* (New York: Duell, Sloan, & Pearce, 1944); S. M. Lipset, P. F. Lazarsfeld, A. H. Barton, and J. Linz, "The Psychology of Voting: An Analysis of Political Behavior," in Gardner Lindzey (ed.), *Handbook of Social Psychology* (Cambridge, Mass.: Addison-Wesley, 1954), pp. 1124–75.

[34] A. C. Kinsey, W. B. Pomeroy, and C. E. Martin, *Sexual Behavior in the Human Male* (Philadelphia: W. B. Saunders, 1948); A. C. Kinsey, W. B. Pomeroy, C. E. Martin, and P. H. Gebhard, *Sexual Behavior in the Human Female* (Philadelphia: W. B. Saunders, 1953).

[35] Study made in Aberdeen, Scotland, by Drs. Dugald Baird and James Walker, as reported in the *New York Times*, June 16, 1954, p. 33. The doctors attributed the differences in obstetrical death rate to differences in diet.

[36] For an interesting and detailed description of differences in the whole pattern of life for the two main classes in an American community, see Robert S. Lynd and Helen M. Lynd, *Middletown* (New York: Harcourt, 1929).

[37] Ralph H. Turner, "Life Situation and Subculture," *British Journal of Sociology*, 9 (December, 1958), pp. 299–320; Louis Kriesberg, "The Relationship Between Socio-Economic Rank and Behavior," *Social Problems*, 10 (Spring, 1963), pp. 334–53.

From the lore of World War I comes a pertinent story of how the lower ranks sometimes influenced the upper: General Pershing was paying his first visit to the front. After he and his party advanced some distance, he asked his aide how far they were from their goal. Down the line went the question, and up the line came the answer, in a whisper, "Five miles." After a further advance, Pershing whispered the same question and received, in a whisper, the reply "Four miles." "Why in the devil," queried the General, "are we whispering?" The question went down the line to a buck private who was guiding the party. He responded, "Because I have a sore throat."

most other fashions and fads.[38] Very rarely, a fashion or cultural trait will be adopted first in the lower class, and then receive increasing acceptance in the upper classes. Whereas most culture traits are transmitted from whites to Negroes in the United States, popular musical forms and themes are regularly adopted by whites from Negroes. Beer-drinking was popular among the lower classes of the United States, probably because it is the least expensive way of imbibing alcohol, long before it became popular with the upper classes.

Class consciousness is distinct from class differences in that it is a concept which takes the point of view of the members of the society rather than that of the observer. There are two bases of class consciousness: (1) the individual's awareness of his membership in a class and the effect of this awareness on his behavior; (2) other people's designation of known members of their society as belonging to certain classes. *Class conflict* is a fourth concept used in the analysis of class. It refers, as the term implies, to activities directed by members of one class against the interests of another class. Class conflict may be overt, that is observable and conscious, or it may be covert, that is below the surface of appearances and scarcely known by most members of the society.

Another concept in this field is that of *status symbols*, a notion which has entered into popular thought in the United States. Status symbols are simply easily observable marks of status, or alleged status. Highly structured societies or groups use status symbols to guide individual behavior which must be differential according to class. Examples are the use of insignia of rank in the armed services, and the different furnishings in the offices of government employees according to their rank. Where race does not obviously distinguish the castes of a caste society, differential clothing or highly visible "caste marks" are required. In less structured settings, informal status symbols are used to distinguish the classes. Style and make of automobile often serve this function in the United States. In the U. S. State Department building it is said that the introduction of

[38] See Chapter 11, Section D.

new, thick rugs in the Secretary's office created a new status symbol—fuzz on shoes and trousers cuffs. "The latest gambit is to pull a large wad of fuzz off one's trousers at a cocktail party and remark sourly: 'If Rusk is going to keep me up there all day, he'll have to do something about that carpet.' An inventive young woman is proposing to sell fuzz in pressure cans, so that those yearning for status can squirt the stuff on their shoes."[39]

For the United States, sociologists have observed that the following traits confer status on an individual: income, occupation, power, family background, nationality background, education, kind of personal associations, and achievement. Some sociologists declare that one or the other of these—income or family background, for example—is basic, and all the others of no consequence. Other sociologists hold that an individual's status is a resultant of all of these factors. Without taking sides on this issue, we shall consider the distribution of each of the traits and changes in them through time. It is to be noted that it is possible to modify one's position with respect to all these traits—even family background and ethnic background are modifiable within two generations—so that change of status is possible. Family and nationality background are the elements of class closest to caste. Studies have shown significant correlations among some of these variables or indices of them, although the correlations reported for the small town studied by Warner and associates are greater than those for the large city studied by Hochbaum and associates (Table 3).[40]

2   INCOME AND CLASS

Income differences in the United States are indicated in Table 17 of Chapter 12, where it may be noted that there are no sharp breaks at different levels to indicate class limits. The curve of income differences is a smooth one with considerable skewing toward the higher level so that there is a much larger differential in amount of income at the higher levels than at the lower levels. These data are for the United States as a whole: there is considerable variation between the different states, cities, and towns. In a residential suburb such as Westchester County, New York,[41]

[39] *New York Times*, February 6, 1961, p. 20. The reference, of course, is to Secretary of State Dean Rusk.

[40] As the table shows, in one respect the two correlations are at about the same (high) level—namely, the correlation of house type and dwelling area.

[41] For a description of this "upper-class suburb," see G. Lundberg, M. Komarovsky, and M. A. McInerny, *Leisure* (New York: Columbia University Press, 1934). For a description of the off-season life of the upper-upper class, see Cleveland Amory, *The Last Resorts: A Portrait of American Society at Play* (New York: Harper, 1948). For a general sociological description of the upper class in one urban area, see E. Digby Baltzell, *Philadelphia Gentlemen* (Glencoe, Ill.: Free Press, 1958).

TABLE 3 · CORRELATIONS BETWEEN SELECTED SOURCES OF STATUS (*In a small town and a large city*)

		Income	Occupational rating	House type	Dwelling area rating
Education	Jonesville	.59	.77	.70	.65
	Minneapolis	.32	.65	.32	.32
Income	Jonesville		.87	.81	.81
	Minneapolis		.50	.35	.26
Occupational rating	Jonesville			.71	.70
	Minneapolis			.45	.45
House type	Jonesville				.74
	Minneapolis				.73

Sources: W. L. Warner, M. Meeker, and K. Eells, *Social Class in America* (Chicago: Science Research Associates, Inc., 1949), p. 172; G. Hochbaum, J. G. Darley, E. D. Monachesi, and C. Bird, "Socioeconomic Variables in a Large City," *American Journal of Sociology*, 61 (July, 1955), p. 34.

most of the residents who commute to New York City would be recognized to be either upper-upper or lower-upper class, depending very largely on their possession of large incomes. Those who serve the families of commuters either as tradespeople or as household servants generally have lower incomes and are therefore considered to be either in the middle- or lower-income classes. In other parts of the country—for example, in communities in West Virginia or Utah—the income differences within the community are not nearly so great as in Westchester County. In these communities people who have the top incomes are considered to be upper class whereas people with the same or even slightly higher incomes in Westchester County are considered to be middle class. The whole range of income is considerably lower and the dividing lines between classes are correspondingly lower. There are cities dominated by one industry, such as Altoona, Pennsylvania, where the income range is not great enough to permit much class distinction on the basis of income. In such communities class distinction tends to be made more on the basis of occupation than on the basis of income. Despite the different bases of class in different communities, Sjoberg finds a certain commonness to them. Referring to the United States as a whole as "the mass society" he says:

The relationship of stratification in the local community to that in the mass society is another point of controversy. However, research findings offer some substantiation for the assumption that there is a parallel relationship between class structure in the local community and that in the mass society and that the social classes of the former are to a considerable degree a reflection of those of the latter, even though regional and local variations exist.[42]

Income differentials in the United States have probably increased considerably since colonial days, although we do not have comparative statistics going back that far. However, the average increase in income differential occurred entirely before World War I; since 1913 the income differential has been declining. The dollar income of the top 1 per cent of income receivers (in 1948 this included those having a family income of $22,000) only doubled between 1913 and 1948, while the rest of the population quadrupled its income and the cost of living went up two-and-a-half times.[43] Between 1940 and 1948 the share in the national income of this 1 per cent dropped from 11 to 6 per cent. A number of influences since 1900 have tended to reduce income differentials. The introduction and extension of income, inheritance, and estate taxes have tended to limit the number of people with extremely high incomes. Minimum wage laws, the continuing development of the factory system, unionization, and the extension of free public facilities have tended to reduce the number of people at the very low-income level. This drift toward the middle-income level from both extremes has also occurred in other Western democratic nations—especially in Sweden and Great Britain. Income, of course, is strongly correlated with the purchases made. But the relationship is not one-to-one. Many studies have shown[44] that the higher the income of a family, on the average, the greater the proportion of income saved. While what Thorstein Veblen called "conspicuous consumption" was characteristic of most of the wealthiest families in the period before World War I, this has declined somewhat. Most obviously, the huge ornate residences of the wealthy have given way to more modest-appearing "ranch houses" and apartments. Certain kinds of fairly expensive household equipment—such as TVs, radios and refrigerators—are owned by almost the same proportion of poor people as of rich people. An interesting example is that of the ownership of television sets. In 1950, when only 18 per cent of American families owned a TV set, among the poorest quarter the figure was 11 per cent as compared to only 24 per cent among the richest quarter of the population.[45] Today the ownership of TV is

[42] Gideon Sjoberg, "Are Social Classes in America Becoming More Rigid?" *American Sociological Review*, 16 (December, 1941), pp. 775–83, p. 776 quoted. One important study showing the similarity of classes in a small community and in the society at large is O. D. Duncan and J. W. Artis, "Some Problems of Stratification Research," *Rural Sociology*, 16 (March, 1951), pp. 17–24.

[43] Simon Kuznets, *Shares of Upper Income Groups in Income and Savings* (New York: National Bureau of Economic Research, 1953).

[44] For example, Kuznets, *op. cit.*

[45] Study by the Industrial Surveys Company, as reported in the *New York Times*, November 13, 1950, p. 39.

To sum it up, America's social structure today and in the proximate future can be perceived as a diamond where the top and bottom are still pretty rigidly fixed, inhabited by upper and lower classes. A working class of the traditional sort also persists but comprises nowadays only a part of the manual workers. Between the extremes, however, classes are disappearing. To be sure, prestige, power and economic differentials persist here too, of course, and prestige differentials tend even to become accentuated as crude economic differences diminish and lose their visibility. But these differentials are no longer the hallmarks of social classes. In the middle ranges of the various rank orders we are witnessing the beginnings of a classless society in a modern industrial economy. It already involves roughly one-half of our population and may well involve more than that in the future although there are no signs that the top and bottom classes are likely to disappear altogether. This is a somewhat different classless society from that envisaged by Marx a century ago, but it is at least a partially classless society nevertheless.

Kurt B. Mayer, "The Changing Shape of the American Class Structure," *Social Research*, 30 (Winter, 1963), p. 468.

practically universal in the communities which have access to a TV station.

The source of income is often important in conferring status. Income from salary and wages is generally more important than income from other sources. In a large institution—such as a factory or university— little attention will be paid to non-salary income in the recognition of status differentials. This is not only because of the obvious high correlation between income and occupation or rank within the large institution but also because of the common principles for evaluating worth which are applied by means of salary differentials. For example, an associate professor with a $6,000 income who has inherited a large fortune will certainly be ranked below a full professor with an $8,000 income, and even below an associate professor with a $7,000 income, even though the latter two do not have any outside income.

3 OTHER FACTORS CONFERRING STATUS
   AND THEIR INTERRELATIONSHIPS

Most of the characteristics conferring status are interrelated, and it is difficult to determine how much each one independently contributes to status by itself and how much it is an influence through the other factors. Income is related to family background since a "desirable" family background opens opportunities for earning larger incomes, and since it often provides an inheritance that contributes unearned income. Income is important for status through its ability to exercise power over other people. The man who can hire people or can give generous sums for charitable or political purposes has an increment of status through the "power" created by this distribution of income. Income is associated with occupation, since the more prestigious occupations generally pay a higher salary, although there are some notable exceptions of poorly paid but prestigious occupations such as those of clergymen or teachers. Other exceptions to the correlation between income and occupation occur through the existence of non-salary income and of managerial occupations that receive moderate salaries but exercise a great deal of power. Income is related to the prestige of people with whom one associates, partly through the need for people of certain occupational levels to associate with each other, and partly through the requirement of a certain degree of income to reach certain expenditure levels demanded in certain social groups.

The major exceptions to the relationship occur in the case of *nouveaux riches*—people who have recently acquired a large income but not the conventional manners or family reputation that sometimes are acquired through generations of wealth—with whom some people who have a high status family background, with or without high income, refuse to associate. But the unaccepted *nouveaux riches* who have not learned good manners are decreasing today, since one newly acquires a large income today only if one has a higher education, and one usually learns manners along with formal education. Income is associated with education because people with high income can purchase a higher education, because people with high income generally insist that their children go through at least the formalities of acquiring a higher education, and because higher education opens opportunities for earning a higher income.[46] There are more numerous exceptions here, however, since a large part of the educational ladder in the United States is free and poor young men who have ability can reach the top of the educational ladder, and since wealthy people occasionally have offspring with such low abilities that they cannot go through college.

Achievement is associated with income through occupation. Persons with the most prestigious occupations are often the ones who can make the most prestigious achievements, and, as we have seen, these occupations are the ones that tend to command high salaries. There are numerous exceptions, however, since certain kinds of achievement, mainly in the arts and sciences, are not remunerated highly in our society. Income is associated with nationality background because of limitations on admittance to prestigious occupations for certain nationality groups and because of the fact that certain nationality groups have not been in the

[46] F. L. Babcock, *The U. S. College Graduate* (New York: Macmillan, 1941); Leonard J. West, *College and the Years After* (New York: Board of Higher Education, New York City, 1952); Ernest Havemann and P. S. West, *They Went to College* (New York: Harcourt, 1952).

United States long enough for their members to accumulate reserves of wealth from which come non-salary income.

Family background contributes to status by virtue of the fact that the achievements and status of one's parents, grandparents, and more remote ancestors contribute to one's own status. Naturally, family background is more important in settled communities than in rapidly changing ones and more important in communities that have had a long existence than communities that are relatively newly established. Family background is probably more important in small towns—where everyone can know everyone else's family background—than in large cities. The small cities and towns of New England are especially characterized by the great weight given to family background in conferring status on their inhabitants.[47] Family background is almost as important in the old South, although the Civil War was a highly disruptive influence on old families in some communities there. In general, family background is of less importance as we move westward across the United States, although a few of the older communities of Utah and California still give a great deal of weight to family background. In Philadelphia, family background has been a most important factor in determining upper class status and is closely associated there with wealth, and until about 1954, with political dominance—which has not been characteristic of other communities. While the "main line" Philadelphians confined themselves largely to successful businesses, they had an unwritten agreement with a corrupt political machine that ran the city.[48]

Family background is becoming less important as time passes, since there is a long-run trend in our society for the extended family to reduce its function of conferring status, and since the other factors conferring status can more easily be attained without family background. In the earlier history of western Europe family background was the major criterion of status, since the society was then emerging from a caste system. Aside from the fact that family background is inevitably connected with ethnic background, the highest degree of relationship between family background and other factors conferring status is that between family background and personal association. That is, the kind of company one keeps, especially in leisure-time situations, is to a considerable extent determined by the family one is a member of. Family background is much less related to income, education, or occupation.

[47] Warner found family background to be the most important factor in the New England town he studied. W. Warner and P. S. Lunt, *The Social Life of a Modern Community* (New Haven: Yale University Press, 1941), pp. 99–110.

[48] Baltzell, *op. cit.* Also see review by Carl Bridenbaugh in *New York Times Book Review*, Nov. 17, 1958, p. 6.

Occupation is a relatively uniform source of status among people of different class levels and people in different parts of the country. This is shown by several studies of the relative prestige of occupations.[49] The major exception to the uniform pattern is that people often place their own occupations higher in the prestige hierarchy than people not in those occupations place them. There is also a greater differential in status attributed to occupations around one's own than there is for occupations in different parts of the hierarchy. Occupation is very important, not only for the relative prestige level which it accords to its members, but also because it determines many other aspects of an individual's life, as we have already had occasion to note in connection with caste. It provides him his own income which permits him to achieve a certain standard of living; it takes up his time for much of the day; it puts him into association with a certain category of people. There is a certain amount of choice of occupation even in one individual's career, that is, one may move from a given occupation to certain other ones. On the other hand, there are certain occupations, notably in the professions, which are more or less closed unless one has the entire background and education for entrance into the occupation. Occupations are not inherited as an obligation under any class system but there is a certain tendency for children to follow the occupations of their parents.

Education is perhaps not so important as income, occupation, and family background in determining one's status directly, but it has certain indirect effects on status which are becoming more important in contemporary society. Education has become a major avenue of social mobility upward. The professions have been assuming a higher position in the occupational hierarchy and they have always required a high degree of education. It used to be possible for an uneducated person to start a business and build it up rapidly if he had ability and luck. With the requirement of a huge amount of capital to start most kinds of businesses and with the increasingly high income tax, it is much less possible to start a highly remunerative business operation now than it used to be. On the other hand, large businesses now take the form of corporations rather than individually owned operations, and corporations are constantly on the search for capable managers to rise in the hierarchy of control. The managers are now drawn almost exclusively from the colleges, and a capable and attractive college graduate of lower- or middle-class background can be chosen almost as easily as a young man of upper-class background, although the latter has certain advantages. While the possibilities of accumulating large amounts of wealth are no longer so likely as they were in the nineteenth century, a larger number of people are able

[49] For a summary of these studies, see Theodore Caplow, *The Sociology of Work* (Minneapolis: University of Minnesota Press, 1954), pp. 39–41, 52–57.

to earn very comfortable incomes by the route of higher education, and there are at least as many chances of becoming a manager today as there were of becoming the owner of a business in the nineteenth century.

The level of educational achievement has generally increased in the United States within the past several generations. Between 1890 and 1960 the proportion of the population aged fourteen to seventeen years that was enrolled in secondary schools has increased steadily from 7 per cent to 90 per cent.[50] Public education itself is not much more than a hundred years old in many of the states, and the level of education that passed as satisfactory is no longer regarded as such today. The lower limit is also being raised as the law sets a minimum educational requirement for all children. The present standards more or less require graduation from elementary school, whereas in the generation completing its education around the time of World War I fully half of the population did not graduate from elementary school.

A special report of the U. S. Bureau of the Census,[51] based on 1956 data, showed that the 10 per cent of American families headed by a college graduate had an average income of about $7,600. The 25 per cent of American families headed by a high school graduate had an average family income of $5,500. The families headed by an elementary school graduate had an average family income of $4,200.

Education as a direct source of status varies somewhat from one group to another. Certain immigrant groups, for example, place a higher value on education for their young than do other immigrant groups.[52] Parents who have themselves achieved a high educational status make greater demands on their offspring for educational achievement than do non-educated parents. Among highly educated people, college education does not so much contribute to status as the lack of it contributes to loss or reduction of status. To a certain extent, self-education is a substitute for formal education. A person is regarded as being educated if he is familiar with literature and history even though he has not spent many years in formal schooling. Self-education is almost in the nature of achievement, which is a separate factor in the conferring of status.

Achievement has long been an important factor in attributing status to a person, although it applies to only a small segment of the population. By its very nature achievement must stand out—if something is very common it is not considered an achievement—and therefore achievement can confer status on only a small proportion of the population. A person

[50] U. S. Office of Education reports.
[51] U. S. Bureau of the Census, News Release, May 5, 1958. Also see C. Arnold Anderson, "Education and Social Stratification," *I Problemi della Pedagogia* (Rome, 1958), pp. 1–17.
[52] J. Whiting and Irving Child, *Child Training and Personality* (New Haven: Yale University Press, 1953).

who has made an unusual and highly valued achievement is in a sense
lifted outside of the status hierarchy. He may have all the other attributes
of low status but people act toward him as though he had the highest
status. The achievements that confer high status vary considerably from
culture to culture and from period to period. Scholarly achievement, for
example, is more important in countries of western Europe than in the
United States where mechanical invention is a very important kind of
achievement. Achievement tends to have a low degree of association with
most of the other factors conferring status, although certain kinds of
achievement require a high level of education and certain other ones are
aided by a certain occupation or income level.

Nationality background is in some ways closer to being a caste factor
than a class factor, as one cannot change his own nationality background
without passing. One can marry outside one's nationality group—itself
an indication that nationality background is to be considered with class
rather than with caste—and thereby change the nationality background
of one's offspring. There is, however, a certain tendency to marry within
one's nationality group, and an even stronger tendency to marry within
one's religious group,[53] although one can readily change one's religion.
Another reason to consider nationality background as a factor in class
rather than caste is that nationalities assume a different status every few
decades in the United States. There is a tendency for nationalities that have
long roots in American history to pass into a general undifferentiated
"nationality" which is generally called "Old Americans." Originally the
"Old Americans" were those whose ancestors came from Great Britain
or France; now they are likely to include all those whose ancestors came
from anywhere in western, central, or northern Europe.

While nationality background can generally be considered as a factor
closer to class than to caste, a few nationalities have a caste-like position
in the United States. This is true of the Greeks, for example.[54] Races
other than white are definitely separate castes in the United States, and
to a certain extent broad religious categories—Protestants, Catholics, and
Jews—are also semi-castes in that there are restrictions against intermarriage among them. While not affecting class itself, passing out of a
nationality group or a religious group is easier than out of a racial group,
and it occurs much more frequently.

In general the class level of a nationality group is roughly related to
the time at which most members of this group were migrating to the
United States. That is, the most recent immigrant groups have a lower

[53] Ruby Jo Reeves Kennedy, "Single or Triple Melting Pot? Intermarriage Trends in
New Haven, 1870–1950," *American Journal of Sociology*, 58 (July, 1952), pp. 45–50.

[54] See the series of articles by J. Mayone Stycos which appeared in *Common Ground* in
1948 under the general title "The Spartan Greeks of Bridgetown."

status than the ones who established residence in this country earlier. This means that the nationalities coming from the north and west of Europe tend to have a higher status than those coming from the south and east of Europe, although there are certain major exceptions. There are some differences in the relative weight of nationality background in the general evaluation of status in different sections of the country. In general, the more newly developed regions pay less attention to this factor than do the older regions.

Religious affiliation is a factor contributing to class in its own right, as well as through nationality. Church affiliation, like membership in voluntary associations,[55] is very important in determining with whom one associates, and frequent associations—even on a "secondary group" level —is one of the most conspicuous characteristics of class. Warner has considered frequency of association, presumably on an equal status level, to be the central characteristic of class. Churches are stratified not only because the local church serves a given community, which generally through ecological processes consists of people having roughly the same income level, but also because through historical processes each denomination has attracted members predominantly from different social classes. The approximate class distribution of the members of the major denominations in the United States is shown in Table 4.

Power is almost a different type of factor conferring status from those we have been considering, since it sometimes supersedes all others and determines status by itself.[56] This is most evident today in the Soviet Union where Communist Party leaders—who often have low amounts of the other status-conferring factors—form the upper class. To a considerable extent power was also central to the top status of the owners of industry in England in the nineteenth century, although wealth was frequently the measure of power. Beatrice Webb, who came out of this class, describes the situation thus:

> For good or evil, according to the social ideals of the student, this remarkable amalgam, London Society and country-house life, differed significantly from other social aristocracies. There were no fixed caste barriers; there seemed to be, in fact, no recognized types of exclusiveness based on birth or breeding, on personal riches or on personal charm; there was no fastidiousness about manners or morals or intellectual gifts. Like the British Empire, London Society had made

[55] See Chapter 10, Section B.
[56] The classic discussion of the relation of class, status, and power is that of Max Weber. See H. H. Gerth and C. W. Mills, *From Max Weber: Essays in Sociology* (New York: Oxford University Press, 1946), pp. 180 ff.; and Max Weber, *The Theory of Social and Economic Organization,* trans. A. M. Henderson and T. Parsons (London: William Hodge, 1947), pp. 390–95.

TABLE 4 · PERCENTAGE DISTRIBUTION OF RELIGIOUS GROUPS BY SOCIAL CLASS[a] (*Ranked according to percentage in upper class*)

Religious groups	Upper class	Middle class	Lower class
National sample	13.1	30.7	56.2
Episcopal	24.1	33.7	42.2
Congregational	23.9	42.6	33.5
Presbyterian	21.9	40.0	38.1
Jewish	21.8	32.0	46.2
No preference	13.3	26.0	60.7
Methodist	12.7	35.6	51.7
Protestant (undesignated)	12.4	24.1	63.5
Lutheran	10.9	36.1	53.0
Christian[b]	10.0	35.4	54.6
Protestant (smaller bodies)	10.0	27.3	62.7
Catholic	8.7	24.7	66.6
Baptist	8.0	24.0	68.0

Source: Polls taken by the Office of Public Opinion Research of Princeton University between November 1945 and June 1946, as reported in: Federal Council of Churches, *Information Service*, 27 (May 15, 1948), Part 2.

[a] Interviewers made the classification "after a careful appraisal of the respondent's dress; home and its neighborhood and furnishings; ownership of home or automobile; occupation; use of luxury items; possession of comforts as opposed to necessities, etc."

[b] The term Christian is presumed to designate the Disciples of Christ Church, but it "may be also that some of the respondents who used this category meant by it only Christian as opposed to non-Christian."

itself what it was in a fit of absentmindedness. To foreign observers it appeared all-embracing in its easygoing tolerance and superficial good nature. "One never knows who one is going to sit next at a London dinner party," ruefully remarked the aforementioned diplomatist. But deep down in the unconscious herd instinct of the British governing class there *was* a test of fitness for membership of this most gigantic of all social clubs, but a test which was seldom recognized by those who applied it, still less by those to whom it was applied, *the possession of some form of power over other people.* The most obvious form of power, and the most easily measurable, was the power of wealth.[57]

A similar characterization of the American upper class could have been made during the years between the Civil War and World War I. With the organization of increasingly powerful trade unions, the trend toward the supplanting of owners by educated managers as controllers of industries, the increasing income of professional people, the income tax, the increasing assumption of leadership in voluntary associations by middle-income

[57] Beatrice Webb, *My Apprenticeship* (New York: Longmans, 1926), pp. 48-49. Quoted by permission of the publisher and of the Webb estate.

people,[58] and possibly other factors, there is no longer such a close correlation between wealth and power. Power remains an important factor in
status, but its greater spread over a larger proportion of people and its
decreasing relationship with other factors in status, probably make it less
central to status in Great Britain[59] and the United States[60] than it used
to be. Some instability may be expected to arise in a society in which
there is too great a discrepancy between status and power,[61] since persons
with more power than status may use their power violently to try to gain
more status for themselves, while persons with more status than power
may use their influence to try to change the society so that persons with
power feel that their power is threatened. This instability, like all social
instability, may not necessarily be evil or harmful.

We have spoken of the factors conferring status separately. The
specific status of a person, however, arises from the peculiar combination
of attributes he has. The factors operate together to confer status, and
seldom is one factor the sole determining influence. Since there are a half-
dozen or so factors, and since they vary somewhat independently of each
other, it is natural that the distribution of status forms a continuum
rather than a series of clearly demarcated, discrete classes.[62] It is likely
that classes are more sharply distinguishable in small towns[63] than in large
cities, since in small towns, where everyone knows each other, family
background—with all its rigidity—can have a greater relative influence
on status, and since large cities offer greater opportunities for social mo-

[58] See Chapter 10.

[59] For a British study on this point, see D. V. Glass (ed.), *Social Mobility in Britain*
(London: Routledge and Kegan Paul, 1954), especially chapter by Rosalind C. Chambers.

[60] Two American community studies consider power to be still highly correlated with
wealth and central to status. R. S. Lynd and Helen M. Lynd, *Middletown in Transition*
(New York: Harcourt, 1937); Floyd Hunter, *Community Power Structure* (Chapel Hill:
University of North Carolina Press, 1953).

[61] See Herbert Goldhamer and Edward A. Shils, "Types of Status and Power," *American
Journal of Sociology*, 45 (September, 1939), pp. 171–82.

[62] This has been the position of, among others, G. C. Homans, G. Myrdal, T. Parsons,
and P. A. Sorokin. Taking the position that classes are discrete units are W. L. Warner
and his followers, C. Wright Mills, and Leonard Reissman (in his *Class in American
Society, op. cit.*). See Gerhard E. Lenski, "American Social Classes: Statistical Strata or
Social Groups?" *American Journal of Sociology*, 58 (September, 1952), pp. 139–44. In the
New England mill town that Lenski studied, local residents did not perceive the status
system as consisting of discrete social classes. In a small community in Pennsylvania,
Duncan and Artis (*op. cit.*) found some "breaks" between occupational groups although
there was considerable overlap. Mayer holds that Warner's own studies do not justify
an assumption of sharp breaks between classes. See Kurt Mayer, "The Theory of Social
Classes," *Harvard Educational Review*, 23 (Summer, 1953), pp. 149–67.

[63] For studies of stratification in small towns, see Wayne Wheeler, *Social Stratification
in a Plains Community* (privately printed, 1949); Harold F. Kaufman, *Prestige Classes
in a New York Rural Community* (Cornell University Agricultural Experiment Station,

bility with all the blurring of class lines that social mobility entails.[64] Within communities of a given size and restricted economic opportunities, however, there may be a trend toward discrete classes, as some factors lose their importance and the remaining factors assume a closer correlation with each other, and as individuals seeking upward mobility find satisfactory opportunities by moving to other communities.

Because any given individual is likely to have a different status in terms of each of the several factors conferring status, there is a phenomenon called "status inconsistency." If a person is high in status as measured in terms of one set of criteria—achieved or ascribed—and also in terms of other criteria, he knows where he stands and others know how to behave with respect to him. If, however, a person is high in status as measured in terms of one set of criteria but low in terms of other criteria, uncertainties and difficulties may easily arise. It is this phenomenon of differing status positions for an individual in differing status systems which has been called status inconsistency. The concept has been found useful in explaining a number of kinds of phenomena, such, for example, as disturbed interpersonal social relationships, unstable self-images, anomalous rewards, social ambiguity, and even stress symptoms,[65] although not all status inconsistency is "bad." Status inconsistency is a likely resultant of social mobility: As one begins to change his status, he is more likely to do so in terms of some status factors than of others.

We shall now turn to a closer examination of social mobility.

D   Social Mobility

Mobility has two meanings: (1) movement from place to place, or horizontal mobility, which we shall consider in Chapter 12, (2) recognized

Memoir 260, March, 1944); A. B. Hollingshead, "Selected Characteristics of Classes in a Middle Western Community," *American Sociological Review*, 12 (1947), pp. 385–95.

[64] G. Hochbaum, J. G. Darley, E. D. Monachesi, and C. Bird, "Socioeconomic Variables in a Large City," *American Journal of Sociology*, 61 (July, 1955), pp. 31–38. The correlation in Minneapolis between the occupational ratings of adult sons in 1950 and of their fathers during their prime was only .35, using the Warner rating scale. Only 30 per cent of the sample had the same occupational ratings as their fathers, about 26 per cent had a lower rating, and 44 per cent had a higher rating.

[65] Everett C. Hughes, "Dilemmas and Contradictions of Status," *American Journal of Sociology*, 50 (March, 1944), pp. 353–59; Gerhard E. Lenski, "Status Crystallization: A Non-verbal Dimension of Social Status," *American Sociological Review*, 19 (August, 1954), pp. 405–13, and "Social Participation and Status Crystallization," *American Sociological Review*, 21 (August, 1956), pp. 458–64; G. H. Fenchel, J. H. Monderer, and E. L. Hartley, "Subjective Status and the Equilibration Hypothesis," *Journal of Abnormal and Social Psychology*, 46 (October, 1951), pp. 476–79; Irwin W. Goffman, "Status Consistency and Preference for Change in Power Distribution," *American Sociological Review*, 22 (June, 1957), pp. 275–81; and Elton F. Jackson, "Status Consistency and Symptoms of Stress," *American Sociological Review*, 27 (August, 1962), pp. 469–80.

change of status, or vertical mobility, which we shall consider here. Mobility can be either upward or downward, although most discussions of mobility emphasize its "social climbing" aspect. Mobility is an essential characteristic of class systems, since it is what primarily distinguishes them from caste systems, but different class systems encourage or tolerate differing amounts of mobility. The ease of attaining or losing those characteristics which the society evaluates as conferring status is the measure of the degree to which mobility is possible or is likely to occur in a society. While this is the basic measure of mobility, there is generally a symbolic aspect to it also. This may range from buying a new car to adopting a new style of speech.[66] Since use of a symbol of social mobility is usually considerably easier than the achievement of more of the characteristics which actually confer social status, symbols of high status are sometimes employed by those who do not have high status. This is roughly equivalent to "passing" in the caste system, although it is more the subject of humor than of emotional revulsion when detected. Much of the well-known behavior pattern of "keeping up with the Joneses" involves adopting the symbolic characteristics of higher status, sometimes appropriate to the higher social status and sometimes not.

Different societies have different means of permitting social mobility. In some societies it is by unique achievement only; elsewhere marriage is one of the few avenues to changing one's social status. In the United States, a combination of changing occupation and gaining an education seems to be the dominant means. These two are intimately related, but insofar as they are separable, education seems to be becoming the more important.[67] In any society, mobility or the lack of it becomes a matter of cultural expectations. For example, studies by Empey, Stephenson, and Caro show that lower class boys prefer and/or expect less prestigious occupational positions than do middle and upper class male high school students.[68]

Most studies of social mobility are made by comparing the occupa-

[66] According to a speech by Professor Benjamin D. Paul of Harvard University (as reported in the *New York Times*, March 24, 1955, p. 33), wives more than husbands emphasize the necessity of symbolic accompaniments of social mobility.

[67] Otis Dudley Duncan and Robert W. Hodge, "Education and Occupational Mobility: A Regression Analysis," *American Journal of Sociology*, 68 (May, 1963), pp. 629–44. For surveys of the literature on American mobility, and of the role of education in it, see Bernard Barber, *Social Stratification* (New York: Harcourt, 1957), pp. 422 ff.; Robin Williams, *American Society* (New York: Alfred A. Knopf, 1957), pp. 78 ff.; Seymour M. Lipset and Reinhard Bendix, *Social Mobility in Industrial Society* (Berkeley: University of California Press, 1959), pp. 76 ff.

[68] Lamar Empey, "Social Class and Occupational Aspiration," *American Sociological Review*, 21 (1956), pp. 703–09; Richard Stephenson, "Mobility Orientation and Occupational Aspiration," *American Sociological Review*, 22 (1957), pp. 67–73; Francis Caro, "Social Class, Formal Education, and Social Mobility," unpublished paper, 1963.

tions of a representative sample of men with the occupational positions of their fathers.[69] Rogoff's study of Marion County, Indiana (which includes the city of Indianapolis) finds that the likelihood of a son being in an occupational group different from that of his father was about the same in 1910 and in 1940.[70] In both time periods about 70 per cent of the men were in occupations different from those of their fathers. On the other hand, the social distance moved in terms of social status was greater in 1910 than in 1940, although this reduction in mobility may have been made up in the prosperous years since 1940. Another study, of Oakland, California, by S. M. Lipset, R. Bendix, and F. T. Malm,[71] shows that, of the sons of fathers who had spent most of their lives as manual workers, 47 per cent were working in non-manual occupations, as compared with 68 per cent of the sons of fathers who had spent most of their lives in non-manual occupations. Manual workers had spent one fifth of their occupational careers in non-manual positions, and white-collar workers one quarter of theirs in manual jobs. This study, as well as one by Scudder and Anderson[72] shows that those who migrate from their home town are the ones most likely to raise their occupational status. Centers'[73] study of a cross-section sample of the American population shows that 35 per cent of the men were in positions that could be considered higher than those of their fathers, while 29 per cent were in positions not so good as those of their fathers. Several nationwide studies of mobility among businessmen indicate that, if anything, upward mobility is increasing slightly in the United States: Warner and Abegglen found

[69] Occupation is used as equivalent to class in studies of social mobility because it is the component easiest to ask about and to compare from generation to generation. A brief review of earlier studies of social mobility is to be found in Natalie Rogoff, *Recent Trends in Occupational Mobility* (Glencoe, Ill.: Free Press, 1953). According to Rogoff, the earliest empirical study of mobility is that of Federico Chessa, *La Trasmissione Ereditaria delle Professioni* (Torino: Fratelli Bocca, 1912). An important, comprehensive early work in English is Pitirim A. Sorokin, *Social Mobility* (New York: Harper, 1927). General analyses of the factors affecting mobility include Sjoberg, *op. cit.*, J. O. Hertzler, "Some Tendencies Toward a Closed Class System in the United States," *Social Forces*, 30 (March, 1952), pp. 313–23; Ely Chinoy, "Social Mobility Trends in the United States," *American Sociological Review*, 20 (April, 1955), pp. 180–86. A comprehensive survey of the literature is contained in S. M. Miller's "Rates of Mobility: A Comparative Analysis," *Current Sociology* (Paris: UNESCO, 1960).

[70] Rogoff, *op. cit.*

[71] "Social Mobility and Occupational Career Patterns: I. Stability of Job-holding" and "Social Mobility," *American Journal of Sociology*, 57 (January, 1952, and March, 1952), pp. 366–74, 494–504. These and other studies of these authors on social mobility have been brought together in Seymour M. Lipset and Reinhard Bendix, *Social Mobility in Industrial Society* (Berkeley: University of California Press, 1959).

[72] Richard Scudder and C. Arnold Anderson, "Migration and Vertical Occupational Mobility," *American Sociological Review*, 19 (June, 1954), pp. 329–34.

[73] Richard Centers, "Occupational Mobility of Urban Occupational Strata," *American Sociological Review*, 13 (April, 1948), pp. 197–203.

that from 1900 to 1950 there had been an increase of 8 per cent in the proportion of executives whose fathers were laborers, and a decrease of 10 per cent in those whose fathers were owners of businesses. Mabel Newcomer found that 7.5 per cent of the executives of 1950 were sons of workers, as compared to only 4.2 per cent for the executives of 1900.[74] Most of the mobility in all studies, however, was to occupational levels adjacent to those of their fathers.[75]

Mobility in the United States in the past has to a certain extent been made possible by the large number of immigrants who, with few exceptions, have been obliged to take positions at the bottom of the occupational ladder, thus pushing upward those who formerly occupied these positions. The offspring of the immigrants, however, experience upward mobility to almost the same extent as offspring of native-born fathers.[76] The decline in immigration during the past thirty years has tended to reduce mobility. On the other hand, it should be recognized that internal migration—especially of Negroes from South to North—and the continuing immigration from other countries in the Western Hemisphere have compensated to a certain extent for the older immigration from Europe.

Differential fertility has been another long-run factor promoting mobility. When people in the upper occupational groups fail to reproduce themselves, their positions can be taken in the next generation by the offspring of those lower in the occupational scale. The recent decline in differential fertility[77] thus also tends to reduce mobility.[78]

The efficiency of economic organization, especially in regard to the technology utilized, is another very important factor in social mobility. The trend toward increasing organizational efficiency and the use of more machinery in production reduces the need for unskilled labor and increases the demand for specialized services, thus tending to shift the occupational distribution upward. The current trend is to step up tech-

[74] W. Lloyd Warner and James C. Abegglen, *Big Business Leaders in America* (New York: Harper, 1955); Mabel Newcomer, *The Big Business Executive* (New York: Columbia University Press, 1955). Bendix and Howton use still other data and come to a similar conclusion; the main value of their work is methodological: Reinhard Bendix and Frank W. Howton, "Social Mobility and the American Business Elite," *British Journal of Sociology*, 8 (December, 1957), pp. 1–13; and 9 (March, 1958), pp. 15–28.

[75] Other studies showing that there is continuing upward mobility in the United States include P. E. Davidson and H. D. Anderson, *Occupational Mobility in an American Community* (Stanford: Stanford University Press, 1937); C. C. North and P. K. Hatt, "Jobs and Occupations: A Popular Evaluation," in L. Wilson and W. L. Kolb, *Sociological Analysis* (New York: Harcourt, 1949), pp. 464–74; Leila C. Deasy, "Social Mobility in North Town," unpublished Ph.D. thesis, Cornell University, 1953.

[76] Rogoff, *op. cit.*

[77] See Chapter 12, Section A.

[78] Elbridge Sibley, "Some Demographic Clues to Stratification," *American Sociological Review*, 7 (June, 1942), pp. 322–30.

nological efficiency: more efficient machines are being substituted for less efficient ones, new sources of power are being made available, industrial engineering discovers new ways to save man power, and automation is now being introduced. Automation is the linking together of the various machines that produce the parts that are necessary for a given product in such a way that a mechanical-electrical process can start with the raw material and end up with the finished product without the use of human labor except to deliver the raw materials and start the process. The effect will be to reduce the need for unskilled and semiskilled labor (as well as changing the nature of the skilled labor needed). While this is causing many short-run dislocations, including unemployment, its long-run effect will probably include upward mobility. Programs of occupational retraining, relocation, earlier and subsidized retirement, and so on, could compensate for side effects of automation.

The trend toward organizational efficiency in manufacturing and commerce, as well as the trend toward combination for power purposes, has moved an increasing proportion of business into the hands of large enterprises. Whereas it was formerly possible for an ingenious, lucky, and hard-working individual, with moderate means, to start a successful and growing enterprise, this is no longer so possible, and this rapid avenue to the top is now more or less closed. On the other hand, it is still fairly easy for an individual to start a more modest but successful specialized service enterprise, and the total number of separate businesses has actually gone up since 1900 in relation to the population (Table 5). The earlier-mentioned study by Lipset, Bendix, and Malm shows that the most frequent way in which upward mobility was accomplished was to set up a small business.[79] Occasionally this is done by manual workers in their spare time while they are still employed.[80] We have already discussed the role of an increasingly available educational ladder as a new avenue to a higher social status. Where the educational ladder is not so available as a means to mobility, as in Great Britain, mobility is more often sponsored by someone already in the elite, rather than resulting from competition among those who would rise in status, as in the United States.[81]

The evidence presented is that there is a good deal of mobility in the United States, and that mobility has probably not declined since 1940. The factors influencing the trend of mobility are working in opposing directions so that they counterbalance each other. The roads to opportunity are somewhat changed but it seems to be about as easy to use them

[79] Op. cit.

[80] Warner Bloomberg, Jr., "The State of the American Proletariat, 1955," Commentary, 19 (March, 1955), pp. 207–16.

[81] Ralph H. Turner, "Sponsored and Contest Mobility and the School System," American Sociological Review, 25 (December, 1960), pp. 855–67.

TABLE 5 · NUMBER OF BUSINESS FIRMS IN OPERATION PER 1,000
POPULATION AND PER 1,000 GAINFULLY OCCUPIED, 1900–1960[a]

Year	BUSINESS FIRMS IN OPERATION		TOTAL POPULATION		GAINFULLY OCCUPIED[b]	NUMBER OF BUSINESS FIRMS	
	No. in 000's	Per- centage increase	No. in 000's	Per- centage increase	No. in 000's	Per 1,000 popula- tion	Per 1,000 gainfully occupied
1900	1,660	—	76,130	—	29,070	21.8	57.1
1910	2,100	26.5	92,270	21.0	37,370	22.8	56.2
1920	2,580	22.9	107,190	14.9	42,430	24.1	60.8
1930	2,950	14.3	123,090	16.1	48,830	24.0	60.6
1940	3,130	6.1	131,670	7.2	52,150	23.8	60.0
1950	4,000	27.8	150,700	14.5	59,590	26.5	67.3
1960	4,658	16.5	180,676	20.0	66,681	25.8	69.9

SOURCES: Kurt Mayer, "Business Enterprise: Traditional Symbol of Opportunity," *The British Journal of Sociology*, 4 (June, 1953), p. 170. Compiled from *Survey of Current Business, May, 1948 and February, 1951*, from *Statistical Abstract of the United States, 1950*, and from *1950 Census of Population, Preliminary Reports*, Series PC-7, No. 2. Figures for 1960 are from *Statistical Abstract of the United States, 1963*, pp. 488, 219, 5.
[a] Data for the business population are 10-year averages centered on the indicated year, except for 1950 which is the year-end figure for that year. Data for the human population are for the enumerated census years.
[b] For the years 1900-30 the figures represent gainfully occupied persons 10 years old and over; for the years 1940 and 1950 the data represent persons in the labor force 14 years old and over.

as it has always been. Indeed, for some groups, such as the Negroes, it is a great deal easier. It is generally believed that upward mobility is a good thing in a society, and we have concurred in this valuation. Before turning from this consideration of social mobility, however, it would be wise to note the costs of a high rate of mobility, as they are wisely pointed out by William Petersen.

A very high rate of social mobility may have harmful consequences, of which we can conveniently distinguish three kinds.

First, even in a rapidly growing economy, a high rate of upward mobility entails some downward mobility; and the consequent *nouveaux pauvres* are a liability in any social system. Typically, declassed people will seek to retain their status by irrational means: it is they who foster race hatred, who give demagogues their first support, who form the vanguard of totalitarian parties. So long as their number is relatively small they constitute a nuisance that can be controlled; but any social program that leads to an appreciable increase in declassed *"lumpen"* ought to include measures to reabsorb them into the social fabric as quickly as possible.

Secondly, a class system that fosters a very wide diffusion of cultural values may well sacrifice some of these values. While a very much higher percentage of young people attend college in the United States than in Britain the level of education at American colleges is, on the whole, decidedly lower. Just recently, for example, Dr. Minard

Stout, president of the University of Nevada, has advocated that it admit any graduate of a Nevada high school, regardless of his academic rating or the kind of courses he had taken in high school. Opening the doors that wide is a first step toward closing them altogether.

Thirdly, rapid social mobility often results in personal maladjustment, if not actual neurosis. This is true both for those who try to climb up the social scale and fail, and for those who succeed. Middle-class Americans are not nearly as happy as their fantastically high standard of living would seem to warrant, for their aspirations are always higher. Instead of enjoying their ample possessions, they strive for higher positions, or gather more gadgets, as new symbols of higher status. The pattern is both to own more and to belittle what one has as hardly comparable with what one *will* have.[82]

E   *Class Consciousness and Class Conflict*

1   THE NATURE AND EXTENT OF CLASS CONSCIOUSNESS AND CONFLICT

Class consciousness refers to the psychological awareness of class and positive identification with own class in a society by members of that society. A society can have marked status differences and even general awareness of these status differences, but unless members of the society also place themselves—individually and collectively—into classes, on the basis of a class containing all people of an approximately equal status, the society would not be said to have class consciousness. Class consciousness therefore requires that the division of the society into classes be fairly sharp, so that people know where they and other people "belong." Class consciousness may be studied under two aspects: (1) class identification, or the tendency of each individual to think of *himself* as belonging to a certain class, to which some other members of the society do not belong;[83] (2) class designation, or the tendency of each member of a society to place *other members* of the society consistently into certain classes and to agree, more or less, with other members of the society as to the status attributes of the classes.

A number of studies have been made of the extent of class identification in the United States, but they do not reach the same conclusion.[84]

[82] William Petersen, "Is America Still the Land of Opportunity?" *Commentary* (November, 1953), pp. 477–86; p. 485 quoted.

[83] Class identification is one kind of "group identification," a concept up to now used in sociology largely in connection with minority groups. See Chapter 17, Section B.

[84] A valuable early analysis is that of Arthur W. Kornhauser, "Analysis of 'Class' Structure of Contemporary American Society—Psychological Bases of Class Divisions," in G. W. Hartmann and T. Newcomb (eds.), *Industrial Conflict* (New York: Gordon, 1939), pp. 199–264.

One type of finding is that an overwhelming majority of Americans place themselves in the "middle class," which would suggest that there is not much class consciousness, since if nearly everyone is in the same class there are really no distinct classes. Among such studies are: a Gallup poll[85] in 1939 which found that 88 per cent of the American people said they were middle class; a Fortune survey[86] in 1940 which showed that 79 per cent held themselves to be middle class; a study by Cantril[87] in 1941 which reported that 87 per cent of the people identified themselves as middle class. An assumption in such studies is that there are three classes—upper, middle, and lower—or the Warner[88] division of these into two parts so that there are six classes—upper upper, lower upper, upper middle, lower middle, upper lower, lower lower.

Centers[89] has challenged the finding that the overwhelming majority of Americans considered themselves to be middle class by asking a cross-section of white adult males to place themselves into one of four classes: upper, middle, working, and lower. By substituting the more respectable but equally specific term "working class" for the more derogatory term "lower class," he got most people to distribute themselves into two classes. His results were that 3 per cent placed themselves in the upper class, 43 per cent in the middle class, 51 per cent in the working class, and 1 per cent in the lower class.[90] The study by Centers then goes on in other ways to indicate that class identification does exist in the United States, and the class identification is more predictive of attitudes on certain social issues than are the objective factors in class that we considered in an earlier section.

Fewer studies have been conducted on class designation, but the findings of one of them[91]—based on a very limited sample—suggest that there is only a certain degree of class consciousness in this sample of Americans. For example, while the average incomes attributed to the different classes are sharply different from each other on the average, the

[85] George Gallup and S. F. Rae, *The Pulse of Democracy* (New York: Simon and Schuster, 1940).

[86] *Fortune* Survey, "The People of the United States—A Self Portrait," *Fortune*, 21 (February, 1940), pp. 21 ff.

[87] Hadley Cantril, "Identification with Social and Economic Class," *Journal of Abnormal and Social Psychology*, 38 (January, 1943), pp. 74–80.

[88] W. Lloyd Warner and P. S. Lunt, *The Social Life of a Modern Community*, op. cit.

[89] Richard Centers, *The Psychology of Social Classes* (Princeton, N.J.: Princeton University Press, 1949).

[90] One per cent more said "Don't know" and the remaining 1 per cent responded "Don't believe in classes."

[91] Arnold M. Rose, "The Popular Meaning of Class Designation," *Sociology and Social Research*, 38 (September–October, 1953), pp. 14–21. Also see Thomas E. Lasswell, "Social Class and Stereotyping," *Sociology and Social Research*, 42 (March–April, 1958), pp. 256–62.

percentage distributions show a good deal of overlap—indicating that there is no popular consensus as to the income range of the classes. There are similar differences, and similar overlap, for the occupations, the educational levels, and the organizational associations of people designated as being in the different classes.

On the basis of information available from studies of class identification and class designation there is at most an incomplete degree of class consciousness in the United States. From other studies there would seem to be much more race and ethnic group consciousness, for example, than class consciousness. Davis and Gardner, who follow the Warner tradition, offer a description of the differing conception of class system found in the different classes:

> Individuals visualize class groups above them less clearly than those below them; they tend to minimize the social differentiations between themselves and those above. This difference in perspective is partly explained by the fact that class lines in the society are not permanent and rigid and that upward mobility is fairly frequent. It is, further, due to the natural tendency in such a status system to identify with "superiors." In view of this situation it is not surprising that individuals in the two upper strata make the finest gradations in the stratification of the whole society and that class distinctions are made with decreasing precision as social position becomes lower.
>
> Not only does the perspective on social stratification vary for different class levels, but the very bases of class distinction in the society are variously interpreted by the different groups. People tend to agree as to where people are but not upon why they are there. Upper-class individuals, especially upper uppers, think of class divisions largely in terms of time—one has a particular social position because his family has "always had" that position. Members of the middle class interpret their position in terms of wealth and time and tend to make moral evaluations of what "should be." Both middle-class groups accept the time element as an important factor in the superordinate position of the "old aristocracy," but for the rest of the society they consider only individual wealth and moral behavior as differentiating factors. Lower-class people, on the other hand, view the whole stratification of the society as a hierarchy of wealth. The lower lowers think that all those above them on the social scale are progressively wealthy and that their own subordination is dependent upon this economic factor alone. While upper lowers have a similar idea of those above them, they frequently add a moral note in explaining the subordinate position of lower lowers.[92]

[92] Allison Davis, Burleigh B. Gardner, and Mary R. Gardner, *Deep South* (Chicago: University of Chicago Press, 1941), pp. 72–73. Copyright 1941 by The University of Chicago.

Many writers have held that there is considerably more class consciousness in certain European countries than in the United States.[93] This is manifest in all sorts of ways. In the Latin countries, where class is based much more on family background than is the case in the United States, few persons in the upper classes will undertake manual labor, no matter how great their economic need, and some members of the aristocracy in Italy will not even accept professional positions. While the French universities have considerably lower fees than even state universities in the United States, and there are various subsidies for the living expenses of students, only a tiny proportion of children of workers go to universities. Worker families seldom even consider sending their children to college. It is quite rare for university students to work at manual jobs while going to college, even if they are desperately poor and even if they have sufficient free time. In England there has been a significant class difference in pronunciation of ordinary speech for a large proportion of the population (although this has decreased since 1940). In Germany one of the reasons why democracy is so weak is that few lower- and middle-class Germans think of seeking positions of leadership except in the trade unions, since leadership is assumed to be a prerogative of the upper class.

Much of this class consciousness in Europe is traceable back to the medieval caste system; only part of it resulted from the separation of owners and non-owners of the means of production that grew up in the Industrial Revolution—which the Marxists hold is the sole source of modern class consciousness. The "bourgeois" capitalists of Europe, especially of the Latin countries, to a considerable extent took over the behavior patterns of the former nobility caste, rather than developing a new set of relationships with the working people as in the United States. The United States started with only a tiny aristocracy and this soon merged with the rising capitalists and managers, so that there is no heritage of class consciousness from medieval caste. Class differences are sharpest and class consciousness strongest in those countries of Europe where medieval culture has hung on longest and strongest, rather than in those countries which have the greatest development of capitalism. This may be the major source of Marx's error of prediction. He held that the communist revolution, built on class consciousness and class conflict, would naturally occur where capitalism had developed far enough; actually the communist revolution has occurred, and the Communists are strongest where capitalism has had most difficulty in getting established because of the life left in the older feudal caste system.

Class consciousness is a prerequisite for class conflict, but conflict by

[93] For an analysis of class consciousness and conflict in Western countries, see Ralf Dahrendorf, *Class and Class Conflict in Industrial Society* (Stanford: Stanford University Press, 1957).

no means always results from class consciousness. Some of the people most aware of their inferior class position, and all its implications for their behavior, are the ones most accepting of it. Comparisons across cultures are difficult, but we may hazard the characterization of Germany as a nation where people tend to be strongly aware of their class and accept and enjoy the privileges and obligations it entails, whereas France is a nation where class consciousness and class conflict go together and interstimulate each other. Both countries present paradoxes. In Germany a worker may be a member of a union and vote Socialist but never feel any desire to offer a challenge to an upper-class judge or military officer; he believes it natural that the latter should occupy positions of leadership. In France members of the upper and lower classes have strong class identifications and have often engaged in bloody conflict with each other, but also have an unusually strong cultural tradition of individualism that makes organization for effective combat difficult and resistance to a potential communist or fascist dictatorship, or absolute monarchy, powerful. Thus, class consciousness and class conflict can co-exist with seemingly incompatible cultural traditions of feudal servility and arrogance and of extreme individualism.

2   TRENDS

In the absence of studies measuring class phenomena for periods longer than a decade or so in the past it is difficult to speak about trends in class consciousness and class conflict. It is possible, however, to describe the changes in several factors influencing class consciousness and conflict, and thereby make an estimate regarding the direction of the trends. We have seen that there is probably as much upward mobility in the United States now as there was before World War I. But it is also probable that not so many Americans *believe* they can rise significantly in social status. Popular literature today is less likely than formerly to stress the unlimited opportunity awaiting the ambitious and intelligent young man in the United States. The Turner thesis about the closing of the frontier and the Marxist thesis about the rich getting richer while the poor get poorer have filtered through the population to a certain extent. In another chapter we reported a few studies showing that a large proportion of lower-income Americans do not expect to start businesses and become "independent."[94]

When people change their expectations from rising in social status to maintaining their initial status, it is likely that they experience an increase in class identification. Much of the change occurred during the 1930's, in connection with one of the most serious economic depressions the world

[94] See Chapter 7, Section A. The defect of these data, of course, is that comparable statistics are not available for earlier periods.

has ever known. While the sharp rise in union membership during the 1930's was due to many factors, it is probable that one of the causes was the increase in class identification, since people who expect to have to remain in a class are more interested in getting the prerogatives of security within that class than if they expect to move up out of the class. Voting behavior became much more class stratified during the 1930's, with the working class largely attaching its allegiance to the Democratic Party, even though the structure of American government and American political system discourages parties from representing a single group's interest.

On the other hand, there have also been certain factors tending to reduce class consciousness in the United States. Around the beginning of the twentieth century the bulk of the rich people ceased to have aristocratic pretensions. Previously, the nobility of Europe had served as a model for many Americans of wealth and old family background. The upper class of the pre-Civil War South considered themselves almost as a caste apart from the "poor whites," and there had not been much of a middle class to cushion the sharp differences between the two groups. The Civil War greatly reduced the tendency toward caste separation of upper- and lower-class whites in the South by seriously weakening the power of the old upper class, by opening the way for lower-class mobility into the upper and growing middle class, and by forcing the upper-class whites to avoid anti-lower-class behavior so as to avoid driving the lower-class whites into a political alliance with the now-free Negroes. On the other hand, the rich people of the North increasingly sought to emulate the European aristocratic model. Some wealthy people began private art collections, occasionally transplanted physically whole castles from Europe or built new castles after a medieval or Renaissance model, occasionally affected a distinctive style of clothing or a distinctive pronunciation, frequently sent their children to private schools or to Europe for their elementary and secondary education as well as their college training, adopted a rigid and elaborate code of manners, and in general held themselves aloof from the rest of American society.[95]

For reasons that are not at all clear this pattern for the American wealthy changed considerably between the 1890's and 1914.[96] Perhaps the "new public relations"—beginning with Ivy Lee's successful effort to change the public stereotype of John D. Rockefeller, which shifted the picture of the large capitalist from an empire-building "robber baron" to a responsible, democratic American—had something to do with convincing

[95] This was the era in which Thorstein Veblen wrote his insightful and biting description of the habits of "conspicuous consumption" among America's wealthy. See his *The Theory of the Leisure Class* (New York: Macmillan, 1899).

[96] Frederick Lewis Allen, *The Big Change: America Transforms Itself, 1900–1950* (New York: Harper, 1952).

The typical income of the American family has undergone a striking change in two major respects over recent years.

The first of these is the increasing prevalence of the double paycheck. In fact, the latest figures of the U. S. Bureau of the Census show that families with two or more earners are now in the majority, outnumbering those with a single earner by more than a million in 1962. By contrast, the one-paycheck families exceeded those with more than one earner by over 6 million in 1950, and the margin was still more than 3¼ million as recently as 1955.

The second change reflects the great extent that thrift has become a common family characteristic. Today there are practically as many families with an extra income, primarily from savings and investments, in addition to one from employment as there are those dependent solely on their earnings.

The proportion is now close to half of all families in each case. The change here has been even more dramatic than in the number of family earners. Census Bureau data show that little more than a decade ago about seven out of ten families had income from earnings alone, a proportion close to three times that of families with earnings and other types of income.

These changes are particularly evident in the higher brackets, which have paced the steady growth in family income over the postwar period. And the dominant factor has been the working wife, whose number is now nearing 14 million, up by three-fifths since the beginning of the Fifties. Working wives, employed either part or full time, now represent one out of every three married women, compared with a ratio of one out of four a decade ago.

The Census Bureau in its recent study reported that the average (or median) money income of America's 47 million families in 1962 rose to a new high of just under $6,000, about $2,700 or four-fifths greater than in 1950.

The Independent Banker, 14 (February, 1964), p. 22.

the wealthy themselves. Many wealthy people gradually abandoned their rigid codes of class conduct, turned part of their art collections over to public museums, dropped distinctive forms of dress and speech, and sought in their public behavior to appear as "typical American," although they did not completely abandon habits of conspicuous consumption.[97] The wealthy were also expected to take an active part in community activities rather than devoting themselves exclusively to their own interests. This shift toward integration of the wealthy into the general American society may be said to indicate a decrease of class consciousness on their part.

The increasing use of education as an avenue of social mobility may have decreased class consciousness just as it has decreased class differences. The educational ladder is freer today than it was in the nineteenth

[97] Extreme examples of conspicuous consumption occasionally are reported in the newspapers, but they seem not to be so typical as they were in the 1890's. For example, in 1947 a publisher held a dinner party at the Waldorf-Astoria Hotel in New York, and had the ice used to chill the cocktails flown 3,300 miles by transport plane from the Mendenhall glacier in Alaska. (*St. Louis Post-Dispatch*, January 15, 1947, p. 1.)

century, a larger proportion of people take advantage of it, and it is more likely to lead to high-status managerial posts as well as to professional positions. Education as an avenue of mobility—as compared to wealth, which was the chief avenue of mobility up to a generation ago—reduces the barriers between the top status class and the next adjacent class, since educated people learn the accepted personal habits of the top class as well as the occupation which raises their status, whereas the *nouveaux riches* did not learn these habits while making money. The achievement of a moderate level of educational attainment (say, high-school graduation) may be a factor in many contemporary workers' conception of themselves as "middle class," even if they also think of themselves as workers.[98]

The increasing level of manual workers' pay—relative to the earnings of white-collar workers and storekeepers, who have traditionally been considered to be middle class—could be a similar factor in some workers' evaluation of themselves as middle class. With their higher income they are acquiring certain possessions—for example, a comfortable home and automobile—which have traditionally been associated with the middle class. On the basis of this principle, some of the non-Marxist socialists who have helped to guide the Scandinavian countries along the "middle way," between capitalism and communism, have held that trade union and government activity for the benefit of the poorer classes has tended to reduce class feeling. The former economic advisor to the Ministry of Social Affairs of Denmark, for example, says:

> . . . the experience of the Northern European countries has shown that it is precisely the activities of the trade unions arising out of this class feeling—including strikes—which help to bring about such improvements in the workers' conditions of life that class feeling is reduced. It may consequently be expected that trade-union activity combined with government measures will ultimately remove the conditions on which the opposition is based, and will thus lead to the disappearance of class feeling. If such a development is to be promoted by means of the feeling of conflict, it must be the task of democracy not to suppress but to guide the activities that have their origin in this class mentality.[99]

[98] There is nothing incompatible between people thinking of themselves both as "middle class" and as "working class." This would explain why several studies have found that most Americans think of themselves as middle class, while Centers's study (*op. cit.*) finds half the American population calling itself working class. It is Centers himself who creates the discrepancy by taking over the Marxist assumption that the workers are the dispossessed class. Actually a large proportion of workers in the United States have material characteristics—such as home ownership or son in college—which tend to make them identify with the middle class.

[99] Joergen S. Dich, "Economic Enquiries as a Basis for Democratic Adjustment of Labour Disputes," *International Labour Review*, 38 (November, 1938), pp. 575–90; pp. 576–77 quoted.

At the opposite end of the scale considerably higher income taxes are cutting down the ceiling on individual wealth, even if they are not decreasing the number of millionaires. Thus the range of income has been decreasing in the past few decades, and this operates as an influence decreasing class consciousness.[100]

The decreasing proportion of foreign-born in the American population, since the immigration laws of 1921 and 1924, is decreasing the proportion of people who might carry over a European conception of class consciousness. Immigrants, too, can seldom escape the negative effects on social status of their ethnic background, whereas their American-born children much more often can. Those who immigrated to the United States when they were adults can feel that they never had an opportunity to use a free educational ladder, whereas their offspring are aware that the ladder is available even if they have not used it. For these reasons the declining proportion of foreign-born in the population may be a factor decreasing class consciousness.

The factors affecting class consciousness thus operate in opposing directions, and in the absence of any long-run direct measure it is impossible to say whether class consciousness is increasing or decreasing. Class conflict is a more overt behavior and changes in it should be easier to detect. Revolution, except for the Civil War, which was a major exception, has been rarer in the United States than in many other countries, and the government has not often been identified with a single class so that efforts to revolt have seldom had the character of class warfare. Still, there were certain events in American history which had some of the characteristics of class warfare—Shays' Rebellion, the march of "Coxey's Army," the Boston police strike, the San Francisco general strike,[101] the hunger marchers on Washington in the early 1930's. These are minor and show no trend.

Industrial strife has had its ups and downs in American history, with short-run variations being greater than any long-run trend. During the mid-1930's there was a decided upswing in the number of industrial strikes, as the number of workers in unions sharply increased. Many of these strikes had the character of real class conflict: the union organizers and many of the workers were desperate, and some of the employers used armed guards or local police to oppose them. In the Minneapolis teamsters' strike of 1934 there was considerable violence and most of the community took sides. In the South Chicago steel strike of 1937 a number of

[100] There are some exceptions. A special income-tax exemption for oil production has created a few new accumulations of unparalleled wealth. The war boom—with its tremendous increase in economic demand and its operation of opportunities for illegal black-market operations—also reversed the trend temporarily.

[101] For a description of general strikes in various parts of the world, see Wilfred Harris Crook, *The General Strike* (Chapel Hill: University of North Carolina Press, 1931).

workers lost their lives and scores of workers and policemen were injured. The sit-down strikes of 1936–37 were temporary seizures of employers' property by disciplined workers.

While the number of strikes has kept at a high level since the hectic days of the mid-1930's (except for the war period when it was considered unpatriotic to strike), the character of the strikes now involves much less of the element of class warfare. Probably none of the recent strikes in the United States have had the character of a "general strike," in which a whole community is tied up because workers in many industries deliberately leave their job simultaneously. Opposition between organized workers and employers remains sharp and cunning, but neither side seems to wish to resort to bloodshed or attempts to destroy the other side completely. The various "unfair labor practices" acts of the federal and state governments since 1935 have reduced the opportunities for use of such all-out tactics. Strikes have taken on something of a ceremonial character in American life. If the union and the company cannot agree on a contract during the annual or biennial collective-bargaining period, the workers go out on strike and remain out until one side or the other is sufficiently weakened to compromise to the point demanded by the other side. Strikes thus have a role in the ongoing process of industrial production and scarcely involve any bitterness or antagonism either during or after the strike. If this characteristic of strikes since 1945 continues, strikes will neither be expressions of class conflict nor contribute to class consciousness.

Aside from the strikes and rare "lockouts" by employers, practically no other conflict[102] in the United States can be considered to be a class conflict. As Anderson points out, "Many, if not most, of the aggressive organizations cut across class boundaries or serve only a faction within a class."[103] This is in sharp contrast with the situation in France and several other continental European countries, where the major cleavages and conflicts are class stratified.

[102] See Chapter 16.

[103] C. Arnold Anderson, "The Need for a Functional Theory of Social Class," *Rural Sociology*, 19 (June, 1954), p. 155.

FOR ADDITIONAL READING

BENDIX, REINHARD, and SEYMOUR M. LIPSET (eds.), *Class, Status, and Power* (Glencoe, Ill.: Free Press, 1953). A collection of readings on social stratification.

DOLLARD, JOHN, *Caste and Class in a Southern Town* (New Haven: Yale University Press, 1937). One of the most penetrating analyses of caste and class in the South.

GHURYE, G. S., *Caste, Class, and Occupation* (Bombay, India: Popular Book Depot, 1961). One of the most recent and comprehensive analyses of caste in India, by one of the leading older sociologists of that country.

LIPSET, SEYMOUR M., and REINHARD BENDIX, *Social Mobility in an Industrial Society* (Berkeley: University of California Press, 1958). Detailed studies of modern social mobility.

MAYER, KURT B., *Class and Society* (New York: Random House, 1955). A brief, sensible analysis of class.

MYRDAL, GUNNAR, with the assistance of Richard Sterner and Arnold Rose, *An American Dilemma* (New York: Harper, 1944). A description and interpretation of the position of the Negro in the United States in terms of caste. A more up-to-date summary of this lengthy work is Arnold Rose's *The Negro in America* (Harper Torchbook ed., 1964).

9 * *Three Types of Human Association: the Crowd, the Audience, and the Public*

The integrated group has been given exclusive attention in preceding chapters as the major form of human association. Whether the organization be formal or informal, based on primary or on secondary relationships, consisting of two persons (as, for example, a married couple) or of a whole society, the basic characteristic of such a group is that each member is able imaginatively to take the role of the other, in advance of action, and so adjust his behavior to that of the other. The members of the group play roles toward each other which permit a high degree of predictability in the behavior of the one toward the other. The basis of this role taking and predictability is common meanings and values which have been communicated to all members of the group.

There are other forms of human association in which people influence each other's behavior and act collectively, but not by means of their expectations and roles toward each other. Among these are what sociologists have labeled the crowd, the audience, and the public. These are very inadequate terms, since they do not suggest the basic characteristic of the association, and since they have a meaning in popular usage that is quite different from that in sociological usage. But we shall follow the traditional usage rather than coin new terms. The crowd, the audience, and the public are each ideal-type concepts. Rarely are they found in pure form. But an element of them may be found in many concrete situations. For descriptive purposes we shall emphasize the pure forms before alluding to the everyday manifestations.

A *The Crowd*

The crowd may be defined as a group of individuals in physical proximity to each other and influencing each other through the mere fact of their physical proximity. A group of individuals is spoken of as a crowd, however, only when that mutual influence of physical presence is rather high. Animal groups, in the forms of herds, packs, or flocks, are crowds in this sense, and the crowd behavior of human beings may be thought of as a type of behavior which they share with other animals. Communication in the crowd is by means of natural signs rather than by means of significant symbols. There are no common meanings and values (that is, no culture, although until the extreme state of the crowd is reached, the participants "remember" some aspects of their culture), and the only thing that can be regarded as common to all members of the crowd is what may be called a "feeling tone." The presence of other individuals is, when perceived through the sense organs of sight, hearing, and touch, stimulating in itself and under certain circumstances may become especially so. We shall emphasize here the circumstances under which the physical presence of others becomes highly stimulating and gives rise to a strong feeling tone.

The writer who first popularized the conception of the crowd was Gustav Le Bon, a French aristocrat who described and evaluated what he saw of street behavior in Paris during the French Revolution of 1871.[1] The occasionally factual sections of Le Bon's book formulated the interests of future writers, but his own work was otherwise rendered almost useless by two serious biases arising from his aristocratic orientation. He believed that political democracy was controlled by street crowds, and that crowd behavior was the typical expression of all group behavior among the masses of the people. Le Bon did not realize that what he was reporting on were some rather rare phases of collective excitement.

A street crowd in revolutionary circumstances does, however, provide one illustration of a very important type of crowd behavior. We call this type the *acting crowd*, or mob, because it is organized for a purpose, and its actions are directed toward the achievement of that purpose. For example, in revolutionary circumstances its purpose is to eliminate at least part of the existing governmental structure. The other major type of crowd behavior is the *expressive crowd*, sometimes known as the orgiastic crowd or dancing crowd because of the emphasis upon rhythmical movement *per se*

---

[1] *The Crowd* (London: T. F. Unwin, 1896). Italian writers—notably Rossi and Sighele —were also early describers of the crowd.

without any goal or purpose in the behavior. A religious revival meeting where emotion and excitement have gotten beyond the control of the participants would be an illustration of the expressive crowd. Another common illustration would be the observers at a football game who are carried away with the excitement of the contest.

1 THE LYNCHING MOB AS AN "ACTING CROWD"

The characteristics of a crowd can be best described in connection with examples. Our first example will be that of a lynch mob, which is one manifestation of the acting crowd. Crowds generally form when a highly organized society—having an "integrated group" mode of relationship— is beginning to break down. Lynchings most often take place in small communities that have a relatively high degree of isolation from the outside world and which have had a high degree of internal integration.[2] Lynchings have generally been found to occur when a problem seriously besets the community, often a problem of economic character, and one with which the community is unable to cope. People have made efforts to solve the problem but their efforts have been frustrated and there is no community-wide agreement or consensus as to the nature of the problem or the best means of solving it. Thus there is restlessness in the community and a feeling that communication is inadequate concerning important community problems. The situation is characterized by what the Yale psychologists[3] would call frustration, in which—because people are blocked in their achievement of a normal goal—some object is searched for upon which the community can react in aggression. The object of collective aggression is called a "scapegoat" since it is a symbolic substitute for the cause of the frustration against which people would normally react (if they were rational and if no extraneous undersirable consequences were to follow).

People not only feel personally dissatisfied but there is a widespread belief that something is wrong with the community in general, that the usual standards are being broken down by forces that are not under control. On a trivial level we can see the same mechanism operating in a committee meeting where things are not going well and there is a good deal of desire to express aggression, held in check by a compulsion to be polite. Tension is gradually built up. Then one person does something which is a bit out of the ordinary, and his act seems to trigger the others to express their pent-up feelings against him. The attack appears concerted, but it

[2] Earle F. Young, "The Relation of Lynching to the Size of Political Areas," *Sociology and Social Research*, 7 (March–April, 1928), pp. 348–53; National Resources Committee, *Our Cities* (Washington, D.C., 1937), p. 16.

[3] John Dollard *et al.*, *Frustration and Aggression* (New Haven: Yale University Press, 1939).

really consists only of like reactions on the part of a number of individuals who feel the same way. The reaction of the group is much stronger than would normally be the case when a person deviates in a minor way. In our example of a frustrated, isolated community a crime may occur and people feel that here at last is a weakness in the community which they can understand—an attack on the customs and integration of the community which they can control. They overreact against the criminal, and if the tradition of law enforcement is not strong in the community, they take the law into their own hands and punish the criminal themselves, not waiting until the normal processes of law determine his punishment, not waiting until the evidence is clear that he really is the criminal. In quite a few cases the community does not even bother to get the real criminal but selects for its object of violence any person who "reasonably" seems to have been the criminal. In 26 per cent of the lynchings of Negroes in the southern states between 1889 and 1933 the person lynched was not even alleged to have committed a crime; he merely appeared to be a convenient victim when the white community became incensed against the local Negroes.[4]

Reaction to news of the crime is not immediate, for a most important "circular process" has to take place before the community transforms itself into a lynch mob. People begin to talk in the streets, over the back fences, in the stores, about the nature of the crime and about the character of the alleged criminal. Details of the crime are embellished and exaggerated. The vicious character of the criminal is developed. Evidence against the criminal is invented during the conversation by people who have no intention of lying. During this circular process of building up excitement and emotion in the community—which may take as much as two or three days—people find themselves being able to communicate with each other adequately about a common problem for the first time in a long while. This is a pleasant experience, as it involves a feeling of once more belonging to the community and being able to solve its problems.

At first people may talk fairly rationally and carry on their everyday business as they talk, but very quickly they are not adding any new facts or new viewpoints to the discussion. They simply repeat what has already been said many times and seem to get satisfaction out of the repetition. Gradually the talk about the crime becomes the center of the whole community's activities, and excitement and emotion grow. People increasingly shut out from their minds any other interests and cut their activities to the minimum necessary to existence. They spend more and more time gathering on the streets to discuss the news and rumors about the crime and the criminal.

[4] Arthur Raper, *The Tragedy of Lynching* (Chapel Hill: University of North Carolina Press, 1933).

During this circular process a change of leadership often occurs in the community. The formal and informal leaders of the organized groups in the community generally have some stake in maintaining the regular community activities and therefore try to hold the crowd down to following the law and group rules and carrying on the everyday processes of community life. But the citizenry is not in a mood for that after a while, and leadership tends to shift to people who in ordinary times have low prestige. These are very often young men who have no great stake in the formal status hierarchy of the community, who are ambitious but have been frustrated in their ambitions, who have the energy and the willingness to engage in irregular behavior. In some lynchings it has been discovered that the leaders were the "drugstore cowboys"—fairly young men who have weak economic positions in the community and who loafed a great deal. These persons are least bound by the formal processes of the community and get most satisfaction out of encouraging unusual behavior. They lead in stimulating excitement, in spreading the rumors and news about the crime, in making suggestions for action. They get satisfaction not only out of being able to talk freely to other people, who are now interested in listening to them, but also out of being leaders when normally they are regarded as inferior or undesirable citizens.

When excitement has reached a high pitch, a large number of people gather on the streets, and the crowd proper has begun to form. They move about in close quarters—a process called "milling"—and there is a mutual physical stimulation which increases muscular tonus. The talk is exciting, even though nothing new is said. Threats and incitement to action against the alleged criminal are freely expressed in an excited tone of voice. Before action can take place most members of the crowd have to reach a psychological state known as "possession." The milling, the loud and exciting noises, the concentration of attention, the increasing rhythm of people's movements stimulate possession. The "possessed" member of the crowd feels himself no longer an individual with his own private concerns and his sense of "free will," but an element of a larger body acting as a unity—in response to forces which he does not understand—to satisfy the "higher" needs of the unit. He loses his sense of "I" or subjective self and feels himself to be a purely responding mechanism. He literally feels as though some force had possession of his body and most of his mind. The crowd member feels himself part of something good and wholesome that is larger than himself, into which he has submerged his individuality, and therefore he does not feel responsible for his actions. It is a very pleasant and exhilarating feeling. It is a feeling of exhilaration that does not often come to a person who leads an uneventful life or who has hitherto been wrapped up in individual problems.

When the crowd begins to move down the street toward its goal, led by persons who are most excited and exciting, few individuals even think of moving away and not participating in what is going on. They may originally have come along simply to watch the excitement, but the process of crowd formation has had its effect on them and willy-nilly they are part of the now acting mob. The leaders initiate the action of destruction or lynching but the crowd aids by its physical presence and its stimulating support. During the action the highest degree of exhilaration and obliviousness to external events is felt by practically every member of the mob. The action is considered to be a collective effort to meet a community problem, and is thus perceived to be for the common good. The individual has a sense of anonymity in the crowd. Temporarily he does not think of himself as James Johnson, storekeeper, member of Kiwanis and of the Methodist Church, father of a family, etc.; he thinks of himself merely as an integral element of the crowd, which he identifies with the whole community. Because of his feeling of being possessed, he does not feel responsible for his actions. Under these psychological conditions mob members go to extremes of physical action such as they would not engage in in ordinary life, much as persons under hypnosis do upon receiving suggestions for strenuous action from the hypnotist.

After the lynching or other type of mob violence is over, some members of the crowd may feel a sense of guilt for having violated the legal or religious code, but nevertheless they also have a pleasant memory of the exciting and exhilarating experience and a sense of rebirth of community feeling. Release and achievement are the major characteristics associated with the memory of the crowd's action. The members of the community retain for a time the sense of mutual understanding which first arose when they engaged in what they perceived as a major collective action to solve a common threat to their collective life as a community. Community integration is so strong after a lynching that seldom is information given to outside law-enforcement officials that would aid in detection of leaders of the lynching.

2   THE REVIVAL MEETING AS AN "EXPRESSIVE CROWD"

The *expressive* crowd differs from the acting crowd only in minor respects, mainly associated with its lack of a specific purpose. The expressive crowd may be illustrated by a description of the typical religious revival meeting.[5] A considerable degree of collective unrest and dissatis-

[5] For other descriptions of the religious revivals as expressive crowds, see Erskine Caldwell, *Journeyman* (New York: Penguin, 1935), pp. 120–32; E. Louis Backman, *Religious Dances in the Christian Church and in Popular Medicine* (New York: Macmillan, 1952); T. K. Oesterreich, *Possession, Demoniacal and Other, among Primitive Races, in Antiquity, the Middle Ages, and Modern Times* (New York: R. R. Smith, 1930).

faction must exist in the community before many people will turn out for a religious revival meeting, just as in the case of the acting crowd. Under normal circumstances, when there are few frustrations in the community and when there is a high degree of mutual understanding based upon the regular meanings and values of the culture, there is little feeling that a religious *revival* is needed. Under normal circumstances in the integrated society religious behavior will be expressed through formal church meetings.

The people who will form the expressive crowd come together at a formalized occasion; that is, when an announcement is made in advance that there will be a meeting for a religious revival. Thus, to a certain extent, people, come knowing in advance what they will experience. They expect some excitement and perhaps a feeling of possession which they identify as a "religious experience." People may not be particularly happy when they arrive, but there is usually some music playing which cheers them up, relaxes them, and makes them receptive before the preacher commences. The preacher often starts off in an ordinary speaker's tone of voice so that there is no immediate change in emotional experience for the audience. But within a matter of minutes he shifts to a strident tone and an exhortatory manner. The unusual loudness, hardness, and cadence of his voice begin to excite people, not only because they are different from those of an ordinary speaker but also because the increased frequency and amplitude of stimuli striking their sense organs tend to stimulate their muscles and glands. From the preacher's standpoint, he is using the tricks of the speaker's trade to prevent people from falling asleep. Early in the service the preacher may call for music several times to "get people into the spirit of the meeting." The songs, while religious in content, have a swinging and invigorating melody. By participating in the singing the audience begins to acquire a sense of solidarity within itself—that is, "the spirit of the meeting"—and to get attuned to the rhythm.

The preacher soon begins to use rhythm and audience participation as an adjunct to his sermon. His own sentences tend to grow shorter and more rhythmical, and he invites audience participation by calls for "Amen" and short phrases as answers to questions. An apparently frequent device used by the preacher is to ask short questions and have the audience shout back stock answers in a regular rhythm. Sometimes a drum is used to beat out the rhythm of the words and of the audience reaction. The rhythm of audience participation stimulates the circular process which is so necessary for crowd behavior. The reaction of the members of the audience is no longer simply to the preacher and to the music but also to each other. As the stimuli come more and more from within the group relative to that from the preacher the audience gradually becomes transformed into a crowd. The stimuli are much more physical than social in nature since people are not giving organized speeches but are simply emitting a few words that have a rhythmical quality and are fairly meaningless in themselves. As people participate collectively in the noisemaking they increase their sense of solidarity as a crowd. Since people are no longer exactly acting as they would in the privacy of their homes or on a public street, the bizarre element in behavior has become more acceptable. People begin to feel a sense of anonymity. "Everyone is doing something strange and therefore it is all right if I act a little odd, too."

Some people are more susceptible than others to the crowd's spirit and reach a state of possession before others do. They provide a kind of leadership in breaking down others' resistance to bizarre behavior and other kinds of inhibitions. Spontaneously they will raise their voices above the others and shout occasionally. Others will push their chairs aside to give themselves more freedom for motion or they will move into the aisles and begin to express with their bodies the rhythm of participation. These sounds and movements are stimulating and exciting in themselves in a physical way, but in a symbolically meaningful way they also suggest that unusual behavior is permissible in the situation. The preacher is one of the first to use body movements. He does not stand up stiffly in front of the podium but sways his body, waves his arms, and sometimes runs up and down a short distance on the stage. As excitement grows, his muscular movements tend to be imitated by members of the audience, perhaps not in such an extreme way but in a more subdued manner, such as the muscular tensions of the members of an audience watching acrobats on a tightrope. Following the lead of the preacher and of the more susceptible members of the audience, even the more inhibited members of the crowd begin to make body motions in time to the rhythm of the words.

Body motion in itself is a stimulant to further body motion and soon chairs and benches are pushed aside so that people can give more sway to their movements. It is then that the circular process takes the form of a dance. The dance, of course, is not one of those ordinarily seen on ballroom or stage floors. It is simply a regularized series of steps and body movements which are repeated over and over again. Each person has his own form of the dance, and the only thing in common among all the people is conformity to rhythm, which has become established for the meeting as a whole. A feeling of exaltation and ecstasy has now claimed most of the people through the dancing, shouting, and singing. Persons most susceptible to the crowd's spirit have already reached the state of possession. They often talk louder than the preacher and pay no attention to him, and sometimes create a rhythmical leadership on their own. By the time possession has taken hold of a person the words that have been establishing the rhythm of the evening no longer have any meaning for them. They are simply a set of repeated noises that sound well together and can be utilized to maintain the rhythm. The words used are very often familiar words from Biblical quotations that are used completely out of context and without relationship to anything that has been said before. During extreme states of possession words will often be abandoned for nonsense syllables. This is the phenomenon known as "glossolalia," or, as the old-time revivalists call it, "speaking with tongues." It consists of a series of meaningless syllables that sound harmonious together. Superstitious people used to think that an angel or devil was speaking through the voice of the possessed person in an other-worldly language. The body movements of possessed persons, too, lose semblance to conventional movements of the human body. More and more they assume the form of wild jerks. Sometimes, in extreme possession, a person will fall to the floor and begin "flopping," or he will beat himself in time to his wailing.

"The jerks" are well described by Peter Cartwright, a clergyman of the early nineteenth century, at which time such "exercises" were common.

> Just in the midst of our controversies on the subject of the powerful exercises among the people under preaching, a new exercise broke out among us, called "the Jerks," which was overwhelming in its effects upon the bodies and minds of the people. No matter whether they were saints or sinners, they would be taken under a warm song or sermon, and seized with a convulsive jerking all over, which they could not by any possibility avoid, and the more they resisted the more they jerked. If they would not strive against it and pray in good earnest, the jerking would usually abate. I have seen more than 500 persons jerking at one time in my large congregations. Most usually persons taken with the jerks, to obtain relief, as they said, would rise up and dance. Some would run, but could not get away. Some would resist; on such, the jerks were generally very severe.
>
> To see those proud young gentlemen and young ladies, dressed in their silks, jewelry and prunella, from top to toe, take the JERKS would often excite my risibilities. The first jerk or so, you would see their fine bonnets, caps and combs fly; and so sudden would be the jerking of the head that their long loose hair would crack almost as loud as a waggoner's whip.[6]

As the circular process of the evening is stepped up, the rhythm of movements and the noise become quicker and quicker. During extreme crowd behavior nearly every participant will be speaking with tongues and flopping or jerking. The group rhythm may be lost but the excitement and noise and movement are so great that they provide extreme stimulation. People are generally not aware of what is happening to them in extreme

---

[6] Quoted by Ernest S. Bates, *American Faith: Its Religious, Political, and Economic Foundations* (New York: Norton, 1940).

states of possession, but until these extreme states are reached there is a feeling that one is gradually being possessed, that is, that one is engaging in behavior beyond his own control, that some sort of force is taking hold of him and making him shout and behave in ways that he would not ordinarily think of doing. Inhibitions are relaxed, but people do not feel responsible for their loss of inhibition. This is a highly pleasant and exhilarating experience. It provides the feeling of ecstasy that is expected in religious experience. The stimulation and the movement go on until the individuals in the crowd are completely exhausted. Exhaustion does not come very quickly, as the human body is capable of much more exertion than one ordinarily engages in, so that extreme crowd behavior may continue for several hours before the members of the crowd literally pass out because of exhaustion.

What are the aftermaths of crowd excitement, after the participants have slept off their exhaustion? For practically everyone there is a memory of exhilaration, emotional excitement, and collective participation. This is especially important for people who have been leading dull and uneventful lives. For some there is also the belief that they have had a truly religious experience; this generally enhances the significance and the value of the memory of the expressive crowd experience. For a few there may be a feeling of disgust at one's self for having engaged in such extraordinary behavior. But those who truly believe that possession is a religious experience will quite frequently be transformed for a long time or even permanently in their personal behavior. They will conform to the expectations for a religious person both in daily life and in frequent attendance at church services. They may even become a "better person"—that is, closer to the cultural ideal or personal ideal of the self[7]—because of the experience. For the group as a whole there is also a change. There has been a significant community event experienced in common, if the revival meeting was a successful one and if a very large portion of the community participated in it. If certain symbols had a conspicuous place in the revival service, such as the name of the preacher or the use of some physical symbol as a cross or star or emblem, these will recall to people's memories the common experience and revive for future occasions the sense of group solidarity which was felt in the original meeting itself.

3   VARIATIONS IN CROWD BEHAVIOR

We have been describing the crowd experience in its extreme form where the whole group becomes possessed in high degree. The crowd may take lesser forms, in which people feel only partially possessed or in which only a few of the members of a group fall under complete sense of possession.

[7] See Chapter 4, Sections E and H.

While extreme forms of the crowd are rather rare, the lesser forms are not completely uncommon. The excitement of a party (especially one at which a little drinking has relaxed inhibitions), of spectators at a football game,[8] of a crowd of people formed in the street to watch an accident, of a number of people trapped in an elevator, has in itself the first elements of a crowd. Closer to full-blown crowds are occasional street demonstrations, such as those which greeted Charles Lindbergh after he crossed the Atlantic in 1927, General MacArthur after he returned from Korea in 1951, King George VI when he visited South Africa.[9] Audiences—such as the one made up of young females who regularly attended the performances of the singers Frank Sinatra,[10] Elvis Presley, and the four Beatles—sometimes become expressive crowds.

Panics are a form of expressive crowd: the panic that seized the visitors to the Cocoanut Grove night club in Boston during a fire in 1942 killed more than a hundred persons.[11] An unusual panic—unusual because it took place over such a dispersed area with the participants not even in physical contact with each other (much of the excitement and feeling tone were transmitted by radio)—was that which followed Orson Welles' dramatic radio broadcast in 1938 of a play about an invasion of men from Mars.[12] Some, though not all, of the "panty-raids" by male college students on women's dormitories in colleges around the country in 1952 had characteristics of crowd behavior, as did the mass fainting of teen-age girls attending a high-school football game in Natchez, Mississippi, in September 1952.[13] Students taught to be aware of the psychological characteristics of the crowd are usually able to detect in themselves the beginnings of the feeling of possession when they are in these kinds of groups. The crowd is a phenomenon of different degrees, and whenever a breaking down of inhibitions, excitement, and the circular process begins in group situations there is some element of the crowd present.

[8] The following item from a college newspaper suggests that books like this one can dampen the ardor of spectators at competitive sports events:

When complaints began to pour in to the University of Washington that there was not enough school spirit at basketball games, one student turned up with this explanation: "How do you expect someone to yell and cheer when there's a sociology professor beside him taking notes of mob behavior?" (*Minnesota Daily*, March 12, 1953, p. 4).

[9] Dan Jacobson, "A Visit from Royalty," *Commentary*, 11 (February, 1954), pp. 181–84.

[10] *Time* magazine, 42 (July 5, 1943), p. 26.

[11] For a survey of the literature on panic, see Anselm L. Strauss, "The Literature on Panic," *Journal of Abnormal and Social Psychology*, 39 (July, 1944), pp. 317–28.

[12] Hadley Cantril *et al.*, *The Invasion from Mars* (Princeton, N.J.: Princeton University Press, 1940). A similar event happened in Russia in 1955, following the publication of a fictional story in a popular Soviet magazine in which "a Martian space ship was supposed to have crash-landed on earth" (*New York Times*, May 1, 1955, p. 80).

[13] *Minneapolis Morning Tribune*, September 13, 1952, p. 1. For a description of a destructive riot by Princeton University students in 1963, see the *New York Times*, May 8, 1963, p. 33, and May 9, 1963, p. 33.

The question is sometimes raised as to whether educated people—
who "ought to know better"—can participate in crowd experience. The
answer is definitely yes. Crowd behavior is a physical reaction which all
the higher animals—including man—are susceptible to under conditions
specific for them. There is variation in individual susceptibility to crowd experience, but this seems to be a function of such physiological factors as reaction time and excitability and of such psychogenic factors as neurotic
susceptibility and strength of inhibition, and these variables have no known
relationship to degree of education and sophistication. The novelist Strindberg gives a striking description of an acting crowd in which most of the
participants, including himself, were educated. The purpose of the mob
was to free some political prisoners, which was not to the rational interest
of the upper class.

> John [Strindberg himself as a young man] tore himself loose; the
> crowd were now driven back by bayonets towards the guard-house
> in the Gustav Adolf market. After them followed a swarm of well-
> dressed men, obviously members of the upper classes, shouting
> wildly, and as it seemed, resolved to free the prisoners. John ran with
> them; it was as though they were all impelled by a storm-wind. Men
> who had not been molested or oppressed at all, who had high posi-
> tions in society, rushed blindly forward, risking their position, their
> domestic happiness, their living, everything. John felt a hand grasp
> his. He returned the pressure, and saw close beside him a middle-
> aged man, well-dressed, with distorted features. They did not know
> each other, nor did they speak together, but ran hand in hand, as if
> seized by one impulse. They came across a third in whom John rec-
> ognised an old school-fellow, subsequently a civil service official, son
> of the head of a department. This young man had never sided with
> the opposition party in school, but on the contrary, was looked upon
> as a reactionary with a future in front of him. He was now as white
> as a corpse, his cheeks were bloodless, the muscles of his forehead
> swollen, and his face resembled a skull in which two eyes were burn-
> ing. They could not speak, but took each other's hands and ran on
> against the guards whom they were attacking. The human waves ad-
> vanced till they were met by the bayonets, and then as always dis-
> persed in foam. Half-an-hour later John was discussing a beefsteak
> with some students in the Opera restaurant. He spoke of his adven-
> ture as though it were something which had happened independently
> of him and his will. Nay, he even jested at it. That may have been
> fear of public opinion, but also it may have been the case that he re-
> garded his outbreak objectively and now quietly judged it as a mem-
> ber of society. The trap-door had opened for a moment, the prisoner
> had put his head out, and then it had closed again.
> His unknown fellow-criminal, as he discovered later, was a pro-

When a circular process and collective excitement in an ordinary group situation provide the background conditions for a crowd, an unexpected incident
can precipitate extreme crowd behavior. A student from a small town in
Minnesota provides an example from an incident that took place at a public
dance hall some years ago:

> Some years ago there was a large dance hall south of our community.
> This pavilion was situated on the shores of a beautiful lake. It was one
> of the most popular spots in the county. The management hired some of
> the top orchestras of the time and reservations had to be made weeks
> ahead of time to insure a party of getting a booth. Many booths were
> reserved for whole seasons. Everyone flocked to this beautiful place of
> amusement. Naturally the owners were coining money and were very
> happy about it.
>
> Suddenly one Sunday evening at about 10:30 p.m., at the height of
> the evening's enjoyment, "something" dropped into the middle of the dance
> floor. An immediate interpretation that passed quickly from couple to
> couple was that the Devil had dropped down out of the rafters! People
> ran screaming—leaving their coats, their scarves and purses! Some never
> returned to claim these articles. The pavilion died. No one showed up,
> no matter what orchestra was engaged. The owner had to board it up
> for years. I have never heard anything talked about as much as this
> incident.
>
> I have never actually met anyone who was there and claimed to
> have seen the "figure" who appeared. But, of course, "everyone" knew
> exactly how he looked, what he wore, and even what he shrieked! I am not
> certain to this day whether there really was something. Was it a shadow?
> Was it some defective light? Or was it someone playing a joke or trick?
>
> But this experience affected the dancers so violently and the rumors
> were so wild that the old pavilion had to close and I never heard of
> a new one being erected. People still talk of the time the Devil appeared
> and continue to relate the tale to their children.

nounced conservative, a wholesale tradesman. He always avoided
meeting John's eye, when they met after this. One time they met on
a narrow pavement, and had to look at each other, but did not smile.[14]

The only thing education might do by way of resisting crowd behavior would be to give people specific knowledge of and insight into the
mechanisms that create the crowd. If an individual were to avoid the
stimuli of the noise and the body movement he might successfully resist
the crowd's influence for an indefinite time even though he were physically
present in it. For example, he might avoid the stimuli occasionally by re-
moving himself every so often from the meeting when he begins to feel excited, or he could close his eyes and stop his ears every so often, or he

[14] August Strindberg, *The Growth of a Soul* (London: Rider, 1913), pp. 76–77.

could distract his attention by forcing himself to concentrate on everyday matters or some kind of problem solving while being present at the meeting. But if even the most educated person is stimulated by the sight and sound of the crowd and has his attention concentrated on it he will soon fall into the circular process of the crowd, and unless he can deliberately make a break or a break is made for him by some pressure pushing him away from the crowd, he will fall into the crowd experience and pattern of behavior as readily as any other person.

A great deal is known about the control of crowds. Charismatic leaders, ranging in motivation from Adolf Hitler to Communist riot-provokers to sports cheerleaders to revivalistic ministers, have developed empirical techniques for transforming audiences into crowds. Military and police leaders have developed empirical techniques for breaking up crowds. These techniques can be readily inferred from the descriptions we have given of crowd behavior. In general, the deliberate creation of a crowd involves bringing a large number of people together in a limited space, exciting them as much as possible with rumors and provocations, having emotional symbols prominently displayed, having stirring and rhythmical music playing, and concentrating their attention. The techniques for deliberate break-up of a crowd are several: (1) Diverting attention from the focus of crowd excitement through providing alternative foci, such as small house fires in various other parts of the town. (2) Forcing attention to one's own comfort and safety, by drenching the crowd with cold water or shooting members of the crowd at random. (3) Breaking up the physical interstimulation among the members of the crowd, such as by driving chained-together armored cars through segments of the crowd. (4) Presenting to the edges of the crowd very powerful symbols of the integrated group, such as crosses, flags, highly respected public figures (Pope Alexander VI is alleged to have stopped a mob invading his palace by standing at the top of a bright staircase with his arms outstretched in the form of a cross). Ordinary verbal pleas to behave sensibly generally have little effect on a crowd that is already somewhat excited, but calm words backed up by the potential use of force may have a calming effect, especially when the crowd is in the early stages of formation.

Here are two descriptions of effective riot control, one from England, the other from the U.S.S.R.

> There were about 1,500 marchers—protesting against the means test, which made the dole harder to get. Police met the marchers south of Bloomsbury Square, just before the parade reached New Oxford St., and the prosperous west end of London. There were about a dozen mounted police, and about 50 on foot. None was armed, except with nightsticks.
>
> The crowd was angry. It could easily be stirred to violence. Had the police been angry, too—or worse, had they been frightened, bungling amateurs, incapable of keeping order except at the point of a gun—there would have been bloodshed at once.
>
> But the police were not angry. Competent men who know their job, and who can handle a situation, seldom get angry. It is the inefficient, the insecure, the badly trained, who lose their heads and make most of the trouble in the world.
>
> The London police were good-natured but unyielding. Even when tin cans and bricks began to fly, they still played the situation down, treating it as less important than it really was.
>
> On the side of the police there was no cursing, no shouting, no shooting, no use of nightsticks. The only weapon used was the weight of the horses' bodies. The mounted police could push their way through the crowd pretty much at will, making room for the men on foot to use their breaking-up tactics.
>
> Several of the police were cut about the face; but the police were the only ones who were bleeding. Even the police who were hurt did not lose their tempers. First and last, whenever officers talked to the rioters it was to tell them not to be foolish, and to assure them that the last thing the police wanted to do was to arrest anyone, but that if this foolish business went on much longer they might have to begin arresting.
>
> Within 10 or 15 minutes the whole thing was over. Finding no violent resistance, nothing on which to feed its anger, the crowd could not keep itself worked up to the riot point. In a short time everyone had quieted down, and groups began to straggle off home, flinging a few parting oaths at the police.
>
> The London police do not think of themselves as a private army,

hired by the rich to assault the poor. They think of themselves as men hired by the community, to help the community keep itself out of trouble.[15]

In November, 1917, after the Bolsheviks had come into power, excesses were no rarity, as is well known; the excited crowds frequently attacked people in the street for no reason, on the strength of simple suspicion aroused by anyone present. The persons attacked ran the risk of being lynched, and in some cases actually were lynched. To obviate this danger an organization of intellectuals in sympathy with the Soviet Government evolved a method of psychological action for such cases. A direct appeal to the crowd was not only liable to be useless but sometimes endangered the life of the person making it. A service was therefore created to which the name of "Fraternal Aid" was given. If anyone was attacked in the street, members of this organization who were witnesses of the attack rushed to the nearest telephone and informed the Fraternal Aid office, where there was always someone in attendance. At once men who were propaganda specialists, and who held themselves at the disposal of the organization, entered a motorcar which was kept always ready, and made at top speed for the point indicated. When they had come as close as they could, they pushed their way at different points into the crowd round the person in peril, and began to take part in the shouting, each independently of the rest, and each trying to attract attention to himself. These men, as experienced agitators, rapidly became new centres of interest for the crowd; they then drew away gradually in opposite directions, trying each to gain a circle of listeners of his own and so to break up the crowd into a number of groups, all of which would completely forget the imperilled man, who could efface himself and escape with his life. The organization was also known as the "Spiritual Aid Service."[16]

A distinction needs to be made between the conditions under which people assemble preparatory to crowd behavior and the conditions under which these assembled people become a crowd. It is hypothesized in this book that the acting crowd is assembled when there is a conscious purpose in mind. That is, people feel there is something wrong going on that they ought to do something about, and so they assemble (perhaps they merely intend to discuss what to do about it; they may or may not intend to engage in overt group activity). Once they assemble, nonsymbolic "circular processes" begin to operate and they are transformed into a crowd in a couple of hours. A suggestion from a "leader" can then send them into action—to lynch, fight, etc. An expressive crowd, on the other hand, is assembled with no conscious purpose among its members, although they may have vague, unfocused feelings of dissatisfac-

[15] Herbert Agar, in the *Chicago Times*, July 8, 1937, p. 17.
[16] Serge Chakotin, *The Rape of the Masses* (London: G. Routledge, 1940), pp. 40–41.

tion. Once assembled, the same nonsymbolic circular processes transform them into a crowd. They have assembled in the first place merely to express themselves, and a suggestion to fight or lynch is not one that they are "ready" for—that is, they are not attentive to such suggestions and so do not hear them, or they find such suggestions surprising and unexpected. However, it is conceivable, though not likely, that an expressive crowd could be transformed into an acting crowd under able leadership.

The first aspect of crowd behavior, the assembling of the crowd and the steps leading up to it, can be explained on a sociological level —in terms of mutual role-taking in which the community comes to an agreement about what is wrong that needs rectifying. One can say that, by sociological processes, the crowd assembles with a purpose (perhaps not specifically defined yet). If one is a psychologist and likes to use the word "motive" here, this is theoretically possible, provided it is understood that this motive is shared by many people and that it has been arrived at through mutual discussion.

A crowd should not be thought of as either good or bad. It is a form of collective behavior that is natural and characteristic of the higher vertebrates. An acting crowd might engage in a "good" action, such as the overthrow of a dictatorial, vicious government, just as readily as it might engage in a "bad" action. The purpose for which the acting crowd comes together is determined before the crowd mechanisms themselves get under way. The expressive crowd, while it has no collective purpose that could be called good or bad, may result in people's behavior becoming more moral and responsible because of the sheer memory of the unusual experience. On the other hand, it may simply be a substitute for more constructive behavior and a way of avoiding the responsibilities of life.

When we speak of the acting crowd as "destructive," it should be understood that the value assumption is the group's own, and not that of the sociologist. The acting crowd intends to destroy what it considers to be bad. This is not to say that the actions of the acting crowd are intrinsically bad. As sociologists we cannot make the value judgment that the government which is toppled by an acting crowd is good or bad, or that the criminal law which is violated by the acting crowd is or is not worthy of civil disobedience. Members of an acting crowd destroy what they think is bad, although they may have a divided conscience on the matter and so have twinges of bad conscience after the act.

Crowd behavior has been called a low form of behavior because it is engaged in by many kinds of animals as well as by man and because it does not involve the higher mental processes or communication through significant symbols. On the other hand, many other forms of behavior are also engaged in by animals and are not regarded as being low. It is not unlikely that our pleasurable responses to music and other forms of art involve some of the same physiological mechanisms that the crowd does. Crowd behavior is biogenic and psychogenic. It is a kind of behavior to be considered as social only in the sense that certain social conditions are more conducive than others toward its occurrence, that it is a collective experience requiring the presence of a significant number of people, and that it has certain social consequences.

B   The Audience and the "Mass Society"

The audience is far more important a phenomenon than most people realize since it occurs very frequently and has numerous effects on behavior. We shall define the term sociologically, to refer to a number of people who act in similar ways because of a common source of stimulation but without much communication with each other.[17] Etymologically the term means "hearers" or "listeners" but we use it to refer to recipients of communications through all sense organs, not only the ear. An almost ideal type illustration of the sociological audience is the audience at a motion-picture theater. People enter the darkened theater at different times and have practically no interaction with each other. They concentrate their attention on the screen, the common source of stimulation, and whatever influence on their behavior that arises out of their experience, either at the moment or after they leave, comes from the screen rather than from each other. The stimulation is one way. Members of the audience usually do not respond to the screen with significant symbols, and even when occasionally they do respond they have no effect on the source of stimulation. The only influence members of the audience have on each other is through the vague feeling that there are other people who are also attentive to the screen; this keeps them from deviating significantly from culturally expected patterns of behavior as they might if they were completely alone. Communication in the audience, therefore, tends to be one way rather than mutual. Members of the audience may act in *similar* ways because of their common stimulation but they do not act together *cooperatively* because there are no bonds among the members.

Whereas members of the crowd have to be in some sort of physical contact with each other in order to have the interstimulation of the circular process, the members of the audience do not have to be in physical

[17] Floyd Allport has used the term "coacting group" to refer to what we call the audience, but his term has unfortunately not been widely adopted. Several sociologists, including the author, have used the term "mass" to refer to what is here called the audience, but that term has been used in so many different ways that it has been a source of confusion. The term audience is not adequate for our purposes either, since it popularly connotes a purely receptive, passive group, whereas it will be shown here that important behavior results from participation in an audience.

"Words hewn on rocks" (see page 3)

Putting a squeeze on history: Workmen strip a finished rubber "squeeze" from the Greek inscription above the entrance to a tunnel leading to the tomb of Mithridates I, King of Commagene in Eastern Asia Minor in the first century B.C. As many as a thousand plaster casts can be made from this single mold for exhibition in museums and universities.

This gold rhyton in the image of a lion of the Achaemenian period, sixth and fifth centuries B.C., is among the masterpieces from the Near East at the Metropolitan Museum of Art.

"What is it?"—a gold drinking vessel from ancient Persia (see page 58)

I

Elston Howard of the New York Yankees argues a call with umpire John Flaherty.

"The use of language as the distinctive characteristic of human relations" (see page 48)

A school dance in the Mexican section of Los Angeles.

Marginal men incorporate two (or more) sets of cultural

meanings and values (see page 151)

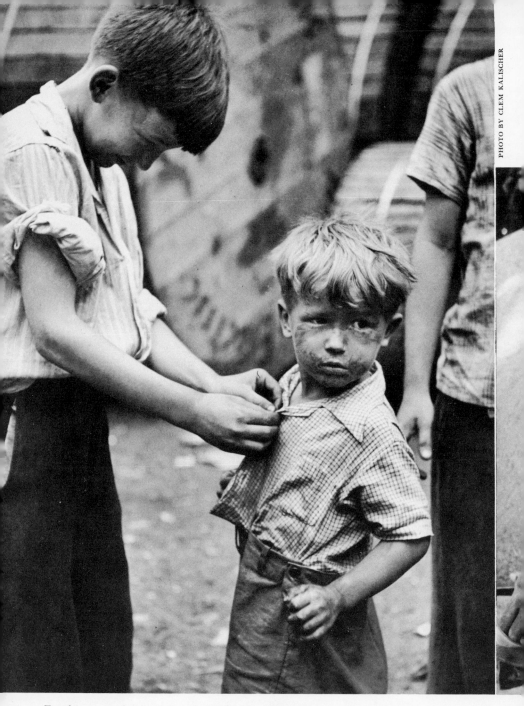

Toughie or angel—they keep big brother or sister busy.

"The child learns . . . from older siblings" (see page 54)

Pueblo Indian children feeding their infant brother.

"The child's relationship to his siblings" (see page 226)

"Institutions have symbols" (see page 179)

First Democratic Donkey—Thomas Nast's cartoon in Harper's Weekly of January 14, 1870. It is aimed at Democratic Press abuse of Lincoln's Secretary of War Stanton after the latter's death in 1869.

First Republican Elephant—Thomas Nast's cartoon in Harper's Weekly of November 7, 1874.
Here Nast depicts the Republicans falling into a political trap as a result of Democratic charges that President Grant was seeking a third term.

Small Indian school in Havasupai Canyon, Arizona (see pages 280-287)

*The elementary schools
are near home.*

COURTESY OF THE BUREAU OF INDIAN AFFAIRS, DEPARTMENT OF THE INTERIOR

PHOTO BY THE AUTHOR

*A Victorian-style house in
Kansas City, later converted to
a mission-flophouse for
homeless men before being torn
down in 1961.*

The nineteenth-century middle- and upper-class home tended to be large,

thus providing extra work for women (see page 436)

Street scene in Ulm, Germany

View of New Ulm's Minnesota street

New Ulm's new post office was modeled after Ulm's town hall but also includes some Dutch architecture.

Ulm, Germany, and New Ulm, Minnesota—culture diffusion and culture contrasts (see page 454)

An office filing and computer machine. One operator can do the work of an office staff with it. (see pages 441-444)

UNIVAC® Computer and Office Machine

"My God, Simpson! That wasn't there when we locked up."

The cartoonist comments on automation (see pages 441-444)

This one-man operated baler with bale-thrower makes it possible to get the hay crop in fast.

Improvements in production have the long run effect
of reducing poverty (see pages 617 and 623)

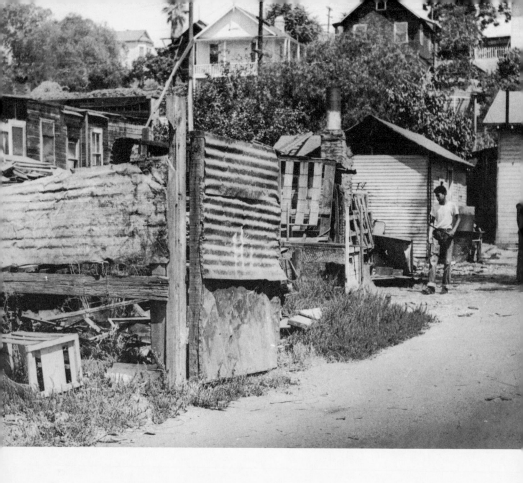

Slum areas of Los Angeles (see pages 604-607)

A recent phenomenon has been return migration from the suburbs

to the central city (see page 540)

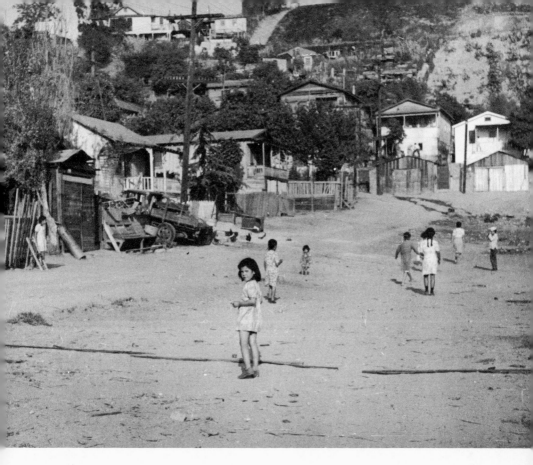

"If we'd joined the exodus to suburbia, we'd be moving back
to the city about this time."

"People have differing values as to what constitutes good housing" (see page 606)

TV in Teepee: Chief White Eagle is shown at left installing a television antenne atop his wigwam in the Iroquois village of Caughnawaga, near Montreal, Canada. The chie prefers his tribal abode to more modern housing, but he doesn't object to a little electronics in the furnishings.

The diffusion of material culture can bring many other social
changes in its wake (see pages 455-456)

*Symbol of a new way in the desert is this
rolling stock of a railroad running from the
coastline to the capital of Saudi Arabia.
The improved means of transportation to
serve local needs was paid for entirely from
oil revenues.*

*Southeast Asian boatman adds a Western
motor and Esso gasoline to his ancient
vessel.*

Advances in technology bring expanded markets (see pages 527-528)

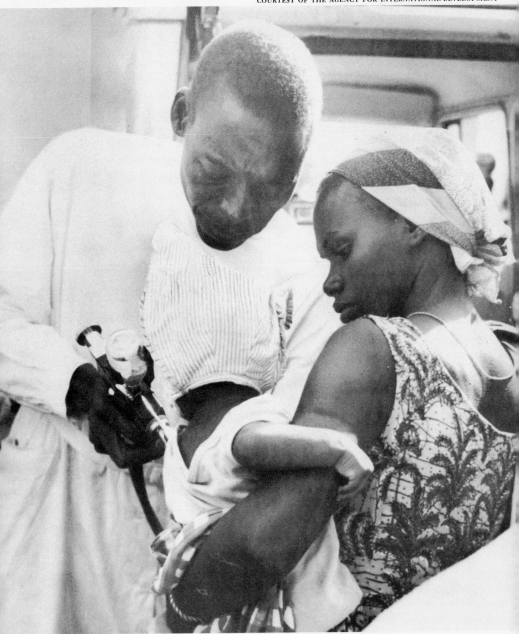

One battle in the war against disease.

An African infant getting an inoculation which will reduce her chances of getting a fatal disease (see pages 490-492)

contact with each other. A radio audience, for example, is scattered widely, perhaps over an entire nation, and yet it fits perfectly the definition of an audience. The formation of audiences and audience behavior are far more frequent than the formation of crowds and crowd behavior, at least in modern society. People who congregate in the street to watch an accident or a steam shovel in operation form an audience. One of the most important kinds of audiences in contemporary American society is that which sees the billboards, car cards, and other forms of advertising. As already indicated, those who receive the communication of all mass media —radio programs, movies, newspapers, magazines, etc.—are audiences.

We may speak of the source of communication in the audience as a "propagandist," because the communication is one way, without implying any derogatory connotation to that term. Since the sociologist is interested in the behavior of people, he is interested in the source of communication merely as a stimulus to a common behavior. Thus the sociologist is primarily interested in the propagandist for his effects on the members of the audience. The propagandist may have the intention of influencing the audience or he may have no such intention. Regardless of the intent, the stimulus provided by the propagandist is an experience to the members of the audience and, especially if it is prolonged or frequently repeated, tends to have an influence on most of the members. The propagandist uses many traditional meanings and values, but he also invents a significant number of new ones which he seeks to impose on the audience.[18]

Members of the audience may not always respond in the same way to the common stimulation since they have different backgrounds and different values. If the propagandist has the intention of influencing the audience toward behaving in a certain way, there is no certainty that the audience will respond in the way he intends. In fact, they may respond in just the opposite way, and we have the phenomenon that social psychologists call the "boomerang effect." If the propagandist is intentionally trying to secure a certain effect, the more he knows of the psychology of audience behavior and of the specific backgrounds and value orientations of the people he is trying to influence the more he can secure behavior in conformity with his intentions.

Members of the audience have certain natural reactions against being influenced by propagandists, and this varies in degree from one person to another. In general the more knowledge that one has of the specific subject matter of the propaganda the more one would tend to behave on the basis of this prior knowledge rather than on the specific content of the propaganda. For that reason, informed people—that is, people who are

[18] Two books that present the techniques of persuasion of an audience are Robert T. Oliver, *The Psychology of Persuasive Speech* (New York: Longmans, 1942); Herbert I. Abelson, *Persuasion: How Opinions and Attitudes are Changed* (New York: Springer, 1959).

informed in the specific subject matter of the propaganda—are less likely to be influenced by the propaganda. Also the person who is trained in critical thinking will tend to be less influenced by the propaganda, since he can subject the communications he is receiving to logical criticism. This does not mean that a person who is a general cynic is less likely to be influenced by propaganda. People who are negative toward all the communications they receive consistently react in just the opposite way as seems to be intended by the propagandist. While their reaction is negative it is nevertheless highly influenced by the propagandist. Many propagandists are aware of the negative and cynical members of their audience and deliberately direct a message to them which has the desired effect on their behavior.[19] They simply give them a communication seemingly designed to secure the opposite effect from the one which is really their intention. The negativist will respond in the opposite way, which is exactly the way the propagandist really wishes him to respond. The propagandist here makes deliberate use of the "boomerang effect." Logical analysis of the merits and demerits of a given piece of propaganda is thus not the same thing as reacting negatively to propaganda.

In addition to specific information and the ability to criticize logically and dispassionately there is another kind of knowledge that aids in resistance to the intention of the propagandist. This is a broad, general knowledge that gives perspective to its possessor. The broadly trained member of the audience may not have enough specific knowledge to contradict the concrete information provided him by the propagandist. Nor may he find anything wrong logically with the message of the propaganda. But, nevertheless, on the basis of his broad training he may recognize that certain things stated by the propagandist are not likely to be so. He needs to check further before he can contradict the propaganda, but he knows how to go about making this further check. A broad knowledge of history, anthropology, psychiatry, and the other social sciences is especially valuable in providing resistance to many contemporary kinds of propaganda. For all the reasons mentioned, educated persons are less likely to be influenced by propaganda than are uneducated persons.

Resistance to propaganda is not solely a rational matter, however. There is another most important factor that may allow completely uneducated people to be resistant to propaganda. One who has a complete set of meanings and values that he finds satisfactory for understanding the world and its events, and is buttressed by a group (usually a community) in his adherence to them because they are common to all members of the group, is not likely to conform to the intentions of a propagandist and is less subject to audience behavior. For these reasons propaganda has probably less

19 Alfred M. Lee, *How to Understand Propaganda* (New York: Rinehart, 1952).

influence on a highly integrated isolated village than it has on a loosely organized city. The "integrated group" mode of relationship resists transformation into the "audience" mode of relationship.

It would be incorrect to think of propaganda as generally bad or the
intentions of the propagandist as always evil or selfish. Propagandists include those who try to get people to behave in a more rational fashion or
in ways that are more beneficial or wholesome for themselves. Consequently, doing just the opposite of what the propagandist desires may be
the most stupid and irrational kind of behavior. Similarly, ignoring all
known forms of propaganda simply because they are propaganda would
tend to make one immune to change and to improvement of any sort. It
would include resistance to any form of education. Listening to suggestions for new modes of behavior, therefore, is not in itself a bad thing.
The mass media are important and valuable sources of common action in
a worthwhile direction in our society.[20] They are dangerous to the individual only when he is subject *solely* to their influence. If he has no specific information, general knowledge, or critical ability to resist them
under any circumstances, then he is simply responding as an automaton
to their influence.

Thus far only the direct positive effect on the behavior of individuals
of being a member of an audience has been considered. There is another,
indirect influence which is important for us to note. Members of the audience are not interacting with each other. They are more or less passive
recipients of communications, rather than active initiators of communications. There is no adequate taking of the "role of the other" among members of the audience, nor is there much opportunity for the interplay of
human emotions. This is another influence that reduces the human character of the member of the audience and makes him more like an automaton. A certain amount of time spent as a member of the audience has no
effects on a person's ability to act as a human being, but if he spends a
very large portion of his time as a member of the audience, he loses something of his ability to have human reactions or human emotions, just as
when he is physically isolated from his fellows.[21]

For example, students of the movies have long noted that those who
are very frequent attenders at movies have less opportunity to participate
as members of a family or a social group. The family and other forms of
intimate association are the developers of the human personality and
human emotions. It has been observed that people who are excessive

[20] For examples of some of the recent research on the mass media, see the two volumes
edited by Wilbur Schramm, *Mass Communications* and *The Process and Effects of Mass
Communication* (Urbana: University of Illinois Press, 1954 and 1962); Charles R. Wright,
Mass Communication (New York: Random House, 1959); Joseph T. Klapper, *Effects of
Mass Communication* (Glencoe, Ill.: Free Press, 1960).

[21] See Chapter 2, Section F.

movie-goers tend to act as though they were living in a dream world.[22] This is not only because they are imagining themselves in the plot of the movie but also because through the course of time they have lost some of their contact with reality, owing to lack of regular human association and human interaction. Some observers have said that the radio has counteracted the effects of the movies by bringing people together in small groups to listen to the radio and providing an occasion for people to comment on the radio programs, to observe each other's emotional responses, and to participate in a collective experience. This is true in so far as attention is not completely absorbed by the mass medium. The radio allows a good deal of independence for the individual since only his ears are attached to the mass stimulation, and even they may be disengaged for direct conversation. With the advent of television, however, the eyes as well as the ears are focused and it is likely that television has almost as much desocializing effect on people as do the movies.

Just as the prevalence of the audience restricts the time available for organized group activities and direct face-to-face conversation, so it restricts the time available for privacy. To the extent that one-way communication absorbs the time of the member of the mass, it prevents him from communicating with himself. Privacy as well as sociable interaction has a certain function in the formation of the human personality and emotions.[23] Extensive thinking and planning can go on only in privacy because the individual must rationally examine the possible consequences of any pattern of behavior and think through all the future contingencies of his own and others' behavior. Past experience is enriched if the individual has the time afterward to go over it in his mind and think through the implications and values of it for himself. In so far as the individual spends his time as a member of the audience, he has less privacy and consequently less time to do any of the above-mentioned things. This again is a question of degree, and one can profitably spend only a certain amount of time in privacy, so that being a member of an audience becomes dangerous to the individual only when he is a member of it for a large part of his waking time.

c   *The Development of Modern Mass Society*

1   THE TREND FROM FOLK SOCIETY TO MASS SOCIETY[24]

Students of society have been aware for some time that there has been a long-run trend since the Middle Ages toward increase in the frequency

[22] Herbert Blumer, *Movies and Conduct* (New York: Macmillan, 1933).

[23] See Chapter 2, Section F.

[24] One of the best sources on the trend toward the mass society, and the reaction to it, is Robert A. Nisbet, *Quest for Community* (New York: Oxford University Press, 1953).

of occurrence of audiences and of behavior based upon audience experience and away from the kind of behavior based on the integrated group. It is because of this that one frequently hears contemporary society characterized as a "mass society," since the term "mass" is a technical equivalent of "audience."[25]

With some exaggeration we can characterize the older society out of which the mass society developed as one based upon the integrated group mode of relationship or what Redfield calls the "folk society."[26] Before the Industrial Revolution, beginning at the end of the eighteenth century, communities had to be somewhat isolated from each other—because transportation was difficult and the main occupation was farming, which took space—and their members were governed by strong adherence to common meanings and values. In their limited circle people were in adequate communication with each other and they had a strong sense of belonging and of loyalty to the community. Their values were clear to them and were believed to be practical as well as "true." People believed they understood the controlling forces of their society, even though modern scientists know that these beliefs had little relationship to reality. Outside influences may have existed in their experience but were regarded simply as beyond their ken and had little challenge for them, little meaning in their daily lives.

The trend toward increasing frequency of occurrence of the audience has been due to several causes. The most obvious one has been the invention of a large number of mass media and of conditions through which these mass media could have a wide audience. To a considerable extent the mass media force the formation of audiences, and before they existed

[25] We use the term "mass society" in a way different from that of some other sociologists. Duncan and Artis and Hatt use it to refer to the general American society, as distinguished from the local community. (O. D. Duncan and J. W. Artis, "Some Problems of Stratification Research," *Rural Sociology*, 16 [March, 1951], pp. 17–29; Paul K. Hatt, "Stratification in the Mass Society," *American Sociological Review*, 15 [April, 1950], pp. 216–22.) Bennett and Tumin use it to refer to a type of social organization where large numbers of people use approximately the same cultural practices. (J. W. Bennett and M. M. Tumin, *Social Life* [New York: Alfred A. Knopf, 1948].) Brown uses the term "cultural mass" in about the same way—to refer to the common elements of culture in a pluralistic society. (James C. Brown, "Cooperative Group Formation: A Problem in Social Engineering," unpublished.) Ortega represents an old tradition among political scientists and publicists in using the term "mass society" to refer to a political situation in which power is held by the bulk of the people as distinguished from one in which power is held by an elite group. (José Ortega y Gasset, *Revolt of the Masses* [London: Allen and Unwin, 1932].) Marx and his followers have referred to the "masses" in this way as meaning the bulk of the population as distinguished from a property-owning or intellectual elite. We use the term "mass society" to refer to a social situation characterized by numerous and frequent formation of people into audiences—in which communication is one way from a leader or propagandist and there is very little interaction among the members.

[26] Robert Redfield, *Tepoztlán: a Mexican Village* (Chicago: University of Chicago Press, 1930). For further discussion of the folk society, see the introduction to Chapter 14.

there was less opportunity for audiences to form. A second influence in the augmentation of the audience has been the decline of the integrated group. With the Commercial and Industrial Revolutions came a good deal of geographical mobility, especially from rural to urban areas.[27] Economic influences broke up a very large number of the old communities and placed people in cities, where it is more difficult to form the highly integrated forms of social existence that are possible in isolated rural areas and small villages.

Coincident with this trend has been the breakup or decline of some of the institutions that formerly buttressed much of the value system of medieval European society. The extended family, which gave the whole community a family-like unity and intimacy, is greatly reduced and has taken on a different form.[28] The church, which taught, interpreted, and expressed the social values, has declined sharply in its influences since the Middle Ages, and here the decline has been more rapid in western Europe than it has in the United States. The Industrial Revolution also weakened the integrating effect of certain institutions by forcing people to segmentalize their lives to a certain extent. The nuclear family no longer provides economic occupations, the primary source of recreation, education for the young. There are now specialized institutions where one works, plays, goes to school, etc., and each of these is distinct from the family. This segmentalization, or division of labor in the broader sense of the term, has further broken up the integrated community in which people once lived in a high degree of mutual interaction with one another. While these changes have released individuals from the tyranny of community pressure to a considerable extent, and have opened up the possibility of greater freedom of thought and action in an individualistic sense, they have also opened the way for the audience to substitute for the integrated community.

Most historians have failed, somehow, to tell us what these drastic changes meant to the average citizen. By far the keenest analysis has come from the pen of an economist and editor, Karl Polanyi.[29] He points out that these changes, especially the "almost miraculous" improvement in the tools of production, were accompanied by "a catastrophic dislocation of the lives of the common people." Before the Industrial Revolution most of the ordinary people had a basic economic security. The feudal serf was treated almost as a slave and had a minimum of legal and political rights. But he "belonged" to a plot of land, and no one could force him off it even though he was not the titular owner. The medieval village

[27] A most important historical description of the initial effects of the Commercial Revolution is Henri Pirenne's *Economic and Social History of Medieval Europe* (London: Kegan Paul, Trench, Trubner, 1936).

[28] See Chapter 6, Section A.

[29] Karl Polanyi, *The Great Transformation* (New York: Farrar and Rinehart, 1944).

also had "common land," out of which a bare living could be eked by sheep raising. The serf and the peasant before the nineteenth century subsisted on an extremely low standard of living, but they felt that there were minimum economic resources on which they could always rely. Then the "enclosure movement" dispossessed most of them of their land and the Commercial and Industrial revolutions transformed a majority from farmers into workers.

At first the sudden uprooting from the basic security of the land was met in England by a sort of minimum-wage law (the Speenhamland Act) whereby a worker who did not earn the minimum would have his wages supplemented up to the minimum by the government. This was a last gesture at maintaining the old security under the new system of industrial capitalism. It failed to work because employers found they could depress wages below the minimum without starving their workers and because workers found that they could loaf on the job without getting fired or lowering their total incomes below the minimum specified by law. After the law was repealed, in 1834, each worker found that his economic security was completely at the mercy of an employer, and each employer had to meet the competition of an impersonal market. Whenever confidence in the employer was shaken, either because of his personal arbitrariness or because he was not competing effectively, there was a drop in the worker's sense of security. Even though the average income per worker rose markedly under industrial capitalism, the *feeling of security* sagged. Each depression, with successively larger unemployment rates, provided a new blow to the worker's feelings that he was economically safe. This led to personal demoralization on the one hand and the demand for security on the other.

The demand for security took two forms: the organization of trade unions and pressure for laws to provide minimum financial security. The growth of unions and farmers' organizations and the passage of social-security laws, minimum-wage laws, relief laws, and the like have compensated somewhat for the basic economic security previously provided by the land. But many workers are not members of effective unions, the unions do not have complete control over firing, the farmers' organizations do not have complete control over pricing, social security payments lag behind the rise in the cost of living, so the economic problem of the mass society remains.

A comparable history could be traced for the businessman. During the Middle Ages his production was protected by guilds and his return by a conception of a "just price." These did not make for efficiency or initiative and so kept his financial return low, but they did give security. When the free-enterprise system developed at the end of the eighteenth century, the businessman had more chances to grow very wealthy, but he also had a greater chance to fail. He was now subject to the vicissitudes of cut-throat competition, of depressions, of fashion in demand for his product, of inventions that would make his product quickly obsolete. So he gradually developed monopolistic combines, "fair trade" laws, techniques to suppress new inventions, and so on. But most businessmen have not completely solved their problems of insecurity, as is evident in their panicky behavior whenever a depression seems to threaten.

Another aspect of transition from folk society to mass society has been studied by Elton Mayo and his followers.[30] While studying industrial fatigue and spontaneous featherbedding in industrial plants, Mayo found that improvements in lighting and rest periods helped to increase worker efficiency. The only difficulty with his early experiments was that *everything* helped; in fact, production stayed high even when all the good things were removed. Interviewing the workers revealed that it had been the sympathetic attention given to the workers while the experiment was going on that had the effect, not the mechanical changes. Similar results have been found throughout industry by Golden and Ruttenberg.[31] They show that even pay raises, bonuses, and profit sharing have seldom, if ever, increased worker output. After extended investigation, the Mayo group came to the following conclusion: When the worker felt he was treated as an impersonal cog in an industrial machine, he did not care much about doing a good job for the employer. But when personal interest was taken in the problems of the employee, when he was consulted on all matters concerning his job, and when rewards and punishments were given out with strict attention to all factors in the worker's situation, his job morale and efficiency rose.

Viewed historically, the factory system under capitalism did transform most workers into impersonal cogs—labor was regarded as an ingredient in production, just as were materials and capital. The worker consequently felt a loss of individuality; he became one of the sheep portrayed so realistically by Charlie Chaplin in *Modern Times*. As a number rather than a man, he felt little incentive, even when a raise in pay might be held out as bait to him. A study by Professor W. Lloyd Warner and his associates of a strike in a New England city during the mid-1930's revealed that the strike had been building up in the workers' minds for eighty years.[32] The strike occurred in a shoe factory, where—eighty years earlier—machine production had replaced skilled hand production. Workers no longer owned their tools; there was little opportunity to exercise skill; there was

[30] Elton Mayo, *Human Problems of an Industrial Civilization* (New York: Macmillan, 1933).

[31] Clinton S. Golden and Harold J. Ruttenberg, *The Dynamics of Industrial Democracy* (New York: Harper, 1942).

[32] W. L. Warner and J. O. Low, *The Social System of the Modern Factory. The Strike: A Social Analysis* (New Haven: Yale University Press, 1947).

no way of knowing how the productive process might next be altered. Ownership changed hands, passing from the enterprising, responsible, paternalistic local leaders to an unknown corporation with headquarters in New York. The new bosses were simply well-paid agents for an impersonal power, and they seemed to care little about the workers or their town. There seemed to be little chance of getting ahead, and there could be little pride in work when the workers' job was so petty. The strike, out of which there developed a union, was simply one manifestation of decades of frustration.

Drucker reports a telling story of what happened in an airplane factory toward the end of World War II.[33] The factory was playing a crucial role in war production, yet the turnover and absentee rates were very high and the production rate low. The workers were "fed up" with war shortages of consumers' goods, the difficulties of transportation to and from work, the inadequate housing, the confusion of working in a rapidly expanding plant. Government officials and plant managers grew frantic as output continued to slip and no appeal seemed to work.

Then the Army put on exhibition a war-battered bomber plane that had been produced at that very factory several years earlier. With it came the crew that had flown the bomber on dozens of missions over Germany and that was now back in the States for a deserved rest. Members of the crew were "guides" to the plane; it was thought they would tell the workers about the bombing flights. It was not expected that many workers would stay after hours to see the plane. But the workers came in droves and most of them asked questions. The questions were pretty much of the same pattern. "My job is to do thus-and-so. Would you please tell me where the part I handle is in the plane, and what does it do?" The workers did not know what they were doing! Naturally they did not see their relation to the war effort. When the part at which each worked was pointed out, its function explained, and perhaps an anecdote passed along as to how that part had once been hit or how it protected a flier, the workers were delighted. It sounds incredible to those who have never felt as these workers apparently did, but production immediately jumped. As far as anyone could tell, the bomber exhibit—or, rather, the workers' discovery of the significance of their job in the total war effort—was the cause. The specialists had regained a conception of the whole, at least temporarily.

Economists and industrial relations experts such as Polanyi, Mayo, Warner, and Drucker have done a good job of analyzing the shift from folk society to mass society in so far as it is manifested in the economic sphere of life. Sociologists, as we noted earlier, have paid a good deal of attention to the consequences of a mass society, but they have not analyzed

[33] Peter F. Drucker, *Concept of the Corporation* (New York: John Day, 1946), p. 77.

the social consequences in historical terms. What happens to the individual, for example, when recreation shifts from the participant form to the passive vicarious form? At present we can only speculate, but certain hypotheses seem likely. When individuals participate in games or other sociable recreation they are obliged to communicate constantly with each other, and adjust their behavior and attitudes to the other participants. Social bonds grow out of such adjustments and readjustments. But when individuals take their recreation by observing other people play, they are not "interacting," they are not adjusting their behavior and attitudes to those of other people. Of course there is a certain amount of interaction within the audience, especially when the individual comes to the sports event with other people. But, on the whole, the interpersonal relations consist largely of the members of the audience observing the players, the players communicating to one another and to the audience, with the audience having only a small reaction back on the players and then not as individuals but as a mass. Modern man, of middle or lower income, has much more time for recreation than did his ancestors, but an increasing proportion of that recreational time is spent in a passive-audience type of situation in which the individual is not communicating with, learning from, or adjusting to his fellows.

2   FACTORS IN THE TREND

Let us be more concrete in examining some of the trends through which the audience has become a more important factor in the life of the modern citizen. In 1790 only 5 per cent of the people of the United States lived in cities; in 1960, 69.7 per cent lived in cities, and the proportion has undoubtedly risen since then. A major adjustment is involved in moving from a rural area to a city, and not enough study has been devoted to the social consequences of this trend, which is still going on. Most urban neighborhoods, especially those in which people with middle and upper incomes live, are not highly integrated in the sense that people know each other and that a common set of stores and other facilities serve all of them. Whereas in rural areas or villages a resident will know all those who live within a radius of several miles, an urbanite may not know his next-door neighbor. There are special occasions in the village when most people will come out at one time and talk to each other—while attending a fair or an auction, or simply while watching the train come through. The absence of these things in the city creates for it a reputation of being cold and unfriendly.

Actually, of course, it is easy to make more friends in the city than in the country, because more people are available and there is a greater possibility of finding those who have congenial personalities. But one makes friends in a different way—by joining a club, a church, a union, or by going to a skating rink or bowling alley. One's friends may live scattered over many parts of a city rather than living close by. For the person who moves from the country to the city it may be difficult to learn that physical closeness of residence is not a necessary basis for association. Consequently, he is lonely and isolated. This is especially significant in view of the fact that many migrants to the city are unattached people rather than family groups, and so do not even have spouses, parents, or children to turn to for companionship. The isolated individual is a member of an audience, not of an integrated society.

The city is heterogeneous, made up of groups of many divergent interests and backgrounds. This diversity, coupled with the large size of the urban population which permits even a well-known individual to walk down most streets unnoticed, creates opportunities for freedom of personal behavior that are rare in villages and that scarcely existed before the great increase in the number of large cities in the nineteenth century.[34] Freedom and diversity have been some of the great attractions of city life, and they have been an essential element in the development of artistic and intellectual activities wherever they have appeared. But freedom imposes a responsibility on the individual to make up his own mind as to what kind of behavior he wishes to engage in. There are fewer standards to which the individual must conform, and the concepts of "right" and "good" are made more relative. To an individual without the training to make up his own mind on such ethical matters, or the strength of character to conform to standards which he thinks proper, freedom may be demoralizing. The demoralized individual is also a member of an audience, not of an integrated society.

The city is also complex, or rather it reflects the complexity of modern life, which impinges on rural areas also. Complexity is confusing to the average individual. Just as industrial relations experts such as Mayo[35] and Drucker[36] have shown that the complexity of machine production confuses and makes unhappy the industrial worker, so could it be observed that the increasing complexity of other aspects of modern life creates new sources of confusion for most citizens.

Take politics, for example.[37] The activities and structures of government are far more complex today than they were a hundred years ago. The government touches the lives of the average citizen at many points. Despite the higher level of formal education, it is probable that the average citizen understands the government less today at those points at which

[34] Louis Wirth, "Urbanism as a Way of Life," *American Journal of Sociology,* 44 (July, 1938), pp. 1–24.

[35] *Op. cit.*

[36] Peter F. Drucker, *The Future of Industrial Man* (New York: John Day, 1942).

[37] William Kornhauser, *The Politics of Mass Society* (Glencoe, Ill.: Free Press, 1959).

it impinges on him. This perhaps explains the widespread belief that corrupt and evil forces have control of the government (even when its head —Roosevelt or Truman, for example—may be widely trusted and respected, and even when there is a popular demand that the government engage in a greater number of activities to aid ordinary people). And a rumor, having no basis in fact, that the Jews are widely infiltrated through the government will be widely adopted as a reasonable explanation of why the operations of government are so mysterious. In the integrated group society of pre-modern times clearly specified powers were known to have control of government and the common people were not supposed to bother their heads with it. In today's democracy the people are supposed to take responsibility for government, but it has become too complicated for them to understand. So they are confused, and feel alienated from their "government" in some ways (not from their flesh-and-blood president, senator, representative, or Supreme Court justice, however). A confused people form an audience also, not an integrated society.

There are other aspects of modern society that give the individual a sense of insecurity and alienation, and social forces are tending to increase these feelings. We can do no more than list them here. First, the functions of women have decreased sharply from the day when a woman was a major helpmate to her husband in breadwinning and when she was the chief educator for a large brood of children.[38] The mechanical revolution greatly reduced and simplified household tasks. Yet society imposes no demands that she seek substitute functions. She can try her hand at a paid job or at social-welfare activity, but usually no one says that she must. And so the modern wife, after her youngest child has started school, is partly functionless, which means that she is likely to raise questions to herself about her very reason for existence and she feels a vague but pervasive dissatisfaction. Since she has related herself to other people at only marginal points, and since she is uncertain as to her own role in society, she is a member of the audience, not of an integrated society.

While the spread of formal education has increased modern man's sophistication, and in one sense helped him to understand the forces which control him, it has concomitantly increased his skepticism regarding the sources of his information. This would tend to decrease false beliefs if the citizen knew how to secure alternative sources of facts and if he could weigh all the evidence and apply the scientific historian's rules of internal and external criticism. But the education of most people has not proceeded that far. They have learned only up to the point that propagandists are all about and that few sources of news are to be trusted. Consequently, some people are generally in as bad a fix as the several hundred women who, in early 1946, while there were still war-induced shortages of many

[38] See Chapter 11, Section B.

consumer goods, waited outside a hosiery store hoping to get a pair of nylons. An hour earlier the proprietor had put up a sign saying "No More Nylons" and had locked his door, as he could not transact other business with hundreds of women milling about in pursuit of nonexistent nylons. A policeman tried to persuade the women to move along. "Really, ladies, there ain't any more nylons today." Responded one of the hopefuls: "I never believe rumors." While this woman had not yet reached the state of bewilderment arrived at when people find out that sometimes it pays to believe signs and sometimes it doesn't, most Americans have arrived at that stage. When people do not know what to believe, and yet feel a need for information, they are members of an audience, not of an integrated society.

While this analysis of contemporary society could be greatly extended, it should be quite clear that folk society has turned into mass society to a considerable extent. Consensus between people on values and ways of behaving hardly exists any longer because tradition and closely knit social structures have been weakened. People have increasingly become mentally isolated from each other, and they are confused by and suspicious of the forces that seem to control them.

The excessive occurrence of the audience in contemporary society, because it causes the separation of the individual and the groups, is the source of several concrete social problems. The core of the difficulty is that the individual finds it next to impossible to communicate satisfactorily with his fellows and consequently cannot orient his own values in relation to those of others or put himself into harmony with society when he is simply a passive member of an audience. As early as 1897 the great French sociologist Émile Durkheim investigated suicide and found its chief modern cause in what he called *"anomie."*[39] This was a sense of estrangement from the values of the social group, and of anonymity from their fellowship. Faris and Dunham, in their brilliant statistical analysis of *Mental Disorders in Urban Areas*,[40] revealed evidence that schizophrenia, the most common type of mental disease, was much more likely to be had by those whose life circumstances prevented them from developing close personal ties with their fellows. Robert Cooley Angell, in a study of how *The Family Encounters the Depression*,[41] demonstrated that a major decline of income resulted in family disorganization only when there were few ties of intimacy and understanding between family members to begin with. Social psychologists such as Fromm[42] and Riesman[43] have been interested

[39] *Suicide* (Glencoe, Ill.: Free Press, 1951; 1st edition, 1897).
[40] R. E. L. Faris and H. W. Dunham (Chicago: University of Chicago Press, 1939).
[41] New York: Scribner's, 1936.
[42] Erich Fromm, *Man for Himself* (New York: Rinehart, 1947).
[43] David Riesman, with the assistance of Reuel Denney and Nathan Glazer, *The Lonely Crowd* (New Haven: Yale University Press, 1950).

in the softening of personality under the impact of the mass society. Riesman traces the trend from a "tradition-directed personality" characteristic
of the integrated society of the Middle Ages to an "inner-directed personality" typical of the commercialization and industrialization period from the
sixteenth to the nineteenth centuries, to the "other-directed personality"
characteristic of the present period. The "other-directed personality" is
described as seeking always to please other people, even at the sacrifice of
other social and personal values. This list of studies could be greatly
extended, but enough has been given to indicate a major conclusion of social
science research into certain contemporary social problems. These problems
in large measure result from the atomization of social groups into mentally
isolated individuals.

3   REACTIONS AGAINST THE MASS SOCIETY

The imaginative layman and social scientist have been aware of this
essential weakness caused by the excessive devlopment of the audience in
contemporary society, but the average man has reacted in a much more
confused and emotional way. There has arisen, for example, a widespread
hatred of city life and a criticism of city life in terms of its evils coupled
with a desire to return to the "neighborliness" of the country. It may be
hypothesized that the city represents—in the minds of these people—the
audience structure of society which urbanization has historically fostered.
This attitude has contributed also to the fascination for movements that
seek to "incorporate" individuals completely and provide them with channels for communication from which there can be no deviation. Thus the
popular reaction to the audience may have dangers for society even more
extreme than those created by the audience itself.

For example, many of the current "isms"—not the least of which are
fascism and anti-Semitism—have their appeal to the masses in terms of
their promise to reintegrate the individual into the social order.[44] They
hold out to the isolated, anonymous modern man an offer to rejoin society,
to regain his sense of social belongingness, and to eliminate his conflict of
values that arises from an unintegrated existence. This is no small offer
to the mass man beset by extreme loneliness and mental conflict. The
mass society we live in today is not and cannot be stable or progressive in an
orderly way. It must run to extreme panaceas: to orgiastic religious movements on the one hand, and to all-explaining, all-dominating dictatorships
on the other hand. Neither of these will solve the problem, since they rely
on false explanations and they maintain the audience condition of society
in order to perpetuate themselves.

There are those who would get rid of mass society by seeking to re-

[44] Paul Massing, *Rehearsal for Destruction* (New York: Harper, 1949); Robert F. Byrnes,
Anti-Semitism in Modern France (New Brunswick, N.J.: Rutgers University Press, 1950).

turn to a folk society. Included among these are the agrarians who would abolish cities and return the populations to farms, the medievalists who would abolish diversity and set up one moral and intellectual authority, the primitivists who would re-establish ancient cultural forms and abolish modern ones. All these people, with their "quest for certainty," see the problems engendered by modern mass society, but do not see the unplanned results of their solutions. The population is now too large and too specialized to return to the farm; the agrarian solution could be achieved only by killing off 90 per cent of the people. The population is now too well educated and too heterogeneous to accept the medievalist solution of setting up one leader to answer all moral and intellectual questions. The population is too sophisticated and too dependent on and adjusted to modern technology to accept the primitivist solution of abolishing modern culture forms. Short of a catastrophic destruction of most of the people and our culture it would appear that the major sources of mass society are here to stay: the large cities, modern machine methods and other types of labor-saving technology, at least an elementary education for most children, people with diverse background and interests, and so on.

Most people seem to feel that these things are not bad in themselves, and the great majority seems anxious to take advantage of them. The question facing most people, then, seems not simply to be how to abolish the mass society, but how to eliminate its unhappy consequences while retaining its beneficent causes. A great deal of thinking and research needs to be done to answer this question. A few suggestions for this will be offered at a subsequent point in this chapter.

Most of the forces creating the mass society reached their full development in the period prior to World War I, although the mass media of communication had a greater impact later on. The counteracting forces that are now to be considered have mainly come into operation in the post World War I period, although the first one is to be traced to the 19th century.

It would seem likely that persons feeling the ill effects of mass society would turn first for psychological compensation to science and education. The belief that scientific knowledge is increasing man's understanding of, and control over, nature more than compensates many people for the loss of dogmatic religion. Recognition that knowledge is available to the masses through public education more than compensates many people for skepticism regarding the teachings of religion. Some people even hope that the development of the social sciences, along with increasing public dissemination of their findings and interpretations, will counterbalance the insecurities created by new physical science discoveries. The whole ideology of "progress," which was developing even as the mass society was developing in the 18th century and which reached its greatest popularity when mass society forces were most rampant in the 19th century, can be seen as a psychological reaction against, or compensation for, the ill effects of the mass society. The appeal of certain mass forms of pseudo-education—such as the Sunday supplement, the vulgarized public lecture, the quiz program, the "believe-it-or-not" column, and science fiction—is not only that they titillate or thrill but also that they seem to provide knowledge, that they do provide psychological compensation for one's feelings of being ignorant. People often say they like these things because they "learn something from them." In so far as there is a demand for serious adult education—through serious but readable books, articles, and radio-TV programs, as well as formal courses—there is even more basis for this psychological compensation.

A second existing institution to which the modern mass man has turned for psychological security is the nuclear family—that is, the family consisting of husband, wife, and children (and occasionally a grandparent). This institution is found throughout most of Western history and in many non-Western societies, even when it sometimes seemed partly submerged by the extended family and the community, and adults—especially women—have generally depended on it for psychological security. The modern features, which we hypothesize are at least partly reactions against the mass society,[45] are a new emphasis on "companionship" between husband and wife and between parents and children. The husband sharing the wife's housework, the wife sharing the husband's job problems, the wife assuming joint control over the family budget and expenditures, both of them seeking to take their recreation together, their increased play with the children, and their efforts to be "pals" with the children—are all modern phenomena.[46] For many adults in our society, the nuclear family provides the only regular source of companionship, the only regular safeguard against loneliness. It thus provides partial compensation for the mass society.

A relatively minor counteracting force to mass psychology can best be mentioned at this point. This is the hobby, including amateur sports and the "do-it-yourself" activity around the home which in recent years has assumed almost the dimensions of a social movement. It has already been suggested that voluntary associations sometimes are formed around a hobby, and the reactive effects of this against the mass society have been noted. But even when the hobby is practiced by unorganized individuals, there are some psychological effects that counteract those created by the

[45] This is not to deny that the modern nuclear family has other causes, but merely to assert that one of its sources of development and strength is the compensation it provides against the mass society.

[46] E. W. Burgess and H. J. Locke, *The Family: From Institution to Companionship* (New York: American Book, 1945).

mass society. In the first place, hobbies offer the opportunity to be creative in ways that ordinary people choose to be and can be creative; these thus offer some reduction in feelings of boredom and uselessness. The "do-it-yourself" hobbies possibly add slightly to economic security. Hobbies also occasionally offer some additional points of social contact—between buyers and sellers of hobby materials, and between hobbyists to compare techniques and results. Some hobbies—particularly sports—require that small groups of like-minded people meet together regularly. Such contacts contribute somewhat to the reduction of loneliness and possibly a little to a reduction of the sense of ignorance. Some hobbies and sports take people out-of-doors a good deal, and there is probably a feeling among many such hobbyists that they are communing with nature if not with other people. Hobbies are probably as old as man, but the use of them has no doubt greatly increased in modern times as leisure time has increased, as there has developed a new emphasis upon consumption, and as hobbies have been found to be somewhat useful in counteracting the negative feelings engendered by the mass society.

Allied with the hobby are certain limited developments toward the "ruralization" of modern society. While the main trend has been toward the "urbanization" of rural society—that is, the extension of mass society to most farming areas—there have also been such counter developments as the rise of the intimate suburban community, the creation of certain "garden" residential communities within the urban complex, the popularization of the summer vacation cabin or "camping" with fairly "primitive" facilities, the spread of gardening as a hobby for city-dwellers, and the intensification of the voluntary association to such an extent that some urban communities now have an integrated character. Further, the process of shifting from primary to secondary relationships in the city seems to have been exaggerated by many sociologists. A sense of identity with the local community in the city does seem to arise in the modern city, even if not to the same extent as in the folk society. Friendship groups do develop in the city, even if not always on a residential basis, but often on an occupational or interest basis. A study by Gregory Stone[47] of a sample of Chicago housewives indicates that a large proportion do their purchasing with "personality" and "ethical" orientations rather than "rational economic" or "apathetic" orientations, and that this was especially true of those most urbanized—that is those who were third-generation city dwellers and who had achieved relatively high economic and education status. The local store is not only a place to shop, it is also a place where one can get to know storekeepers and to discuss things with them. There are a good many friendly, primary relationships that develop in the large city

[47] Gregory Stone, "Sociological Aspects of Consumer Purchasing in a Northwest Side Chicago Community," unpublished M.A. thesis, University of Chicago, June, 1952.

and one can gain a sense of personal identity with an urban neighborhood and even with a city as a whole,[48] and this may be increasing as the urban population is more likely to be urban-born rather than migrants displaced from rural and village backgrounds.

There have been special forms of reaction against the economic insecurity created by the mass society. These can be considered under three heads: (1) government activity to provide a minimum social security and put on brakes to economic depression; (2) the formation of "monopolies" and other structures to hedge against the vicissitudes of the free market; (3) adjustments in the technology of mass production. There are several economic aspects of these three phenomena with which we have no concern, including the question as to whether they are *effective* in the long run in reducing economic insecurity. Our assumption is simply that they are partially *motivated* by the desire to reduce economic insecurity. Businessmen have created corporations to limit their liability in case of failure, formed combines to control the market and keep out competitors, entered into agreements to prevent the free use of inventions, distributed their investments so that all would not be likely to go bad at the same time, imposed contracts on their corporations to pay them a secured income for life, and bribed politicians so that control of natural resources and transportation routes could be assured. Workers have formed or joined trade unions to raise wages, set arbitrary but impartial rules for promotion and lay-off, set restrictions on job entry, pressured politicians into voting for minimum wage laws and for old age and unemployment insurance laws, sought to get guaranteed-annual-wage contracts, developed medical insurance and pension funds. Some of these measures make for economic inefficiency; most of them work against the economic interests of the other group and of consumers, many of them increase the economic insecurity of those who are not organized, but they do increase the economic security of those directly involved—at least in the short run, where they can see it.

While the quest for economic security has undoubtedly been the primary motive for these developments, they have had certain consequences which also limit the psychological effects of the mass society. These have occurred because the businessmen's combines and the workers' unions are also voluntary associations, and have all of the effects of the voluntary association in counteracting the psychology of the mass society. While some union leaders allow very little or no participation on the part of the rank-and-file members in the actual running of the union, there is more participation of other kinds in most unions. At the lowest level of making routine complaints to the employer in the name of the union, most unions allow rank-and-file activity. Most unions have social affairs; all

[48] Joel Smith, William H. Form, and Gregory P. Stone, "Local Intimacy in a Middle-Sized City," *American Journal of Sociology*, 60 (November, 1954), pp. 276–84.

unions distribute membership cards, buttons, labels and other material symbols which help members to identify with one another; most unions distribute literature to their members which helps them to learn what is going on in the union and even to interpret events in the larger society; some unions have an educational program for their members; some unions encourage their members to serve on committees or as shop stewards; some unions provide aid to their members in dealing with the government (e.g. giving advice regarding income tax or social services, the law, the housing market, and many of the other large impersonal institutions of modern society). There are non-material psychological "rewards" for union membership: seeing the union representatives talk as equals to the boss, reading about occasional union successes in the daily newspapers, referring to other union members and union leaders as "brothers." Businessmen's associations usually provide even more of this sort of thing, especially those activities which involve actual distribution of power. All such activities—even the purely symbolic ones—help to counteract the psychological concomitants of modern mass society.

Economic alienation has also resulted from increased technological specialization. As writers from Marx to Friedmann and Drucker[49] have pointed out, the trend after the Industrial Revolution was for the worker not to control his tools, not to be able to "see" a complete production process, not to be able to control the pace and "rhythm" of his work, not to have his employer pay attention to his human personal needs. While this trend perhaps continues in some countries which are belatedly adopting "American efficiency" techniques in accord with the pre-World War I advice of Frederick Winslow Taylor, in the United States itself at least there is a significant countervailing trend. While the assembly line system of production continues to be used in many factories, it is often now arranged so that the worker can control its speed and skip parts coming to him without damaging the whole system. Automation is bringing a system of production in which the worker avoids "mechanical" jobs and spends his time in the more "creative," less boring jobs of inspection, repair, and adjustment of highly complicated machines. The long-run trend for the skilled worker to be replaced by the unskilled worker has been reversed not only by the small increase in skilled workers but also by the large increase of semi-skilled workers. The American efficiency expert today is usually very much aware—some would say "too much" aware, from the standpoint of the worker's independent political development—of the "human" and the social relations needs of the worker. Factory managers also pay increasing attention to the worker's orientation to the plant and his understanding

[49] Georges Friedmann, *Problemes Humains du Machinisme Industriel* (Paris: Gallimard, 1946); Georges Friedmann, *The Anatomy of Work* (New York: Free Press of Glencoe, 1961); Peter F. Drucker, *The Future of Industrial Man* (New York: John Day, 1942).

of the production process. Thus, to a considerable extent, the most recent technological developments, and the newer attitudes of "modern" managers have combined to reverse the alienation consequences of the 18th and the 19th centuries' technological revolution. There is also a long-run trend—called by Colin Clark[50] a shift from secondary to tertiary occupations—from factory work in general to the less boring service, clerical and professional occupations.

Since one major source of the mass society was the recurring deep economic depression and unemployment, the apparent partial control of this phenomenon by government since 1940 has also tended to limit the mass character of the society. To the extent that the average man believes he will not be cut off from the goods and services made available by the economy, and in fact finds himself claiming an expanding amount of these, he is less likely to feel economically alienated from the society. Another way of looking at this phenomenon is from the political standpoint: The government—through its increased controls over the economy and its increased protection of the individual against economic vicissitudes—has made itself something of a partner of the "little man" in his economic struggle for existence, and while this may reduce economic and other freedoms in the long run it also reduces modern man's alienation from his government and his society.

Two major forces reducing the impact of the mass society are: (1) the public, which is considered in the next section, and (2) the voluntary association, which is considered in Chapter 10.

We have examined a number of social forces and institutions—mostly modern at least in so far as they have significance for the bulk of the population—which have developed against the historical trend toward the mass society. In the United States, and in such other industrially developed nations as Sweden and Britain, they have perhaps even stopped or reversed the trend. In the past ten or twenty years, there have been complaints against too much integration and too much conformity in these countries. This does not mean that the social problems created by the mass society have been solved: there remain the extreme victims of the mass society (the isolated and the unorganized) which the counteracting forces have not reached; there remains the fact that economic recession has not been completely controlled; there remains the fact that the voluntary association, the nuclear family, and the other institutions do not completely counteract for many of those they partially reach the feelings of loneliness, ignorance, helplessness, uselessness, and insecurity created by the mass society. Still, these counteracting forces have developed and they have been gaining greater significance.

[50] Colin Clark, *The Conditions of Economic Progress* (London: Macmillan, 1940), pp. 337–73.

D   *The Public*

1   THE NATURE OF THE PUBLIC

The concept of the public first began to take form in the writings of the university president A. Lawrence Lowell[51] and the publicist Walter Lippmann,[52] although it was first distinguished from the crowd in the writings of the French jurist Gabriel Tarde.[53] The concept later received more explicit formulation in the writings of the sociologists Ferdinand Töennies,[54] Robert E. Park,[55] and Herbert Blumer.[56]

The public is a huge informal discussion group. When any problem arises or when anything happens that concerns them collectively, members of the public talk the matter over, argue it out in such a way that everyone's attitude is influenced by everyone else's. That does not mean that the resulting "public opinion"[57] is completely unanimous; it simply means that every person understands the other's point of view and has somehow given it consideration. It also does not mean that everyone is considering the same subject or pursuing the same line of cultural development; there are many publics, each with a different interest, and one may join or leave them freely and voluntarily. While there is this element of volition in membership, the public—for any specific issue—is a definite enough group with adequate communication between its members. There is thus no social isolation, no sense of loneliness, no unsatisfied longing to belong to some group or movement. While all the members of a public are subjected to the same influences, including propaganda, the influences are conflicting in their effect and are not taken at their face value and so are not directly determining. Members of a public do not respond directly to outside stimuli as members of an audience do; rather, they evaluate every influence to see how it fits in with their knowledge, beliefs, and expectations. The public has a culture and a set of ideals with which to make these evaluations.

Leadership of the public tends to shift. Anyone who sets forth a distinctive and interesting point of view, or sometimes merely an important fact, draws attention of other people, and for a while the discussion centers

[51] *Public Opinion and Popular Government* (New York: Longmans, 1913).

[52] *Public Opinion* (New York: Harcourt, 1922).

[53] *The Laws of Imitation* (New York: Holt, 1903).

[54] Ferdinand Töennies, *Kritik der Oeffentlichen Meinung* (Berlin: Springer, 1922).

[55] Robert E. Park and Ernest W. Burgess, *Introduction to the Science of Sociology* (Chicago: University of Chicago Press, 1924), pp. 791–96.

[56] Herbert Blumer, "Collective Behavior," in Alfred M. Lee (ed.), *New Outline of the Principles of Sociology* (New York: Barnes and Noble, 1946), pp. 185–93.

[57] For valuable discussions of the nature and origin of public opinion, see William Albig, *Public Opinion* (New York: McGraw-Hill, 1939); Alfred M. Lee, "Public Opinion in Relation to Culture," *Psychiatry*, 8 (February, 1945), pp. 49–61.

around what he has to say. When someone else has a more attractive point of view or bit of information to express, the leadership of the public shifts to him. Some persons are adept in forms of expression and hold leadership of the public for considerable lengths of time if they keep attuned to what is of public interest; they are not innovating leaders—as propagandists of the audience often are—but rather the well-known type of "leaders who follow."

Leaders of the public tend to be one of three types of persons. First are those who articulate well a certain point of view, and who achieve a social position in the integrated group which gives them access to large numbers of people to whom they explain their point of view. Second are the experts who have knowledge, or alleged knowledge, which large numbers of people happen to be greatly interested in at the moment. Third are the "ecological leaders"[58] who happen to be located in social positions where they are likely to have brief conversations with large numbers of diverse people, and who serve as channels for transmitting the diverse points of view and facts which they hear (such as storekeepers, postmen, traveling salesmen, etc.).

Clearly the public is the only kind of stable society that is possible in modern Western civilization, since the isolation and unbroken tradition required by the folk society can no longer exist. The public can exist for a long time only in a democracy, since it requires freedom of expression and freedom of belief. Much of American, British, Scandinavian, Swiss and Dutch society has been that of the public type, and this helps to explain the long devotion to democracy that has characterized these nations. Some of the central European nations—notably Germany, Austria, and Italy—have less of a tradition of free discussion and therefore urbanization and secularization in them have created the audience rather than the public. When modern democratic governments developed in these countries, they proved at first to be unstable. Some of the eastern European nations have never ceased to be folk societies, at least in their rural areas, and an authoritarian type of government that does not too strongly violate local traditions is satisfactory to them. As they modernize, the latter become mass societies with totalitarian control from their progagandists.

2   THE TOTALITARIAN SOCIETY

The distinction between the audience and the public is a most important one for the analysis of contemporary society. In the first place, it should be noted that while both may exist in a democratic society, the audience, when it is the dominant form of group in a society, is such an unstable and unsatisfying condition that it is actually conducive to totalitarianism. But dictatorship provides only superficial satisfaction to the needs created

[58] This term will not be fully understandable until one reads Chapter 13.

by mass society. While the totalitarian state provides something for the people to belong to, it still keeps people apart and out of communication with one another. No dictatorship can survive if the common people form publics and freely discuss their situation, their culture, and their ideals. For if they do so, they threaten the dictatorship, or at least prevent it from doing what it wishes to do.

Fascism, therefore, sets up the strongest barriers to certain kinds of communication among citizens and yet tries to create the illusion that they are fully integrated members of an understanding and protective state. The dictator must subject his people to frequent propaganda and expect them to respond to it directly. Thus every totalitarian state in these days of high average education and easy means of communication must be a mass society, even though it may have a camouflage of stability. The mass society is no more stable under dictatorship than it is under democracy. Fascism eventually turns out to be a mirage. While it recruits members in its early stages because it seems to be a way out of the mass society, it becomes an extreme form of the mass society once it has achieved power and is seeking to keep people in line.

The Soviet communist dictatorship has been much cleverer than the fascist in avoiding some of the unpleasantness and ill effects of the mass society.[59] The communist leaders know that a sense of participation in the processes of government and a *feeling* of being free to discuss the matters relevant to political affairs are important for the satisfaction and mental health of the ordinary citizen. They therefore outline a set of discussion topics that are considered by them to be of greatest significance and yet which can be discussed without endangering the leadership in the exercise of power. To make sure the discussion does not take a "dangerous" turn, they specify in great detail what are the "right solutions" at which the discussion should eventually arrive.

Every adult and adolescent in the Soviet state is urged and pressured into being a member and attending the meetings of a small discussion group composed of people who work or live in the same place. The discussion topics are handed over to a trusted group leader who is a member of the Communist Party, and with every sort of moral pressure people are encouraged to discuss the topics and to arrive at the predetermined solutions. In one sense the discussion is free, or at least gives the appearance of being free, since any kind of argument can be raised if it is properly refuted when it does not lead to the predetermined conclusion. There

---

[59] Some of the better sources on what is going on within the Soviet Union are the publications of the Russian Research Center of Harvard University. See especially Alex Inkeles, *Public Opinion in Soviet Russia* (Cambridge: Harvard University Press, 1952); A. Inkeles and R. A. Bauer, *The Soviet Citizen* (Cambridge: Harvard University Press, 1959); Robert Campbell, *Soviet Economic Power* (Boston: Houghton, 1960).

is considered to be only one right answer and all deviations from it show incorrect thinking. In addition to engaging in the discussions, the average member of the Soviet state is urged to participate in all sorts of activities for the physical, mental, and moral improvement of the community and the society at large, as specified by the communist leaders. This high degree of community participation and interpersonal communication removes much of the sense of isolation which is the basis of the problems created by the mass society. There is a great deal of friendly sociability in these activities and the individual citizen perhaps gets the feeling of participating in the important activities of his time. He is generally unhampered by the state unless he consistently refuses to be convinced of the right solution of all the social problems as specified by his leaders. He is aware that there is a threat of power in the background pushing him into conformity with the line specified by the Communist Party, but his more immediate sensation is one of not being isolated and of belonging first to the small group and through it to the whole communist state which considers itself not only national but international.

In the discussions the Soviet citizen is given full "explanations" of the forces controlling the social world. These explanations stem from basic Marxist theory, and while they seem utterly bizarre and unrealistic to the outsider whose mind is not completely adapted to the framework of communist theory, the Soviet citizen learns through long practice to work his thinking through to an acceptance of these explanations. Through his extensive participation in community activities and through the "election" of lower party leaders, the Soviet citizen is given the impression that he is one of the controllers of the Soviet state. Of course he is given only a choice of voting for the "right" candidate or not voting at all, and of participating in the "right" activities as determined by his leaders or not participating at all. A great deal of community and other pressure is used on him to participate and to vote and talk and think in the "right" way.

The Soviet state by these means avoids the *appearance* of being a mass society and tries to give its citizens the *feeling* that they are not simply an audience for the leaders. Actually, however, the Soviet state is still one large audience because there is no connection between the tremendous amount of communication and participation at the lower level and the ultimate control of important activities and even of social values by the top leaders. The important communications are still one way, from the top down, and the only thing that is characteristic of the audience and is avoided in the Soviet state is the block against the intercommunication of the members of the audience. The leaders pay attention to the discussion at the lower level only in so far as they are interested in measuring the current amount of deviation from the party line which they specify, although there is some evidence that the leaders are beginning to modify their policies in accord with a growing public opinion.[60] Premier Nikita Khrushchev's 1956 denunciation of the excesses of control by his predecessor, Josef Stalin, somewhat accelerated the movement toward developing incipient publics.

The basic fact that the state is one large audience, however, is apparent only to the more sophisticated people and to those who are themselves within the middle or upper levels of the party hierarchy. They are the ones who are aware of the huge, impersonal, audience-controlling mechanism that the Soviet state is, and they are the ones who not infrequently become prey to the diseases of the mass society. For the ordinary citizen who has never been aroused to what is going on around him or has never shown any willingness to deviate, the satisfactions of the small group discussions and the community participation may be quite enough to keep him happy and to give him a sense of rootedness and belonging and a belief that he understands the mechanism of the state and has a share in its control. Whether the average Soviet citizen will ever realize that these are delusions cannot be predicted. It is quite possible that the avoidance of the sharpest weaknesses of the mass society will leave him sufficiently satisfied to avoid questioning whether he has any voice that actually does reach through to the top of the Soviet hierarchy. The people of Russia also have roots in a pre-communist folk society which was a highly integrated social organization, and this serves to give the Soviet society a stability based on the past stronger than would normally occur in a more modernized and industrialized society. There are changes going on in Soviet society, especially since 1956, which are permitting some development of public opinion, particularly through a reduction in the "terror" which previously inhibited even private conversation between friends and family members.

The purpose of considering the Soviet system of community participation and group discussion was to clarify the distinction between audience and public. Despite appearances to the contrary, the Soviet system has not been a true example of the public. The public can provide an antidote to the mass society, and the Soviet leaders have attempted to gain some of the advantages of the structure of the public as distinct from that of the audience. But the true public can exist only when there is diversity of opinions and backgrounds, when there are freedom and complexity, and when the sources of information are manifold. Yet it avoids isolation and confusion and puts people on the road toward resolution of mental and valuational conflicts.[61]

[60] Inkeles, *op. cit.*
[61] Kornhauser, *op. cit.*

3   THE DEMOCRATIC SOCIETY

The "public" is only a word, of course, and therefore it does not "do" any of these things. What is meant is that the conditions which create the social relationship known as the public are also the conditions which eliminate some of the characteristics of the social relationship known as the audience. The main condition is that of free and constant communication. If people can talk over their divergent points of view, and vicariously share their divergent experiences and sources of information, their confusion will diminish and they will have a clearer understanding of the forces that move society. If, through this communication, they can relate themselves to one another despite their initial differences, not only will they cease to feel isolated, but also they can develop a sense of participation in the political process. The achievement of a consensus in a political discussion usually results in a demand for expression of that consensus in some sort of political action.

Free discussion does not necessarily result in the elimination of divergence and the creation of uniformity. In the first place, diversity arises in our society naturally, and it would take a ruthless dictatorship to eliminate it. Second, discussion seldom results in unanimity of opinion (witness our presidential elections which involve a maximum of discussion but practically never a majority of more than 60 per cent). Third, the deviation of minor groups in a society will be tolerated only if there is some understanding of the causes of deviation of those groups and of the exact nature of the deviation. Fourth, if minor groups wish to participate in the processes which affect the society as a whole, and to see that their point of view and interests get represented, they must relate themselves to other groups and work cooperatively with them. Finally, the existence of minor groups with divergent ideas and culture forms depends on the preservation of democratic government, and democratic government requires at least a minimum of understanding and cooperation among its citizenry. Diversity thus fosters intellectual and cultural development only if there is adequate communication through most of the society.

4   MEANS OF DEVELOPING THE PUBLIC

Let us assume that this hypothesis is correct, that the solution for the difficulties created by mass society is the attainment of a "public" state of social relationships in which discussion is free and constant, and that no major issue is settled without a public opinion having been formed about it. How, then, can this social condition be achieved? Until further studies are made, no one can say. But some hypotheses may be offered which have a basis in general sociological knowledge.

1 A major block to communication from the standpoint of the individual is a feeling of insecurity. All efforts to promote security, especially job security, will reduce these paranoid tendencies in people that block their communication with others.

2 Discussions take place most freely and constantly if people are in groups that have a definite purpose and time for discussion. These are called voluntary associations and are discussed more fully in the next chapter. If means can be found for encouraging people to join functional groups —such as civic-improvement organizations, political clubs, unions, and recreational associations—our society will shift from the audience to the public mode of human relationship. New kinds of voluntary interest associations could possibly be developed.

3 Attachment to neighborhood would be another way of stimulating the public. Recently city planning has taken the line of developing neighborhood units with all necessary facilities and space for recreation. More attention needs to be given to the social side of these "housing projects." Also, people in the older city blocks might be encouraged to take advantage of the benefits of cooperation to get advantages for themselves which they could not afford as individuals. All such activities would promote group attachment on a neighborhood basis and would also help to eliminate some of the major "evils" of city life.

4 On many important issues people do not have access to the facts, or to the arguments for different points of view. Newspapers in many localities do not provide this information or see the need for providing it. Provision of basic information regarding important issues, in readable and easily accessible form, would seem to be an aid to discussion.

5 New ways of disseminating information need to be devised. Adult educators have been working on this problem for a long time but have not yet found enough ways to make adult education interesting.

6 Civic groups need to put pressure on newspapers to gain more adequate representation of issues and even honest reporting. At present newspaper adequacy and point of view seems to be determined almost solely by owners, editors, and advertisers.

7 There is too much cynicism about the possibility of making contact with differing groups. One of the characteristics of a leader is that he is not cynical regarding possibilities. Some group leaders have worked out effective techniques for making contacts between their group and members of other social classes and races.

8 Training in public speaking could be made available to members of functional groups who feel they need it. One of the most popular courses in most labor-education programs is public speaking. The major reason the class members give for selecting the course is that they sometimes

feel the urge to express themselves at a union meeting but are afraid they will make fools of themselves.

These are simply suggestions for promoting more effective communication. Any of the suggestions may be wrong, and together they may be ineffective, as future experimentation would show. But they represent the sort of thing about which we must think and be inventive if we are to solve the problems created by the mass society. The alternatives seem to be either to continue to drift in a mass society, with its pain for the individual and its danger to culture, or to turn to some form of totalitarianism, with its loss of liberty for the individual and its placing of culture in rigid molds. Since the mass society is inherently unstable, if there are no efforts to combat the alienation of modern man, totalitarianism is our destiny. Unfortunately, too many seem to be willing to give up and accept totalitarianism as the way out of the mass society.

E *The Interrelation Among the Forms of Association*

The concepts of integrated group, crowd, audience, and public are, as mentioned earlier, merely ideal types (Table 6 summarizes their characteristics as ideal types). They are seldom found in pure form in any concrete behavioral situation. People seldom act collectively solely on the basis of traditions which they use to predict the behavior of others in guiding their own actions. On the other hand, this basis of the integrated group is seldom completely lacking except in the most extreme crowd situations. Similarly, an element of stimulation that comes out of the physical interaction characteristic of the crowd occurs in many situations in which human beings are found together. The passive acceptance of external stimuli characteristic of the audience is, of course, part of all social situations; one cannot avoid being a member of an audience to a certain extent in every situation. While the independent thinking and rational discussion of the public are sometimes difficult to distinguish from the traditional thinking of the integrated group, careful observation would probably discern an element of them in all human group situations except that of the extreme crowd.

While elements of all four of the bases of collective action are to be found in most concrete group situations, their frequency and importance vary sharply from time to time. This is not only true within any one culture, but is also true between different periods and between different cultures. The small isolated community and the society with strong traditions and values tend to have a minimum of audience behavior and even very little of the public. Crowds tend to increase in frequency during periods of transition and of social unrest arising out of group frustrations.

TABLE 6 · SUMMARY DESCRIPTION OF FOUR FORMS OF ASSOCIATION

	Integrated group	Crowd	Audience	Public
1 Conducive situation	Social stability, history of no barriers to communication.	Collective frustration, within hitherto stable community.	Traditional meanings and values inadequate to explain or "control" new situations; barriers to interpersonal communication but facilities for mass communication.	Social change. feeling of need for new meanings and values; no barriers to communication.
2 Nature of communication	Multilateral, face-to-face, using traditional meanings and values.	Multilateral, through "natural signs" that express emotions.	Unilateral, through mass media using both traditional and new meanings and values (new ones not common).	Multilateral, "rational," often face-to-face, using both traditional and new meanings and values, with the new ones becoming commonly understood.
3 Basis of concerted action	Expectations for other's behavior on the basis of traditional meanings and values.	The "circular process" and "possession."	Similar stimuli.	"Rationally" agreed-upon meanings and values.
4 Nature of leadership	Stable and formal; supports *status quo;* from persons of high prestige.	Unstable; advocates unusual behavior; from persons of low prestige.	Unstable; from persons who wish to influence behavior of others and have access to mass media.	Unstable; from all interested segments of the community, especially those with information or ability relevant to public's interest.
5 Duration	Indefinite number of years, often decades or centuries.	A few hours or days.	Could be indefinite, but tends to be transformed into something else.	Indefinite number of days or years, sometimes decades or centuries.
6 Behavioral products	Slight and graduate extensions of traditional meanings and values.	Entirely new symbols which tend to become traditional and which can be powerful influences on behavior; memories of an exhilarating experience; perhaps some guilt feelings.	Changed individual habits.	Constant developing of new meanings and values. Sometimes crystallizes into a voluntary association.

The audience and the public both tend to increase in frequency as the integrated society declines, and yet the audience and the public have a certain degree of inverse relationship to each other.

There is a correlation, although this should not be considered as a necessary or causal relation in all instances, between the form of the government and the form of collective action dominant in a society. The society characterized by integrated groups has historically been associated with monarchy and aristocracy. The audience reaches its peak in the modern dictatorship, especially of the fascist variety, although it is known to have frequent expression in modern democracies as well. A public can exist only under constitutional and democratic forms of government.

A certain functional relationship between the four forms of association should also be mentioned. The crowd and the audience tend to be unstable groups and to give way to the other forms readily. The usual consequence of crowd behavior is a memory of new collective meanings that become part of the basis of organized group activity. The audience is sometimes stampeded into becoming a crowd, as in a panic, where an audience is turned into a crowd within a few minutes upon evidence of an apparent threat to life, which immediately starts an intense process of circular interaction. The audience can become a public even more readily if people begin to talk to each other and to exchange ideas, information, and points of view. The public tends to be a stable form of group, just as is the integrated society, but occasionally such a high degree of consensus is reached on a topic through discussion that there is no longer a need for further discussion of it and it takes on an accepted and traditional meaning. Some of the products of the public, therefore, contribute to the integrated group. The voluntary association is typically a public well on the road to becoming an integrated group.[62] These are the most usual sequences from one form of association to the other, although the other possible ones occasionally also occur.

Historically, Western society has moved from the domination of the integrated group in the Middle Ages, through periods of frequent crowd activity, to a phase of mass society reaching its high point in the 19th and early 20th centuries. At present, the public seems to be contesting the audience as the dominant mode of human relationship. The audience readily gives rise to totalitarian dictatorships. The public can be stable, but it can also become encrusted into voluntary associations which, in advanced stages of development, take on more the character of integrated groups than of publics. If such a return to a domination of the integrated group were to occur, which does not seem likely at the moment, it would be reminiscent of what happened to Europe in ancient times: Greece and Rome emerged from integrated group dominance, through periods of

[62] See Chapter 10.

crowd activity, degenerating into audiences and totalitarian dictatorships (with only very brief periods in which publics flourished). Eventually, by the 4th and 5th centuries A.D., the integrated group mode of relationship once again emerged dominant. Of course, it must be remembered that in all these phases, some basic amount of integrated group relationship continues to provide the basic structure of the society.[63]

[63] See Chapter 5.

FOR ADDITIONAL READING

BERELSON, B., and M. JANOWITZ, *Reader in Public Opinion and Communication* (Glencoe, Ill.: Free Press, 1953). A collection of readings on the public and public opinion.

BLUMER, HERBERT, "Collective Behavior," in A. M. LEE (ed.), *An Outline of the Principles of Sociology* (New York: Barnes and Noble, 1946). A summary statement on the crowd and the public.

CANTRIL, HADLEY, *The Invasion from Mars* (Princeton, N.J.: Princeton University Press, 1940). A study of one of the most extensive examples of crowd behavior in recent times. Reports on what happened after Orson Welles's realistic radio drama of a Martian invasion.

LANG, KURT, and GLADYS ENGEL LANG, *Collective Dynamics* (New York: T. Y. Crowell, 1961). A systematic textbook on collective phenomena.

MERTON, ROBERT K., *Mass Persuasion: The Social Psychology of a War Bond Drive* (New York: Harper, 1946). An analytic study of a specific instance of mass behavior.

TURNER, RALPH H., and LEWIS M. KILLIAN, *Collective Behavior* (Englewood Cliffs, N.J.: Prentice-Hall, 1957). A broad-ranging text, with readings.

10 * Voluntary Associations

A   Conditions for Development

A voluntary association develops when a small group of people, finding they have a certain interest (or purpose) in common, agree to meet and to act together in order to try to satisfy that interest or achieve that purpose.[1] Frequently their action requires that they urge other like-minded persons to join them, so that some associations may become very large and extend throughout the whole country. In the United States they have absolutely no formal contact with the government unless they incorporate, which obliges them to conform to certain minor laws of state governments (and unless, of course, they commit an offense against the general criminal law, which is naturally extremely rare). In fact the "due process" clause of the 14th Amendment of the United States Constitution has been interpreted to protect the independence of voluntary associations from state government restrictions, just as the 1st Amendment has always been interpreted as protecting voluntary associations from federal government restrictions.[2] A good example of the limitation on state action occurred in 1958 when the Supreme Court supported the refusal by the National Association for the Advancement of Colored People to open its membership lists to state inspection in accord with an Alabama statute. Mr. Justice Harlan, speaking for a unanimous court, declared that the Alabama statute would limit "the right of members to pursue their lawful

---

[1] Voluntary associations are usually defined so that their purposes do not include profit making for the members. But many voluntary associations do create economic benefits for their members—for example, the consumers' cooperatives or mutual-aid societies that provide sickness or death benefits for members.

[2] David Fellman, *The Constitutional Right of Association* (Chicago: University of Chicago Press, 1963).

> In modern democracies and to some extent in all inclusive societies on the scale
> of modern states, men exercise their influence and voice their aspirations through
> delegated powers operating through functionaries and leaders, through lobbies,
> party organizations, religious denominations and a variety of other organized
> groups having a complex internal organization of their own.
>
> Louis Wirth, "Consensus and Mass Communication," *American Sociological Review*,
> 13 (1948), p. 8.

private interest privately and to associate freely with others in so doing."[3]
In France and Italy, on the other hand, the national government sets
certain restrictions on voluntary associations, and sometimes directs the
activities of associations whose purposes are for the benefit of the public.[4]

As social structures voluntary associations have distinct features of
formal leadership, specialized activity, rules for operating, place and time
of meeting, and so on. An important distinction among them must be specified. Some associations act only to express or satisfy the interests of their
members in relation to themselves—these include the recreational and
sport associations, the social and hobby clubs, the professional societies, etc.,
which may be especially numerous in the modern democracies but which
are also found in large numbers in all literate and in some preliterate
societies. Other associations are directed outward; they wish to achieve
some condition or change in some limited segment of the society as a
whole. These are rarely found outside the modern democracies, for reasons
we shall examine later. The former associations may be called "expressive" groups and the latter "social-influence" or "instrumental" groups—
for lack of better terms.[5] It is with the latter type that we are primarily
concerned in this chapter.

Since the social-influence groups have a specific and limited purpose,
they also tend to have a limited life. When the purpose is accomplished, or

[3] John Marshall Harlan, "Text of Supreme Court Decision Upholding NAACP in
Alabama Case," cited in full in the *New York Times*, July 1, 1958, p. 18.

[4] Arnold M. Rose, *Theory and Method in the Social Sciences* (Minneapolis: University of
Minnesota Press, 1954), Chapter IV; Arnold M. Rose, "On Individualism and Social
Responsibility," *European Journal of Sociology*, 2 (Summer, 1961), pp. 163–69.

[5] A test of the validity of this distinction, using ratings by both group members and
outsiders, has shown that the dichotomy is widely accepted and can be measured. See
Arthur P. Jacoby and Nicholas Babchuk, "Instrumental and Expressive Voluntary
Associations," *Sociology and Social Research*, 47 (July, 1963), pp. 461–71. Sherwood Fox
suggests another way of classifying voluntary associations—according to which groups they
serve: Majoral associations serve major institutions such as business or education; minoral
associations serve important minorities, such as women's clubs or hobby clubs; and medial
associations mediate between major parts of the population, such as social welfare groups.
See David L. Sills, *The Volunteers* (Glencoe, Ill.: Free Press, 1957), p. 79.

the need which gave rise to the association changes, the association usually dies. Since change is rapid in the United States, and many social problems get solved while new ones continually arise, the turnover in voluntary associations of the social influence type is great. Even when an association continues in full vigor, there can be a large turnover in its membership. Members join and leave an association for a great variety of personal reasons, including a belief that the purpose of the association needs, or does not need, to be accomplished.

We may consider briefly the sense in which these associations are voluntary. Voluntary associations are presumably those into which an individual may freely choose to enter and from which he may freely choose to withdraw. But such a statement is a mere tautology: voluntary implies free choice. "Voluntariness" may be placed in a continuum and thus "voluntary" and "involuntary" become polar terms in an ideal-typical dichotomy. There is no clear-cut, realistic line of division between the two. In this sense, the term "voluntary" can only be defined in terms of "involuntary." The mentioned dichotomy implies a psychology: The assumption is that man, a rational creature, in certain circumstances weighs the advantages and disadvantages of joining a certain group or participating in a collective enterprise and, on the basis of the outcome of this deliberation, joins this group. Such a group would be a "voluntary" association. Conversely, an "involuntary" organization would be one which the individual is compelled to be a member of because of external pressures. The involuntary organizations are usually the ones an individual is born into or must join to survive in the society: the state, the family, the economic system, the school system, the church, the army (where conscription is the law), and perhaps others.

As a matter of fact, ignoring the metaphysical implications, there is seldom free will in the psychological sense considered above. Formal and informal means of social control, or social forces, in effect dictate that certain individuals are going to join certain "voluntary" associations. In those cases when the individual does reflect on the advisability of joining an association or participating in a certain sphere of activity, he may not be "free" in his choice because there are overwhelming advantages to the one choice or another which dictate his decision. On the other hand, certain "involuntary" associations may never be joined. For example, the youth may become a tramp (or a perpetual "student") and never join or participate effectively in the great involuntary association of the economic system to provide a living for himself. In a secular order such as our modern, urban, democratic, free-enterprise society, in a sense, it becomes quite possible for anyone to withdraw from any involuntary association except a jailhouse. One can leave his family, his church, and even his state and the economic system.

This discussion of the logical meaning of "voluntary" and "involuntary" is really not essential to an analysis of voluntary associations. The reason is that "voluntary" associations is a concept (however lacking in precise formulation it might be) in sociology, and in that universe of discourse it has a meaning that cannot be understood from its constituent words. It is evident that the formulations of lists of voluntary associations in various societies would reveal that there are certain universal criteria of involuntary associations (though not of voluntary associations). Thus voluntary acquires a residual meaning. The general criteria of involuntary associations are: (1) when the individual is physically forced to join an association it will be called involuntary; and (2) when the individual is born into the association it will be called involuntary. Like all social phenomena, voluntary associations are not entities that have a place in some ultimately real classification. The term is merely a concept determined both by conventionality and usefulness.

Some preliterate societies, notably those of West Africa, Central Australia, parts of Melanesia, and a few American Indian tribes, have certain kinds of voluntary associations.[6] The African associations are most developed, and a consideration of them will tell us something of the limited nature of voluntary associations in preliterate societies. The African associations are mostly secret orders, bearing some resemblance to fraternal associations in our own society. Most of them are for one sex only, although some include both sexes. They have sociable, magical, religious, mutual-aid, and political functions, the first three being expressive and the latter two having social influence implications. "As mutual-aid protective associations the secret orders of West Africa pay special attention to the interests of their members as against the world at large. They collect private debts from delinquent creditors on behalf of their members. They punish other transgressions against the brotherhood as well."[7] As political associations the secret orders assist the king in the application of the sanctions that uphold the tribal laws.

Thus the African secret orders are extensions of the government. They carry on some of the central functions of government where the latter is apparently too weak to perform them itself. They do not, as in our society, seek to *change* a very limited aspect of the government or society at large. They are thus not social-influence associations in our limited sense of the term, but are a basic arm of an "involuntary" organization, the state. The same is true of the "military societies" found among some of the American plains Indian tribes; their nearest equivalent in our society is the Army, a branch of the government even when made up of

---

[6] The material of this paragraph has been taken from E. Adamson Hoebel, *Man in the Primitive World* (New York: McGraw-Hill, 1949), pp. 305–07.

[7] *Ibid.*, p. 307.

volunteers. In most preliterate societies that have voluntary associations at all, the associations have purely expressive functions.[8] The typical voluntary association of those primitive societies which have any associations at all is likely to have religious, magical, socializing, or sociable functions. The smallness and homogeneity of the population in most preliterate societies restrict the absolute number of associations of any kind.[9]

Voluntary associations of the social-influence type are to be found primarily in societies that are urban and democratic in general character. In the Middle Ages of Western society, to exemplify an alternative, when the church and state had resolved their differences, few individuals could be members of any formal organization other than the church and state; and these were coterminous both with each other and with the community.[10] One of the most characteristic features of the shift from medieval to modern times is the rise of groups with specialized interests and divergent activities *within* the community. But not even in all modern communities are there a significant number of voluntary associations. Strictly speaking, in a modern totalitarian society there are no groups but the state (or, more precisely, the party or social movement that controls the state).[11] All the individual's affiliations are determined in some way by the state, and these affiliations exist ultimately to carry out the purpose of the state.

Even within our primarily urban and democratic society we may note wide variations in the complexity and diversity of group structures in any given community. In a relatively homogeneous rural community, at one ex-

[8] Robert H. Lowie, *Primitive Society* (New York: Boni and Liveright, 1925), Chapters 10 and 11; Hutton Webster, *Primitive Secret Societies* (New York: Macmillan, 1932); Alexander Goldenweiser, *Anthropology* (New York: F. S. Crofts, 1937), Chapters 19 and 20; E. D. Chapple and C. S. Coon, *Principles of Anthropology* (New York: Holt, 1942), Chapter 17.

[9] Scholars who specifically discuss the "paucity" of associations in preliterate societies include Robert Redfield, "The Folk Society," *American Journal of Sociology,* 52 (1947), pp. 293–308; and Robert M. MacIver, "Interests," *Encyclopedia of the Social Sciences* (New York: Macmillan, 1935), Vol. 8, pp. 144–48.

[10] There were religious and knightly orders, of course, but these had the same characteristic tendency to be at once a community, a governmental unit, and a religious unit. In the late Middle Ages the guilds developed, but they did so in response to the urbanization and differentiation of society—which we hold to be among the characteristic conditions for the rise of voluntary associations. See Louis D. Hartson, "A Study of Voluntary Associations, Educational and Social, in Europe During the Period from 1100 to 1700," *Pedagogical Seminary,* 18 (1911), pp: 10–31.

[11] The establishment of modern totalitarian regimes has regularly been attended by the destruction or "integration" of voluntary associations, especially those that sought to have some influence on the society—less so of those that were purely expressive, sociable, or recreational in character. The church—which represents a loyalty alien to the state—is likely to become a problem for the totalitarian state, and may even be a source of resistance unless it is assimilated into the state's interest in some way.

treme, most people tend to go to the same church, to be members of the same occupational (agricultural) organization, to participate in the same sociable activities, and to send their children to the same schools. While there are different organizations for the various activities, and while there is some differential participation in the groups according to age and sex, there is still no large number of groups with divergent membership and interest in a homogeneous rural community. There is less likely to be relatively much diversity of interest and attitude among the groups where all the members of the community belong to the same groups. While we need to learn much more regarding the conditions under which voluntary group differentiation develops, we may take it as a close approximation to the facts that the development of voluntary associations with diverse ideas as to how the society should be changed occurs primarily in the modern urban democratic society. The term "urban" is to be understood in its sociological sense, not in terms of the census definition: many villages in the United States are urban, and there is a trend toward their becoming more urban. To put our observations in general terms: The existence of a significant number of social-influence associations in the community seems to require that the population be somewhat heterogeneous in background and interests, and that no one instutition, such as the church or state, be successful in dominating the entire life of most individuals.

B   *Numbers and Structure*[12]

No one knows how many associations there are in the United States, or how many people belong to them. But the number is known for some local communities where special studies have been made, and extrapolating from these would lead us to estimate that there are well over 100,000 voluntary associations in the United States.[13] A count of the voluntary associations—exclusive of the governmental, the specific church affiliated, and the strictly occupational—in Minneapolis and St. Paul, by the Minnesota Council of Adult Education, turned up some 3,000 organizations, of which some 450 were engaged in an effort to influence or educate the adult population. A list of organizations in a small New England city (50,000 inhabitants) prepared by the local council of social agencies in-

[12] Except where otherwise specified, the description in the rest of this chapter will be limited to the United States. Where sources are not specified, information comes from an unpublished study of voluntary associations in Minneapolis and St. Paul, conducted by Arnold M. Rose and John E. Tsouderos in 1953 and 1954.

[13] Fox has compiled a list of 5,000 *national* associations alone in the United States, but makes no claim that it is complete. Sherwood Dean Fox, "Voluntary Associations and Social Structure," unpublished Ph.D. thesis, Harvard University, December, 1952.

cluded some 300 associations.[14] In 1924 there were almost 3,000 voluntary organizations in a group of 140 rural villages.[15] Warner's "Yankee City" (population, 17,000) had 357 associations when it was studied in the early thirties.[16] Boulder, Colorado, a city of 12,000, had 245 associations in the early 1940's.[17] In 1935 there were 200 associations among the 7,500 Negroes of Natchez, and 4,000 associations among the 275,000 Negroes in Chicago.[18]

A fairly complete study of voluntary associations was made for the city of Detroit in 1951, where 63 per cent of the population belonged to some organization other than a church. About half of those belonging to non-church organizations belonged to two or more. The types of organizations adhered to were as follows: occupational associations, 37 per cent; fraternal and social clubs, 21 per cent; church-connected groups, 9 per cent; athletic and other recreational associations, 8 per cent; youth-serving groups, 8 per cent; welfare organizations, 7 per cent; neighborhood improvement associations, 5 per cent; women's clubs, 2 per cent; political clubs, 2 per cent; community centers, 1 per cent; nationality groups, 1 per cent; other groups, 3 per cent.[19]

Another systematic study was made in Bennington, Vermont (population, 8,000), in 1947.[20] The proportion belonging to some voluntary association was 64.2 per cent; 24.6 per cent belonged to only one association, 15.9 per cent to two associations, 8.6 per cent to three associations, 15.1 per cent to four or more associations. The last group of 15.1 per cent held 50.7 per cent of the total memberships. In this small town, 20.4 per cent of the memberships were in church groups; 16.8 per cent in fraternal associations; 10.8 per cent in business, civic, service, or improvement associations; 9.5 per cent in "cultural" groups; 9.4 per cent in youth-serving groups; 9 per cent in athletic or hobby groups; 8.5 per cent in sociable groups; 5.5 per cent in professional or scientific groups; 4.9 per cent in military, political, or patriotic groups; 4.2 per cent in cooperative,

[14] Arnold M. Rose, "Communication and Participation in a Small City as Viewed by Its Leaders," *International Journal of Opinion and Attitude Research*, 5 (Autumn, 1951), pp. 367–90.

[15] Edmond deS. Brunner and J. H. Kolb, *Rural Social Trends* (New York: McGraw-Hill, 1933), pp. 102, 244, 372.

[16] W. Lloyd Warner and P. S. Lunt, *The Social Life of a Modern Community*, Yankee City Series, Vol. I (New Haven, 1941).

[17] F. A. Bushee, "Social Organization in a Small City," *American Journal of Sociology*, 51 (1945), pp. 217–26.

[18] Gunnar Myrdal, with the assistance of Richard Sterner and Arnold Rose, *An American Dilemma* (New York: Harper, 1944), pp. 952–55.

[19] Detroit Area Study of the University of Michigan, *A Social Profile of Detroit* (Ann Arbor: University of Michigan, 1952), pp. 13–16.

[20] John Carver Scott, Jr., "Membership Participation in Voluntary Associations," unpublished M.A. thesis, University of Chicago, September, 1948.

mutual-benefit, or protective associations; and 2.3 per cent in labor unions. At the time of the study the average duration of membership had
been ten years, but of course most persons had not ended their membership at the time of the study. Frequency of attendance per membership
averaged .84 times a month for the men and 1.23 times a month for the
women.

There have been a few studies of membership in voluntary associations
using polling techniques and national samples, but the results have been
so different and the techniques of getting the data so questionable that
these studies do not provide reliable information.[21] The National Opinion
Research Center in 1955 used a schedule of 136 questions, and the next
to the last one was "Do you happen to belong to any groups or organizations in the community here?" From the answers to this question, the
authors concluded that only 36 per cent of American adults belong to
voluntary associations. Using a less representative sample, the same inadequate procedures of interviewing, but a somewhat more relevant questionnaire, the American Institute of Public Opinion in 1954 found 55 per
cent of adult Americans belonging to voluntary associations. Using a still
less adequate sample and an equally inadequate questionnaire, but better
interviewing techniques, the Survey Research Center at the University of
Michigan found that 64 per cent of adult Americans belong to at least
one voluntary association. The very discrepancy between the three figures
should make us suspicious of all of them, and it cannot be concluded that
the true figure is somewhere in between.[22]

A public-opinion study provides some comparable data for France.[23]
A representative cross-section sample of adults in that country showed
that 41 per cent belong to any kind of association, including the trade
unions and other occupational associations (30 per cent), the semi-
official veterans' organizations (3 per cent), and the political parties
(5 per cent). Other types of associations claimed the following proportions of the adult population: "cultural" associations, 6 per cent; fraterni-
ties and social clubs, 4 per cent; religious associations, 2 per cent; others,
2 per cent.

There are some published data for other countries also. Zetterberg

---

[21] The studies are first reported in Charles R. Wright and Herbert Hyman, "Voluntary
Association Membership of American Adults: Evidence from National Sample Surveys,"
American Sociological Review, 23 (June, 1958), pp. 284–93. A more comprehensive analysis
of the same data is Murray Hausknecht, *The Joiners* (New York: Bedminster, 1962).

[22] The breakdowns reported by the authors, for various categories of the population, may
have some significance for comparative purposes, but even this is hard to gauge when
non-response is obviously so great.

[23] Unpublished data provided the author by M. Max Barioux, director of *Service de
Sondages et Statistiques*, Paris. The constituent figures add to more than 41 per cent since
an individual could belong to more than one type of association.

reports that 51 per cent of a national sample of Swedes belong to at least one association exclusive of membership in churches, unions, cooperatives. If membership in these associations were to be included, then "virtually every adult Swede belongs to an association."[24] In Guadalajara, Mexico's second largest city, Dotson found that 41.6 per cent of the men and 32.2 per cent of the women belonged to one or more associations, and that the upper classes were more participant than the lower classes.[25] For two neighborhoods in the city of Rome, Italy, Rose found a membership rate in voluntary associations (exclusive of unions and political parties) of 21.1 per cent among the men and 8.6 per cent of the women.[26] In an isolated rural community of Southern Italy, Banfield found no participation or associations whatsoever.[27]

There seem to be urban-rural differences in voluntary association membership although there is no consensus about their direction. The NORC national survey found that more residents of highly urbanized counties belong to organizations than those living in less urbanized but similar areas.[28] On the other hand, Hausknecht, also using national data, finds a larger proportion of members in small communities. He attributes this to the fact that a large metropolitan area offers many alternatives to voluntary associations for leisure time activity. He suggests that membership in a small town group gives the individual a sense of power which also helps to account for the higher rate.[29] A study in Flint, Michigan showed that 43.1 per cent of those living in the central city belonged to voluntary associations while only 24.7 per cent of those living in the fringe areas were members.[30]

While the number of associations in a community naturally appears to be a function of the number of inhabitants of that community, this is not entirely the case, for many of the associations are regional or national and have affiliates in small communities as well as large ones, thus raising the relative number of associations in the small communities.[31] Even when

[24] Hans L. Zetterberg, "National Pastime: Pursuit of Power," *Industrial International 1960–61* (Stockholm, 1960), pp. 105–07, 156–68.

[25] Floyd Dotson, "A Note on Participation in Voluntary Associations in a Mexican City," *American Sociological Review*, 18 (August, 1953), pp. 380–86.

[26] Arnold M. Rose, *Indagine sull'Integrazione Sociale in due Quartieri di Roma* (Rome: Istituto di Statistica, Universita di Roma, 1959), p. 34.

[27] Edward Banfield, *The Moral Basis of a Backward Society* (Glencoe, Ill.: Free Press, 1958).

[28] Wright and Hyman, *op. cit.*, p. 290.

[29] Hausknecht, *op. cit.*, p. 18.

[30] Basil G. Zimmer and Amos H. Hawley, "The Significance of Membership in Associations," *American Journal of Sociology*, 65 (September, 1959), p. 198. In this study, the definition of voluntary association excluded unions, church and church groups, and PTAs.

[31] In a representative sample of voluntary associations in Minneapolis and St. Paul, 59 per cent had a national affiliation, 11 per cent had a state affiliation, while 30 per cent were purely local.

the association is national or regional, there tends to be a great deal of local autonomy, with some exceptions, because of the voluntary nature of the membership. The officers of the central or parent body, usually elected by a congress of representatives from the local associations, secure a minimum degree of similarity among the local associations by demanding conformity to a small list of "basic principles." The major exception to this structural principle of complete democracy and local variation is found among the trade unions. The greater degree of centralizations and uniformity among trade unions is made necessary by the conflict activity of these associations, but even here the deviation from principle is not great. American unions, especially those that have developed in the American Federation of Labor as distinguished from the Congress of Industrial Organizations, have much more local autonomy than do European unions.

While the relationships of the local affiliates of a national association with each other tend to be democratic, democracy is not always the governing principle *within* the local association. The reason is easy to understand. Some people have more interest, more time, more drive, more ability, than others, and they tend easily to take over control.[32] Any person who wishes to, however, can usually join the leadership of most voluntary associations, if he is willing to spend the time and assume the responsibilities. And those who do not wish to become leaders exert an ultimate control over the latter by voting against them at the annual elections or simply by resigning from the association, which—if done by sufficiently large numbers—kills the organization and permits the formation of a new one with the same purpose but with new leaders.

The leaders of voluntary associations are different from the average citizen, but these differences are only in degree and not in kind, according to a study of voluntary association presidents in Minnesota.[33] They tend to be better educated: 75 per cent have gone to college compared to 25 per cent of the general population. They usually hold professional or managerial positions and feel themselves to be members of the upper or upper middle class. They tend to participate in more voluntary associa-

[32] In the Minneapolis–St. Paul study about half of the top leaders had been in office longer than two years. Sixty-four per cent of them spent more than ten hours a month in association affairs. In Great Britain until recently leaders in most types of voluntary associations came from the upper classes apparently because there was an upper-class tradition of responsibility for leadership and because some upper-class people gave money to associations in return for being elected to the office of honorary vice-president even though they did not participate in the activities of the association. The situation has been changing, especially since World War II, and an increasing number of functioning leaders are drawn from the middle and lower classes. See Rosalind C. Chambers, "A Study of Three Voluntary Organizations," in D. V. Glass (ed.), *Social Mobility in Britain* (London: Routledge and Kegan Paul, 1954), pp. 385–87.

[33] Arnold M. Rose, "Alienation and Participation: A Comparison of Group Leaders and the 'Mass,'" *American Sociological Review*, 27 (December, 1962), pp. 834–36.

tions than the rest of the population. Group presidents in this study tend to be more socially integrated and more satisfied with the democratic process than the average person. Leaders also must have time to devote to voluntary activity and the special skills necessary for leadership. Some have a temperament that impels them to become leaders to satisfy a personal need.[34]

While only a small proportion of the population is very *active* in the association, a very large proportion—at least in the towns and cities—are *members* of the associations. Several studies show, however, that Americans of middle and higher incomes are more likely to join associations than are people of lower income.[35] A study by Bottomore shows that this is true in Great Britain, and a study by Bo Anderson shows that the generalization holds for Sweden also.[36]

Lower-income people are, however, likely to be attached to a trade union, to a church, and to informal but fairly stable friendship groups (including kin groups) for recreation, and these perform some of the same functions that the more typical voluntary associations perform for other classes.[37]

To a certain extent an association tends to draw members from a

[34] Sills, *op. cit.*, pp. 33–34.

[35] R. S. and H. M. Lynd, *Middletown* (New York: Harcourt, 1929); Warner and Lunt, *op. cit.* (1941); W. G. Mather, "Income and Social Participation," *American Sociological Review*, 6 (June, 1941), pp. 380–84; Herbert Goldhamer, "Some Factors Affecting Participation in Voluntary Associations," unpublished Ph.D. thesis, University of Chicago, 1943; Bushee, *op. cit.* (1945), pp. 217–26; Mirra Komarovsky, "The Voluntary Associations of Urban Dwellers," *American Sociological Review*, 11 (December, 1946), pp. 686–98; Scott, *op. cit.* (1948), pp. 14–18; I. D. Reid and E. L. Ehle, "Leadership Selection in Urban Locality Areas," *Public Opinion Quarterly*, 14 (Summer, 1950), pp. 262–84; Floyd Dotson, "Patterns of Voluntary Association Among Urban Working-Class Families," *American Sociological Review*, 16 (October, 1951), pp. 687–93; Walter T. Martin, "A Consideration of the Differences in the Extent and Location of the Formal Associational Activities of Rural-Urban Fringe Residents," *American Sociological Review*, 17 (December, 1952), pp. 687–94; Odell Uzzell, "Institution Membership and Class Levels," *Sociology and Social Research*, 37 (July–August, 1953), pp. 390–94; John M. Foskett, "Social Structure and Social Participation," *American Sociological Review*, 20 (August, 1955), p. 433; Wendell Bell and Maryanne T. Force, "Social Structure and Participation in Different Types of Formal Associations," *Social Forces*, 34 (May, 1956), p. 35; Wright and Hyman, *op. cit.*, p. 288; Morris Axelrod, "Urban Structure and Social Participation," *American Sociological Review*, 21 (February, 1956), pp. 13–18; John C. Scott, Jr., "Membership and Participation in Voluntary Organizations," *American Sociological Review*, 22 (June, 1957), pp. 315–26.

[36] One difference between the Western European and American lower classes is that the former have some tendency to belong to political organizations—probably because their unions urge them to belong to the Labour Party. See Thomas B. Bottomore, "Social Stratification in Voluntary Organizations," in D. V. Glass (ed.), *op. cit.*, pp. 381–82; Bo Anderson, "Some Problems of Change in the Swedish Electorate," unpublished study, Department of Sociology, Uppsala University, Sweden, 1960.

[37] F. Dotson, *op. cit.*; Nicholas Babchuk and C. Wayne Gordon, *The Voluntary Association in the Slum* (Lincoln: University of Nebraska Press, 1962), p. 116.

limited class range and from a given religious, ethnic, or racial group, so that a given community will have several associations with the same function but with a different composition of membership.[38] Of course some kinds of associations have a narrower class range than do others.

Other significant differentials in participation have been reported in a variety of studies, although sometimes the conclusions of these studies are at variance with one another. Most of the studies report that more men than women participate in voluntary associations.[39] Participation is related to religious affiliation in that Protestants and Jews are more frequently members of voluntary associations than are Catholics.[40] Married people are more likely to participate than are single persons.[41] There have been a variety of findings concerning Negro and white participation in voluntary associations.[42] One national study finds that the two groups have the same proportion of participation, another comes to the conclusion that whites have more participation, while a third indicates that Negroes participate more. A study of Lincoln, Nebraska, where there is only a small proportion of Negroes, reports that Negroes participate more than do whites.[43] Married couples with one child are less likely to participate than married couples with no children or with two or more children.[44] Newcomers to a community are likely to participate less than do the natives, but within five years of migration to a large city the newcomers are as likely

[38] Mhyra S. Minnis, "The Relationship of Women's Organizations to the Social Structure of a City," unpublished Ph.D. thesis, Yale University, 1951; August B. Hollingshead, "Trends in Social Stratification: A Case Study," *American Sociological Review*, 17 (December, 1952), pp. 679–86.

[39] Previously cited studies of the following authors report greater participation by men than by women: Lynd and Lynd (p. 527), Brunner and Kolb (p. 262), Warner and Lunt (p. 335), Goldhammer, Komarovsky (p. 685), Scott (pp. 7, 9). Another study reporting greater male participation is G. A. Lundberg, M. Komarovsky, and M. A. McInerny, *Leisure, A Suburban Study* (New York: Columbia University Press, 1934). Authors reporting greater participation by women than by men are Bushee (pp. 220–21), Mather (p. 381). In the working class, lower-middle and upper class, men participate more; in the upper-middle class, more women participate; see Alfred Hero, "Voluntary Organizations in World Affairs Communications," unpublished study prepared for the World Peace Foundation, 1958, pp. 50–51. Under the age of forty years, men participate more, over forty, women do; see Hausknecht, *op. cit.*, pp. 32–33.

[40] Warner and Lunt, *op. cit.*, p. 346; Goldhamer, *op. cit.*, p. 29; Scott, *op. cit.*, pp. 14–18; Hausknecht, *op. cit.*, p. 52. Komarovsky (*op. cit.*, p. 696) found no religious differences.

[41] Komarovsky, *op. cit.*, p. 695; Scott, *op. cit.*, pp. 14–18; Wright and Hyman, *op. cit.*, p. 292; Hausknecht, *op. cit.*, p. 35. Goldhamer found this to be true among men, but not among women (*op. cit.*, pp. 34–35). Bell and Force found that marital status had no effect on participation (*op. cit.*, p. 34).

[42] Hausknecht, *op. cit.*, pp. 51–52.

[43] Nicholas Babchuk and Ralph V. Thompson, "The Voluntary Associations of Negroes," *American Sociological Review*, 27 (October, 1962), p. 652.

[44] Scott, *op. cit.*, p. 18; N. L. Whetten and C. C. Devereux, Jr., *Studies of Suburbanization in Connecticut: I. Windsor, A Highly Developed Agricultural Area*, Storrs Agricultural Experiment Station Bulletin No. 212 (1936).

to participate as much as anyone else.[45] Home owners are almost twice as likely to belong to voluntary associations as are renters, possibly because owners feel they have more of a "stake" in the community.[46]

There are several studies reporting on participation in voluntary associations as related to age. These studies generally show that social participation declines at the later ages despite the increased leisure time following upon retirement. In McKain's[47] study, about one-half of those past 65 years of age reported that they gave less time to organizations than they did when they were 50 years of age, and only 1 per cent said that their social activity had increased. Havighurst[48] corroborates this finding and adds to it:

> Formal associations lose attractiveness as age changes from 40 to 70, though not among women until they reach the sixties. Informal groups are most attractive to men in the 50 to 60 group but are equally attractive at all (middle) ages for women.

On the other hand, in Scott's[49] study of a representative sample of adults of the New England town of Bennington, Vermont, there was no consistent relationship between membership and age. Those under 25 years of age reported an average of 1.75 memberships, those between 25 and 39 reported an average of 1.46 memberships, those between 40 and 54 years reported an average of 1.98 memberships, while those 55 years and older reported an average of 1.48 memberships. Among men alone, membership in voluntary associations did not fall with age, whereas it did markedly so among the women. Studies by Goldhamer,[50] by Freedman and Axelrod,[51] and by Anderson and Ryan[52] also correlated age with membership in voluntary associations. The Goldhamer study indicates that young adults aged twenty to thirty are, among all age groups, least likely to participate. Foskett finds just the opposite, that this young age group participates the

[45] Basil G. Zimmer, "Participation of Migrants in Urban Structures," *American Sociological Review*, 20 (April, 1955), pp. 218–24. Those who are upper class and come from other cities are the quickest to join voluntary associations in their new home community.

[46] Hausknecht, *op. cit.*, p. 47.

[47] W. C. McKain, "The Social Participation of Old People in a California Retirement Community," unpublished Ph.D. dissertation, Harvard University.

[48] R. J. Havighurst, "The Leisure Activities of the Middle-aged," *American Journal of Sociology*, 63 (1957), pp. 152–62, at p. 160.

[49] J. C. Scott, "Membership and Participation in Voluntary Associations," *American Sociological Review*, 22 (1957), pp. 315–26.

[50] H. Goldhamer, "Some Factors Affecting Participation in Voluntary Associations," unpublished Ph.D. dissertation, University of Chicago.

[51] R. Freedman and M. Axelrod, "Who Belongs to What in a Great Metropolis?" *Adult Leadership*, 1 (November, 1952), pp. 6–9.

[52] A. Anderson and B. Ryan, "Social Participation Differences Among Tenure Classes in a Prosperous Commercialized Farming Area," *Rural Sociology*, 8 (1943), pp. 281–90.

most. He suggests that this is due to the lower average educational and income level among the elderly.[53] Hausknecht, using national samples, corroborates Scott's finding that association membership reaches a peak around age 40.[54]

Participation normally means attendance at general meetings (from once a week to once a year),[55] attendance at committee meetings (which convene irregularly, depending on the amount of activity), and the performance of the activity prescribed by the association. Membership in a single association can take as little or as much of one's time as one is willing to devote to it. Reasons for participation or non-participation in voluntary associations vary with the individual as well as with the structure and purpose of the organization. Often upper and middle class people join organizations to further their careers, to make business connections, or as a mark of status. Some large, absentee-owned corporations push their employees into joining community groups so that the company may maintain a favorable public image and so that it can keep tabs on the organizations to keep them from adopting programs that would work to the corporation's disadvantage.[56] Some people, because of their high status in the community, are pressed into participation in fund drives so that organizations can take advantage of the prestige of their names.[57] Middle class women may join voluntary associations to help in their adjustment to life after their children are grown.[58]

The reasons for not joining voluntary associations or being inactive members are just as varied. Lack of time because of job or family obligations, which our society defines as more important than voluntary association membership, are reasons individuals often give for their inactivity. Also, membership in many organizations may lead to little participation in some of them.[59] Especially among lower class people, shyness and lack of self-confidence are also important reasons for lack of participation.[60] Those with less education may not understand how voluntary association activity could affect community policies which have a bearing on their lives. The

[53] Foskett, *op. cit.,* p. 435.

[54] Hausknecht, *op. cit.,* pp. 33–34.

[55] In the Minneapolis–St. Paul study, 13 per cent of the associations had had no membership meetings during the previous year; 43 per cent had 1 to 3 meetings; 31 per cent had 4 to 24 meetings; 13 per cent had 25 or more membership meetings during the year.

[56] For example, to push for enlarged welfare programs that would increase taxes; see Roland J. Pellegrin and Charles H. Coates, "Absentee-owned Corporations and Community Power Structure," *American Journal of Sociology,* 61 (March, 1956), p. 415.

[57] Foskett, *op. cit.,* p. 437.

[58] Joan W. Moore, "Patterns of Women's Participation in Voluntary Associations," *American Journal of Sociology,* 66 (May, 1961), p. 598.

[59] Sills, *op. cit.,* pp. 35–36.

[60] Hero, *op. cit.,* p. 6.

structure of some organizations encourages inactivity. If there is too much bureaucratization, people will lose interest in an organization.[61] The larger the group, the larger the proportion of apathetic members it is likely to have. This is because a large group tends to be more heterogeneous and therefore have less consensus about what group activities should be.[62] Individual personality and status as well as the structure of the group thus have a bearing on whether or not the individual will be an active participant in a voluntary association. Most associations require their members to pay annual dues, which is usually a small amount except in unions and businessmen's associations. The association usually has other sources of income, and each has its effect on the contributors' psychological involvement and on the extent of the association's activities.

1 Solicitation of voluntary contributions from both members and non-members is usually moderately successful in a culture where "philanthropy" is an accepted cultural trait, even among poor people,[63] and where most contributions can be deducted in calculating income taxes. Practically all American cities also have a "Community Fund," which is a voluntary association whose purpose is to collect contributions once a year, from as many citizens as want to contribute or can be pressured to contribute, for the purpose of distributing these funds to "worthy" associations of many types. These community funds are growing in favor because most people do not like to be bothered by many smaller drives, sometimes conducted by obscure organizations.

2 Legacies and special gifts sometimes are given by interested wealthy people.

3 Money-raising events are likely to produce funds even in hard times; these latter operate on the principle of *quid pro quo:* an association will provide a dinner, or sell all sorts of objects at a bazaar or rummage sale (where the merchandise is provided gratis by members), or offer amusement at a card party or carnival. The labor and materials going into these are provided by the members, and the money earned goes into the treasury of the association to carry on its regular work. Some of the bigger associations—and this includes practically all of the national ones—have enough money to hire

[61] Sills, *op. cit.,* p. 331.

[62] Hero, *op. cit.,* p. 3.

[63] An extensive study by the Russell Sage Foundation in 1950 revealed that contributions to voluntary associations and philanthropic causes of all sorts were part of nearly every family's expenditures, and that the lower-income groups devoted as large a proportion to this purpose as did the middle- and upper-income groups. See Frank Emerson Andrews, *Philanthropic Giving* (New York: Russell Sage Foundation, 1950).

professional workers to help carry on the functions of the association and, incidentally, to help in the money raising.[64]

The purposes of associations are as diverse as can be imagined.[65] The only thing they have in common is that the purposes are limited, and practically never will an association act for a purpose different from the original one which brought the members together. The reason is easy to understand: people who have one interest in common are not necessarily likely to have another interest in common, and any effort to act on a second purpose is likely to split the association. Thus the association is the opposite of all-encompassing: it does not seek to involve the individual in all his interests or in all aspects of his life. Therefore it is quite the opposite of a family, of some churches, and other religious institutions (such as a monastery), or of the Communist Party. The specific nature of the purposes of voluntary associations gives to American culture a characteristic which was originally known as "cultural pluralism" (although that term has recently been distorted to refer solely to religious and nationality diversity). In its original meaning—as stated by Dewey, Cooley, and Kallen—cultural pluralism referred to the encouragement of all kinds of group differences characteristic of American life and especially to those group differences that one voluntarily chooses to cultivate. Most individuals are encouraged to be "culturally plural" as they are encouraged to belong to several associations, with quite different purposes and often with different memberships.

In order to determine some of the social psychological bases for the formation of voluntary associations we may pose the question as to what other means have been used historically to satisfy the two needs for self-expression and satisfaction of interests through collective action. Again, we have to turn to history for a complete answer, but an impressionistic observation would suggest that other historical societies have relied on the family, either the immediate family or the extended family (*grosse Familie*), on the church, or on the community as a whole for the satisfaction of these needs. This leads us to the observation long made by sociologists that in contemporary American urban society the extended family, the church, and the community are relatively weak social structures and that many people do not belong to them at all. The hypothesis is sug-

[64] In the Minneapolis–St. Paul study, about half the associations had at least one paid employee; often this was only a clerical worker.

[65] In the Minneapolis–St. Paul study, 43 per cent of the associations had as primary purpose some sort of benefit or activity intended for their own members; 44 per cent directed their activity toward the public at large; 10 per cent were principally engaged in charity or some form of aid to needy individuals; the rest were principally engaged in coordinating the activities of other organizations.

gested, then, that because the American extended family, church, and community are weak, each individual is obligated to turn relatively frequently to voluntary associations for self-expression and satisfaction of his interests, if these two needs are to be met at all.[66] If this is the case, the voluntary association would tend to contribute to the democratic character of American society, since strong family systems, churches, and communities tend to be totalitarian in their influence over the individual, whereas voluntary associations distribute and diversify power and influence.

If our hypothesis is correct, it is likely that another psychological satisfaction served in other societies mainly by the immediate family, and secondarily by the extended family, church, and community, is also being inadequately provided by them in our society. This is the provision of a sense of security, which may be thought of as the defense of the individual against reduction of his need satisfaction by outside forces, as distinguished from attainment of satisfaction in a positive sense. That we are on the right track in our psychological analysis of the motives for joining groups has been suggested by several studies of trade unions, reform groups, fraternal organizations, and even churches.[67]

Certain students of the labor movement have attempted to explain the rise and rapid development of trade unions in such a way that their analysis has relevance as a more general hypothesis for explaining the historical proliferation of all kinds of voluntary associations in contemporary society. We have already considered Polanyi's[68] historical analysis of the breakdown of the pre-Industrial social system and how it left a gap that unions and businessmen's organizations sought to fill.[69] Tannenbaum[70] goes one step farther than does Polanyi. He holds that the union movement grew up in reaction to the segmentalization as well as the insecurity of modern life to re-establish a "sense of community" which

[66] Of course there exist those victims of the mass society who do not get their needs for self-expression and achievement of interests satisfied. For them, the family, church, and community are weak or otherwise unsatisfactory, but they have not joined voluntary associations.

[67] A by-no-means-exhaustive list of such studies would include Arnold M. Rose, *Union Solidarity* (Minneapolis: University of Minnesota Press, 1952), Chapter III, Section D; Albert Blumenthal, *Small Town Stuff* (Chicago: University of Chicago Press, 1932); William Gellerman, *The American Legion as Educator* (New York: Teachers College, Columbia University, 1938); C. F. Marden, *Rotary and Its Brothers* (Princeton: Princeton University Press, 1935); E. W. Bakke and C. Kerr, *Unions, Management and the Public* (New York: Harcourt, 1948); Charles W. Ferguson, *Fifty Million Brothers* (New York: Farrar and Rinehart, 1937); Noel P. Gist, "Structure and Process in Secret Societies," *Social Forces*, 16 (March, 1938), pp. 349–57; Edward D. Starbuck, *The Psychology of Religion* (New York: Scribner's, 1908), pp. 28 ff.; Lundberg, Komarovsky, and McInerny, *op. cit.*; Sills, *op. cit.*; E. Wight Bakke, "Why Workers Join Unions," *Personnel*, 22 (July, 1945), pp. 37–46.

[68] Karl Polanyi, *The Great Transformation* (New York: Farrar and Rinehart, 1944).

[69] See Chapter 9, Section C.

[70] Frank Tannenbaum, *A Philosophy of Labor* (New York: Alfred A. Knopf, 1951).

prevailed in pre-Industrial times. He views unions as a means of regaining the security, recognition, and self-expression for the worker which had been lost because of the growth of modern capitalism and the Industrial Revolution.

This approach to economic organizations could be applied to other kinds of voluntary associations: the declining influence of the community (and the extended family and the church) resulted in psychological insecurity, segmentalization of personal relations, reduction of intimacy, and alienation from once-powerful values. The voluntary association is a new kind of institution crescively established to fill the gap left by these social changes. Kluckhohn has suggested this in a succinct passage:

> Mass economic upheaval following upon unprecedented economic growth; lack of attention to the human problems of an industrial civilization; the impersonality of the social organization of cities; the melting pot, transitory geographic residence, social mobility, weakening of religious faith—all of these trends have contributed to make Americans feel unanchored, adrift upon a meaningless voyage. . . . Why are Americans a nation of joiners? In part this is a defense mechanism against the excessive fluidity of our social structure. Because of the tension of continual struggle for social place, people have tried to gain a degree of routinized and recognized fixity by allying themselves with others in voluntary associations.[71]

Another writer sees the voluntary association as a means of correcting inequalities of status in the different spheres of an individual's life. He joins a voluntary association to provide status in areas where he feels he is weak.[72]

Once a voluntary association is formed, it may undergo one of several processes of development. Some associations die shortly after they are created; others continue indefinitely without developing; still others have a growth in structure and function. Chapin has provided a succinct description of the growing association, emphasizing bureaucratic tendencies:

> A group of citizens meet informally to consider some problem or need. After a few conferences, a chairman is selected. As the problem under discussion is broken down into its elements, various committees are appointed: executive, ways and means, publicity, program, survey, etc. Soon the business of calling conferences and notifying interested persons becomes too arduous for volunteer pri-

[71] Clyde and Florence Kluckhohn, "American Culture: Generalized Orientations and Class Patterns," Chapter XX of L. Bryson, L. Finkelstein, and R. M. MacIver (eds.), *Conflicts of Power in Modern Culture* (New York: Harper, 1947), pp. 249–50.

[72] S. N. Eisenstadt, "The Social Conditions of the Development of Voluntary Associations —A Case Study of Israel," unpublished manuscript, Eliezer Kaplan School of Economics and Social Science, Hebrew University, Jerusalem, Israel, p. 27.

vate citizens and the half-time services of an executive secretary is provided. He soon finds it necessary to have a clerk-stenographer. She needs a typewriter, chair, desk, and filing cabinets. Supplies of stationery, postage, telephone, and other items of equipment are purchased. As the work of the new organization, branch, section (or whatever the name of the new unit may be) grows in volume, it is systematized by establishing membership requirements and dues. A constitution and bylaws are adopted at some stage of its development. The organization may be incorporated if it is an independent entity and not a department of some larger whole. A full line of officers may be chosen: Chairman of the Board, President, Vice-Presidents, Secretary, Treasurer, etc. As the funds accumulate and a bank account is established, the Treasurer is bonded and an annual audit is required.

Meanwhile the organization finds more office space necessary. A full-time executive secretary is engaged. Additional clerks are needed. Office equipment is increased by additional typewriters, chairs, desks, filing cabinets, and other equipment. Then an office manager is chosen. As time passes, and the full-time staff grows in size, vested interests in "the job" appear. Some staff persons become more concerned with the perpetuation of their job and guarding their "rights" than in the function and purpose of the organization. Rules and policies are worked out to cover sick-leave allowances, vacation time, termination pay, and pensions. Along with the expansion of staff hierarchy there goes an expansion of committees of all sorts, so that the dignity and status of office take on added prestige and social position is sought for by interested persons. As the length of line organization increases, the problems of communication between different status levels become more acute. All these tendencies are signs that point to the formalization of the organization, which was originally quite innocent of bureaucratic trends and characteristics.[73]

c *Kinds of Voluntary Associations*

To bring into consideration how the voluntary association relates an individual to the general society, let us enumerate some of the associations to which a middle-class American man and woman in a moderate-sized city might belong. The man might belong to a sports club or hobby club, which helps its members organize teams for playing baseball or basketball,

[73] F. Stuart Chapin, "The Growth of Bureaucracy: An Hypothesis," *American Sociological Review*, 16 (December, 1951), p. 835. Similar observations were made by Charles Perrow, "The Analysis of Goals in Complex Organizations," *American Sociological Review*, 26 (December, 1961), p. 862.

or for providing materials for the hobby. The sports club also has the purpose of putting pressure on the local government to provide fields and houses where these games can be played. If he is a war veteran, the man might belong to one of the big veterans' organizations, which provides many types of non-athletic recreation and entertainment for him. The veterans' organizations also put pressure on government to obtain special privileges for soldiers and veterans, and occasionally the leaders speak on general political subjects. Whether he is a member of a veterans' organization or not, the average middle-income man may belong to a very similar organization known as a "lodge" or fraternal association. This provides recreation, entertainment, and fellowship, and occasionally does a "good deed" for the community as a whole, but seldom puts pressure on government. The fraternal associations are declining somewhat, but a smaller, less formal, type of social club seems to be taking their place.

Our average man is also likely to belong to an occupational group: to a labor union if he is a factory worker, to a trade association if he is a businessman, to a farmers' organization if he is a farmer, to a professional association if he is in one of the free professions. These groups seek to defend the occupational interests and improve the occupational status of their members. In doing so, they oppose each other and even the society as a whole, since they occasionally stop the functioning of the whole occupational group and they often put pressure on government to get laws or administration of laws favorable to the occupation. Only recently have some of them—mainly the unions—expressed any interest in government in general, but even this is very rare: their main concern with government is primarily in relation to improving conditions of work in their particular occupation.

The average man is also likely to belong to some kind of benevolent, social-improvement, or "charitable" association. For people in the lower-income classes, this association is usually connected with the church. In the middle- and upper-income classes, people also tend to belong to one or more such associations organized independently for its social-welfare purposes. The activities of the voluntary associations for social welfare are supplementary to those of government. These functions are too numerous to describe adequately, but a few examples will give their general character. One exists to collect money to subsidize intelligent but poor boys and girls at a university. Another collects money to subsidize scientific research on cancer. Another has its members help blind children in after-school hours. Another directs a neighborhood recreational house for children. Another sews sheets for the public hospital. Another works to integrate recent immigrants into American community life. And so on. For each "underprivileged" group in nearly every community there is one or more voluntary associations—whose members are anybody, often including a few "underprivileged"—to assist them.[74] Each of these functions is carried on by the government (federal, state or local), but the association also helps in a supplementary and personal way.

Some of these social-improvement associations shade over into social-reform[75] associations. One of the latter has as its purpose giving out propaganda to get a better law on procedures governing the adoption of orphan children. Another distributes information about the United Nations and about international affairs for the betterment of international understanding. Another collects money to send a public-school teacher to an annual institute for the modernization of teaching techniques. Another watches the local government to see that tax money is not "wasted." And so on. For every way in which a dozen or more people in the community think the community should be changed there are one or more associations working in some manner for that change. While there are hundreds of thousands of social-reform associations across the country, only a minority of the population belongs to at least one, although some individuals belong to several. In general, there is a connection between one's income level and one's membership in social-reform associations: poor people usually belong to none, and rich people tend to belong to many.

Women belong to somewhat the same types of associations as men do, but there are some differences. Only a third of the women have occupations other than housewife and so are not so likely as men to belong to occupational associations. Very few women belong to sports clubs, veterans' associations, or "lodges," although there exist female counterparts of the men's fraternal associations. Women, however, tend to be more participant than are men in the informal social clubs, the social-improvement associations, and in some kinds of social-reform associations. There is one type of association that many women, but few men, join: the "self-improvement" or "educational" association. Specific examples would be a club that invites speakers to talk on various subjects, a music-appreciation club, a book-reviewing club, or a "recent political-events discussion club." Men have something of this in their service clubs—Rotary, Kiwanis, Lions— but the latter also have the function of integrating the business and professional interests of a community. In many cities a few men as well as a

[74] Chambers traces the development in Great Britain of social-service associations. Originally created by the privileged to help the underprivileged, they have—as in the United States—increasingly included some of the lower classes among their members and even leaders. Judging from Chambers's observations, this trend may have developed further in Britain than in the United States. See Chambers, *op. cit.*, Chapter 14.

[75] The term "social reform" is used here to refer to any kind of social change, regardless of direction or value. While most social-reform associations in the United States would be judged to have mildly "liberal" purposes, some could be said to have "conservative" or "reactionary" purposes.

few women will form musical societies (orchestras, choruses, chamber-music sections, etc.). The participants of all these self-improvement groups come almost entirely from the middle-income groups, and only a minority of even this class is involved.

Young people belong to many types of associations, and these exist for children of eight years of age and upward, of all socioeconomic classes. Many are connected with school life, but many others are outgrowths of the church, the local community, or any other institution to which young people may be attached. Children of high-school age will belong to sports groups, scout groups, religious groups, self-educational groups (for example, nearly every high school and college has its "French Club"), sociable or fraternal groups, hobby groups, school or community improvement groups. College students have an even broader range of associations, for these include many of the adult types, many of the children's type, and still others peculiar to American university life.

In addition to the general types of associations mentioned there are special types to which only a small segment of the population belongs. College graduates, for example, may belong to their college alumni associations, which are for the purpose of supporting their old university. Scientists belong to scientific societies, which have some of the characteristics of other occupational associations but are also devoted to the discovery of new knowledge. Last, but not least, those particularly interested in politics may belong to a local club of their political party. Even though only a small proportion of these persons ever run for political office, they provide much of the direction in politics—especially local politics—and of the detailed work in election campaigns.

D   *Some Specific Associations*

In order to get a more coordinated picture of the voluntary associations, let us examine a few of them in some detail. Our first example is the Parent-Teachers Association (PTA).

The public schools in the United States are usually controlled by locally elected boards of education, and the relatively large funds which they administer are raised through general taxation. Thus the administration of the public schools is part of local government. The principals and teachers of a public school are hired experts, usually employed under some civil-service regulations, which set standards for hiring and limit reasons for dismissal. The state and federal governments indirectly set some standards through their control over certain of the funds available to the public schools that conform to their standards. Community pressure groups have an influence on the conditions under which the public schools are run just as they have on other branches of government. In some communities teachers form unions to enhance their economic bargaining power and to maintain the standards of their profession.

In this cross play of power forces on the public schools it is not surprising that voluntary associations of parents would also form to exert some influence on the administration of public schools, especially when certain well-organized pressure groups of a community often wish to reduce school expenditures in order to keep down taxes. Parents of children in the schools have the opposite motivation in order to provide a good education for their children and find it desirable to organize to form a contrary pressure group. Shortly after the public schools were set up in the United States during the nineteenth century, parent-teachers groups began to form in various communities to obtain what they considered to be the best available education for their children. Today a substantial majority of local communities have parent-teachers associations that are loosely linked together into a national organization. The major activities and powers are local, however, just as the public schools themselves are locally controlled. Thus the parent-teachers associations vary considerably in size, power, and activity from community to community. Perhaps the most important influences of the PTA's are the least observable ones. Through their mere existence, even if they are dormant, they serve as a counterbalancing force for other pressure groups in the community that might engage in efforts to detract from the effectiveness of education. Second, PTA's inform their members concerning political issues affecting the schools, and—while the PTA's do not endorse candidates for the school boards—this political education serves to guide parents and their friends into informed voting for school-board members. PTA's are thus indirectly often effective instruments in the election of a qualified and sympathetic board in contradistinction to just anybody who might wish to run for public office. While the continuing work of the PTA's is probably not of so great importance as these two major functions, they nevertheless have an impact on the public schools and it will be instructive to examine the detailed characteristics of a single Parent-Teachers Association (organized in an elementary school district in Minneapolis, Minnesota).

While only about half of the parents of the children in this school are active in the association, and these mostly the mothers rather than the fathers, and while the teachers belong largely because they feel an implicit pressure to do so, the PTA is quite important. The PTA meets once a month (except during the summer) and has a program consisting of a speaker giving an "educational" talk, a discussion of the current problems of the school and of the association, and a social coffee hour for the purpose of acquainting parents and teachers with each other. The discussion is based on the committee reports, for the active work of the PTA is done by its committees, although the membership as a whole has to vote on important projects. During one recent school year this PTA did the following things: the Community Participation Committee successfully petitioned the City Council to provide a "warming house" at the local skating rink, collected a sufficient number of men and dollars to provide the necessary sponsorship for a local Boy Scout troop, and cooperated with the program of the local Neighborhood House (which provides recreation facilities for all people in the neighborhood, regardless of age and class). The Health Committee disseminated information to parents about proper diet, teeth care, and inoculation of children, and debated the advisability of starting a sex-information course at the school. The Political Committee was active in a successful city-wide campaign to get the voters to approve a new bond issue for the schools (which meant higher taxes even for those who had no children). The Human Relations Committee co-operated with a city-wide program to increase understanding among the different races and nationalities in the city (a program directed at the parents as well as at the children). The School Patrol Committee supervised a group of the older children who were granted the privileges of policemen to stop traffic when children were coming to, or leaving, school (in a few communities where the streets are dangerous the parents themselves take turns directing traffic during the hours when children are going to school and coming home). The Hobby Committee encouraged children to have hobbies and has organized a large hobby show to display the products of hobbies of all family members together; this show attracted a great deal of neighborhood attention and encouraged fathers and mothers to help their children with hobbies. The Ways and Means Committee responded to the teachers' appeal for a restroom in the school where they might have coffee or lie down during the day. They organized a large food "bazaar" to which parents freely brought food delicacies that were sold to anyone who would buy them. The money was used to buy floor tiles, curtains, a bed, coffeepot, etc., and some of the men in the PTA volunteered to lay the tiles and paint the old furniture. The previous year this committee raised enough money to buy the school a new motion-picture projector when the old one wore out and the City Board of Education did not have enough money to buy a new one. The Hospitality and Membership Committee welcomed newcomers into the neighborhood, if they had children, and urged them to join the PTA. It had teas for the newcomers (and for other mothers whose children were just beginning school) to introduce them to the old-timers. The Music Committee helped the teachers with a music-appreciation program for children.

In general, the PTA will set up a new committee to perform any function that is felt to be needed by enough parents, or by a reliable educational or community leader. Dues for the PTA are only 50 cents a year, but of course parents generally spend additional money on the food bazaar, the scout donations, and other associated activities. As previously mentioned, members give as little or as much of their time as they want to devote to the association. While most parents nominally belong to the association, only about half the mothers and perhaps 5 per cent of the fathers come to the monthly meetings, a good number of these are occasionally active in the committees, and perhaps 2 or 3 per cent are consistently very active (the latter are the "leaders" and are accorded respect and prestige by the community as a whole).

The second type of voluntary-association activity that will be described also illustrates how social change arises from organized effort. Its purpose is to remove race prejudice from American thoughts and actions and to compensate for the hardships faced by minority peoples because of this prejudice. While one of the most important of the associations—the National Association for the Advancement of Colored People (NAACP)—was begun in 1909, and a few others were begun in subsequent years, the main development has come since 1943, and the members of independent associations now reach into the thousands, with perhaps almost a hundred being organized on a national scale with numerous local branches. Such a complex activity—that delves into a central element of American culture—would take volumes to describe adequately;[76] obviously we cannot even scratch the surface of the question in the short space we can devote to it. Our approach will be to make a few general statements about the strategy of the activity and about its effects.

The outside observer might wonder why Negroes and other discriminated-against minorities have not become disaffected, since they are so relatively underprivileged in the United States. The answer lies partly in the possibility of change through voluntary activity. As the late Walter White, general secretary of the NAACP and an outstanding Negro, put it:

> In America, organizations like the NAACP are free to criticize all that which displeases them—including the government. . . . We prefer to take our chances, and fight to realize our aspiration in the framework of our democracy, whatever may be its faults, for the progress we make is real.

The progress, so defined, is made by those who work for it—that is, the members of the association—and it is a substantial achievement, even if there is much left to challenge the workers. No one who has closely fol-

[76] The description of the associations which work for the passage of a Fair Employment Practices Act (FEP) alone has required a book: Louis C. Kesselman, *The Social Politics of FEPC: A Study in Reform Pressure Movements* (Chapel Hill: University of North Carolina Press, 1948).

lowed the facts of the American race problem up to 1940 would believe
that so much social change could be accomplished in the twenty-five years
since then.

Each association has had a different strategy, as each has been made up
of people with different backgrounds and different conceptions of social
structure. The NAACP has taken advantage of the fact that the Constitution of the United States theoretically prohibits any discrimination by
the government. It has successfully brought a large number of cases of
discrimination into the courts, and has thereby established legal precedents
that have made the laws and the courts a protection for minority groups.
The Urban League has propagandized businessmen, with considerable success since 1940, to give Negroes a fair chance to secure good jobs, and it is
now working to make better homes available to Negroes. The Anti-Defamation League (organized by Jews), the American Jewish Committee, and
the National Conference of Christians and Jews have for many years coun-
tered verbal attacks on minorities with better verbal defenses and have
used various techniques to combat specific discriminations. The American
Jewish Congress, the March-on-Washington Committee (now disbanded
after a short period of great achievement in 1941–42 and again in 1963),
the Congress of American Indians, and other groups have used the mass-
protest demonstration effectively. The Congress of Racial Equality has
borrowed the non-resistance, direct-participation techniques of Gandhi
to discourage customers from using restaurants, swimming pools, etc., until
those establishments stopped discriminating against minorities. These techniques have been successfully copied by the Southern Christian Leadership
Conference, founded by the Rev. Martin Luther King, and by the Student
Nonviolent Coordinating Committee. Many organizations—few more successfully than the Japanese American Citizens' League—have maintained
lobbies in Congress and the state legislatures. The community associations
use a variety of techniques, depending on the situation, the militancy or
conservatism of their members, and the means available to private associations. Some of the most successful long-range reforms are being made in
the education of the youth. Most children are now being taught that
prejudice and discrimination are wrong and that equality and fraternity
with all groups should be put into concrete practice. Many youngsters have
responded positively to this effort: they say and do things in a democratic,
equalitarian fashion that shocks their prejudiced parents.

Let us be more concrete by describing the activities of a single association: the Mayor's Council on Human Relations of Minneapolis,
Minnesota, as it functioned up to 1963. It was a group of twenty-seven
persons selected by the mayor from nominations made by the dominant
organized groups in the city (businessmen, the unions, the minority

organizations, the League of Women Voters, etc.) and by the older members of the council itself.[77] Once named, the members were completely independent of the mayor as they could not be dismissed by him and they got no funds from the city government. They got funds by contributions from the organizations nominating the members, by solicitations of ordinary citizens who favored their activities, and by an annual dinner at which some outstanding community and national leaders spoke to citizens willing and able to pay $10 for admission. Most of the money went to pay the salary of an energetic young man who spent full time with the Council's activities and gave them the benefit of continuous attention and expert knowledge. The rest of the money paid for a secretary and for propaganda that the organization distributed in the community. The members usually met once every two weeks, at lunch, and their committees met at least that often again.

Some of the committees were very active and successful; others were relatively passive. The Housing Committee sought to prevent real estate companies and landlords from refusing to rent or sell houses and apartments to minority persons. The chairman of this committee was himself a leading realtor in the city, and he made some remarkable dents in the prejudices of his fellow realtors. The Health and Hospitals Committee sought to prevent hospitals from segregating minority persons into special rooms and wards, and, through the chairmanship of a woman of strong will, it changed the policies of more than a fourth of the hospitals in the city. The Education Committee had early success in getting the public schools and the university to institute policies of complete non-discrimination in hiring teachers, in making job recommendations, and in securing rooms for students, and to institute an "intercultural education" program. It later worked to improve the teaching of better intergroup attitudes in the elementary and secondary schools—both private and public—and to encourage minority youngsters of ability to secure a higher education (one of the greatest problems is that Negro, Indian, and Mexican children do not get enough encouragement at home to continue in school). The Employment Opportunities Committee helped to obtain the passage of a city law making it illegal to refuse to hire qualified minority persons. Since a branch of the city government then took over the job of stopping discrimi-

[77] This manner of becoming a member of an association is quite unusual. It can be questioned whether the Mayor's Council should be called a voluntary association because the membership is so limited and because of its connection with city government. We have chosen to consider it a voluntary association because: (1) one can easily refuse the appointment or resign at any time; (2) it operates just like any voluntary association where membership is more open; (3) many kinds of voluntary associations put some limitations on membership, although rarely as restrictive as in the case of the Mayor's Council; (4) the governmental connection of the Mayor's Council is fairly nominal.

nation in employment, and since two other voluntary associations had this same interest,[78] the Employment Opportunities Committee disbanded, and all problem cases coming to the Council's attention are turned over to the other associations. The Committee on Churches, although headed by a brilliant and active Japanese-born Episcopalian minister, made little headway in its chief project of getting churches to welcome members of other races. In the Northern states the churches were at first among the most resistant of community institutions to change their non-equalitarian policies with respect to minorities. The Special Problems Committee handled "incidents" as they arose. When it was learned that a policeman had struck a Negro prisoner who was not resisting him, its protest to the chief of police secured a suspension of two weeks (without pay) and a transfer to another district for the offending policeman. When a salesman at a hat store asked a Negro customer to move to the back of the store where she would not be seen, the Council's protest to the manager secured a formal apology and a promise that the practice would not be repeated.

The group instituted a special course of instruction for policemen so that they might know how to handle equitably and without tension all disturbances and crimes involving minority persons. Special committees were set up to handle new problems as they arose. When the United States decided to expand its Army in 1950, and the heads of the Army (although not of the Navy and Air Force) made clear the intention to retain Negroes in segregated units, the Minneapolis Council set up a committee to work with similar committees from all over the country to protest this racial discrimination. Two of the members flew to Washington at their own expense to interview the Secretary of the Army and the Chief of Staff (the civilian and military chiefs of the Army, respectively) in an effort to get them to change their policy. With two other members of the Council, later added to this new committee on Armed Services, they drew up a detailed and factually based protest and sent it to the United States Senator from Minnesota, with a request that he transmit copies to the Secretary of Defense and his subordinate chiefs of the Army (the Senator not only did so, but volunteered to provide the council with all information on future developments). The changes forthcoming from the Army were slow but steady, and the Minneapolis group continued its interest in this national problem until it was eliminated.

[78] The Urban League (for Negro social welfare) and the Joint Committee on Equal Employment Opportunity (made up of delegates from 75 other community associations which operate by personally talking to employers about discrimination and by encouraging all citizens to indicate to their tradespeople their support of non-discrimination in employment).

E   *Voluntary Associations and the Distribution of Social Power*

Power in our society is differentially distributed in several ways. Class and ethnic group affiliation have long been among the most important traits associated with the holding of power. Classes and ethnic groups are not, of course, formally organized as such in our society, and the exercise of power usually requires formal organization. The formal organizations in our society having a concentration of power are political parties, occupational or industrial groups, and what we have called social-influence groups. The upper class and the ethnic groups of western European origin held their power by their frequent membership in and control of these formal organizations. Over the last two decades or so the situation has been changing somewhat. Now, a significant proportion of the lower classes is organized into labor unions; an increasing proportion of middle-class people is assuming leadership in the social-influence associations; the ethnic minorities have organized their own social-influence groups; and all of these are taking a stronger interest in politics. Thus power has become more widely distributed through greater participation in voluntary associations.

Let us consider some examples of the influence of voluntary associations over the community as a whole. There are groups such as the Farm Bureau Federation which have the ear of many congressmen; there are groups such as the League of Women Voters, which—by informing their members on a variety of issues—exercise influence on the political attitudes of many people; there are specialized action groups such as the American Civil Liberties Union, which bring cases before the courts and secure judicial precedents for future legal cases. Groups that attract members mainly for sociable or recreational purposes, such as the American Legion, also function as political-pressure groups. Even the fraternal organizations, which are predominantly sociable in their function, provide an avenue of influence for members who have political interests. In a largely decentralized democracy such as ours, many political activities—in the broad sense of that phrase—take place in non-governmental groups.

Very few of the great number of organizations having informal political power in our society have attracted membership from the lower-income classes. Low-income people have been too poor to pay membership fees, too ignorant to know how to conduct themselves in group settings, or too apathetic to have any interest in organized group activities. As a consequence, members of the lower-income population have not had the power and influence which go with membership in these groups. The pattern of non-participation has not changed significantly in recent years, nor is there any immediate prospect of its changing. Even the rising educational level of lower-income persons, the increasing leisure time available to workers, and the disappearance from the American scene of unassimilated immigrants have not yet resulted in appreciable increases in participation in those voluntary associations that have informal political power.

Lower-income people have been joining labor unions in large numbers since 1935, however, and these associations have had an increasing power. The rank-and-file members control the policies of their unions only in a very broad sense. Most members are apathetic as long as the union gets them economic benefits, and so policy making is left largely in the hands of union leaders. Union leaders come mostly out of the lower-income population, although their incomes are now at the levels of the middle class and occasionally of the upper class. They seek to represent the lower class in the various power associations in the community. For example, when a group is formed to improve the street lighting system of a city or work for more adequate housing or to make certain that legal rights are protected, it is now frequently considered necessary that "labor" be represented. Union leaders influence many voters; hence they are accorded attention by politicians and those seeking to get certain laws passed. Labor leaders find themselves increasingly requested to participate on boards and committees of both voluntary and governmental organizations. While occasionally the person invited is not a functioning union leader but merely a figurehead, while some labor leaders are not democratically elected as heads of their organizations, and while by no means all workers are organized into unions, when labor leaders become representatives in community-wide groups they usually express the workers' point of view.

Thus there are the beginnings of representation of the lower-income classes in a large number of the organizations that together make up the informal government of our society. But this is the mere beginning of a trend. The more important observation is still that the large proportion of lowest-income people in our society do not participate in voluntary associations and that they therefore have little contact with persons of other classes and little power in the community as a whole. The lower-income person is effectively, although not legally, segregated in his neighborhood, his church, and possibly his labor union. The situation creates weaknesses in the social structure not only because a large section of the population is not getting the power and personal satisfaction obtainable from social participation, but also because leaders of this very class can gain enormous political power for themselves by representing the huge amorphous lower class in political parties. What might happen, at the extreme, is that the lower-income classes, who are not active in the many voluntary associations (outside of unions and farmers' organizations) that *distribute* informal power in the community will, by virtue of their large numbers, create a formal government out of contact with—and therefore hostile to—these voluntary associations. Because the lower class in our society has the characteristics of what we have called an audience or mass, they lend themselves to the centralizations of power. Such a government—even though democratically selected by universal suffrage—might become so centralized as to be semi-totalitarian.

F   *Functions*

To consider what the numerous diverse facts about American voluntary associations might mean, we shall suggest some of the functions they perform in the social structure.[79]

The power distributing function. From the standpoint of the society as a whole, as we have seen, they distribute power and are sort of semi-permanent forms of the public in counteracting tendencies toward an audience mode of relationship in our society.[80] Through the voluntary association the ordinary citizen can acquire as much power in the community or the nation as his free time, ability, and inclinations permit him to, without actually going into the government service, provided he accepts the competition for power of other like-minded citizens. A consideration of the varied activities and achievements of the social-influence types of associations would support that. Political power, or influence, in the United States is not concentrated in the government, but is distributed over as many citizens, working through their associations, as want to take the responsibility for power. As Goldhamer says:

> It is precisely this function of expressing and enforcing the wishes of its members that has characterized the activities of many American organizations. In this way these organizations appear to revive once more, in varying degrees, the participation of citizens in the governmental process.[81]

[79] This chapter attempts to give a description of voluntary associations only as they have developed in the United States. Certain other democratic nations—Great Britain, Switzerland, and the Scandinavian countries—also have large numbers of voluntary associations which apparently have many of the same characteristics. Even those democratic countries such as France, that do not have a large part of their citizenry active in social-influence association, nevertheless tolerate the associations. Thus the description contained in the chapter is by no means unique to the United States, even though our specific information is so limited. The functions claimed for voluntary associations can also be achieved by other social mechanisms some of which are suggested in the chapter on social change. Frenchmen, for example, have other means of gaining understanding of, and satisfaction with, democratic processes, and other means of instituting social change. Actually, as we have already suggested, the voluntary association is often inadequate to fulfill the functions attributed to it, as it often does not incorporate many people and it often functions inefficiently and ineffectively.

[80] See Chapter 9.

[81] *Op. cit.,* p. 509.

And Oscar Handlin comments:

> Only through the action of non-political, voluntary associations could men check the state's power without directly opposing it. As long as men are free so to act, they cannot be reduced to the blankness of the subjects of totalitarian regimes.[82]

An alternative interpretation of these facts is that Americans participate extensively in voluntary associations because they find it difficult or unpleasant to get into politics.

Pressure groups or lobbies are prime examples of voluntary associations functioning to distribute power. The purpose of these groups is to influence legislation and executive action either directly or indirectly. Although the public views lobbying as evil, those connected with the legislative process look upon lobbyists as experts who are often their only source of technical information. Pressure groups tend to have the most influence when public interest on an issue is low. The scope of influence of a given pressure group is limited only to the one area in which the group has an interest or special knowledge.[83]

The orienting function. Those who thus participate become aware of how social, political, and economic processes function in their society. They learn how things are done in at least the limited sphere in which they operate. The voluntary association informs its members on matters occurring in the society at large which affect the association's purpose. This does not make the members satisfied in the sense that they always like what they learn about, but it makes them satisfied in the sense that they understand some of the complex social mechanisms that control them. As society grows more and more complex, the average citizen is usually less and less able to understand the devious controls within it, and this creates dissatisfaction. The voluntary association provides him an avenue for understanding some of the controls, and thus provides him with a degree of social satisfaction. By working in voluntary associations, people also learn exactly what is wrong with the power structure of the society, from the standpoint of their own values, and this gives them something definite to work toward, rather than leaving them with a vague and delusive feeling that, because "something" is wrong, only a complete revolution can change it. In like measure, the opportunity to engage in something creative, even if only in a hobby association, provides a compensation for the deadening effect of working on a simple repetitive task on the modern production

[82] Oscar Handlin, *The American People in the Twentieth Century* (Cambridge: Harvard University Press, 1954).

[83] Bernard C. Cohen, *The Influence of Non-Governmental Groups on Foreign Policy Making* (World Peace Foundation, 1959), p. 12.

line.[84] The association that does most about this is the trade union, which seems to the worker to provide him with a significant measure of control over his working conditions, gives him a sense of economic and personal security since it protects him from being fired arbitrarily, and even directly provides him some recreations, social-reform activities, and other creative opportunities. Many intellectuals overlook the fact that there are many compensations for, controls over, and satisfactory adjustments to, the monotony of work on the factory production line. Not the least of these is participation in voluntary associations. The present difficulty— which has certainly not been solved in the United States—is that many people do not take advantage of their opportunities, because they do not see that their needs for understanding the "mysterious" social mechanisms and their need for creative activity can be satisfied by participation in the associations. While they are constantly propagandized to join, the propaganda is far from being always successful.

Hausknecht feels that the orienting function of the voluntary association is less important today than it used to be. Since people have more education now, they have a better idea of how society functions. Many volunteer associations do not help members learn about democratic methods since they are democratic in name only. Most church and social organizations, because of the restricted nature of their aims, provide little opportunity to see how society operates. Finally, he points out that even if voluntary associations do help orient the individual to society, those who most need this kind of education, the lower class and city dweller, according to his statistics, are least likely to join voluntary associations.[85]

The social change function. The voluntary associations offer a powerful mechanism of social change; they are the organizational form of the reform movements that we shall consider in the chapter on social change. As soon as a felt need for some social change arises, one or more voluntary associations immediately spring up to try to secure the change. Not only do they operate directly on the problem, but their attention to it also makes the government concerned about the problem, as a democratic government has to pay attention to the interests of alert voters. It may take decades to effect the change completely, but movement toward that change is likely to occur in small steps all along the way. Sometimes the change is never completely achieved because the needs behind it disappear or are converted into other needs, but it would be hard to find a need for a specific social change that existed as long as a hundred years

---

[84] No one has described this as well as the French sociologist Georges Friedmann (*Problèmes Humaines du Machinisme Industriel* [Paris: Gallimard, 1946]; *Où Va le Travail Humain* [Paris; Gallimard, 1950]).

[85] Hausknecht, *op. cit.*, pp. 111–12.

ago in the United States and that still exists today substantially unsatisfied. The associations and the other mechanisms of change are thus usually successful in achieving their purposes in the long run.

Sometimes voluntary associations try to block social change, emanating from some other source in the society, when their leaders view it as harmful to their members. One example of this might be the resistance of the private child welfare associations when the government steps into their field.[86]

The social cohesion function. Most voluntary associations act to tie society together and to minimize the disintegrating effects of conflict. While they are themselves sometimes conflict groups, associations practically never carry their conflicts to the extreme of tearing the society asunder. This is largely because some people belong to more than one association. One association starting a serious fight with another risks losing some of its members who are members of, or friendly toward, the other group. The most serious conflicts come about where there is no overlapping of membership, such as in labor-management disputes.[87]

The function of personal identification. In so far as we live in a mass society,[88] the individual tends to feel anonymous and a mere number in the pull and haul of large scale social forces. The voluntary association often gives him the feeling of identification with some smaller group that he can fully comprehend and influence in major ways. It thus functions as the small rural community used to function. Many members of voluntary associations today find that their memberships and activities in the association help materially to give meaning and purpose to their lives.[89] This effect on these members is what is meant by the voluntary association having the function of personal identification.

The function of social and economic advancement. Many people join clubs and other voluntary associations to enhance their social status. As they gain access to the more exclusive clubs, sometimes they gradually relinquish their memberships in the ones that were easiest to get into.[90] In some clubs—especially the social clubs for businessmen and lawyers and the so-called "service clubs," like Rotary, Kiwanis, etc.—a good deal

[86] Bernice Boehm, "The Voluntary Association and Social Change," unpublished paper prepared for the author's social psychology course in the spring of 1955.

[87] Hans L. Zetterberg, "Voluntary Association and Organized Power in Sweden," Bureau of Applied Social Research, Columbia University (October, 1959), p. 12.

[88] See Chapter 9, Section C.

[89] Studies providing some evidence on this point include Arnold M. Rose, "Life Satisfaction of Middle-Class, Middle-Aged Persons," *Marriage and Family Living*, 17 (February, 1955), pp. 15–19; Arnold M. Rose, "Group Consciousness Among the Aging," in A. M. Rose and W. A. Peterson (eds.), *Older People and Their Social World* (Philadelphia: F. A. Davis, 1965).

[90] John R. Seeley, R. Alexander Sim, and Elizabeth W. Loosley, *Crestwood Heights* (New York: Basic Books, 1956).

of "business" is transacted, which is important for the economic advancement of the members. Minority group persons—Jews, Negroes, Orientals, etc.—excluded from these clubs sometimes find it difficult to compete with those to whom membership is accorded. Offices in welfare and civic clubs are often considered a testing ground for young potential executives and managers.[91]

A final word about this often-ignored aspect of modern democratic social life. The voluntary association is characteristically a voluntary activity, and to make it anything but voluntary would destroy its basic functions as we have listed them. It is true that informal community pressures occasionally push people into associations that they have no desire to join. Such people, with the few exceptions who change their minds once in the association, are seldom satisfied with, or effective workers in, the association. They neither share the power, understand it, nor effect social change. They are the "paper" members, from whom dues cannot be collected, and they almost invariably drop out of the association. This leads us to a broader observation: there is no value in participation *per se;* it is only when the individual spontaneously feels the need for participation that it performs any of the above functions for him. This implies, further, that the effective voluntary association is one in which not only membership is voluntary, but the type of activity also voluntary in that the members choose their goals and the means for obtaining them. Few things would wreck an association faster than to impose a goal or a means of action on the members. In other words, pluralism of ends and means is a necessary component of voluntarism in democracy.

Even worse than forced participation would be to encourage the individual to participate in a group activity that could not possibly have any effect, because the sources of power in the society were beyond the influence of that association's activity. If, say, all political power were lodged in a government, and the individual citizens were encouraged to be active in associations that were not allowed to influence that government, the individual's frustrations and lack of understanding of the power processes would be compounded. Fortunately, for the United States and other Western democracies, participation in the associations is voluntary and the associations are able to compete for their share of real power in the society.

[91] Unpublished study by Professor Aileen Ross of McGill University.

FOR ADDITIONAL READING

GIST, NOEL P., *Secret Societies: A Cultural Study of Fraternalism in the United States,* (Columbia, Missouri, 1940). Human behavior in fraternal groups.

HAUSKNECHT, MURRAY, *The Joiners* (New York: Bedminster, 1962). Analysis of nationwide surveys of members of voluntary associations.

ROSE, ARNOLD M., "Voluntary Associations in France," Chapter IV of *Theory and Method in the Social Sciences* (Minneapolis: University of Minnesota Press, 1954). A study exemplifying the viewpoint of this chapter.

SILLS, DAVID L., *The Volunteers* (Glencoe, Ill.: Free Press, 1957). A systematic study of the members of one voluntary association.

11 * Social and Cultural Change

Social change is the development of new meanings and values, or the substitution of new ones for old, and thus it involves changes in the characteristic behavior patterns in a society. Individuals and subgroups in a society vary considerably in the meanings and values they hold, as we have seen,[1] and since individuals and subgroups are constantly in the process of developing and dying, there are constant little uncoordinated changes in the culture of any society. For example, a child learns a skill from his father, but he does not learn to exercise this skill in exactly the same way in which his father did. This we shall not consider to be social change for the purposes of this chapter. Social change will be conceived as a fairly large-scale change in a number of related meanings and values, affecting the behavior of most people who occupy a certain role or a number of related roles. Social change thus has a direction, even if we cannot say that it has a purpose, and it involves a culture and not merely the behavior of a small number of individuals.

Writers of past generations who discussed social change often thought of it in terms of "progress." Today, whether because of scientific objectivity or because of skepticism, we are unwilling to think of change as progress.[2] Progress means change with a positive valuation placed on it; it is "good" by definition. Change, on the other hand, is neutral; it might

[1] See Chapters 1, 2 and 9.

[2] One of the most serious modern efforts to deal with progress in scientific terms is that of Hornell Hart, "Is Progress a Scientific Concept," *Sociology and Social Research*, 13 (1929), pp. 303–14. A sophisticated, modern anthropologist's view of progress and evolution is that of Julian Steward, *Theory of Culture Change* (Urbana: University of Illinois Press, 1955). Also see A. L. Kroeber, *Configurations of Culture Growth* (Berkeley: University of California Press, 1944); Leslie A. White, *The Evolution of Culture* (New York: McGraw-Hill, 1959).

be good or bad depending on the way one looks at it—depending on the evaluation one adds to it. Philosophers who thought of social change as progress often concentrated exclusively on the material culture, particularly on technology, for new techniques and other material inventions usually increased man's control over nature and permitted him to satisfy more of his needs and desires with less expenditure of human energy.

It was also thought that increase in knowledge about human behavior and social life would reduce social problems and thus increase human happiness. In analyzing this point of view we must recognize two facts about it: (1) It involves the value premises of efficiency and happiness—which are values in our culture but are not absolute values that must be highly regarded in all cultures. (2) It provides only a partial picture of what happens when there is social change. New technology may be used to hurt or destroy men more efficiently as well as to help them; new knowledge about human behavior and social life may be used to enslave men or make them miserable instead of happy. We wish only to raise these philosophic issues, not to deal with them systematically. "Progress" must continue to be a subject for philosophers; sociologists can only study "social change."

Some people have the impression that the normal and natural condition for society is stability, and that change results from some external push. Sociologists make the assumption, on the other hand, that change is as natural and normal in society as stability. It may require just as much of a "push" to stop change as to start it. In discussing social change, therefore, we are as much concerned with the barriers to change as we are with the causes of change. It is probably also true that when most people think of change, they think of it in terms of material culture. Sociologists are, of course, as much interested in change in non-material culture as in material culture.

Some societies change at a more rapid rate than do other societies, and some institutions within a society change at a more rapid rate than do other institutions in the same society. Therefore, it is necessary to look not only for the external causes that channel change in one direction rather than another but also to examine the inherent flexibility or changeability of the social structure being changed.

A   Theories of Social Change

Since ancient times philosophers have been advancing theories of social change, and in recent decades sociologists have been adding to the list. We cannot possibly present all of these theories, but shall have to confine ourselves to mentioning some of them and giving a more detailed explanation of three theories that have a good deal of support from

There is an evident tendency for growths in distinct activities to be associated in time, but no clear indication that a successful growth in one activity must be accompanied by growths in other activities. In other words, successful activity growths in one culture may be few or solitary; and many civilizations have failed to attain high achievement in one or another activity. That, on the contrary, growths tend to occur associated may be attributed to the fact that distinctive success in one activity presupposes a high degree of cultural energy, and once this is aroused it is unlikely to remain restricted to a single activity. But again, there is no reason to believe that once such cultural energy is aroused it must necessarily spread to all possible fields of cultural activity, since it is notorious that civilizations differ in their interests and emphases.

Alfred L. Kroeber, *Configurations of Culture Growth* (Berkeley: University of California Press, 1944), p. 842.

Thus, if a cultural base at any one time or in any locality be described generally, it is seen to possess certainly a limiting value in regard to the inventions possible. . . . The old saying that "necessity is the mother of inventions" is only a half truth. . . . It is nearer the truth to say that the existing culture is the mother of inventions. . . .

. . . the facts of the growth of material culture seem to indicate a development by jumps. There will be a period of stability or of relatively slight change. Then occurs a fundamental invention of great significance which precipitates many changes, modifications and other inventions which follow with relative rapidity for a time. These rapid changes are then followed by another period of relative stability—unless another fundamental discovery be made.

William F. Ogburn, *Social Change* (New York: B. W. Huebsch, 1922; rev. ed., Viking, 1927, 1950), pp. 82–83, 107–08.

empirical research and are regarded highly by contemporary social scientists. Some theories of social change are based upon an assumption that change is a result of immanent or inherent factors in the nature of man or of society. Most of these theories assume that society moves in cycles, that is, that it is constantly moving toward one extreme and then reversing itself and moving to another extreme. Others keep a cyclical conception but add an optimistic twist to it by saying that society moves forward as it moves from one extreme to another. The combined movement thus results in a *spiral* pattern of change.

Such cyclical and spiral theories of social change have received more support from philosophers than they have from sociologists, although one outstanding sociologist—P. A. Sorokin—has formulated a cyclical theory with a great deal of support from empirical data.[3] Some writers seek the causes of change in non-social factors. These are often scholars in the fields of geography and biology but are rarely sociologists. Some geographers, for example, have held that social change is the result of changing climatic conditions or of movements of people to areas where geographic conditions are different from those of the area from which they came.[4] A biological theory of social change is that the gene composition of our population is changing as a result of the differential birth rate in the various social classes or of racial intermarriage.[5] While these are undoubtedly factors in certain social changes they do not satisfactorily explain most of the changes we see in the social world about us and therefore we shall not be concerned with them here.

The theories to which we shall give more detailed attention will be those which find the cause of change in certain social conditions. Through studies of specific social changes, each theory has a great deal of support in empirical fact. But as a statement of the general causes of social change none of the theories is sufficiently verified. We should regard each theory as calling attention to important sources of social change rather than as an explanation of *the* cause of change. There is probably no one factor, or consistent set of factors, that is responsible for all social changes in all societies. Nor could one factor, operating by itself, be considered as the sole cause of any one single change.[6] The theories draw attention to what logicians call "sufficient causes" rather than to all the "necessary causes" —that is, to all the conditions that must exist before the sufficient cause can operate to effect the change. In ongoing social life everything is linked up in some way with everything else, and the full causal description of anything is practically everything else. Thus, in searching for causes in a practical sense, we must limit ourselves to the "sufficient" causes.[7]

While we shall try to account for each cause of social change as it develops in human history in its unplanned or unintended form, it should be understood that each cause may be deliberately planned for. By organized and deliberate planning, most changes can be instigated and —if the human and material resources are available—achieved. But this

[3] Pitirim A. Sorokin, *Social and Cultural Dynamics* (New York: American Book, 1937–1943), 4 vols.

[4] See, for example, Ellsworth Huntington, *Main Springs of Civilization* (New York: Wiley, 1945). For an account of the effort to explain social phenomena as due to geographic causes, see P. A. Sorokin, *Contemporary Sociological Theories* (New York: Harper, 1938).

[5] See, for example, Raymond B. Cattell, *The Fight for Our National Intelligence* (London: P. S. King, 1937).

[6] Our discussion of the causes of migration is relevant here. See Chapter 12, Section B.

[7] The theoretical position we hold in respect to social causation is stated by Gunnar Myrdal, with the assistance of Richard Sterner and Arnold Rose, *An American Dilemma* (New York: Harper, 1944), Appendix 3.

must be done *through,* and by means of, one or another of the causes of change we discuss in this chapter. This may be extremely difficult and often impossible, because the resources are not available, or because the conditions for initiating one of the causes of social change are not attainable. Nevertheless, the theoretical possibility of planning social change must be recognized.[8]

B   *Technological Invention as a Source of Social Change*

1   THE TECHNOLOGICAL THEORY

The technological theory of change has been most clearly enunciated by William F. Ogburn and by S. McKee and Laura Rosen.[9] The first premise of this theory is that inventions are created largely out of known elements in the culture. A new combination of known techniques or a slightly new technique added to a number of older ones results in an invention. Thus inventions are cumulative in character. The more techniques and tools available in a society, the more techniques and tools can be invented. Ogburn speaks of the cumulation of culture over time as taking the form of the constantly accelerating compound-interest curve. The cumulative character of inventions causes social change within a given culture to have a tendency to increase in amount regularly, although there would naturally be a leveling off or a plateau when a culture reaches the end of its creativity for one reason or another. The development of a given invention out of previous discoveries makes an invention almost inevitable, Ogburn holds, as evidenced by the fact that many important inventions are independently created almost simultaneously by several inventors.[10]

A second assumption of the theory is that certain inventions cause economic changes in a society. New techniques make for higher productivity and for changed ways of producing or distributing the goods and services "needed" in a society. These changes in economic structure include such things as the relocation of industries, the rearrangement of workers from family groups to small specialized groups of handworkers to attendants of a conveyor belt; the shortening of the working day due to a new technique of production; and so on. A third assumption is that social

[8] Social scientists' views and research concerning planned change may be found in Warren G. Bennis, Kenneth D. Benne, and Robert Chin, *The Planning of Change: Readings in the Applied Behavioral Sciences* (New York: Holt, Rinehart and Winston, 1961).

[9] William F. Ogburn, *Social Change* (New York: B. W. Huebsch, 1922; rev. ed., Viking, 1927, 1950); S. McKee and L. Rosen, *Technology and Society* (New York: Macmillan, 1941). Also see Stuart Chase, *Men and Machines* (New York: Macmillan, 1929).

[10] W. F. Ogburn and D. S. Thomas, "Are Inventions Inevitable," *Political Science Quarterly,* 37 (March, 1922), pp. 83–98; Alfred L. Kroeber, *Anthropology* (New York: Harcourt, 1948), pp. 341–43.

structure and customs must adjust to the economic pattern of production, distribution, and consumption, and that society changes as a result of this adjustment process. Thus a social or cultural change is a function of a technological invention as mediated through changes in economic structure.

Some inventions may be repressed, of course, so that they have no influence on the social structure.[11] The repression may be deliberate, as when manufacturers of certain kinds of cloth buy up the patents controlling a process for making a new, improved kind of cloth, in order to prevent the manufacture and sale of the latter in competition with the cloth which their factories are equipped to produce. Or the repression may occur simply because the invention fails to interest anyone—it is out of accord with fashion or the "climate of opinion" in some way which is not completely understood as yet. For example, Gregor Mendel's discoveries about biological inheritance were ignored for about a generation but have now become the basis of the modern science of genetics and the modern practice of developing hybrid plants and animals. The technique of measuring the growth of population by means of the net reproduction rate —which we will explain and utilize in the chapter on population—was published in 1884, but it was not adopted by any other demographer until 1928; whereas today practically all students of population use it.[12] The common zipper was more or less ignored for almost twenty-five years after it was invented in 1891, despite the fact that the customary alternatives were the clumsy hooks and eyes and the buttons and buttonholes, and despite the fact that the inventor gave it a strong promotional campaign.[13] There are probably hundreds or thousands of valuable discoveries—fully described in the published literature—which lie ignored and unexploited to this very day. And even today valuable inventions are being reported that will be ignored in the future. In other cases there is a lag in the modification of economic structure resulting from the invention or in the modification of the social structure resulting from the economic change. This circumstance gives rise to the phenomenon that Ogburn has so aptly called "cultural lag."[14]

Some proponents of the technological theory of change emphasize the increased *energy* provided by improved technology, rather than the eco-

---

[11] Hornell Hart, *The Technique of Social Progress* (New York: Holt, 1931); S. C. Gilfillan, *The Sociology of Invention* (Chicago: Follett, 1935); B. J. Stern, "Resistances to the Adoption of Technological Innovations," in National Resources Board, *Technological Trends and National Policy* (Washington, 1937).

[12] R. Boeckh, *Statistisches Jahrbuch der Stadt Berlin* (Berlin, 1884), p. 30; Robert R. Kuczynski, *The Balance of Births and Deaths* (New York: Macmillan, 1928).

[13] *New York Times*, February 21, 1947, p. 18.

[14] Ogburn's 1922 statement on "cultural lag" has long been seen as oversimplified. A much more sophisticated discussion is to be found in Robert M. MacIver and Charles H. Page, *Society: An Introductory Analysis* (New York: Rinehart, 1949), pp. 575–80.

> The thesis is that the various parts of modern culture are not changing at the same rate, some parts are changing much more rapidly than others; and that since there is a correlation and interdependence of parts, a rapid change in one part of our culture requires readjustments through other changes in the various correlated parts of culture. For instance, industry and education are correlated, hence a change in industry makes adjustments necessary through changes in the educational system. . . . When the material conditions change, changes are occasioned in the adaptive culture. But these changes in the adaptive culture do not synchronize exactly with the change in the material culture. There is a lag which may last for varying lengths of time, sometimes, indeed, for many years.
>
> William F. Ogburn, *Social Change* (New York: B. W. Huebsch, 1922). Cited from revised edition, Viking, 1927, pp. 200–1.

nomic changes consequent to it. The anthropologist Leslie A. White, for example, enunciates what he calls "the basic law of cultural evolution": "Other factors remaining constant, culture evolves as the amount of energy harnessed per capita per year is increased, or as the efficiency of the instrumental means of putting the energy to work is increased."[15] The sociologist Fred A. Cottrell has devoted a whole book to an analysis of the relationship of the production of energy to cultural development and change.[16]

In addition to the mechanical inventions proper, advocates of the technological theory of social change recognize a number of other agents of change which affect the energy level available to a society: the discovery or depletion of natural resources, disasters which destroy significant amounts of the resources or capital equipment or working force of a society, drastic population movements which increase or decrease the productivity of a society, disease epidemics which destroy a significant portion of the working force of a society. All of these forces operate in a society almost like mechanical inventions to change the energy level and productivity of that society.[17]

Technological change exerts a varying influence on the course of general social and culture change in different periods of history. At the present time, the influence must be seen as of paramount importance, because of the problem of modernizing the "underdeveloped" countries, because of the recent breakthrough in using "automation" for industrial production and clerical service, and because of the imminent substitu-

[15] Leslie A. White, *The Science of Culture* (New York: Farrar, Straus, 1949), pp. 368–69. The anthropologist Julian H. Steward develops this idea as the modern theory of evolution of culture: *Theory of Culture Change, op. cit.*

[16] Fred A. Cottrell, *Energy and Society* (New York: McGraw-Hill, 1955).

[17] *Cf.* Abbott P. Herman, *An Approach to Social Problems* (Boston: Ginn, 1949), pp. 55 ff.

tion of cheap nuclear energy in place of the traditional fuels. It is some-times said that the Western world is now undergoing a second or third "Industrial Revolution" and many of the economically underdeveloped countries are moving from the donkey age to the age of automation in a few decades. The social consequences of technological change are tre-mendous, and many of them are little understood. Studies of the effects of past technological changes will help us understand what is occurring today.[18]

Some examples will now be given to clarify the theory of technological change as the source of social change.

2   EXAMPLE: THE COTTON GIN AND RACE RELATIONS

Our first example will involve examining the widespread social effects of a single technological invention, as mediated through changes in the economic system. The invention was that of the cotton gin by Eli Whitney in the United States in 1793. Prior to this invention cotton was a rare source of cloth and the Western world clothed itself primarily in wool and linen. The cotton gin was a very simple device, run at first by hand and later by steam and electric power, which permitted the separation of the cotton seeds from the cotton boll at a much more rapid rate than by hand alone. The cotton gin, even in its earliest form, could do the work of eight men during a given amount of time. The saving of time was sufficient to make it cheaper to produce cotton cloth than woolen or linen cloth. The cheapness and practicality of cotton cloth caused it to be rapidly substi-tuted for woolen and linen cloth in many parts of the world.

The cotton plant could not be grown in most parts of Europe since it required a hot, humid climate and a good deal of flat land. Cotton growing was feasible in parts of Egypt and Asia but most feasible in the southern areas of the United States. Cotton was grown and ginned in the southern states and territories and then shipped to mills in England, and later in New England, where it was manufactured into cloth and clothing. Improvements in transportation and commercial organization about the same time made the process of transportation a feasible one for the heavy and numerous bales of cotton. The rapid growth in the population of Europe in the early nineteenth century made it essential to seek a new source of clothing, as the raising of sheep for wool required more space than there was available in the fields of Europe. Hence everything was

[18] There are many studies of automation, but few by sociologists. Among those by economists and industrial engineers, see Walter Buckingham, *Automation: Its Impact on Business and People* (New York: Harper and Row, 1961); G. G. Somers, E. L. Cushman, and N. Weinberg (eds.), *Adjustment to Technological Change* (New York: Harper and Row, 1963). The nearest to a sociological survey of contemporary technological influence is to be found in Francis R. Allen *et al.*, *Technology and Social Change* (New York: Appleton-Century-Crofts, 1957).

just right for the creation of a tremendous economic demand for cotton.

The hitherto-sparsely settled areas of South Carolina, Georgia, Alabama, Mississippi, and Louisiana became rapidly filled with people who set themselves down there largely to grow cotton. A host of service enterprises developed to serve the cotton growers: those who would arrange for the ginning and transportation of the cotton; those who would sell to the cotton growers the necessities for their farms, for their homes, and for themselves; those who would provide luxuries and entertainment. Many people grew wealthy by growing cotton or by providing the cotton growers with the necessary materials and services. With its tremendous increase in population, the South took on a new political significance in the nation as a whole. Whereas in 1790 it appeared that population growth would be more rapid in the North than in the South and hence that political dominance would move from rural Virginia to urban New England, the great increase in population in the South owing to the rise of cotton strengthened the position of the Southern bloc in Congress.

The possibilities of gaining wealth by growing cotton created a tremendous new demand for slaves to grow the cotton. It had been found practically impossible to get white laborers to engage in the tedious and extremely tiring job of picking cotton, and slaves were found to be the cheapest and most practical source of labor. Thus, even though the federal government abolished the importation of slaves after 1809, the smuggling of slaves after that year brought more Negroes into the country than had been brought in legally during the previous 150 years. Some wealthy families of Virginia, in which state most of the sales of the slaves of the United States were to be found in 1790, found a new source of economic support in raising slaves for sale to the cotton plantations farther south. The increasing profit found in the slavery system killed the Abolitionist movement in the South, which had been growing during and shortly after the Revolutionary War. The ideology of liberty, equality, and democracy, which had been spreading throughout the Western world, found itself in conflict with the slave system now so profitable and widespread in the southern states.

In order to keep their liberal democratic philosophy and at the same time their slaves, the wealthy southern planters developed a modified ideology which insisted that true democracy had to be based upon leisure and upon a division of labor between those engaged in leisure and those engaged in work. Hundreds of books, pamphlets, speeches, and sermons were written and discussed throughout the South in the early decades of the nineteenth century, justifying in various ways the slave system. The effort to justify slavery and to reconcile it with democracy took several forms.

One was a copy of the ideology and social structure of ancient Greece, which seemingly had successfully resolved the opposition between slavery and democracy. The copying of the ancient Greek culture by wealthy Southerners extended even to borrowing the style of architecture of ancient Greece and the names of several of the Greek cities. The plantation owners also hoped to create a high development of literature, art, and music, but in this they were less successful than their model. A second ideology adopted by the early nineteenth-century Southerners—mostly by the less educated among them—was a religious justification of slavery: the Bible was scoured for passages that might suggest the propriety of slavery. A third ideology was most important of all since it has lasted to the present day. This was the ideology of racism, which started in the writings of some of the early biologists. The doctrine of race superiority and inferiority developed gradually into a whole philosophy of social life and into the basis of the new social structure of caste which we have examined in an earlier chapter.[19]

Thus we observe some of the populational, occupational, architectural, ideological, and social-structural changes which resulted ultimately from the invention of the cotton gin in 1793. It has to be recognized that other events had to occur before this technological factor could manifest itself in the widespread social changes we have mentioned.[20]

3 EXAMPLE: THE INDUSTRIAL REVOLUTION AND THE POSITION OF WOMEN

Our second example of the invention theory of change will consider a relatively restricted social change as arising from a group of technological inventions. It has already been pointed out that the invention of certain machines of production in the late eighteenth and early nineteenth centuries substituted a factory system of production for a domestic system of production. The changing functions of the family as a consequence of this change in the economic system have already been commented upon.[21] The changes we wish to note now are those involving the differentiation of the social roles of men and women arising from their occupational specialization and their spatial separation which in turn developed out of production in a factory as distinct from production in the home.[22]

With the Industrial Revolution men lost many of their family func-

[19] See Chapter 8, Section A.

[20] Such other events are referred to, in logic, as "necessary causes." The technological factor has been presented as a "sufficient cause."

[21] See Chapter 5, Section C.

[22] The following paragraphs are taken from Arnold M. Rose, "The Adequacy of Women's Expectations for Adult Roles," *Social Forces*, 30 (October, 1951), pp. 69–77.

tions, but they acquired new civic ones at the same time, so that there did not seem to be a decrease of function. They no longer helped with food and clothing preparation, and their educational function for their children dropped to a minimum. But now they voted for governmental officers, joined businessmen's associations or unions, participated in social-welfare activities, and occasionally went to war. Most important of all, men established a new routine of work to earn the family's living. This gave their lives meaning and fixed their roles. Every boy learned that he would certainly grow up and work at an occupation. He might not do many other things, but work he must, unless he were one of the very small number of very wealthy people who did not care to work.

The change in the social role of the middle-class woman after the eighteenth century was quite different. In the first place, her change of functions was slower and not quite so complete. She gave up working in the home shop at the same time as her husband did, but she still had all the housekeeping and child-raising tasks. In fact, at first she had more as the nineteenth-century home became larger, and as fewer children died in childbirth or infancy. But gradually housework became simplified, there were all sorts of labor-saving devices, fewer children were born, and the schools took over part of the task of raising and educating them. These losses of functions transpired so slowly in the last 100 years that most women did not realize that they were occurring. Certainly most women were not in a position to plan in advance for changes in their life roles when the changes could hardly be seen, much less foreseen. In fact, many failed to see the changes that had taken place long after they occurred. Writers, clergymen, public speakers, and even some advertisers assumed that woman's only significant role was in the home long after she had acquired many new roles outside the home.

A second major difference between men and women, in their modern modification of roles, is that there was much more opposition to women acquiring new functions. Many organizations and interest groups worked to keep women in the home. The struggle for woman's suffrage was long and bitter after the men had acquired the vote, and women are still far from wholly accepted in politics. The virtual exclusion of women from many of the higher status occupations, from leadership in mixed organizations, and from positions as publicists, is still not very far behind us. This opposition has made it much more difficult for women to acquire new roles. The fact that a significant proportion of women themselves opposed these extensions of their functions indicates that they were not convinced that new social roles would be desirable for them.

A third major difference between men's and women's change of roles is that new roles for women have never become clear and definite. The old economic functions (e.g., clothes making) once made an imperious demand on women's time, but they have sharply declined. Even the continuing functions connected with child rearing begin to decline when the children start school, and usually disappear completely before the average woman reaches the age of forty-five.[23] No new strong demands on time and interest take their place. The modern woman has a choice between career and marriage, or she can work out some combination of them almost by herself. Since she has a choice, she may later question whether the goals she chose are the ones she *really* wants. A man has no such choice facing him: he *must* get an occupation (and he usually expects to have marriage and family life, too). Other people measure his success in terms of achievements in his occupation, whereas even if a woman is a success in what she sets out to do, public acclaim will not be at all universal. The woman who has chosen marriage also has to choose which social clubs and civic organizations she wishes to join, or whether she will join any at all. A man, on the other hand, has to pick many of his "voluntary" organizations on the basis of what is best for his occupation. There may even be a union, a businessmen's association, or a professional organization which he is *obliged* to join, and yet which demands much of his free time and provides him a good deal of his social life. A woman has to *decide* how much time she will devote to her housework within the limits imposed by necessity and by the budget. She can take the time necessary to do a thorough job or she can continue for a long while with superficial straightening up; she can be very quick and efficient or she can dawdle and string out the work so that she is never finished. A man usually has no such decision to make; in most occupations, regardless of how efficient or inefficient he is, a strong sense of what is proper, group pressures, and even the law serve to keep him from working many more, or considerably fewer, than forty hours a week.

For these and probably other reasons the modern woman's role is much less definite and specific than modern man's. There are many individual exceptions, of course, although most of the exceptions tend to be outside the middle class. The relatively greater indefiniteness of woman's roles is reflected in her expectations for her future from the time she leaves childhood. Vagueness and inconsistency in expectations are often manifested in apparent lack of seriousness in college and in insufficient or unrealistic planning for adult roles. Thus we can trace the development of certain sex differences in contemporary Western culture to a series of related technological changes.

[23] The median age of mothers at the time of bearing their *last* child, in the United States in 1960, was 25.8 years. Paul C. Glick, D. M. Heer, and J. C. Beresford, "Social Change and Family Structure: Trends and Prospects," unpublished paper presented to AAAS, December 29, 1959.

c   *Science, Technology, and Automation*

1   THE DEVELOPMENT OF SCIENCE AND TECHNOLOGY

In the great explorations of remote parts of the earth that lasted into the early part of the twentieth century, isolated peoples were discovered whose technology was exceedingly primitive and who had nothing that resembled science. This was especially true of the tribes of central New Guinea, Australia, and of some of the South Sea islands, among whom it was reported that not even the wheel was known and who dipped their mouths in pools of water in order to drink rather than using drinking vessels. Yet it was not lack of intelligence or other ability that kept them so backward technologically. Many of these tribes had elaborate kinship systems and complicated religious beliefs. Some of their grandchildren today, who have been thoroughly exposed to Western technology, have no difficulty in using this technology. Indeed, the New Zealanders of Western ancestry have so westernized the Maori, the native inhabitants of their island, that some of the latter have become inventors and scientists in the Western style. It is the purpose of the present section to examine the causes of their earlier technological backwardness,[24] and thereby to illuminate the explanation why technology and science did develop in the Mediterranean basin, in China, and in India in ancient times; in the Arab world in our Middle Ages; and in Europe and North America in modern times.

The concept of *surplus energy* or *surplus product* is of primary importance in this explanation.[25] There are certain minimum requirements for life by way of food, clothing, shelter, which man must produce in order to stay alive and healthy. If all of his productive time and energy is spent in obtaining these, there is no time or energy left for science and invention. A harsh climate; a geographic setting lacking in materials such as wood, working metals, and edible plants; a topography that cuts a people off from trade with others are among the influences which can prevent man from having any time or energy left after satisfying his basic animal needs. On the other hand, a too-beneficent nature can create an absence of challenge to invention, as all basic needs are satisfied practically without effort. For example, the Indians who originally inhabited California were among the most primitive in North America, whereas those who inhabited

---

[24] Varying analyses of the causes of the contemporary technological backwardness of some countries have been offered by David C. McClelland, *The Achieving Society* (Princeton, N.J.: Van Nostrand, 1961); Robert S. Morrison, "The University and Technical Assistance," *Daedalus*, 11 (Spring, 1962), pp. 319–40; Everett E. Hagen, *On the Theory of Social Change* (Homewood, Ill.: Dorsey, 1961).

[25] The leading sociological study of "surplus energy" is Fred Cottrell's *Energy and Society, op. cit.*

What were the main factors that made possible Japan's rapid emergence as a modern industrial society? I shall not dwell on the historical roots of modern Japan, which laid the basis for industrialization. . . . I shall rather single out some features which, I believe, are significant to an understanding of Japan's dynamic growth since the end of World War II.

One vital element lies in Japan's trained, skilled and industrious labor force. Universal education has given Japan one of the highest literacy rates in the world. Japan understood long ago that the road to modernization lies in education; that schools came before steel mills as the *true* status symbols of a modern industrial society—a lesson which many developing countries have yet to grasp.

A second critical factor has been Japan's high rate of savings and investment (which we have called the surplus product). Total domestic investment has averaged nearly a third of gross national product over the entire postwar period, climbing as high as 42 percent in 1961. (By comparison, gross private investment in the United States amounted to 9 percent of GNP.) This heavy investment in new plants and new equipment has made possible rising labor productivity. This, in turn, led to major gains in wages and real income, while keeping Japan's production costs competitive in world markets.

Edward G. Posniak, *Japan in the World Economy* (Washington, D.C.: United States–Japan Trade Council, 1964), p. 5.

the cold Great Lakes region and the hot jungles of Yucatan were the ones who developed the highest Indian civilizations of North America.

Whereas nature tends to set outer limits on the possibilities for creating the original surplus product necessary for the development of science and technology, man's social organization sets the actual conditions for its creation. The establishment of autocratic governments that were able to extend their political rule over other people and make slaves of them was one of the ancient social forces that erected a surplus product for the autocrats. Most of them used the surplus product simply to build monuments for their personal glorification, but others used it for engineering developments that enhanced their surplus energy. The means of food acquisition has always played a role in the erection of surplus product: Hunting, gathering, and pastoral activity have required that those who used these means of getting their food live a nomadic life, and a nomadic life has never allowed the accumulation of a surplus product. Even if nomads do accumulate a small surplus of food, they merely take it easy before moving on, for they must abandon all unnecessary baggage when they migrate.

Equally important is the belief system of a people, particularly their religion. Some primitive religions enjoin a "tampering with nature" which prevents invention and the curiosity that leads to science. The Hindu religion today prohibts the killing or eating of "sacred cows," and these animals roam the streets and roads of India, eating the surplus food, without contributing anything to the economy. Max Weber, the great German sociologist of an earlier generation, thoroughly explored the intellectual climates created by the leading religions and found great variations among them in the encouragement and hospitality they gave to science and technology. He even held that there were differences between Catholicism and Protestantism in this matter, finding that the emphasis upon work and saving the surplus product were conducive to the accumulation that aided the development of technology.[26] Catholic beliefs encouraged that a good deal of the surplus product go to the church, whereas Protestantism tended to reject elaborate church edifices, large monasteries and convents, and indulgences, and kept the wealth in the hands of private entrepreneurs, who encouraged invention to enhance their wealth further.

The belief system of a society that favors universal education and that specifies which social groups should be given greatest prestige and power has much to do with the development of science and technology. It has already been suggested that the entrepreneurial class is more favorable to these things than are the clergy. The contrast between ancient Greece and Rome suggests that the intellectual class is more favorable than the military. However, the experience of medieval China shows that a distinction must be made here between the humanistic scholar and the innovating scientist. In general, though, the extension of education to as many people in the society as possible seems to be associated with rapid scientific technological development.

As we know it today, science got its start in 15th century Italy and other parts of Europe,[27] although they benefited from the written heritage from the ancient Greeks and medieval Arabs. Since then, science has expanded enormously both in scope and intensity, aided both by government and by independent entrepreneurs. A significant percentage of the surplus product of our society is devoted to science, and scientists have considerable prestige. Technology's modern boom started later than that of science—in the late eighteenth century—but its speed of development today is fully as great.

Science and technology have both beneficial and harmful effects on mankind. Knowledge and its application can be used for both good and ill. The great means for increasing productivity and controlling disease have also caused the development of deadly weapons and the obsolescence

[26] Max Weber, *The Protestant Ethic and the Spirit of Capitalism,* trans. Talcott Parsons from *Gesammelte Aufsätze zur Religionssoziologie,* Vol. 1, Chapter 1 (New York: Scribner's, 1930).

[27] For a consideration of additional causes of the rise of science in post-medieval Europe, see Gerard De Gre, *Science as a Social Institution* (New York: Random House, 1955).

of working skills. It would be a lengthy and complicated history indeed to trace these considerations through. Rather we shall merely illustrate some of the benefits and difficulties created by science and technology by a consideration of the effects of the modern developments known as the "industrial revolutions," with special emphasis on automation and nuclear energy.

2   AUTOMATION AND ITS SOCIAL CONSEQUENCES

An industrial revolution may be said to consist of a relatively sudden and major increment in productivity with its radical consequences for industry and society as a whole. In this sense, we may distinguish three industrial revolutions since the end of the eighteenth century in England. Prior to this period, the technological equipment of Western society had remained substantially unchanged—with a few exceptions, such as the introduction of gunpowder—since Roman times. While social organization had drastically changed during this period, the only change that involved a marked increase in productivity was the great extension of the economic market, known as the "Commercial Revolution," in the period following the fifteenth century. The *first* industrial revolution—beginning in the 1770's—involved the introduction of a few simple productive machines— such as the spinning jenny and the cotton gin—and the extended use of water and steam power. Probably the major economic consequence of the first industrial revolution was the factory system of production, as distinguished from commercial production in the small family-run shop. The *second* industrial revolution began in England about a century later with the use of electric power. This permitted the introduction of increasingly complex machines and the relocation of factories. The *third* industrial revolution began in the United States after the beginning of the twentieth century and has not yet spread to all countries in Western society. It did not involve technological improvement so much as changes in the use of manpower. Its goals were specialization and mass production, and its chief industrial manifestation was the assembly line.

Each of these industrial revolutions was followed by a series of drastic social changes, largely unanticipated, all involving a great deal of dislocation and human hardship and all eventually raising the standard of living and making possible a great growth of population. The main outlines of these changes are known to most informed citizens, and the details have been the objects of careful study. If this knowledge can now be used to help predict the future directions of social change, it is possible for instrumentalities of our society, both governmental and private, to plan now to avoid some of ill effects on people and their institutions that will otherwise probably ensue.

In one sense we have been living in one continuous, accelerating industrial revolution since the end of the eighteenth century, because technological and organizational invention has been continual and multiplicative. Each invention has had its effect on human behavior and society as it came into widespread use. But the effects of most of these inventions have either been small, when considered by themselves, or they accelerated trends already well under way. The concept of "industrial revolution" is here reserved to periods in which the adoption of new techniques of production have caused both rapid, large increments in productivity and radical changes in social institutions and human relations generally. The technologists now tell us that the means of dramatically increasing productivity are within our grasp and are of a sort that can have a profound influence on society because of certain characteristics. Thus, while certain technological improvements—such as the improvement of gadgets for reducing household work—will continue trends already well under way, it is justifiable to speak of a new industrial revolution.

The mere fact that we have been living in a society which has been experiencing steady technological and other social changes suggests that the current changes will not have the impact of an industrial revolution first hitting a static society. There is nothing in our analysis which suggests —as a few physical scientists ignorant of social science have suggested—that our society will have extraordinary difficulties in adjusting to the coming changes or that there will be widespread disorganization. For example, we shall observe later that there will be relocation of factories and hence large scale migration of workers. But the scale on which this will occur will probably be no different, relatively speaking, than the speed and scope of migration after the Civil War or during World War II. Our society is so structured that it will not fall apart at the seams if the rate of internal migration should once again be stepped up, although we shall suggest that there are ways to ease the hardships arising from migration. Also, none of the coming changes are likely to be so drastic or so quick that they will have people any more confused or bewildered than they have been. Change is a normal condition in any society, and even rapid change is characteristic of our society; neither the current engineering changes[28] nor the consequent social changes are likely to be extraordinary in their extent or speed, although in some cases they will be different from what we have experienced previously.

The technological means of this new revolution are the following: 1) the use of energy from fissionable materials which are easily transportable;[29] 2) the processes of machine production collectively called "auto-

[28] John Diebold, *Automation: The Advent of the Automatic Factory* (New York: Van Nostrand, 1952), pp. 148–52.

[29] Other new sources of energy may become available. In the late 1940's a technique was discovered for harnessing the energy coming from the sun without the mediation of plants.

mation." The use of a new source of energy involves no basic change in the *manner* of production, although it will have profound impact on the cost, location, speed, and other characteristics of production. Automation has at least three *generalized* types of effect on the manner of production, according to George B. Baldwin and George P. Schultz, industrial economists of the Massachusetts Institute of Technology:

1   The linking together of conventionally separate manufacturing operations into lines of continuous production through which the product moves "untouched by human hands." This first development, which depends primarily on mechanical engineering for its adoption, we shall refer to simply as "integration", a term already in wide use in the metal working industries. It is also called "Detroit Automation" in honor of the industry in which it got its start. "Continuous automatic production" is another and perhaps more descriptive term being used.

2   The use of "feed-back" control devices or servo-mechanisms which allow individual operations to be performed without any necessity for human control. With feed-back, there is always some built-in automatic device for comparing the way in which work is actually being done with the way in which it is supposed to be done and for then making automatically any adjustments in the work-process that may be necessary. This second development we shall refer to simply as "feed-back" technology; it is dependent primarily not on mechanical but on electrical engineering knowledge and techniques.

3   The development of general and special purpose computing machines capable of recording and storing information (usually in the form of numbers) and of performing both simple and complex mathematical operations on such information. We shall refer to this aspect of automation as "computer technology", a technology that rests primarily on new developments in electrical engineering.[30]

Automation is not entirely new. Tustin notes that for hundreds of years a few examples of true automatic control systems have been known. A very early one was the arrangements on windmills of a device to keep their sails always facing into the wind. It consisted simply of a miniature windmill which would rotate the whole mill to face in any direction. The small mill's sails were at right angles to the main ones, and whenever the latter faced in the wrong direction, the wind caught the small sails and rotated the mill to the correct position.[31] And Diebold points out that:

If this source becomes commercially usable, it should have substantially the same effects we note for the use of atomic energy. Energy from atomic fusion may also become available.

[30] George B. Baldwin and George P. Schultz, *Monthly Labor Review*, 78 (February, 1955), pp. 165–69.

[31] Arnold Tustin, "Feedback," *Scientific American*, 187 (September, 1952), p. 48.

The present efforts to apply feed-back to industry are directed toward adapting it to existing machinery and processes. But the new technology of control in terms of actual rather than expected performance makes it possible to build entirely new types of production machines—machines which still perform a bundle of functions but are quite different from those we now have.

Feed-back provides industry with a very powerful new tool for the design of machinery. A man has two hands, two eyes, and ten fingers with only limited dexterity. He can control only a limited number of variables at one time. All too many of our present machines have been built around these limitations. In some cases this has hampered design greatly and has led us into inefficient ways of production. With intelligent use of the feed-back principle and of the automatic control devices which this principle makes possible, we should be able to achieve entirely new types of automatically controlled machinery. This has a far greater significance than simple fitting automatic controls to our present machines. It is difficult to foresee what forms these new families of machinery will take, but we do know the areas of industry in which mechanization has been least successful—machine setup, materials handling, product inspection, and assembly. It is clear that the new technology has much to offer toward the automation of all these tasks as well as toward the automation of the office. It is equally clear that industrial automation will not be complete until all of these functions have been made automatic.

John Diebold, *Automation* (New York: Van Nostrand, 1952), pp. 88–89.

In 1784, before the industrial revolution had really begun, Oliver Evans built an entirely automatic factory just outside Philadelphia—a continuous process flour mill. Evans' mill made use of all three basic types of powered conveyors in a continuous production line. No human labor was required from the time the grain was received at the mill until it had been processed into finished flour. And in Paris, in 1801, Joseph Marie Jacquard exhibited an automatic loom controlled by punched paper cards, similar in many ways to the punched cards used in modern office equipment. Jacquard's loom became so popular that by 1812 there were eleven thousand operating in France alone.[32] Still, only a segment of industry is already automatized, and recent scientific discoveries now make possible a great new extension of automation.

Automation will not affect all industries, and even those in which it can be used are not likely to make 100 per cent use of it. Some industries are more amenable to automation than others[33]—notably those engaged

[32] Diebold, *op. cit.*, p. 1.

[33] "In an excellent unpublished paper entitled Automatism in the American Society, a physical scientist, Richard L. Meier of the University of Chicago lists the industries he believes ripe for automation. They are (by U. S. Bureau of the Census categories): bakery products, beverages, confectionary, rayon, knit goods, paperboard containers, printing, chemicals, petroleum refining, glass products, cement, agricultural machinery, miscellaneous

in part production and assembling, those engaged in processing (e.g., of chemicals, flour, oil), and those relying heavily on bookkeeping (e.g., insurance, banking, public utilities). Industries already largely automatic (e.g., canning, oil processing), those in which production requires constant judgment or irregular variation (e.g., slaughtering, construction), and those producing goods the demands for which are continually subject to changes in taste and fashion (e.g., outer garment making) will be least affected by the trends toward geographic decentralization and concentration of ownership. Agriculture, mining, transportation, service, retailing will be little affected by automation directly.

Most factories that automatize will not adopt it completely. The engineers say that it often is feasible to automatize, say, 80 per cent of a plant's equipment, but the remaining 20 per cent would be so expensive to automatize that it is not likely to be done. Thus, automation will not come immediately or completely in the near future. As far as the use of nuclear power is concerned, it first became possible to produce it at competitive cost in 1964,[34] and it will be a decade before it is widely used.

The above-mentioned technological changes are the "givens";[35] we shall now consider their probable social consequences assuming that they are adopted to a significant extent during the next twenty or thirty years. The probable effects will be considered on the following areas of social life: the structure of industry, the labor market, the lives of workers, education, government, international relations, and what might be called the "mental life of the society."

Industry will be less and less dependent on difficult-to-transport fuels, such as coal, oil, and water power, and on large supplies of unskilled manpower, and so will be more mobile and hence more likely to decentralize geographically. Present needs to be close to sources of raw materials and to markets will remain, of course, so that the decentralization will probably not be drastic. Investment in real estate and plain inertia will probably keep it from being rapid. But some decentralization will gradually occur to avoid the high land costs, high taxes, congestion, difficulty in disposal of waste products, and other desirable features of large indus-

machinery, communications, limited price retailing, and some miscellaneous items" (Diebold, *op. cit.*, p. 149).

[34] Announcement by President Lyndon Johnson, June 9, 1964.

[35] The best single general work on automation is John Diebold's *Automation* (*op. cit.*). The issue of *Scientific American* for September, 1952 (Vol. 187) has reliable authors. For a well-selected bibliography on atomic energy and automation, see *Saturday Review*, 38 (January 22, 1955), pp. 51–52. For discussions of the effects of automation, see also Frederick Pollack, *Automation: A Study of Its Economic and Social Consequences* (New York: Praeger, 1957); Harold B. Jackson and Joseph S. Roucek (eds.), *Automation and Society* (New York: Philosophical Library, 1959); Walter Buckingham, *Automation: Its Impact on Business and People* (New York: Harper, 1961).

trial cities. A second influence of automation on location of industrial areas arises from the fact that there will be no advantage to moving where there is a large supply of cheap, unskilled labor—namely, the South. Skilled workers and good schools for training skilled workers are more readily available in the North and West, and wages for skilled workers show little regional differential. With the advantage of the large Northern markets, it is thus likely that industries which automatize will stay in the North or move there.

A reliable economist, Wassily Leontief, has made a careful study of the costs of automation and finds it relatively inexpensive, hence capable of being introduced rapidly.

> The estimated cost of complete instrumentation of a new modern plant to automatize it as fully as possible today ranges from 1 to 19 per cent (depending on the industry) of the total investment in process equipment. The average for all industries would be almost six per cent. . . . six per cent is far from a formidable figure. Furthermore, the investment in instruments would not necessarily mean a net increase in the total plant investment per unit of output. On the contrary, the smoother and better balanced operation of self-regulating plants has already shown that they can function with less capitalization than a non-automatic plant of identical capacity. And much existing equipment can readily be converted from manual to automatic control. It therefore seems that the automatization of our industries, at least to the extent made possible by present technology, is likely to advance rapidly. The mechanization of the 19th century required heavy capital investment and proceeded slowly; the new technology, unhampered by such vast capital requirements, can be introduced at a much faster pace.[36]

On the other hand, it takes some time for the changeover and larger firms will be better able to take the time and put up the capital immediately. The larger firms will be better able to take advantage of the possibilities of decentralization. Also, as a prediction poll among owners of industry makes clear, the larger firm owners are more psychologically prepared to automate as soon as it become technically feasible.[37] Thus there may be some tendency for automation to encourage concentration of ownership, unless the government steps in to compensate small firms with loans, information, and other aid.

The most general long-run effects on workers will arise out of needs for new kinds of skills and out of the sharply lessened need for unskilled labor. To keep employed, many unskilled or semiskilled workers will re-

[36] Wassily Leontief, "Machines and Man," *Scientific American*, 187 (September, 1952), p. 152.

[37] Henry Bund, "I.R. II: Yes or No?" *Saturday Review*, 38 (January 22, 1955), p. 21.

quire training, and some kinds of skilled workers will have to be retrained. Without new training, many industrial workers will find themselves unemployed or forced to shift into the expanding service occupations.

Most workers discharged from one job or industry will be required in another. But they will be needed with a new skill and perhaps in a new location, so that extensive temporary unemployment is likely. The problem for industry will increasingly be to find a sufficient number of properly trained workers, while the problem for workers will be to acquire new skills.[38]

There are likely to be certain changes in the labor market that will affect the level of unemployment. First, there will be some continuation of the trend to prolong the period of education, although the colleges are still insufficiently financed to handle the expected increase in the number of college-age youth, much less a higher proportion attending college. Second, during the period of transition to automatic production, a certain proportion of workers will have to be withdrawn from the labor market temporarily for re-education. Thirdly, and most important, a large proportion of the present unskilled and semiskilled workers will be needed in the rapidly expanding service industries (where, incidentally, most of them will be wearing "white collars" rather than overalls).

The trend toward requiring new skills will work special hardships on older workers, for whom an educational investment will net a smaller total payoff, and hence who are less likely to be given the opportunity to obtain retraining. Untrained older workers will either be downgraded in jobs, or retired earlier if pensions become available at an earlier age. On the other hand, if the worker is retrained to operate the automatic machinery, his age of retirement may be later than it is now because of the shortage of skilled workers that will last for many decades and because the work will be physically easier than it is now. Some kinds of women workers will also find it harder to obtain the unskilled employment they have sought while awaiting marriage or which they seek occasionally to supplement the family budget or to fill their idle hours after their children have grown up, mainly because unskilled and incidental clerical and factory jobs will be greatly reduced in number.[39] Women are also less likely to be offered training as machinists and maintenance workers which will be the jobs mainly available in automatized factories.

The general upgrading of the average skill levels of workers may be expected to have some effect on unions. Skilled workers have traditionally

---

[38] For example, "in Washington recently there were several hundred empty jobs in the printing trades with no one around to do the work—and no program in operation to train unemployed individuals for these posts." Ben B. Seligman, "Automation and the State," *Commentary*, 37 (June, 1964), pp. 52–53.

[39] Jobs as waitresses and saleswomen are unaffected by automation.

favored strong unions, and with a tendency on the part of workers to seek protection from the continuing dislocations of automation, they will probably move into the unions in increasing numbers if the unions show the organizing skills to attract them—as they have in Sweden. Unions will probably also be strengthened by their increasing functions: At the present time some union leaders have noted a slackening of union loyalty[40] as unions are unable to provide many new advantages to their members; new kinds of dependence of members on unions will probably revive "solidarity" to a certain extent. On the other hand some traditional enemies of unions will disappear: piecework pay, incentive systems, the speedup, and other features associated with individual production. Also, as part of the long-run trend associated with increasing productivity, the service industries will hire a steadily increasing proportion of the labor force,[41] and this element has traditionally been the hardest to unionize, although it may become less so if it is increasingly recruited from persons previously unionized. Union contracts can be expected to develop new kinds of provisions concerning seniority, incentive systems, layoff and other security provisions.[42]

The changes already noted, if they come to pass, will have a great effect on the daily lives of ordinary people. The changes in location, jobs, skill, training, and retraining are obvious. There will also be a shift of workers from one industry to another, as some industries are automatized while others are not, and as new industries are created to satisfy new "needs." The great increase in productivity may be expected to have two types of profound effects on the average man: 1) real incomes and the standard of living will probably be sharply raised, and 2) hours of work will probably be sharply reduced.[43] These changes will, of course, have innumerable secondary effects which can be guessed but not predicted

[40] Total union membership went down slightly from 1956 to 1964, but then started to rise again. *New York Times*, June 1, 1964, p. 1.

[41] Colin Clark, *The Conditions of Economic Progress* (London: Macmillan, 1940).

[42] In fact many labor disputes today focus on the questions of job security and fringe benefits equally with the ever-present demand for higher wages and shorter hours. The longshoremen's dispute on the West Coast, for example, was concerned mainly with job security as automation increasingly eliminated jobs. Even white-collar professions, teachers and government employees, for example, have been actively struggling in disputes where the issues of fringe benefits and better working conditions take precedence, as in the recent teachers' strikes in New York and elsewhere.

[43] It is difficult to predict the extent of the rise of wages and reduction in working hours, as they will be a function, not only of increase in productivity, but also of 1) the extent to which the proceeds of increased productivity are transmitted throughout the economy; 2) the probable increase in economic demand; 3) the change in the age structure of the population. Still, a responsible economist has predicted a four-day work week with a 20 per cent increase in average income by the 1970's. (George L. Ridgeway, director of economic research for International Business Machines Corporation, *New York Times*, March 27, 1955, p. 82.)

with any accuracy. Two are especially worthy of speculation. 1) The continuation of the rise in the standard of living will reduce still further the consumption differentials between the classes, especially as automatically produced goods will be of higher quality.[44] The lower income groups will be able to afford more of the luxuries now available only to the wealthy.[45] 2) There will be a great flowering of leisure-time activities for the "common man." Present trends suggest the great variation in this development: not only will there be more recreation and social "participation" of the usual types, but there will be more small "sideline" service businesses, "do-it-yourself" improvements around the home, gardening, "creative art" work. Since many people are not adequately prepared for spending large amounts of leisure time, the sudden increase of it will also probably cause some boredom and dissatisfaction. New small industries and occupations will arise to cater to the increased leisure of the population; some of this will undoubtedly be exploitative. This refers to the United States; no attempt is made to predict the effects of the increase in leisure time in less industrialized countries.

Education will necessarily be greatly affected by automation. Industries that automatize will usually be compelled, if they wish to get adequate workers quickly, to train workers in the new skills required. But the training of the youth in preparation for their life careers will probably continue to take place in the kinds of schools now in existence. Already there are pressures to change these schools to meet the needs of the new industrialization. 1) At the secondary school level, there will be strong need for providing good technical training. Since teachers adequately trained in these fields are now decreasing in number because of the relatively low salary scale, not only will salaries be raised (by federal or industry aid plans) but differential salaries by fields may be expected to appear. 2) At the university level, the rise of engineering, natural science and social science may be expected to be continued at the expense of the humanities and "education." The humanities can continue to perform their vital function in general education only by increasingly serving as adjuncts to science majors rather than so much as majors in their own right. It is increasingly recognized that managers and engineers need the breadth that the humanities provides. Higher education will continue to be increasingly important for social mobility. Leadership in industry, government, and civic life generally will depend increasingly on ability to understand, al-

[44] The higher quality resulting from automation is stressed by William Newberg, Vice President of the Chrysler Corporation, in a speech on January 11, 1955. The economist Yale Brozen predicts that automation will raise wage rates generally, even on jobs that are not automated. See Yale Brozen, "The Economics of Automation," *The American Economic Review,* 47 (May, 1957), pp. 339–50.

[45] As now, the "excess" income of the wealthy will be spent outside of personal consumption.

though perhaps not to practice, the newer technology and the social readjustments that it entails.

The effects on government of the changes in technology will be secondary in the sense that they will be contingent upon the changes in industry and labor predicted above. If there is geographic decentralization of factories and people, the numerous physical and cultural services now provided by city governments will have to be provided by state and federal government, or by new metropolitan or regional authorities not yet in existence. Already the movement to the suburbs is straining the cities' ability to collect taxes to provide the services which suburbanites insist on using. If ownership of industry is concentrated in a decreasing number of firms, government controls on these firms may be expected to multiply. Since the new "monopolies" will not be inefficient or restrictive of output, but the contrary, the new government controls will move in the direction of the pattern set by the Federal Communications Commission and the Securities and Exchange Commission rather than to the old-fashioned "trust-busting" set up by the Sherman and Clayton Acts.

Increased "social security"—as protection for non-earning during unemployment, retraining periods, and old age—is already being recognized as a necessity for personal and social stability. Social security will be increasingly necessary as there is increasing technological unemployment and loss of incidental privileges from jobs long held, in the form of pension rights, vacation rights, seniority generally, and so on. Probably not all of the compensating security benefits will be organized by government, as some unions have already been moving toward forcing industry to provide severance pay and a "guaranteed annual wage."[46] Government will take a new role in education, under the pressure of industry and workers alike. Federal aid to education will be enacted, and in the coming years it will have to become a major part of school revenues. It is even likely that the federal government will provide increasing funds to private colleges, as it has already begun to do in the form of research subsidies, scholarships and fellowships, and agricultural extension work. "Industrial extension" activities, including workers' education, can be predicted as a federal government activity in the near future.

Internal migration policies will probably become necessities for industrialized countries, representing a development which democratic nations have never embarked on before. These can be kept within the democratic framework by being voluntary for the worker. There always has been a tremendous personal and social waste in migration, which government could inexpensively obviate. With the relocations required

---

[46] The United Automobile Workers Union has, thus far, done more to call attention to and plan for the social consequences of the new technology than any other social organization.

by the coming technological changes, industry as well as workers will find a federal migration aid service almost essential. Information on job opportunities, job requirements, and wage levels can parallel the crop reporting service the federal government has long provided. Small loans to pay for transportation of families and household goods cannot be provided by the usual lending agencies, limited as they are by their collection facilities and by state law, so that a federal agency will probably have to be set up for this purpose. Aid in finding housing and in helping migrants adjust to new communities will be social services that will be greatly in demand. These and other related innovations can best be serviced by a Division of Migration Service in one of the existing departments of the federal government.

The dynamics of international relations are so complex that it is hazardous to speculate on the influence of the coming technological changes on them. Still, there are bound to be significant effects. One of the major factors in world politics today is the discrepancy in productive capacity between the industrialized nations and the so-called "underdeveloped" nations. The new technology will increase that gap. We speak of India, Africa, and China struggling to "catch" up with the Western industrialized nations; the first impact of the newer technology will leave them far behind in a relative sense. Automation will require relatively large amounts of capital and specialized skills, which these countries and others even more technologically backward do not have. If, on the other hand, capital and skill-training are given to them by countries which can easily provide them, they will be able to move from their present pre- or early-industrial stage to ultra-modern times in one quick step. Their cultures, their intellectuals, and their government bureaucracies may resist such gifts or loans, but these may not be able to resist the popular demand for a higher standard of living. The biggest task, of course, will be to train a sufficient number of engineers, workers, and business executives to handle the new production, but if this is done it will result in new contacts and new understandings between the technologically advanced and underdeveloped nations.

The technologically-backward countries have an advantage in not having a large capital investment in the technology of the first, second, and third industrial revolutions. Such an investment may hold the advanced countries back unless they are willing to scrap much of their present "wealth," as England was held back when her capital commitments to the first and second industrial revolutions prevented her from taking advantage of the third. Some engineers estimate that 70 per cent of all machine tools in use in the United States in 1955 were outmoded;[47] that is quite a large

[47] A. H. Ruskin, "Automation Parts Industry on Eve of Fantastic Robot Era," *New York Times,* April 8, 1955, p. 14.

investment to scrap, but it is now occurring. Another way in which automation will fit in especially well with the underdeveloped nations arises
out of the fact that most of their towns and cities are small and scattered.
Automatic production does not need the large industrial cities developed
in the past 150 years in Western countries. In this one respect, automation
will obviate the dislocations caused by extreme urbanization, and still allow
the benefits of industrialization to come to the underdeveloped countries.

The new source of energy will also help the underdeveloped countries
when it becomes available at competitive prices: fissionable materials
(and materials that are likely to become fissionable as science works at
them during the coming decades) are much more scattered over the earth's
surface than are coal and oil, and in any case are much more cheaply
transported. In general, the coming industrial revolution will be more
exportable to Asia, Africa, and South America than the early industrial
revolutions were (the training of personnel remaining a major block), and
hence the long run may see a narrowing of the productive capacity between
technologically advanced and underdeveloped nations. Even technologically advanced countries short on coal and oil—like Italy and Japan—
will be helped by a shift to atomic energy, and the prospects are for a
lessening of the differential in productivity that has characterized the world
since 1775.

To speak of the effects of the coming industrial revolution on the
"mental life" of man is even more speculative, because no one is certain
just what this mental life consists of. But a base unmeasured does not
mean a base non-existent, and dynamic phenomena can sometimes be more
readily charted than static ones. We have heard much of "alienation from
work" and the meaninglessness of specialized jobs in the total productive
process as a consequence of the machines, the assembly line, and the "industrial engineering" of the previous industrial revolutions. The coming
industrial revolution may be expected to move in the opposite direction.
The new worker will typically be a skilled and technically educated worker,
not an unskilled or semiskilled worker such as the earlier industrial revolutions called for. The worker in an automatized factory will be able to
"see" a given productive process from beginning to end. His job will be
to control, tend, and repair the machines, rather than being forced to let
the machines set the rhythm of his work.[48]

On the other hand, machines will be much more complex; hence
science and technology will be as much a "mystery" as ever to those not
oriented to science. Whether the mysterious forces be perceived as benevolent or malevolent will, of course, depend on the degree of adjustment the
worker is allowed or helped to make to the new economy, the amount of

[48] Bernard Karsh, "The Meaning of Work in an Age of Automation," *Current Economic
Comment*, 3 (August, 1957), pp. 3–13.

extra-economic trouble science and technology cause him, the degree of control he retains over his personal fate, and the satisfactoriness of the explanation of science and technology given to him. The American and English people, at least, are now being psychologically prepared for automation, and if those who provide clear explanations dominate over those who give vent to scare stories, the process of mass adjustment to the concept of automation will be much easier.

There will probably be fewer of the heavier, dirtier, and more boring jobs in automatized factories than in equivalent contemporary plants, and factory work generally will be cleaner and safer. Many workers will be able to wear "white collars" instead of overalls. Thus, labor will not be so deadening and humiliating to the spirit as it sometimes is now. Diebold goes so far as to say:

> In an odd and entirely unexpected way, automation may bring us back to the human and psychological values of the self-respecting craftsman. Electrical and mechanical repair work, instrument adjustment, and general mechanical tinkering can provide challenges, pleasures, and satisfactions very much like those enjoyed by the swordsmith or cabinetmaker of old.[49]

And the engineers, Brown and Campbell, make this more specific:

> Even in the most robotized of the automatic functions there will be many men, and they will have interesting and responsible jobs. They will be freed from the timing, nerve-racking or even boring jobs of today's mass manufacturing. To win this freedom, however, they will have to upgrade themselves in skill and sophistication. The new controllers and instruments will call for a higher level of precision of repair and maintenance. A $50,000 controller cannot be hit with a hammer if the shaft doesn't fit into the hole on the first try. Men who have heretofore thought of electronic equipment as simply a metal chassis with tubes will become conversant with switching, flip-flop, peaking, and other circuits. They will have to judge when to repair and when to throw away rather than stop production. We have here a paradox: Today we cannot afford not to have lots of control, because a half-day shutdown of a plant may mean a $100,000 loss in potential sales.
>
> These robots are not hurting the workman—they merely coax him none too gently into taking more responsible jobs, making bigger decisions, studying and using his mind as well as his hands.[50]

On the other hand, the really unpleasant jobs characteristic of the mining and slaughtering industries will probably not be capable of being

[49] *Op. cit.*, p. 164.
[50] Gordon S. Brown and Donald P. Campbell, "Control Systems," *Scientific American*, 187 (September, 1955), p. 64.

automatized in the next few decades. But hours of work will go down in all industries, and this may make even the most unpleasant of occupations more bearable. The mental life of the worker of the future will be much more determined by what he does during his leisure time than what he does during his working hours. As his job ceases to dominate his time, political, family, religious, "cultural" (in the narrow popular sense) activities can take on greater significance for the average citizen. It is difficult to see how a democratic state can channel leisure-time activities, except by making desired facilities—sports, other recreational, artistic and cultural facilities—more freely available. But whatever forces mold the leisure hours of the future citizen will mold the future to a greater extent than any other set of factors.

If the social consequences of the technological changes occur as we have predicted them, the net prognosis over the long run seems to be for a happier people, provided the upsets of the transition do not panic people into a frightened reaction which will destroy democracy along with the modern technology. Planning and a little intelligent activity on the part of public and private organizations can reduce the incidental hardships greatly. This can be done by greater investment, both by private business and by government, in the production of goods and services that people want and need, and by efforts to eliminate and compensate for the unemployment created by technological advancement.[51]

D   Culture Contact as a Source of Social Change

Let us turn now to a second theory of social change, the theory of social contact and cultural diffusion. This theory, in brief, holds that major changes in a society occur as a result of contact with other societies. In part the theory arises out of an older anthropological conception of the central importance of diffusion of cultural elements. Some of the early diffusionists carried their ideas to an extreme form, holding that if similar cultural traits were to be found in widely separated societies then there must have been an earlier contact between these two societies which could be traced historically.[52] In other words, they did not acknowledge the existence of independent invention.

[51] The specific character of this unemployment and the special difficulties it creates will be considered in Chapter 15, Section D.

[52] Fritz Graebner, *Methode der Ethnologie* (Heidelberg, 1911). For discussions of the earlier anthropological theory and research on diffusion of culture, see Robert H. Lowie, *History of Ethnological Theory* (New York: Farrar and Rinehart, 1937); Alexander Goldenweiser, "Cultural Anthropology," in H. E. Barnes (ed.), *History and Prospects of the Social Sciences* (New York: Alfred A. Knopf, 1925); A. L. Kroeber, "Diffusionism," *Encyclopedia of the Social Sciences* (New York: Macmillan, 1932); G. Elliot Smith *et al.*, *Culture: The Diffusion Controversy* (New York: Norton, 1927); Melville Herskovits, *Man and His Works* (New York: Alfred A. Knopf, 1938), Chapters 30–31.

The modern theory is much less extreme. It recognizes the possibility of independent invention. When people with divergent cultural backgrounds come in contact there may be borrowing from one culture to another of certain elements of the culture, and there also may be new independent invention resulting from the stimulation of people with different ideas coming in contact with another people.[53] In a society as complex as ours, and having so many contacts over time and space with other cultures, most of the individual elements have been borrowed, although the unique synthesis has been developed here.[54]

The early anthropological research traced the patterns of past diffusions of culture complexes across societies, and the early sociological research had to do with the influence of the metropolis on its satellites, the effectiveness of natural and legal boundaries as barriers to diffusion, the flow of innovation in "concentric circle" waves across the country. Modern anthropological research has shifted to "acculturation" or ongoing rather than historical intergroup contacts.[55] Modern sociological research studies the influence of mass communications,[56] the acceptance of new farm practices,[57] the rate of acceptance of educational innovations,[58] the acceptance of new health practices,[59] the acceptance of new products following advertising campaigns,[60] and the spread of other cultural practices or

[53] The theory probably has its roots in the writings of anthropologists. Among sociologists, the work of Thomas and Znaniecki, Park and Miller, Chapin, and Wirth are important. See W. I. Thomas and F. Znaniecki, *The Polish Peasant in Europe and America* (Boston: Badger, 1918–19), 5 vols.; R. E. Park and H. A. Miller, *Old World Traits Transplanted* (Chicago: University of Chicago Press, 1921); R. E. Park, "Human Migration and the Marginal Man," *American Journal of Sociology*, 33 (May, 1928), pp. 881–93; L. Wirth, "Culture Conflicts in the Immigrant Family," unpublished M.A. thesis, University of Chicago, 1925; L. Wirth, *The Ghetto* (Chicago: University of Chicago Press, 1928); F. S. Chapin, *Cultural Change* (New York: Century, 1928); R. V. Bowers, "The Direction of Intra-Societal Diffusion," *American Sociological Review*, 2 (December, 1937), pp. 826–36; Edgar C. McVoy, "Patterns of Diffusion in the United States," *American Sociological Review*, 5 (April, 1940), pp. 219–27.

[54] Linton has an interesting discussion of this: Ralph Linton, *The Study of Man* (New York: Appleton-Century-Crofts, 1936), pp. 326–27.

[55] R. Redfield, R. Linton, and M. J. Herskovits, "Memorandum on the Study of Acculturation," *American Anthropologist*, 38 (January, March, 1936), pp. 149–52.

[56] J. T. Klapper, *The Effects of Mass Communication* (New York: Free Press of Glencoe, 1960), Part I.

[57] Herbert F. Lionberger, *Adoption of New Ideas and Practices* (Ames: Iowa State University Press, 1960); Everett M. Rogers, *Diffusion of Innovations* (New York: Macmillan, 1962).

[58] Walter Cocking, *The Regional Introduction of Educational Practices* (New York: Teachers College, Columbia University, 1951).

[59] Steven Polgar, "Health and Human Behavior: Areas of Interest Common to Social and Medical Sciences," *Current Anthropology*, 3 (April, 1962), pp. 159–79.

[60] *Public Opinion Index for Industry, The Tastemakers*, Vol. I (Princeton, N. J.: Opinion Research Corporation, April, 1959).

> The service of diffusion in enriching the content of individual cultures has been of the utmost importance. There is probably no culture extant to-day which owes more than 10 per cent of its total elements to inventions made by members of its own society.
>
> Ralph Linton, *The Study of Man* (New York: Appleton-Century-Crofts, 1936), p. 326.

products.[61] [In their comprehensive survey of the research on diffusion, Katz, Levin and Hamilton define the process of diffusion as the acceptance, over time, of some specific item (an idea or practice), by individuals, groups or other adopting units, linked to specific channels of communication, to a social structure, and to a given system of values.[62]]

The theory of culture contact assumes that societies in isolation tend to have stable cultures and that people in them believe that the ways in which they have always carried on their lives are satisfactory and unchangeable. The theory has some miscellaneous propositions associated with it. For example, anthropologists have found in their studies that the material aspects of culture diffuse more readily than non-material aspects, that culture patterns including mores resist diffusion more than do other culture patterns not including mores, that cultural elements diffuse more readily when the donating and receiving societies have had some history of contact and when the receiving society is not highly integrated, and that elements of an alien culture which fit into existing patterns of culture are more readily accepted than elements of an alien culture which conflict with existing patterns of culture. In accord with the last-mentioned principle, the meaning of a material culture object may change when it is adopted in another culture.

> Minor items of material culture may remain wholly constant in form but be given entirely altered use, meaning, and function in the accepting culture. The external appearance of the result is often ludicrous in the eyes of the donors. An explorer may give a used film spool to a native, who receives it with delight, puts it through the slit in his ear-lobe, and proudly struts his beauty. The form of the spool is unaltered, but its use becomes that of an ear labret, its meaning aesthetic, and its function that of prestige enhancement and ego gratification. The spool is culturally acceptable because it readily fits into the context of the native culture in a positive way.[63]

[61] For a systematic survey of modern research on diffusion, see Elihu Katz, Martin L. Levin, and Herbert Hamilton, "Traditions of Research on the Diffusion of Innovation," *American Sociological Review*, 28 (April, 1963), pp. 237-52.

[62] *Ibid.*, p. 240.

[63] E. Adamson Hoebel, *Man in the Primitive World* (New York: McGraw-Hill, 1949), p. 480.

Traditions can sometimes actually promote changes under the impact of contact with an alien culture. For example, when medical science was brought by Westerners to India, the Hindu custom of forbidding women to have close contact with men not their husbands acted to encourage women to study medicine so that women doctors would be available to serve women patients. Today about a fourth of all medical students in India are women, a proportion higher than in the United States and in many countries of western Europe.[64]

[Another important sub-hypothesis of the theory is that change arises from social contact partly through disorganization of existing values of the society. People are no longer so sure as to what is right and proper when they are confronted with two or more sets of cultural values, and they thereby become more willing to accept new ideas and new values.] [When one culture comes into contact with another culture, change does not come about simply because an alternative is presented but also because people are forced to realize that alternatives are possible and that values may be relative to a given people or a given culture. [Thus people placed in contact with other cultures become oriented toward change. They become willing to accept new ideas, new values, and new ways of life. They become inventive, not only technologically, but also in terms of social structure and social behavior patterns.

[A frequently cited example of the important role of culture contact in social change is that of the changes following the breaking down of the barriers to travel at the end of the Middle Ages.[65] The first traders with distant lands brought back tales of strange ways of living as well as wonderful material goods. Those who had participated in the Crusades could never fully accept the simple, unchanging, and narrow outlook which characterized their home villages. The Renaissance—that embodiment of rapid change following the relative stability of the Middle Ages—received its first and highest development in those areas which were in ready contact with other cultures, namely, the cities of Italy and of the Low Countries along the North Sea. Other historical evidence gives strong support to the theory: the fact that cities where cultures mix are more susceptible to change than isolated rural areas; the fact that coastal cities that have contacts with overseas lands change at a faster rate than do inland cities; the fact that population elements that have a wide range of cultural

---

[64] This is also an example of the unanticipated consequences of social change arising out of certain demands of the existing social structure. Merton has revived for sociologists the eighteenth-century term "serendipity," coined originally by Horace Walpole, as a label for this phenomenon. (Robert K. Merton, *Social Theory and Social Structure* [Glencoe, Ill.: Free Press, 1949], pp. 98–101.) Many natural scientists have long used the term "serendipity" to refer to unsought-for findings of research.

[65] A most perceptive description of these changes is that by Henri Pirenne, *Economic and Social History of Medieval Europe* (London: Kegan Paul, Trench, Trubner, 1936).

contacts (for example, the more educated people, people who travel a good deal) are known to be the inventors, innovators, and fashion leaders.

Social change arising from culture contact is apparently not reversible, despite deliberate efforts to reverse it and even when the culture contact is withdrawn. This does not mean that the culture which is changing always moves toward greater similarity to the other culture. Even the resistances and the reactions against the other culture create changes, although these do not bring the two cultures into greater harmony with each other. Numerous examples of this can be drawn from one of the most important changes going on in the world during the past two centuries. This is the spread of Western culture and the stimulus coming from Western culture, to Oriental, African, and primitive cultures. While the West has borrowed many things from these cultures, the main direction of influence has been from the West to the others. In recent years Western representatives in many of the other societies have either been pushed out or they have voluntarily withdrawn, but the influence toward change created by the West continues apace.

Striking cases of this occurred when American troops were stationed in out-of-the-way parts of the world during World War II. In 1944 United States Navy units were sent to Port Barrow, Alaska, one of the northernmost inhabited spots of the world, to construct large-scale naval installations and later to explore for oil. The Eskimos there were living in essentially a stone-age culture when they were employed as workers earning $400 to $600 a month.[66] From sod huts they moved into modern settlements of new homes, and in many other ways they adopted the culture of the United States. Then suddenly, in 1953, the Navy moved out, and the Eskimo community—which had grown from 400 to over 1,000 by attracting other Eskimos from settlements along the Arctic coast—was left stranded. The Eskimos took collective action: they helped to persuade the Alaska Airlines that Point Barrow was an interesting tourist spot during the summer months; they subscribed $35,000 to build a two-story modern hotel with windows facing the Arctic Ocean; they subscribed more money to build a clean, modern restaurant that served whale steak and other Eskimo delicacies and they constructed a motion-picture theater; they put on sale fur moccasins, ivory bracelets, and other curios; they planned conducted tours by outboard-motor-powered umiak (walrus-skin-hulled boat); one of them began writing a column for the *Fairbanks Daily News-Miner*. In the summer of 1954 nearly 300 tourists came and each stayed two or three days. By continuing their primitive hunting for food, and using the income

[66] This description is taken from a *New York Times* article of November 21, 1954 (p. 27), and from personal conversations with Dr. Robert Spencer, an anthropologist who spent almost six months studying these Eskimos.

> The slow cultural advance of societies which are left to their own abilities is well illustrated by the conditions in isolated human groups. Perhaps the outstanding example is the Tasmanians. These people were cut off from the rest of mankind at least 20,000 years ago. When they reached their island they seem to have had a culture which, in its material development at least, corresponds roughly to that of Europe during the Middle Paleolithic. They were still in this stage when Europeans first visited them during the eighteenth century. During the long period of isolation they had no doubt made some minor advances and improvements, but their lack of outside contacts was reflected in a tremendous culture lag. To cite a much less extreme example, the culture of some of our own isolated mountain communities still corresponds in many respects to that of the pioneers of a century ago. The first settlers of these isolated regions brought this culture with them, and their unaided efforts have contributed little to it. In general, the more opportunities for borrowing any society has the more rapid its cultural advance will be.
>
> Ralph Linton, *The Study of Man* (New York: Appleton-Century-Crofts, 1936), pp. 328–29.

from tourists for cash purchases, this community was able to continue to live in a modified modern American style.[67]

Sometimes it is only a few members of the preliterate society who make the permanent jump to modern civilization. In 1942 the Japanese invaded Netherlands New Guinea and quickly overwhelmed the primitive Papuans, who could resist them only with spear and fire.[68] The tribe of 200 persons we shall consider previously had very little contact with the outside world: their dwellings were palm-thatched huts set on stilts, and they lived largely on fish and coconuts. Herman Wormsiwor was then a boy of thirteen years who served the Japanese and learned not only their language but their modern industrious ways. When the United States Army invaded the area three years later, Wormsiwor joined it, acting as a guide and general handyman for an ammunition company. When the Army moved on, some soldiers smuggled the now-seventeen-year-old Papuan onto a ship going to Japan. He worked for the American Air Force there as an interpreter of Japanese, achieving a United States civil-service rating and a commendation. Meanwhile, he saved his money and took courses in economics, Japanese, and English at the International Students Institute in Tokyo. After nine years he returned to his native land, but found that he could not accommodate himself to the primitive life of his tribe. So he set up a trading cooperative for his people at the harbor at Biak, just fifteen

[67] For a detailed study of rapid social change in a "primitive" society, see Margaret Mead, *New Lives for Old: Cultural Transformation-Manus, 1928–1953* (New York: Morrow, 1956).

[68] This account is taken from an article by Robert Alden in the *New York Times*, January 20, 1955, p. 6, and February 13, 1955, p. 9.

miles from where he was born. "The natives contribute the goods they can provide—copra, seashells (for buttons), wild pigs, and a gluelike substance that comes from trees. Mr. Wormsiwor trades these products with the Dutch and local Chinese merchants for rice, cigarettes, sugar, and anything else that the natives want."[69] His equipment—a wartime warehouse, an old jeep, a rusty safe, office supplies—is crude, but he uses fairly modern business practices. In effect, he is a Western small businessman living at the edge of his native tribe. Other natives have remnants of American military equipment—in one village the walls of the homes are adorned with checkerboards, charts showing how to disassemble German anti-tank mines, and pictures of pin-up girls—but they have only the faintest idea of American culture. The marks of the war are disappearing, weeds are over-running the once-busy air strips, and the rotting hulks of amphibious landing craft are flaking away, but one native carries on a brisk business in American style with considerable knowledge of American ways.

Culture contact can bring in its train culture conflict, if the individuals involved are obliged to live their daily lives in a different culture from which they were raised or if they find it necessary to have regular contact with persons from another culture. We shall consider conflict in another connection,[70] but let us here simply consider the possibilities for social change arising out of culture conflict. A most important situation of this type is that of an immigrant's children who have been raised by their parents according to one set of cultural standards and very early in life come in contact—through their playmates and school associates—with a quite different set of cultural norms. Some of these children are quite unable to choose between the two sets, or even feel comfortable by acting completely in conformity with either one of them. Such persons have a culture conflict within themselves, and sociologists have called them "marginal men" because they are living at the edge of two cultures simultaneously

[69] *Idem.*
[70] See Chapter 16.

but are not completely part of either one.[71] The dissatisfaction and restlessness of these persons often lead them to innovate, to seek to become leaders of reform movements, to create special institutions or new ways of life for themselves which sometimes serve as patterns for the whole society. There is little doubt that marginal men contribute a disproportionate amount of change to society, in comparison to persons who know but one consistent set of cultural norms. Conflicts between any kinds of groups, not only nationality and culture groups, is stimulating and is likely to lead to innovations, if only in self-defense.[72]

Thus far we have been talking of culture contact as introducing something new, but it must also be remembered that innovation and cultural diffusion also destroy the older way of life. It is also to be considered as social change when a social practice declines and nothing takes its place. An example may be taken from the recent decline of the collective agricultural settlement (*Kibbutz*) in Israel.[73] While there are several reasons for this decline, one of the most important is the immigration to Israel after 1933 of an urbanized population from Europe that was neither able nor willing to go into agricultural work and to live a simple, collective life. Contact with advanced urbanized societies quite generally brings dissatisfaction to isolated rural societies and sometimes results in the gradual decay of certain social institutions in the latter.

E   *Social Movements as a Source of Social Change*

1   THE THEORY OF SOCIAL MOVEMENTS

A third theory of social change holds that it is a function of a social movement.[74] The theory, in brief, is this: A number of people feel a similar need due to some inadequacy in the social structure that prevents them from receiving adequate satisfactions of a certain type. They feel restless because of this dissatisfaction. Through talking among themselves, some of them realize that the need they feel is one common to many of them and in fact common to others who are not aware of the similarity of their

[71] Everett V. Stonequist, *The Marginal Man* (New York: Scribner's, 1937). In the preface to this book, Robert E. Park defined the marginal man as "one whom fate has condemned to live in two societies and in two, not merely different but antagonistic, cultures" (p. xv).

[72] Lewis A. Coser, "Social Conflict and the Theory of Social Change," *British Journal of Sociology*, 8 (September, 1957), pp. 197–207.

[73] From an unpublished paper, "The Decline of the Collective Settlements in Israel," by Samuel Koenig, delivered to the American Sociological Society, September 4, 1952. The *Kibbutz* is a collectively owned and collectively operated type of settlement founded by Jews in Palestine after 1909, as a means of carrying on economic and social life under the threat of marauding Arabs and as a means of putting into practice a socialist ideal.

[74] This theory has been best expressed by Herbert Blumer; see his "Collective Behavior" in A. M. Lee (ed.), *New Outline of the Principles of Sociology* (New York: Barnes and Noble, 1946).

problem to that of others. The discussions lead to a common understanding, whether correct or not, that the need can be satisfied by making some change in the social structure, sometimes by passing a law, and sometimes by making a more extensive change in the cultural way of life. A process of public opinion formation occurs, in which more and more people believe that this need can be satisfied by making some change in the social structure. Also the intensity of the belief and the interest in doing something about solving the problem increase in a certain, although perhaps very small, proportion of the public.[75] In general, the structure of a movement is at first amorphous; later it may take on organization, a body of traditions, division of labor, rules, and a specific hierarchy of social values.

The change created by a social movement is often in the nature of an innovation that is like an invention (or series of inventions), except that it occurs in the non-material structure of the society rather than in its material means. For example, the founding in 1909 of the first collective settlement (Kibbutz) in Israel was such an innovation in the way of living and involved a number of deliberate and accidental experiments to develop to a point of widespread usefulness, just as any material invention does. Many of the reforms in government developed by social movements—such as the social-security system adopted in many Western countries—are similar social inventions.[76] Since economic depressions are generally periods of widespread dissatisfaction, it may be said that depressions are a stimulant to social change by means of social movements, just as periods of economic prosperity are stimulants to social change by means of inventions.

Under a dictatorial government, those highly motivated to change conditions may take the risk of seeking to gain the sympathetic ear of government officials. If they fail, and their motivation is very high to make the change which they believe to be necessary, they usually become revolutionary leaders. Under a democratic government the process of formation of a social movement is quite different, and most of our description of the theory will indicate how it applies to a democratic society. The leaders who are highly motivated to make the social change do not move toward revolution in a democratic society unless they become convinced that it is impossible to convince the majority of the people that the social change is desirable. Thus revolution is likely to occur in a democratic society only if, among other things, a minority believes that it cannot acquire access to the channels of public opinion or that, if it does gain access, it cannot convince the masses of the correctness of its plan for social change. In other words, if change—whether "good" or "bad"—is easy to effectuate by peaceful means, revolutions are not likely to occur.

[75] See Chapter 9, Section D.

[76] One of the best descriptions of the development of a series of social inventions, in Sweden, is contained in Alva Myrdal, *Nation and Family* (New York: Harper, 1941).

In the United States and in many of the other democracies access to the channels of public opinion is readily available to any determined group, and, if the change desired is not too radical, usually some converts can be acquired by an effort of communication. There are some political democracies, however, where the general atmosphere is one of hopelessness concerning the possibility of convincing large sections of the population, either because reform leaders believe that the masses are too stupid or illiterate or because they believe that people would never go against the dominant tradition or the wishes of those in power. Also in some political democracies channels of public opinion are not readily accessible to even well-organized groups. Under such circumstances revolution can also develop. These conditions occur to a certain extent in the political democracies of Italy and France, where the desire for social change often takes a revolutionary form.

We know very little about the factors associated with the success or failure of social movements.[77] A systematic comparative theory is needed, both within one given society and across societies. When dealing with the failure of a given movement, it should be understood that this is failure in terms of the explicit goals of the movement: an "unsuccessful" movement may still be a considerable force for social change of the unanticipated kind. Of course, even successful movements have social effects considerably beyond what they were intended to have. Sometimes schisms develop within a movement over its divergent effects.

2   REFORM MOVEMENTS

In the Scandinavian, Anglo-Saxon, and American democracies, on the other hand, desire for social change is much more likely to take the form of a movement for social reform rather than revolution. Those who are highly motivated to secure the social reform do not organize secretly to seize control of the channels of communication and of political power. Rather, they organize openly into voluntary associations[78] the purpose of which is generally to convince the public, or key sectors of it, that their goals should be formally and generally adopted. While many voluntary associations are plagued with high turnover of membership and an inefficient administration, their efforts to secure social change are usually rewarded by at least small successes. This is because they can gain some access to the channels of public opinion without too much difficulty and because they work continuously, even if haphazardly, to effectuate the changes, whereas most of the rest of the population is at first apathetic and unconcerned.

[77] C. Wendell King, *Social Movements in the United States* (New York: Random House, 1956).

[78] For a fuller discussion of voluntary associations, see Chapter 10.

Not all of the efforts to seek social changes are motivated by a desire to improve conditions for society as a whole. Many of them, on the contrary, are motivated solely by the desire to enhance the power or wealth of the individual members of the group, who find that their individual selfish interests can best be achieved by cooperative efforts. Such groups as businessmen's associations, trade unions, and professional organizations generally have as their primary function the increase in their economic bargaining power as opposed to each other or to the community at large. When groups of this type seek to get the government to pass a law or grant an administrative change that will benefit the members of the group, they are known as "pressure groups." Some voluntary associations work for the benefit of their own members, but not at the expense of non-members. Such, for example, would be the various self-education groups or organizations as the Parent-Teachers Association. Whether working for their own selfish interests or for the benefit of the community as a whole, whether they actually do some good for the society or not, the voluntary associations of the action type are creators of social change in a democracy.

Jerome Davis[79] summarizes succinctly the typical life cycle and rationale of a reform movement, although his statement is oversimplified.

> Every social movement tends to traverse a cycle of change. First of all, there arises a tangible need, and some individual or group begins to voice this need more or less publicly. Second, propaganda and agitation result. Third, there follows a growing consciousness of this need in a small or large group. Fourth, they organize. Fifth, concerted action and strong leadership develop and new converts are won. Sixth, if the movement is successful it becomes institutionalized —becomes the pattern of the majority, and group control sets in. Anyone who does not conform to the new pattern code is disciplined. Seventh, eventually bureaucracy, inflexibility, and reaction become dominant. When this occurs someone usually feels a new need and either the institution changes to meet that need or in time it is superseded. This cycle could be applied to the movement for the abolition of slavery or to the prohibition drive in our own country. It may be asked why institutions tend to become fossilized. It is because they are products of the past. The very function of an institution is to give stability to society. Institutions are like the great steel beams and giant metal ribs of an ocean liner. They knit our social life together. Leaders of institutions are usually prosperous and comfortable once their goal is achieved; inevitably they tend to conservatism and reaction. This attitude is reinforced by the natural conservatism of the common people and of the dominant group. Neither will lightly jeopardize present welfare for a radical change. Furthermore, the institu-

[79] *Contemporary Social Movements* (New York: Century, 1930), pp. 8–9.

tion, through its control of the mediums of thought and expression, consciously tries to inculcate an attitude of loyalty and pride towards the institution, which further conserves and preserves that institution.

Blumer[80] finds it convenient to distinguish between three types of social movements: the general-purpose movement, the specific-purpose movement, and the expressive movement. The social movement with a general purpose—such as the labor movement or the peace movement— arises out of a gradual and general shift in people's conception of themselves and of their relation to society. Under these new values people develop ideas about what their place should be in society that do not conform to the actual situation. These ideas are at first vague and the early activities of a social movement are therefore tentative and uncoordinated. Nevertheless, the young general-purpose movement has a direction and it spreads into many areas of life. It grows by fits and starts—sometimes having decades of relative stagnation and even retrogression—but the changed attitudes of people inevitably bring them back to a concern with changing the structure of society. Stimulus for increased activity usually comes from articulate leaders and from published writings. The leaders do not set the direction of the movement, but they help to state the goals and to break down individual resistance to change. Both the leaders and the literature tend to be vague and utopian.

A social movement with a specific purpose, because it has a well-defined goal, develops an organization and a pattern of activities. The initial unrest becomes crystallized through agitation and intense communication so that the movement can take form. While the leaders at the inception of a specific social movement are of the type called "prophets" or "reformers," these are gradually replaced by "politicians" and "administrators." The early leader's function is to jar the people loose from their customary ways of thinking and to specify for them the goals that will realize their new desires. He does not create the goals, but he translates the needs and values of the people into concrete and practicable terms. That is, he helps to create new meanings without creating new values.

As people become aroused and accept the goals set up for them, they develop a loyalty to the goals and to each other. This may be termed the morale of the movement, since the strength of the feeling determines the extent to which the members of the movement can be counted on to work for the goals and to avoid being disheartened by obstacles. The growth of a body of defense doctrine, myths, a tradition of success in action, close association of members and ceremonials, also increase morale.[81]

While voluntary associations of the social-influence type are characteristic features of reform movements in urban democratic society, other

---

[80] *Op. cit.,* pp. 199–220.
[81] For a fuller discussion of morale, see Chapter 17.

types of societies have other means of achieving reforms by means of deliberate efforts. Dictatorships use force and "encouragement." For example, Soviet Russia has organized an atheistic movement and a Stakhanovite movement (to get people to work harder). The Turkish dictatorship of Kemal Ataturk changed the alphabet and educated the population to use it almost by fiat. The old, complicated Arabic script was replaced with a Latin alphabet, and millions took lessons. Every book was reprinted and every public sign changed. In less-industrialized societies reforms can be initiated by traditional leaders and carried through by informal groups.[82]

3   REVOLUTIONARY MOVEMENTS

Revolutionary movements are quite often like reform movements in their initial stages, although the dissatisfactions that give rise to them are usually much more profound and widespread.[83] The motivations of those who join revolutionary movements must be strong enough to resist the dominant power and often even the dominant tradition of the society. The major distinction of the revolutionary movement from the reform movement is that its aims are not specific but cover a wide range of goals covering many areas of social life. The revolutionary movement is always directed against the government, whereas the reform movement is only occasionally so directed. Reform movements never go much beyond legal limits in seeking to achieve their goals, although some reform activities have involved a certain amount of violence and even bloodshed.[84]

Revolutionary activities, on the other hand, always have something of the character of warfare about them. They involve the war of a discontented element of the society against the holders of political power. As a kind of warfare, revolutions never hesitate to use violence. On the other hand, there have been some bloodless revolutions when the group in power has voluntarily surrendered before the revolution got too far under way, and there was a transfer of power from the group in control to the new group without violence or bloodshed. If violence is employed, it may range from the spontaneous crowd kind of violence that we considered in an earlier chapter[85] to the organized military warfare such as we found in

---

[82] Such reforms are not frequent by American standards; but they do occur occasionally.

[83] For a fuller description of the conditions giving rise to revolutions, and the characteristic features of revolutions themselves, see Lyford P. Edwards, *The Natural History of Revolution* (Chicago: University of Chicago Press, 1927); Crane Brinton, *The Anatomy of Revolution* (New York: Norton, 1938); Rex D. Hopper, "The Revolutionary Process," *Social Forces,* 28 (March, 1950), pp. 270–79; Pitirim A. Sorokin, *Social and Cultural Dynamics* (Boston: Porter Sargent, 1957), especially Chapter 35.

[84] For example, the reform involved in desegregating the public schools of the South has involved and probably will continue to involve a certain amount of violence.

[85] See Chapter 9, Section A.

the Civil War in the United States or the Spanish Revolution of 1935–39. In addition to violence, a revolutionary movement is characterized by the use of other means to achieve its goal: slogans, fanatic but expert leadership, ringing public addresses that influence a much larger audience than that which is in immediate attendance, highly organized structure, use of mass media of communication, usually underground formulation of manifestos, and the creation of complex ideologies to support and justify the goals of the movement.

Edwards[86] and Brinton[87] have independently worked out a scheme of "typical" stages in the development of revolution, which Gorrow finds he can readily synthesize in the following way:[88]

> Revolutions are found to progress through the following consciously planned typical stages: (1) unrest, (2) the defection of the intellectuals, (3) the emergence of an economic incentive and social myth, (4) the outbreak, (5) the rule of the moderates, (6) the rise of the radicals or the accession of the extremists, (7) the reign of terror, and (8) the return to normality and reaction.

After a revolution has reached the turning point, and the victory of one side over the other has been decided, the leaders of the opposition group are usually eliminated from the society. In milder revolutions this elimination has occurred by means of exile, but in many revolutions imprisonment and execution are the common treatment of the opposition leaders. If the revolution has been successful, a series of radical changes are generally made in the society in an effort to satisfy the needs which gave rise to the revolutionary movement. Some, but not all, of these radical changes generally have to be modified shortly, partly because they are untried and hence often unworkable and partly because they do not jibe with the rest of the structure of the society and have to be changed so that the society can continue to function. This does not mean, however, that the society ever returns to its condition before the revolution. While all societies are in constant change, there is no doubt that revolution accelerates change and often sets it off in new directions. The leadership of a successful revolution also changes after a few years in power, since successful leaders of the violent stages of a revolution are people who have aptitudes and skills as agitators or military innovators whereas the organizers of new social structures have to be good as administrators, and these two types of abilities are seldom to be found in a single person. Because of these two types of changes a revolutionized society might become quite stable within a few years after its "terror" stage.

[86] *Op. cit.*
[87] *Op. cit.*
[88] Bernard J. Gorrow, "The Comparative Study of Revolution," *Midwest Sociologist,* 17 (Spring, 1955), pp. 54–59.

If the revolutionary group fails, on the other hand, and its leaders are wiped out, it is unlikely that no social changes will be made and that the society will continue in its old ways. The motive forces and the needs that gave rise to the revolution in the first place are still present, and the successful party in power usually finds it expedient to attempt a series of reforms to satisfy those needs and to appease these forces. The changes are not nearly so drastic as would occur if the revolutionary party had been successful, but the success of the old government in power sometimes leads to a number of changes that make further motivation to revolution unnecessary and undesired. This is by no means always the case, however, and if the successful government does not make radical changes to satisfy the needs that gave rise to the revolution, the seeds of the revolution remain, and when new leaders arise and the unsuccessful forces have regained their strength the revolution may once again break out. Such seems to be the situation in Spain and several countries of Latin America today.

4   EXPRESSIVE MOVEMENTS: FADS AND FASHIONS

A third kind of social movement, the expressive movement—which is best represented by fashions and fads—does not have the organized character of the reform and revolutionary movements.[89] In expressive movements, people's needs are very vague and their motivations are hardly conscious. Instead of there being a public recognition that a certain change in government or social organization would satisfy their needs, people simply have vague feelings of restlessness that take overt form in a non-specific desire for more color in their clothing, for example, or an inexplicable "need" for sharp lines and jagged edges rather than rounded curves, which now appear ugly. Expressive movements develop new forms of behavior in which people can symbolically relieve their tension and unrest.

The specific form of a fashion may be set by a group of fashion designers, in women's clothing, for example, but the experience of these people—whose economic situation is often improved by a change in fashion —is that only a small proportion of the changes they design are successful in "catching on."[90] The upper classes, who are more able economically to discard the old elements around them and to adopt the new fashions, are generally the pace setters in fashion, whereas the middle and lower classes cannot afford to follow them until after a period of months or

---

[89] Only a small part of the valuable literature on fashions is strictly scholarly. One of the best studies is that of Alfred L. Kroeber and Jane Richardson, *Three Centuries of Women's Dress Fashions* (1940). The more popular literature that is worth reading includes Elizabeth Hawes, *Fashion Is Spinach* (New York: Random House, 1938); Elizabeth Burris-Meyer, *This Is Fashion* (New York: Harper, 1943); M. D. C. Crawford, *The Ways of Fashion* (New York: Putnam's, 1941); Russell Lynes, *The Tastemakers* (New York: Harper, 1954).

[90] Crawford, *op. cit.*, pp. 16, 149, 249; Roy Sheldon and E. Arens, *Consumer Engineering* (New York: Harper, 1932), pp. 127–28.

years.[91] In some cases, the better-educated people lead in adopting a fashion because they are more accessible to the scientists, writers, or other professional people who set off a fashion—in child care, for example. On the other hand, certain fashions—such as those involved in juke-box playing and drinking Coca-Cola—are more likely to begin in the lower classes and spread from them into the middle- and upper-income groups.

Expressive movements are just as much related to the general condition of society as are reform and revolutionary movements. A society will have a period in which it goes in for fashions and fads at a much more rapid rate than it does in another period. In general a society that is organized mainly in the form of an audience[92] has many more expressive movements than a society that takes the form of an integrated group. The dissatisfactions and needs that give rise to expressive movements, however, are much less clear both to the participants in the society and even to outside observers. The needs themselves are not specific but rather consist of a vague restlessness or *Weltschmerz*. The specific fashions seem to satisfy members of the society, at least temporarily, probably because of their symbolic significance—unconscious meanings that tie them in a not-at-all-obvious way to real problems within the society—and because they offer evidence of change at a time when change seems to be desired for its own sake rather than for any specific purpose. For example, it may be that the nineteenth-century fashions of large complicated "Victorian" houses, with their ornate "dust-catching" furniture and large, ruffled hoop- and petticoat-supported dresses were expressions of the "need" of Victorian women to find new "functions" in house and dress care when their eighteenth-century functions declined as a result of the Industrial Revolution and its concomitants.

A fashion movement does not develop a social structure, leadership, division of labor or morale, but it belongs under the category of social movements by virtue of the fact that it removes dissatisfaction with an existing social situation. It "changes" the situation, but only symbolically. People express their unrest in something new which seems objectively to have little to do with the cause of the unrest. But the mere creation of something new serves subjectively to change the old situation.

Not all fashion movements involve new behavior patterns in the sense that they have never before been followed. Some of them copy, in great detail, the discarded behavior patterns of an earlier period, as in the case of the 1953–54 fashion among teen-age British youths to wear "Edwardian" clothing.[93] The costume involves tight trousers, brocaded vests, high-

---

[91] On the other hand, modern women clothes' designers depend on being copied by the mass producers; see Hawes, *op. cit.*, pp. 108–09; Paul M. Gregory, "Fashion and Monopolistic Competition," *Journal of Political Economy*, 56 (February, 1948), pp. 69–75.

[92] See Chapter 9, Section B.

[93] Peter D. Whitney, in the *New York Times Magazine*, June 6, 1954, pp. 17 ff.

buttoned jackets with narrow lapels, velvet collars, and sleeves with turned-back cuffs. Hair is worn long, with a crest effect or a pompadour. The outfit is used for dress purposes by children of both the lower and the middle classes. Behavior toward girls typically is courtly and respectful. Explanations of the fashion are varied, but one hypothesis interprets it in terms of the youths' efforts to recapture the security, elegance, vitality, and optimism of their grandfathers' generation.

Expressive movements become more frequent not only when there is increasing dissatisfaction with the social order, but also when social movements with general or specific purposes are not feasible. The latter are not feasible when people cannot imagine ways of overcoming their problems (because the problems are so complex) or when social pressures—including restricting governments—do not allow them to act to overcome their problems. Not enough is known about expressive movements to provide adequate scientific support to the points we have mentioned about them; but there can be little doubt that expressive movements give us our most important clues to the hidden, unconscious characteristics of our society. The changes they bring about seem to have no relationship to any specific obvious "need" of the society, but they create important—and sometimes lasting—changes nevertheless.

There is an expressive element in most reform and revolutionary movements, usually in the form of a "mystique," or an attribution of inevitability and naturalness to the direction and goal of the reform or revolution. As Marcus points out,[94] there is assumed to be an Idea behind history, and the facts of history are merely weak expressions of the immanent and permanent "reality." The disjointed facts of history are given meaning by this Idea, the believers in which assume they have found the "laws" of history. These laws, of course, require the success of the reform or revolution which the espousers of the Idea are in favor of. The existence of a mystique at a given epoch of history usually results in a similarity among all the reforms and revolutions taking place in that epoch, because to gain support they must all be in accord with the same Idea—which decrees their inevitable success.

F *Law and Social Change*

1   LAW AS A MEANS OF EFFECTING SOCIAL CHANGE

The theories of social change that we have thus far considered focus attention on what are believed to be the initial stimuli to social change. Relatively little attention has been given to the specific means by which change is effected in concrete cases. In a sense all the social processes,

[94] John T. Marcus, "The Mystique: Movement and Order," *American Journal of Economics and Sociology,* 19 (April, 1960), pp. 231–39.

especially the means of social control, that we considered in the early chapters of this book constitute the means of effecting social changes. To provide an illustration, this section will discuss law as such a means. The different theories of social change would give differential roles to law. The technological theory would relegate it to a very minor position, considering only perhaps how the patent law of a country stimulates or inhibits inventions, and how ideology changed by means of economic modification reflects itself in new laws. On the other hand, the social-movement theory would give a central role to law as an instrument of social change; both reform and revolutionary movements usually concentrate their efforts on changing laws, and often count it as their key victory when such a change in law has been achieved. The woman's suffrage movement, the social-security movement, the Negro March-on-Washington movement, and many other reform movements, went so far as formally to disband their organizations when laws embodying their goals were put into operation.

In considering law at this point we by no means limit ourselves to statute law formally enacted by legislatures or other bodies that the society recognizes as its law-creating bodies. We also include executive orders, rulings of administrative bodies, customary practices of law-enforcement agencies, and—perhaps most important of all—judicial decisions that serve as precedents for future judicial decisions. Law is to be defined in the broad sense as "social control through the systematic application of the force of politically organized society."[95] We shall consider only those laws which are enforced to some significant degree.

The first important way in which law is a means of social change is in its role as a protector of innovators, minorities, and dissenters. There is, in Western democratic cultures at least, an accepted value endorsing majority rule and another accepted value limiting it. It is essential, of course, for any political democracy to endorse and practice majority rule, and our Western democratic cultures accept it for the election of political leaders. But they also have the value that there is a significant area of individual freedom which governments should not invade. Voltaire could even have been speaking for modern democratic government when he said, "I do not agree with what you say, but I will defend to the death your right to say it." This value has been extended in the United States to a defense of minority group rights, although Voltaire probably would not have favored such an extension.[96] If individuals have certain rights inde-

[95] Roscoe Pound, as quoted by A. R. Radcliffe-Brown, "Primitive Law," *Encyclopedia of the Social Sciences* (New York: Macmillan, 1933), Vol. 9, p. 202.

[96] Voltaire was opposed to group interests that intervened between those of the government and those of the individual, for the groups he was able to observe—the guilds and the religious *congrégations*—deprived the individual of his rights. He is quoted as saying, "When society is well governed, there is no need for private associations." (*Larousse du XX⁰ Siècle* [Paris: Librairie Larousse, 1928], I, p. 396; my translation.)

pendent of the state, they can expect recognition of these rights when they form into groups or categories. It is on this value that minority rights are defended in the United States.

An important but curious evidence of the simultaneous acceptance of the values of majority rule and minority rights can be seen in the public reaction to President Franklin Roosevelt's efforts to "pack" the Supreme Court in 1937. Roosevelt was undoubtedly one of the most popular presidents in recent times, and most of his legislative measures seemingly had the strong support of the majority of the people. Yet a good number of the new laws were declared invalid by the "nine old men" on the Supreme Court, all of whom had been appointed by previous Republican presidents and had life tenure and many of whom had openly acknowledged their allegiance to a now-unpopular social and economic philosophy. After some four years of rebuff by the Court, Roosevelt felt he could save his legislative program only by making additional appointments to the Court, and he sought legislative permission to do so. While there was widespread criticism of what the Court had done and none of Roosevelt's opponents on the Court had a personal following among the people or among the congressmen, there was a strong protest against Roosevelt's attack on the Court as an institution, and he suffered his first major legislative defeat.[97] The basis of support for the Court was, in part, a sentimental respect for a traditional institution, but it was also a widespread belief that the Court must be maintained as a protector of minority rights against the majority.

Thus the law and law-enforcement institutions are protectors of minority groups and as such are protectors of innovators. Whether social change comes from the adoption of a new technology, of elements of an alien culture, or of the goals of a reform or revolutionary movement, there is always a section of the society—a minority group—that adopts the change first and then by example or influence passes it along gradually to other members of the society. It is the law which, in Western culture, permits the innovator to function.

To realize the importance of this fact in our society we have to compare it with the situation that prevails in societies where the law does not express the social value of individual freedom and minority rights. In most of the preliterate cultures law seems to express only the demands of the society on the individual; law protects the society from the individual but not the individual from the society. In such a situation, innovation is not only not aided by the law but is often suppressed by the law. Innovation can come only as a result of the weakening of social values and social bonds, often as a result of essentially *illegal* activity. In the modern dic-

---

[97] It was not a complete defeat, however, since some of the anti-Roosevelt members of the Court offered to resign so as to permit the president to appoint new judges who would be more favorable to his policies.

tatorship the law is an instrument to gain conformity from the masses to the will of the leaders of the state. Social change may be directed by these leaders and the law is usually one of their instruments for achieving it, but this always involves a social change that is planned for, never one that arises spontaneously from the needs and the experiences of people. An important source of innovation and social change is thus inevitably stifled by the modern dictatorship.

Western democracies, however, do not rely solely on innovations introduced by minority groups under the protection of laws safeguarding individual freedom as a source of social change. They also use planning and law as instruments to translate the plan into social reality. Sociologists and perhaps the public generally are still prone to think of the law as a repressive force, as criminal law, when actually the great bulk of contemporary legislation consists of positive acts to make certain social changes possible. Quite often these laws contain no clauses providing sanctions against nonconformity; they simply set up certain facilities or provide funds and expert personnel to be used by any citizen who wishes to participate in the activity which the legislation envisages as desirable. Participation by the individual citizen under these circumstances is a voluntary matter, and he need consult only his own interests to join in an activity that may result in far-reaching social changes. Even if the majority of the members of the society were opposed to joining personally in this activity, they might still be willing to see a law enacted making it possible for a minority to participate. It sometimes occurs that the majority—observing the benefits accruing to the minority by participating in the activity— themselves choose to take advantage of the opportunities provided by the law, and the social change has thereby become much more pervasive.

In democracies where there is a strong tradition of local government —notably Switzerland, the United Kingdom, and the United States— laws may be effectuated by local majorities to govern themselves even when the great bulk of the country is opposed to such laws. Many of the most important reforms in the United States were enacted by certain states and cities long before they had any chance of acceptance by the rest of the nation. Foreign visitors who probe beneath the surface standardization in American life are often startled to discern the great variety of local experiments in social change in various corners of the country. Even socialism, supposedly taboo in a nation devoted to free enterprise, is not unknown in some of the states that have large numbers of descendants of Scandinavian immigrants. Sometimes these experiments prove successful in the eyes of those Americans who have not adopted them, and they spread from one state to the next until the whole country has adopted laws to compel their acceptance. The nineteenth century saw this occurring for legislation providing, for example, for compulsory education, compensation for industrial accidents, and restrictions on child labor. The twentieth century is now seeing it go on in regard to legislation providing for non-discrimination in employment and the scientific treatment of the mentally ill.

Equally important, in democratic society, is the direction given to social change by the minority of the population consisting of the political leaders and the leaders of communication. If the society is operating dominantly in terms of the *audience* mode of interaction, they provide direct control of social change through legislation and propaganda favorable to the legislation. In the long run they may abuse their power for their personal advantage, but in the short run the diversity and opposition of interests among them may keep the changes in line with the whole society's needs. If the society is operating dominantly in terms of the *public* mode of interaction, the political and communications leaders serve as originators and disseminators of new ideas. If these ideas are in accord with the higher ideals of the society, as they often are, the leaders who propagate them can evoke a public opinion favorable to the enactment and enforcement of laws embodying the ideas, even though current customs of the masses are not in conformity with them. In pluralistic modern democratic society—in which people tend to belong to many groups and publics—an innovation in law is typically met with by a variety of reactions; some are opposed, some are favorable, but most are indifferent or only mildly hostile. If the majority of opinion leaders are behind the change, the opposition remains a minority, and most of the people gradually accommodate themselves to the change. This is perhaps the most important way by which laws create social changes in a democracy.

2   THE SOCIAL CONTEXT IN WHICH LAW INFLUENCES
     BEHAVIOR

The question as to whether law can change behavior may be considered in a broader context. Social causation is seldom a direct one-to-one relationship; it is much more often a multi-variabled interaction in which effect reacts back on cause and modifies it just as cause creates effect. One of the best descriptions of this process is that by Myrdal, who calls it "dynamic cumulative causation" or "the vicious circle mechanism." Describing it in relation to the status of the American Negro, he writes:

> If, in actual social life, the dynamics of the causal relations between the various factors in the Negro problem should correspond to our hypotheses, then—assuming again, for the sake of simplicity, an initially static state of balanced forces—*any change in any one of these factors, independent of the way in which it is brought about, will by the aggregate weight of the cumulative effects running back and forth between them all, start the whole system moving* in one di-

rection or the other as the case may be, with a speed depending upon the original push and the functions of causal interrelation within the system.

Our point is not simply that many forces are "working in the same direction." Originally we assumed that there was a balance between these forces, and that the system was static, until we introduced one push coming in at one point or the other. When the system starts rolling, it is true that the *changes in the forces*—though not all the forces themselves—work in one direction; but this is because the variables are assumed to be interlocked in such a causal mechanism that a change of any one causes the others to change *in the same direction,* with a secondary effect upon the first variable, and so on.

We may further notice that the "balance" assumed as initial status was not a stable equilibrium at all—of the type which is tacitly assumed in the notions of "maladjustment," "adjustment," "accommodation," "social lag"—and, further, that in our scheme of hypotheses there is not necessarily assumed to exist any new "balance," or "equilibrium," or "harmony," toward which the factors of the system "adjust" or "accommodate." In the utilization of this theoretical model on problems of actual social reality, the initial state of labile balance, which we assumed for simplicity in our demonstration, will, of course, never be found. What we shall have to study are *processes of systems actually rolling* in the one direction or the other, systems which are constantly subjected to all sorts of pushes from outside through all the variables, and which are moving because of the cumulative effect of all these pushes and the interaction between the variables.[98]

We cannot assume from this principle, however, that there is any direct or immediate carryover from changes made in one area of life into other areas of life. Studies showing changes in attitudes toward minorities created by legal or other policies affecting one institutional setting do not show equivalent changes in attitudes in other institutional settings.[99]

For reasons we have already examined there is a better chance that law will receive an initial push than public opinion or many basic social institutions, although this is not always true. New laws, because they have force and prestige behind them, are more likely to reach and affect a large number of citizens quickly than are other institutions. Laws generally control behavior where it may be readily observable; less often do laws

[98] Myrdal, *op. cit.,* p. 1067.

[99] For evidence see Dietrich C. Reitzes, "Collective Factors in Race Relations," unpublished Ph.D. thesis, University of Chicago, 1950; Arnold M. Rose, *Union Solidarity* (Minneapolis: University of Minnesota Press, 1952), Chapter V; John Hope III, unpublished study of Packinghouse Workers Union, Fisk University, 1952; *Journal of Social Issues,* 8, *1* (1952) and 9, *1* (1953).

seek to control behavior in purely private situations such as the home, and still less often do they seek to control attitudes. Thus, laws are more likely to achieve changes in what may be called "external behavior." However, changes in external behavior are, after a period of time, usually followed by changes in attitude. As Morroe Berger[100] points out,

> While it is true that the province of law is "external" behavior, it is also true that in an urban, secular society an increasing number of relations fall within this province. Thus the range of behavior that can be called "external" is enlarged. At the same time, law can influence "external" acts which affect or constitute the conditions for the exercise of the private inclinations and tastes that are said to be beyond the realm of law. "Are not our most private feelings and beliefs," asks Felix S. Cohen, "molded, in part at least, by our personal contacts, our economic circumstances, our education, our opportunities for recreation and work? And in all these fields of activity does not the law again and again intervene, for better or for worse?"[101]

Another writer makes the point more forcefully:

> I believe that the reduction or elimination of discrimination will inevitably lead to the reduction of and make for the elimination of bias and prejudice. I submit that external attitudes and behavior influence internal convictions and emotions of normal men and women. This conclusion rests basically upon my conviction that a life of mental reservations, of hypocritical compliances and hidden hostility is a burden unbearable for the majority of decent human beings.[102]

That the change in attitude is only partial and not wholehearted at first does not make it any the less a change. There are no laws, and very few customs, that have complete and wholehearted acceptance, and enforcement is always a matter of degree. Attitudes toward laws, like attitudes toward any social object, are neither monolithic nor dichotomous, but reflect different distributions covering a wide range. Poll data show that when an opinion is not solidly structured, the passage of a law on the subject of the opinion gains it immediately about 10 per cent of the population in the direction of acceptance.[103] Increasing enforcement tends to shift the opinion further along, as people have a tendency to adjust their opinions to their behavior—in other words, to rationalize what they

---

[100] Morroe Berger, *Equality by Statute* (New York: Columbia University Press, 1952), p. 172.

[101] Felix S. Cohen, *Ethical Systems and Legal Ideals* (New York: Falcon, 1943).

[102] Shad Polier, "Law, Conscience and Society," *Lawyers Guild Review*, 7 (1946), p. 491.

[103] Hadley Cantril *et al.*, *Gauging Public Opinion* (Princeton: Princeton University Press, 1944), p. 228.

must do.[104] People always fear and resist new situations somewhat, especially those that come upon them suddenly, such as those created by the judging of a court decision. But the majority very quickly finds new directions for behavior, new securities, new meanings and values, in the new situation.

All this should not lead us to exaggerate what law can do. Legislators in a political democracy can step far ahead of their constituencies only when the issue is too minor for the constituencies to be aware of or concerned about it, or when they expect that the opinion of the majority of their constituency will have caught up with them before the next election. The deviations of legislators from the majority of their constituency are not always in the direction of the trend of social change but may actually be "reactionary" in the literal sense, as is well known. Judges and administrators are limited in several additional ways in effectuating social change, as Frank and Maslow point out: (1) legal and administrative procedure is slow and often cumbersome with red tape; (2) it is limited to the instant case; (3) it is subject to circumlocution—to devices for appearing to comply with orders without actually doing it; (4) it is limited by fear—whether based on good estimation or not—that the orders "may be publicly and contemptuously disregarded."[105] We have given cursory attention to other factors reducing the influence of law on general social change: the demagogues, whether sincere or not, can sometimes gain more influence over the passive masses of people than can the prestige of the law and of society's leaders; there seems to be little carry-over from changes resulting from a law governing one area of human behavior to other areas of behavior; there exists a minority of persons, who have been studied under the label of "authoritarian personalities,"[106] who resist change in any form.

Democratic societies are mostly law-abiding, and they provide a variety of means for changing the law. Under these two conditions, and under other conditions which we have examined in the course of this section, it can be expected that law would be a major means of effecting social change. The exact process by which this occurs—namely, the relation of the abstract law to individual behavior—needs to be further investigated.

[104] See, for example, the interesting study by Gerhart Saenger and Emily Gilbert, "Customer Reactions to the Integration of Negro Sales Personnel," *International Journal of Opinion and Attitude Research*, 4 (1st issue, 1950), pp. 57–76.

[105] John P. Frank, with comment by Will Maslow, "Can the Courts Erase the Color Line," *Journal of Negro Education* (Summer, 1952), pp. 304–16.

[106] T. W. Adorno *et al., The Authoritarian Personality* (New York: Harper, 1950).

G   *Social Change and Individual Motivation*

Most theories of social change do not touch the problem of individual motivation. They find the causes of social change in broad impersonal forces, such as the cumulation of material inventions, the contact of diverse cultures, the shift in control of means of production, and so on. The social changes themselves are frequently conceived of as broad trends in society and culture, such as the growth in power of the federal government, development of a universal and secular school system, the rise of trade unionism. Students of social change have tended to ignore the individual, although they would all certainly agree that social change works through the individual—its causes impinge on him and its effects are manifested as changes in his actions.

One of the unintentional results of ignoring the individual in studying social change is to think of change occurring in some sort of mechanical fashion. It is assumed that there is cause and effect, and that there is a simple relation between them. This assumption of a mechanism in social change occurs even when the theory is a most complicated one. The assumption occurs because the social change is studied and theorized about without reference to the individual.

If a social change is thought of as occurring mechanically, it also tends to be thought of as inevitable. A theory of social change gets its support from illustrations from history; thus, with hindsight, changes that did actually occur seem to have occurred "naturally" and inevitably. For any chapter of a history book, except one on the most recent period, the following chapter is already known. Because he develops his theory of social change on the basis of knowledge about the past, the theorist is generally able to "confirm" his theory with evidence from the past. Whether the *future* will confirm predictions based on his theory is another matter. Even if the future should confirm a theory of social change, in a given prediction, there is no reason to introduce an assumption of inevitability. Something *might* have intervened, even if it *actually* did not. It was not inevitable, for example, that women's roles became less clear cut after the Industrial Revolution; part-time or full-time occupations outside the home might have become expected for women just as they did for men. There is probably more freedom in the early stages of a given social change than in the later stages. Ogburn, in discussing the social effects of a technological change, says that "Man appears to be the master in the particular use he makes of the machine, but he seems not to be able to control all the derivative results of its creation and manufacture."[107] This may be a little extreme, but it suggests that man is in a better position to decide whether

[107] William F. Ogburn, with the assistance of Jean L. Adams and S. C. Gilfillan, *The Social Effects of Aviation* (New York: Houghton Mifflin, 1946), p. 9.

and how he will use a machine than he is to control all of the adaptations he makes once he has used the machine.

The investigation of the relation of a social change to an individual undergoing it or experiencing it will help to avoid the introduction of a hidden assumption of inevitability. To the individual, few things appear inevitable, even if they are so. A choice always seems to be open to him, and for most types of social changes, he actually does have a choice. All theories of social change assume that he will make his choice one way rather than another. But the process of making this decision should, nevertheless, be of interest to the student of social change. We need to know, for example, how a woman felt when the Industrial Revolution and its concomitants reduced her functions and made her role less clear cut, and we need to learn why so few women at first did anything about this change. The social forces are evaluated as ends and means in the mind of a "conscious agent" and are integrated by the individual in what MacIver calls a "dynamic assessment."[108] He provides the following example:

> How does the decline of religious authority combine with urban congestion and the improvement of contraceptives in the lowering of the birth-rate? The suggested answer is that in *the dynamic assessment all the factors determining conscious behavior are brought into a single order.* The external factors enter not as such, but as considerations affecting or relative to the pursuit of ends.[109]

Quite often a social change occurs when some key persons make decisions which affect a large number of their subordinates. Many of these decisions do not seem worthy of being dignified with the name of "social change" until they are seen in the perspective of history. But from the perspective of history it can be seen that most social changes were once problems for solution to a number of individual persons. While decisions of "great men" have unquestionably been guided and even determined by broad social forces, it is still of considerable interest to find out how these forces influenced these men, and how the personalities of the men may have modified the influence of the forces.

Seldom does it occur that a decision is made on the basis of one influence only, even though it seems to be so. A research staff preparing a report is often disappointed when the report brings no "results." A propagandist is seldom so successful as to have a given piece of propaganda change people's attitudes in the direction he desires. A policy-maker or the "man in the street" is seldom actuated by selfishness alone or idealism alone. Social change generally requires a large number of fairly independent variables operating simultaneously toward a common goal. In-

[108] Robert M. MacIver, *Social Causation* (Boston: Ginn, 1942).
[109] *Ibid.*, p. 298.

dividuals have to combine and to effectuate these variables in their behavior because the social change comes about. We need to know more about how this takes place.

Motivation is usually complex. Not often can we find a single specific cause for an individual's action. This does not mean that cause-and-effect relationships do not control men's actions, but simply that the cause has a many-faceted origin. Nor does it mean that a man's action cannot be influenced by passing him a bit of information or propaganda. It merely means that one influence usually must be commingled with others before it has any effect. One influence may stimulate others to influence an individual in approximately the same way, and it is this combined pressure that causes him to change in a given direction. In any case, the pressure to social change must be seen as operating through individuals to be thoroughly understood. Only recently have experiments been undertaken to study pressures toward change on the individual,[110] but unfortunately the kinds of pressures studied are often not the ones which historians and sociologists have found to be most significant in the broader perspective. The opportunities for significant research along these lines are tremendous, and until this research occurs our knowledge about social change —especially about how change operates through individuals—will be inadequate.

[110] The researches of Kurt Lewin and his followers are most valuable here.

FOR ADDITIONAL READING

ALLEN, FRANCIS R., HORNELL HART, DELBERT C. MILLER, WILLIAM F. OGBURN, and MEYER F.' NIMKOFF, *Technology and Social Change* (New York: Appleton-Century-Crofts, 1957). A broad-ranging survey of the influence of technology on society, with concrete studies.

EDWARDS, LYFORD P., *The Natural History of Revolution* (Chicago: University of Chicago Press, 1927). An effort to determine the typical sequence of events in the development of a revolution.

ETZIONI, AMITAI, and EVA ETZIONI (eds.), *Social Change: Sources, Patterns and Consequences* (New York: Basic Books, 1964). A collection of articles which include studies as well as theoretical discussions.

OGBURN, WILLIAM F., *Social Change* (New York: B. W. Huebsch, 1922; rev. ed., Viking, 1927; 1950). A classic analysis of change from the technological point of view.

12 * Population

There is a tendency for all specialists to concentrate on the relationship of factors within the frame of reference of their specialization and to neglect other factors which strongly influence some of the things they study but which are intrinsically studied in another specialization. Sociologists are no exception to this tendency, and we shall therefore be emphasizing throughout this book the interrelationship of strictly sociological variables, even though biological, geographical, economic, and other influences affect strongly some of the social behaviors we shall be considering. Fortunately for sociologists in one way, their discipline has historically come to include the study of two sets of phenomena which are not logically part of their central subject matter, any more than economics and political science are part of sociology. These two sub-disciplines are demography—or the study of population, its distribution, its characteristics, and the factors in its growth and decline—and human ecology—or the study of "how men relate themselves to one another in order to live in their habitats."[1] This chapter and the following chapter will consider some of the distinctive contributions of these two sub-disciplines and suggest some of the ways in which they are related to the central subject matter of sociology. This consideration should somewhat reduce the specialist's bias inherent in a book of this type.

Before there can be the interrelations among people to form groups and group products there must be people. People are differentially distributed over the face of the earth, and their concentration, distance, and proximity influence the character of their interaction. Populations are growing, declining, or remaining stationary, and this fact influences people's outlook on life, the stability of their culture and social organization,

[1] Amos H. Hawley, *Human Ecology: A Theory of Community Structure* (New York: Ronald, 1950), p. 74.

the relations with neighboring populations, and so on. Populations have different birth rates, and these affect the relative concern of people with the socialization of children, the relative amount of the population's resources and time devoted by adults to themselves, the functions of some of their social institutions, and so on. Populations have different sickness, accident, and mortality rates, and these affect their concern with disease and death, their attitude toward the cheapness or worth of life, their expectations for old age, and many other things.

Populations have different age distributions, and these—at least in our culture—influence the relative liberalism or conservatism of people's attitudes, the structure of families, the amount of time different segments of the population have for participation in organized group activities, and so on. Populations have different rates of immigration and emigration, and these influence the amount of social change they experience, the degree of consensus about meanings and values within a given society, the number and kinds of problems in connection with intergroup relations, and other social matters. Each demographic factor thus affects a number of purely social phenomena, and sometimes the influence is in the other direction as well.

A   The Distribution and Growth of Population

1   THE GEOGRAPHIC DISTRIBUTION OF PEOPLE

People are very unevenly distributed over the face of the earth. Their relative concentration in an area is a function of the amount and balance of accessible natural resources; the state of industrial arts in the culture of the permanent residents of the area or of the people exploiting the natural resources of the area; the balance of births and deaths in the area and of migration to and from the area; the level of living of the population; and the past history of all the preceding factors. Population statistics are very inadequate for large parts of the globe—particularly for Africa, Asia, and South America—but they are sufficiently accurate to give us a general picture of the distribution and concentration of people.

The best estimate of the world's population in 1962 was 3,115,000,000.[2] More than half the population of the world—concentrated into 10 per cent of the world's land area—is in eastern and southern Asia, including parts of China, India, and Japan. Another fourth of the world's population is in Europe, comprising 6 per cent of all land. The area of concentrated population in North America—stretching from the Atlantic Coast to the Great Lakes region—holds 5 per cent of the world's population.

[2] "Population and Vital Rates for 127 Countries," Information Service, Population Reference Bureau (Washington, D.C.: September, 1962).

Population density is greatest in European countries—outside of Norway, Sweden, Finland, and parts of Russia—and in eastern and southern Asia. Population density is lowest in Australia, Brazil, the Sahara and Arabian deserts, and Canada. Densities are greatest in river valleys and along coasts, lowest in deserts, frozen wastelands, jungles, and mountains. Two kinds of locations have the highest population density: cities in any kind of cultural-economic circumstances and regions with fertile soil intensively cultivated. In the latter there is generally a low standard of living, if the agriculture is for direct use rather than for trade. The economic life of cities is generally based on production for trade, and the standard of living can be quite high despite the population density. Table 7 presents some important demographic and social facts about the ten largest countries.

The cultural factors in the distribution of population can be most readily seen in the differential rate of growth of the population of different countries and of different sections within a country. Within approximately a century the United States has multiplied its population sixfold, China did not change appreciably[3] until the Communist government encouraged population growth after 1950, and Ireland has fallen to half its former size. With technology fairly static, as was the case in most periods of world history before the year 1700, population tends to reach a point of stability. While statistics of past periods are inadequate, there is evidence that the population of Europe did not grow materially between 1300 and 1700,[4] nor in Japan between 1650 and 1865.[5]

There have been periods in pre-modern history—notably in the ancient Roman Empire—when population underwent a rapid growth, but none have been so rapid as that which occurred in Western society following the Commercial and Industrial Revolutions.

Since 1650 the population of Europe has more than quadrupled, and Europe has sent scores of millions to populate the Americas, Australasia, and parts of Africa. Table 8 shows the relative growth of population in the continents of the world since 1650. The great growth was made possible by the changing technology and the increase in international trade. The expectation now is that the world's population will not grow quite so rapidly in the future as it has in the past. Woytinsky[6] estimated in 1953 that the population would reach 3,250,000,000 by the year 2000 and become stabilized eventually at around four billion. Among the factors considered in predicting the future rate of population growth are an increasing

[3] Ta Chen, *Population in Modern China* (Chicago: University of Chicago Press, 1946), pp. 4–5.

[4] R. R. Kuczynski, *Population Movements* (Oxford: Oxford University Press, 1936), p. 23.

[5] Ryoichi Ishii, *Population Pressure and Economic Life in Japan* (London: P. S. King, 1937), pp. 5–16.

[6] Wladimir S. and Emma S. Woytinsky, *World Population and Production: Trends and Outlook* (New York: Twentieth Century Fund, 1953).

TABLE 7 · SOME IMPORTANT SOCIAL FACTS ABOUT THE TEN LARGEST COUNTRIES
(Approximate figures for 1954 and 1962)

Country	1962 Population	Density per square mile	Average length of life	Average calory consumption per day	Per capita income	Dominant language	Dominant religion
China (Mainland)	716,000,000	123.1	30	2,030	$ 27	Chinese	Buddhist
India	448,000,000	312.7	32	1,700	$ 57	Hindi	Hindu
U.S.S.R.	221,000,000	24.9	52	3,020	$ 308	Russian	Christian
United States	187,000,000	43.1	68	3,130	$1639	English	Christian
Indonesia	96,000,000	185.8	32	1,880	$ 25	Indonesian	Moslem
Pakistan	96,000,000	224.2	30	2,020	$ 51	Urdu and Bengali	Moslem
Japan	95,000,000	309.3	58	2,100	$ 100	Japanese	Buddhist
Brazil	75,000,000	15.2	37	2,340	$ 112	Portuguese	Christian
West Germany	55,000,000	266.7	61	2,640	$ 462	German	Christian
United Kingdom	53,000,000	537.8	68	3,100	$ 773	English	Christian

Source: Various United Nations Publications. 1962 population estimates from Information Service, Population Reference Bureau, "Population and Vital Rates for 127 Countries" (Washington, D.C.: September, 1962).

knowledge of contraception, a broadening desire for a higher standard of living, and increasing pressure on resources. But Woytinsky is already being proved wrong, for the population of the world—especially in Asia— is growing much more rapidly than he predicted. Mass ignorance of contraception, religious resistance to the spread of contraceptive knowledge, Communist policies favoring population expansion, and failure to recognize the relationship between population, research, and standard of living —all these are combining to build up the world's population explosion.

2   BIRTHS

Changes in the size of a population are a function of the number of births, of deaths, and of in-migrants and out-migrants. We shall consider each of these factors in turn. *Fecundity*—that is, the capacity for having babies—is limited both by biological and environmental influences. A woman can bear children only during certain years of her life, and women vary somewhat in their hereditary capacity for having children. Insufficient or inadequate diet is an important environmental factor that can reduce fecundity below its hereditary potential. Accidents, certain diseases, and deliberate sterilization operate with the same effect. There is no scientific evidence whatever to support the popular idea that modern life—with its fast pace and tensions—has any influence on fecundity.[7]

Fertility—or the actual bearing of children—is always a good deal below fecundity. Pure chance is probably the most important reason for

TABLE 8 · ESTIMATED POPULATION OF THE WORLD AND ITS SUBDIVISIONS, 1650–1960

AREA	POPULATION (in millions)						
	1650	1750	1800	1850	1900	1950	1960
Total	545	728	906	1,171	1,608	2,400	2,995
Asia[a]	330	479	602	749	937	1,320	1,733
Europe[a]	100	140	187	266	401	541	587
Africa	100	95	90	95	120	198	254
North America[b]	1	1.3	5.7	26	81	166	199
Central and South America[b]	12	11.1	18.9	33	63	162	206
Oceania	2	2	2	2	6	13	16

Sources: Data for all years except 1950 and 1960 are from A. M. Carr-Saunders, *World Population* (Oxford: Clarendon Press, 1936), p. 42. These estimates are a revision of those by Walter F. Willcox. Data for 1950 are from the United Nations *Demographic Yearbook, 1951*, Table 1A, p. 103. Data for 1960 is from the United Nations *Demographic Yearbook, 1961*, Table 2, p. 120.

[a] The population of the USSR is distributed as three-fourths to Europe and one-fourth to Asia.

[b] "North America" includes only Canada and the United States. Mexico is grouped with Central and South America.

[7] This idea was supported by certain scholars of past generations—notably by Herbert Spencer—but no informed person regards it as scientifically tenable today.

this, as a certain concatenation of biological events has to take place—the ovum must be in a certain place, glandular secretions of the female must be of a certain sort, etc.—before a child can be conceived and born, and the chances of all these events occurring at the appropriate times are not particularly high. Restrictions on the frequency of or occasions for sex relations further reduce fertility. Nearly every culture includes values that restrict sex behavior, for a few years after puberty, outside of marriage, during certain periods devoted to religious ceremonials, during menstruation, or under other culturally defined circumstances. Regular sex relations are missed because of the absence of suitable or available sex partners. There is also deliberate prevention of conception by some artificial device or technique, and nearly every society knows of and practices some kind of voluntary contraception.

> In order to understand the fertility rates of any civilization one must know its institutions, the social definitions which prevail with regard to sex behavior outside of marriage, and the age and conditions of marriage. One must know the value the society places upon children, the restraints placed upon sex relations within marriage by religion, economic pressures, and taboos, and the extent to which the group has developed techniques and established moral doctrines which permit or forbid it to interfere with the normal course of nature with regard to conception and reproduction.[8]

Effective fertility can be further distinguished from simple fertility, since foetuses can be destroyed—deliberately[9] or accidentally or because of disease or malnutrition—before they are born. Finally, infants and children can die before reaching the childbearing age, and thus their contribution to the effective biological population is as though they had never been born.

The fecundity of populations is extremely difficult to measure, and is more or less unknown except with range of a sizeable error. There is much more knowledge about fertility since the law in most contemporary civilized societies requires that births and stillbirths be reported. The simplest

[8] Paul H. Landis and P. K. Hatt, *Population Problems* (New York: American Book, 1954), p. 157.

[9] Deliberate killing of foetuses is called *abortion*. Although it is against the law in many countries, it is practiced to a significant degree by people who do not have adequate access to contraceptive techniques. Although no reliable data on the total number of abortions are available, a study made during the depression—when the abortion rate was high—estimated that the ratio of abortions to births in urban districts in the United States was 1 to 2.5, and in rural districts 1 to 5. George W. Kosmak, "Pathological Aspects of Reproduction," *Annals of the American Academy*, 188 (November, 1936), pp. 78–83. Sweden is one of the few Western countries that permits legal abortion, after a board of medical experts ascertains that there is a significant health reason for it, that birth would endanger either the mother or the child.

measure of fertility is the *crude birth rate,* which is the number of births occurring in a year within a population, divided by the size of that population (multiplied by a round number constant, such as 1,000, to eliminate the decimal point). Table 9 represents the crude birth rates for selected countries, and from it a considerable variation may be seen. Birth rates are highest in Asia and southern Europe, lowest in northern Europe, North America, Australia, and New Zealand. Kuczynski states that

> Probably there never was a country with a birth rate exceeding 65. On the other hand, it is very rare, so far, for the birth rate to fall below 10, as it did in France in 1916. Actual birth rates, as a rule, lie between 13 and 55.[10]

In general, birth rates have fallen with the dramatic changes in the social structure associated with the transition from subsistence agriculture to crop specialization and intensive commercial agriculture and with industrialization and urbanization, until very recently.[11] Thompson and Whelpton[12] have estimated that in 1800 and 1810 there were approximately 55 births per year per 1,000 white persons in the United States—which meant that the average woman had an average of about eight children— and that this rate had fallen to about 43 by 1850 and to about 30 by 1900. Alva Myrdal[13] lists the long-run causes of the decline in the birth rate as follows: (1) Children are no longer an economic asset and are more expensive to raise; (2) there is "an increasing disposition to weigh rationally the motives and actions in one's own life"; (3) some people have become more habituated to modern techniques of contraception; (4) there is more economic and other insecurity. This author feels that "the change in childbearing cannot be explained by any change in the technical feasibility in birth control"; because effective techniques were known before the modern techniques were invented and the old-fashioned techniques are still the main ones used.

In general, birth rates went up during and after World War II. France, for example, which had a birth rate of 14.6 in 1938, raised its birth rate to 21.0 in 1947.[14] The United States, which saw its lowest birth rate—16.7 births per thousand population—in 1936, raised its birth rate to 27.0 in 1947 (although it fell again to 21.8 per 1,000 population in 1963).[15] This

[10] Robert R. Kuczynski, *The Measurement of Population Growth* (New York: Oxford University Press, 1936), p. 102.

[11] Kurt Mayer, "Fertility Changes and Population Forecasts in the United States," *Social Research,* 26 (Autumn, 1959), pp. 347–66.

[12] Warren S. Thompson and P. K. Whelpton, *Population Trends in the United States* (New York: McGraw-Hill, 1933), p. 263.

[13] *Nation and Family* (New York: Harper, 1941), p. 51.

[14] *St. Louis Post-Dispatch,* August 19, 1948, p. 3B.

[15] *New York Times,* January 31, 1964, p. 2.

TABLE 9 · POPULATION MEASURES FOR SELECTED COUNTRIES, 1960 OR 1961

	Crude birth rate 1	Crude death rate 2	Natural increase 3
New Zealand	27.1	9.0	18.1
Australia	22.8	8.5	14.3
Netherlands	21.2	7.6	13.6
Norway	17.5	9.1	8.4
Denmark	16.6	9.6	7.0
Sweden	13.9	9.8	4.1
Germany	18.2	10.9	7.3
Canada	26.0	7.7	18.3
England and Wales	17.4	12.0	5.4
United States	23.4	9.3	14.1
Austria	18.5	12.0	6.5
France	18.4	11.0	7.4
Finland	18.4	9.0	9.4
Italy	18.8	9.4	9.4
Bulgaria	17.8	8.1	9.7
Portugal	23.6	10.7	12.9
Hungary	14.0	9.6	4.4
Poland	20.7	7.6	13.1
Chile	35.4	11.9	23.5
Japan	16.8	7.4	9.4

Source: United Nations *Demographic Year Book, 1961*, Summary Vital Statistics, Table 3, pp. 121–25.

should not be understood to mean that large families were becoming popular again but that the trend toward a smaller number of children per family has been halted and slightly reversed, that we moved out of a period of depression into a period of prosperity, and that we have been in a temporary period in which an unusually large proportion of our people are in the childbearing ages. A significant exception to the recent upward trend in the birth rate is provided by Japan. The crude birth rate fell from 34.3 in 1947 to just over 23 in 1953 and to below 17 by 1960. This was a result of deliberate government policy. To relieve population pressure, Japan passed a Eugenics Protection Law in 1949, which legalized contraception and permitted sterilization and abortions for social and economic reasons. The birth rate has been falling in the United States again since the 1950's apparently because the war and post-war surge had stopped, and because some women had had their babies at a younger age and considered that they had as many children as they wished to have.[16]

[16] *New York Times*, June 2, 1964, p. 33.

The crude birth rate is a function, not only of fertility, but also of the proportion of women in the population and of the proportion of persons of childbearing ages, and it gives no indication of effective fertility since it ignores the deaths of children. Various *refined birth rates* can be calculated to take account of variations in these influences.[17]

3   DEATHS

The *span of life* is a biological concept referring to the total number of years a "normal" man has to live unless he is killed by accident, design, or disease. In folklore it has been considered that man's span of life is "threescore and ten," but now we know that individuals vary considerably in span of life and that seventy years is rather on the low side for the average man, although we have no knowledge as to what the exact span of life really is. Dublin believes that the life span of the average man is about 100 years. Dublin, Lotka, and Spiegelman cite one case of a man who lived 146 years.[18] It is likely that the span of life has been changing slightly as the genetic composition of the population has changed.

The *average length of life* is a much more readily measurable concept. It is the average age of death of all persons in a given population dying in a given year. It has been used to indicate the average chances of living to a certain age on the part of people born in a certain year, but it does not really indicate that because it is calculated from the age of death of people born in different years. In 1960 the average length of life for white males in the United States was 67.4 years, for white females 74.1 years, for non-white males 61.1 years, for non-white females 66.3 years.[19] In Egypt, to take a country near the other extreme, the average length of life for males is only 31 years, for females it is 36 years.[20] Since the length of life is influenced by accident, design, and disease, the differences between the four are probably due to these factors. In our society men are more likely to have accidents, to be murdered or executed, and to acquire the

[17] Among the refined birth rates are: (1) the *net reproduction rate,* which is the number of girl babies born—during the course of time—to a cohort of 100 average girl babies traced through from their birth to the end of their child-bearing period; (2) the *specific birth rate,* which is the number of births for a given age-sex category; (3) the *gross reproduction rate,* which is the sum of the age-specific female birth rates by five-year-age periods (this tells how many female children will be born per thousand mothers during their lifetime, not corrected for deaths, as in the net production rate); (4) the *fertility ratio,* which is the number of children (usually under five years of age) in the population per one thousand women aged fifteen to forty-four.

[18] Louis I. Dublin, in E. V. Cowdry (ed.), *Problems of Aging,* 2nd ed. (Baltimore: Williams and Wilkins, 1942), p. 109; L. I. Dublin, A. J. Lotka, and M. Spiegelman, *Length of Life,* rev. ed. (New York: Ronald, 1949), Chapter 1.

[19] Metropolitan Life Insurance Company, *Statistical Bulletin,* 44 (July, 1963), p. 2.

[20] Robert R. Martin, "Some Observations Concerning Population Problems in Egypt," *Alpha Kappa Deltan,* 25 (Winter, 1955), pp. 24–28.

fatal diseases, than are women. The main reason is that men lead a less sheltered life than do women. In our society Negroes are more likely than are whites to meet death by accident, design, and disease primarily because of their lower accessibility to schools, hospitals, and good jobs.

The death rate is measured very much as is the birth rate. The *crude death rate* is simply the number of deaths occurring in a year within a population, divided by the size of that population (and multiplied by 1,000). Kuczynski gives us some idea of the range found for the crude death rate:

> At the time of the Black Death (1348), the death rate may have reached several hundred in one country or another. In many cases, many death rates have been recorded which exceeded the highest recorded birth rate. It may suffice to mention as an example the 1868 death rate of Finland which amounted to 78, and which was due to a famine. In 1932, according to the *Statistical Year-Book of the League of Nations,* the death rate varied between 29 in Egypt and 8 in New Zealand; but this compilation does not include such countries as China, which probably had a higher death rate than Egypt.[21]

The crude death rate for the United States in 1961 was 9.3.[22] The death rate is inversely related to the average length of life, so that the long-run trend has resulted largely from the gradual improvement of techniques for the prevention and cure of disease. The average length of life in the United States in 1690 was approximately thirty-three years. Even by 1850 it was only forty years. The first great discovery to raise that figure significantly was sanitation, especially in the care of infants. Keeping food and water clean; reducing contact with diseased persons; killing off disease-bearing insects, rodents, and other animals; cleansing the body—these simple practices were not followed widely until the nineteenth century, and even then only in Western society. Knowledge of the disease-producing capabilities of bacteria and the possibilities of killing them with heat, cold, and certain chemicals were part of the nineteenth-century discoveries—partly associated with the names of Lister and Pasteur—that reduced the death rate through sanitary practices.

The discovery of preventive antitoxins and vaccines was the second major discovery, which all but wiped out such communicable diseases as smallpox, diphtheria, and whooping cough at the beginning of the twentieth century in Western society. New techniques for controlling the carriers of disease reduced sharply the incidence of such diseases as typhoid fever and malaria. The most recent important discovery to raise materially

---

[21] Robert R. Kuczynski, *The Measurement of Population Growth* (New York: Oxford University Press, 1936), p. 160.

[22] United Nations, *Demographic Yearbook, 1961.* Summary Vital Statistics, Table 3.

TABLE 10 • TEN LEADING CAUSES OF DEATH IN THE
UNITED STATES, 1960 (*rates per 100,000 population*)

1	Disease of heart	369.0
2	Malignant neoplasms, including neoplasms of lymphatic and hematopoietic tissues	149.2
3	Vascular lesions affecting central nervous system	108.0
4	Accidents	52.3
5	Certain diseases of early infancy	37.4
6	Influenza and pneumonia except pneumonia of new born	37.3
7	General arteriosclerosis	20.0
8	Diabetes mellitus	16.7
9	Congenital malformations	12.2
10	Cirrhosis of liver	11.3

the average length of life has been that of sulfa drugs, penicillin, and other antibiotics, which have a powerfully destructive effect on bacteria and viruses already in the human body. The next future sharp drop in the death rate must be at the expense of the degenerative diseases—primarily the heart diseases and cancer—since these are by far the most important causes of death in the United States and other Western countries today (see Table 10).

Still, the United States has not taken advantage of all the best knowledge available to cut down its death rate. Economically depressed elements in the American population still have sharply higher disease and death rates than do the better-off people. Certain other countries have made more successful efforts to apply available medical knowledge concerning the prevention and cure of disease to all elements of their populations, and their lower death rates can be remarked in Table 9. The situation is not improving: the United States fell from 5th to 11th place among countries with a low infant mortality rate, between 1950 and 1962.[23] In 1962 on the average, 25.3 of every 1,000 live babies died in their first year of life in the United States. The Netherlands and Sweden tie for having the lowest infant mortality rates—15.3 infant deaths per 1,000 live births. Other countries making a better showing than the United States are Norway, Finland, Australia, Denmark, New Zealand, Switzerland, the United Kingdom, and Ireland. In life expectancy at birth for males in 1960, the United States ranked in only the 13th position, although for females it was in 7th position.

On the other hand, most of the countries outside Western culture have death rates a good deal higher than the United States. Because of the spread

[23] *New York Times*, November 26, 1963, p. 42.

of medical and sanitary knowledge, their death rates are also falling and their catastrophic epidemics are being brought under control.[24]

The total population of the world can grow either through an increase in the birth rate or a decrease in the death rate. The simplest measure of this growth is the *rate of natural increase,* which is the birth rate minus the death rate. The rate of natural increase indicates the number of people being added to the population in a given year for each 1,000 people already in the population. This is a crude rate of change in the population, since it does not take into account the age distribution of the population. Table 9 gives the rate of natural increase for selected countries.

The phenomenal growth of the world's population over the past three centuries has been largely due to a decrease in the death rate, because the birth rate has also fallen—although not so soon and not so rapidly as the death rate. Different parts of the world have had a different pattern of relationship between the birth rate and the death rate in their growth over the past three centuries. In western Europe and North America the death rate began to fall slowly in the seventeenth century, and the birth rate remained constant until around 1850, when it also began to fall.

The death rate is still falling, although at a greatly decelerated pace —with most of the recent progress being made following important medical discoveries. It may be expected that the death rate will rise slightly for a while as the population ages. None of the medical or sanitary discoveries thus far has raised the span of life, although expected future discoveries on how to prevent the degenerative diseases may have this effect. The birth rate remained fairly much at its age-old high level until around 1850, when it also began to decline. The major factor in the decline was a new orientation toward life on the part of the masses of western Europeans and Americans. They perceived that they could raise their personal level of living if they had fewer children. Techniques of contraception easy to use and more effective were added to the ones known by most people, and their use gradually spread throughout the population.[25] The birth rate fell more or less steadily until about 1940.

Since then there has been an upturn in the birth rate, but it is still too early to determine whether this is a result of a cultural change in attitude toward having children or merely a temporary response to the prosperity and peace following fifteen years of depression and war. It is likely

[24] See, for example, Kingsley Davis, *The Population of India and Pakistan* (Princeton, N.J.: Princeton University Press, 1951), pp. 33–37.

[25] Ancient methods of contraception—widely practiced even by industrially backward peoples of the world today—include having intercourse during the so-called "safe period," *coitus interruptus,* the post-coital douche, and the use of a physical pessary. Modern methods include use of the condom, the diaphragm (with or without chemical accessories), and certain hormones usually taken orally.

that both factors have been operative, and that the birth rate of Western countries will remain at its relatively high plateau.

Outside of western Europe and North America, the death rate did not begin to turn downward substantially until the nineteenth century, and in a country such as China—which retains a primitive technology and has had frequent political upheavals—it has not yet started to fall. In several of the countries whose death rates began falling early in this period—for example, countries in eastern Europe—the birth rate has also begun to decline. But in certain other countries—for example, Indonesia and Asiatic Russia—the birth rate has remained at its old high level and the population is growing rapidly. It cannot be predicted whether those nations will follow the European pattern of deliberately reducing their birth rates, but it can be predicted that those nations will soon reach the limits of population pressure on present use of resources unless their birth rates begin to decline or they are able drastically and continuously to change their technology or to send their excess populations outside their national borders. India has just begun to reduce its birth rate, at the same time as it is improving its technology, and it seems likely to follow the European pattern, as Japan has for several decades.

4   DIFFERENTIALS IN THE BIRTH RATE

There are differences in the pattern of reproduction within a population. One of the most consistent of these differences—across time and across cultures—is an urban-rural difference in the birth rate. Within any given culture, cities tend to have a lower birth rate than do rural areas.[26] A few exceptions can be noted, as in France for a period before World War I,[27] and in the movement of Italian peasants to American cities,[28] but the differential is otherwise quite general. It existed in colonial times in the United States.[29] In 1957, the number of children ever born per 1,000 American women was 1,504 in the cities, 1,881 in rural nonfarm areas, and 2,275 in rural farm areas.[30]

Another differential in birth rates is important in our society but is by no means universal. This is the differential in the fertility of the socioeconomic classes. The lower classes in our society have had a higher

[26] A. J. Jaffe, "Urbanization and Fertility," *American Journal of Sociology*, 48 (July, 1942), pp. 48–60.

[27] *Revue d'Economie Politique* (March–April, 1929), as cited by Enid Charles, *The Twilight of Parenthood* (New York: Norton, 1934), p. 114.

[28] Arnold M. Rose, "The Influence of Immigration on the Birth Rate," *American Journal of Sociology*, 47 (January, 1942), pp. 614–21.

[29] Clyde V. Kiser, "Differential Fertility in the United States," in National Bureau of Economic Research, *Demographic and Economic Change in Developed Countries* (Princeton, N.J.: Princeton University Press, 1960), pp. 77–116, at 78.

[30] *Ibid.*, p. 83, based on *Current Population Reports* of the U.S. Bureau of the Census, Series P–20, No. 84, pp. 9–10.

fertility rate than the upper classes. While earlier sources of vital statistics are inadequate, it seems that the differential has existed at least as far back as 1800.[31] In 1935 the net reproduction rate among urban whites in the United States was less than half as high in families having an income of over $3,000 a year as it was in families having an annual income of less than $1,000.[32]

The same phenomenon could be discerned in an educational differential. For white women living in cities in the United States in 1935 those who had some college education had a net reproduction rate of 52, while for those who had never gone beyond the sixth grade the net reproduction rate was 97. Since World War II this differential has partly evened out. The fertility ratio among married women college graduates rose 34 per cent between 1940 and 1947, whereas it rose only 13 per cent among wives with less than five years of schooling.[33] The reasons for this equalization seem to be that people in the lower socioeconomic classes have become more sophisticated about birth control, that the educated people have responded more to wartime and postwar prosperity, and that people in the upper socioeconomic classes have changed their attitude toward children.[34] A special study of college graduates by the Population Reference Bureau reflects this change of attitude:

> Married graduates of the class of 1944 already average more children, only 10 years after graduation, than graduates of the class of 1921, 25 years after graduation. A smaller proportion of the class of '44 is childless.
>
> With 15 more years of family building ahead of them, there is even a possibility that members of the class of 1944 will replace themselves in the new generation. An average of 2.1 children per graduate is necessary to accomplish this.
>
> Men of the class of 1944 now average 1.70 children per graduate and women average 1.39. For the men that is a 67 per cent gain in fertility over men of the class of '36 who reported an average of only 1.02 children 10 years after graduation. Women of the class of

[31] A. J. Jaffe, "Differential Fertility in the White Population in Early America," *Journal of Heredity*, 31 (September, 1940), p. 411.

[32] Bernard D. Karpinos and Clyde V. Kiser, "The Differential Fertility and Potential Rates of Growth of Various Income and Educational Classes of Urban Population in the United States," *Milbank Memorial Fund Quarterly*, 17 (October, 1939), p. 376.

[33] U.S. Bureau of the Census, *Current Population Reports—Population Characteristics*, Series P-20, No. 18, June 30, 1948, p. 6. See also study by the Population Reference Bureau, as reported in the *New York Times*, June 6, 1955, p. 29.

[34] Kurt Mayer (*op. cit.*) disputes the psychological factor in the change and holds that the United States has restored its structural equilibrium and homogeneity of population which account for both the rising birth rate and the decline of differential fertility.

1944 increased 46 per cent over women of 1936 who averaged only 0.95 child.[35]

Whether there has been a permanent reduction of the class differential in the birth rate cannot yet be said. The likelihood is that this is the case, for the differential was probably simply part of the general downward trend in the birth rate, with the rural population lagging behind the urban and the lower classes lagging behind the upper classes in the use of modern techniques of contraception. As the upper classes dwelling in cities reach a lower limit in their birth rate, or even begin to raise their birth rate, the lag can be expected to be made up and the differentials disappear. On the other hand, we must recognize that the more educated people respond more in their birth rate to depression and prosperity than do poorly educated people, and therefore part of the recent equalization has been because of the current prosperity.

There is also differential fertility by race and religion. The racial differences largely reflect the class differences: in 1957, the number of children ever born per 1,000 women in the United States was 1,637 among whites and 1,990 among nonwhites, and the differentials have been widening.[36] Whereas at the peak of immigration to the United States in 1910, foreign-born white women had considerably higher fertility than did native-born women, the differential has disappeared today. The religious differential is considerable: the number of children ever born per 1,000 married women 45 years and over in the United States in 1957 was 2,218 among Jews, 2,753 among Protestants and 3,056 among Catholics. Within the Protestant group the range was considerable: for example, the Presbyterians had a fertility rate of 2,188 as compared to the Baptists' 3,275. When age differentials were held constant, the fertility difference between Catholics and all Protestants disappeared, which means that in the future there no longer should be any fertility difference between the two groups, although this equality is made possible partly by the larger proportion of rural residents and Negroes among the Protestants.

B   *Migration*

1   MIGRATION IN A WORLD CONTEXT

Migration has always been a major source of population change, although its pattern has changed markedly. Most ancient migrations, and migrations in preliterate societies, were by small groups, whereas most modern mi-

[35] "College Study Report," *Population Bulletin*, 10 (June, 1954), p. 1.
[36] Clyde V. Kiser, "Differential Fertility in the United States," *op. cit.*, pp. 83 ff.

gration is by individuals or families.[37] There have been some forced migrations in recent years of whole categories of a society—as in the Nazis' movement of slave labor or the expulsion of the Sudeten Germans from Czechoslovakia after World War II, but the migrants disperse as individuals or as families after reaching their destination. Migration has had periods of increase and of decrease throughout history, but in general there has been more migration in modern times than in ancient or medieval times.

Migration does not, of course, add to or subtract from the total population of the world, but it can have an effect on total population by involving the movement of people from areas where they are likely to reproduce less to areas where they are likely to reproduce more, or vice versa. The westward movement of people across the United States in the nineteenth century undoubtedly increased the population of the country more rapidly than it would have grown if there had been no migration. The general modern trend of migration from rural to urban areas has thus far operated to reduce the total birth rate. Since voluntary migration is usually from areas of poorer economic opportunity to areas of greater economic opportunity, such migration usually lowers the death rate of the migrants.

The effect of migration on the birth rate of those who do not migrate —either in the area from which the migrants leave or in the area to which the migrants go—is not so clear. This was a subject of great debate in the United States between 1890 and 1940, but no convincing evidence has yet been adduced that there is any effect. The issue was first publicly raised in 1891 by Francis A. Walker, then Commissioner of Immigration, who contended that immigration had made no difference in the size of the American population because immigrants had merely taken the place of additions to the native stock, which otherwise would have kept up its higher birth rate. This point of view has been statistically refuted by Willcox and Carr-Saunders, who prove that the increase in numbers by immigration was much greater than required to offset the lower birth rate.[38] Of course it is clear that the age distribution and cultural characteristics of the migrants have an influence on the birth rates of the exporting and importing countries: since a disproportionate number of modern immigrants have been in the childbearing ages, their departure has temporarily lowered the birth rate of the exporting country and temporarily raised the birth rate of the receiving country. But these facts

[37] Warren J. Thompson, *Population Problems* (New York: McGraw-Hill, 1942), pp. 372 ff.

[38] See Francis A. Walker, "Immigration and Degradation," *Forum*, 11 (1891), pp. 642 ff.; Walter L. Willcox, *International Migrations* (New York: National Bureau of Economic Research, 1931), Vol. II, pp. 93–107; A. M. Carr-Saunders, *World Population* (Oxford: Clarendon Press, 1936), pp. 204–05.

seem to have no significant or consistent influence on the birth rate of
the non-migrating people of either country.

Europe has been the great exporting continent of the world, in population as in culture and manufactured goods. A significant exception has
been France since 1815; in the twentieth century France has even gone so
far as to become a population-importing country. During the economic
prosperity of the late 1950's and the 1960's, many European countries
imported population. The "new continents" of North and South America
and Australasia have also been regular importers of population. Africa—
as a developing continent in recent centuries—has had an excess of immigrants over emigrants, although a significant proportion of the population of the Americas came from Africa. Asia—in prehistoric and ancient
times the greatest exporter of population—has been relatively stable in
modern times. A significant number of Indians have gone to South Africa
in the past seventy-five years, and Japanese have gone to lands in and
bordering the Pacific Ocean (including those in South America), but
these migrations have been relatively small compared to the others mentioned. Much migration from Asiatic countries is to other countries in
Asia. A considerable proportion of Asiatic emigrants return to their native
countries.[39]

2   MIGRATION AND THE UNITED STATES

The United States has had immigrants from all the countries of Europe,
as well as from Central Africa, Mexico, and a thin sprinkling from the
Orient (Figure 3 shows the main countries from which the antecedents of
the white population in 1920 had come). On the other hand, the United
States has contributed people only to some of its small territories, such
as Guam and the Virgin Islands. This does not mean that there is no
formal emigration from the United States, since a significant proportion
of those who have migrated to the United States have returned to their
countries of origin. In 1911 the U.S. Immigration Commission estimated that 40 per cent of the new immigrants returned to Europe and
that two thirds of those who went remained there.[40]

Migration to the United States was at first slow, with most of the
immigrants up to 1840 coming from Great Britain, the Netherlands,
Central Africa, France, and Spain (most of the people from the latter
two countries having settled in territories that were later annexed to the
United States). There were also early sprinklings of Poles, Swedes, and

---

[39] Thompson, *op. cit.*, pp. 376–77; S. W. Kung, *Chinese in American Life* (Seattle:
University of Washington Press, 1962), Chapter 1.

[40] U.S. Immigration Commission, *Abstracts of Reports of the Immigration Commission*
(Washington, D.C.: Government Printing Office, 1911), p. 24.

FIGURE 3 · WHITE POPULATION BY COUNTRY OF ORIGIN, 1920

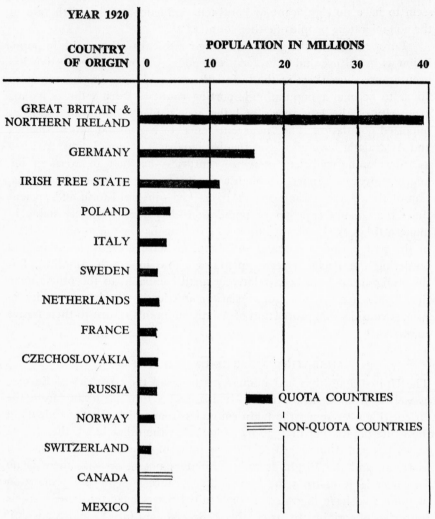

Mexicans are included with whites in accordance with the classification of the 1920 census. Their number here appears large in comparison with the estimated number of persons of Mexican descent in 1920 published in the 1930 census, since this latter estimate does not include such persons born in the United States of native born parents, of whom there were large numbers in the southwest.

Source: Estimates made by Joseph A. Hill of the Bureau of the Census, reported by Warren S. Thompson and P. K. Whelpton, "The Population of the Nation," in *Recent Social Trends*, by The President's Research Committee on Social Trends (New York: McGraw-Hill, 1933), Vol. I, p. 20.

Germans. As shown in Table 11, a significant jump in the immigration rate occurred during the 1840's when a great crop failure hit Ireland, which already had a heavy pressure of population on resources, and when the failure of a revolution convinced many German liberals that there was no hope for democracy in their country. The Irish and German migration kept up, and was soon joined by the beginnings of immigration from China and the Scandinavian countries. Immigration from Europe had a slight setback during the Civil War period, while immigration from Africa ceased altogether.

In the 1870's the great immigration from Italy and Poland began, and was soon augmented by heavy immigration from Russia, the Austrian Empire, and the Balkan countries. While immigration from China all but ceased, and even took a reverse direction by the end of the nineteenth century, the first decade of the twentieth century saw a small but significant migration from Japan to the West Coast of the United States. The drop in immigraion during the 1890's was owing primarily to economic depression, while that during the second decade of the twentieth century was because of war. In general, immigration followed the business cycle—that is, in prosperous times there was considerably more immigration than when economic conditions were depressed, even if the depression also affected the countries of emigration.[41] The all-time high of immigration occurred during the period just before World War I, when some years saw more than a million persons coming to American shores to establish permanent residence.

Agitation to stop the free flow of people into the United States began before the Civil War but made little headway until the depression of 1873. The first restrictions were written as though directed against criminals and prostitutes (Act of March 3, 1875) but actually they were used only against the Chinese, whether they came into the proscribed categories or

TABLE 11 • ESTIMATED NET IMMIGRATION TO THE UNITED STATES BY DECADES, 1770–1960 (*in thousands*)

1770–80	20	1870–80	2,580
1780–90	40	1880–90	4,964
1790–1800	50	1890–1900	3,689
1800–10	62	1900–10	6,243
1810–20	71	1910–20	2,225
1820–30	123	1920–30	3,335
1830–40	493	1930–40	–46
1840–50	1,420	1940–50	1,789
1850–60	2,558	1950–60	2,975
1860–70	2,074		

Sources: Victor S. Van Szeliski, "Population Growth Due to Immigration and Natural Increase," *Human Biology*, 8 (February, 1936), p. 27. The figures for the 1940's and 1950's are taken from U.S. Bureau of the Census, *Current Population Reports*, Series P-25, No. 278 (January 29, 1964), p. 7.

[41] Harry Jerome, *Migration and Business Cycles* (New York: National Bureau of Economic Research, 1926); Dorothy S. Thomas, *Social and Economic Aspects of Swedish Population Movements, 1750–1933* (New York: Macmillan, 1941), pp. 166–69.

not.[42] By 1883 the law openly set restrictions on the immigration of Chinese laborers. Agitation against and opposition to free immigration increased until by the end of World I it was overwhelming.

The laws of 1921 and 1924 cut immigration sharply and employed the national-origins clause which discriminated against all but persons from countries in the Western Hemisphere and from northwest Europe. In 1930 President Hoover by executive order further limited immigration, especially of Mexicans and Canadians. As a result of all the limitations on immigration there were a number of years since 1930 when emigration from the United States exceeded immigration. Beginning in 1943, Congress passed a series of laws that permitted token immigration of a few hundred Orientals, but the policy of heavy restriction of immigration and of restriction on a nationality and racial basis (which all but barred immigration from Asia, Africa, and eastern and southern Europe) was reaffirmed in the McCarran-Walter Immigration Law of 1952. Since then, there has been only a slight relaxation of the law to permit some refugees from Communism to enter the United States.

Many other nations of the world have recently set up barriers to immigration, and some—especially in eastern Europe and Asia—have set up barriers to emigration. There were a number of forced migrations consequent to the ending of World War II and the creation of the independent nations of India and Pakistan. Also, a few countries—notably Australia, New Zealand, Israel, and Canada—have been encouraging the individual immigration of skilled workers from Europe. Several European countries have been importing workers from other European countries, and there are refugees migrating from East Germany to West Germany. But on the whole, the era seems to be one of relatively little international migration.

Internal migration—that is, migration within the political boundaries of a nation—continues at the high rate to which it was stimulated by the Industrial Revolution.[43] About half the population of the United States changed residence during the seven years following April, 1940,[44] which were years of war and postwar adjustment. About one sixth of these moved to a new state, more than a sixth stayed in the same state but moved to a new county, and the rest changed residence within the same county. In the more recent and typical year from April 1, 1960, to April 1, 1961, 20.0 per cent of the people of the United States 1 year old and

[42] U.S. Immigration Commission, *Statistical Review of Immigration 1820–1910* (Washington: Government Printing Office, 1911), p. 366.

[43] The most comprehensive work on internal migration within the United States is Henry S. Shryock, Jr., *Population Mobility Within the United States* (Chicago: Family Study Center, University of Chicago, 1964).

[44] Census Bureau report, quoted in the *St. Louis Post-Dispatch*, April 15, 1948, p. 1.

over changed residence, and 9.0 per cent crossed a county line in this movement.[45] Much of the mobility is from rural areas to cities and villages. In 1790 only 5 per cent of the population was urban; in 1960, 69.7 per cent was urban. Between 1940 and 1950 alone the farm population dropped about 25 per cent, although many of these people moved merely to nearby villages. Young adults are generally more mobile than older persons.

Much of the interregional migration within countries has been simply a coincidental aspect of the country to city migration. In the United States, for example, the migration from the South to the North has been largely, although much less completely for the Negroes than for the whites, a movement of rural people to take advantage of job opportunities in the industrial cities.[46] Almost the same could be said for the migration from southern to northern Italy, or from Brittany to the central and eastern departments of France.

At first the westward movement in the United States, which has historically been the most important direction of internal migration for whites, was mainly to rural areas but more recently it has been to the cities. While some of the white residents of the Southwest were descendants of early Spanish settlers who came up from Mexico, an increasing proportion of the inhabitants of the whole West had previously lived in the East. By 1930 about five million persons born east of the Mississippi River were living somewhere west of that river.[47] Between 1940 and 1960 alone California grew 128 per cent, and the states that followed it in having the most rapid growth in population due to net in-migration were, in order, Nevada, Florida, Arizona, Oregon, and Washington.[48] Sometime in 1960, California became the most populous state in the union.

3   THE CAUSES OF MIGRATION

The causes of migration are never simple, except in the case of a forced migration when a direct political motive is clearly discernible. A number of factors are taken into consideration by the individual who decides to migrate, and the combination of factors considered and the weights

[45] U.S. Bureau of the Census, *Current Population Reports—Population Characteristics,* Series P–20, No. 118 (August 9, 1962), p. 1.

[46] Negro migration was also predominantly northward (at least until 1940, after which it increasingly turned westward). But the motivation for the migration was to escape the southern caste system as well as to seek better job opportunities. See Gunnar Myrdal, with the assistance of Richard Sterner and Arnold Rose, *An American Dilemma* (New York: Harper, 1944), Chapter 8.

[47] National Resources Planning Board, *The Problems of a Changing Population* (Washington, D.C., 1938), p. 83.

[48] Landis and Hatt, *op. cit.,* p. 401. Figures for 1960 taken from U.S. Bureau of the Census, *Census of Population: 1960, U.S. Summary,* Vol. I, Part 1, Table 15.

assigned to each are probably different for each person who makes such a decision. The single most important factor in modern history seems to be the presence of considerably greater economic opportunities in the place of immigration as compared to the place of emigration. This differential cannot be measured solely in general economic terms but must also be measured in personal and psychological terms—that is, an opportunity must be perceived as such for an individual and it must be an opportunity that will fit him before the individual decides to move.[49] If an individual is fairly well satisfied with his present situation, he often will not migrate even if economic opportunities are considerably better somewhere else. This is why lower-income people migrate more than middle-income people, even though the latter could also improve their economic position greatly by migrating.

Certain conditions facilitate migration, and their absence retards migration, even when the search for economic betterment is the chief motive for migration.[50] The establishment of a "tradition of migration" is a most important factor of this type. If a person knows of others who have successfully migrated from his area to another, he is more likely to migrate than if he is one of the first to migrate. A line of communication informs him of economic opportunities available and eases his anxieties about the difficulties of adjustment to the new location. This is why most migrations are for short distances.[51] People who are less attached psychologically to their communities are more likely to migrate than those who are more attached. Thus influences that make people more sophisticated or that disturb the social integration of communities are stimuli to migration. Purely personal events abet an economic influence. The precipitating cause of the migration of an individual might be such an event as the spurning of a young man by his sweetheart, or the death of a mother who was too old to be moved.

For many migrants—although probably not the majority—the main motivation is not economic. There can be many personal reasons for wishing to break with one way of life and to try another. A large number of the young men and women who move from rural areas to cities are as much attracted by the possibilities for greater freedom and a more varied

[49] The psychological factor is not only a factor in successful migration, but also in unsuccessful migration. Of the estimated 60 million people who left Europe in the nineteenth century, 20 million returned. Most of these perceived the new opportunities incorrectly, although some had always intended to return after earning some money. (A. M. Carr-Saunders, *World Population* [Oxford, 1936], pp. 49–50.)

[50] A major study of the causes of migration in the United States is Peter H. Rossi, *Why Families Move: A Study in the Social Psychology of Urban Mobility* (Glencoe, Ill.: Free Press, 1955).

[51] Samuel A. Stouffer, "Intervening Opportunities: A Theory Relating Mobility and Distance," *American Sociological Review*, 5 (December, 1940), pp. 845–67; Arnold M. Rose, "Distance of Migration and Socio-Economic Status of Migrants," *American Sociological Review*, 23 (August, 1958), pp. 420–23.

life as they are by the job opportunities. In the United States Negroes migrating from South to North go partly because they want to escape the restrictions and dangers of the southern caste system. A good proportion of the immigrants from Europe to the United States came to gain political and religious freedom. Some Jews managed to leave Nazi Germany during the 1930's and go to many other parts of the world in order to escape the deprivation of their civil liberties and the threat to their lives. This was also true of the Hungarians who left their country after the unsuccessful revolt of 1956. Some Frenchmen move to the Côte d'Azur and some Americans move to California or to Florida because they like the climate better and are not economically tied down. Some people move to take advantage of social opportunities, such as to be near certain desirable schools, near relatives, near persons who can confer social prestige, and so on. Reasons for migration are thus both very numerous and often complex.

c   *The Composition of the Population*

There are an indefinitely large number of elements that might be considered when we examine the composition of a population. Population experts have traditionally emphasized certain biological differentia—such as age, sex, and race—and certain broad social differentia—such as nativity, religion, education, marital status, occupation, and income. Since better statistical information is available for these variables than for others that might equally well be examined we shall follow the traditional interest.

1   SEX AND AGE

The sex composition of the population is measured by the *sex ratio,* which is the number of males for every hundred females (in other words, the number of males divided by the number of females multiplied by 100). Nature, unhampered, tends to produce approximately the same number of males and females. In the United States a slightly larger number of males than of females are born every year, but the death rate of males is greater. In 1960, the sex ratio for those under five years of age was 103.[52] As age increased, the sex ratio fell until those aged 25 to 29 years constituted 97 men for every 100 women, and for those over 85 years of age the sex ratio was only 64.

For all persons in the United States, regardless of age, the sex ratio was 97.3 in 1963.[53] This represents a drop from earlier periods when there

---

[52] U.S. Bureau of the Census, *Census of Population: 1960, U.S. Summary,* Vol. 1, Part 1, Table 45.

[53] Calculated from U.S. Bureau of the Census, *Current Population Reports,* Series P–25, No. 276 (November 19, 1963), p. 2.

PROPORTION OF TOTAL POPULATION GAINFULLY EMPLOYED, 1960

Canada	37 per cent
Netherlands	37 per cent
Belgium	39 per cent
United States	40 per cent
Italy	41 per cent
France	43 per cent
United Kingdom	46 per cent
West Germany	50 per cent

The variation is to be explained largely in terms of:
1 the proportion of married women working,
2 the proportion of older people who are retired,
3 the proportion of unemployed in the total labor force.

UNESCO publications.

were many more men than women in the United States, owing not to the fact that more males were born and remained alive but to the fact that immigrants included many more men than women. As immigration remains all but cut off, and as the discrepancy between men's and women's length of life increases, we may expect the sex ratio to continue to fall for a while in the United States. The greater resistance of women to disease in civilized and industrialized countries, as well as the greater incidence of wartime deaths among men, has created a low sex ratio in most western European nations.

Countries that are still receiving significant numbers of immigrants and countries that are medically backward enough to have a high female death rate at childbirth are the ones with a high sex ratio. For example, Canada has a sex ratio of 103.6, and Ceylon has a sex ratio of 113.0.[54] On the other hand, countries with high health standards that are losing population, and countries badly hurt by war, have a low sex ratio. For example, Scotland's sex ratio in 1945 was 92.4 and France's was 86.1.[55]

The sex ratio is markedly different in different parts of a country. Urban sex ratios are generally lower than rural ones, although the functions and ages of a city vary this principle. In the United States in 1960

[54] United Nations, *Demographic Yearbook, 1949–1950* (Lake Success, 1950), Table IV. The figure for Canada is for 1949, that for Ceylon is for 1946.
[55] *Ibid.*

the urban sex ratio was 94.0, the rural non-farm was 103.3, and the rural farm was 107.2.[56] This differential was greater at the older ages than at the younger ones. For those sixty-five years of age and over, the urban sex ratio was 75.7, the rural non-farm was 93.5, and the rural farm was 117.3.

The age composition of a country is a function of the recent history of its birth rate and death rate, as well as its immigration and emigration during the past generation. The age and sex composition of a population are best described by means of a *population pyramid,* which consists of two bar charts, one for males and the other for females, placed back to back, with the length of the bars indicating the percentage of the population in a given age category. The whole takes the rough form of a pyramid when the highest ages are placed on the top and the youngest ages at the bottom, as is shown in Figure 4.

The shape of the pyramid indicates several things about the age-sex composition. Asymmetry indicates an unbalanced sex ratio—reflecting recent migration and/or war deaths. A broad base and a narrow peak indicate a population with high birth and death rates. A base with the lowest bars narrower than the next highest bars indicates a falling birth rate. In the population pyramid for the United States (Figure 4), the trough in the age groups twenty to thirty-five years indicates the falling birth rates of the 1920's and the 1930's. The long bars toward the bottom indicate the rapid increase in the birth rate since the return of prosperity

FIGURE 4 • AGE PYRAMIDS FOR THE TOTAL POPULATION OF THE UNITED STATES, 1950 AND 1963[a] (*in millions*)

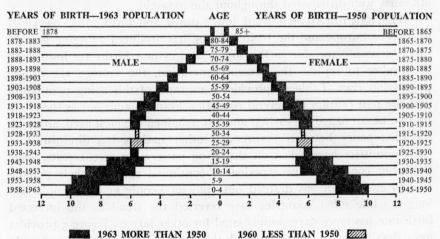

a Total resident population. Alaska and Hawaii included in both years.
Source: U.S. Bureau of the Census, *Censuses of Population, 1950 and 1960.*

56 Calculated from U.S. Bureau of the Census, *Census of Population: 1960, U.S. Summary,* Vol. 1, No. 1, Table 65, p. 199.

TABLE 12 • PERSONS SIXTY YEARS OF AGE AND OVER PER 1,000
TOTAL POPULATION IN SELECTED WESTERN EUROPEAN NATIONS,
1850–1961

Nation	1850	1900	1947	1957–61
Belgium	89	95	156	176
Denmark	82	99	131	133
England	72	75	152	166
France	101	124	160	170
Germany	70	78	138	—
Norway	88	109	137	114
Switzerland	79	93	142	132
The Netherlands	77	92	116	96

Sources: Alfred Sauvy, "Social and Economic Consequences of the Aging of Western European Populations," *Population Studies*, II (June, 1948), p. 115; United Nations *Demographic Yearbook, 1961*, Table 5, pp. 138 ff.

(and also reflect the resumption of child-bearing after the war and possibly a new attitude favorable to slightly larger families). These long bars at the base of the pyramid have been the basis for the prediction of an increasingly heavy college enrollment beginning around 1963. The effects of the heavy immigration to the United States in past decades can scarcely be seen in the population pyramid today, as they could be formerly. Migrants are predominantly young adults, and they first expand the lower central parts of the pyramid. As they age, their children increase the lower parts of the pyramid, and they themselves move into the upper part. A generation after a heavy migration the migrants and their descendants are fairly well distributed throughout the pyramid.

The long-run trend toward lower death and birth rates, especially in western Europe and the United States, has produced an *aging population*. As people are able to live longer and as new births are insufficient in number to replace the present generation, the average age of the population rises. Table 12 provides a measure of this aging population over the past century for several countries. France stands out as the country that began to age the earliest and has remained the most aged, although the discrepancy between France and other nations has diminished as other countries have taken on the aging pattern. In recent years, some European countries have experienced continued aging of their population as emigration has drained out younger people and as people live longer, while other countries have reversed the trend as the increased birth rate has more than compensated for other factors. Figure 5 provides more details on the extent to which the American population has "aged" since 1850.

An aging population represents both a longer length of life and a failure to reproduce sufficiently to maintain the population at its existing size. Even if the birth rate should resume its ability to reproduce the preceding generation, as in most countries after World War II, the population will continue to age for a number of years. An aging population has certain predictable consequences for a nation. Economically, it means that a smaller proportion of the population will be in those ages that can support the total population. Just one illustration reveals the significance of this fact. If we consider that the population aged sixty-five years and over pay less taxes than those in the age group 25–64 years, because they are mostly retired and have more tax exemptions, the tax rate must have increased about 80 per cent from 1900 to 1950 to maintain the same total income for the government solely as a result of the relative increase of people in the ages past sixty-five years.

This is by no means all, for government services to older citizens are greater than to citizens in the age range twenty-five to sixty-five, and as the former groups increase their proportion in the population the government must spend more just on keeping up its usual services. It is impossible to calculate a percentage representing this increase, since government expenditure statistics do not permit this kind of breakdown, but it is likely that government expenditures have increased 50 per cent between 1925 to 1950 as a result of this factor alone. This loss of govern-

FIGURE 5 • PER CENT DISTRIBUTION OF TOTAL POPULATION BY AGE, UNITED STATES, 1850 TO 1960

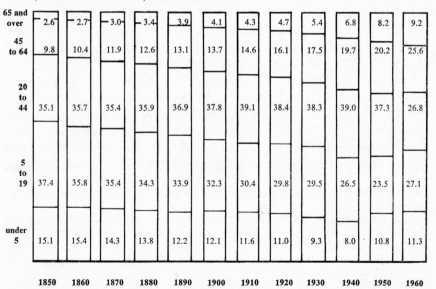

	1850	1860	1870	1880	1890	1900	1910	1920	1930	1940	1950	1960
65 and over	2.6	2.7	3.0	3.4	3.9	4.1	4.3	4.7	5.4	6.8	8.2	9.2
45 to 64	9.8	10.4	11.9	12.6	13.1	13.7	14.6	16.1	17.5	19.7	20.2	25.6
20 to 44	35.1	35.7	35.4	35.9	36.9	37.8	39.1	38.4	38.3	39.0	37.3	26.8
5 to 19	37.4	35.8	35.4	34.3	33.9	32.3	30.4	29.8	29.5	26.5	23.5	27.1
under 5	15.1	15.4	14.3	13.8	12.2	12.1	11.6	11.0	9.3	8.0	10.8	11.3

Source: Decennial censuses of the United States, as compiled in "Changing Pattern of the American Population," Metropolitan Life Insurance Company, *Statistical Bulletin* 33 (May, 1952), p. 2. Data for 1960 are directly from U.S. Census Reports.

ment income and increase of government expenses due to the larger number of the elderly was made up by increased productivity and higher taxes.

Aging has consequences other than economic. Older people tend to be somewhat more conservative in their politics and general point of view than do younger people,[57] and an increasing proportion of the aged in a population tends to set it in a conservative direction (except in so far as they seek more social services from the government for themselves). The aged make a greater demand on medical services than do younger adults, and thus the need for doctors, nurses, hospitals, etc., is growing more rapidly than is the population. Older people have different recreational habits than do younger adults, and so the recreational facilities of a country change as its population ages. Older people find it difficult to learn new skills, hence an aging population is not so flexible in making industrial changes as a young population. These and dozens of other implications of our aging population have been described in the literature or speculated about.[58]

2   RACE, NATIVITY, AND RELIGION

There are few nations of the world that are racially homogeneous. Even Sweden—which is often said to be an example of a Nordic nation—has a population in which only some 15 per cent meet the anthropologist's criteria of the Nordic race.[59] Tens of thousands of migrations have mixed up the races at least to a certain extent in all nations. Some populations, of course, have a more racially heterogeneous background than others. Spain is a country whose history reports a great admixture of peoples, including Negroes, but these were fairly thoroughly amalgamated before the present century. In Brazil the process of amalgamation of Portuguese, Indians, and Negroes is quite visible at the present time. Some countries retain conspicuous racial differences in their populations through thousands of years —as in the case of India, by means of its caste system.[60]

The United States still has considerable racial heterogeneity, although one cannot judge this fact by appearances alone. The 1963 Census reports that 89.0 per cent of the population is white, 10.5 per cent is Negro, and 0.5 per cent is of a number of other races.[61] This distribution, however,

---

[57] As evidenced in public opinion polls; also see Dublin, Lotka, Spiegelman, *op. cit.*, pp. 257–60.

[58] See, for example, Clark Tibbitts (ed.), *Handbook of Social Gerontology* (Chicago: University of Chicago Press, 1960); Kimball Young, *Personality and Problems of Adjustment,* second ed. (New York: Appleton-Century-Crofts, 1952), Chapter XX; Otto Pollak, *Social Adjustment in Old Age* (New York: Social Science Research Council, 1948).

[59] Myrdal, *op. cit.,* p. 114.

[60] For a brief description of India's caste system, see Chapter 8.

[61] Computed from *The World Almanac and Book of Facts for 1963* (New York: World Telegram and Sun, 1963), p. 254.

is based largely on the judgments and guesses of census takers, and often does not reflect the true distribution of racial ancestry. There are very few people left in the United States who are of pure Negro ancestry—practically every "Negro" has at least one white ancestor, and a significant proportion have some Indian ancestry. American "whites" include significant numbers who have some Negro ancestry, especially among those whose ancestors came to the United States before the American Revolution. In the whites' case, the Negro ancestry is often unknown or forgotten, occasionally deliberately hidden. Negroes are defined by the census takers as persons who appear or are reported to have some Negro ancestry. Mexicans are reported by census takers as whites, even though by ancestry they are amalgamations of Indians and whites. Thus the true racial composition of the population is unknown except for the clues afforded by history.

Turning now to certain social characteristics of the population, we note briefly that nativity is a reflection of recent international migration. In 1960 only 5.4 per cent of the American population was foreign-born—a smaller proportion than any other recorded in the history of the country.[62] In earlier periods, of course, the proportion of foreign-born was much larger.

Statistics on religious affiliation are less adequate than most statistics, since most countries—including the United States—do not ask about religious affiliations in their censuses. In Sweden it is assumed that if a person is not registered with any other church he is a Lutheran. This would seem to make the great majority of the population Lutherans, but actually only a small proportion of the Swedish people attend the Lutheran Church. Similarly, France is often called a Catholic country, but a map of France prepared in 1947 by two sociologists sympathetic to the Catholic Church and based on reports by priests shows that the larger part of even rural France consists of "parishes indifferent to Christian traditions" and that there are some "mission areas" which do not even have parishes.[63] In the United States, recent estimates are that 34.2 per cent of the population have no church affiliation. Table 13 shows the distribution of the population by religious affiliation.

[62] U.S. Bureau of the Census, *Census of Population: 1960, Detailed Characteristics, United States Summary, Final Report,* PC (1)–1D, Table 162, p. 366.

[63] Fernand Brulard and Gabriel Le Bras, in *Cahiers du Clergé Rurale,* no. 84 (November, 1947), and reprinted in *Population,* Vol. 3, No. 2 (April–June, 1948), pp. 310–11. The *Institut Français d'Opinion Publique* has asked cross-section samples of the French population about church attendance: only 33 per cent attend mass habitually, 55 per cent do not (4 per cent adhere to a non-Catholic religion, and 8 per cent give no answer).

TABLE 13 · MEMBERSHIP IN RELIGIOUS BODIES, UNITED STATES, 1962

Name and number of church bodies	Inclusive membership	Percentage of total population
Adventist Bodies (5)	372,972	.20
Armenian Church	155,000	.08
Baptist Bodies (28)	21,643,490	12.09
Brethren (German Baptists) (4)	250,227	.13
Brethren (River) (3)	8,698	.004
Buddhist	60,000	.03
Christian Churches (Disciples of Christ) (2)	4,029,046	2.24
Churches of God (11)	485,010	.27
Churches of the Living God (2)	45,922	.02
Churches of the New Jerusalem (2)	5,854	.003
Eastern Churches (20)	3,001,751	1.67
Evangelical United Brethren Church	756,596	.40
Evangelistic Associations (9)	66,717	.03
Friends (8)	128,495	.07
Jewish (8)	5,509,000	3.08
Latter Day Saints (5)	1,846,841	1.02
Lutheran Bodies (11)	8,356,656	4.66
Mennonite Bodies (12)	164,440	.09
Methodist Bodies (21)	12,739,925	7.15
Moravian Bodies (2)	67,807	.03
Old Catholic Churches (5)	159,961	.08
Pentecostal Assemblies (12)	404,611	.22
Polish National Catholic	437,411	.24
Presbyterian Bodies (10)	4,361,344	2.43
Protestant Episcopal Church	3,317,870	1.85
Reformed Bodies (6)	507,751	.28
Roman Catholic Church	43,847,938	24.49
United Brethren Bodies (2)	22,214	.01
United Church of Christ	2,056,696	1.14
Other Churches	3,035,769	1.77
Total Protestant Churches	64,929,941	36.21
Total Inclusive Membership	117,946,002	65.78
Non-Church Population	61,377,173	34.22
Total (1960 population)	179,325,657	100.00

Sources: National Council of the Churches of Christ in the U.S.A., *Yearbook of American Churches, 1964* (New York, 1964), pp. 273–75. The total population for 1960 is taken from U.S. Bureau of the Census, *Census of Population: 1960, Detailed Characteristics, U.S. Summary, Final Report*, PC (1)–1D, Table 155, p. 349.

3   EDUCATION AND MARITAL STATUS

The educational level of practically all nations has been advancing during the past century. In Western culture during the Middle Ages, formal education—even the teaching of reading and writing—was limited to a very small section of the population. Private schools were established during the Renaissance but reached only those children whose parents could afford them. The compulsory public-school system is fairly much a development of the post-Industrial Revolution period, and has been extended in countries outside Western culture. Still, in the United States, 8.4 per cent of the population twenty-five years of age and over have had four years of school or less, and thus are practically illiterate. Only 7.7 per cent have completed college.

The great recent extension of public education, coupled with the fact that higher education is still not completely free, creates certain differentiations in educational status within our population. Older people have, on the average, lower educational attainment than those who have received their education recently. Richer people have higher education attainment, on the average, than have poorer people. Since urban areas have more school facilities—especially for higher education—than do rural areas, and since urban areas have more occupational outlets for educated people than do rural areas, urban areas have people of higher educational attainment, on the average, than do rural areas. Since the southern states in the United States lagged behind the North in establishing a free, compulsory public-school system, Southerners have lower educational attainment than have Northerners, on the average. Since most American Negroes were raised in the South, and since the Negro schools in the South are inferior to schools for whites, and since Negroes are poorer and have more pressures on them to leave school at an early age, the educational attainment of Negroes is lower than that of whites, on the average. Educational attainment in the United States and some of these differentiating influences are shown in Table 14.

The marital status of the American population has shown significant changes in the period since 1890 (Table 15). Due primarily to the lower age of marriage, the proportion of single people in the population has markedly declined and the proportion of married people has markedly increased. The proportion of divorced persons has increased, although the figures available are not reliable because of the tendency of divorced persons to report themselves as single or widowed. Widows have consistently remained much more numerous than widowers because of the higher death rate among males than among females and because of the greater tendency of widowers to remarry. Single males are more likely to be found on farms than in cities, since young women leave the farm at a

TABLE 14 · YEARS OF SCHOOL COMPLETED BY PERSONS 25 YEARS OLD AND OVER, UNITED STATES, 1960

Years of school completed	Percentage of population who have completed indicated number of years of school							
	Among all persons 25 years of age and over	Among those 25–29 years	Among those 65–74 years	Among persons living in urban areas	Among persons living in rural non-farm areas	Among persons living in rural farm areas	Among natives of native parentage, white	Among non-white
None	2.3	0.7	6.6	0.5	1.0	1.7	1.2	0.9
1–4 grades of elementary school	6.1	2.2	12.9	1.9	2.9	6.2	5.2	5.8
5–7 grades of elementary school	13.9	6.7	21.9	6.2	8.9	13.8	13.4	14.1
8 grades of elementary school	17.6	8.0	26.4	7.4	9.6	18.3	17.1	9.7
1–3 years of high school	19.3	21.9	12.2	21.4	21.1	18.1	19.2	27.9
4 years of high school	24.3	38.5	10.1	32.6	34.4	32.1	23.7	26.2
1–3 years of college	8.8	12.0	5.9	15.3	7.8	7.0	9.5	8.2
4 or more years of college	7.7	10.0	4.0	14.7	14.3	2.8	10.7	7.2
Total	100.0	100.0	100.0	100.0	100.0	100.0	100.0	100.0
Median school years completed	11.3	9.0	11.1	11.0	9.2	10.4	12.0	9.0

Source: U.S. Bureau of the Census, *Census of Population—Educational Attainment, Final Report*, PC (2)–5B, Tables I, II, pp. 1 ff.

more rapid rate now than do young men. The young women who remain on farms have a greater likelihood of getting married than those who migrate to cities. Partly because of the different locations of eligible single men and women, about 10 per cent of the population never gets married.[64] There are significantly more divorced persons in cities than in rural areas.

These patterns which we have found characteristic of the United States should not be assumed to be true of other countries. In Ireland, for example, the age of marriage has been getting higher over the past century, hence the proportion of single persons in the population has been increasing. In Ireland 41.6 per cent of the females and 62.4 per cent of the males were unmarried at ages thirty to thirty-four, as compared to 13.2 per cent and 21.2 per cent for the two groups in the United States for a comparable year.[65] In Italy and many other countries of heavy emigration it is the young males who emigrate from the rural areas in greater numbers than the young females, and so the sex distribution of single persons is considerably more weighted on the female side than it is in the United States.

4   OCCUPATION AND INCOME

The occupational distribution of populations varies even more widely than does the marital-status distribution, since the occupational distribu-

TABLE 15 • MARITAL STATUS OF PERSONS 14 YEARS OLD AND OVER, UNITED STATES, 1960 (*Percentage Distributions*)

Sex and marital status	All persons 1890	All persons 1960	Urban residents 1960	Rural non-farm residents 1960	Rural farm residents 1960	Non-whites 1960
MALE						
Single	43.6	25.0	24.1	26.0	29.5	30.5
Married	52.1	69.5	70.2	68.7	66.2	62.6
Widowed and Divorced	4.0	5.5	5.7	5.3	4.3	6.9
FEMALE						
Single	34.1	19.0	19.4	17.2	20.0	22.0
Married	54.8	66.0	64.4	69.8	71.1	60.6
Widowed and Divorced	11.0	15.0	16.2	13.0	8.9	17.4

Source: U.S. Bureau of the Census, *Census of Population: 1960, Detailed Characteristics, U.S. Summary, Final Report*, PC (1)–11, Table 175, pp. 423 ff.

[64] Arnold M. Rose, "Living Arrangements of Unattached Persons," *American Sociological Review*, 12 (August, 1947), pp. 429–35.

[65] *International Vital Statistics*, pp. 436–39, as reported in Landis and Hatt, *op. cit.* Data for Ireland are for 1926; for the United States, 1930.

TABLE 16 · OCCUPATIONAL DISTRIBUTION OF THE EMPLOYED POPULATION OF THE UNITED STATES, 1960

| | Percentage of employed persons in indicated occupational groups among | | | | | |
| | | | MALES | | FEMALES | |
Occupational group	All persons	Non-whites	All	Non-white	All	Non-white
Professional, technical, and kindred workers	11.9	5.3	10.3	3.9	13.0	7.5
Farmers and farm managers	3.9	2.9	5.5	4.4	0.6	0.7
Managers, officials, and proprietors, except farm	8.4	1.8	10.7	2.3	3.7	1.2
Clerical and kindred workers	14.4	6.4	7.0	5.0	29.6	8.5
Sales workers	7.2	1.6	6.9	1.5	7.8	1.7
Craftsmen, foremen, and kindred workers	13.2	6.4	19.5	10.2	1.2	0.7
Operatives and kindred workers	18.0	19.6	19.5	23.5	15.4	12.8
Private household workers	2.7	14.0	0.1	0.7	7.9	34.2
Service workers except private household	8.4	16.8	6.0	13.7	13.4	20.7
Farm laborers, except unpaid, and foremen	1.8	4.9	2.4	6.6	0.6	2.3
Farm laborers, unpaid family workers	0.4	0.5	0.4	0.5	0.6	0.6
Laborers, except farm and mine	4.8	12.1	6.9	19.3	0.5	1.0
Occupation not reported	4.9	8.2	4.8	8.4	5.7	8.1
Total	100.0	100.0	100.0	100.0	100.0	100.0

Source: U.S. Bureau of the Census, *Census of Population: 1960, General Social and Economic Characteristics*, PC (1)–1C, Tables 87–89, pp. 216–19.

tion is primarily a function of the pattern of the economy, which has almost indefinite variation, while the tendency for adults to get married is an almost universal culture pattern. Not all adults have a gainful occupation, especially in an industrially advanced country such as the United States. In 1960, about 5.1 per cent of the labor force was classified as unemployed; 0.9 per cent of the adult population were inmates of institutions; 5.8 per cent were enrolled in schools; 24.7 per cent were keeping house; 6.9 per cent were retired.[66] Table 16 shows some occupational characteristics of the gainfully employed population of the United States. A comparison of the successive pairs of columns shows that the non-white minorities in the United States are heavily represented in the service and laboring occupations and have low representation in the professional, technical,

[66] U.S. Bureau of the Census, *Census of Population: 1960, General Social and Economic Characteristics, U.S. Summary, Final Report*, PC (1)–1C, Table 82, p. 213.

managerial (non-farm), and clerical occupations.[67] Most women are not gainfully employed, but among those who are there is a higher representation of professional, technical, clerical, and service workers and a lower proportion of farmers, managers, and manual workers, than among men.

The income distribution of the American population in 1960 is shown in Table 17. While there were some people with very high incomes in the United States, these made up only 12 per cent of total population (if we call $10,000 and over per family unit a very high income). These high-income people were slightly more concentrated in the northeastern states (primarily in and around New York City) than in other sections of the country. While there were also families with extremely low incomes, the income distribution—except at the extremes—was not so great. This can be seen from the fact that the median income—that is, the income level which half the families exceeded and the other half failed to reach—was about $4,791 while all but a small percentage received under $10,000. This is a ratio of but four to one.

While we have no comparable data for earlier periods in the United

TABLE 17 · CUMULATIVE PERCENTAGE DISTRIBUTION OF FAMILIES AND UNRELATED INDIVIDUALS BY INCOME LEVEL IN 1960, UNITED STATES

Total money income level	*Cumulative percentages of families and unrelated individuals with indicated income level among*						
	All U.S. families and unrelated individuals	*Urban and rural non-farm residents*	*Residents of north-eastern states*	*Residents of north central states*	*Residents of southern states*	*Non-white residents of southern states*	*Residents of western states*
Under $1,000	12.8	13.4	4.1	4.5	9.3	21.3	3.5
Under $2,000	23.3	24.5	9.3	11.1	20.6	43.9	8.8
Under $3,000	32.5	33.2	16.0	18.6	31.9	62.7	15.5
Under $5,000	52.5	65.3	36.0	38.2	54.1	85.3	33.5
Under $7,000	71.8	74.0	60.7	62.6	75.5	93.9	60.1
Under $10,000	88.0	88.0	82.6	84.2	89.6	98.2	83.3
Total	100.0	100.0	100.0	100.0	100.0	100.0	100.0
Median Income	$4,791	$5,199	$6,191	$5,892	$4,465	$2,322	$6,348

Sources: U.S. Bureau of the Census, *Census of Population: 1960, General Social and Economic Characteristics, U.S. Summary, Final Report*, PC (1)–1C, Table 95, pp. 225 ff.; *Census of Population: 1960, Detailed Characteristics, U.S. Summary, Final Report*, PC (1)–1D, Table 268, p. 747.

[67] This is a result of the now-declining caste system; see Chapter 8, Section B.

States, or for other countries,[68] general information suggests that the variation is decreasing somewhat within the United States and that it is lower in the United States than in many other civilized countries. (Income variation may have reached a low point around 1950; since then it has increased slightly again.) In recent decades Great Britain and the Scandinavian countries have made great efforts to reduce variation in income and they probably have less variation than does the United States. But most other countries have retained older patterns of having huge income variations.

Another change reflected in Table 17 is the practical absence of difference in income between rural and urban families, especially if we consider that there is greater concentration of farms in the South and the South's income is generally lower than in the rest of the country. In preceding decades farmers had lower income than did city and town people. In the South it is primarily the Negro population that has the low income, as we can see by comparing the two columns in the table representing the South. Poor whites in the South have a lower income than do people in the lower-income half of the population in other parts of the country. But when we glance at those with incomes of $7,000 and above, we see that there is about as large a proportion of white Southerners as there is of residents of the north central states. That is, the South—considering either the region as a whole or only the whites in it—has a larger income variation than do other sections of the country. This is a more accurate characterization of the South than the one commonly heard, "The South is the poor section of the country."

[68] There are no comparable data because a question on income was first asked in the 1950 census, and it is next to impossible to translate purchasing power of incomes of other countries into American dollars as of 1950 or 1960.

FOR ADDITIONAL READING

LANDIS, PAUL H., and PAUL K. HATT, *Population Problems* (New York: American Book, 1954). A textbook.

MYRDAL, ALVA, *Nation and Family* (New York: Harper, 1941). A report on how Sweden reversed the downward trend in its birth rate.

PETERSON, WILLIAM, *Population* (New York: Macmillan, 1961). A textbook.

ROSSI, PETER H., *Why Families Move* (Glencoe, Ill.: Free Press, 1955). A study in the social psychology of urban mobility.

THOMPSON, WARREN S., *Population Problems* (New York: McGraw-Hill, 1954). A textbook.

13 * The Human Community: Urban and Rural

Man's relationship to his fellow men is influenced by his natural habitat, and the study of this influence is the subject of a branch of sociology called *human ecology*.[1] Human geography is interested in the influence of the habitat on men, but not particularly on the interrelations among men. Thus, human geography is distinct from human ecology, although it is closely related. Hawley has elaborated on this distinction:

> Human ecology is therefore something different from human geography. Geography treats men and their activities in their visible aspects and so far as they may be regarded as distributed phenomena. It does not concern, except incidentally, the interrelations among men. Human ecology, which is also interested in the relations of man to his geographic environment, fastens its attention upon the human interdependences that develop in the action and reaction of a population to its habitat. In other words, while geography views the adjustment of man from the standpoint of modifications of the earth's surface, human ecology makes a detailed analysis of the process and organization of relations involved in adjustment to environment. This brings us to a second point of distinction between the two disciplines. Geography involves a description of things as they are at a point in time; its interest is in distribution rather than development.

[1] The most comprehensive brief survey of studies in human ecology is that of James A. Quinn, "Topical Summary of Current Literature on Human Ecology," *American Journal of Sociology*, 46 (September, 1940), pp. 191–226. There are two outstanding textbooks in the field: Amos H. Hawley, *Human Ecology: A Theory of Community Structure* (New York: Ronald, 1950); James A. Quinn, *Human Ecology* (New York: Prentice-Hall, 1950). We consider ecology in a framework of urban and rural sociology, in which fields there are many valuable textbooks. Some of the leading textbooks in rural sociology are Alvin Lee Bertrand, *Rural Sociology; An Analysis of Contemporary Rural Life* (New York: McGraw-Hill, 1958); John Harrison Kolb, *Emerging Rural Com-*

Ecology, on the other hand, is evolutionary. It undertakes to describe the developmental process as well as the form of man's adjustment to his habitat. Human geography and human ecology thus constitute diverse approaches to the question of man's relation to environment; the one proceeds by way of environment, the other by way of organism.[2]

The whole habitat has some influence on interrelations among men —the geographical opportunities and limitations, the presence of plants and the lower animals, and the presence of other men and their economic activities. Man in this total habitat may be called the *human community,* and it is to be noted that this ecological definition of community is different from a popular one or even a sociological one.[3] The term "human" is

---

munities; Group Relations in Rural Society (Madison: University of Wisconsin, 1959); John Harrison Kolb and Edmund de S. Brunner, *A Study of Rural Society* (Boston: Houghton Mifflin, 1952) ; Charles Price Loomis and J. Allan Beegle, *Rural Sociology, The Strategy of Change* (Englewood Cliffs, N.J.: Prentice-Hall, 1957); Lowry Nelson, *Rural Sociology,* second ed. (New York: American Book, 1955); Everett M. Rogers, *Social Change in Rural Society; A Textbook in Rural Sociology* (New York: Appleton-Century-Crofts, 1960); Walter L. Slocum, *Agricultural Sociology; A Study of Sociological Aspects of American Farm Life* (New York: Harper, 1962); Thomas Lynn Smith, *The Sociology of Rural Life,* third ed. (New York: Harper, 1953). Some of the leading textbooks in urban sociology are Nels Anderson, *The Urban Community; A World Perspective* (New York: Holt, 1959); Richard Bruce Andrews, *Urban Growth and Development, A Problem Approach* (New York: Simmons-Boardman, 1962); Egon Ernest Bergel, *Urban Sociology* (New York: McGraw-Hill, 1955); James M. Beshers, *Urban Social Structure* (New York: Free Press of Glencoe, 1962); Leonard J. Duhl (ed.), *The Urban Condition; People and Policy in the Metropolis* (New York: Basic Books, 1963); Ephraim Gordon Ericksen, *Urban Behavior* (New York: Macmillan, 1954); Elizabeth Geen, Jeanne R. Lowe, and Kenneth Walker, *Man and the Modern City* (Pittsburgh: University of Pittsburgh Press, 1963); Noel Pitts Gist and L. A. Halbert, *Urban Society,* fourth ed. (New York: T. Y. Crowell 1956); Scott A. Greer, *The Emerging City: Myth and Reality* (New York: Free Press of Glencoe, 1962); Paul K. Hatt and Albert J. Reiss, Jr. (eds.), *Cities and Society; The Revised Reader in Urban Sociology,* second ed. (Glencoe, Ill.: Free Press, 1957); James Alfred Quinn, *Urban Sociology* (New York: American Book, 1955); Svend Riemer, *The Modern City; An Introduction to Urban Sociology* (New York: Prentice-Hall, 1952); Thomas Lynn Smith and C. A. McMahan, *The Sociology of Urban Life, A Textbook With Readings* (New York: Dryden, 1951).

[2] Amos H. Hawley, *Human Ecology,* Copyright 1950, The Ronald Press Company, p. 72.

[3] Sociologists have used the term "community" in divergent ways. Töennies used it to refer to a highly integrated, intimate group of people living together. (Ferdinand Töennies, *Gemeinschaft und Gesellschaft;* trans. C. P. Loomis, *Fundamental Concepts of Sociology* [New York: American Book, 1940]). MacIver has used it to refer to small concentrations of people in distinction to a society as a whole (Robert M. MacIver, *Society* [New York: Rinehart, 1937]). In this chapter we mainly follow Park in using an ecological definition of community (Robert E. Park, "The Urban Community as a Spatial Pattern and a Moral Order," in E. W. Burgess [ed.], *The Urban Community* [Chicago: University of Chicago Press, 1925]). For an analysis of the theoretical and methodological problems in the study of "community," see Albert J. Reiss, Jr., "Some Logical and Methodological Problems in Community Research," *Social Forces,* 33 (Octo-

used in conscious preference to the term "social" as we are here not concerned with man's adjustment to other men based on mutual expectations but with man's adjustment to other men based on living in a common habitat.

It was Darwin who first set the problems of ecology, although his concern was exclusively with plant and animal ecology rather than with human ecology. Incidental to his concern with the evolution of species, Darwin observed that there is a "web of life" in which organisms are mutually adjusted or are in the process of becoming mutually adjusted through a "struggle for existence" (which we include in our concept of competition) within a physical environment that sets certain conditions for the adjustment.[4] Thus the basic relationship among creatures as far as the ecologist is concerned is *competition,* not in the narrow economic sense but in the broad biological sense. Competition is behavior considered not for its direct effect of the one who acts on other individuals, but its indirect effect on them through modification of the common habitat. The central role of competition among ecological processes suggests the close relationships of ecology and economics. Economics shares with ecology the study of all those phenomena determined by the fact that men must live in space and use material goods, both of which are scarce and so must be competed for. Ecology differs from economics in that it is not concerned with the pricing and distribution of these scarce goods, but with their effect on men and their spatial distribution. We shall again quote Hawley to draw the distinction between the two fields:

> Although the terms derive from a common origin, the disciplines differ both in problem and approach. Economics is concerned with the efficiency, as measured in units of cost, of the interrelations required in a given task of production, and with the changes in those producing relationships resulting from changes in costs. The point of view may be characterized as that of an entrepreneur planning and managing the production and sale of goods or services. This is in contrast to ecology in which attention is directed more to the form or pattern of human sustenance relations, the process of development of such patterns, and the factors that affect their development. The ecological viewpoint is that of individuals and groups seeking position in a developing system of relationships.[5]

---

ber, 1954), pp. 51-57; Henry Zentner, "Logical Difficulties in Relating the Concepts Community, Society, and Institutions," *Alpha Kappa Deltan,* 28 (Winter, 1958), pp. 28–36. In Sections E and G of this chapter, and in Chapter 14, we shift to MacIver's definition of community.

[4] Charles Darwin, *Origin of Species* (London: J. Murray, 1859) and *Descent of Man* (London: J. Murray, 1871).

[5] Amos H. Hawley, *Human Ecology,* Copyright 1950, The Ronald Press Company, p. 73.

From the above it may be discerned that human ecology deals with merely an aspect of human behavior. That aspect may be of small or great importance, depending on the situation, but it is part of every human situation and never the whole of any situation. In thus dealing with an abstraction from behavior, human ecology can never fully explain any human behavior or situation. It is thus more appropriate to speak of an "ecological aspect" of a behavior or a situation than of an ecological behavior or an ecological situation. An ecological influence never operates in a vacuum, and cultural influences may direct or deflect an ecological influence.[6]

A   Competition and the Structure of the Community

Competition is an impersonal process whereby an individual (or a group) modifies his environment to meet his needs and thereby affects the need satisfaction of other individuals (or groups) in the same environment. An individual takes up space and thus restricts the space available to others; an individual takes up desirable space (desirable from an economic, esthetic, prestige, or any other basis) and thus forces other individuals into less desirable space; an individual uses goods of which there is a limited quantity and thereby restricts the amount of goods available to others; an individual secures a certain economic position and thus prevents other people from obtaining that particular position—these are examples of competition.

While competition implies struggle, even though it be of an impersonal sort, it also makes for order.

> Competition is the term in social theory which associates the fact of struggle with the formation of order. It is the key word in an account . . . of how rivalry for prestige and income, for power and wealth, comes to promote organization.[7]

A certain habitat, with a given state of the industrial arts and of the division of labor, can support a certain number of people at a certain standard of living. Within the framework of a culture these people can support only a certain number of institutions of different types. A larger concentration of population can support certain institutions—such as an

[6] This, we take it, is the significance of Firey's and Form's studies which involve a critique of "pure" ecology. See Walter Firey, *Land Use in Central Boston* (Cambridge: Harvard University Press, 1947); William H. Form, "The Place of Social Structure in the Determination of Land Use: Some Implications for a Theory of Urban Ecology," *Social Forces,* 32 (May, 1954), pp. 317–23.

[7] Walton Hamilton, "Competition," *Encyclopedia of the Social Sciences* (New York: Macmillan, 1932), Vol. 4, p. 141.

art museum or a university—which a smaller concentration of people cannot.

Thus there is a certain balance between the number and variety of institutions, the size of the population, and the economic potentialities of the habitat, within any given cultural framework. This balance is created by competition. A discovery of new resources in an area, or an invention that permits greater exploitation of existing natural resources, or an improvement of economic organization (including transportation) that permits a more efficient use of existing resources and technology, tends to raise the standard of living in the area and to attract immigrants. As the population becomes wealthier and as new people come into the area, people increase the number and variety of their institutions and other cultural facilities. There is an increased demand for stores, recreational and amusement facilities, educational institutions, etc. New schools and churches are built, either to accommodate a growing population or to make them more accessible and "better." As new people come into the community, a wider range of voluntary associations is developed since there are more people available with certain specialized interests. A growing small town reaches a point where it can afford to establish a community center; a growing large town reaches a point where it can afford to establish a symphony orchestra, a museum, a stadium. The small core of leaders that want to build each of these new facilities—whether publicly or privately owned—can be considered as competing for spare money and time of the town's inhabitants. When enough money and popular interest are accumulated, the facility can be built.

There is also competition for space. Each house, each enterprise, each community facility takes up a certain amount of space. Even without the growth of population, changes in the community affect the utilization of space through competition. The building of a railroad spur line to a village makes it profitable, efficient, and sometimes even necessary for the local shippers and receivers of goods to build or rebuild at least some of their facilities near the railroad. If one or two leading families of a town build homes in a certain area this may attract most new homebuilding to that section of town. If a smoky or noisy factory settles in one section of a town, competition for space for new homes in that immediate area, and the sales price of existing homes, goes down as people avoid settling there and as the residents who can afford it try to leave.

In larger cities, merchants specializing in a certain product—such as wholesale clothing or used cars—may find it expedient and profitable to settle near one another so that customers can "shop around." Thus they out-compete potential owners or renters of the land and structures of the area who have different purposes. Each institution seeks the space most necessary to the efficient carrying on of its functions, and obtains that space if it can out-compete other institutions that seek the same space. Hughes indicates why a newspaper seeks to locate itself near the center of a city.

> A newspaper, one of the most characteristic of modern institutions, is usually printed in a building near the center of a city. News must be gathered and distributed quickly. Reporters gather much of it in the nearby heart of the city where happen so many of the things that make news. Reports of world events also come quickly to the city where are focused so many means of rapid communication. The papers are distributed by screaming trucks and shouting newsboys to the masses, who crowd the nearby streets at certain hours of the day. Quick postal and express services carry papers in all directions to the more distant parts, where families receive and read them. Much of the advertising revenue, which is so large a part of the newspaper's income, comes from department stores. The area from which local news is gathered and to which it is distributed corresponds rather closely to the area from which people come to shop in the stores near the newspaper's office.[8]

When the town or city government enacts zoning ordinances, restricting the use of certain districts to certain purposes, that does not eliminate the competition for space but merely channels it along certain lines. Nor is competition eliminated in a socialist society. If certain potential users of a piece of land have a greater need or a greater desire for that piece of land than do other potential users, they express that greater need or greater desire to the public official or board that decides allocations, and the land is usually given to them if such an allocation does not conflict with the zoning principles set up by the government. Competition under socialism is presumably less expressed through monetary pressure than through social, moral, or personal pressure, and the pressure is directed less at an existing owner than at a public official; but it is still competition.

Competition for space and for markets to buy and sell tends to give an area a characteristic human use. Certain areas are used primarily for certain economic uses, other areas are used primarily for residential purposes. Rich people competing for land to build homes in an area out-compete poor people, and so the homes built take on a characteristic expensive appearance. Yet once a residential area begins to deteriorate, the well-to-do flee from it and leave it to be taken over by poorer people. No single rich person feels that he could move into a blighted area, no matter how good a location it is in terms of accessibility to desirable surroundings. Competition to extend a new use into a piece of land tends

[8] Everett C. Hughes, "Institutions," in Alfred M. Lee (ed.), *New Outline of the Principles of Sociology* (New York: Barnes and Noble, 1946), pp. 249–50.

to occur within a given period of time so that the whole area has a development characteristic of that period and that use. Thus an area acquires distinctive and identifying traits—by way of function, appearance, and composition of population—which set it off from adjacent areas. Local government boundaries—of a state or province, city or village, ward or district—are seldom coterminous with the boundaries of the area we are describing. In ecology, therefore, it is useful to speak of *natural areas* as distinct from political areas.

Certain natural areas influence conditions in certain other natural areas—for example, a city attracts truck gardening rather than wheat farming in nearby rural areas, and a factory requires a workingman's residential district within easy commuting distance. We can thus speak of the *dominance* of certain uses of land, or of certain natural areas, over other land uses or areas. The extension of dominance of a city over surrounding areas varies with the type of activity under consideration: the area served by a city's leading department store is likely to be far smaller than the area served by the city's leading newspaper. The latter, incidentally, provides one of the most extensive delineations of what is called the *metropolitan community*—that is, the city and the surrounding suburbs, villages, and farm land which the city dominates.[9] The extent of dominance by one area over other areas varies with each specific service the dominant area performs. Thus the size of a community is always arbitrary, and depends on the service under consideration.

Natural areas change when a new potential user out-competes a current user for the land occupied or when a current user is no longer interested in the area and abandons it to anyone who will have it. This change in land use is spoken of in ecology as *succession*.[10] If the new potential user comes into the area by outcompeting the current user, the process is called *invasion*. If an area is restricted to a given use by law or by the organized and conscious pressure of all current users, the restriction is known as *spatial segregation*. There are three kinds of spatial segregation in American society: limitations on the encroachment of industry into residential areas by law, limitations on the kinds of structures that can be built in a given area by law (so that apartment buildings cannot be built in areas of single-family homes, for example), and restrictions on the sale or rental of residential property to Negroes and other minority groups by private agreement of property owners. Segregation is not itself an ecological

[9] R. E. Park and C. Newcomb, "Newspaper Circulation and Metropolitan Regions," in R. D. McKenzie (ed.), *Readings in Human Ecology* (Ann Arbor: George Wahr, 1934), Chapter VIII.

[10] Robert E. Park, "Succession, An Ecological Concept," *American Sociological Review*, 1 (April, 1936), pp. 171–79.

process, since it is deliberate and not competitive, but it shapes and limits the competition. For example, it restricts a growing Negro population into a limited area and thus causes high rents and overcrowding in that area.[11]

B *The Location of Settlements*

Open country is settled largely on the basis of its agricultural productivity and its accessibility to a market, within the limitations set by the pressure of population or resources and by the values of a culture. (There are, of course, reasons for settlement in an area other than economic advantage.) There are, in general, two types of agricultural settlement: that where the farmers live in small villages and disperse each day in several directions to cultivate their fields, and that where the farmers live in isolated homesteads each on his individual farm. The former type of settlement was necessary in the Middle Ages as a means of protection against enemy armies and outlaw gangs, and has largely remained as the typical form of agricultural settlement in Europe. The latter type of settlement has become typical of the United States as a result of individual pioneering when the frontier was open.

When population increased in the farm-village type of settlement, population density increased until it reached a natural limit as farmers could go out only so far from the village to work their fields. Where new land was available, a part of the village split off to start a new village, or to settle in a city. When population increased in the individual-farmstead type of settlement, some of the young adults moved away (to new farms or to cities) or the farms were split into smaller units. The specific changes made were decided on in terms of the values of the culture. When population declined, as a result of emigration or disaster, half-empty villages or empty, isolated farmsteads were the results. Such villages can be found in parts of southern Italy today, and the ruins of such farmsteads can be seen in parts of Vermont.

When commercial farming replaced self-sufficient farming, the European farm village readily served as a collecting and distributing point for the local farmers. In the United States, however, the commercial village developed to take on this function. The village was located on a railroad line, along a river, or at some other point with transport facilities to the outside world and yet within hauling distance of the farms it served. Before the invention of motor vehicles, villages were distributed at such distances throughout American agricultural territories so that each farmer could make a "team haul" from his farm to the village, sell his produce,

[11] Luigi Laurenti, *Property Values and Race* (Berkeley: University of California Press, 1960); Davis McEntire, *Residence and Race* (Berkeley: University of California Press, 1960).

and/or purchase his supplies, return to his farm, all between sunup and sundown.[12] These villages had their characteristic institutions. At the minimum they had a railroad station or other terminal facility for transportation to and from the outside world, they had storage facilities adapted to the local farm products, they had at least one general store (which sold a wide range, but very limited selection, of articles), a post office, earlier a place to water and feed horses and later a gas station, sometimes a barbershop, a saloon-restaurant, a church, and often some specialty shops such as a shoemaker's shop. These villages usually grew or declined with the prosperity or extension of the agricultural territory they served.

Villages were established for other reasons, of course, than merely to serve agricultural communities. Some villages developed in frontier country in the United States to serve a similar commercial function for fur traders, cattle herders or sheep grazers. The territory served was generally much greater than that serving an agricultural area. Villages also grew near mines, but these were functionally more like the European villages since their purpose was primarily residential and social rather than commercial. Transportation villages grew up at the crossroads of two arteries of transportation—river, railroad, lake—to serve the secondary commercial function of shifting goods and passengers from one to the other. Railroads passing through isolated areas had to have watering places established every so many miles, and villages grew up at these points to service the railroads.[13] Other villages grew up as county seats to serve certain governmental functions, and still other villages grew up to serve tourist or resort areas.

Some of the villages increased in population until they were large towns and cities. Or the trend could go in the opposite direction, as the function for which the population center was established gradually disappeared. Hawley cites some historical cases of the declining city:

> This is not to say, of course, that once a center is established it is a permanent and immutable fixture thereafter. The rise and fall of centers is a familiar phenomenon to students of history. Changes in route patterns, whatever may be their cause, alter the advantages offered by existing locations, leaving some centers to recede into insignificance and sometimes extinction, and enabling others to rise to new heights of dominance. Many an ancient center, the victim of a river's change of course or of a new alignment of trade routes, is known now only through the researches of archaeologists. The once-important cities of the Euphrates-Tigris Valley—Nineveh, Babylon,

---

[12] C. J. Galpin, *The Social Anatomy of an Agricultural Village*, Agricultural Experiment Station of the University of Wisconsin, Research Bulletin 34 (Madison, 1915).

[13] W. F. Cottrell, "Death by Dieselization," *American Sociological Review*, 16 (June, 1951), pp. 358–65.

Some of the most striking examples of declining cities in modern times have been western mining centers:

Mark Twain's Virginia City on the Comstock lode rose over night from nothing to several thousand souls. The population of Storey County, Nevada, in which the Comstock lode lies, increased to 16,000 at the census of 1880. In 1930, the census enumerator recorded 667 souls left to guard a camp that in its time had produced nearly 400 million dollars in gold and silver. In 1877 the site of Leadville, Colorado, was occupied by a village of 200 people. Three years later the population had increased to 14,820, and at the last census it had fallen again to 3,771. Cripple Creek, in the palmy days, claimed 45,000 inhabitants, and even the unimpressionable census taker recorded 29,002 people in Teller County, of which it is the center, in the year 1900. By 1930 the official count for Teller County had fallen to 4,141, and the depression revival of gold mining had brought it up to perhaps 7,500 today (1936).

Carter Goodrich *et al.*, *Migration and Economic Opportunity* (Philadelphia: University of Pennsylvania Press, 1936), p. 271.

Baghdad—are today but subordinate towns. The same applies to Tyre and Sidon, leading commercial points on the Mediterranean seaboard in ancient times. Cairo, located close to the site of ancient Memphis, has superseded it as the principal center of the Nile Valley; while Rome, after a recession, has regained its prominence as a center of political, ecclesiastical, and commercial functions. Athens and Constantinople have declined; Naples and Genoa have gained at the expense of Florence and Pisa; Milan has displaced Venice; and the list of such changes could be extended indefinitely.[14]

A small number of villages developed into great cities, usually because they were strategically placed to serve a major function. When people were competing in several villages to perform a given commercial function, for example, those competitors would be most successful who worked in the village best located in terms of transportation routes. In this sense it may be said that villages competed with each other to become cities. Each kind of city—according to its major function—has different reasons for its location at a given type of place. The commercial cities—which include most of the largest cities of the world today and which have attracted such other activities as finance and scholarship—are almost invariably built at a natural transfer point from one type of transportation to another. This includes natural harbors, where land and sea transportation routes meet (e.g., London and New York); the meeting point of two

[14] Amos H. Hawley, *Human Ecology*, Copyright 1950, The Roland Press Company, p. 244.

rivers (e.g., St. Louis and Coblenz); the outlet of a navigable river into a navigable lake (e.g., early Chicago and Geneva).

Industrial cities develop where some large source of raw materials for industry is near some large power supply or some major artery of transportation. The latter reason sometimes brings a major industry to an already-established commercial city: for example, Chicago attracted the meat-packing industry because it had superior transportation and commercial facilities and yet was not too far from the Midwestern hog-raising farms. Pittsburgh became a great steel-producing city because it had important transportation routes and was also in the heart of a great coal-mining area. Essen, Germany, is quite comparable to Pittsburgh. Lyons early acquired most of the silk industry of France because it had two rivers and was near the heart of French silkworm culture.

Capital cities of nations or states are usually established at points most accessible to the largest number of people in the territory governed.[15] Thus capital cities are located somewhere near the geographic or the population center, at the time the capital city is chosen. A major exception occurred when Tsar Peter I changed the capital of Russia from Moscow to St. Petersburg so as to encourage contact with Western nations. Being unconcerned with this, the Communists returned the capital to Moscow when they seized power in 1917. When the boundaries of a nation change, the location of its capital may also be changed to bring it closer to the new center. An outstanding example of this occurred when the capital of Turkey was moved from Constantinople to Ankara in 1920.

c   *The Expansion of Settlements*

Adam Smith enunciated a basic law of ecology as well as of economics when he stated that an increase in division of labor extends the market. Specialization in production undertaken to increase efficiency requires that one seek new markets to sell one's product and to buy one's needs. Thus economic progress means increased interdependence, greater influence of the impersonal competitive type over a wider area. Improvements of transportation facilitate the same effect (see Table 18). These have been the long-run characteristics of modern economic development, at least until national autarchy was developed as an ideal in some countries after World War I. The medieval economy was based on village isolation and self-sufficiency. By 1914 the economy was world-wide, and there was a high de-

---

[15] This is an illustration of an ecological principle of "median location," which holds that settlements are made at a median location with respect to the area it serves and the areal resources it utilizes. See James A. Quinn, "The Hypothesis of Median Location," *American Sociological Review*, 8 (April, 1943), pp. 148–56.

TABLE 18 • SPEED, AVERAGE LOAD, COST PER TON MILE, AND MAXIMUM DISTANCE OF HAUL FOR DIFFERENT TYPES OF TRANSPORTATION

Type of transportation	Speed: miles per day	Average load: tons	Cost per ton mile[a]	Maximum distance with full load of food or fuel: miles
Human porter	15– 20	.03	$0.10 –$1.00	300
Horse team	15– 20	1.40	0.07 – 0.25	675
Pack animal	15– 25	.14	0.10 – 1.00	500
Liberty ship (10,000 tons)	250	12,000.00	0.001– 0.005	110,000
Motor truck (12 tons)	250– 600	——	0.02 – 0.08	40,000
Railroad (Steam and diesel)	400–1,000	2,500.00	0.007– 0.05	13,000–85,000
Airplane (July, 1943)	4,000–6,000	9.00	0.14 – 0.33	3,000– 6,000

Source: *Atlas of World Maps,* Army Service Forces Manual, M–101 (Washington, D.C., 1943), 23. Adapted from Hawley, *op. cit.,* p. 352.

[a] Costs in all parts of the world approximated in U. S. currency.

gree of interdependence. With each extension of the market it was possible for people in any area to buy products made or grown in a greater variety of other areas and to buy them more cheaply.

Table 18 shows the lower prices for goods and the greater distance from which they can feasibly be brought made possible by improvements in transportation alone. Not only did these developments make for an increase in the variety of products available to all people in the world economy, but they also made it possible to sustain a much larger population. The tremendous multiplication of the population of the Western world that we noted in the previous chapter was made possible by the extension of the market. While division of labor and specialization were tied up with diversification of available economic products, increased prosperity, and increase in population, they also entailed new dangers: a threat at any point in the line of trade was felt all along the line; any cutting off of a market endangered the prosperity and even the population of the rest of the world; any return to a lower level of specialization hurt a greater number of people. Thus modern economy is more damaged by war, nationalism, and organized movements to return people to the farm than any less interdependent economy would be.

The extension of the market has had other effects, happy and unhappy, on the people whom it touched. These are outside the realm of the ecological, but we may list a few of them: the expansion of the range of culture contact, the opening of people's minds to new cultural possibilities, the breaking up of ancient tyrannies and superstitions, the dissolution of cultural values, imperialism, occasionally the subordination of non-economic interests to economic ones. Whether the net economic effect of these changes be considered good or bad, it should be recognized that it would take almost as long to return to a medieval type of economy as it took to get out of it, and the amount of human suffering resulting from this return would far exceed the total amount of suffering that resulted from the expansion.

Thus far we have regarded the modern extension of the market from the broadest possible angle. We need now to examine it from progressively closer perspectives. The extension of the market made necessary the formation of whole new types of communities. Transportation or commercial communities had to be established along the routes of world and national transportation. Specialization in production required concentrations of population in industrial cities. People had to be sent out from commercial and industrial centers to facilitate the marketing of goods and to acquire raw materials. Improvements in agricultural technique as well as specialization in commercial crops sharply reduced the proportion of the population needed to produce the food and other agricultural requirements of the population. Thus the extension of the market has resulted in a great redistribution of population, some of the characteristics of which we noted in the preceding chapter. National boundaries set limits on this

TABLE 19 · SAME DISTANCE, SHORTER TIME TO GET THERE

	1938		*1964*	
	Miles	*Hrs./Min.*	*Miles*	*Hrs./Min.*
New York-Albany	150	4/41	154	2/49
New York-Philadelphia	88	2/44	97	1/49
New York-Washington *(via. Phila.)*	229	7/09	238	4/30
New York-Harrisburg	169	5/00	176	3/42
New York-Pittsburgh *(via Harrisburg)*	370	11/04	373	7/15
New York-San Francisco	3,038	101/00	3,031	66/10
Cleveland-Toledo	113	3/30	110	2/00
Toledo-Detroit	55	1/38	62	1/05
Toledo-Chicago	234	7/07	245	4/28
Detroit-Chicago	267	8/06	267	4/49
Washington-Chicago *(via Pittsburgh and Toledo)*	702	20/57	708	13/29
New York-Chicago *(via Harrisburg, Pittsburgh, and Toledo)*	840	25/7	849	15/54

Source: *The Christian Science Monitor,* July 6, 1964, p. 4.

redistribution for economic purposes, especially when there are tariffs or other barriers to trade and when there are barriers to international capital investment and to the movement of commercial travelers.

As noted, the multiplication of cities has been the most distinctive feature of the modern extension of the market. Despite the great attention given to cities by historians of the ancient and medieval periods, only a very small proportion of earlier populations lived in cities. And most ancient and medieval cities were small by modern standards.

> Very few early cities achieved populations of 100,000 or more and this order of magnitude was probably of temporary duration in most instances. At the birth of Christ there were approximately twelve cities of 100,000 population in the Mediterranean area. It is said that Carthage at one point in its history attained a population of 700,000, and Rome may have surpassed the 500,000 mark. One or two such agglomerations also may have appeared in Asia in ancient times, notably at Peiping. Nevertheless, the populations of the areas containing these great cities were preponderantly rural.
>
> The reasons for the relatively small amount of urban settlement in early times are to be found in the simple techniques of production and the clumsy transportation facilities then in existence. Since the yield from the soil over and above the day-to-day requirements of the producers was very slight, the proportion of non-agricultural workers that could be maintained in cities was correspondingly small. The number of city dwellers was further held in check by a lack of quick and inexpensive transportation. Without such facilities the distribution of food, a product which is both bulky and perishable, is closely restricted. This partly explains the much greater growth of early cities located on water routes as compared with inland cities.[16]

In 1800 there were only twenty-one cities of 100,000 or more population in the world.[17] By 1940 there were about 720 cities of this size. London was the first city in history to reach a population of one million, in 1802. At the present time at least 61 cities have reached that size, of which five are in the United States.[18] It is Asia which has had the largest increase in large cities: In 1900 there was only one Asian city with over 1 million inhabitants; by 1955 there were 28 such cities. If we consider total metropolitan areas of over 1 million in 1955, Europe led with 34;

[16] Amos H. Hawley, *Human Ecology*, Copyright 1950, The Ronald Press Company, p. 371.

[17] Adna F. Weber, *The Growth of Cities in the Nineteenth Century* (New York: Columbia University Press, 1899).

[18] Population Reference Bureau, Inc., "The World's Great Cities," *Population Bulletin*, 16 (September, 1960), p. 119.

Asia followed closely with 32; North America had 27, for a world total of 108.[19]

Another way to examine the transformation resulting from the extension of the market is to note the shift in the economic activities of people. Table 20 shows the distribution of workers in the United States by industry groups since 1820. Agriculture has undergone a steady relative decline. At first manufacturing and commerce were the activities that commanded an increasing proportion of the labor force. Commerce (including trade, transportation, and communication industries) continues to grow, but manufacturing reached a relative plateau after 1900. Professional service and public service have been the newly expanding industry groups. Such a pattern of development has been found by Colin Clark to be characteristic of all economically developed nations.[20] His theory of the "morphology of economic growth" holds that the first effect of expansion is to increase agricultural and mining employment as new territories are added. But the demand for the products of agriculture and mining is inelastic, and increasing efficiency of production reduces the relative needs for labor in them. The second stage then occurs with the diversification of production through manufacturing. But again technological development causes a plateau to be reached in the proportion of manufacturing workers. Expansion finally takes place in professional and public service, and can continue indefinitely as technological improvement continues to affect agriculture and manufacturing.

As a city grows, both the amount and the variety of service activities increase. Each increase in size affords greater opportunity for specialization. Both the immediate urban population and the dependent rural and small-town population create the demand for governmental service, higher education, health and recreational facilities, and marketing service. Specialization intensifies dependence. As a city grows, the rural areas around it change character somewhat. Heavy and spoilable foods are best raised in areas close to a city so that their transportation to the consumer is feasible. Thus a growing city has an increasing proportion of its surrounding agricultural area devoted to truck and dairy farming. The growing city is increasingly able to provide the goods and services the farmers nearby need, and thereby both expands the "needs" they can satisfy and reduces the role of the nearby village in satisfying them. Farmers and villagers develop a hierarchy of commercial centers to which they go to shop. These movements have been described for the residents of Irwin, Iowa, for example:

[19] *Ibid.,* p. 128.
[20] Colin Clark, *The Conditions of Economic Progress* (London: Macmillan, 1940), pp. 337–73.

TABLE 20 · PERCENTAGE DISTRIBUTION OF EMPLOYED WORKERS BY INDUSTRY GROUPS, UNITED STATES, 1820–1960

Industry	1960[a]	1950[b]	1940[c]	1920[d]	1900[d]	1880[d]	1860[d]	1840[d]	1820[d]
All Industries	100.0	100.0	100.0	100.0	100.0	100.0	100.0	100.0	100.0
Agriculture, forestry, fisheries	6.7	12.4	18.8	25.6	36.8	48.9	59.7	68.6	71.9
Mining	1.1	1.7	2.0	2.6	2.0	1.5	1.6	0.3	0.3
Manufacturing and mechanical (includes construction)	33.6	32.0	28.0	30.8	27.0	24.1	18.4	14.6	12.2
Transportation and communication	6.8	7.8	8.4	7.4	18.7	12.2	7.4	3.8	2.5
Trade (includes finance, repair)	24.7	24.7	16.7	10.2					
Public service	4.9	4.4	3.9	1.8	—	—	—	—	—
Professional service	11.4	9.3	10.5	5.2	4.2	3.5	2.9	2.7	2.8
Domestic and personal service	6.0	6.2	11.7	8.1	10.6	9.3	9.5	9.6	10.0
Clerical	n.a.	n.a.	n.a.	7.5	—	—	—	—	—
Other (includes recreation)	4.8	1.5	—	0.8	0.7	0.5	0.5	0.4	0.3

[a] From U.S. Bureau of the Census, *U.S. Census of Population: 1960*, Vol. I, *Characteristics of the Population*, Part 1, *U.S. Summary* (Washington, D.C., 1964), p. 563.

[b] From U.S. Bureau of the Census, *U.S. Census of Population: 1950*, Vol. II, *Characteristics of the Population*, Part 1 (Washington, D.C., 1953), pp. 1–103.

[c] From U.S. Bureau of the Census, *Sixteenth Census of the United States: 1940*, "Population: United States Summary" (Washington, D.C., 1943), p. 10.

[d] From P. K. Whelpton, "Occupational Groups in the United States, 1820–1920," *Journal of the American Statistical Association*, 21 (September, 1926), S.No. 155, p. 340.

n.a.—not available.

Irwin as a village is a retailing, local produce, service, and residence center. The goods and services available in the village are generally those for which there is frequent call and which are of relatively low cost. Shopping excursions are often made by Irwin people to Harlan, the county seat, a town of 3,500, and to Manila, Dennison, and Manning, where a greater variety of goods and services are available. Less frequent trips are made to Omaha and Council Bluffs. Sales of farm produce, particularly of livestock, are made in the metropolitan center, as are purchases of livestock for feeding, men's and women's clothing, furniture, household utensils, and other goods and services of a somewhat special character. Council Bluffs and Omaha newspapers and radio stations supply the town with news and entertainment and exert great influence through the control devices of propaganda and advertising. Styles, fashions, and fads flow out into the locality from these cities.[21]

[21] Edward O. Moe and Carl C. Taylor, *Culture of a Contemporary Rural Community: Irwin, Iowa* (Washington, D.C.: U.S. Bureau of Agricultural Economics, 1942), Rural Life Studies No. 5, p. 48.

The increasing dependence of rural people on the city in this manner probably tends to segmentalize their loyalties in a manner much like that noted by sociologists for city dwellers.[22] Interest in local government, neighborhood groups, and such local institutions as the church must decline when rural people make regular trips to large urban centers. The larger a city, the more efficient do its transportation services tend to be: only the largest cities can afford subways and frequently running public-transportation facilities of any type. The competition for desirable sites is so great that few competitors can afford to pay for the land best suited to their economic functions. Consequently, they pool their resources and build upward; the result is the skyscraper. Homer Hoyt has described this growth in Chicago:

> A large demand for office space sprang up from the new manufacturing concerns that were locating in or near Chicago at this time. Other tenants were secured from the increasing numbers of people who were entering the real estate business, and from promoters of enterprises for the World's Fair, who sought to enhance their prestige by having an office in these popular skyscrapers. Doctors and dentists found that it paid to have an office in high buildings near the State Street stores. Department stores discovered that people preferred to ascend in elevators rather than walk a block to a side street. Thus vertical rather than lateral expansion became the order of the day, and some of these structures paid handsome returns, for a time, even on their common stock.[23]

Pressure on the central business district of a growing city further expresses itself in the distribution of some of its functions to outlying districts. Especially facilities for consumers—such as motion picture theaters and department stores—are likely to decentralize, and outlying business districts grow up with most of the consumer facilities possessed by the central business districts.

Improvements in the transportation facilities of cities have permitted great extensions in the size of metropolitan communities. Within the city, the removal of public transportation lines from crowded streets to subways and elevated lines and the substitution of rapid busses for slow streetcars have made for more rapid movement. The building of highways from the center of a city to its outskirts has permitted more people to live in suburbs while they work in the center of the city, but these have also increased the downtown traffic and parking problem. Suburbanites are more and more turning to the suburban railroad, even when they

[22] Louis Wirth, "Urbanism as a Way of Life," *American Journal of Sociology,* 44 (July, 1938), pp. 1-24.

[23] Homer Hoyt, *One Hundred Years of Land Values in Chicago* (Chicago: University of Chicago Press, 1933), p. 152. Copyright 1933 by the University of Chicago Press.

own cars, to get them to the city's center. Since these railroads reach out in only a few directions from the city, the direction of suburban development has been somewhat limited, but the total number of people that can be accommodated in suburbs has hardly been limited yet.

Considering non-occupational purposes, a high degree of access to the city's facilities on the part of people who prefer to live in suburbs has been furnished by the automobile, the telephone, radio, and television. Since suburbs have been attractive to people because they are less congested, cleaner, and sometimes cheaper for those who prefer to live in single-family houses, they have grown rapidly around cities. In the decade between 1930 and 1940, while American cities proper grew only 5 per cent in population, the areas surrounding them grew 15.8 per cent.[24] This process continued, and in the decade 1950–1960, while the population of the central cities in the Standard Metropolitan Statistical Areas (total population 112.9 millions) grew by 10.8 per cent, the population of the surrounding areas rose by a phenomenal 48.5 per cent.[25] In the five largest metropolitan areas during that decade, the population of the central cities rose only 1 per cent, whereas the increase in the suburban ring was 71 per cent. In 1960 only 51.4 per cent of the total population included within all the metropolitan areas actually resided in the central cities.[26] There are some exceptions to the trend—notably Los Angeles and Miami. In some metropolitan districts the central district has actually declined in population, while the suburban areas have more than made up for the center's loss.[27]

The growth of suburbs causes some serious institutional difficulties. The movement of population—especially of high-income receivers—outside the city limits reduces the possibilities for the city government to tax people to maintain the city facilities which they use. On the other hand, the governments of most suburban communities govern too few people to support extensive public-health facilities, flood-control programs, etc. The multiplicity of governments in areas immediately surrounding cities results in conflicts over jurisdiction, ineffective and inefficient use of police power and fire control, inequitable distribution of tax burdens, etc. The loss to the city by outward movements consists not only in inability to tax suburbanites who use city facilities, but in a less intensive use of land in

[24] Amos H. Hawley and Don J. Bogue, "Recent Shifts in Population: The Drift Toward the Metropolitan District, 1930–40," *Review of Economic Statistics*, 24 (August, 1942), p. 145.

[25] U.S. Bureau of the Census, *Census of Population: 1960*, Vol. I, Part A (Washington, D.C.: Government Printing Office, 1961).

[26] U.S. Bureau of the Census, *Census of Population: 1960. Standard Metropolitan Statistical Areas.* PC(3)–1D (Washington, D.C.: Government Printing Office, 1961).

[27] Howard W. Green, *Movements of Families Within the Cleveland Metropolitan District 1933* (Cleveland, 1934), pp. 18–19.

various parts of the city. Old buildings are not soon replaced by new ones with higher valuation, and vacant lots are left unused while sidewalks, sewers, and streets have to be maintained in front of them. The solution would seem to be a single government for a metropolitan area, but differential tax burdens, local loyalties, and the crossing of state boundaries by metropolitan districts prevent this development.

Suburban populations typically include a significant over-representation of children and a significant under-representation of older people, who remain in the central city.[28] The large number of children in areas of new residence means that there must be a very heavy expenditure for education, which generally is the most costly item for local government. Central cities have much lower expenditures for education, at least until they have to rebuild worn-out schools, but they have another problem of greater seriousness—the culturally deprived child.[29] Children who come from families where there is little motivation to get an education, whose backgrounds are primitive and involve a paucity of the opportunities available in modern society, become psychologically and sociologically incapable of getting much out of school. They often become problem children, prone to delinquency and even drug addiction. The large Northern cities tend to segregate these children—partly because they are de facto segregated by their residential concentration in certain areas, partly out of deliberate design, and partly because they can do nothing else, being cut off by political boundaries from the culturally advantaged children whose families have migrated to the suburbs.[30] If the central cities have fewer expenditures than do the suburbs for education, they have more for law enforcement. They also have more expenditures for the relief of older people, who typically do not move out to the suburbs nearly as rapidly as do younger families.

Another problem created by the dispersion of the urban population to the suburbs is that involving the transportation of large numbers of people from homes in the suburbs to the downtown areas for work, shopping, or entertainment. Only a few American cities have followed the European pattern of expanding the mass transit system to cope with the needs of a burgeoning metropolitan population to move around rapidly and freely. The more typical American response has been to rely on the

[28] Otis D. Duncan and Albert J. Reiss, Jr., *Social Characteristics of Urban and Rural Communities, 1950* (New York: Wiley, 1956), pp. 117–33. A useful summary source on the problems of, and created by, the movement of population to the suburbs is William Dobriner (ed.), *The Suburban Community* (New York: Putnam, 1958). An interesting cultural analysis of suburban life is Sylvia F. Fava, "Suburbanism as a Way of Life," *American Sociological Review*, 21 (February, 1956), pp. 34–37.

[29] Frank Riessman, *The Culturally Deprived Child* (New York: Harper, 1962).

[30] Arnold M. Rose, *De Facto School Segregation* (New York: National Conference on Christians and Jews, 1964).

There is no official definition of a suburb provided by the Bureau of the Census, nor has the term received much systematic attention by sociologists. A rough "content analysis" of the relevant literature reveals that suburbs are (1) communities (2) outside the central city and politically independent of it (3) culturally and economically dependent upon the central city, and (4) in general, highly specialized communities particularly along familistic and residential lines. Accordingly, a working definition of the suburb might be: *those urbanized, residential communities which are outside the corporate limits of a large central city, but which are culturally and economically dependent upon the central city.*

The rural-urban fringe is conceived in a somewhat different light. Some variety in language exists, but Blizzard and Anderson's definition is typical: "From an operational point of view in research, the rural-urban fringe has usually been designated at that area of mixed urban and rural land uses between the point where full city services cease to be available and the point where agricultural land uses predominate."* Thus, suburbs are conceived of as urbanized communities, while the rural-urban fringe is seen as a land belt surrounding the central city containing mixed urban and rural uses of land. It is that area where city and country come together. . . .

William M. Dobriner (ed.), *The Suburban Community* (New York: Putnam, 1958), p. xvii.

* Samuel W. Blizzard and William F. Anderson, "Problems in Rural-Urban Fringe Research: Conceptualization and Delineation," The Pennsylvania State College Agricultural Experiment Station, Progress Report 89 (State College, Pa., November, 1952), mimeo, p. 11.

private automobile. The results of the latter are the building of city freeways which disperse the population still more, the clogging of roads and streets, the transformation of valuable downtown land into parking lots and parking ramps, the pollution of the city air with gasoline fumes (sometimes taking the form of poisonous smog). Taking into consideration all the values of health, speed and ease of transportation, the maintenance of urban facilities (for example, cultural centers, big department stores, first-run movies, etc.), the maintenance of city neighborhoods, the sustenance of big newspapers (as compared to suburban neighborhood shopping newspapers), the automobile is the least efficient and the most destructive means of transportation when large numbers of people in the large cities try to rely on it exclusively, yet it has become the dominant mode of intra-urban transportation in most American cities. At the extreme is the case of Los Angeles, which some observers have claimed to no longer be a city, but a collection of suburbs connected by freeways and stifled by smog. Rather belatedly, the federal government in 1963–65 began to see the need to stimulate the only practical and efficient alternative—rapid mass transit. But in only a few cities—like San Francisco and Boston—were local leaders sufficiently perceptive and influential enough to see the need to encourage the means whereby the mass of the people would shift their transportation medium from the automobile to mass transit. (Of course, a huge city like New York had perforce grown up with an efficient mass transit system.) The greatest question in the mid-1960's for the large cities of America was whether they would choke themselves with traffic, smog, and urban decay in the interest of permitting each individual to battle the transportation problem for himself.

Other institutions have difficulties of a different sort resulting from the dispersion of the urban population. A church once located among the dwellings of its parishioners sees them scattered in all directions, while persons belonging to another denomination enter the neighborhood. A recreational center or school built in the heart of a residential area finds itself being surrounded by commercial enterprises while its clientele moves away. Commercial enterprises that serve a transient trade—such as a gas station that makes a heavy investment in underground gasoline tanks and "greasing palaces"—find themselves on streets that no longer serve the through traffic.

There are limits to the expansion of the metropolitan community.[31] We have already referred to the difficulties of commuting to the center of the city from too far out in the suburbs and to the high cost of maintaining urban facilities—such as water mains, sewers, paved streets, public-transportation facilities—in sparsely settled areas. In earlier times the difficulty of bringing sufficient quantities of food to huge concentrations of popula-

[31] A new term has come into existence since the mid-1930's to distinguish the far-out areas from the built-up suburbs—"the rural-urban fringe." See the box on page 536 for definitions.

When compared with central cities, the suburbs have higher fertility ratios, higher percentages of married persons, lower percentages separated, higher percentages in primary families, higher socio-economic status in the labor forces, higher median income, lower median age, a higher percentage of mobile families and a higher level of educational achievement. When the suburbs are compared with independent cities, many of the same tendencies persist. Duncan and Reiss, in a study of suburbs and independent cities, found the suburbs contained a smaller proportion of the nonwhite population, slightly larger households, higher proportions of married males, higher proportion of males in the labor force than independent cities, a higher socio-economic status, higher percentages in the white-collar occupations, craftsmen, foreman and similar occupations, a higher percentage of college-age persons enrolled in school, higher median family income and a higher percentage of home ownership.

William M. Dobriner (ed.), *The Suburban Community* (New York: Putnam's, 1958), p. xvi.

tion was a limiting factor in city growth, but today—with well-organized and speedy transportation systems, equipped with refrigeration facilities—that is not so important. The maintenance of a sufficient water supply, however, has proved to be a burden to several contemporary cities and may yet serve as a limiting factor.

Also of importance in limiting urban expansion—especially in western Europe and in the eastern states of the United States—is the competition of adjoining metropolitan areas for space and for workers and buyers living in the intervening zones. It is not only a question of the time and cost of transportation to one city's center rather than another's, but also of the relative merits of the marketing facilities available in the two centers. The diffusion of many of the city's services—especially facilities such as public libraries, department stores, beauty salons, and other service enter-prises—to suburban centers reduces the area's dependence on the city's central business district.

D   *The Pattern of Growth in the Modern City*

Certain characteristic developments take place within a city as it begins to grow, although the pattern of internal change varies with the functions of the city. Most of the research has been done on commercial cities that have had their main development in the past century or two, and we shall therefore describe the pattern of internal development for this type of city. It would be a mistake, however, to assume that the pattern of recently developed commercial cities is the pattern for all cities, as several writers seem to assume. A commercial city has its start near the point where its major arteries of transportation meet—at the harbor, at the crossing of two rivers or of two railroad lines. Here the transportation facilities must be placed, and commercial establishments are located nearby to service them. Homes are placed at convenient spots not too far from where people work.

When the town grows, the new commercial users of land can out-compete the residential users, and they need to be located near the already-established commercial enterprises. So commercial enterprises crowd out the first area of residential settlement. Those who can afford it build new homes in adjacent territory, which now becomes completely residential. They leave their old homes to be inhabited by poorer immigrants, to be converted to commercial uses, or to be torn down and the land sold to a commercial user. This drawing-away process occurs from two types of commercial encroachment. One is circular, that is, away from the center of the town; the other is radial, that is, along the major arteries of trans-portation as they leave the center of the town. Richard Hurd was probably the first to note that city growth was both central and axial, as he called them: "A continual contest exists between axial growth, pushing out from the center along transportation lines, and central growth, constantly following and obliterating it, while new projections are being made further out on the various axes."[32]

As job-seeking migrants enter the town they settle in the area of lowest rents since they are poor. This is the area infiltrated by commercial and sometimes manufacturing enterprises. Status differentiation[33] begins to develop rapidly in a growing town. The area of first settlement acquires the reputation of a lower-class area, and people who can afford it move out to other residential areas. But people who leave the lower-class areas are not happily accepted as neighbors by those who are already living in the second residential zone: the latter consider themselves to be upper or upper middle class and do not accept the pushers from below. They move out and form a third residential zone. In American cities, until very recently, there has been an ethnic factor greatly strengthening the status differentiation. A given ethnic group has migrated to the United States predominantly within a few decades, and therefore it is often predominantly a single ethnic group that answers the call for workers in a growing city at a certain period of time. Thus the escape of a middle class from a lower class, and an upper class from a middle class, is also usually a matter of ethnic differentiation as well as of status differentiation.

At the same time, industry moves outward as it seeks to expand and to settle along the major arteries of transportation—railroads, rivers, and highways—as they leave the city.[34] These transportation routes are essential to bring raw materials to the factories and help to distribute their products to regional and national markets. Yet most factories remain near the city to get its labor supply, part of its market, and its attraction of several transportation routes. Along with the settlement of factories at the outskirts of the city grow up residential areas of workers who work in the factories. Often only the larger factories can afford to settle along the major transportation arteries and still be close to the city. Smaller plants—those employing fewer than 100 workers, say—are forced to distribute themselves in the less desirable territory away from the major transportation routes, and so they round out an industrial suburb.[35]

And so a city grows—in modified concentric circles away from the center and in sectors according to the type of population and land use

[32] Richard M. Hurd, *Principles of City Land Values* (New York: The Record and Guide, 1903), p. 39.

[33] See Chapter 8, Section C.

[34] Maurice R. Davie, "The Pattern of Urban Growth," in G. P. Murdock (ed.), *Studies in the Science of Society* (New Haven: Yale University Press, 1937); Walter Firey, *op. cit.*

[35] Leo G. Reeder, "A Note on the Burgess-Davie, Firey Differences Regarding Industrial Location," *American Sociological Review*, 18 (April, 1953), pp. 189–91.

that got started moving outward in a given direction from the center of the city.[36] But a number of factors interfere with these two patterns of growth. Natural barriers are almost inevitably present since the commercial city is usually built at the edge of a sea, lake, or river, and these prevent growth in their direction. Social barriers also operate: an upper-class residential area built along a lake shore or riverbank succeeds in retaining this choice location against the encroachment of commerce and slums; zoning ordinances channel industry away from certain desirable areas; certain institutions (hospitals, for example) become surrounded by slums but retain the fine appearance of their immediate surroundings; some cities spread out to such great distances that commuting becomes difficult and a segment of the suburban population moves back to a renovated center of the city. Finally, certain people have a sentimental attachment to a certain piece of land and retain it long after it is efficient or even pleasant to retain it for its old use.[37] These and other modifying forces do not change the essential pattern that underlies the growth of a modern commercial city.

E. W. Burgess, who formulated the concentric-zone elements in the theory of urban growth just presented, postulated five concentric zones in the mature city, recognizing the many sources of distortion noted above.[38] Burgess made his observations of American cities in 1923, and therefore could not be aware of the recent "return to the center" that has begun in the largest cities when commuting to the suburbs became too difficult. The five zones are:

1 A central business district, containing terminal facilities for the major transportation routes out of the city, major shopping and entertainment facilities designed to serve the whole city and not just one segment of it, offices of the most important commercial and financial enterprises servicing the economic activity of the city, other kinds of offices that are attracted by the central and prestigious location and that can afford to pay the high rents.

2 A zone of transition, containing factories that were early attracted to the growing commercial city, warehousing and storage facilities,

[36] These two patterns of growth have been emphasized in two different theories of city growth—that by Burgess and that by Hoyt—but it is likely that both theories are correct. Ernest W. Burgess, "The Growth of the City," in R. E. Park (ed.), *The City* (Chicago: University of Chicago Press, 1925); Homer Hoyt, *The Structure and Growth of Residential Neighborhoods in American Cities* (Washington, D.C.: Federal Housing Administration, 1939).

[37] Firey, *op. cit.*

[38] The most complete statement of the zonal hypothesis by Burgess is in his "Urban Areas," in T. V. Smith and L. D. White (eds.), *Chicago: An Experiment in Social Science Research* (Chicago: University of Chicago Press, 1929), pp. 114–23. A summary of the criticisms of the zonal hypothesis is contained in James A. Quinn, *Human Ecology* (New York: Prentice-Hall, 1950), pp. 116–37.

wholesale establishments, slum housing, "shady" entertainment spots, hobohemia, old residences "converted" into rooming houses or into commercial offices, colonies of some recent immigrants (including a few well-to-do members who prefer to live near their compatriots), and some vacant lots where old houses have crumbled but no new use has yet been made of the land.

3   A zone of workingmen's homes, including lower-class residences and a few factories that also settled early at the edge of the growing city.

4   A zone of middle-class residences, including both single-family homes and apartments for middle-class people, and secondary shopping centers.

5   A zone of commuters' residences, including a large proportion of upper-class homes. Occasionally the late establishment of a factory in the cheap land outside the city develops an industrial suburb here that includes many workingmen's homes.

While far from perfectly fitting the facts, these zoned concepts aid considerably in understanding the distribution of population and land uses in cities that have developed in modern times. The separation between zones is not usually sharp but rather gradual, and certain characteristics—both ecological and social—increase or decrease with a certain regularity as we move outward from the center of the city. These latter effects of a dominant natural area are called gradients.[39] Some urban gradients that fit in with the Burgess zonal hypothesis are the decreasing age of structure as we move outward from Zone II, the decreasing proportion of foreign-born in the population, the increasing proportion of married adults, the increasing income per family, and many others. Indices of social disorganization have also been shown to form characteristic patterns when plotted on maps of the city. In most instances, Zone II is found to have the highest rates, which irregularly go down as one moves outward toward the edge of the city. This has been found to be true for crime and juvenile delinquency,[40] physical and mental disease,[41] and suicides.[42]

[39] Ernest W. Burgess, "The Determination of Gradients in the Growth of the City," *Publications of the American Sociological Society*, 21 (1927), pp. 178–84.

[40] H. W. Green, *Population Characteristics by Consensus Tracts, Cleveland, Ohio, 1930* (Cleveland: The Plain Dealer Publishing Co., 1931); C. R. Shaw, *Delinquency Areas* (Chicago: University of Chicago Press, 1929); National Commission on Law Observance and Enforcement, *Report on the Causes of Crime* (Washington, D.C.: U.S. Government Printing Office, 1931); R. C. Fletcher, H. L. Hornbeck, and S. A. Queen, *Social Statistics of St. Louis* (1935).

[41] H. W. Green, "Cultural Areas in the City of Cleveland," *American Journal of Sociology*, 38 (1933), pp. 356–67; Kansas City Tuberculosis Society, *Report* (1935); R. E. L. Faris and H. W. Dunham, *Mental Disorders in Urban Areas* (Chicago: University of Chicago Press, 1939); S. A. Queen, "The Ecological Study of Mental Disorders," *American Sociological Review*, (1941), pp. 201–9.

[42] Ruth Cavan, *Suicide* (Chicago: University of Chicago Press, 1928); Calvin Schmid,

The ecological forces tend to create one-class communities, as we have seen. Land values, competition among alternative uses, age of existing dwelling units, need to be close to certain facilities, and sheer individual choice tend to inhabit a given community with people on a given-income level. To these factors have recently been added the policy of government. As government has moved into housing construction, it has tended to follow the existing ecological patterns in planning a project for use by people of a given-income level. Some of the government projects have been very large and thus have tended to increase the class segregation. Sharp has described the situation in England:

> The recent and present segregation is even more regrettable than that of the 19th century, bad as that was: for this has arisen not from the actions of individuals, but from activity by government itself, and it has occurred on a far larger scale than any segregation hitherto. As a result of governmental activity in the housing of the working classes, we have now in every town or city in the country whole estates devoted entirely to the housing of one particular wage-earning group of population. Around the great cities we have enormous one-class communities (if they can be called communities) the like of which the world has never seen before; Becontree, one of a score of London County Council housing estates, where no less than 120,000 working-class people live in one enormous concentration; Norris Green, one of many Liverpool Corporation estates, housing 50,000 working-class inhabitants; and so on and so on in Leeds, Manchester, Birmingham, and all the rest of the big and little towns in the kingdom.[43]

E   Some Characteristic Residential Areas Within American Cities

Many of the sociological studies of American city characteristics were undertaken by students at the University of Chicago, as a result of the stimulation of R. E. Park and E. W. Burgess, and hence much of the information relates to the city of Chicago.[44] There is a danger in over-generalizing from one city to all American cities. In this section we shall

Suicides in Seattle, 1914–1925 (Seattle: University of Washington Press, 1928); C. Schmid, "Suicide in Minneapolis, Minnesota: 1920–1932," *American Journal of Sociology*, 39 (1934), pp. 30–48; R. E. L. Faris, *Social Disorganization* (New York: Ronald, 1948); Jack P. Gibbs, "Suicide," in R. K. Merton and R. A. Nisbet, *Contemporary Social Problems* (New York: Harcourt, Brace, 1961), pp. 222–61.

[43] Thomas Sharp, *Town Planning* (New York: Penguin, 1942), p. 86.

[44] A summary of many of the studies carried on at the University of Chicago over fifty years is contained in Ernest W. Burgess and Donald J. Bogue (eds.), *Contributions to Urban Sociology* (Chicago: University of Chicago Press, 1964).

describe certain kinds of urban areas, recognizing that the general features of the area are characteristic of many American cities but that certain details are limited to the city described.

The homeless-man areas of Chicago, described by Nels Anderson in 1923,[45] were three in number, located at the edge of the central business district. They stretched westward along Madison Street, southward along State Street, and northward along Clark Street. The first of these was inhabited largely by migratory hoboes and casual laborers who stayed only a short time in the city, mostly in winter. The second area was the lodging-house area for older, down-and-out men who seldom left the city. The third area, smaller than the others, attracted radicals and intellectuals among the hoboes. Most of the men—there were practically no women among them—lived in lodginghouses of varying quality. Some were cheap hotels, where small private rooms were available. Others were converted residences, where cots for several men would be set up in each of the erstwhile family rooms. Still others were flophouses—perhaps former stores, warehouses, or meeting halls—where men would rent sleeping space on the floor. The city had one municipal lodginghouse and there were some semi-philanthropic lodginghouses, providing small cells each with a cot and perhaps a chair. Numerous cheap restaurants—generally advertising "home-cooked meals"—dotted the areas. There were also many colorful but tawdry amusement spots: cheap movie houses, burlesque shows, houses of prostitution, penny arcades, and taverns, open or secret, depending upon the current law. Special-service facilities were established for the population. Employment agencies offered short-time jobs to unskilled workers; barber colleges provided free or cheap haircuts, secondhand clothing shops enabled a homeless man to buy suits and coats cheaply and to sell his overcoat in the spring, religious missions sought to appeal to the men's spiritual needs (and often provided free food and shelter). An open-air forum for soapbox speakers, bohemian clubs, bookshops, and a "Hobo College" appealed to the intellectual and radical elements in the population.

The major areas of segregated Negro residences in Chicago and New York have been described by Frazier.[46] The Chicago "Black Belt" was a thin strip, three quarters of a mile wide and more than five miles long, stretching straight south from the edge of the central business district. The area could be divided into seven zones which roughly paralleled, in a contracted form, the concentric zones of the city as a whole, with an exception for a shopping and amusement section in Zone III. Whereas the

[45] Nels Anderson, *The Hobo* (Chicago: University of Chicago Press, 1923).

[46] E. Franklin Frazier, *The Negro Family in Chicago* (Chicago: University of Chicago Press, 1932); and "Negro Harlem: An Ecological Study," *American Journal of Sociology,* 43 (July, 1937), pp. 72–88.

This ecological and statistical evidence shows that the alcoholic psychoses have their highest rates in and near the center of the city. In this sense the patterns of their rates are quite similar to those patterns found in the schizophrenic series but unlike the patterns found in the manic-depressive series. In the alcoholic psychoses the rates by housing areas for the different nativity classifications indicated that there was some relationship between liability to the psychosis and the fact that the person does not live in a community primarily populated by his own nativity or racial group. The distribution of drug addicts, while representing a definite selection of cases, shows a pattern similar to the alcoholic psychoses. Not only do high rates occur in the zone of transition but also the bulk of the cases are to be found in this zone. The fact that the next highest rate for drug addiction is in the apartment-hotel and hotel area would seem to indicate that drug addicts tend to select the more mobile areas of the city where their habits and activities are less likely to be scrutinized.

R. E. L. Faris, and H. W. Dunham, *Mental Disorders in Urban Areas* (Chicago: University of Chicago Press, 1939).

Chicago area spread outward in one direction from its source near the center of the city, New York's Harlem area spread outward in all directions from its source at 125th Street and Seventh Avenue (although the rate of growth was inhibited on the west side by an exclusive white residential district). Frazier found five concentric zones within Harlem that were differentiated much as American cities generally are differentiated. For example, the percentage of non-residential structures, of lodging and rooming houses, of single adults, of families on relief, generally decreased from Zone I to Zone V. The central zone had the largest proportion of business establishments, but also—unlike complete cities—the largest proportion of religious institutions, political clubs, and recreational centers.

An upper-class residential area of Chicago, known as the Gold Coast, was described by Zorbaugh in 1929.[47] This was a small area, about twenty blocks long and two blocks wide stretching along the lake front from the northern tip of the central business district. It was separated from the business district proper by a street of expensive shops, hotels, and attractive office buildings. The area contained the residences of more than a third of all the persons listed in the social register, with most of the others living in exclusive suburbs. Residences were of three types: huge single-family mansions, modern apartment buildings with apartments of seven to ten rooms apiece, and expensive hotels sometimes having small apartments as well as single rooms. There were few commercial establishments in the area, except for restaurants and an occasional drugstore or dress shop in the hotels, but there were many restaurants, shops, and service establish-

[47] Harvey W. Zorbaugh, *The Gold Coast and the Slum* (Chicago: University of Chicago Press, 1929).

ments on adjoining streets away from the lake. Some exclusive clubs were located in the area and a secluded area of the beach was used as a harbor for small boats.

A residential area of Los Angeles, occupied mainly by middle-class white American families, was described by McClenahan in 1929.[48] The area originally consisted of single-family homes, but a good number of these had been remodeled to accommodate two families, and some apartment buildings had been built. No stores or factories were permitted in the area, by zoning ordinance, although a number of business establishments were located on the boundary streets. Offices of doctors and dentists could be established within the area. A total of 92 stores and service establishments were spatially available. These included 12 professional offices—of physicians, dentists, attorneys, druggists, music teachers, artists; 13 shopkeepers providing personal service—cleaners, barbers, florists, shoe repairmen, and tobacconists; 18 grocery and food markets; 12 clothing stores; 10 household-equipment stores; 9 manufacturing and wholesale centers; 5 automobile repair or service stations; 3 restaurants; 1 bank; 1 real-estate office; 1 post office; and 7 miscellaneous establishments. Most of the inhabitants went outside the area for their recreation, and many of them had most of their friends in other neighborhoods. There were churches and a school in the area, but many of the adults and some of the children went outside the area to attend church or school. The residents belonged to many voluntary associations, but only a few of these had most of the membership among dwellers of the area.

The west end of Boston, inhabited mainly by Italian-Americans, was described by Herbert J. Gans as of 1962.[49] Whereas other writers on the immigrant emphasized the bewildering transformation that peoples undergo in migrating from the old world to the new, Gans emphasizes that much of the old country's social system was retained. Migrants from a given town or village in Italy would tend to settle together in the same American city. They held the same type of unskilled and poorly paid occupations in the U.S. as they did in Italy (except that few went in for farming). The extended family continued to function as the matrix of social life. The public authorities were consistently defined as an enemy, including the school which kept children from work and from contributing to the family income. It is only in superficial aspects of life—acquiring a taste for cars, sports, and the mass media—that the Italian immigrant became quickly acculturated. Even the second-generation Italian, attached to his own age group (often in the form of a gang), remained resistant to the broader American society and leadership. For example, the child who adopted the

[48] Bessie A. McClenahan, *The Changing Urban Neighborhood* (Los Angeles: University of Southern California, 1929).

[49] Herbert J. Gans, *The Urban Villagers* (New York: Free Press of Glencoe, 1963).

behavior patterns demanded of him by school teachers or settlement house workers ran the risk of losing his gang's support. The peer group offered much by way of warmth, friendship and social entertainment. To be left without close and constant companions was the scourge of the west ender's life. Teen-agers, for instance, who were outgoing and aggressive when together, were found to be quiet and docile when confronted individually. Aspirations for career, wealth, prestige, individual development were usually sacrificed to the demands for conformity from the group. Of course, a few got professional educations and became leaders in the community as lawyer or physician. For most, with poor elementary educations, there was little opportunity for the American type of success anyway. The west end had little crime or drug addiction, even though the rest of Boston thought that it did. Buildings were old, but kept in good condition. Yet the neighborhood was called a slum, and it was razed in an urban renewal program in 1963. That caused the break-up of the social community as well.

F The Cultural Setting of the City

We have emphasized that ecological factors are abstractions and do not determine the location, growth, and structure of settlements all by themselves. To support this assertion it is desirable to consider cities in a variety of historical cultures: the differences reveal unique amalgamations of ecological and cultural factors.

Davis[50] points out that cities did not begin in human history until sometime between 6000 and 5000 B.C., considerably later than most of the basic institutions (such as the family, the church, or the government) or of such other aspects of social organization as stratification. Their origin required a technological development that made possible both an agricultural surplus (so that each agricultural worker could produce more than his family needs) and transportation facilities to bring food to the non-producing cities. Technological advances by themselves were not sufficient: there must also be highly fertile land (as in the alluvial valleys of Egypt, Mesopotamia, and India) and sufficient social organization—especially in terms of commerce and government—to make trading possible and reliable. Davis estimates that the ancient cities of Babylon, Ur, Erech, Mohenjo Daro, and Harappa held between 5,000 and 25,000 people, and that the Egyptian cities of Tel el-Amarna and Thebes were not much larger. There were many dangers to the early cities. Non-urban barbarians often swooped down on them and if they did not destroy them physically, they damaged

[50] Kingsley Davis, "The Origin and Growth of Urbanization in the World," *American Journal of Sociology*, 60 (March, 1955), pp. 429–37. For another history and cross-cultural comparison of cities, see Population Reference Bureau, Inc., *op. cit.*, pp. 109–30.

the structure of commerce and government that made cities possible; disease was a deadly threat until sanitary practices were adopted and a start was made on medicine; despotic monarchy occasionally exploited the working population so drastically as to cut down on its productivity so essential to urban life.

The Graeco-Roman civilization that flourished between 600 B.C. and A.D. 400 made possible much larger cities. Davis[51] attributes this to "iron tools and weapons, alphabetic writing, improved sailboats, cheap coinage, more democratic institutions, systematic colonization—all tended to increase production, stimulate trade, and expand the effective political unit." Athens held a population of between 120,000 and 180,000 in the fifth century B.C. Rome and Byzantium, based on a huge empire with a much more effective political organization, achieved a population of perhaps three times this size.

The loss of this political organization and of trade over a wide area reduced the cities of western Europe to small towns once again, and cities of more than 100,000 people did not arise again until the Renaissance restored trade in the thirteenth century.[52] Perhaps the largest city in the Western world in the fourteenth century was Gubbio, Italy, the center of the textile trade. Today it is a depopulated shell. Even with the Renaissance, cities grew slowly until the Industrial Revolution that began at the end of the eighteenth century. The pre-Industrial city was cramped and internally sharply divided into neighborhoods occupied by the different social classes.[53] The "business district" was not yet the center of the town; this function was more often held by the cathedral. Because the Industrial Revolution has developed most rapidly in Western culture, most of the urbanized areas of the world today are in Western culture. Table 21 shows that the most urbanized regions of the world today are Australia–New Zealand (included under Oceania), United States–Canada, and Europe.

Even within this culture area cities differ considerably in their ecological structure because of historical circumstances. Cities such as Paris and Rome, for example, have no clearly demarcated central business district, there is dense building distribution right up to the edge of the city, there are few skyscrapers.[54] Historical buildings and monuments are widely

---

[51] *Op. cit.*, p. 432.

[52] A basic source on medieval cities is Henri Pirenne, *Medieval Cities* (Princeton: Princeton University Press, 1925).

[53] Gideon Sjoberg, "The Preindustrial City," *American Journal of Sociology*, 60 (March, 1955), pp. 438–45.

[54] Paris has been the subject of one of the best urban studies ever to have been made: Paul H. Chombart de Lauwe *et al., Paris et l'agglomération parisienne* (Paris: Presses Universitaires de France, 1952), 2 vols. Also see Georges Friedmann (ed.), *Villes et Campagnes* (Paris: Librairie Armand Colin, 1953).

TABLE 21[a] · PERCENTAGE OF WORLD'S POPULATION
LIVING IN CITIES, BY REGIONS

	In cities of 20,000 plus	In cities of 100,000 plus
World	21	13
Oceania	47	41
North America (Canada and United States	42	29
Europe (except U.S.S.R.)	35	21
U.S.S.R.	31	18
South America	26	18
Middle America and Caribbean	21	12
Asia (except U.S.S.R.)	13	8
Africa	9	5

[a] Kingsley Davis, "The Origin and Growth of Urbanization in the World," *American Journal of Sociology*, 60 (March, 1955), pp. 429–37.

scattered throughout the city and help to limit the use of some areas for industrial purposes. Each city that can trace its origin to the pre-Industrial era is sharply different from every other city.

> French cities show a much greater variety of forms [than do American cities]. . . . Thus only one of our large cities has a radial plan; none, to the writer's knowledge, shows the separated sector plan, the fish-bone plan, a system of related terraces, a regular elliptical plan, or even a ribbon pattern. . . . We are unfamiliar, in the United States, with the double street, the covered street, or the stairway street. Much the same thing may be said of the numerous forms of the public patio, the park, the promenade, the patio, the river-front quai, the bridge, the hillside terrace. . . .[55]

Each city in Europe is so unique that it is almost possible for a well-traveled person, who might be set down in any European city without any advance indication of where he was, to look at the structure and color of the buildings and streets in a quarter he has never been in before and guess accurately what city he is in.

Among the 3,166,164 members of the Yoruba people of Nigeria, Africa, 34 per cent lived (in 1931, the date of the last census) in sixteen cities each containing at least 20,000 inhabitants.[56] In 1952 the largest of these cities, Ibadan, contained 459,196 inhabitants. These people are more urbanized than the French, the Swedes, or the Canadians, yet their economy is still based essentially on agriculture. Farms surround the city, extending as

[55] Theodore Caplow, "Urban Structure in France," *American Sociological Review*, 17 (October, 1952), pp. 544–49.

[56] All information on the Yoruba is taken from William Bascom, "Urbanization Among the Yoruba," *American Journal of Sociology*, 60 (March, 1955), pp. 446–54.

much as fifteen miles outside it, and most city dwellers are farmers. "Families whose farms are more distant may have farm huts, where they spend several days at a time during the height of the farming activity, but they maintain a residence in the city and regard it as their real home." The Yoruba also engage in specialized crafts and trade in addition to farming. The cities are densely crowded, but there are no tall buildings. Some Yoruba cities are metropolitan, serving as governmental and military centers; other cities are "provincial."

In Southeast Asia only about 7 per cent of the huge population live in cities of 100,000 or more.[57] Most of the cities are quite large and have a multiplicity of functions and attractions that give them dominance over their region or country. Governmental, commercial, and industrial functions are concentrated in the great cities of Rangoon (Burma), Bangkok (Thailand), Manila (the Philippines), Singapore (Malaya), Saigon (South Vietnam), Hanoi (North Vietnam), and Jakarta (Indonesia), while most of the rest of their countries are agricultural except for a few small provincial towns and cities (an exception is Surabaya in Indonesia). These cities are young; in 1800 they were either non-existent or were small towns. The European and Chinese traders and government offices were largely responsible for their growth. The Chinese quarters are largely made up of "shophouses," a two-or-more-story building with shops on the first floor and with residential flats and cubicles behind and above, constructed in continuous rows and back to back. The European quarters are mostly very "modern" and luxurious. The two sections are often physically separated into an "old city" and a "new city" with the natives living in slums at the edge of both. Bangkok is an exception in having a fully-developed old native section centering on an ancient castle. Since their countries have obtained their independence from European empires, they are assuming a more native character and their relations with the hinterlands are becoming closer.

The cities of India are somewhat like those of Southeast Asia except that there are many of them and they have a large indigenous population.[58] In 1951 about 7 per cent of the Indian population lived in seventy-three cities of more than 100,000 inhabitants apiece. Five of these cities—Calcutta, Bombay, Delhi, Madras, and Hyderabad—each had more than one million people. Indian cities are not only growing very rapidly but theye are the temporary homes of a large migrant population of casual laborers, who return to their villages when they have earned a little money each year. Many of the larger cities were created by Europeans—Calcutta and Madras by the British, Bombay by the Portuguese—but the bulk of the

[57] All information on Southeast Asia is taken from Norton S. Ginsburg, "The Great City in Southeast Asia," *American Journal of Sociology*, 60 (March, 1955), pp. 455–62.

[58] All information on Indian cities is taken from Robert I. Crane, "Urbanism in India," *American Journal of Sociology*, 60 (March, 1955), pp. 463–70.

population is native. India had large cities before the Westerners arrived; they were centers of government and handicrafts. Most of these have declined in favor of the European-built cities since the Europeans wiped out the crafts and installed their own government and trading practices. The new cities have separate "modern" sections for the Europeans and large native sections for their servants and factory workers.

G Some Rural Community Structures

We have already given considerable attention to rural communities dependent on urban ones, and to rural villages serving as trading centers for a farming area. The purpose of this brief section is to note some ecological variations in rural communities.

Pioneer families in the younger days of the United States were often more or less self-sufficient and had little interaction with others because they were so spatially isolated. Family groups live isolated lives in African and Asiatic deserts, although most of them are not agricultural but pastoral. There are some more closely settled communities—such as Landaff, New Hampshire—where spatially dispersed farm families do little trading, participate only slightly in local institutions, and have few social contacts with other families.[59]

The so-called "nucleated" agricultural village can be illustrated by El Cerrito, New Mexico.[60] Each family is almost self-sufficient economically, having farm land adjacent to the village and pastures for grazing a little farther away. There are few trade contacts with the outside world because there is no surplus product, and there is little trade within the community since each family produces the same product. There is a great deal of social interaction within the village, however, and thus people save time by living in the village even though the men have to walk out to their fields every day. There are community institutions—church, school, areas for playing games—that knit the community together ecologically as well as socially.

The town-centered farm communities to which we have already referred may be illustrated by Galpin's classical study of Elkhorn, Wisconsin.[61] Galpin measured the areas around the town receiving each of seven services furnished by the town. Through a considerable area surrounding

---

[59] Kenneth MacLeish and Kimball Young, *Culture of a Contemporary Rural Community: Landaff, New Hampshire* (Washington, D.C.: U.S. Bureau of Agricultural Economics, 1942), Rural Life Studies No. 3.

[60] Olen Leonard and C. P. Loomis, *Culture of Contemporary Rural Community: El Cerrito, New Mexico* (Washington, D.C.: U.S. Bureau of Agricultural Economics, 1941), Rural Life Studies No. 1.

[61] C. J. Galpin, *op. cit.*

the town, rural families enjoyed all seven services. In the next zone, irregularly concentric, families received only six of the seven services. Similarly, with increased distance from Elkhorn City along any radial line the number of services tended to decrease until, at what Galpin considered the outskirts of the community, farmers received only a single one of the seven services through the city. These farmers were often at the edge of another community, whose center provided them with other services. A resurvey of Elkhorn by Kolb and Polson showed that, although the various service areas had changed in size and shape from 1913 to 1929, and the services had changed their order of importance, the community still retained its gradient pattern.[62] The changes resulted mainly from improved transportation facilities that made Elkhorn City more accessible to all but permitted distant farmers to shift to competing town centers for their services.

The Old Order Amish community of Lancaster, Pennsylvania, illustrates a type of rural area characterized by a cultural milieu that differs markedly from that of surrounding localities and may be called a "culture island."[63] The community consists entirely of farmers distributed fairly compactly through open country. The basis of cohesion is membership in a religious sect and in the institutions associated with the church. Non-Amish people are scattered through the area but have a minimum of contacts with the dominant Amish. Although the Amish maintain economic relations with town merchants to whom they sell produce and from whom they purchase certain supplies, the town is not culturally dominant and only slightly ecologically dominant. Towns with caste segregation exhibit a somewhat similar cultural isolation. While not spatially separated, the Negro and white communities of Harmony, Georgia, have separate sets of local institutions, and each visits exclusively within its own circle.[64] The two communities are somewhat integrated ecologically, however, since both tend to use the same economic institutions.

H   *Conclusion*

In this chapter the human community was examined from the angle of impersonal competitive relations of human beings in a habitat. Competition tends to bring people into balance with each other and with their

[62] J. H. Kolb and R. A. Polson, *Trends in Town-Country Relation* (Madison: Agricultural Experiment Station of University of Wisconsin and U.S. Department of Agriculture, 1933), Research Bulletin No. 117.

[63] Walter M. Kollmorgen, *Culture of a Contemporary Rural Community: The Old Order Amish of Lancaster County, Pennsylvania* (Washington, D.C.: U.S. Bureau of Agricultural Economics, 1942), Rural Life Studies No. 4.

[64] Waller Wynne, *Culture of a Contemporary Rural Community: Harmony, Georgia* (Washington, D.C.: U.S. Bureau of Agricultural Economics, 1943), Rural Life Studies No. 6.

habitat in a given cultural and technological-economic framework. People tend to settle and to increase their numbers in certain spots depending on the potentialities of that location. The major functions of the settlement —generally economic functions in modern society—give a characteristic form to a settlement and a characteristic pattern to its relationship to surrounding areas.

Extension of the market in modern times has created an ecological interdependence throughout most of the world. For purposes of analysis, however, it may be preferable to examine small interdependent regions, such as a metropolitan community. A city has a certain dominance over its hinterland, for both trade and cultural influence. Communities of different size and function have a web of relationships with each other and with the isolated farmer. The city itself has a variety of natural areas, each with its own specialized function, and forming a systematic pattern when viewed from either a temporal or spatial aspect. This ecological approach to the study of human communities is a highly abstract one and is not intended to give more than a facet of a picture of social reality.

Ecology deals with the characteristics, structure, and development of communities when sheer competition is operating. Many things modify this sheer competition. Firey has called attention to the cultural factors in this modification. Of increasing importance are the political factors, including the deliberately planned modification to serve some stated human purpose.[65] City planners propose many ways of changing the "natural" ecology of a community—to make it more beautiful, habitable, or convenient for business or industry—and politicians occasionally put their plans into operation. To be successful in achieving its goals, whatever they may be, community planning must be based on realistic knowledge of ecology—as indicating the community structure and trends from which the plan is to create a deviation. The resulting community is an amalgam, then, of the natural ecology, the induced plan, the culture, the social organization, and the social psychology. In the next chapter, we turn to some illustrations of the latter factors.

[65] City planning—or, in a broader sense, community planning—is an applied field in which the sociologist, the geographer, the economist, the political scientist, and the architect cooperate. For some examples of sociological contributions to city planning, see the articles by Frank L. Sweetzer and Mel Ravitz to *Alpha Kappa Deltan*, 28 (Winter, 1958), pp. 42–51; Henry Fagin, "Problems of Planning in the Suburbs," in *The Suburban Community, op. cit.*, pp. 362–71; various chapters in Coleman Woodbury (ed.), *The Future of Cities and Urban Redevelopment* (Chicago: University of Chicago Press, 1953); and Basil G. Zimmer, *Rebuilding Cities* (Chicago: Quadrangle, 1964).

FOR ADDITIONAL READING

FIREY, WALTER, *Land Use in Central Boston* (Cambridge: Harvard University Press, 1947). A study of Boston which criticizes the concepts of ecology.

HAWLEY, AMOS H., *Human Ecology: A Theory of Community Structure* (New York: Ronald, 1950). A textbook on ecology based on a systematic theory.

NELSON, LOWRY, *Rural Sociology* (New York: American Book, 1952), Part II. This textbook on rural society includes a consideration of the physical basis of the rural community.

QUINN, JAMES A., *Human Ecology* (New York: Prentice-Hall, 1950). A textbook on ecology.

SJOBERG, GIDEON, *The Preindustrial City* (Glencoe, Ill.: Free Press, 1960). The most systematic sociological study of cities outside of the contemporary Western world.

14 * The Public Life of a Community

In the preceding chapter we defined the "human community" in ecological terms and considered such aspects of an agglomeration of people as their location in geographical space and their differential distribution within this space. In the present chapter we shall consider the "social community" to be an agglomeration of people larger than a family living in spatial proximity to each other and interacting in various ways.[1] We shall concentrate on such readily observable sociological characteristics of life in communities as people's channels of communication and participation in collective activities.

MacIver and Page[2] hold that the major defining element of a community is the presence of "community sentiment," that is, an "awareness of sharing a way of life as well as the common earth." There are many elements in this sentiment: (1) a common interest in what belongs to us, as members of a community, and what we belong to—that is, the obligations and responsibilities that hold us within an accepted social order; (2) a "we-feeling," whether based on interest or on sentiment; (3) a "role-feeling," or recognition by each member that he has a function to fulfill in the reciprocal exchanges of the social scene; (4) a "dependency-feeling," which involves both a physical dependence for the satisfaction of physical wants and a psychological dependence for the satisfaction of spiritual and other social needs. These elements are present not only in the small, intimate community, but also in the pluralistic, multi-group community increasingly characteristic of the modern world.

---

[1] The classic study of the community in this sense is that of Robert M. MacIver, *Community: A Sociological Study* (London: Macmillan, 1917).

[2] Robert M. MacIver and Charles H. Page, *Society: An Introductory Analysis* (New York: Rinehart, 1949), pp. 8–11, 291–309; quote from p. 10.

An indefinitely large number of classifications of communities could be presented, and various sociologists have found several classifications useful. One of the most valuable is that which considers communities to lie along a "folk-urban" continuum,[3] provided it is recognized (1) that rural communities in an industrialized country such as the United States have much more in common with urban communities in the same country than they do with those communities that anthropologists have labeled "folk communities," and (2) that certain cities whose main functions are religious—such as Mecca, Benares, Lhasa—have a folk quality.[4] The continuum is based on several characteristics that *tend* to be associated with each other but are not perfectly associated. At the extremes, the continuum has "ideal types"—that is, hypothetical cases with exaggerated characteristics, which are never found in real life but which are useful for understanding the nature of the differences.

Let us now consider the characteristics of the folk-urban continuum in ideal type terms. First, the community functions of members (except for those based on sex and age differences) can be more or less identical or they can be based on a high degree of division of labor, with the specialized activities of one person fitting gearlike into the activities of various other persons. Durkheim, in analyzing the basis of cohesion or solidarity of a society, called the former situation one of "mechanical solidarity" and the latter situation one of "organic solidarity."[5] In the folk community relations between members of the community tend to be "primary"—that is, intimate and based on considerable knowledge of the other person—while in the urban community relations between non-family members tend to be "secondary"—that is, formal and limited to a mere segment of total social life.[6] This characteristic requires that the folk community be relatively small and not have much individual migration. Because the folk community is so intimate, and because attitudes within

[3] Robert Redfield is the social scientist chiefly responsible for these terms although the concepts underlying them antedated his work. See his *Tepoztlan, A Mexican Village* (Chicago: University of Chicago Press, 1930); "The Folk Society," *American Journal of Sociology*, 52 (January, 1947), pp. 293–311. The German terms of Ferdinand Töennies, *Gemeinschaft* and *Gesellschaft*, are used almost as frequently and with the same meaning. See his *Fundamental Concepts of Sociology (Gemeinschaft und Gesellschaft)*, translated and supplemented by Charles P. Loomis (New York: American Book, 1940). For a critique of the classification, see Horace Miner, "The Folk-Urban Continuum," *American Sociological Review*, 17 (October, 1952), pp. 529–37.

[4] Howard Becker, *Through Values to Social Interpretation* (Durham, N. C.: Duke University Press, 1950), p. 68.

[5] Emile Durkheim, *The Division of Labor in Society* (1st edition, Paris: Felix Alcan, 1893; latest American edition, Glencoe, Ill.: Free Press, 1947).

[6] While it was Cooley who first systematically described the "primary group" and pointed out its significance for the formation of personality, it was Robert E. Park who first drew the distinction between primary and secondary contacts. (See C. H. Cooley, *Social Organization* [New York: Scribner's, 1909], Chapter 3; Robert E. Park and Ernest

> The folk society is seen in contrast to the modern city. The vast, complicated, and rapidly changing world in which the urbanite and even the urbanized country-dweller live today is enormously different from the small, inward-facing folk society, with its well-integrated and little-changing moral and religious conceptions. At one time all men lived in these little folk societies. For many thousands of years men must have lived so; urbanized life began only very recently, as the long history of man on earth is considered, and the extreme development of a secularized and swift-changing world society is only a few generations old.
>
> Robert Redfield, "The Folk Society," *American Journal of Sociology* (January, 1947), p. 303.

it are so likely to spread to all members, its values tend to be "sacred"—that is, having a high moral significance and compelling character. In the urban community each individual is much more independent and the values of the society therefore are likely to be "secular"—that is, being relatively permissive for the individual, rational in character, and not considered as so essential to the community as a whole.[7] This characteristic tends to prevent the development of science and rapid technological innovation in the folk community, and also tends to make it especially ethnocentric. Becker speaks of the sacred-secular continuum in much the same way as Redfield does of the folk-urban continuum, and he defines the sacred and secular ideal types of society in the following way:

> A sacred society is one that elicits from or imparts to its members, by means of sociation, unwillingness and/or inability to respond to the culturally new as the new is defined by those members in terms of the society's existing culture. Otherwise put, a network of sociation that develops, among the personalities weaving and woven by it, a

W. Burgess, *Introduction to the Science of Sociology* [Chicago: University of Chicago Press, 1921; 2nd edition, 1924], pp. 284–87.) S. C. Lee notes that the term "primary group" was first used as the title of a chapter, "The Primary Social Group," in A. W. Small and G. E. Vincent, *An Introduction to the Study of Society* (New York: American Book, 1894), but these authors did not develop the concept. (S. C. Lee, "The Primary Group as Cooley Defines It," *Sociological Quarterly*, 5 [Winter, 1964], pp. 23–34.)

[7] It is Howard Becker who has been mainly responsible for developing the concepts of "sacred" and "secular," although he credits Robert E. Park with suggesting the concepts to him. See Becker's "Of Sacredness and Secularity: as Linked with the Tightness and Looseness of Societies," unpublished paper delivered at Fisk University, April 1, 1955, p. 1. The sacred-secular continuum should be sharply distinguished from the sacred-profane continuum that the anthropologists use. The latter refers to what a society considers to be holy or sinful, and both extremes of this continuum belong to what Park and Becker call "sacred."

high degree of resistance to change, particularly in their social order, is a sacred society.

A secular society is one that elicits from or imparts to its members, by means of sociation, willingness and ability to respond to the culturally new as the new is defined by those members in terms of the society's existing culture. Stated in another way, a network of sociation that develops, among the personalities weaving and woven by it, a high degree of readiness and capacity to change, particularly in their social order, is a secular society.

Formulated differently: a society that incorporates and sustains an impermeable value-system is sacred; one that embodies a permeable value-system is secular.[8]

In sum, the typical mode of relationship among the members of a folk community is that which we have called in an earlier chapter the "integrated group," while the typical modes of relationship in an urban community are the "audience" and the "public."

No two communities are exactly alike, even within a given culture. In the United States the range is so great that it is not appropriate to speak of a "typical" community.[9] While there have been numerous excellent sociological studies of communities in several of the countries of the Western world, the communities chosen for analysis cannot be said to be representative. Yet communities are complicated social structures, and it is not possible to give any adequate portrayal of the range in a limited space by giving a part of the story of one community and a different part of the story of another community. For these reasons it is desirable to illustrate the public life of communities by presenting a moderately comprehensive description of a single community, to which we shall give the fictitious name "Easterntown."[10] The community chosen is considerably closer to the urban ideal type than it is to the folk.[11] Most of the information about

[8] *Through Values to Social Interpretation, op. cit.,* pp. 252–53. For a late statement by Becker on the sacred and secular, see his "Current Sacred-Secular Theory and Its Development," in H. Becker and A. Boskoff (eds.), *Modern Sociological Theory, in Continuity and Change* (New York: Dryden, 1957), pp. 133–85.

[9] The general problems of community study have been dealt with by Albert J. Reiss, Jr., "A Review and Evaluation of Research on Community," unpublished memorandum, 1954; by Irwin T. Sanders, *The Community* (New York: Ronald, 1958); and by Roland L. Warren, *The Community in America* (Chicago: Rand McNally, 1963).

[10] This description is taken from my "Communication and Participation in a Small City as Viewed by Its Leaders," *International Journal of Opinion and Attitude Research,* 5 (Fall, 1951), pp. 367–90.

[11] For descriptions of comparable communities in other Western countries, see I. Gadourek, *A Dutch Community* (Leiden: Steufert Kroese, 1956); William M. Williams, *The Sociology of an English Village: Gosforth* (London: Routledge and Kegan Paul, 1956); and the study of Auxerre, France, by Charles Bettleheim and Suzanne Frère. For

the community comes from interviews with thirty-three community leaders, some of whose specific observations will be referred to at various points in the description.

A   Extent of Organization

There was a good deal of diversity of judgment on the part of the community leaders as to whether most of the townspeople were organized into groups. Some of this diversity was caused by different standards of what a group was: apparently there is a lot of purely nominal affiliation with the unions, with churches, and with lodges that some of the interviewees refused to consider as group participation. But even if active membership alone is considered, there is still apparently a good deal of diversity of opinion. Several of the people who spoke of the paucity of group participation explained it in terms of typical New England individualism and lethargy. Said one of the town's few publicists:

> Easterntown is very characteristic of New England. The people are individualistic. They are not as great joiners as in the Midwest, not even for social clubs. Easterntown is a little more organization-minded than the rest of New England. Only a minority of the population of the city is of old New England stock: since the city is mainly industrial it has attracted workers from all over the east and a large proportion of the population is first or second-generation foreign-born.

One civic and social leader, a woman, held that women were inclined to join civic and social organizations but that men were not. None of the men's groups serves the function of encouraging political interest like the very active League of Women Voters. The women have vitalized the Parent-Teachers Association, which recently has become a power in school affairs. There are a number of women in the city who are active in all sorts of civic organizations and activities. Another woman leader, as well as a minister, said that the "top" group in the population belonged to everything, but there were many who did not belong to any group. The minister felt that it would do no good to organize any more groups since the same joiners would join them, and the apathetic people would remain apathetic.

---

studies of more rural communities in other European countries, see Conrad M. Arensberg, *The Irish Countryman* (New York: Macmillan, 1937); Irwin T. Sanders, *A Balkan Village* (Lexington: University of Kentucky Press, 1949). Comparable studies of villages in the United States include H. C. Nixon, *Possum Trot: Rural Community, South* (Norman: University of Oklahoma Press, 1941); James West, *Plainville, USA* (New York: Columbia University Press, 1945).

He pointed out that Easterntown had every *type* of organization that a much larger city would be expected to have, and in that sense was well organized, but he was the one who said that "90 per cent of the people do not belong to anything but a church and maybe the union."

A public official said that group participation was a function of age. He said there were few groups for young adults—there were plenty of clubs for older people and several organizations catering to children all the way up to age eighteen. The most serious gap was for young women, since the town boasts of a YMCA but no YWCA. A minister made the same observation, and stressed the lack of organizations for young married couples.

Most of the interviewees felt that the city had good leadership, and that lack of leadership would not be an explanation of low group participation. It should be recalled, however, that those making these observations were community leaders themselves. Several people pointed out that there was a natural reserve of leadership in the large number of engineers working for the town's largest industry, and their college-trained wives. In the past few years this company has been encouraging its people to lead in civic activities. One interviewee regarded it as evidence of good and available leadership that there was always someone willing to lead a drive for funds for some civic enterprise. A public official who had a lot to do with civic boards and committees said that civic-minded people could always be found to work on these volunteer organizations, although there is a scarcity of qualified people willing to run for public office. The volunteer members of these boards and commissions are broadly representative of all classes and occupations, but they are an "interlocking directorate." The use of the same leaders to serve on a great variety of civic organizations was noted by several of the interviewees. One person noted that the circle of leaders had been expanding somewhat recently.

Despite the fact that the same people serve on all the committees and boards, many interviewees decried the lack of integration of these organizations. Said one civic leader:

> The community is overorganized and there is no need for further groups. The main problem is that of pulling these groups together for common interests and for civic benefit. We need a Community Council.

A lawyer felt that civic interest would be best served by a Citizens' League, the purpose of which would be to secure good candidates for public office. As noted, several persons stressed the need for social and recreational organizations for young adults. One interviewee felt that there could be more organizations which attracted the poor, but said that the Park and Recreation Commission was trying to aid there. Another, a member of the

Easterntown Discussion Council, said that that organization was trying to integrate people who were not affiliated with anything, but said that the success was small in relation to the total need. A banker pointed out that lower-income people frequented taverns, which, in essence, were very much like social clubs for the higher-income groups. One interviewee who was familiar with the situation said that there was need for more groups and more leaders in the Polish community. The older Poles, especially, were not affiliated with anything but the church. Both Poles and Negroes were kept out of certain organizations because of their nationality and race. The Masons and the Eastern Star lodges have segregated units for Negroes.

A minister felt that the major organizational need of the community was for a community center with recreational and social facilities. He felt that the community wanted this, but that it was so passive it made no real efforts to get it. He held that the passivity of Easterntown was due to the paternalism of the old mill owners, who created such things as the Museum and the Boys' Club, without encouraging the community to do things for itself. Most of the mills had been wiped out by the depression and by competition from the South, but the townspeople were still passive. The company representing the big new industry does not do anything for the city. In common with many other interviewees, this minister pointed out that many of the engineers and scientists working for this company came from outside the city and did not care to become integrated into it. They formed their own social circle and even had their own organizations, and thus contributed to the community's passivity and lack of integration. The engineers are in professional associations that have local branches; there is the Stanley Club for their social life, the Athletic Association mostly for the workers, and three golf clubs.

Several of the interviewees felt that there were too many organizations in the city already, and that there could well be a decrease without anybody being cut out. This attitude was especially expressed by those who felt that they themselves were on too many committees and organizations. These people pointed to the fact that there are almost 300 organizations in the city.

B   *Channels of Communication*

The *Eastern County Evening Star,* published six days a week, is the sole paper edited locally. According to its editor, it has a circulation of 25,000, which means that nearly every family in Easterntown, and in some of the surrounding small towns, gets the paper. Most of the community leaders seemed to be aware of this, and felt that the *Star* was most influential because everyone read it. Most of the interviewees felt that it was a good paper, in that it had a wide coverage of the news and presented issues fairly in the editorial columns. Several people pointed out that the editorials and the letters-to-the-editor column were unusually widely read, although how they would know this was not indicated. All but three out of the 33 interviewees said that the *Star* had more influence than the radio. These three felt that the radio was more important among the lower-income groups, since these people kept their radios on all day. However, representatives of the Negro and Polish groups, which are among the poorest in the city, said that among their groups the *Star* was more influential than the radio, even though most of the homes had radios.

There is a significant sale of out-of-town newspapers in Easterntown, partly because the *Star* is an evening newspaper and people want a morning paper, too. The *New York Daily News* and a Boston tabloid sell quite well, as also do the *New York Times* and *New York Herald Tribune*. For several months during the time of this study, a strike prevented production of newspapers in another nearby New England city, but ordinarily they were quite popular too.

The only criticism that came out against the *Star* was that its news was almost a direct copy from the *New York Times* and *Herald Tribune*, according to one minister. Most of the interviewees felt that the *Star* reported local news very adequately, and also participated actively in most community activities.

There are two radio stations in Easterntown: WBCE has been established for many years; it was formerly owned by a member of one of Easterntown's leading families but in recent months it was bought by an engineer. WDEF was begun only two months before this study took place; it is owned by the publisher and editor of the *Eastern County Evening Star*. A Hooper Audience Study carried on in 1944 showed that Easterntown was somewhat more radio-minded than average: 30 per cent of the sets in Easterntown were "in use," as compared to a national average of 24 per cent. The survey also showed that WBCE led its competitors for listenership:

	8–12 A.M.	12–6 P.M.	6–10 P.M.
WBCE	66.9	47.9	38.1
Station A	14.6	30.3	30.4
Station B	9.3	5.7	1.0
Station C	3.3	1.8	2.3

The second most popular station was a large one broadcasting from a city in New York State. WBCE's overwhelming lead in the morning was explained in terms of Easterntown's need to listen to the radio for news in the morning, since there was no morning paper. A Broadcast Measurement Bureau study showed that 87 per cent of all families with radios listened sometime in the morning, and 85 per cent listened sometime in the evening—a very high listenership.

Most of the community leaders felt that the radio stations gave enough time to local news and local activities that needed publicity, although a couple of persons felt that this had happened only recently when WBCE got competition from WDEF, and one person said that some of the time given over to local news was purchased by local merchants to advertise their businesses. The station manager of WBCE said that his report to the Federal Communications Commission for 1946 indicated that 40 per cent of the time on WBCE is devoted to "local" programs. Some of these were not locally originated, but simply received local sponsorship. WBCE is affiliated with one national and one regional network.

Some of the interviewees felt that the chief difficulty with local programs was that few local groups took the time or had the ability to plan a good program. A couple of persons mentioned the local discussion groups held on the air, especially the one dealing with the city-manager plan that was being discussed for Easterntown. One of the priests felt that local civic groups could not get radio time. A few of the interviewees felt that the radio was not influential since it did not give time for people to think over what was said on it: it went too fast while people could take their time with the newspaper. A few others also made such general criticisms as "The trouble with radio is that it does not give details and most of the commentators spend most of their time with their own opinions. The newspapers stick to facts and give details." Still, one of the most important influences in the town, according to several interviewees, was the daily radio commentary by Fulton Lewis, Jr.

Only a minority of the community leaders mentioned sources of information and opinion other than the newspaper and radio. Even the ministers did not feel that the churches were important, although a few respondents felt that the Catholic Church was a significant influence on its members. One or two mentioned the library and museum. A couple mentioned lectures and discussions, especially the biweekly lectures of the Council of Social Agencies, to which representatives of all community organizations were invited. One person mentioned gossip. An engineer and a minister pointed out that the big new industry distributed a paper to its workers, and the union representative indicated that almost 9,000 copies of the union weekly newspaper were distributed to its members. Significantly, only one person mentioned organizations as channels of communication, and he indicated that this had only recently become so. This was probably because only such small organizations as the Progressive Citizens' Association or such specialized organizations as the veterans' groups were concerned with civic or political matters.

c   *Issues and Cleavages*

There was considerable variation in what the community leaders felt that people in the community were talking about. Many of them said that issues were a function of what group one happened to be with. Many of the community leaders admitted that they were not in a position to know what the average informal conversation in Easterntown was about. Some felt that gossip and sports were the most frequent topics of conversation, but others held that Easterntowners were a serious lot. Among topics mentioned were the current issues of communism, international relations, the Taft-Hartley labor law, and the local city-manager plan. Topics of conversation that had a longer standing included housing, the schools, the high cost of living, racial and religious group relations, and labor relations. Local civic problems getting some attention are a possible recreation center and veterans' memorial, garbage disposal, pure water, the cultural programs carried on at a nearby town and by the museum, local recreation programs, unaccepted (that is, privately owned) streets. Leaders of lower-income groups said that jobs and job security were among the most important topics of conversation.

Undoubtedly the most seriously felt cleavage in Easterntown is between religious groups. Easterntown is in Massachusetts where there has been a long-standing feud between the old residents, who are Protestant, and the more recent immigrants, who are Catholic. In recent years this feud has been accentuated, in conformity with trends throughout the country. A few of the community leaders denied its existence even when asked, but most spontaneously mentioned it as the most important cleavage, and a few mentioned it as the most important problem in Easterntown. As several interviewees pointed out, the cleavage goes into areas of life other than religion. One man said that in Easterntown until the war they had always thought of Catholics as workers, and Protestants as businessmen. The war, of course, greatly expanded large industry, and great numbers of Protestants migrated to the town as workers too. In politics, most of the Protestants voted Republican, and most of the Catholics, especially during the New Deal, voted Democratic. Social clubs were pretty well separated by religion. No Catholics joined the Masons, and only Catholics joined the Knights of Columbus. Since service clubs and recreational clubs were stratified by class, they were also pretty well stratified by religion, although there were exceptions. According to one interviewee, civic organizations tended to be Protestant only, except for those that were deliberately intended to be representative, such as the Council for Social Agencies, the Red Cross, and the Easterntown Discussion Council. The PTA's were an example of how this worked out: many of the middle- and upper-income Catholic families sent their children to parochial schools and so were not in the PTA's. In lower-income Catholic families that sent their children to public schools, the mothers were apathetic toward PTA's. However, it is to be noted that there are exceptions: the present chairman of the PTA for the whole city is a Catholic woman.

With respect to feeling against Jews, most of the interviewees said that it seldom took outward form in Easterntown, but it lay just below the surface of appearances. The anti-Catholic feeling of Protestants drew the latter a little closer to the Jews, in the sense that the Jews were in all the formal organizations that Protestants were in. The Jewish temple is in the Protestant Council of Churches, which recently has been reacting against the Catholics. In the informal social groupings, however, there was some drawing of the line. One Jewish community leader said the banks, utilities, insurance companies, and the city hall very seldom hired Jews. The large new industry does not have Jews on its managerial or engineering levels, but it has Jewish chemists and a large number of Jewish manual workers. According to this informant, there is no residential segregation against Jews, although there is one new housing development in which no Jews have bought, and there is a whole section near a suburb which will not admit Jews. Some of the tourist homes will not admit Jews. Newspaper ads sometimes indicate preference for non-Jews, usually in such indirect ways as mentioning proximity to a church. There are now two Jews in minor elective posts in the city government, and a prominent Jewish merchant was mayor of Easterntown many years ago. While a few anti-Semitic incidents stirred up quite a bit of anxiety on the part of the Jewish community, they are not too significant as their perpetrators do not have a respected position in the community. Much more serious is the non-acceptance of Jews at certain informal social functions, the talk about the unpleasant business practices of some Jewish merchants, and the concern about alleged habits of Jewish summer visitors.

The investigator made special inquiry about reactions to the summer visitors, since Easterntown is a tourist center and many of the visitors are Jews from New York. At present, tourism takes several distinct forms: there are children's camps around the lakes just north of the city; there are those who come to attend the music, dance, and art festivals which are held in several of the small towns nearby; and there are those who simply pass through Easterntown on their motor tours of New England. It is to be noted that none of these types of tourists are "summer residents." They do not own fine homes as the summer visitors of a generation ago used to. They do not sink any roots into the community, and seldom have informal or intimate contact with the members of the community. It was unanimously stated by the community leaders that the summer visitors had no effect on the city except in so far as they brought money to the hotels, restaurants, tourist homes, gas stations, and some stores. A few of the interviewees noted that the summer visitors created cultural opportunities for Easterntown: the festivals would not be able to come to Eastern County unless the summer visitors supported them.

But, on the whole, Easterntown thinks of the summer visitors as a nuisance, except in terms of what money they bring to the town. They overcrowd the restaurants, the hotels, the streets, the parking spaces, the recreation spots. They are said to be "very demanding," and their propensity for slacks and shorts is interpreted as disrespect for "hicks." Some of the interviewees were quite positive in saying that they disliked Easterntown in summer, and went away when they could. This situation creates something of an antipathy toward the summer visitors, who are identified as Jews, but who are actually probably an approximate cross-section of upper-middle-class New Yorkers (except for the children at the camps and the parents visiting them, who are almost entirely Jewish). One of the interviewees, a prominent businessman and otherwise seemingly liberal, expressed his personal reactions thus:

> A minority must always remember that it is a minority and should follow the majority in dress and manners. They can do what they want to when they are among themselves, but when they are with the majority they should act as the majority does. A minority must remember that it is a minority and conduct themselves accordingly.

Still, the position of permanent Jewish residents is quite favorable: many are recognized civic leaders, and against few has there been very harmful discrimination.

The position of Negroes is much worse. Easterntown's Negro community, numbering about 700 as compared to about 1,700 Jews, has a most unenviable economic status in the community even though it has been established for generations. It is an anomaly among Negro communities in the United States, although of a type found elsewhere in small towns in New England, in that it seems to be completely isolated from the rest of Negro America. It was established by freedmen and runaway slaves before the Civil War, and the ancestors of most of the present inhabitants were living there before 1880. Thus members of the community have few relatives and friends outside the city. They took over the outward forms of becoming New Englanders, such as joining the Congregational Church (which is still the only Negro church in Easterntown), and were pleased to consider themselves as New Englanders rather than as identified with the masses of Negroes. The overwhelming majority of the Negroes have consistently voted Republican, whereas most Northern Negroes broke sharply with the Republican Party during the 1930's.[12] While they always had all the legal and political rights that Negroes always have in the North, socially they were completely ostracized by the white community and economically they were relegated to the bottom position. Aside from the one minister, the leading Negroes hold positions of elevator operator and bell-hop. The war and the FEPC also made a difference in that the large new industry brought two Negro chemists to Easterntown along with about 250 other workers and their kin. Negroes are not segregated in the formal sense: they live in various sections of the city when they are servants in the homes of those sections. They are found in several of the schools, depending on where they live. If they are not Congregationalists, they go to the "white" church of their choice. They are in the Boy Scouts, Girl Scouts, YMCA, and the League of Women Voters. But in anything relating to the economic sphere they are discriminated against. In the high school, for example, they are strongly discouraged from taking any vocational course that will fit them for any but the most lowly of occupations. It has only been recently, after a year's effort on the part of the Community Relations Committee, that they were finally accepted for nurses' training by the three Easterntown hospitals. Since World War II, the large new industry has hired Negroes in other than menial jobs. But only one of the smaller factories in Easterntown does that, and some of the small plants will not hire Negroes at all. There are no Negro schoolteachers.

The coming of the well-educated, aggressive minister, the integration of Negroes into jobs and unions at the large new industry, the renewal of contact with Negroes in the outside world through reading the Negro press and the recent establishment of a branch of the National Association for the Advancement of Colored People, all are beginning to stir the Negro population in Easterntown, and they may soon be expected to demand a higher economic and civic status. Some of the whites are already reacting against this in a mild way: they do not like to be told that they have to specify in advance the wages they are willing to pay when they want to hire a Negro maid; they talk about the present Negro minister as being too aggressive and always inserting the Negro side of the issue whenever any public discussion is going on. The Community Relations Committee was set up during the war, after some intergroup trouble in Boston led the governor to urge each local community in Massachusetts to set up such a

[12] Gunnar Myrdal, with the assistance of Richard Sterner and Arnold Rose, *An American Dilemma* (New York: Harper, 1944), Chapter 22.

committee. It is composed mostly of white Christians, some of whom themselves have "mild" prejudices against Negroes and Jews, and it has acted very slowly. Its main achievement thus far has been to get the three hospitals to agree to take Negro girls for nurses' training, during a time of extreme shortage of nurses.

There are other cleavages in Easterntown. We shall reserve discussion of management-labor relations until the following section. There are other cleavages along class lines. Antagonism between the economic levels is not, in itself, given too much attention. Class cleavage rather takes such forms as an antagonism between Ward 3 and other sections of Eastern-town, and as an antagonism between "old Easterntowners" and the new residents. Ward 3, of course, is where all the well-to-do people live. Its demands for streets, water supply, and other physical improvements are somewhat greater than those of other areas of the city since its houses are more spread out. This is the source of a certain amount of friction on the governmental level. But, more important, Ward 3 stands symbolically for the upper classes. People do not talk about the "rich," the "well-to-do" or the "upper-income levels," but they do talk about what Ward 3 thinks, about what Ward 3 is going to do, and about who is moving into or out of Ward 3.

The distinction between old Easterntowners and the newcomers is not strictly along class lines, because many a well-to-do person has been resident in Easterntown for only five, ten, or fifteen years and dislikes the old Easterntowners as much as do the poorer people. And there are some poor or middle-income people whose ancestors have lived in Easterntown for generations. But these people do not think of themselves as old Eastern-towners, for this term connotes snobbishness and upper-class position. The old Easterntowners are those whose parents belonged to the paternal-istic upper class and who now hold themselves aloof from most civic activity since it now means getting into politics or into other forms of competition. They also hold themselves aloof from newcomers, regardless of the latter's wealth, education, or ability. A leading businessman who had lived in Easterntown only about ten years described the old Easterntowners thus:

> Certain names are like red flags to bulls. These hated people usually come from the old families. They are non-productive people who have influence regardless of merit because of their family back-ground. The hard-working, self-made people don't get recognized socially. Newcomers to the city generally know more about the city than those old families. For example, I was walking down the street with ————, and I stopped to talk to many people whom he did not even know, although he has lived here all his life. Another young

man of an old Easterntown family wanted to run for public office, but I had to advise him against it because of his family's unpopularity.

There are also nationality cleavages in Easterntown, although according to the community leaders these were more important in the past than they are today. However, social contacts are still based largely on nationality background. There are nationality clubs for the Italians, Poles, Scots, French, Germans, Russians, and Greeks. An Italian leader indicates how the feeling of nationality has declined:

> When I came to the United States as a boy I had to fight my way with the Irish in Easterntown. I made alliances with other Italian and Jewish boys to battle the Irish. Now, there is very little feeling of foreign ancestry. Some of the nationalities have organizations but they are not strong except for the old people.

This man felt that the conflict between Protestants and Catholics was really a reaction of the Protestants to the obstreperous Irish. A leader of the Polish community revealed a similar feeling of nationality cleavage in his discussion of schools. Although a very religious Catholic, he seemed quite satisfied with the fact that the great majority of the Polish children went to public schools rather than parochial schools, as he felt the parochial schools were dominated by the Irish Catholics. There is a continuation school that meets between four and five-thirty every day to teach Polish children the Polish language, and that was better, he thought, than having a straight parochial school with no Polish language. That Old Americans also have some anti-nationality feeling was adduced from the fact, mentioned by a couple of interviewees, that Old American parents would not send their children to a school in which there were many Italian children even though it was a well-equipped school and had a lot of room, and the alternative was to send their children to an old, poorly equipped, and overcrowded school. Still, the young Italians are resisting an effort to start an Italian parochial school—they want to be integrated into the community.

D   *Industry and Labor Participation*

There are two divisions of the large new manufacturing company represented in Easterntown. The largest is a section of the regular electrical equipment production division and the other is the headquarters of the entire chemical division. They employ 10,000 to 12,000 people normally, but during the war employment mounted to 16,000. Until about a year and a half before the study, this company was an impersonal force: it never interfered with the community, it never helped the community. Its top managers, engineers, and scientists were usually outsiders who kept to themselves and were socially estranged from the community. Many of them did not stay very long but were transferred after a few years to one of the other plants belonging to the company. The chief attitude of the community toward the company is that toward a job provider, and the chief concern has been about the company's business falling off so there would be fewer jobs. All the community leaders were aware of the dangers of having the city so economically dependent on one industry and several told of unsuccessful efforts to encourage small industries, non-competitive with the company, to settle in Easterntown. From what these people said, the company seems to have encouraged Easterntown's desire to diversify its industry. Still, it was the company's ability to outbid for labor that helped to drive some of the textile mills out of Easterntown (although the depression and the new southern competition were factors, too). The company has paid fairly decent wages, and its conditions for work have been good, so all the community leaders have said. It did discriminate against Negroes until the war, and no Jew holds a top managerial post; still, the company was not felt to discriminate much even by the leaders of the minority groups. Practically everyone felt, and said the groups they represented felt, that the company was a good employer.

The two locals in the company plants were organized in 1940 by a large CIO international union. The question as to whether there is Communist domination of this union has been a source of anxiety for the workers and, indeed, for the whole community, although most of the leaders interviewed felt that there were no Communists in the local leadership. A few thought the chief organizer was a Communist, since he was sent out by the national office. The business agent, and of course the presidents, were Easterntowners, and were rather highly thought of by the community leaders. Practically all of the community leaders said that industry-union relations were good, but a few hedged and said they were good only on the surface or temporarily. The most frequent description of the company's general manager is that he is a liberal, civic-minded man, and of the business agent is that he is a good, capable man who sometimes gets wrong ideas from his national office.

The chief problem for the unions is low attendance of members at meetings and other evidences of lack of interest in the unions. Although all shopworkers are unionized and so are most of the eligible white-collar workers, everyone understands that this does not mean that all the workers are sold on unionism. The business agent frankly admitted that he was engaging in an educational campaign to get the workers out to union meetings. The hall in which union meetings are held would not hold anything like the entire membership, and apparently it is not often filled. An attendance of one or two hundred union members is usual at the average meeting. When the Taft-Hartley bill was up before Congress, the union distributed leaflets to all workers to dramatize the alleged dangers of the bill and urged all of them to attend a gate meeting. Since a gate meeting is held for a short time as the workers are leaving the factory, 3,000 workers attended, according to the business agent. From the union leaders' standpoint, low attendance is due to "a feeling that the union will take care of them anyhow, even if they don't participate." From the standpoint of those critical of the union, low attendance is due to the workers' dissatisfaction with domination by the leaders and a feeling that the company has been very fair with them. According to one of the community leaders who would be in a position to know, there is an opposition group within the union which is instigated by the Catholic Church in its opposition to Communism. While most of the workers are Catholic, the opposition apparently has not yet developed much popular support.

Although some of the community leaders said that Easterntown is a "one-company town," they seemed to be thinking in an economic rather than a political sense. Only one or two of the leaders said that the company was a dominating influence over the city, although several others said that Easterntowners would never do anything to offend the company and would build streets, water mains, etc., where the company wanted them to. Practically all the community leaders spontaneously asserted that until the present general manager arrived on the scene about two years ago, the company was very cold toward civic problems. Since then there seems to be a new public-relations policy: the company will sanction a civic drive (as for the new hospital) and allow collections to be deducted from the payroll, it will contribute financially to civic enterprises, it encourages townspeople to visit the plant, it disseminates company news through the newspaper and radio, it works with the local school system to develop vocational courses, and so on. The new policy is "public relations conscious." Some attribute the new policy to the personality of the new manager, others attribute it to the strike. In April and May of 1947 the company conducted a secret public-opinion poll in Easterntown to determine community attitudes toward the company.

There are several smaller, but not insignificant, industries in Easterntown, chiefly engaged in the manufacture of paper and cloth. Some of these plants are unionized; others are not. The carpenters, plumbers, milkwagon drivers, musicians, and other groups are in AFL unions. The major group of workers not in a union, outside of those in some of the mills, are the store clerks.

E   *Educational, Recreational, and Fraternal Organizations*

Easterntown has twenty-four public schools, including the one high school and the junior high schools. Some of the schools are one-room affairs with only three or four grades taught in them. There are four parochial schools on an elementary level, and one Catholic high school. There are no colleges in town, although there is a state teachers' college in a nearby city. The public schools are a great source of controversy, and the differences of opinion are reflected in the statements of the community leaders. The opposition points to the one-room houses which they say should be combined, to the lack of playgrounds, to the lack of auditoriums or gymnasiums (except for the large auditorium in the high school), to the lack of diversity in the curriculum, to the fact that few high-school graduates do well in college so that most parents plan at least a couple of years of prep school if they are going to send their children to college, to the inadequate vocational training in the high school so that industry has to get its trained people from outside the city, to the poorly trained and low-paid teachers. The proponents of the school system point to the fact that in Massachusetts the local school systems get no help from the state, to the efficiency and lack of corruption in the school system, to the excellent vocational-guidance system that was introduced a few years ago, to the raise in teachers' pay last year with special incentives for those teachers who improved their education (and to the large attendance of teachers at the summer school for teachers), to the plans now under way for improving the vocational training. The opposition feels that the school system is too slow in making changes. The superintendent and his backers feel that the opposition has a lot of half-baked ideas. There is more criticism of high-school training than of elementary-school training, although the physical plant of the high school is quite good.

The organized opposition comes from a volunteer committee led by some engineers' wives that was started last year to survey the schools and compare them with schools in other cities. This committee secured the support of the Taxpayers' Association, and is now planning to merge with that organization. But they had little effect on the school system since they did not get a sympathetic ear from the superintendent or the school board. Another organization working to bring about changes in the school system, although much less radical in its demands, is the PTA. In the year prior to the study the PTA became quite active; this was observed by most of the community leaders. Whereas at the beginning of the year it had only seven branch PTA's organized, it added five more during the year, and another one was being organized. This means that thirteen out of twenty-four schools are organized. Besides working to effect changes in the schools, the PTA sponsors lectures and forums for the education of its own members.

For adult education, Easterntown has the aforementioned extension courses for teachers during the summer, vocational courses given at the high school in the evenings, cultural courses at the museum, orchestra concerts during the summer, string concerts in the winter, lectures sponsored occasionally by various groups, the Easterntown Discussion Council with about twenty-eight local discussion groups, the Great Books Discussion program with two groups in the city, naturalization and literacy training courses. Before the war there was a forum meeting regularly, but during the war attendance declined and it was abandoned. The Easterntown Discussion Council's program, which is only about a year old, has largely taken its place. There are some special groups with educational programs, such as the College Club and the Engineers' Association. Some community leaders mentioned specific lacks in the current adult-education program. Others said that the town was saturated with adult education: there were too many things to do. They pointed to a drop in the sales of tickets to lectures in the past few years. One interviewee said people were sick of being talked *at;* they wanted to talk themselves.

Easterntown has a well-stocked and well-staffed library with one of the highest circulation rates for a city of its size in the country. The library is publicly supported. The Eastern County Museum, on the other hand, was originally endowed by one of the paternalistic mill families, and is kept up by subscriptions. The museum is for both art and science, and temporarily for history, too. Besides the permanent exhibits, there are special exhibits each month, classes for youth and adults in art and science, educational movies, summer art school, concerts in both summer and winter, summer drama, extension activities to the schools of the county (traveling exhibits and three "Nature" instructors). An attendance of 80,000 was counted for the year 1946, but of course this includes duplicate visits and summer visitors.

On the whole, Easterntown is a fairly cosmopolitan city. The region in which it is located is a mecca for cultural and recreational activities, and the great as well as the unimportant are among the visitors. Easterntown is not very far from New York and Boston, and its residents go to these cities frequently.

Among Easterntown's public-recreation facilities are twelve summer playgrounds, one beach, two wading pools, ten baseball diamonds, eight softball diamonds. There are twenty-nine baseball teams in the city, including 434 children and adults. One of the parks has facilities for professional boxing and wrestling and professional baseball. During the year

1946 there were 135,000 paid admissions to baseball games during the summer and autumn. The parks and playgrounds are supervised only during the winter and summer, which are the big tourist seasons. At times the majority of people using the public recreational facilities are out-of-towners. In general the public recreational facilities are very heavily used. There is no building for recreation, and thus no table games or other facilities for recreation for the middle-aged and old. There are, however, city-wide events throughout the year: Winter Carnival, Halloween Celebration, City Marble Tournament, Easter Egg Hunt, Playground Mardi Gras, Diaper Derby. There is a publicly supported teen-age center.

Easterntown has a full range of fraternal organizations. They were formerly more popular than they are now. The upper-class men no longer find them so attractive, but prefer the golf club, the Stanley Club, or some other place where they can either be with persons of their own class or with their entire families. Lower-income people often cannot afford to join the fraternal organizations. Thus they are mainly institutions for the middle-income groups, and even among them the popularity of lodges has declined because there seems to be a trend for families to have social life as units. Most of the lodges have women's auxiliaries.

The activities of the lodges are mostly social—for the entertainment of the members—according to all the interviewees. Occasionally they take up a pet civic cause, such as supporting the boys' club, or sponsoring "I am an American Day," or helping a needy and worthy family. But they do not participate in civic affairs actively, and they do not educate their members in civic affairs. They never interfere in politics, but one interviewee pointed out that membership in one or more of the lodges helps political candidates get elected to office. The service clubs—Rotary, Kiwanis, Lions —are more concerned with civic affairs than are the fraternal organizations. But even they have limited activities. One member reported that these groups would rather have a speaker sent out by some propaganda agency, because he came free, than a good speaker for whom they would have to pay. All these organizations, including the lodges, send two representatives apiece to the biweekly luncheon lectures sponsored by the Council of Social Agencies. These meetings do something to hold all groups in the town together.

F   Political Interest

Easterntown's city government is headed by a mayor and a council of eleven members, one from each of the seven wards and four elected at large. The city secured a non-partisan charter in 1934, which provides that each of these persons be elected as individuals rather than under party labels. The charter sets a maximum limit on salaries at $5,000 per year for the Mayor and $400 per year for each of the councilmen. The Mayor, however, has held that $4,000 per year is enough for himself, and each of the councilmen gets only $250. Since the position of councilman is demanding in terms of time and patience, since it requires one to stick his neck out, and since the pay is insignificant, it was an almost unanimous complaint of the community leaders that qualified people could not be induced to run for the City Council. Only one or two of the councilmen claimed the respect of these community leaders. The Mayor, who has been in office since 1938, seems to be universally respected as honest, but sometimes criticized as old-fashioned. The chief concern now is that the Mayor, a man in his seventies, will soon retire, and no other qualified person can be induced to run for his position. In the last election he was opposed by a man who all the interviewees who mentioned the incident regarded as unqualified, and who ran for the position out of personal animus.

Since the Mayor receives only $4,000 a year, most of the other city officials receive less than he does, and this is a source of complaint among them. One official pointed out that the starting salary for his assistants was only a little over $1,500 and he could not get qualified people to work for this sum. Several of the city departments depend almost entirely on part-time or volunteer workers. Another weakness of city administration that was voiced by one official was that there was no coordination among its members: there are no channels whereby one can learn what the other is doing, and there are never any staff meetings.

A deeper political problem, voiced by many community leaders outside the ranks of the public officials, is that things appear to be all right on the surface but problems are accumulating and will someday reach a crisis. There are problems of old and poorly equipped schools, sewage, water supply, etc. City government has been run cheaply recently, and there is a surplus in the city treasury, but that is because things do not get done unless they are routine. The fault is essentially the public's: it is quite satisfied to have things go along smoothly without looking ahead. A confidential survey was recently made which showed that the physical needs of the city now, that will eventually demand attention, would cost $7,000,000 to set right. The entire city budget for one year is $4,000,000 and the surplus is only about $1,000,000, according to one city official.

According to most of the community leaders, Easterntown's interest in state and national elections is fairly typical. But its interest in local politics is very low. One of the reasons given by the community leaders is the fact that things seem to be running smoothly and there is no corruption. Another reason given is that under the non-partisan charter an individual party affiliation is not given, and there is no rivalry between parties to stimulate interest. One of the factors increasing interest in state politics, according to a few of the community leaders, is that the Catholics and ethnic groups tend to be Democratic, while the Protestants and old Americans tend to be Republican. The struggle of these two groups for political control of the state creates interest. Of course this is not always the basis of political cleavage: occasionally large sectors of the Italian and Polish population will vote Republican, and one minister said that some Catholics reacted against attempted political control by their Church and voted for Protestants. This splitting of party lines is much more common in local politics when people frequently do not know a candidate's party affiliation. In the most recent election the city went slightly Republican, but in previous elections it was slightly Democratic.

Several persons mentioned that the League of Women Voters has been working to increase interest in politics, but they said it had had little success. Recently the League came out in favor of a city-manager plan for Easterntown to meet the need created by the possible retirement of the mayor. Despite the mayor's endorsement (of a slightly variant plan), the excellent publicity and endorsement through the press and radio, and the discussion in several organizations, community leaders interviewed a few weeks after the plan was first announced seemed to feel that the plan had little chance of success. Not enough voters would turn out to fulfill the requirements for changing the charter. This was regarded as another evidence of the community's apathy toward local politics.

The description of this single American community could be greatly extended. But enough has been given to illustrate some aspects of a community as a group of people living in spatial proximity to each other and interacting in various ways with each other.

FOR ADDITIONAL READING

ANDERSON, ELIN L., *We Americans* (Cambridge: Harvard University Press, 1937). A study of nationality cleavage in a small New England city.

BERNARD, JESSIE, *American Community Behavior* (New York: Dryden, 1949). A textbook on the community.

HUNTER, FLOYD, *Community Power Structure* (Chapel Hill: University of North Carolina

Press, 1953). A study of a large southern city from the standpoint of power relationships.

LYND, R. S., and H. M. LYND, *Middletown* (New York: Harcourt, 1929). One of the earliest and most influential of community studies.

MACIVER, ROBERT M., *Community: A Sociological Study* (London: Macmillan, 1917). A classic theoretical analysis of community.

WARREN, ROLAND, *Community in America* (Chicago: Rand McNally, 1963). A recent text.

15 * Social Problems

A Definition and Classification of Social Problems

1   THE NATURE OF A SOCIAL PROBLEM

A social problem is generally defined as a situation affecting a significant number of people that is believed by them and/or by a significant number of others in the society to be a source of difficulty or unhappiness, and one that is considered to be capable of amelioration.[1] Thus a social problem consists of both an objective situation and a subjective social interpretation. The social problems of long standing in the world today include overpopulation, extreme poverty, juvenile delinquency, crime, chronic alcoholism, suicide, mental disorder, mental deficiency, divorce, desertion, intergroup prejudice and discrimination, industrial conflict, inadequate housing and slum neighborhoods, unemployment, chronic dependency, corruption in government. Several others are included by different authors, but any list must be recognized as arbitrary since no one has made a systematic study of public opinion to determine which situations are widely recognized to be social problems.

Some problems of a generation or so ago have disappeared—either because changed social conditions have eliminated the problem situations, or because the situations are no longer defined as problems. A problem such as slavery has largely disappeared from the world mainly because it is recognized to be less efficient than labor-for-hire under modern conditions and because it goes against most modern cultural values. A problem such as that formerly created by public drinking places—"saloons"—has largely

---

[1] A number of questions can be raised, and have been raised, about this typical definition. For example, how many are a "significant" number? If the persons affected are influential, cannot they be few in number and still be the source of a social problem? Obviously we cannot go into these and similar questions in this introductory text.

disappeared because it is no longer defined as a problem. That is, some people continue to drink in public places more than is good for their health, and excessive drinking continues to be thought of as a problem, but people no longer consider the public drinking place itself to be the source of difficulty. Another behavior formerly defined as a social problem but no longer considered to be such—except in so far as it has lately been recognized as a hazard to health—is smoking by women and youth.

Whatever may be the specific causes of social problems, there are always involved situations and human behavior considered to be out of accord with one or more social values. People who are thus acting in opposition to the social values may not be doing so voluntarily, or be aware of this implication of their behavior, but nevertheless their actions are a manifestation of the inability of the values to control people's behavior in all relevant situations and are therefore a threat to the future effectiveness of the values. This basic point takes us back to our first discussion of values as those elements of culture that encourage or demand certain kinds of behavior from members of the society possessing this culture. Values, along with meanings, permit coordinated behavior (or, as we have called it, "integrated group behavior") among members of a society. When a segment, large or small, of the society no longer accepts certain of its values, or finds other values to oppose to these, social problems result. This point of view is an old one in sociology, although by no means do all sociologists accept it. It was stated by Durkheim in his explanation of the anomic and egoistic forms of suicide; it was restated by Thomas and Znaniecki in their discussions of forms of social disorganization among immigrants to the United States; it has been used in numerous other studies of specific problems[2] and by several textbooks in social problems.[3]

This orientation toward social problems suggests several significant classifications of social problems:

[2] For example, R. C. Angell, *The Family Encounters the Depression* (New York: Scribner's, 1936); R. E. L. Faris and H. W. Durham, *Mental Disorders in Urban Areas* (Chicago: University of Chicago Press, 1939); Gunnar Myrdal, with the assistance of R. Sterner and A. Rose, *An American Dilemma* (New York: Harper, 1944).

[3] M. Elliot and R. E. Merrill, *Social Disorganization*, fourth ed. (New York: Harper, 1962); John F. Cuber, William F. Kenkel, and Robert A. Harper, *Problems of American Society: Values in Conflict* (New York: Holt, Rinehart, and Winston, 1964); R. E. Merrill, H. W. Dunham, A. M. Rose, and P. W. Tappan, *Social Problems* (New York: Alfred A. Knopf, 1950); R. E. L. Faris, *Social Disorganization* (New York: Ronald, 1948). Other recent textbooks on social problems include R. K. Merton and R. A. Nisbet (eds.), *Contemporary Social Problems* (New York: Harcourt, Brace and World, 1961); Earl Raab and G. J. Selznick, *Major Social Problems*, second ed. (New York: Harper and Row, 1964); Harry C. Bredemeier and Jackson Toby, *Social Problems in America* (New York: Wiley, 1960); R. R. Dynes, A. C. Clarke, S. Dinitz, and I. Ishino, *Social Problems* (New York: Oxford University Press, 1964); Paul B. Horton and Gerald R. Leslie, *The Sociology of Social Problems*, second ed. (New York: Appleton-Century-Crofts, 1964); Marshall B. Clinard, *Deviant Behavior* (New York: Rinehart, 1959).

1   Some of the problem behavior opposing the values arises "voluntarily" through the personalities of the individuals performing it while other kinds of problem behavior are imposed "involuntarily" on the individuals performing it. Crime is an example of the first type, and cyclical unemployment of the second type. The words "voluntarily" and "involuntarily" are put in quotation marks as the distinction between them is a matter of degree, or sometimes a matter of legal definition.[4]

2   Some of the people creating problems by behavior in opposition to certain social values do so as individuals whereas others do so in groups. Mental disorder is an example of a problem involving the first type of behavior, and most kinds of crime the second type. This needs a little explanation, as all social problems must involve a significant number of people, and it is difficult to tell when a significant number of people are a number of individuals or a number of groups. The distinction can be made by pointing out that a group requires common meanings and values of its own, and it is when these meanings and values are contrary to those of the larger society, and the members of the group act in accord with them, that a social problem of the second type exists.

3   Some of the problem behavior involves simply opposition to one broad social value or to a consistent set of broad social values. Other problem behavior involves opposition between two values or two sets of values. Suicide is an example of the first type, and intergroup prejudice and discrimination, at least in American culture, is an example of the second type. The values opposed to each other in intergroup relations in the United States are, on the one hand, fair play, free competition, liberty, equality, and, on the other hand, self-advancement, support for one's own group, defense against the attack of, or rising power of, another group believed to be dangerous to one's own group, maintenance of what is conceived to be the "highest" civilization.

4   Closely allied with the above is the distinction between problems resulting from disorganization of all social values—such as mental disorder, suicide and alcoholism—and problems resulting from conflicts between groups holding different values—such as most crime,

---

[4] As we have indicated elsewhere in this book, the distinction between voluntary and involuntary is a tricky one. Here, as elsewhere, we take the viewpoint of the law, and do not mean to infer that voluntary behavior is not caused or determined by specifiable forces. As indicated above, voluntary activities are determined *through* the medium of the individual's personality, while involuntary forces act regardless of the individual's personality. But this is not always an adequate distinction, as even in cyclical or technological unemployment, where the individual loses his job through no fault of his own and as a result of impersonal forces, the individual still has the "choice" of migrating to a distant spot to get a job, or he can go into submarginal jobs or submarginal farming. The distinction needs to be made, but we cannot go into all its subtleties here.

racketeering, and ethnic conflict.[5] We shall have more to say about these causes in subsequent sections. Here we merely wish to note that the first type involves the weakening of both current values, or norms, and of the valued ideals toward which people are striving. The second type may involve a conflict between ideals and norms, as in the case of the old drinking-prohibition problem or other problems believed to have strong moral implications.

2   THE CAUSES OF SOCIAL PROBLEMS

The consideration of social problems in terms of behavior not in accord with social values is part of the definition of social problems. This behavior does not "explain" social problems. The causes have to be looked for in a variety of biogenic, psychogenic, and sociogenic factors in behavior as well as in various social structures that direct individual behavior. Generally, no one cause is sufficient to explain all the varied individual manifestations of a social problem. For most problems we do not know all the causes, even in the case of a specific individual's manifestation of a social problem when his heredity, his life history, and the environment surrounding him are well known. In this situation we can only describe the extent, distribution, and manifestations of some of the problems, and offer some of the more widely accepted theories in explanation of them.

Before doing this, however, we shall examine some of those elements in the causation of social problems arising from their definition in terms of behavior not in accord with some social values. People are more likely to act out of accord with the social values of their culture in times of rapid social change than in times of social stability. The reasons for this are: (1) sometimes values are no longer helpful in guiding people to adjust to the changed situations they must face; (2) individuals internalize one set of meanings and values in their childhood and then are expected to conform to another, somewhat conflicting, set during adolescence and adulthood; and (3) in times of change people are likely to get out of communication with each other—communication that would allow them to modify their meanings and values to meet the changed situation.

Some kinds of changes our society has been undergoing during the past two centuries—toward increased literacy and increased concern for the welfare of the entire people—have increased the number of social problems not by changing situations but by changing *definitions* of situations. Pre-modern Western society had much higher incidence of poverty, disease, brutality, ignorance, danger to life and property from preventable accidents and from brigands than has modern society. Yet they were not

[5] Arnold M. Rose, "Theory for the Study of Social Problems," *Social Problems,* 4 (January, 1957), pp. 189–99.

> Preliminary to any self-determined act of behavior there is always a stage of examination and deliberation which we may call *the definition of the situation*. And actually not only concrete acts are dependent on the definition of the situation, but gradually a whole life-policy and the personality of the individual himself follow from a series of such definitions.
>
> But the child is always born into a group of people among whom all the general types of situation which may arise have already been defined and corresponding rules of conduct developed, and where he has not the slightest chance of making his definitions and following his wishes without interference. Men have always lived together in groups.
>
> W. I. Thomas, *The Unadjusted Girl* (Boston: Little, Brown, 1923), p. 42.

considered as problems, but as part of the order of nature and hence not reducible. Modern science, education, and democratic values have caused us to redefine these situations as social problems and have helped us to reduce their objective manifestations. Social problems arising out of redefinition in this way probably result in a reduction of human misery, although they may have resulted also in increased sensitivity to and heightened awareness of unpleasant conditions. In general, situations seem to be more readily interpreted as social problems than social problems are reinterpreted as "not problems." Once people define a situation as a problem, they do not seem to be inclined to forget about it. This may be a characteristic of our particular culture, with its trends toward secularized explanations of conditions, increasing scientific knowledge, and probably increasing concern about individual welfare. Of course even in our society certain problems get "defined" out of existence. We have suggested that certain aspects of the "saloon" problem and certain aspects of the race problems (e.g., the former belief that Negroes are biologically incapable of working with machines) have thus been redefined as not problems, and most people have ceased to be concerned about them. It seems to be extremely difficult to start a social movement to redefine a problem as not a problem, but there have been many reform and revolutionary movements that have succeeded in getting a public definition of a given situation as a social problem.

The absence of change can also be a source of social problems. The deliberate withholding of new scientific knowledge that could relieve suffering, increase productivity, or otherwise aid people in satisfying their needs operates to maintain social problems in our society which we need not maintain. There is the phenomenon of "cultural lag"[6] in which some parts of culture fail to change in adjustment to changes in other parts of culture, and this can create problems. For example, the migration of

[6] See Chapter 5, Section C.

numerous unattached adults to cities in response to job opportunities made available by the Industrial Revolution was not accompanied by the building of housing specially adapted to the needs of unattached people, with the result that most unattached people live as "roomers" in housing inadequate to their needs.[7]

Several social problems of our society could be eliminated by widespread acceptance of new definitions of the problem situation. For example, part of the problem of rehabilitating mental patients discharged from mental hospitals as cured is that many people in the home communities will not accept them in work or social relations; they are still regarded as "crazy," which puts such a strain on them that sometimes they have to return to the hospital.[8] Many of the problems of intergroup relations in our society are based on prejudice—that is, a derogatory attitude toward, and false beliefs about, a group by members of another group. The causes of this are complex, but if the definition of groups toward which there is prejudice could be changed (even without eliminating all the causes which gave rise to prejudice in the first place), many—though perhaps not all—of the problems of intergroup relations could be eliminated. Actually, both of the kinds of problems we have mentioned as examples are now in the process of being eliminated by just the kind of redefinition we have been speaking of.

Efforts to impede this redefinition—that is, to prevent change—are efforts to maintain the problems. There are many kinds of reasons why some people impede the changes that reduce social problems. First, while the problem behavior opposes certain values, it may maintain other values, and some efforts to impede change may consist of a sincere effort to maintain these other values. People who oppose the reduction of race prejudice, for example, may sincerely believe they are preventing the destruction of important social values.

Second, there are purely selfish motives for opposing social change. Personal advantage is a major motivation for some people who oppose efforts to reduce race prejudice. Personal advantage is a major motivation also for those who own slum property, bringing in high rents relative to cost, and who oppose public housing projects which would wipe out slums and give decent housing to those who could never otherwise afford it. Appeal may be made to the value that the government should not compete with the private construction industry, but the underlying motivation has nothing to do with this propaganda appeal, as may be seen from the fact that the private construction industry has no interest in the slum area

[7] Arnold M. Rose, "Living Arrangements of Unattached Persons," *American Sociological Review*, 12 (August, 1947), pp. 429–35.

[8] Howard E. Freeman and Ozzie G. Simmons, *The Mental Patient Comes Home* (New York: Wiley, 1963).

and that the appeals are made by the slum property owners rather than by the private construction industry.

Third, some opposition to social change arises from simple ignorance. This is probably the source of the failure to build sufficient housing specially designed to meet the needs of unattached persons. It is only gradually being realized that 10 per cent of all city dwellers are permanently unattached and that another significant, although changing, percentage are temporaily unattached, and that most of these people would prefer to, and could afford to, have living arrangements other than those of "roomers."[9]

When values are not sufficiently strongly held or are not shared by all members of a society, people do not completely know how to act toward one another. The roles they play toward one another do not mesh, and the society may be said to be "disorganized," although this should be recognized to be a matter of degree, not an absolute state. Thus "social disorganization" has sometimes been used in sociology as synonymous with "social problems." The term "social pathology" has also been employed, in an effort to suggest the similarity between disease of the bodies of living creatures and "disease" of societies. This should be understood to be merely an analogy, although there are certain points of similarity. Disease in a physical organism hampers the functioning of that organism, and social problems hamper the functioning of society as the members of the society see it. A disease generally attacks only one segment (or organ) of a living creature but thereby affects the whole organism, while a social problem generally affects only a segment of society but thereby has a detrimental influence on the whole society.

The analogy can easily be overstretched, however, as there are many basic differences between a physical organism and a society and between the disorders of each. A physical disease has certain objective symptoms, whereas a social problem exists only when the members of a society define a situation as a problem in terms of their own values. A physical disease has a definite pattern of origin and development, whereas a given social problem can originate and develop in several diverse ways. A physical disease usually involves destruction of some tissue, whereas a social problem need not always involve destruction of some people.

There are several influences that reduce the control of values over people's behavior. All of these thereby contribute to social problems, but some of them also reduce social problems by reducing the difficulties people have in their social settings. Migration, for example, creates social problems by isolating individuals who migrate, by reducing family and neighborhood controls over deviant behavior, by placing together people who hold divergent sets of values. But it also relieves social problems in

[9] People who favor the reduction of a social problem such as race prejudice may, of course, be characterized in these same three ways.

that individuals leave areas where they are not able to make a living or where they are the objects of discrimination and move to areas where economic and social opportunities are greater. In general, migration has been increasing in modern times, although we do not have adequate comparative statistics.[10]

The economic mobility made possible by the free-enterprise economic system and the Commercial and Industrial Revolutions has also had the mixed effect of both creating and resolving social problems. Changes in the economic system since the Industrial Revolution released individuals from their bondage to a single job, permitted a rise in occupational status, and markedly increased the average level of living. But they also created the possibility of unemployment and rapid economic losses.

Unemployment is both an economic and a personal problem. On the one hand it causes poverty, and all the problems that poverty entails. On the other hand it may cause a crisis in one's conception of one's self and in family and neighborhood relations. Even when one is not unemployed, the possibility that one might become so creates feelings of personal insecurity. During the depression of the 1930's there were ten to twelve million unemployed in a total American working population of some fifty million. During the brief recession in the spring of 1954 unemployment rose to four million in a working force of some sixty-two million. The lowest unemployment record of recent decades, except for the war years, was achieved in the summer of 1952, when only 600,000 Americans were reported out of work. Some of these were voluntarily unemployed but reported themselves as unemployed to take advantage of their unemployment insurance. Nevertheless, unemployment is a constant problem in modern society, although of varying magnitude from year to year.

Changes in the material circumstances of people, such as immigration or unemployment, may create social problems in themselves by making it impossible for significant numbers of people to satisfy their material needs. But they also tend to create social problems by preventing people from carrying out their expected roles in relation to each other. For example, when a father who has been the sole breadwinner of a family is no longer able to support his family because he cannot find work, sometimes the mother or the older children take on that role. If the family is not flexible enough to readjust quickly to this changed role relationship— for example, by the father assuming many household tasks and accepting the greater independence of the working children—the family is likely to disintegrate.[11]

The inability to carry out expected role relationships arises from a

[10] See Chapter 12, Section B.
[11] Angell, *op. cit.*; R. S. Cavan and K. H. Ranck, *The Family and the Depression* (Chicago: University of Chicago Press, 1938).

number of different circumstances besides changes in material conditions. The institutions of a society are practically never so perfectly adjusted to each other in their functions and operations that they do not compete and conflict. Political corruption often arises from the fact that a person elected to public office has not only a role to play in that office but has a conflicting role to play in the dominant political group which put him into office.[12] Two ideologies within a culture may also be in conflict and the individuals who behave toward other people on the basis of either one of them thereby create a social problem. In the United States the conflict between the ideology of the American creed and the ideology of racism is the source of many of the problems of race relations. Finally, the inability of certain individuals to learn their roles, or to learn under what circumstances they should be carried out in behavior, is a source of social problems. Neither the feeble-minded nor the psychotic person is able to comprehend the roles which others expect of him under most circumstances.

3   THE REDUCTION OF SOCIAL PROBLEMS

One of the defining characteristics of social problems is that people believe they can be eliminated. If a situation causes difficulty or misery for people, but is thought of as incapable of being changed through deliberate effort, it has the position in that society of an "act of God" or part of the order of nature rather than a social problem. Of course some people may be pessimistic and feel that their society does not have the ability or resources to solve the problem; but still if they think that they know what actions could conceivably solve the problem, this meets the definitional requirement of a social problem. Then, too, people may not be sure that they know the solution for a social problem, but still have faith that further study or thought would elicit the appropriate techniques.

The kinds of action believed likely to reduce or eliminate a social problem have a great range. Some would have individuals change their behavior, and this could be accomplished through rational persuasion, emotional exhortation, mass propaganda, or some other manner of communication directed toward individuals whose behavior is considered to be the source of the problem. Others believe that the solution must occur through change of individual behavior but believe that individuals whose habits are already formed are not likely to change their behavior. These advocate an effort to educate or indoctrinate children in a certain way so that the next generation would not grow up with the problem behavior.

Still another approach to the reduction of a social problem is through the use of experts who would treat the social pathology much as a physician treats individual pathology. In some cases it is considered necessary to make a study first, and this involves the use of social-science research

[12] Lincoln Steffens, *Autobiography* (New York: Harcourt, 1931).

experts as well as practicing experts. The latter include psychiatrists, social workers, group organizers, group workers, group administrators, educators, and other specialists who deal with people and social structures. Some people believe that it is beyond the scope of a social scientist, as a scientist, to make recommendations that would alleviate or reduce a social problem. This is a bias that arises out of a misconception of the role and actual activities of scientists. The scientist should not state that a given condition is bad, and should be reduced or eliminated. But once a condition is considered by others to be a problem—and the scientist can do research to ascertain whether people generally or in certain groups consider it to be a problem—he can study and test means for reducing the problem just as he would study or test anything else. If he then finds that one means is better than another—in the sense of being more effective, or costing less, or having the least harmful side effects (the judgment about harmfulness again has to be made by the public)—he is quite justified in recommending the better means.

Another approach to the reduction of social problems is through legal prohibition of the problem behavior—that is, the provision of punishment by the government. Sometimes punishment by incarceration is accompanied by efforts to reform or "rehabilitate" the offending individual. The government, or other organizations, can deal with certain problems directly by physically eliminating the conditions that seem to give rise to the problem behavior. Slum living can be attacked by the construction of housing projects; chronic alcoholism can be attacked by prohibition of the sale of liquor. The "great experiment" of Prohibition of the sale of intoxicating liquors in the United States from 1919 to 1933 failed to stop excessive drinking, because many people failed to obey the law, and because violations of the law created new problems—such as those of poisonous liquor and corruption of law-enforcement officials. But if this one experiment in changing people's behavior by legislation failed, many others—conducted with greater attention to sociological and psychological factors—have been successful.

Still another kind of effort to reduce social problems is to change the social structures through which social behavior takes place. If conflict among groups is believed to be caused by the fact that there is no occasion for friendly contact among them, situations may be contrived in which members of the group come together in sociable settings.

The above listing of means believed capable of reducing social problems is by no means exhaustive, and no one has ever claimed that each is equally applicable to all social problems. There has never been an adequate scientific test of any of the techniques, except in very limited circumstances, and it is quite possible that some have no effect whatsoever.

But in general social scientists know a great deal more about how to reduce social problems than is currently being put into practice. Social
scientists can suggest means that are likely to reduce social problems by
removal of their causes or at least their supporting conditions. But social
action lags behind social knowledge for reasons varying from ignorance
to deliberate resistance to change. Some relevant possible approaches to
solutions will be considered in connection with the following discussion
of some of the concrete social problems.

This introductory survey of sociology obviously cannot examine all
social problems, even major ones. The nature of social problems, their
social causes, and techniques of dealing with them will be illustrated by a
consideration of a few selected social problems. The remainder of this
chapter will take up delinquency, the population "explosion" and
poverty, some of the problems of older people and inadequate housing.
Other chapters take up other social problems in different contexts. Chapter
8 considers "caste" as an aspect of social organization; with the introduction
of democratic and equalitarian value premises—held by a very large segment of our society—caste in the United States can be considered a social
problem. Chapter 16 examines conflict which, under certain conditions
and certain values, is a social problem. Chapter 17 takes up low morale of
groups.

B   *Problems of Delinquency*

1   THE SOCIAL SETTING OF DELINQUENCY

The values defining the role of the modern child are not consistent or clear
cut. Parents are not at all certain as to how they should act toward their
child—how much "pressure" they should put on the child, for example—
and their behavior is therefore often inconsistent. People other than
parents differ from parents in their conceptions of how children should
behave, and their influence on children is both considerable and diversified.
There is inconsistency of viewpoint concerning the proper functions in
relation to the child of the school, the church, the recreational center, the
formally organized children's associations (such as the Scouts), the social
agency, the juvenile courts, and the police. The delinquent child, who by
definition is considered as one behaving in opposition to certain social
values, is to be understood partly in terms of such conflicting social values.

The universal function of parents is to socialize their children—or at
least to do a major share of the job of early socialization—and one of the
essential aims of socialization is to create in the child an understanding
and acceptance of certain social values. A juvenile delinquent is fre-

quently nothing more than an incompletely socialized child.[13] At a tender age the child will not be expected to understand and accept the social values governing the privacy of property and the inviolacy of the person, and he may be completely forgiven for behavior which would be defined as crime if he were older. But an older child is expected to know better— even if he actually does not—and if he commits a crime he is socially defined as a juvenile delinquent. On the other hand, some parents set too high and too rigid a standard of conformity for their children. The child is physically, mentally, and emotionally capable of doing only certain things at certain ages, and not until he is an adult can he be expected to act completely like an adult. Parents who set too high or too rigid a standard may simply provoke rebellion or negativism, which might take the form of violation of social expectations in such a way as to label the child a delinquent.

A third source of parental influence leading a child to delinquency is inconsistency in the parents' own values or behavior. They may never have been incarcerated as criminals, but they believe they can (and do) "get away" with certain violations of the law. They do not want their children to be "criminals" but they also teach their child to wink at the law. The child may violate the law in ways different from his parents, but he may not see the difference.

A fourth kind of family situation leading to delinquency occurs when the parents socialize their child, but in such a way that he is completely maladapted to the culture of his friends or of his school. This occurs in a significant proportion of immigrant families, where the parents teach the youngster the ways of behaving that would be proper in their native lands, but which the child finds sharply inappropriate when he becomes a member of a play group or school. He may come to reject a large part of the meanings and values of his parents, and in doing so violates certain laws.

Fifth, parent-child conflict can occur on levels other than that of cultural values regarding proper behavior, and the child's reactions to his parents also take a delinquent form. For example, parents—through some quirk in their own personality—may deprecate a child, try to give him the feeling that he is inferior in some way. The child may react by trying to hurt his parents, and thereby commit a delinquent act. Some especially serious forms of delinquency have this source.

It is the larger society that defines a child's behavior as delinquent. This it does formally through the laws and the law-enforcement agencies— that is, the juvenile courts and the police—and informally through turning over a child as a delinquent to the police or approving the apprehension of a delinquent child by the police. Not all children who commit infrac-

[13] Arnold M. Rose, "Incomplete Socialization," *Sociology and Social Research,* 44 (March–April, 1960), pp. 244–50.

tions of the law are brought to the attention of a court unless the crime is an especially serious one (the same can be said of adult violators of the law).

Assuming that the child is known by members of the community as one who has committed a not-too-serious crime (say the theft of some merchandise from a store), the child generally will not be brought to the attention of the police and the courts if the child is considered to be too young to know better, if the child is believed to have committed his first offense and that a reprimand might prevent reoccurrence of the crime, if the parents are influential and/or wealthy and use their power to "persuade" other members of the community (or the police) not to arrest the child. Local communities differ, of course, in what they perceive to be a criminal act; some communities are apathetic or antipathetic toward law enforcement and practically never bring a delinquent child to the attention of the police.[14] Porterfield has shown that the behavior of children brought before the juvenile court had been engaged in by almost all among a representative sample of college students, but that practically none of the latter had ever been brought to the attention of the police or the courts.[15]

The juvenile courts are a modern development. Only gradually have different nations and states come to regard a crime committed by a child as requiring a different treatment from a crime committed by an adult. In France not until 1952 did this principle receive full legal recognition. But legal recognition alone does not completely change policy, and many juvenile courts still manifest their criminal-court origins. They use punishment frequently, they are authoritarian in determining by themselves what shall be done to a delinquent child, when not using formal punishment they assume an air of sentimental benevolence.

Some juvenile courts have fairly well broken away from this older tradition. The judges of juvenile courts usually are specially informed about children's problems, and they generally have a staff of social workers who are trained in handling children's cases. The larger cities in the United States have juvenile sections in their police departments, and they have changed police philosophy, in so far as it concerns juvenile offenders, in the direction of avoiding arrests and court petitions. They use dis-

[14] The extent to which crimes occur that are not brought to the attention of the police or the courts was studied in a rural community in Illinois. See Thomas C. Esselstyn, "Crime and Its Control in the Hinterland," Ph.D. thesis, New York University, February, 1952.

[15] Austin L. Porterfield, *Youth in Trouble* (Austin: Leo Potishman Foundation, 1946). These statistics should not be read to mean that the true crime *rates* of the students and the charged delinquents are the same. The students were asked if they had *ever* committed these acts, while the charged delinquents had undoubtedly committed many criminal acts other than those for which they were currently charged.

cussion, admonition, persuasion, warning—with both children and parents—and sometimes sponsor positive programs of leisure-time activities. These new practices are generally followed only with the less serious offenders.

Juvenile delinquency is not clearly defined in the United States. Following British common law, it includes all those behaviors by children, which, if they were engaged in by adults, would be regarded as crimes. In addition, many states include as delinquent behavior various specific children's offenses such as truancy and running away, as well as several vaguely defined offenses such as "incorrigibility," "willful disobedience," and "bad associates." On top of this the juvenile courts and juvenile sections of police departments are inclined to give attention, advice, and protection to children who have committed none of these offenses, but whom the judges or police personally believe might be aided by this attention. The personal preferences of the judges are—for good or for evil—more important than the law in the handling of all but the most serious cases of juvenile delinquency. Many cases of delinquency are handled by agencies other than the police and the courts, even when the local community is aware of the case and is willing to have it handled by public authority.

Thus much of what is legally and publicly recognized as juvenile delinquency is not handled as the law directs. In the city of Washington, D.C., an effort has been made to collect data on all the non-official handling of delinquents by public agencies, and the results show that a significant proportion of offenses are handled in this way. In this city only 5 per cent of the known truancy offenses and 24 per cent of the known sex offenses are handled by the juvenile court, as compared to 80 per cent of the known stealing offenses and 99 per cent of the known traffic violations.[16] These percentages would, of course, vary drastically from city to city, and even within a given city they vary from time to time as the administrative practices of a number of agencies change.

The variations in local practices extend to the matter of the age at which an offender ceases to be regarded as a juvenile delinquent and is regarded as a criminal. The control of juvenile courts applies to offenders only up through the age of sixteen in six states and in parts of two others, but through the age of twenty-one (at least in some cases) in seven other states (see Table 22). To further complicate the matter, there is concurrent jurisdiction of the juvenile and criminal court over certain ages, and the distinction is over certain types of crime, which are sometimes ill-defined in law. In addition, certain types of crime are under the exclusive

[16] Edward E. Schwartz, "A Community Experiment in the Measurement of Juvenile Delinquency," *National Probation Association Yearbook* (Washington, D.C., 1945), p. 173.

jurisdiction of the criminal court in some states, no matter what the age of the child. These variations reflect, in part, differences in social values at various times and places.

2   THE INADEQUACY OF THE STATISTICS
AND THE METHODS OF RESEARCH

Because of all the factors mentioned above, statistics on delinquency collected from official sources are highly inadequate. Nevertheless, there are certain conclusions that can be drawn from them which are generally true, even if the specific figures are inaccurate. One is that girls commit fewer offenses of most types than do boys. In the case of those offenses for which girls appear in court more frequently than boys—mostly sex offenses—the reason is that the behavior is more likely to be ignored or excused in boys rather than that boys engage in them less. Reasons for the sex discrepancy—which applies to adults as well as to children—can only be inferred from a general knowledge of our culture. While laws represent cultural expectations for behavior, there is nevertheless a subsidiary cultural expectation that boys will violate the law in minor ways and that they will risk an approach to the dividing line between legal and illegal behavior frequently. This subsidiary expectation applies much less to girls. This expectation is transmitted to children even by law-abiding parents, but to a greater extent by peer groups.

Other reliable conclusions that may be drawn from the official statistics are suggested by Table 22. These are data on arrests, rather than on court petitions or complaints, and thus do not show the large number of court cases that are brought in by parents, social agencies, and other petitioners. The considerable proportion of juvenile cases taken to court for recalcitrance, running away, and truancy do not appear in arrest statistics. Even so, the data show the relatively low rates of serious offenses charges against younger children as compared to the high rates for youths from seventeen to twenty-four. Auto theft and burglary (entry into and theft from closed property) are the most frequent charges against those under eighteen, while larceny (theft from open property), robbery (theft from person), suspicion, drunkenness, and rape join it in frequency for the older youth. Juvenile-court statistics (not shown) indicate that acts of carelessness or mischief are second to stealing (all forms: larceny, burglary, robbery from persons, automobile theft) as reasons for complaints resulting in court action.[17]

No other conclusions can safely be drawn from the official statistics, despite the fact that many experts and laymen use such statistics or even

[17] U.S. Children's Bureau, *Social Statistics* (Washington, D.C., 1945), p. 11.

TABLE 22 · COUNTY ARRESTS OF PERSONS UNDER 18, UNDER 21, AND UNDER 25 YEARS OF AGE, METROPOLITAN AND RURAL COUNTIES, UNITED STATES, 1962

Offense charged	118 metropolitan counties;[a] 1962 estimated population 13,183,000				921 rural counties; 1962 estimated population 16,375,000			
		Percentage				Percentage		
	Total	Under 18	Under 21	Under 25	Total	Under 18	Under 21	Under 25
TOTAL	219,265	18.1	29.6	41.4	273,211	13.4	27.1	40.1
Criminal Homicide								
(a) Murder and nonnegligent manslaughter	479	6.9	23.6	38.4	672	7.3	17.1	29.0
(b) Manslaughter by negligence	321	5.0	18.1	33.6	553	5.4	17.5	37.4
Forcible rape	904	14.5	38.1	63.7	1,036	10.4	33.8	57.2
Robbery	2,668	17.1	41.6	65.0	1,519	14.3	33.8	59.6
Aggravated assault	4,423	10.6	24.0	38.2	4,790	5.6	17.1	33.9
Burglary—breaking or entering	13,744	47.4	66.6	79.6	16,798	40.2	63.6	79.0
Larceny—theft	15,848	42.7	58.9	70.3	19,825	28.3	52.1	66.8
Auto theft	5,264	57.9	76.0	85.6	5,878	51.0	69.4	80.9
Other assaults	12,603	6.7	15.7	29.7	10,578	5.0	16.7	32.8
Embezzlement and fraud	5,444	.9	4.8	17.6	8,229	1.6	7.6	22.6
Stolen property; buying, receiving, etc.	704	20.7	38.8	54.3	1,329	17.6	38.2	55.6
Forgery and counterfeiting	2,032	5.7	17.2	33.0	5,127	5.4	18.3	35.4
Prostitution and commercialized vice	400	.8	7.0	37.0	295	9.2	19.0	40.3
Other sex offenses (includes statutory rape)	3,561	17.9	32.7	46.6	3,357	13.3	29.6	45.6
Narcotic drug laws	3,129	4.3	22.4	52.4	759	9.6	34.0	51.1
Weapons; carrying, possessing, etc.	1,801	23.5	39.4	52.7	2,207	8.6	24.5	42.9
Offenses against family and children	7,911	.5	5.6	20.1	10,140	1.2	8.5	24.7
Liquor laws	6,468	23.1	60.7	67.9	14,836	18.7	60.1	71.4
Driving while intoxicated	12,537	.7	5.0	14.8	24,300	.7	5.3	15.8
Disorderly conduct	14,635	15.9	30.9	44.4	18,634	8.6	24.3	41.2
Drunkenness	46,182	2.1	7.1	15.4	60,544	1.8	7.3	16.2
Vagrancy	3,455	7.0	22.7	37.8	5,435	6.5	16.9	28.0
Gambling	2,177	1.2	4.3	11.9	1,591	.7	4.0	14.7
All other offenses, except traffic	47,875	27.2	37.1	48.9	50,782	23.5	37.1	50.4
Suspicion	4,700	39.4	58.4	71.4	3,997	19.3	36.9	52.3

Source: J. Edgar Hoover, Director, Federal Bureau of Investigation, Crime in the United States: Uniform Crime Reports—1962 (Washington, D.C.: U.S. Department of Justice, 1963), p. 102.

less reliable newspaper reports to observe that children of low economic status, foreign parentage, Catholic religion, Negro race, broken homes, and slum environment are more likely to be delinquents than other children. All we can infer from the statistics is that children with one or more of the above-mentioned characteristics have a greater *risk* of being arrested and/or brought to court than do other children. Delinquencies committed by children in other categories are much more likely to get handled by parents, private psychiatrists, and non-official social agencies, although we have no systematic evidence on the extent of this practice. Children in the first-named categories are much more likely to grow up to become adult offenders who are brought to court for theft, assault, drunkenness, etc. But it is quite possible, although the evidence is practically non-existent, that children in other categories grow up to become embezzlers, black marketeers, smugglers, defrauders, and other kinds of "white-collar" criminals. We do know that people in the upper-income categories who commit minor crimes are less likely to get arrested, brought to court, or convicted than people in the lower-income categories who commit similar crimes, although the discrepancy in official treatment is probably not so great for adults as for children.

Finally, we must face the possibility that the treatment of delinquent children influences markedly their future adult behavior. Numerous case studies suggest that police apprehension and court experience define a child to himself as a social deviant,[18] that incarceration in a detention home brings him in contact with habitual older delinquents who teach him a criminal's orientation to society as well as specific tricks of the trade, and that labeling of him as a delinquent by his community and by a police record places limits on his opportunities to deviate from a career of delinquency and crime.[19] Tappan represents the opinion of a considerable number of contemporary criminologists when he says that "in an unknown but considerable number of cases, adult crime is mainly the product of our conventional handling."[20] We have been in the habit of regarding delinquency as deviant behavior. Actually, from what evidence is available—admittedly poor—it is just as likely that *most* young children labeled as delinquents are engaging in "normal" or average behavior.

Methods of research into the causation of delinquency have been

[18] Here it might be wise to review Cooley's conception of the self as a "looking glass." See Chapter 2, Section E, of this book, or Cooley's original discussion on pp. 183–85 of his *Human Nature and the Social Order* (New York: Scribner's, 1902; rev. ed., 1922).

[19] See, for example, the life histories of criminal careers published by Clifford Shaw, under several titles.

[20] Paul W. Tappan, in R. E. Merrill (ed.), *Social Problems* (New York: Alfred A. Knopf, 1950), p. 203.

inadequate from a scientific standpoint.[21] One procedure has been to examine the life history of single cases. This may provide an adequate picture of the motivations of, and influences on, this single delinquent child (assuming that the method of getting information is an adequate one), but the pattern of development for one child is seldom duplicated in other delinquents, and no statistical check is made on the relative incidence among delinquent and non-delinquent children of the factors deemed crucial. Detailed psychiatric case studies seem to indicate that the factors deemed crucial in the etiology of delinquency do not operate in isolation. A given experience or personality trait (e.g., the breaking up of a home, rejection by a parent, aggressiveness) plays a role in leading to delinquency only in connection with a host of other experiences or traits of the individual. One psychiatrist holds that an especially disturbed child will "steer" his companions into delinquency even though they have only the vaguest tendencies in that direction:

> There are some youngsters who, because of mental disturbance, are not able to have fun in the usual way. They feel they must do something for "fun" and enter into fantastic things. Sometimes it is heavy drinking, using narcotics, or sexual excesses. Delinquent "fun" is frequently aggressive—destructive, but aimless.
>
> There may be feelings of confused aggression in several members of the gang, which are not expressed in serious anti-social acts until a particularly disturbed kid comes along and channelizes it into a particular way. He talks it up or acts it out, and the others—or some of them—accept it as an outlet for their confused feelings.[22]

The usual statistical approach, even when it avoids the previously mentioned pitfalls offered by the official statistics, also has serious limitations. Correlations do not prove causation; it is difficult to measure some of the most likely factors and so statistical studies tend to concentrate on easily measured variables; many studies fail to use comparable control groups so as to determine whether the incidence of a given factor deemed causative of delinquency is not also found in the same proportion in the non-delinquent population; statistical studies operate on the unstated premise that causative factors operate as independent variables whereas actually it is likely that they operate in interrelationships whose total effect is law violation. What are needed are long-time studies, using designs for experimental research, with adequate samples of the population. Such studies have not yet been made, and until they are, our information about

---

[21] A good critique of the methods of research in studies of the etiology of delinquency is contained in Paul W. Tappan, *Juvenile Delinquency* (New York: McGraw-Hill, 1949).

[22] Milton H. Horowitz, senior psychiatrist in charge of the Boys' Adolescent Ward at Bellevue Hospital, as quoted in the *New York Times*, May 22, 1955, p. 83.

the causation of delinquency rests on the inadequacies of our methods, the biases of the investigators, and the selectiveness of official statistics as much as it does on real information about delinquents.

3   THE CAUSES OF DELINQUENCY

In considering some of the outstanding theories and researches regarding the etiology of delinquency, we find the distinction between biogenic, psychogenic, and sociogenic influences most useful.[23] Early studies looked for biological traits associated with criminality,[24] but there have been repeated and scientifically adequate demonstrations that all the physical and inherited mental-deficiency traits once claimed to be characteristic of criminals are found with about the same incidence in non-criminal populations. The two outstanding types of contemporary explanations of delinquency and crime are those that place the primary explanation on personality development and those that place the primary emphasis on social environment. This is not to say that certain constitutional factors— such as thyroid deficiency or excess, brain deficiency or damage, body height, etc.—may not help shape the significant personality development or social environment, but since these latter arise from a whole variety of factors, it is considered that they should be studied directly for their influence on delinquency, rather than going back to their history or biological limitations.[25]

Both types of contemporary theories distinguish predisposing factors from precipitating factors, and recognize the latter to be significant social experiences of a great range of types outside the possibilities of prediction except in so far as they are related to the predisposing factors. Thus, the research effort is concentrated on discovering the predisposing factors, recognizing that these are not ultimate causes or "necessary" causes in the logical sense, but simply proximate and sufficient causes. This is to say that most researchers on delinquency do not concern themselves with all the background or limiting conditions that must be present before delinquency can occur, but only with those personality drives and social conditions that lead a child unfailingly to delinquency (perhaps provided that

[23] See introduction to Chapter 4.

[24] For example, Cesare Lombroso, *Crime, Its Causes and Remedies* (Boston: Little, Brown, 1911). The later study of E. A. Hooton claiming to discover a significant relationship between body characteristics and crime seem to this author to have been adequately refuted by the critics. See E. A. Hooton, *Crime and the Man* (Cambridge: Harvard University Press, 1939).

[25] Periodically there are reports that a new physiological cause of crime is discovered. For example, an article in the *New York Times* for September 28, 1952 (p. 34), states that studies were being made in England which showed that crimes were committed when the sugar content of the blood was low. Generally, no comparisons are reported for non-criminals, and no consideration is given to the influence under discussion as a mere contributory or correlative condition.

a "final straw"—or precipitating factor, such as unusual opportunity to commit a theft undetected—be present).

a The Personality-Development Theory

The characteristic interest of those who hold to a personality-development theory of juvenile delinquency is a description of the personality traits of the delinquent as compared to the non-delinquent. This may be developed as a clinical picture[26] or as a systematic statistical comparison using a variety of personality-measurement devices.[27] The findings of one of the most recent and most carefully designed studies of the latter type depict delinquent girls, on the average, as more psychopathic, more paranoid, more schizophrenic, and more manic than the girls who do not run afoul of the law-enforcing agencies. They find that the average delinquent boy is more psychopathic and manic than the average non-delinquent boy. This does not mean that the delinquents are so extremely psychotic or psychopathic as to be considered as clinical or legal cases, but simply that many of them have mild tendencies in this direction.

Not all studies directed at determining the distinctive personality traits of delinquent children have found significant personality differences between delinquents and non-delinquents,[28] but this may simply be due to inadequate instruments or procedures. Those who look for or find distinctive personality traits as the source of delinquency do not have exactly the same ideas as to the development of these personality traits. Some investigators make no effort to explain the development, others employ one or the other of the psychoanalytic theories of disturbances in child development, still others use non-analytic theories. One of the most widely held theories traces the source of the personality deviation to the lack of acceptance of and affection for the child by the parents; this is held to develop in the child feelings of insecurity, inadequacy, withdrawal, frustration, and rebelliousness.

b The "Broken Family" Theory

The search for the cause of the delinquent personality in family relations brings us close to the social-environment theories of delinquency.

[26] For example, Maude A. Merrill, *Problems of Child Delinquency* (Boston: Houghton Mifflin, 1947).

[27] For example, S. R. Hathaway and E. D. Monachesi, "The Minnesota Multiphasic Personality Inventory in the Study of Juvenile Delinquents," *American Sociological Review*, 17 (December, 1952), pp. 704–10; S. R. Hathaway and E. D. Monachesi, *Adolescent Personality and Behavior* (Minneapolis: University of Minnesota Press, 1963).

[28] Forty-two per cent of the 113 studies investigating personality differences between criminals and non-criminals showed significant differences. See Karl F. Schuessler and Donald R. Cressey, "Personality Characteristics of Criminals," *American Journal of Sociology*, 55 (March, 1950), pp. 476–84.

Emotional insecurity, as a source of continuing maladjustment, generally is traced to unsatisfactory intrafamilial relationships. Some investigators consider the problem a specific function of the "broken family"—that is, one where one or both of the parents are not present to aid in the raising of the child. The question might be considered whether it is the separation of the parents that is so important, or the incompatibility and discord of the parents which led to their separation. It might be that separation of the parents eases the tension that led the child into delinquency in some cases. Other investigators believe that any seriously unsatisfactory sort of relationship with one or both parents can cause a development toward delinquency. The problem remains—even if we should arrive at completely satisfactory statistical differences between delinquents and non-delinquents in the incidence of relevant personality traits—as to why so many people who have the same kind of unsatisfactory family backgrounds do not develop the same personality traits, and that many who do still do not wind up as juvenile delinquents but find some more socially approved outlet for their feelings of frustration or rebelliousness. Further, there are a few delinquents who do not have a background of unsatisfactory family relationships.

The family is not only the creator of most psychogenic personality traits in the child, but is also one of the most important sources of sociogenic influences. The family can directly transmit a delinquent role to the child, as in the case of a family whose members are mostly criminals.[29] Attitudes toward the personal property of others, toward the law and law-enforcing agents, toward other semi-coercive institutions—such as the school and the church—toward society generally, receive their early development in the family. The community has the same formative influence, especially the play group, which is the part of the community closest to the child. In American society the family tends to decrease in importance as a formative influence as the child grows older, and the community tends to increase in importance. It has been shown that delinquencies are seldom committed by individual children, but usually by children in groups, or gangs, at least in areas where large numbers of delinquents are reported to the police or the courts.[30] The central question for those who seek a social explanation of delinquency is: What is there in the nature of a society which permits or encourages families and other groups to raise children oriented, in some respects, toward what are regarded as viola-

[29] In his *Brothers in Crime* (Chicago: University of Chicago Press, 1938), Clifford Shaw presents the case of a child whose delinquent career began at the age of three years, when he was pushed through a transom of someone's house so he could open the door to allow his teen-age brothers to burglarize the house.

[30] Clifford Shaw and Henry D. McKay, *Juvenile Delinquency and Urban Areas* (Chicago: University of Chicago Press, 1942).

tions of the laws?[31] The question is not why do *certain* children engage in delinquent behavior, but why does society consider some of the behavior of *all* of its children as delinquent? The sociologist's answers are in terms of the weak attachment of people to what are formally declared to be the values of the society. The conditions under which persons and subgroups in a society fail to internalize the values of the larger society have already been discussed.[32]

c The "Differential Association" Theory

The most important social theory of the causes of delinquency has been that of the so-called "Chicago school"—as enunciated by Burgess, Sutherland, and Shaw, although there are some important differences among these writers.[33] They start with the premise that, in one degree or another, people are partially detached from the values that apply to the society as a whole—some of which values have been inherited from an earlier period when Western society was more integrated, and others of which have recently been formulated as laws but which have not been fully accepted as values. The people who commit crimes have certain meanings and values opposed to those of the larger society of which they are a part. As Sutherland (who calls this explanation the "differential association" theory) puts it: "A person becomes delinquent because of an excess of definitions favorable to violation of law over definitions unfavorable to violations of law."[34] The theory applies—except for its basic premise—only to Western society, and, more specifically, to the United States, although with slight modifications it could be extended to other Western countries.

Delinquency is found in significant amounts among children in all social classes, but in the middle and upper classes the family and the community save all but the more serious offenders from police or court recognition of the delinquents. Since the children are not labeled as delinquents, and are not exposed to an organized tradition of crime, they seldom grow up as professional criminals. But the pattern of violating the law "when you can get away with it," and when the community regards it as not too disreputable to do so continues into adult life. Tax evasion, "black mar-

---

[31] A volume which comprehensively follows this theme is Milton L. Barron, *The Juvenile in Delinquent Society* (New York: Alfred A. Knopf, 1954).

[32] See Section A of this chapter, and Section D of Chapter 2.

[33] The fullest statement of the position summarized in the following paragraphs is to be found in Edwin R. Sutherland, *Principles of Criminology*, fifth edition prepared by Donald R. Cressey (Philadelphia: Lippincott, 1955); and in Daniel Glaser, "The Differential Association Theory of Crime," in Arnold M. Rose (ed.), *Human Behavior and Social Processes* (Boston: Houghton, 1962), pp. 425–42.

[34] *Ibid.*, p. 78. While Sutherland did take into account personality and other characteristics, he considered them to be related to crime only to the extent that, in the dynamics of an individual's development, they are conducive to acquiring an excess of definitions favorable to the violation of law.

ket" violations, illegal use of child labor,[35] violation of other laws regulating the conditions of work, fraudulent claims for legal interests and for
merchandise, smuggling, bribery, traffic-law violations, and even fraud
and embezzlement,[36] are fairly common behaviors in the middle and upper
classes. People who commit these crimes do not think of themselves as
"criminals," even though they are usually aware that their actions are
contrary to law. A survey of 1,698 persons—mostly in the upper-income
category—elicited the fact that 99 per cent of them anonymously admitted
that they had committed crimes for which they had never been apprehended.[37] Practically all of them provided rationalizations for their behavior, but these would have carried no weight in court.

A housewife over sixty, admitting to false testimony, added this
statement: "It made no difference in the outcome, and I did it to spare
someone pain." An artist made this comment on the same question:
"It was a divorce action and I'm a gentleman." A doctor, admitting
to taking a car without permission, penciled in the word "emergency."
A businessman who opened someone else's mail appended this explanation, "Tried to keep my son from making a fool of himself, but he
did it anyway." A girl student justified illegal opening of somebody
else's mail with the explanation, "She (roommate) opened my mail
first." A minister who confessed to making false statements about a
commodity that he sold commented, "I tried truth first but it's not
always successful." Annoying letters were sent by a social worker to
her husband, by a student to his teacher, and by a salesclerk to his
boss . . .

A farmer faced with the issue of whether or not he had been guilty
of assault without provocation wrote "no" in the designated space, but
added the comment, "Thrashed a lot of men in my time but they all
jolly well deserved it." A woman artist decided to call herself guilty of
assault but with the qualifying phrase, "Threw ash tray at an unbear-
able cad.". . .

Persons in the lower-income groups do not have quite as much opportunity to commit these kinds of crimes, and they generally have a different pattern of personal development. One might distinguish two types
of lower-income people—although the differences between them should
not be exaggerated. One grows up in fairly integrated working-class and
rural districts where tendencies toward delinquency are early inhibited by

[35] In 1952 the National Child Labor Committee estimated more than 2,000,000 American
children of school age were employed illegally (*New York Times,* November 27, 1952, p.
33).

[36] Donald R. Cressey, *Other People's Money* (Glencoe, Ill.: Free Press, 1953).

[37] James S. Wallerstein and Clement J. Wyle, "Our Law-Abiding Law-Breakers,"
National Probation (April, 1947), pp. 107–112. The sample was not controlled to be
representative, but the study is nevertheless revealing of the manner in which people
who do not regard themselves as criminal look upon their criminal acts.

family and community and where opportunities for the upper- and middle-class types of crime are scarcely available. This is probably the most law-abiding section of our population, although it should be recognized that it includes just as large a proportion as in any other class who violate the sex laws, who destroy public property, and who generally do not regard law violations as bad. These "respectable" lower-income people are quite like middle- and upper-income class people except that they do not have nearly as many opportunities to violate the law, although their opportunities are now increasing as the income-tax requirements are extended down to their income level and as increasing economic prosperity permits them to buy automobiles and household equipment on which there are laws governing usage.

The other sector of the lower-income class provides the bulk of the current inhabitants of our prisons and reformatories. It is not poverty that leads them there, since most poor people do not get to jail, since the high level of American prosperity has not reduced their crime rate, since—to repeat—their proclivity for delinquency is not greater than among those in the other classes. The etiology of their criminality is an exceptionally sharp cleavage in values and an especially sharp attention to their criminality on the part of the police and the courts. In a different sense from that of the upper-class people mentioned above, they have more "opportunities" to commit crimes of theft, burglary, and robbery than do people in other social categories.[38] In an unusually large proportion of cases their parents were immigrants to large American cities—from foreign countries or from poor southern rural areas. The parents usually have strong sets of values, but often these diverge from the values dominant in the larger American society. The children of the immigrants soon become aware of this divergence, and a large number of them thereby lose respect for their parents, considering them as ignorant, stupid, and "green." With controls from the parents unusually weakened, the pressures of the immediate neighborhood become all the more important in providing guides for the behavior of the youth.[39] The most important of these pressures are gangs of

[38] A theory of "opportunity" as a source of delinquency and crime, as a variation of the differential association theory, has been advanced by Richard A. Cloward and Lloyd E. Ohlin: *Delinquency and Opportunity: A Theory of Delinquent Gangs* (Glencoe, Ill.: Free Press, 1960).

[39] The diversity of values to which a child in such circumstances is exposed is a manifestation of the "conflict of cultures" that we considered in connection with social change. (See Chapter 11, Section C.) Sutherland clearly relies on a "conflict of cultures" interpretation of crime. He states that the reason a person fails "to follow a prescribed pattern of behavior is due to the inconsistency and lack of harmony in the influences that direct the individual . . ., the conflict of cultures is therefore the fundamental principle in the explanation of crime." (E. H. Sutherland, *Principles of Criminology* [Philadelphia: Lippincott, 1934], pp. 51–52.) For a careful evaluation of this point of view, see Thorsten Sellin, *Culture Conflict and Crime* (New York: Social Science Research Council, 1938).

youngsters who have a tradition of delinquency passed along in them from older youths to younger children, generation after generation.[40] This is true regardless of what ethnic group happens to occupy the immigrant neighborhoods. In the past generations, the Germans, Swedes, and Irish used to furnish the largest proportion of delinquencies known to the police; then came the Italians and Poles; and now it is the Negro and Mexican groups, with a significant sprinkling of native white children whose parents have immigrated from isolated southern areas.

Most of the boys, and some of the girls, go into these delinquent groups. Those boys who do not go into the delinquent gangs become social isolates and furnish a significant proportion of the schizophrenics sent to mental hospitals.[41] In the delinquent gangs, members learn the techniques and traditions of such crimes as larceny, robbery, and burglary, and—as they grow older—of the "rackets" and gambling. The police and the courts are very familiar with these gangs, and often their efforts to reform or punish the delinquents have the effect of encouraging the criminal pattern of development. The provision of recreational facilities often simply provides the delinquent gang with a place to meet regularly; and incarceration provokes resentment against the law, a conception of oneself as a criminal, and contact with more experienced criminals. The programs of most detention institutions include little by way of positive rehabilitation, despite many verbal statements of good intentions.[42] Thus, a good number of these youngsters graduate into an adult career of crime. According to various studies, from 65 to 85 per cent of the youngsters committed to state training schools are caught in law violations after their discharge.[43]

d   Modification of "Differential Association": The Delinquent Subculture Theory

Significant empirical verifications of Sutherland's theory of differential association have been presented by Cressey, Short, and Wheeler.[44] But these

[40] For a general consideration of the "peer group" as transmitter of culture and specific patterns of behavior, see Chapter 6, Section E.

[41] H. Warren Dunham, "The Interrelationship of Criminal Behavior and Schizophrenic Psychosis," unpublished Ph.D. thesis, University of Chicago, 1941.

[42] Tappan, in Merrill, *op. cit.*, pp. 235–76, especially p. 239.

[43] *Ibid.*

[44] Donald R. Cressey, "Application and Verification of the Differential Association Theory," *Journal of Criminal Law and Criminology,* 43 (May–June, 1952), pp. 43–52; Donald R. Cressey, "Role Theory, Differential Association and Compulsive Crimes," in Rose (ed.), *Human Behavior and Social Processes, op. cit.,* pp. 443–67; James F. Short, Jr., "Differential Association with Delinquent Friends and Delinquent Behavior," *Pacific Sociological Review,* 1 (Spring, 1958), pp. 20–25; James F. Short, Jr., "Differential Association as a Hypothesis: Problems of Empirical Testing," *Social Problems,* 7 (Summer, 1960), pp. 14–25; Stanton H. Wheeler, "Social Organization in a Correctional Community," unpublished Ph.D. thesis, University of Washington, Seattle, 1958.

1 White-collar criminality is real criminality, being in all cases in violation of the criminal law.

2 White-collar criminality differs from lower class criminality principally in an implementation of the criminal law which segregates white-collar criminals administratively from other criminals.

3 The theories of the criminologists that crime is due to poverty or to psychopathic and sociopathic conditions statistically associated with poverty are invalid because, first, they are derived from samples which are grossly biased with respect to socioeconomic status; second, they do not apply to the white-collar criminals; and third, they do not even explain the criminality of the lower class, since the factors are not related to a general process characteristic of all criminality.

4 A theory of criminal behavior which will explain both white-collar criminality and lower-class criminality is needed.

Edwin H. Sutherland, "White-Collar Criminality," *American Sociological Review*, 4 (February, 1940), p. 12.

tests have revealed some of the weaknesses of the theory. To correct these, Daniel Glaser has broadened Sutherland's theory somewhat and has relabeled it "differential identification."[45] He states the basic principle: "A person pursues criminal behavior to the extent that he identifies himself with real or imaginary persons from whose perspective his criminal behavior seems acceptable."

A more drastic revision, which attempts to reconcile differential association theory with personality theories of the source of delinquency and crime, have come from those who analyze what they call "the delinquent subculture."[46] Albert Cohen explained the delinquent subculture as

a system of beliefs and values generated in a process of communicative interaction among children similarly circumstanced by virtue of their positions in the social structure, and as constituting a solution to problems of adjustment to which the established culture provided no satisfactory solutions. These problems are largely problems of status and self-respect arising among working-class children as a result of socially structured inability to meet the standards of the established culture. The delinquent subculture, with its characteristics of nonutilitarianism, malice, and negativism, provides an alternative status

[45] "Criminality Theories and Behavioral Images," *American Journal of Sociology*, 61 (March, 1956), pp. 433–44. Glaser has provided perspective to his reformulation in his "The Differential-Association Theory of Crime," in Rose (ed.), *Human Behavior and Social Processes, op. cit.*

[46] This concept was first systematically set forth by Albert K. Cohen in his *Delinquent Boys: The Culture of the Gang* (Glencoe, Ill.: Free Press, 1955). A more advanced statement by the same author is Albert K. Cohen and James F. Short, Jr., "Research in Delinquent Subcultures," *Journal of Social Issues*, 14, 3 (1958), pp. 20–37.

system and justifies, for those who participate in it, hostility and aggression against the sources of their status frustration.[47]

This does not mean that the delinquents do not learn the values and beliefs of the larger society, which is against criminal behavior, but that they have also learned to neutralize these values and beliefs. Further, there is not merely one delinquent subculture, but several, which Cohen and Short characterize as follows:

1 The parent male subculture, which is held by a large section of the working-class in the United States. It has been described as non-utilitarian, malicious, negativistic, versatile, and characterized by short run hedonism and group autonomy.

2 The conflict-oriented subculture. It is a culture of large groups, which are openly at war with the larger society and with other gangs. The gang has a territory, or "turf," to defend or extend, and a reputation, or "rep," to maintain. Although fighting occupies but a small portion of the gang's time, "heart" or courage in fighting is the highest value and the most important determinant of the position of gang members within the gang as well as that of the gang among other gangs. While the gang does not hesitate to use brutality, there is a code of fairness in its actions. Most of the time of the members is spent in drinking, sex, gambling, stealing, and vandalism.

3 The drug addict subculture. The addict avoids the more violent forms of delinquency and prefers income-producing forms of delinquency, which are essential to the support of the expensive drug habit. The addicts are also members of gangs, either as marginal figures of gangs of the first variety, or as members of all-addict groups which pretend aesthetic amenities of clothes and music.

4 Semi-professional thief subculture. The members of these groups also engage in utilitarian, systematic, and pecuniary crime, and begin to learn it at a very early age. But they are not drug addicts, and do not engage much in irrational violence.

5 Middle-class delinquent subculture. Boys of middle-class family backgrounds who are in delinquent gangs emphasize deliberate courting of danger (avoidance of being "chicken") and a pseudo-sophisticated, irresponsible, "playboy" approach supposed to emulate adult roles—centering around sex, liquor and automobiles. They avoid the malice, bellicosity, and violence of lower-class subcultures.

6 The female delinquent subculture. While a few girls are to be found in the dominantly male subcultures already described, most delinquent girls follow another pattern: When unattractive or unskilled girls, especially in the lower class, despair of respectable

[47] Cohen and Short, *op. cit.*, p. 20.

marriage and social mobility, they abandon their reputation for chastity and thereby gain male attention and male favors, albeit within unstable relationships which further lower their value on the marriage market. These girls also form gangs to sustain each other in their sexual activity, and they range in emphasis from pseudo-sophistication to hoodlum orientations. Many become engaged in prostitution and drug addiction.

Implied in the two general theories of the causes of delinquency are two different approaches to the reduction of delinquency. Those who hold to the personality development theory would prevent the problem by creating more wholesome family situations for children to grow up in—through educating parents to be more affectionate and permissive toward their children, through discouraging family breakups, and through shifting children into good foster homes when the natural families are incurably unwholesome. They would treat children who have already developed into delinquents with some form of psychotherapy, much as neurotics and psychotics are treated. Those who hold to the "differential association" or other sociological theory of the causation of delinquency would seek to reduce the problem by changing the culture of the neighborhoods or gangs from which the delinquents derive their values and "definitions" or by shifting these children to different cultures. Trained youth workers have gone into areas of high delinquency to reorganize the gangs, or even the whole community, to engage in more law-abiding activities. Or they seek to restructure the delinquent's values while he is in detention so that he moves into a new world of occupation or education when he is released rather than into his old world of delinquent gangs. These various techniques of "treating" delinquents have had a certain degree of success, but none of them has been applied with the comprehensiveness to make a sizeable dent in the problem—especially since delinquency in recent years is increasingly becoming manifest in all social classes rather than mainly in lower-income classes.[48]

In sum, there is evidence that both personality and social environmental influences contribute to delinquency. But none of the existing studies can be regarded as conclusive or final.

c *Housing as a Social Problem*

1 VALUES REGARDING HOUSING

Different persons would perceive the housing problem in the United States in somewhat different ways. For most it probably means an in-

[48] For a brief survey of various techniques used to reduce delinquency, and studies of their effectiveness, see U.S. Children's Bureau, *The Effectiveness of Delinquency Prevention Programs* (Washington, D.C.: Government Printing Office, 1954).

sufficient number of dwellings, with consequent overcrowding and use of overaged structures or a price for housing in excess of the purchasing power of a large number of consumers. For others it means "substandard" housing in such quantity and concentration as to constitute a "slum." For still others it means the construction of housing that does not meet certain standards of comfort, convenience, or beauty. People are affected by a housing problem directly, when their housing wants are inadequately satisfied, or indirectly, when they face the undesirable social consequences flowing out of the poor housing from which other sections of the population suffer.

In one very fundamental sense the housing problem is an economic one, that is, a function of some inadequacy in the distribution of income or of the supplies, labor, and land necessary to build satisfactory housing. In a closely related sense, the housing problem is also a political one, since the availability of satisfactory housing is also a function of zoning and planning by government bodies, of taxes that affect construction and real estate, of interest rates and other credit policies, of public housing policies, of the cost and availability of governmental services (such as provision of water, sewage and garbage disposal, fire protection, etc.), of regulations on quality, rent, and even total cost, and of the general government framework in which economic variables affect housing function. The housing problem is to be analyzed as a sociological problem in terms of the size and concentration of the population seeking housing, desires for spatial proximity and segregation in various respects, customs concerning what constitutes a residential family or unit and what is to be considered as adequate or good housing, the reactions of people to their failure to achieve their aspirations for adequate housing, the consequences for behavior of various kinds of housing arrangements and facilities.

Average housing conditions are probably better now than they have ever been before in history, although parts of the United States have housing conditions poorer than the average of most countries at many other times in history. But this does not mean that poor housing is considered to be less of a problem in Western civilization today than in other cultures at other times.

Men have lived in caves, in crude temporary camps, in crowded and unsanitary towns and cities, and some of them at least have survived to tell the tale. In part, housing under these circumstances did not loom large as a social problem because its adverse effects upon other phases of life, such as health, order, safety, and welfare, were not clearly perceived. In part, too, the objective conditions which we would now regard as poor housing did not come to be considered as problems because not very much was actually demanded or expected in the way of housing. The absence of the necessary material resources, the technology, and the knowledge of how to improve the situation, together with the absence of high standards or norms, tended to make housing a matter of indifference.

In the modern world, however, where men have access to the technical information and where, in consequence of democratic ideas, education, advertising, and propaganda, situations which would otherwise not be regarded as problems become problems, housing is likely to be prominent in any inventory of community issues. Cultural and political doctrines have imbued men with conceptions as to their rights, social responsibilities, and expectations, so that the claims for decent housing on the part of individuals and the corresponding obligations of the community become vocal. Thus we have come to assume that certain minimum standards of housing are necessary and desirable objectives to be striven for, and have come to look upon the failure to reach these standards as social problems.[49]

People have differing values as to what constitutes good housing, but they also have certain common values that can be attained only in housing of certain minimum standards. A good number of the purely personal values of people in Western culture are sought in the home, although there is some variation in this respect. Sociability, for example, is largely a home matter for most people in the United States and Britain, whereas the Frenchman is more likely to seek sociability in such institutions as the café. Among the other important values that most Western people seek in their homes are shelter, warmth during cold weather (and, for some, shade during hot weather), privacy, food preparation and consumption, family life, all of the activities associated with the toilet and the laundry.

Convenient and comfortable houses also achieve other values: easy access to place of work (either by walking or public transportation); closeness to everyday shopping facilities, schools, and churches; good transportation to central shopping, recreational, cultural, and meeting places; congenial neighbors (although this is not considered so important in a city where one is likely to choose his friends from different neighborhoods); attractiveness and suitability of the house and the surrounding neighborhood; improvement or maintenance of family prestige; achievement of these values at relatively low cost. Certain physical features of the residential structure may make it desirable or undesirable, and this is partly a function of the nature of the structure. For example, relatively sound-proof walls will usually be considered desirable in multiple-dwelling structures, several toilets are more necessary where the dwelling unit covers two or three floors than where it is all on one floor.

Individuals vary, of course, in what they believe to be important in

[49] Louis Wirth, *Contemporary Social Problems* (Chicago: University of Chicago Press, 1939), pp. 25–26. Copyright 1939 by Louis Wirth.

a home. Some would sacrifice many other things to get a fireplace, a workroom, garden space, closeness to certain friends or relatives, a movie theater, or one of a hundred other things. In an earlier chapter we considered the forces that bring people to certain regions or localities.[50] In these different regions and localities different values may be uppermost in the selection of adequate housing. This may be a function of climate; in warm climates, for example, it is not important to have a central heating system but it is important to have windows arranged to permit good cross-ventilation. The economic cost of space may make a difference in what one looks for in a desirable home. In New York City, for example, one does not seek a garden with his residence, but in certain other cities—not to speak of rural areas—this is considered almost a necessity. Then there are important cultural differences, which are a function not only of national origin, but also of regional and class background. In some groups, a large kitchen is considered desirable, since much of the family living takes place in the kitchen. But there are housewives in our society who greatly prefer a tiny kitchen so they can move quickly from stove to sink to refrigerator, and the kitchen is used for little else but cooking.

The standards listed in the preceding paragraphs are not all that people have in mind when they make choices concerning housing, but they are probably the most important ones and they illustrate the nature of the relevant values. Housing problems may be defined as significant deviations from these standards that affect significant proportions of the population. There are no systematic data that measure all housing problems, although most architects and city planners can provide farily complete descriptions of the housing problems in their areas. The untrained observer, if he looks about an area systematically, can also get a fairly good idea of its housing problems. A student, knowing generally the values of a local culture, can see, simply by walking around a neighborhood without even entering people's houses, such problems as insufficient open space, poor garbage-disposal facilities, crumbling and ugly houses, such discomforts and dangers to health as open walls, outside toilets, public bathhouses, uncared-for streets and yards. He can even get a rough idea if there is overcrowding by noting the number and age distribution of people who come in and out of houses during various hours of the day and relating this to the size of the houses. But more systematic observation and measurement are necessary to get more information about housing problems.

2   BAD HOUSING

For the United States as a whole, the most complete information at the present time comes from the census of housing (1960) conducted by the United States Bureau of the Census. Some of the salient summary facts

[50] See Chapter 12, Section B.

from that source are shown in Table 23. If residences built before 1930 be considered as "old," 46.5 per cent of all dwelling units in the United States could be considered as old in 1960. It is always somewhat arbitrary to fix standards of suitability. A criterion of sufficient amount of dwelling space often used is .75 persons per room (not including bath)—which is 1½ rooms per person. By this criterion over 42 per cent of renter-occupied, and about 30 per cent of owner-occupied, American dwelling units did not have sufficient dwelling space. The *quality* of dwelling units was judged by the census takers. They judged a unit to be dilapidated "when it had serious deficiencies, was run down or neglected, or was of inadequate original construction so that it did not provide adequate shelter or protection against the elements or endangered the safety of the occupants."[51] According to this criterion 5.0 per cent of all units were dilapidated in 1960 and another 13.8 per cent were judged to be deteriorating. Of those not reported dilapidated, 12.8 per cent had no hot water, 11.7 per cent lacked other plumbing facilities, and 7.1 per cent had no running water. In addition, it is to be noted that 13.2 per cent of all dwelling units did not have private flush toilets, and 21.6 per cent did not have telephones. Housing conditions have been improving under the long prosperity starting just before World War II, but it is obvious from these figures that a significantly large proportion of the American people are still living in inadequate housing.

Most of the above facts about housing problems in the United States refer to those features which are a function of poor construction, age, or inadequate care. There are many kinds of housing problems, not covered by the available statistics, which are functions of changing cultural standards of beauty and comfort. The importance of the latter is not to be denied, but it is more difficult to measure them and to analyze causes and prescribe cures for them. Thus when we now come to a consideration of how housing problems developed, we shall again emphasize the more easily observable problems.

In its causation, the housing problem is essentially an economic problem. If there were unlimited wealth, people could build the kind of houses they needed and wanted, and the only problem would be over who would get the most desirable locations. If tastes changed, people would demolish their old houses and build new ones. But the economic causes of the housing problem are more complicated than the mere insufficiency of wealth. Housing is a fairly expensive investment. Most of those who buy houses have to obtain a loan and pay interest on that loan. In doing so they have to meet the restrictions of their creditors, and the money they pay in interest cannot be diverted to improvement of the house. Most

[51] U.S. Bureau of the Census, *Census of Housing: 1960.* Vol. I, *General Characteristics, Part I, U.S. Summary* (Washington, D.C.: Government Printing Office, 1963), p. xviii.

TABLE 23 · HOUSING CONDITIONS IN THE UNITED STATES, 1960

	U.S. total	Urban	Rural non-farm	Farm
A Age of Dwelling Units				
YEAR BUILT				
1959–March 1960	3.8	3.7	5.2	1.4
1955–58	10.7	10.5	12.8	4.4
1950–54	13.0	13.5	13.0	7.6
1940–49	14.8	14.4	16.7	11.7
1930–39	11.2	10.9	11.8	11.2
1929 or earlier	46.5	47.0	40.5	63.6
TOTAL	100.0	100.0	100.0	100.0
B Persons Per Room				
OWNER OCCUPIED				
0.50 or less	46.7	46.7	44.6	52.1
0.51–0.75	23.5	24.3	22.0	21.2
0.76–1.00	21.2	21.6	21.4	16.8
1.01–1.50	6.6	6.0	8.4	7.1
1.51 or more	2.0	1.4	3.6	2.8
RENTER OCCUPIED				
0.50 or less	34.1	35.4	29.5	29.2
0.51–0.75	23.6	24.1	21.2	21.5
0.76–1.00	26.2	26.5	26.0	22.4
1.01–1.50	10.0	9.1	13.5	13.6
1.51 or more	6.1	4.9	9.8	13.3
C General Condition and Plumbing Facilities				
SOUND	81.1	85.4	71.9	69.7
With all plumbing facilities	74.0	81.4	58.2	50.9
Lacking only hot water	0.8	0.6	1.5	1.2
Lacking other plumbing facilities	6.3	3.4	12.2	17.6
DETERIORATING	13.8	11.2	19.2	22.6
With all plumbing facilities	7.8	8.1	7.2	7.2
Lacking only hot water	0.6	0.5	0.7	0.5
Lacking other plumbing facilities	5.4	2.6	11.3	14.9
DILAPIDATED	5.0	3.4	8.9	7.7
TOTAL	100.0	100.0	100.0	100.0

TABLE 23 • (continued)

	U.S. total	Urban	Rural non-farm	Farm
D *Water Supply*				
Hot and cold piped water				
inside structure	87.2	94.9	70.3	65.3
Only cold piped water inside	5.7	4.0	9.7	9.5
Piped water outside	1.0	0.5	2.2	2.2
No piped water	6.1	0.6	17.8	23.0
TOTAL	100.0	100.0	100.0	100.0
E *Toilet Facilities*				
Flush toilet, exclusive use	86.8	94.2	71.4	62.0
Flush toilet, shared	2.7	3.9	1.0	0.4
Other toilet facilities or none	10.5	1.9	27.6	37.6
TOTAL	100.0	100.0	100.0	100.0
F *Telephone Available*				
Yes	78.4	83.1	67.1	64.2
No	21.6	16.9	32.9	35.8
TOTAL	100.0	100.0	100.0	100.0

Source: U.S. Bureau of the Census, *1960 Census of Housing,* Vol. I, Part I, *U.S. Summary* (Washington, D.C., 1964), Tables 9, 11, 12, 13. Figures are rounded to the nearest tenth.

homeowners do not participate in the original planning of their houses; they bought (or inherited) a completed house that had already been lived in, and such a house always had "something wrong with it."

Those who rent houses or apartments are even less likely to get what they want. Since any improvement a renter makes in the house does not belong to him (and may even result in raising the rent), he has little incentive to make any but the most inexpensive, short-term improvements. Further, the landlord's interest is not the same as the renter's interest. When an improvement is to be made, the landlord has to consider not only the desires of the present renter and the rent now paid, but he must also consider the future value of the dwelling unit and the general popularity of the improvement for potential future renters. If an area is going down in value, the landlord is usually bound to lose money if he makes any but the most trivial of improvements for his present tenants because he is not likely to be able to maintain the rate of rent for long. If an area is going up in value, the landlord is also likely to lose money if he makes any major improvements for his present tenants, as the latter soon may not be able to pay in rent what the dwelling unit is worth, and then the landlord would like to attract a "better class" tenant who can afford to pay the new standard rate of rent. Even if the area or property is not moving either down or up, the landlord has to consider the permanency of the present tenant before he can afford to make expensive improvements in the unit. A new tenant may want things to look different, and he will certainly be attracted if new and fresh repairs are made for his occupancy.

3   THE SLUM

A concentration of very bad housing in an area constitutes a *slum*. Sometimes whole towns are slums—especially those towns built for workers in a single heavy industry. Slums are found in poorer agricultural districts. But most slums are in large cities, and there they are concentrated at the edge of the central business district[52] and in factory areas. Sometimes slums were built as such—to provide dwelling units for the largest number of workers in the smallest amount of space at the cheapest cost. This was quite common in past generations, but is not often done today because there has been a change in policy by both employers and the government. The Scandinavian countries, the Low Countries, Great Britain and several British dominions, the United States, Germany and, to a lesser extent, the other European countries have been experiencing a strong trend toward building attractive and healthful, if modest, living areas for industrial workers.

Another important kind of slum arises out of deterioration and poor upkeep of what was once a desirable residential neighborhood. Quite often a slum will exist in what was a few decades earlier a wealthy single-family home district. Such a district ceased to be popular for some reason, perhaps because it was invaded by business, and the homes were bought up by real-estate speculators. Since few middle-income or lower-income families wanted so much space and since few could afford the upkeep on such large houses, the owners "converted" each of the houses into a number of small "apartments." Since the homes were not planned for such use in the first place and since not too much investment was put into their conversion, the resulting units were often inadequate: common toilets, inadequate kitchen equipment stretched out along the wall of a living room, very large rooms broken up into smaller ones by cheap partitions were among the characteristics of these converted apartments. The houses are not kept in repair as the tenants were often in no position to enforce their requests and repairs would be relatively expensive in these large,

[52] For an explanation of why slums are generally to be found at the edges of central business districts, see the discussion of the concentric-zone theory of urban growth in Chapter 13, Section D.

aging houses. Some of the tenants were especially careless, and the depredations they committed remained for succeeding tenants to cope with. The lack of care is characteristic of the grounds as well as the buildings, and turns an attractive neighborhood into an ugly one as well as bringing in dirt, rats, and other vermin.

The physical deterioration of an area is often accompanied by social deterioration, although this is not true when impoverished members of a single ethnic group occupy most of a slum area and make an integrated community out of it. Perhaps most of the poor people coming to a slum area to live want to get out as soon as they can afford it; they feel no responsibility for the condition of their homes or the neighborhood. Some are people of low intelligence, low morality, or low standards, and their presence discourages the more capable and more responsible citizens from taking action for the social or physical improvement of the neighborhood. The lack of community responsibility and organization makes it easy for local government to neglect the area in providing services and improvements. For reasons only partly connected with the poor housing, slum areas are also areas of concentration of other social problems: dependency and unemployment, disease, alcoholism, truancy, delinquency, crime, schizophrenia and the organic mental disorders, family disorganization, illiteracy, illegitimacy, suicide, mental deficiency.[53] Inadequate housing may be a direct cause of some of these things, such as disease and family disorganization. Studies of slum populations transplanted to low-cost housing projects show that they have relatively low rates of tuberculosis, infant mortality, adult criminal offenses, juvenile delinquency, fires, home accidents, and communicable childhood diseases.[54]

But the transplanted families are only a selection of all persons living in slum areas and do not include single persons, transients, very large families, families unwilling to move into projects, or many persons without steady employment. Public housing projects get the slum families with the lowest social problem rates, and the question remains as to whether these particular families are "improved" by their movement into the projects. A controlled study by F. Stuart Chapin[55] shows that some rehoused families gained in social participation and social status, but not in "mo-

[53] For a summary of the studies showing these relationships, see Jay Rumney and Sara Shuman, *Cost of Slums* (Newark, N.J.: Housing Authority of the City of Newark, 1946), Part III. See also Ernest R. Mowrer, *Disorganization: Personal and Social* (Philadelphia: Lippincott, 1942).

[54] John P. Dean, "The Myths of Housing Reform," *American Sociological Review*, 14 (April, 1949), p. 284. The studies cited were made in Gary, Newark, Philadelphia, and Pittsburgh.

[55] "An Experiment on the Social Effects of Good Housing," *American Sociological Review*, 5 (December, 1940), pp. 868–79.

rale." Another careful study by Naomi Barer[56] shows that some rehoused families had a lower delinquency rate and a reduction in tuberculosis after entrance into a project than they had previously. These studies seem to indicate that improvement in housing reduces manifestations of social problems, although many people feel that the slums move along with their former inhabitants into the new housing projects.

4   THE CAUSES OF THE SHORTAGE OF ADEQUATE HOUSING

A consideration of the causes of the housing shortage requires several levels of analysis, not all of which are primarily of concern to the sociologists. On the technological level, the fact of primary importance is that very few persons in our society are capable of building their own houses, and that construction usually requires the employment of many persons with diverse skills. In most Western countries there is no shortage of the chief materials used in housing construction, except in wartime. On the other hand, some of these construction materials are fairly expensive, and there are various barriers against the use of cheaper but adequate substitute materials such as plywood. Local political authorities, following dominant opinions, often refuse to license the construction of houses that are to have exterior finishes or a style of construction that is different from the already-built homes in the area. Sometimes contractors or unions in the construction industry refuse to work with less expensive materials or with changes in design that require less labor. It is an industry that is highly resistant to modern machine methods, and there is a strong tradition in favor of low capital investments. Thus there is technological conservatism in the building industry that raises the cost of construction and changes the desirability of the finished product from the standpoint of the consumer.

The construction industry is made up of a huge number of uncoordinated entrepreneurs and yet it has aspects of a monopoly. Each entrepreneur is a specialist in a skilled trade—foundation, digging, carpentry, bricklaying, plumbing, electrical work, etc.—except for the contractor who serves as coordinator and intermediary between these specialized entrepreneurs and the consumer. The "consumer" may be the one who plans to live in the house or to act as landlord in renting the units, or he may represent a housing development organization (either specially organized for this business or having funds for investments arising out of some other business). The "consumer" has to hire a contractor, unless he already has a contractor working for him as part of his business operation. He may or may not also hire an architect, who is a professional designer

---

[56] "Delinquency Before, After Admission to New Haven Housing Development," *Journal of Housing* (December, 1945–January, 1946), p. 27; "A Note on Tuberculosis Among Residents of a Housing Project," *Public Housing* (August, 1945), p. 133.

of buildings and who directs the contractor. Most contractors have "contracts" with at least one of each of the specialized entrepreneurs who hire the workers, skilled and unskilled, who do the work. There are many middlemen and wholesalers, and they have paid little attention to standardization of materials. The coordination of these many independent operators is a difficult and time-consuming task, and if there is an especially heavy demand for any one of them, the whole operation may be held up. Not infrequently there are jurisdictional disputes about which craft is to do a certain task, and this may also hold up construction.

Since the work of any single specialized entrepreneur is essential to the total job but involves only a small part of the total expense, and since the specialized entrepreneurs seldom come into direct contact with the consumers, it is relatively easy for the specialized entrepreneurs to set high prices for their services and rigid conditions for their work. In many communities plumbers will insist, for example, on using pipes of a certain thickness, even when this precludes the use of thin walls since the pipes must fit into these walls. If the bricklayers have a rule about using a certain ratio of unskilled to skilled workers, they will often not deviate from it even though an architect's innovation reduces the relative need for one or the other category. The purpose of these rules is to stabilize and protect the demand for the services of the specialized entrepreneurs in a labor market which is highly subject to the vicissitudes of seasonal and cyclical variations in demand. To this end also the unions of skilled workers set heavy restrictions on entrance to the trades. A very large proportion of construction workers are elderly, and there has not been much stimulus for them to learn new and more efficient techniques of work. The whole organization of the building industry prevents taking advantage of the economics of mass production and standardization that characterize other modern industries. The effect of all these factors on housing is unnecessarily high cost and inflexibility of design.

In pursuing our analysis of the causes of the housing problem let us now turn to some long-run causes. The United States especially, among Western countries, has had a mobile and rapidly growing population. The urbanization due to rapid industrialization has been the main force in redistributing people. Rural areas have been declining in population, while urban areas have been growing at greatly different rates. Thus there has been a heavier demand for housing than would be true if the population were not stable. The speed with which some of the housing, especially that for workers, was constructed in the late decades of the nineteenth century and the early decades of the twentieth century did not result in a high-quality product. Since then there has been a rise in living standards, not to speak of changes in housing fashions, which made what was originally low-quality housing seem even less desirable. The situation became especially acute during the 1940's when the population increased at an accelerated pace, when war production created considerable mobility and raised average incomes, and when the country had passed through a decade of economic stagnation during which there had been very little construction.

Such cultural factors as the demand for individual units, the organization of city land into square blocks, the possibilities for speculation in land and houses, the determination of the nature of the house by the contractor and consumer without a view to the interests of the whole community, the slow assumption of controls over patterns and quality of construction by government, conservatism in tastes regarding housing styles and construction materials have all led to a pattern of housing construction which is far from being efficient, adequate or esthetic. The most important of these factors in the United States has been the *laissez-faire* relation of government toward housing. This country has lagged behind most European countries in setting minimium housing standards (although it has probably now caught up in this regard) and in helping to support housing construction. With some minor exceptions, mostly during World War I, government aid to housing did not get under way until the 1930's and then it affected only a small proportion of dwelling units as compared to what occurred in Scandinavia and England. The United States adopted two major programs of governmental aid. One was a guarantee of capital loans for private construction, which facilitated borrowing and investment (in the case of loans to war veterans it also reduced the interest rate). The second was an outright subsidy to local communities for the purpose of building housing projects with low rents for low-income families. There were also programs which combined both of these principles—for example, where the government provided a partial subsidy, but private groups retained ownership. The latter is used in constructing certain types of housing for the elderly, where the owner is a non-profit organization, such as a church or fraternal association. During World War II the government also built some projects to house middle-class war workers, and later sold these projects to private corporations. The program of guaranteeing loans (by the government's Federal Housing Administration) has been widely accepted, even though its administration has been attended by some corruption, because it does not change established practices of builders or banks.[57] It has been responsible, however, for making it more difficult for minority groups to get adequate housing, since it practically refused to guarantee loans to minority persons until about 1950.[58] After then, the federal

---

[57] A few experts have criticized government guarantees, since they protect the lenders rather than the owners, and since they permit owners to saddle themselves with heavy obligations out of proportion to their incomes.

[58] The rationale of the Federal Housing Administration was that minority areas were

government continued to lend money to builders who deliberately refused to sell or rent any of their units to Negroes, which included the great majority of builders. In late 1962 President Kennedy signed an Executive Order which would restrict the lending of money with government guarantees if the housing affected was not available for lease or purchase by minority groups. Political considerations limited the coverage of this Order to only about a third of the 90 per cent of all housing units covered by such loans.

The program of subsidizing low-cost housing, on the other hand, has met much opposition from large parts of the construction industry, the banks, the real-estate profession, and large taxpayers. Neighborhood opposition to specific projects also developed in some local communities, largely on the ground that some of the projects mixed races and classes. The program became much smaller after World War II because of the persistent opposition, although it probably would be revived if there should be another major economic depression. A large share of the subsidized housing for low-income persons since 1955 has been restricted to rental units for those past the age of 65 years. Most Americans are not sufficiently impressed by the need of government support to provide housing for low-income persons, even though it can be shown that the lowest current rentals for private housing constitute more than the standard 20 per cent of incomes[59] for a significant portion of the American people, unless this is presented to them as a device to stop a depression.

Probably most Americans today consider the insufficiency and inadequacy of housing to be due to temporary factors such as the dislocations caused by World War II and the increased marriage and birth rate which followed it. Actually the problem is a chronic one and is not yet on the way to being solved, although some of the extreme hardships of the postwar years are being eliminated. The main reason is the archaic organization of the industry, which we have already considered. Second, residential construction is not generally a good investment except for those building for their own personal use: the ownership of real property involves responsibilities that are not found in other forms of investment; the owner is beset by high real-estate taxes, petty government restrictions, and changing tastes and patterns of land use; the return on capital comes slowly since a building is expected to last a long time. Third, the majority of the American people have not accepted government aid and cooperative ownership, which have served to solve the housing problem in certain other Western countries. There are numerous other lesser

---

too run down to justify loans and that other areas would be hurt if minority persons moved into them. See Charles Abrams, *Forbidden Neighbors* (New York: Harper, 1955).

[59] Twenty per cent of income devoted to housing has become a standard, though arbitrary, maximum accepted by specialists on housing and consumers' budgets.

reasons why the housing problem is not on the road to solution; among them are the lack of influence of city-planning agencies, the absence of control of land speculation and the difficulty in assembling land parcels for large-scale construction, the over-dependence of local government on real-estate taxes. As an easily observable social problem, the housing problem has been with us for a long time and will continue to be with us much longer.

D   *Poverty as a Social Problem*

1   THE ANATOMY OF POVERTY THROUGHOUT THE WORLD
For two-thirds of the world—the underdeveloped nations—there is a great poverty because population growth is moving ahead of economic growth, and the political and social structures either are unable to cope with the problem sufficiently or they contribute to it directly by stimulating the birth rate or by diverting the economic resources. Of course, the problem and prospects are not the same for all the nations of Asia, Africa and South America. Japan is a nation that has already become industrialized and is solving its population problem. Some of the other politically stable countries of Africa and Asia—Malaysia, Nigeria, Turkey and Israel, for example—seem to be moving along the same lines. The great nation of India is struggling desperately to follow suit, but its population and poverty have such huge dimensions that the prospects do not seem good. The chances for the Latin American countries to overcome these problems will apparently depend on whether they have stable governments with rational policies (Uruguay and Mexico have had the greatest success in this regard) and whether the Roman Catholic Church can develop a policy which permits a fall in the birth rate.

Poverty for the masses of the people in all these countries is grinding and terrifying. It is generally worse than before they came into contact with the scientific and technological "advances" of the West, for disease regularly took its toll—especially of infants—and there were not so many mouths to feed. Furthermore, the early stages of industrialization, which uproots country people and sends them to the city, often makes the poverty seem worse than it was before, because it concentrates the poor people together and makes them more aware of their social problem. Practically all of these countries have a hereditary upper class who have always taken the economic "surplus" for their own luxuries, and when they continue to do so in the face of increasing poverty, the contrast is all the more shocking. The situation is naturally conducive to political revolution, which is now being encouraged by the international Communist movement. Some nations are struggling to gain political reform before the Communists are able to seize control. In some cases—Egypt and Indonesia, for example—the political reform takes the form of putting into power extremely nationalistic and imperialistic leaders who exploit their peoples' woes with demagoguery and depredations against equally poor neighbors. In other nations—Tanganyika and Venezuela, for example—reformist leaders seem to be more bent on solving their economic and social problems than on fooling their people or compounding the problem with imperialist ventures. In still other nations—Haiti and Iraq, for example—the reform takes on the character of reaction in which the established upper class seeks to maintain its privileges through more repressive control of its impoverished masses. Finally, there are the nations —Cuba and British Guiana, for example—in which the reform leaders join the international Communist movement and use even more repressive measures to bring their countries into modern industrialism. Thus, political upheavals of various sorts follow in the train of the great problems of poverty and population explosion.

Political reforms in these countries often include two special kinds of developments which are efforts to solve other long-standing problems— the removal of colonialism and the redistribution of agricultural land. The period of great industrialization and population growth in Europe in the nineteenth century saw a search for new markets and sources of raw materials in the backward countries of Africa and Asia. As recently as 1940, most of the land area of the world was under the political control of Great Britain, France, Belgium, the Netherlands, and even the less economically developed European nations of Spain and Portugal. The years since World War II have witnessed the removal of the political tutelage of these European nations from most of Africa and Asia, the major exception being the retention of Angola by Portugal. In some cases, bloody revolt and destruction of property attended the removal of colonialism, as in the case of the Belgian Congo and Algeria. This kind of revolution compounded the problem of poverty. Even where the removal of the imperial power was peaceful, as in most of Negro Africa formerly under the control of Britain and France, the new native leaders were insufficiently trained for political and economic leadership to run their countries efficiently. This tended to retard economic growth and compound the problem of poverty, although hopefully this lack of skill and experience will shortly be overcome.

Often the colonial powers, and even more frequently the native aristocracies, held the greatest source of wealth—the agricultural land—in a few hands. Reform movements in these underdeveloped countries usually made a major effort to redistribute the land into the hands of the peasants. If done carefully—as in the case of Mexico and Japan[60]—the land

60 Clarence Senior, *Land Reform and Democracy* (Gainesville: University of Florida Press, 1958); R. P. Dore, *Land Reform in Japan* (London: Oxford University Press, 1959).

reform reduced poverty. But in other cases, land reform disrupted the organization of agricultural production and distribution and increased poverty, at least temporarily. Land reform has been one of the great incentives held out by Communist leaders to the peasants of underdeveloped nations, but in most cases—notably that of China—this has simply meant the transfer of control of the land from the hands of the traditional aristocracy to the new bureaucracy making up the apparatus of the State, and it is doubtful if the peasants are any better off than they were under the old regimes. Whatever increased wealth the Communist governments have been able to develop out of industrialization has gone into armaments and military ventures rather than into a higher standard of living for their people (we are here referring to the Communist underdeveloped countries, not to the Communist nations of Europe which in some cases have recently bettered the standard of living).

If poverty is the single most salient fact and problem of the approximately 70 underdeveloped countries of the world, it has not ceased to be a problem in the industrialized nations. Only Sweden seems to have achieved the combination of high productivity and constant redistribution of wealth so that a class of poor people does not regularly replenish itself. All the other Western nations have a very poor class ranging in size from one-fourth to two-thirds of its total population. In the Soviet Union, this poor class includes most of the agricultural population and a large proportion of the urban working population especially outside the largest cities. The upper class in the Soviet Union—which includes most of the higher government employees, the intellectuals, the military leaders and the managers of the state-owned enterprises—have a high income, but their ability to transmit their wealth to their offspring is largely limited to providing them with exceptionally good opportunities to enter the upper class also. No good statistics on occupational distribution exist for the Soviet Union, but it is likely that the upper class there is about as large as that for Western Europe or the United States. It is the middle class which is much smaller in the Soviet Union, since it consists largely of skilled or otherwise trained urban workers. The excess of wealth—which in other Western countries would go to support a large middle class of small managers, semiprofessionals, and many farmers, as well as skilled workers—goes into the State, especially into its military and foreign operations. Thus, there is a much larger proportion of poor people in the Soviet Union than in most Western countries.

Italy is another Western nation with a large proportion of poor people—largely because the southern third of the nation is economically underdeveloped and because unemployment is endemic in the country. Northern Italy, however, follows the pattern of most of the rest of Western Europe in its high productivity and rapid economic growth. These countries would have no unemployment if it were not for the immigration of the dispossessed from Southern Italy and North Africa (into France). Spain and Portugal have much poverty but they are more similar in their economic and political structures to North Africa than they are to the rest of Western Europe—that is, they are economically underdeveloped and politically autocratic. Ireland, too, is an exception: like South Italy it is predominantly agricultural and has too high a birth rate (despite late marriage) for its economic opportunities.

Most of Western Europe and the United States have poverty concentrated in the unskilled population (both rural and urban) and in certain categories which might be called "the unemployables." In general, the United States has fewer unskilled than does Western Europe, and they are somewhat better off. But the United States has a much larger proportion of unemployables. About a fourth of the American population could be classified today as unemployable, and most of these are very poor.[61] (See Figure 6.)

2   THE "EXTRA" PEOPLE: THE UNEMPLOYABLES

It is difficult to define "unemployable" precisely. An unemployable person is one who is unemployed because the economic structure is such that no job opportunity can be found for all in his condition. Unemployability can and usually does exist side-by-side with a shortage of labor, which is not true for mere "unemployment." The distinction is based on the economist's distinction between "structural" and "cyclical" unemployment. In the latter, which occurs during periods of economic depression, the unemployment lasts only a few months or years, until the cycle moves once again into prosperity. But structural unemployment will last indefinitely unless the basic structure of the economy is changed; usually this requires deliberate government action.

Structural unemployment in the United States has come about largely because of technological advance since about 1950. A secondary factor—the unwillingness of employers to hire Negroes except for agricultural labor or service occupations—has existed since shortly after the Civil War. But as discrimination against the Negro has been sharply diminishing, he has been increasingly faced with the depredations of technological unemployment, along with the unskilled white youth, the elderly, and inhabitants of "dis-

[61] The best sources on poverty in the United States are Michael Harrington, *The Other America: Poverty in the United States* (New York: Macmillan, 1962); J. N. Morgan, M. H. David, W. J. Cohen, and H. E. Brazer, *Income and Welfare in the United States* (New York: McGraw-Hill, 1962); Leon Keyserling *et al., Poverty and Deprivation in the United States* (Washington, D.C.: Conference on Economic Progress, 1961); Gabriel Kolko, *Wealth and Power in the United States* (New York: Praeger, 1962); Robert J. Lampman, *The Share of Top Wealth-Holders in National Wealth* (Princeton, N.J.: Princeton University Press, 1962).

FIGURE 6 • INCIDENCE OF POVERTY

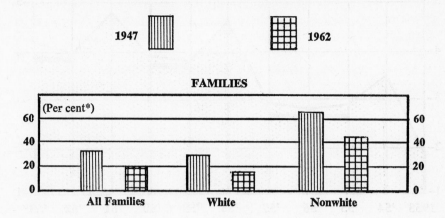

1947   1962

FAMILIES

(Per cent*)

All Families   White   Nonwhite

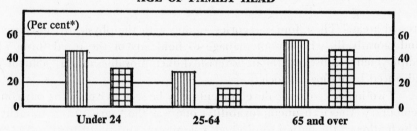

AGE OF FAMILY HEAD

(Per cent*)

Under 24   25-64   65 and over

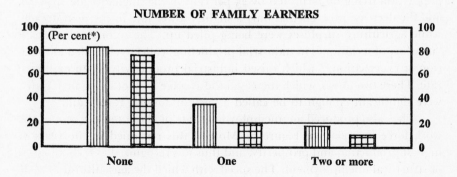

NUMBER OF FAMILY EARNERS

(Per cent*)

None   One   Two or more

* *Per cent of families with given characteristics that are poor. Poor families are defined as all families with total money income of less than $3,000 (1962 Prices).*

Source: U.S. Department of Commerce, Department of Labor, and Council of Economic Advisors.

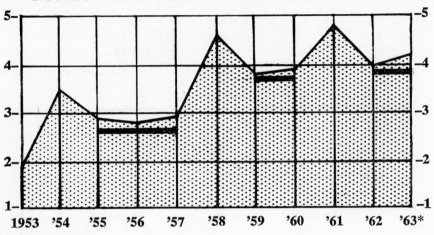

FIGURE 7 · RISING TREND OF UNEMPLOYMENT (*in millions*)

1953 '54 '55 '56 '57 '58 '59 '60 '61 '62 '63*

*Average, first 8 months, seasonally adjusted
Source: U.S. Department of Labor.

tressed areas." These four categories—along with the physically, mentally, and morally ill, who cannot manage to hold any of the usual forms of employment—constitute the impoverished unemployables of our "affluent," advanced technological society.

Two major economic developments may be seen as causes for our contemporary American unemployability: one was the "agricultural miracle" which allowed the nation to produce a significant surplus of food and fiber with a diminishing number of farmers. The proportion of the American population living on farms fell by 25 per cent in the single decade 1940–50, and the decrease proceeded at only a slightly lower rate in the next decade, while agriculture surpluses were being piled up. The second cause was a "new" set of techniques in industrial production, collectively called automation or cybernation,[62] which raised industrial productivity at an explosive rate. These two forces, which increased the average level of living materially, were significant enough to be called a "new industrial revolution."

They also produced an unemployment rate of about ten per cent of the work force by 1960 (see Figure 7). Most of this remained in the years of highest production and prosperity, and thus was recognized as technological or structural unemployment. The speed with which the agricultural miracle

[62] The term "automation" seems to have been coined by John Diebold in his *Automation: The Advent of the Automatic Factory* (New York: Van Nostrand, 1948). The term "cybernation"—a combination of "cybernetics" (invented by Norbert Wiener to refer to the study of communication and control in man and machines) and "automation"—was coined by Donald N. Michael in *Cybernation: The Silent Conquest* (Santa Barbara: Center for the Study of Democratic Institutions, 1962). Most of those using the term "automation" included the operation of computers as well as the automatic production of goods, so the term "cybernation" seems superfluous. It is part of the ethos of discussion of modern technology, however, to coin new terms and to use startling phrases.

and the new industrial revolution had come upon the American economy was recognized as one cause, but others were soon perceived: (1) The American economy had become somewhat "rigid" with inflexible prices and wages, so that the excess labor did not get absorbed by expanding "demand" for goods and services and lowered wages. (2) The high prosperity of most of those who remained employed resulted in increased inelasticity of demand—people were not expanding their expenditures as fast as their incomes, although increased government expenditures were making up the difference. (3) The new techniques of industrial production required a *higher* skill level for workers than the jobs from which these workers had been displaced; thus the displaced workers could not be absorbed even if wages fell. (4) The skill level of labor in the newly automated establishments was so high that it could not be economic to re-train some of the displaced labor for jobs in these transformed industries.

The employment picture promises to become even grimmer in some respects: (1) The new industrial revolution is just beginning—new sources of productive energy and newer kinds of machines are just around the corner for American industry. (2) About 2½ million persons presently on farms are not needed there. More than enough agricultural products to meet the current demand can be raised without their labor. (3) The other nations with purchasing power sufficient to buy American products have recovered enough from wartime devastation to meet many of their needs without American imports (this is a matter of degree for each nation, of course, and is a function of American prices and of the possibilities of reciprocal trade). Thus, exporting industries are beginning to lay off workers. (4) If the much-hoped-for disarmament program should materialize, the decreased government demand for armaments will throw additional millions of workers out of jobs.

Thus unemployability has recently become a serious problem in American society, and promises to become increasingly serious. In saying this, however, we must recognize that "unemployability" is not for the most part an absolute; it is purely relative to the characteristics of the job-seeking population and to the jobs available. A person who has characteristics which make him unemployable today was not likely to have been so ten years ago, and need not be so next year. In one sense, practically no one is intrinsically unemployable: If the handicaps of the most unlikely person are adjusted and an appropriate niche can be found for him, the unemployable becomes employed. Still, in terms of existing personal characteristics and of existing job opportunities, it is useful to recognize that there is unemployability and that it is growing today largely because of technological advances.

Let us examine the characteristics that currently are associated with unemployability, in a general way. One is residence in an area where the only major industry has sharply declined or becomes automated. Major examples are cotton-growing areas of the South, coal mining areas of West Virginia, Kentucky, and Alabama, and iron-mining areas of northern Minnesota. The problem of these areas is not merely that the former industry has declined but that no new industry has arisen in them to take the place of the old. This problem is likely to increase as a reduction of tariffs cuts off the protected market for certain inefficient industries (for example, textiles) located in areas where there are no other major industries. Within these areas are thousands of able-bodied potential workers, some even with skills that are in demand elsewhere. A second category of unemployables is that of older persons—roughly fifty years of age and over—who are able-bodied, but have been displaced from their jobs by automation and other technological advances, and are not considered to have sufficient working years left to be "worth" retraining. The third category consists of youth who, for one reason or another, have not finished high school and hence do not have enough basic education to be considered good risks for advanced training for skilled jobs which are available. Both the amount of basic education deemed necessary for giving specialized training to these youth, as well as the maximum age at which a displaced older person is deemed "worth retraining" is a function of the availability of other, "higher quality" labor. A fourth category of unemployability consists of members of minority groups who, despite their good health, usable skills, and favorable age, are not hired because of racial prejudice on the part of employers, unions, or customers. Because of Fair Employment Practice laws in seventeen states of the North—which include the large bulk of minority persons in the North—most of this kind of unemployment now occurs in the South, but not all. A fifth category consists of persons with physical, mental, or moral handicaps (including alcoholics, drug addicts, hermits, "psychopaths" and "sociopaths") who seek work at least occasionally, but are employed generally only in times of great labor shortage, such as in World War II. This category is so heterogeneous that it might best be considered in terms of its component elements rather than as a group: The physically handicapped person who can be rehabilitated and trained for a specialized skill job should not properly be put into the same category as a person who has no real motivation to accept regular employment. Still, the policy considerations that apply to all those people are sufficiently similar to justify treating them as a single category. Also, perhaps needless to say, there is a certain amount of overlap among all five categories.

Not only does unemployability cause poverty, the destruction of personal ambitions, and economic waste. It is also a major source of other kinds of social problems—such as crime, family disorganization, mental disturbances and suicide. The problem of structural unemployment—except that caused by racial discrimination—is so relatively new in the United

States that little has been done yet to cope with it. Most of the governmental efforts have been of the sort developed during the 1930's to deal with cyclical unemployment, and of course, these are bound to be insufficient.

E   *Older People in a Changing Society*

The elderly have always been part of society, and debilities and handicaps have always characterized them, but they have only recently been considered a social problem. This recent shift in attitude toward the aging has two sets of causes: (1) Changing objective conditions affecting the aging have made their debilities and handicaps both more severe and more salient. (2) The public has recently come to recognize that it is possible and feasible to alleviate some of the difficulties facing the elderly. These two sets of social changes will be the subject of our analysis. Together they make of aging a contemporary social problem.

While population statistics for earlier periods of history are generally faulty, it is likely that the proportion of the elderly—defined as those over 65 years of age—did not vary significantly from the figure of 4.1 per cent which was found for them in the year 1900 in the United States. But from that year until the present, the elderly have formed a steadily increasing percentage of the population; in 1960 they accounted for 9.3 per cent of the population. Thus, the elderly are relatively about twice as numerous as they were 60 years ago—twice as salient.

One major reason for this change, of course, is that there has been a major improvement in medical knowledge and preventive medicine. One category of diseases—the acute, infectious illnesses—has been virtually wiped out as a cause of death. This has led to a new problem of medical care for the elderly. They now usually survive the infectious diseases to acquire the chronic diseases—the deadly heart diseases and the cancers, as well as the handicapping arthritis and rheumatism—all of which cost much more in medical care, in nursing care and hospitalization. Whereas one formerly typically died of influenza or pneumonia after only a week or two of illness, and it was relatively inexpensive to die, today there are usually expensive and long-drawn-out medical costs attached to both living and dying as an elderly person. In the National Health Survey of July, 1959, to June, 1960, it was found that 77 per cent of the elderly population had one or more chronic illnesses.[63] In the short span of years between 1901 and 1955, according to another study, the proportion of persons over 65 years having one or more chronic diseases rose from 46 per cent to over 81 per cent.[64] At about the same time, the costs of medical care rose with extraordinary sharpness: Despite a half-day average reduction

[63] U.S. National Health Survey, Series B, No. 31 (Table 2).

[64] Metropolitan Life Insurance Company, "Major Aspects of American Morbidity," *Statistical Bulletin*, 41 (August, 1960), pp. 1–3.

in the length of hospital stay, the cost of the average hospital confinement rose from $148.64 to $279.91 between 1952 and 1962, a rate of increase about six times as great as that for all other living costs.[65]

This combination of circumstances has created one major facet of the contemporary social problem of the aging: the high cost of illness and death. It is estimated by the President's Council on Aging that, in 1961, only about 14 per cent of those past 65 years of age had total incomes of more than $3,000 a year[66] which might reflect the minimum amount of savings large enough to permit them to pay for a year's siege of chronic illness. Of course, those who are very poor (about 15 per cent) get their medical costs paid for by the Old Age Assistance (OAA) program.[67] But that leaves the large "middle class"—those who have enough saved and have pensions big enough to take care of all their ordinary living expenses, including ordinary medical costs—with insufficient funds to pay for medical care for a long-drawn-out chronic illness. About half of them have some kind of private medical insurance, but seldom does this cover the full costs of care for a chronic illness. The cost of medical insurance is rising rapidly: between 1952 and 1962, it rose 120 per cent, which is eight times as fast as all other living costs and three times as fast as wages.[68] Further, this private insurance is not economic: the high benefits to the elderly subscribers result in high insurance rates for middle-aged and younger subscribers. So far, the insurance companies have succeeded in convincing a sufficient number of younger persons to purchase medical insurance at rates considerably higher than their medical risks would warrant, but there is no economic reason for this and eventually it is likely that younger people will demand lower rates or cease to subscribe for health care insurance. Even by 1964, only about half the elderly were getting the benefits of private medical insurance. Thus there is a great challenge to our society to devise methods to take care of the new medical care costs of the bulk of our older citizens.

[65] Report by the Martin E. Segal Company, *The Machinist* (November 7, 1963), p. 3.

[66] President's Council on Aging, *The Older American* (Washington, D.C.: Government Printing Office, 1963), p. 9.

[67] Until the passage of the Kerr-Mills Act (1960), only a few states gave complete medical care free to those on OAA. Title 1 of the Kerr-Mills Act provided for generous federal subvention of medical care for OAA clients, and most states adopted this by statute. Thus, the figure of 15 per cent represents the approximate proportion of those over 65 on OAA. About 28 of the states (Fall, 1963) have also adopted Title 2 of the Kerr-Mills Act, providing partial medical care for the "medically indigent." But, in all but 3 or 4 of these states, the coverage is so limited—both in number of persons reached and in amount of medical care provided—that it can be said that Title 2 scarcely provides any additional medical care for the elderly. *Medical Assistance for the Aged: The Kerr-Mills Program, 1960–1963*. Report by the Subcommittee on Health of the Elderly to the Senate Special Committee on Aging (Washington, D.C.: Government Printing Office, 1963).

[68] Martin E. Segal Company, *op. cit.*

Another great need created by the changing health situation, which has been neglected during all the concern about medical costs, is that for improved preventive and diagnostic health services. If the chronic diseases cannot yet be cured, they can be partly avoided by better health habits and by earlier diagnosis. These will require organized effort.

Almost as dramatic in changing the lives of older Americans as the increase in their life expectancy has been the increase in compulsory and voluntary retirement from occupations. "Retirement as it is known today was relatively uncommon in 1900 and the difference between life expectancy and work life expectancy was a scant 3 years."[69] Even as recently as 1950, only 83 out of every 1,000 men 64 years old left the labor force before they were a year older. Today the retirement rate between 64 and 65 is 234 per 1,000—nearly a three-fold increase in about one decade.[70] The decline in the number of self-employed men has been a major factor in this shift: farmers, small storekeepers, and independent artisans are far less numerous, relative to the general growth in the population, than they were just a few generations ago. Further, the industries which hire the great bulk of employed Americans have established compulsory retirement ages, for both blue-collar and white-collar workers. The drive to have a continual accession of more vigorous, more recently trained, and more efficient workers has undoubtedly been a major reason for this, but there has also been the belief that a person in his 60's has worked long enough and should have the privilege of retirement. With the increasing availability of Social Security and pensions, the elderly seem to be more willing to retire.[71] With the simultaneous improvement in the health conditions of the elderly, they are now likely to have a considerable number of years ahead of them upon retirement, and many of them are physically and mentally vigorous. The average length of life for white men who have reached 65 years today is 12.9 years, while for women, it is 15.9 years.[72]

While this is the length of life for the "average person" just retiring from a gainful occupation, the situation for the woman whose chief life roles have been those of mother and homemaker is more complicated. The average woman of today has completed the task of raising her children when she is in her mid-40's. Modern household appliances and the use of manufactured clothing and many semi-prepared foods have greatly dimin-

[69] U.S. Department of Labor, *Manpower Report No. 8, The Length of Working Life for Males, 1900–60* (Washington, D.C., July, 1963), pp. 7–8.

[70] *Ibid.*, pp. 11–12.

[71] Harold Ohrbach, "Social and Institutional Aspects of Industrial Workers Retirement Pattern," unpublished paper presented to the International Gerontological Seminar, August 6–9, 1963.

[72] For non-whites in the United States, the expectation of life at 65 years is 12.7 years for males and 15.2 years for females (Metropolitan Life Insurance Company, *Statistical Bulletin*, 44 [July, 1963], p. 2).

ished the task of the homemaker. Thus, in a sense, the non-employed woman reaches retirement at about the age of 45. An increasing number of these women then seek gainful employment, but not all of them find appropriate jobs.

Thus, a combination of social changes has created a situation for the aging which Ernest W. Burgess has called "the roleless role" and which Elaine Cumming calls "disengagement." While Cumming considers disengagement inevitable and desirable, a more appropriate interpretation would be that it is an unintended product of recent social changes which our culture has not yet devised means to compensate for.[73] The retired of today, healthier and more vigorous than the retired of a generation ago, are seeking new roles, and this is a major challenge to our society. Some resist retirement from their regular occupations, but with the shortage of job opportunities today even for younger workers they are not likely to be very successful.

Some older people do find marginal, part-time work—in selling, babysitting, the crafts, etc.—which keeps them happily busy while it adds to their usually meager income. But most older people are searching for non-remunerative activities, and the past decade, especially, has seen a tremendous development of these. Some take the form of individual hobbies and "do-it-yourself" activities around the home. Still others take the form of increased participation in the regular, non-age-graded voluntary associations throughout the society, such as the church organizations, the social welfare organizations, political parties, and the fraternal-recreational associations of many types.[74] But a new type of activity for the elderly is springing up which might become the characteristic solution for the increased leisure-time problem for the retired in our society. This is the association exclusively for the elderly.[75] Some of these are organized by non-elderly social workers or by welfare-minded citizens; still others are organized by the older people themselves. Some grow out of existing social structures—such as churches—while others are formed *de novo* without a parent organization. Most of them have recreational-sociable activities, but some have purposes beyond meeting the needs of the participants themselves—such as visiting the home-bound, sewing for institutions, seeking a reduced bus-fare, propagandizing for medical care for the elderly. Some of these associations have a formal structure, while others are so informal as to be nothing more than a fairly regular coming-together of congenial

[73] Arnold M. Rose, "A Current Theoretical Issue in Social Gerontology," *The Gerontologist,* 4 (March, 1964), pp. 46–50.

[74] Arnold M. Rose, "The Impact of Aging on Voluntary Associations," in Clark Tibbitts (ed.), *Handbook of Social Gerontology* (Chicago: University of Chicago Press, 1960), pp. 666–97.

[75] Arnold M. Rose, "The Subculture of the Aging: A Topic for Sociological Research," *The Gerontologist,* 2 (September, 1962), pp. 123–27.

people. Obviously, these associations have been formed to meet a need among their elderly participants. Whether they are structured enough, or offer enough activity, to meet the need satisfactorily is something almost completely unknown, as there have been practically no evaluative studies of these associations.[76] That they should be successful is a challenge to our society.

In this time of cultural transition for the elderly, it is difficult for them to know what to do. They have to take initiative and make major decisions for themselves when the culture does not offer clear-cut guide lines for appropriate behavior. Problems of income, employment, housing, medical care and leisure-time activities arise, toward a solution for which the elderly have no guidance in the general standards of our society. In the larger cities, social work agencies exist to provide help in the more severe cases. But the problems of most older people are not severe enough for them to be directed to the welfare agencies, or they feel they would be losing their independence if they were to go to the welfare agencies. What is needed, and now occasionally provided, is a regularly-repeated educational series of lecture-discussions on the typical problems faced by older people. Persons informed of the extensive body of gerontological research conducted during the past decade or so, and who are skilled in leading discussions, are needed to present programs in the existing neighborhood organizations for the elderly and making these programs available also to those who are not members of these organizations. Periods of rapid social change create new needs and new opportunities for adult education.

While the health and employment changes affecting the aging have resulted from great impersonal forces impinging on the entire society, the changes in housing for the elderly are more a result of deliberate and specific planning. Of course, this is not true of the reduction of the number of farms in our society, but even many of the elderly farmers who have moved into village and town homes have done so out of their own choice. Voluntary choice has also been the major factor in the movement of a significant number of Eastern and Middle Western retirees into states like Florida, Arizona and California. After the migration, the dwelling places tend to be smaller than they were before the migration. Some are even trailers, hotel rooms, and small units in settlements specifically designed for the aging.

Throughout the United States, we are copying the Europeans in providing—with both private and public funds[77]—apartments and small

[76] A first study along this line is Arnold M. Rose, "Group Consciousness Among the Aging," to be published in A. M. Rose and W. A. Peterson (eds.), *The Aging and Their Social World.*

[77] Publicly-aided housing for the elderly got under way after 1956; by 1962, 550 million dollars was spent by the federal government for this purpose. President's Council on Aging, *op. cit.,* p. 44.

homes designed to meet the special needs of older residents. These can be entered without climbing stairs, and, if not on ground level, are serviced with elevators (large enough, usually, to accommodate a movable bed as well as standing passengers). The hallways and rooms of these modern dwelling places are fitted with handrails or grab bars at strategic spots. The doors are opened with levers rather than knobs, to meet the needs of the arthritic. Electric wall outlets are three feet off the floor so they may be reached without bending. The bathrooms, especially, have equipment which shows they are intended for use by the elderly—having shelves and lighting fixtures which can be reached without stretching or standing on ladders, having faucets that can be opened with levers instead of knobs, having handrails near the tub and toilet, and sometimes being equipped with a sitzbath instead of ordinary tub. While many of the basic furnishings in these dwelling places are as new as the structures themselves, the inhabitants are encouraged to bring in a few items of furniture from their old homes in order to give them a feeling of continuity with their past. Because the units are small, there are many common rooms in the complex, for recreation, for entertaining, for laundry use and sometimes even for everyday eating. There are also outdoor balconies and gardens where one may sit in the sun. The complexes themselves, while inhabited excusively by older people, are usually located in the midst of family residential areas, unless they are in the so-called retirement towns, like St. Petersburg. Generally, they are located near downtown or other shopping areas, or near medical facilities such as hospitals so that physicians can gain ready access to their numerous elderly patients. It is evident that a great deal of thoughtful planning has gone into the location and construction of dwellings for the elderly.

But it is still only a minority of the older people who live in this modern kind of private dwelling or its publicly-owned equivalent. About five per cent are obliged by poor health to live in nursing homes or other kinds of institution, and this proportion has been slowly growing with the increasing availability of nursing homes and the greater need for them to serve the chronically ill. Three-generation dwelling under one roof is almost as common as it ever was. But whereas it previously took the form of a younger family living in the grandfather's large home, now it is likely to be the case of a widowed grandmother added to a young family's limited quarters.[78] The largest number of older people continue to dwell by themselves in large, old homes, in which they raised their families or could have. Such dwellings are not suited to elderly inhabitants, unless they have been converted into rooming houses and provide both income and

[78] Geneva Mathiasen, "A New Look at the Three-Generation Family," unpublished paper presented at the 87th Annual Forum, National Conference on Social Welfare, June, 1960.

a small apartment for their aging owners. The old houses are too large and too difficult to maintain for an older person or couple. They often have stairs and shelves which cannot be reached except on a ladder. Even the apartments among the older dwellings do not have equipment for the safety and convenience of elderly inhabitants. If, as usual, they are inter-mingled with units in which younger families dwell, the younger adults do not associate much with their aging neighbors,[79] and their children often create a nuisance with noise and thoughtless behavior from the stand-point of the older folks. It is an obvious need and challenge to our society to move older people into modern housing units particularly designed to serve their special requirements. This is actually being accomplished steadily, although some would question whether it is being done rapidly enough.

Low income has been a chronic dilemma for the elderly, as their energy declines and their skills become outmoded. As noted, this has become ac-centuated by the decline in self-employment and the increase in compulsory retirement of employees. Our society has met the problem with relative directness: the Social Security retirement insurance program was in-augurated in 1935 and by now has been extended to most segments of the population. As recently as January, 1953, only 3.5 million older Americans and their dependents were collecting Social Security checks. Just ten years later—in January, 1963—12.7 million collect such payments, almost four times as many.[80] At the current rate of increase, about 95 per cent of the elderly will be covered by Social Security by the year 1980. This is supple-mented by the Old Age Assistance program to meet the basic needs of the minority not covered, or insufficiently covered, by Social Security. Of those receiving old-age assistance, 43.8 per cent are also receiving Social Security benefits, but not enough to provide for all their living costs.[81] That OAA does not meet the basic needs of all is shown by the fact that twenty states require a 5-year residence, and three more states require between 1 and 5 years' residence, before allowing an elderly person to be eligible for OAA.[82] However, the income of the elderly is augmented by the fact that many industries have inaugurated pension programs, usually with con-tributions from both employers and employees.

There remain two major unsolved problems. One of the problems of the contemporary economy, especially salient since 1945, has been the steady rise in the cost of living. Income from Social Security and from private

---

[79] Irving Rosow, "Local Concentration and Social Contacts of Older People," un-published paper read at Sixth International Congress of Gerontology, Copenhagen, August, 1963.

[80] President's Council on Aging, *op. cit.*, p. 43.

[81] U.S. Department of Health, Education and Welfare, *Aging*, No. 111 (January, 1964), p. 28.

[82] *Ibid.*, p. 46.

pension plans thus becomes progressively insufficient to meet even the minimum needs of the retirees. The Old Age Assistance program—based on concepts of "government relief" and the "means test"—is both an inefficient and socially unhealthy means of providing income to the elderly; it has been useful as a stopgap until the Social Security system could come into full operation and it serves as a continuing foundation program for the socially disorganized welfare client. But the Old Age Assistance program should not be used to supplement the income of a retiree who has earned his own income all of his working life because inflation has eroded the purchasing power of his life savings and his Social Security insurance. Social Security income should be shifted from fixed dollar payments to purchasing-power payments, which would require federal government subsidy to the program during periods of inflation. This would not only be psychologically beneficial to the retiree, but would also relieve the pressure on state and local governments now hard pressed to maintain the Old Age Assistance program and not able to benefit from inflation in the way that the federal government does.

The second problem of sustaining the income of the elderly also arises out of large-scale impersonal social forces which the individual worker cannot control. This is the effect on jobs of the continuing technological revolution—sometimes called "automation." The worker in manufacturing, construction, and certain clerical occupations frequently finds his employment threatened by technological improvements which increase the economic efficiency and wealth of the society as a whole. If he is past the age of about 45 years it is seldom economically worthwhile to retrain him for the new positions in automated industries. In a small way, our government has embarked on programs to accommodate such displaced workers in service occupations with low skill requirements, and has lowered the age at which Social Security payments may begin. But these efforts fail to meet the employment needs of the older worker displaced by automation and of the retiree who begins his Social Security benefits after a period of unemployment which resulted from no inadequacy on his part. This is a large part of the major challenge to our society to adjust to the disruptions created by rapid technological progress.

Thus far, we have examined the many objective social changes affecting the aging which have made their natural debilities and handicaps more severe and more salient, and which provide challenges to a civilized society to take the organized and rational action necessary to alleviate the additional hardships created for the elderly by these changes. We shall now turn to some more speculative observations about the changing public image of the aging in American society, both on the part of the aging themselves and on the part of the less-elderly public. Generally speaking, the culture of the United States has put a very low value on aging. Until very recently, no privileges or titles of honor were conferred on the elderly because of their age, as has been true in many other cultures. The aging have not been assumed to have special wisdom or other admired characteristics, but, on the contrary, are widely considered to be "old-fashioned" and to have other undesirable characteristics. Ours is a youth-centered society, in which the aged are an anti-model. In addition to the natural debilities and objective deprivations of old age, the elderly have had to suffer neglect and negative regard. Many have tried to avoid acknowledging their age, at least until they have achieved some remarkable age such as 90 years, and the word "aged" has not been considered a polite appellation.

There are some evidences now that this is changing. Since the 1930's the government has been paying attention to the economic needs of the aging, since the 1950's to their housing needs, and since 1960 to their medical needs. Especially since 1950, churches, private voluntary associations, and social welfare agencies have been giving attention to the recreational, educational, and sociable needs of the aging. A great number of conferences, lectures, and discussions are being devoted to the problems of the aging. The private citizen is being urged to pay more attention to the elderly, and to perform little services for them, such as driving them to meetings. Politicians are paying more attention to the large number of elderly voters (estimated at 17 per cent of the national electorate). Thus, there is evidence that the United States is becoming more "aging conscious," and is less inclined to ignore the elderly even if it does not evaluate them highly.

Among the elderly themselves there seems also to be a change in self-image. Perhaps as a result of all the public attention to their problems, they are beginning to become aware of themselves as a group. They are starting to think of their problems less in individual terms and more in collective terms. Those who are taking advantage of the new opportunities to meet together show some interest in protesting against some of the discriminations under which the elderly have long lived and in taking positive action to reduce their handicaps. They show more of a tendency to share each other's company—to have more age-graded social relations—and to exhibit pride in such achievements as hobbies and performances of skill (for example, the "life begins at 80" activities). There are some among them who are urging the elderly to use their significant voting power to gain political benefits for the elderly as a group. In sum, there is evidence of a nascent "aging group consciousness" among the elderly.

If both these phenomena—the "aging consciousness" in the general public and the "aging group consciousness" among the elderly themselves—should grow to significant proportions, American culture will be significantly changed. Already there is considerable evidence of an "aging subculture" growing among the elderly, regardless of their consciousness of it. New values concerning social status, personal worth, sex, interpersonal relations, and other important aspects of life are emerging among the elderly. Especially as a result of their growing numbers and salience, this is bound to have some impact on general American life.

It is evident that we are living in a period of great social change for the elderly, and that this will offer new opportunities and new challenges to American society which are not yet clear.

FOR ADDITIONAL READING

ELLIOTT, MABEL, and FRANCIS E. MERRILL, *Social Disorganization* (New York: Harper, 1950). A textbook on social problems.

HARRINGTON, MICHAEL, *The Other America: Poverty in the United States* (New York: Macmillan, 1962). The first of the recent spate of books to recall to Americans that there is still considerable poverty in this country.

MERTON, ROBERT K., and ROBERT A. NISBET (eds.), *Contemporary Social Problems* (New York: Harcourt, Brace and World, 1961). A rather sophisticated analysis of fourteen social problems, with a theoretical interpretation, each chapter being written by a different author.

SUTHERLAND, EDWIN H., and DONALD R. CRESSEY, *Principles of Criminology* (Philadelphia: Lippincott, 1955). An influential textbook on criminology.

TIBBITTS, CLARK (ed.), *Handbook of Social Gerontology* (Chicago: University of Chicago Press, 1960). The most comprehensive survey of the social situation and problems of older people.

16 * Social Conflict and Its Accommodation

A   Conflict and the Social Order

1   THE NATURE OF CONFLICT

Conflict may be defined as activity intended to hurt others physically or mentally or to deprive others of liberty (or property) and as activity designed to prevent one from being so intentionally hurt or deprived by others. Conflict among human beings may be considered social since common values are either the object of contention or are the basis on which individuals join forces in their conflict activities against others who do not share these values but somehow block the first group from realization of their values.

Some species of lower animals fight in groups—for example, ants live in colonies that function as a unit for offensive and defensive purposes. But this is a function of their instincts rather than a result of common agreement. They cannot live or fight long when in isolation, and the colony is never broken up when they fight among themselves. For the lower animals conflict always involves physical violence. This is far from always true among human beings. During the course of history humans have engaged in all forms of conflict, including some subtle ways in which the victim is not even aware as to who his mental torturers are. Social conflicts very often last over periods of time, sometimes even beyond the life of the men who begin them. Men have developed elaborate institutions to perform their conflict more effectively for long periods of time. A most obvious example is an army, which is an institution designed to engage in conflict (offensive or defensive) among nations. Somewhat less obvious as conflict institutions are trade unions and businessmen's associations, public-relations firms and lobbyists, certain community-improvement and protective associations, the "defense organizations" established by minority groups, pressure groups of all sorts.

The distinction between conflict and competition has already been suggested.[1] Competition is an impersonal process and requires no contact between those opposed to each other. Conflict is personal, although not always selfish, and requires a point of contact—often a violent one—between the contenders. Competition determines the ecological order and some aspects of the economic order. Conflict is an important basis of social organization—although not the sole basis, as such theorists as Gumplowicz would claim—as well as the more obvious basis of such forms of social disorganization as war, feuds, factionalism, race riots, and other forms of intergroup violence, showdown battles between management and labor or between any two other vested interests.

The forced subordination of individuals and groups by a person or group with power to do so has probably more often been the way societies have been organized throughout history than by consensus or agreement.[2] Sometimes an apparent agreement is achieved by coercion. Whether the conflict is overt or hidden, individuals and groups can be coerced into co-operation to keep the necessary activities of the society going. Conflict makes it possible to readjust norms and power relations within societies or groups in accord with the ever-changing needs of their individual members or subgroups. Conflict has varying degrees—ranging from all-out effort at extermination, in which any tactic may be used, to a ceremonial opposition fully under the control of mutually recognized norms. Any conflict a degree or more away from the extermination extreme involves some social organization.

While we shall here be emphasizing the "naturalness" of conflict and its place in the social order, we must also recognize that conflict can also be considered as a source of certain social problems and as itself a kind of social problem. War between nations, race conflict, and opposition between organized labor and management have sometimes been analyzed in terms of the general processes governing social conflict. In attempting to explain crime, some sociologists have emphasized the role of the gang as a conflict group rather than any individual motivation to criminality.

[1] See Chapter 13, Section A.

[2] The leading exponent of this idea among sociologists has been Georg Simmel. See *The Sociology of Georg Simmel*, edited and translated by Kurt H. Wolff (Glencoe, Ill.: Free Press, 1950), e.g., pp. 201–07. Also see Lewis A. Coser, *The Functions of Social Conflict* (Glencoe, Ill.: Free Press, 1956); Irving Louis Horowitz, "Consensus, Conflict and Cooperation: A Sociological Inventory," *Social Forces*, 41 (December, 1962), pp. 177–88. A general social science approach to conflict is that of Kenneth E. Boulding, *Conflict and Defense* (New York: Harper, 1963).

In the preceding chapter we saw that there are alternative theories of the causes of social problems, but at this point we can readily recognize that for many social problems conflict is at least an accessory or manifestation.[3]

2   CONFLICT AS A BASIS OF SOCIAL ORDER

It may not be so obvious why conflict is a basis of social order and co-operation until we recognize that conflict may settle how valued objects or symbols are to be distributed. On the individual level this can be clarified by an analogy between the "pecking order" among hens and the rivalry among men. Allee describes the interesting manner in which hens determine their personal status through a limited combat that zoologists call "pecking":

> In (some) animal groups leadership may be expressed by the arrogation of certain rights and privileges. This is very well illustrated in the organization of a flock of domestic hens. Such groups, again, are an open not a closed society, but the newly admitted members must fight for any privileged standing which is accorded them in the community. The ranking of the hens is indicated by their reactions when another member pecks or threatens to peck them. A given hen will submit to pecking by certain individuals without showing resentment, and will in turn treat others similarly without their making protest. Hens with such power are said to possess the "peck right" over those submitting to the pecking and the group is said to be organized according to the "peck order." The ranking is obtained by combat or by passive submission and newcomers can escape the bottom ranks only by fighting.
>
> The "peck order" within a given flock may be a single series in which "A" pecks "B" which pecks "C" which pecks "D" and so on to "Z" which, oddly enough, may have the right over "A" gained in some encounter when "A" was ill or otherwise below par. A revolt or a fight may upset or confirm the existing order. It is usual, however, for birds inferior in the "peck order" to fight less fiercely against those high above them than they do against those of approximately their own rank or lower. It is also generally true that a hen that stands high in the "peck order" is less likely to be vicious in her attacks on those below her than is a hen standing relatively low in this order.
>
> Hens with chicks are more likely to revolt successfully against their positions in the flock organization than are those without or the same hen when her chicks are removed. A cock introduced into the flock stands at the apex of the "peck order." High position in the flock

[3] An overall survey of conflict—considering both its organizational and disorganizational effects—is to be found in *Conflict Resolution*, 1 (June, 1957). See, especially, the summary article by Raymond W. Mack and Richard C. Snyder, "The Analysis of Social Conflict—Toward an Overview and Synthesis," pp. 212–48.

If . . . a fight simply aims at annihilation, it does approach the marginal case of assassination in which the admixture of unifying elements is almost zero. If, however, there is any consideration, any limit to violence, there already exists a socializing factor, even though only as the qualification of violence. Kant said that every war in which the belligerents do not impose some restrictions in the use of possible means upon one another, necessarily . . . becomes a war of extermination. It is almost inevitable that an element of commonness injects itself into . . . enmity once the stage of open violence yields to another relationship, even though this new relation may contain a completely undiminished sum of animosity between the two parties.

One unites in order to fight, and one fights under the mutually recognized control of norms and rules.

Georg Simmel, *Conflict*, trans. Kurt H. Wolff (Glencoe, Ill.: Free Press, 1955), pp. 26, 35.

involves the right to peck without being pecked in return, to eat without being disturbed by those of lesser rank and bestows general independence from social interference. Other birds are said to show essentially similar flock organization.[4]

The process is different among humans, but sometimes the results are similar. In a boys' gang,[5] the most aggressive (who is sometimes the strongest, sometimes the cleverest) becomes the leader by telling or showing the others what to do. The leader selects lieutenants, who assert themselves over the other boys—the followers. If anyone challenges the leader or his ideas, he persuades or ridicules him into conformity, or, failing that, beats him up (or gets another member of the gang to beat him up) and forcibly ejects him from the group until he is willing to "knuckle under" and conform. If the leader does not do these things, and the challenger persists successfully in asserting himself and his ideas over the others, the challenger becomes the leader. Similar patterns are often found among groups of adults. Whyte,[6] for example, reports a hierarchy shown in Figure 8 among a gang of young men in an Italian section of a large American city. "Doc" is the leader and Mike, Nutsy, and Angelo are the lieutenants who transmit his influence to the seven followers. Danny and Long John are close friends of Doc, but do not assert their authority over the others. The pattern of dominance and submission is not so explicit as the diagram suggests, but it can be observed in the men's behavior and found to predict the influence

[4] Warder Clyde Allee, *Animal Life and Social Growth* (Baltimore: Williams & Wilkins, 1932), pp. 154–56.

[5] See Chapter 6, Section E.

[6] William F. Whyte, *Street Corner Society* (Chicago: University of Chicago Press, 1943).

relations among them. Conflicts between groups as well as between individuals help to establish their relative status in the social order.

There are many ways in which conflict contributes to social organization. Conflict with out-groups increases the internal solidarity of an in-

FIGURE 8 • THE MEMBERS OF DOC'S GANG

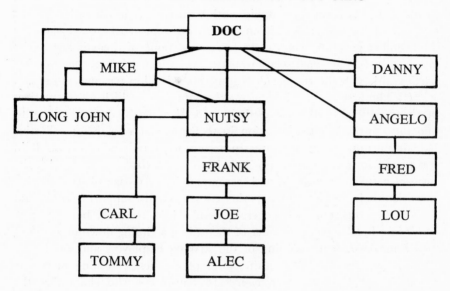

group and sharply sets off group boundaries, as sociologists since William
Graham Sumner have observed. Conflict with out-groups usually motivates
an in-group to clarify its goals and values.[7] When there are two or more
interest groups, and there is no conflict, it means that the accommodation
among them works out to the disadvantage of all but those on top; whereas
overt conflict can lead to compromise and even agreement for the accommodation of all interests. Especially in a loosely organized society, with
many crisscrossing interests and influences, and with some shared values that
cut across lines of cleavage, the presence of many little conflicts prevents
any one large conflict from dominating the relations of sizable groups and
thus tearing the society apart.[8] In other ways, conflict channels hostility
and reduces tension, which, if they persisted over long periods of time,
could be completely disruptive. Finally, as we have noted in an earlier
chapter,[9] conflict is stimulating and promotes inventiveness and innovation,
both in self-defense and in providing access to alternative sets of ideas.

[7] D. Kahn-Freund, "Intergroup Conflicts and Their Settlement," *British Journal of
Sociology*, 5 (1954), p. 201.

[8] This seems to have been first observed by Simmel, and reiterated by Coser, *op. cit.*,
pp. 41–44.

[9] See Chapter 11.

B Conflict in Industrial Relations

Business management and organized labor are in opposition to each other for certain values (for the money difference between sales income and cost of supplies and equipment), although they are often in harmony concerning the value of high total sales and productive efficiency. This opposition puts them into conflict with each other, although the conflict only occasionally becomes violent, as during some strikes or lockouts.[10] The conflict generally takes three forms and none of them is *necessarily* attended by bad personal relations between representatives of the opposing parties, although the conflict does sometimes develop personal animosity.

(1) The first of these is *collective bargaining,* in which representatives of the opposing parties argue their respective needs, desires, strengths, and the "justice" of the situation in so far as it favors them; collective bargaining now generally results in a contract, but it may also result in the second form of conflict. (2) This is an *overt display of power,* in the form of a strike or lockout, with accompanying stoppage of work, picket lines, denunciatory propaganda, other efforts to enlist support from neutral sources, boycotts, etc.; this generally results in a contract, but may also result in a break up or surrender of the union, a closing down of the business firm, or permanent firing of the striking employees and the hiring of new employees. (3) The third form of conflict, becoming more frequent, is the *pressing of grievances* by employees who claim that the management has done them some injustice as defined by the contract; this generally results in some agreed-upon settlement or in arbitration, in which an impartial third party judges the case. All of these forms of conflict define the status of the employees and the union on the one hand, and the management and the owners on the other hand, in their relationship to each other. The history of labor relations shows that, as each of the contending parties accepts the continuing existence of the other, extreme and unlimited violence drops to almost nothing while the three above-mentioned forms of industrial conflict continue.

A cross-cultural study of the incidence of strikes by Ross and Hartman[11] shows three different patterns. In most Northern European countries, strikes are infrequent and typically short; in Mediterranean and Asiatic countries they are extremely widespread but short; and in the United States and Canada, they are relatively frequent and relatively long. In

[10] For an analysis of how sociologists have studied industrial conflict, see R. C. Sorenson, "The Concept of Conflict in Industrial Sociology," *Social Forces,* 24 (1951), pp. 263–67. The best modern source on industrial conflict is A. Kornhauser, R. Dubin, and A. M. Ross, *Industrial Conflict* (New York: McGraw-Hill, 1954).

[11] Arthur M. Ross and Paul Hartman, *Changing Patterns of Industrial Conflict* (New York, Wiley, 1960).

CONFLICT WITH OUT-GROUPS
INCREASES INTERNAL COHESION

The group in a state of peace can permit antagonistic members within it to live with one another in an undecided situation because each of them can go his own way and can avoid collisions. A state of conflict, however, pulls the members so tightly together and subjects them to such uniform impulse that they either must get completely along with, or completely repel, one another. This is the reason why war with the outside is sometimes the last chance for a state ridden with inner antagonisms to overcome these antagonisms, or else to break up definitely.

The fighter must "pull himself together." That is, all his energies must be, as it were, concentrated in one point so that they can be employed at any moment in any required direction.

The well-known reciprocal relation between a despotic orientation and the warlike tendencies of a group rests on this informal basis: war needs a centralistic intensification of the group form, and this is guaranteed best by despotism.

Georg Simmel, *Conflict*, trans. Kurt H. Wolff (Glencoe, Ill.: Free Press, 1955), pp. 87, 88, 92, 93.

the Communist countries, strikes are prohibited, and the information which has leaked out about strikes which have occurred there has not been systematic. In both North America and Northern Europe, strikes and lockouts have been sharply declining in frequency and duration, when compared with total employment and union membership. This change has been related to more flexible employer policies, more active government programs to prevent strikes, and a shift in union philosophy from seeking long-range solutions to short-run gains.

There is nothing unnatural or abnormal about industrial conflict, and it is likely to continue as long as we have a free society.[12] In fact, the only presently conceivable way to eliminate industrial conflict is to stop it by force, which would require the establishment of a dictatorship in the government. Richmond has stated well why industrial conflict must be expected in a free, modern society:

A study of the nature and origins of conflict from the sociological point of view suggests that conflict is an inevitable concomitant of

[12] The "naturalness" of conflict was perhaps first emphasized by Simmel and has been re-emphasized in recent years by Jessie Bernard. See Georg Simmel, "The Sociology of Conflict," *American Journal of Sociology*, 9 (1904), pp. 490–525; G. Simmel, *Conflict*, trans. K. H. Wolff (Glencoe, Ill.: Free Press, 1955); J. Bernard, "Where Is the Modern Sociology of Conflict?" *American Journal of Sociology*, 56 (1950), pp. 11–16; Coser, *op. cit.*; Harold Sheppard, "Approaches to Conflict in American Sociology," *British Journal of Sociology*, 5 (1954), pp. 324–42.

change. Only in a completely static society can conflict be altogether eliminated. . . . The preoccupation with psychological aspects among those concerned with "human relations in industry" has led to an unrealistic avoidance of the problem of conflict or to naïve assumptions concerning its elimination. There has been a tendency to assume that there is no real conflict of interests between labor and management and that the adoption of the right kind of technique by an enlightened personnel department will create a state of harmony in which workers and management alike will collaborate in the pursuit of the manifest objectives of the organization. Such an approach fails to recognize that conflict, as understood in the sociological sense, can exist independently of the subjective reactions of the members of a group. Friendly relations may exist between the man on the bench and the Works Manager or the Chairman of Directors, but this does not alter the fact that the interests of the employee in maintaining his job are not the same as the interests of the employer in employing him, as will be quickly shown at a time of trade depression. Conflict in this sense is embedded in the institutional structure of society and is not removed, however enlightened the management. In this particular case the production of particular goods or services represents the manifest purpose of the organization—the shared collective goal. The employer and those associated with the management have additional goals arising out of the need to maximize efficiency, reduce costs, and maintain profit levels and dividends. The employees, on the other hand, are concerned with the security of their employment, the protection or increase in the size of their wage packet, and a number of other personal and social satisfactions derived from their occupation.[13]

There are three forms of society in which industrial conflict of the types outlined above do not occur: (1) the dictatorship, which uses force to prevent and suppress internal conflict, but which is far from completely successful against the subtler forms of conflict, such as featherbedding, ca'canny, and the speed-up;[14] (2) the society in which there are no employees or slaves since productive property is either individually or communally owned and worked;[15] (3) the society functioning on the basis of strict traditional norms governing relations among all men, in-

[13] Anthony H. Richmond, "Conflict and Authority in Industry," *Occupational Psychology*, 28 (January, 1954), pp. 24–33.

[14] "Featherbedding" or "slowdown" is deliberate withholding of effort on the part of the worker. "Ca'canny" is deliberate slackening by workmen in rate of production. The "speed-up" is action on the part of the manager to increase the worker's production by having him work faster or harder than "normal."

[15] Such societies are found among certain preliterate tribes of Oceania and the Americas, and among certain "utopian" groups with Western culture.

cluding relations between employers and employees.[16] The last-named type of society, which approximates the "integrated group" relationship described in an earlier chapter,[17] was characteristic of Western culture in the Middle Ages.

When employer-employee relations, under the impact of the Commercial and Industrial revolutions, shifted from traditional mutual obligations based on status to deliberate, constantly changing agreements of the "contract" type,[18] the stage was set for the formation of organizations of workers and employers and for conflict between them. What happened specifically was that when it was no longer part of society's "rules" that employers protect their employees, the latter started to protect themselves, which in effect meant conflict with employers. The industrial history of the late eighteenth and early nineteenth century is replete with instances of individual workers protesting their hard lot, getting fired for doing so, and then forming organizations called unions so that the employer would find it difficult to fire all or most of his help. Other aspects of trade unionism came later, but the first motivation in every democratic Western country was to avoid arbitrary action by the employers. Unions also have found themselves in conflict with government and have sought special privileges from government. Even earlier, merchants and professional men had organized themselves into loose but effective federations to protect and promote themselves against government and against competition from potential rivals, foreign competitors, and the consuming public. They prevented the free utilization of inventions and sought government aid to protect and increase their markets.

c   *Conflict Among Religious and Racial Groups*

1   RELIGIOUS CONFLICT

Another illustration of conflict as part of the normal social organization may be seen in the relations among religious sects. Certain religions, such as Hinduism, consider themselves as flexible and compatible with other forms of religious belief. Other religions, such as Mohammedanism, consider themselves to be the only true religion and thus incompatible with any system of beliefs that claims to rival them. The latter religions are

---

[16] Such societies—which include most of those in the second category but include others as well—occur in relatively isolated parts of the world where they do not come in frequent contact with the dynamic civilizations.

[17] See Chapter 5, Section A.

[18] It was Sir Henry Maine who emphasized the importance of the shift in economic relations from status to contract. See his *Village Communities in the East and West* (London: J. Murray, 1871); *Ancient Law* (London: J. Murray, 1863), p. 165.

inevitably sources of conflict, for they oppose all rival religions for the loyalty and adherence of people.

Western culture, of course, has been closely associated with Christianity. In the Middle Ages only one form of Christianity was dominant in Europe, Roman Catholicism. Orthodox Christianity, with which Roman Catholicism had had a serious break in the earlier centuries of the Christian era, was the religion of people who were geographically separated in eastern Europe and Asia Minor. Judaism was held by only a small proportion of Europeans, and Roman Catholics alternately went through periods of exterminating Jews who refused to be converted and periods of protecting them as God's appointed outside witnesses of the veracity of Christian belief. A number of "heresies"—such as the Waldensian and Albigensian movements—developed in Europe in the Middle Ages, but they were ruthlessly suppressed by military force. Individual heretics and infidels were commonly tortured and killed. From the eleventh to the thirteenth centuries there were the Crusades, an almost continuous series of wars between Christianity and Mohammedanism, ostensibly for control of the Holy Land. The greatest religious conflict did not arise, however, until Roman Catholic Christianity was challenged in its own territory by a series of religious movements collectively known as Protestantism. Following the publication of Martin Luther's *Theses* in 1517, there was a series of wars between the Catholic and Protestant monarchs that were among the bloodiest known in history. These wars ended in a stalemate, and, while the Roman Catholic Church has never considered its Christian rivals as equals, it has never since attempted to bring them back into the fold by force.

This does not mean that religious conflict has ceased.[19] It was transferred from the international level to the local level, and shifted its tactics from the use of violence to the use of argument and propaganda. In a few countries where the Catholic Church is closely connected to the government —notably Spain, Portugal, and some South American countries—Protestants and Jews are sometimes not allowed to carry on the full range of church activities, such as missionary work, education, holding advertised "public" services, etc.—but they are seldom physically molested by the government or by Catholic Church authorities. In some countries where a Protestant church has been "established"—notably England and Sweden until very recently—the government gave certain privileges to the established church which made it somewhat difficult for other churches to operate as effectively. There has been a significant diminution of Catholic-Protestant church conflict especially since the papacy of John XXIII, beginning in 1958.

[19] For a discussion of contemporary religious conflict, see the *Journal of Social Issues*, 12 (1956), especially the introductory essay by D. J. Hager.

In the United States, where the government is deliberately separated from all churches, the churches carry on their conflict on an equal status basis. Church conflict in the United States is largely between the Catholic Church and the Protestant churches as a group, and sometimes between the smaller, newer, fundamentalist sects and the older, larger, Protestant denominations. In addition to the running verbal arguments over theology, the conflict occasionally erupts into policy matters that affect the daily lives of people. For example, the Catholic Church not only considers contraception a sin, but has advocated laws that prevent the sale or dissemination of information about birth control to any citizen (Massachusetts and Connecticut—with large Catholic populations—have retained such laws, although they were originally passed when those states were controlled by Protestants). Protestant groups have prevented the extension of privileges provided by government for the health and welfare of school children—such as free milk, school bus service—to children who attend parochial schools. In Community Chest councils and other groups where funds are allocated for social-welfare purposes there is often a good deal of bickering between Catholic and non-Catholic leaders as to how much money is to be distributed to the Catholic institutions. Certain political issues—such as over the fitness for office of Alfred E. Smith or Joseph McCarthy or over the question of naming an American ambassador to the Vatican—find the American people divided partly along religious lines. Somewhat similar political divisions are found in the Netherlands, where the population is almost evenly divided among Catholics and Protestants. Religious tension in the United States has diminished considerably since the election of President John F. Kennedy in 1960. There was virulent antagonism against Kennedy in some groups because of his Catholic affiliation, but his separation between religion and government in his activities as President disarmed some of his religious opposition.

2   RACE CONFLICTS

Race conflict has some characteristics in common with religious conflict. The study of "race relations" is generally considered to encompass the investigation of the nature of social contacts between racial, religious, nationality, and cultural groups. The term is in ill repute among social scientists since many of the groups clearly have no racial distinctions whatsoever, and even those that have are not pure races in the scientific sense of being biological entities with distinctive inborn traits and a separate ancestry. Terms now coming to take the place of "race relations" are "intergroup relations" and "ethnic group relations."

While ancient and medieval scholars observed biological and cultural differences between peoples, and reported on frictions that occurred when two groups came in contact with each other, the concern over race relations is a modern phenomenon. One reason is that in ancient times people usually lived in societies that were relatively more homogeneous as to race, religion, and culture than they are today. More important, however, is the fact that the problems of contact, friction, and prejudice between freeman and slave, Greek and barbarian, Roman citizen and colonial were thought of as political or status problems, rather than as problems of race or human relations. Until the eighteenth century biological differences were practically never a basis of intergroup hatred. Certain types of cultural distinctions did form the basis of intergroup conflict, but it was not uncommon for persons from despised cultures to change their habits and thereby gain acceptance. Perhaps most noteworthy of ancient prejudices within one society was that displayed between the Jews and the Greeks. These developed into open clashes in the first century B.C. and seem to have been caused by the aggressive promulgation of opposed religions and by Greek jealousy of the favoritism shown by the dominant Romans toward the Jews.

During the Middle Ages in Europe race and nationality hatred remained practically unknown. Some prejudice existed on the basis of culture differences, but the new basis of intergroup conflict was religion. Once established, Christianity became more intolerant than any of its predecessors had been.

Modern times were ushered in by a renewal of contact between white Europeans and people of other races. Attitudes at first were diverse and individual, but the fact of racial differences was made much more apparent. This alone did not make for race conflict or prejudice, and even after the slave trade in Negroes grew up there was no evidence that slavery rested on any doctrine of racial inferiority. Negroes were simply a weak people, and whites with no power could be enslaved as well as Negroes. Some churches, however, soon gave added sanction to Negro slavery by pointing to the need for Christianizing the heathen by means of enslavement—at least the churches explicitly denied any opposition to slavery. The concept of race itself seems to have been a concomitant of the growth of biological science as it developed in the eighteenth century. Following the classification of species of animals, biologists such as Linnaeus, Buffon, and Blumenbach separated mankind into races.

As soon as the notion of racial differences became widespread and sanctioned by science, some writers took this to mean that some races were superior and others were inferior. There was a social "need" for this kind of pseudo-science to serve as a justification for slavery, since slavery became much more economically profitable while ideological currents associated with the American and French revolutions, as well as the whole philosophy of the Enlightenment, gave people the impetus to abolish slavery and recognize the equality of man. While there was this popular "need" for a racist justification, historical evidence also seems to indicate that the writings of some early biologists and pseudo-biologists served as propaganda to further encourage race prejudice.

The period from 1830 to 1880 saw the development of the racist theories, especially in two nations, Germany and the United States. With the development of these theories, relations between groups became much more strained and took the form of open conflict and severe persecution. The doctrines spread to eastern Europe, to the British Empire, and to some other parts of the world, but—except for short periods—they have never been quite so virulent in producing race conflict as in Germany and the United States (and, more recently, in South Africa). Some European nations—such as the Scandinavian countries, the Low Countries, and Italy—have a minimum of race prejudice and conflict. Race prejudice scarcely appeared in South America and the Orient (except for Japan, which was greatly influenced by Germany and where racism was encouraged by an empire-seeking autocracy).

Anti-Semitism, as a racial doctrine, began in Germany and Austria after the end of the Napoleonic wars.[20] It was used for political purposes, to rationalize the movement for national integration and the expansionist aims of the allegedly superior "Teutonic" or "Aryan" race at the expense of all lesser peoples (including the French and the British). Many of the latter were supposed to be dominated by Jews. A whole pseudo-science grew up to support the doctrines, and groups and political parties were formed to express their hatred of Jews. The movement continued, with ups and downs, until it was taken over by Hitler as one of his major devices in strengthening his control over Germany and as one of his major weapons in weakening other nations. While Germany and eastern Europe had seen a good deal of organized violence against Jews between 1870 and 1933 they now went in for mass murder and torture. Practically all of the Jews in Germany proper were killed by 1945, and only a few emaciated thousands were left in the other countries directly under German control. It is estimated that the Germans and their allies killed four to six million Jews between 1938 and 1945.[21]

Czarist Russia imported anti-Semitism from Germany in the 1880's as a political device for getting popular support behind a shaky and corrupt government. The device worked, at least to the extent of getting anti-Semitism well distributed throughout the submerged and embittered

[20] A history of racist ideology in Europe is given in Erich Voegelin, *Die Rassenidee in der Geistesgeschichte* (Berlin: Junker und Dünnhaupt, 1933). Also see Friedrich O. Hertz, *Race and Civilization* (New York: Macmillan, 1928); Hannah Arendt, *The Origins of Totalitarianism* (New York: Harcourt, 1951), Chapter 2.

[21] Kurt R. Grossman, "The Final Solution," *Antioch Review*, 15 (March, 1955), pp. 55–72 (figures cited are on pages 65–66). Also see Office of U.S. Chief of Counsel for Prosecution of Axis Criminality, *Nazi Conspiracy and Aggression* (Washington, D.C.: Government Printing Office, 1947).

Russian masses. When the Communists came to power they sought for a while to eliminate discrimination and prejudice against Jews, but events, especially after World War II, revealed that the Communist government also was finding anti-Semitism a useful device for gaining popular support.

The United States has had many problems of intergroup relations (see Table 24).[22] The Negro problem has long been with us; the problems associated with Indians and European immigrants used to be formidable but are now declining; for some years there have been significant problems involving Orientals; the period between the two world wars saw a serious growth of anti-Semitism. In Chapter 8 we analyzed the caste system between Negroes and whites in the United States as an almost institutionalized form of group conflict. Once developed to govern Negro-white relations, caste increasingly tended to dominate other racial and ethnic group relations in the United States until World War II. Since then caste has greatly weakened in the United States, and conflict between racial and ethnic groups has taken a more open but less virulent form. We can give only the briefest space in this book to a consideration of the position of minority groups.

From the earliest days of American history there was a good deal of prejudice and discrimination against Indians, as well as open war. But the strongest antagonism and overt conflict were manifested in the nineteenth century. After all the Indian tribes had been beaten, or compromises were made with them in which most of their land rights were taken away in exchange for regular payments in cash or goods, Indians were restricted to reservations where they had very little contact with the general white population. Gradually a distinction was made between the Indian as an individual and the Indian as a member of a tribe. They are not obliged, as individuals, to remain in this completely segregated setup, but ownership of land, the regular payments from the United States Government, and a desire to retain their ancestral way of life, keep many of them there. Many other Indians, however, have preferred to leave the reserva-

[22] For surveys of intergroup relations in the United States, see Maurice R. Davie, *Negroes in American Society* (New York: McGraw-Hill, 1949); R. A. Schermerhorn, *These Our People* (Boston: Heath, 1949); E. F. Frazier, *The Negro in the United States* (New York: Macmillan, 1949); Paul Walter, *Race and Culture Relations* (New York: McGraw-Hill, 1952); Brewton Berry, *Race Relations* (New York: Houghton Mifflin, 1958); G. E. Simpson and J. M. Yinger, *Racial and Cultural Minorities, An Analysis of Prejudice and Discrimination* (New York: Harper, 1958); Edward C. McDonagh and Eugene S. Richards, *Ethnic Relations in the United States* (New York: Appleton-Century-Crofts, 1953); James W. Vander Zanden, *American Minority Relations* (New York: Ronald, 1963); Charles F. Marden, *Minorities in American Society* (New York: American Book, 1952); G. Myrdal, R. Sterner, and A. Rose, *An American Dilemma* (New York: Harper, 1944); A. M. and C. B. Rose, *America Divided* (New York: Alfred A. Knopf, 1948); A. Rose, *The Negro in America* (New York: Harper Torchbook, 1964); Peter I. Rose, *They and We: Racial and Ethnic Relations in the United States* (New York: Random House, 1964).

TABLE 24 · SIZE OF MINORITY GROUPS IN THE UNITED STATES, 1960–1963

		Year	Number	Per Cent
1	Roman Catholics (42,876,665) a Exclusive of Catholics enumerated below: Mexicans, other Latin Americans, Negro Catholics, Indian Catholics, Puerto Ricans, Spanish-speaking Americans living in the Southwest	1960	38,231,210	21.32
2	Negroes (including 64,569 foreign-born and 703,443 Catholics)	1960	18,848,619	10.51
3	Jews	1963	5,365,000	2.99
4	South-Western Spanish Americans	1960	3,464,999	1.93
5	Mexicans a Foreign-born	1960	572,564	0.32
	b Native-born whites with one or both parents from Mexico	1960	1,152,274	0.64
6	Indians (including 129,070 Catholics)	1963	546,228	0.30
7	Foreign-born from Balkan nations with few Roman Catholics (Greece, Turkey, Bulgaria, Rumania)	1960	324,173	0.18
8	Puerto Ricans	1960	855,724	0.47
9	Whites from Central and South America and West Indies a Foreign-born	1960	801,152	0.45
	b Native-born white with one or both parents from Latin America	1960	1,312,437	0.73
10	Japanese (including 109,175 foreign-born)	1960	473,170	0.26
11	Chinese (including 99,735 foreign-born)	1960	236,084	0.13
12	Mennonites	'59–'61	162,135	0.09
13	Minor Asian groups (including: 201, 746 Filipino; 1,976 Korean; 27,538 other Asians)	1960	249,040	0.14
	Subtotal (all minorities except for Catholics not excluded in 1a)		34,363,599	19.16
	Total (all minorities, including Catholics)		72,594,809	40.48
	Total Population of the United States	1960	179,325,657	

Sources: Felician A. Foy (ed.), 1964 National Catholic Almanac (Garden City, N.Y.: Doubleday), Negro Catholics, p. 516, Indian Catholics, p. 517; Benson Y. Landis (ed.), Year Book of American Churches for 1963 (National Council of the Churches of Christ in the USA), January, 1963, Roman Catholics, Jews, p. 248, Mennonites, p. 253; U.S. Bureau of the Census, U.S. Census of Population: 1960, Subject Reports, Persons of Spanish Surname, Final Report PC (2)–1B, South-Western Spanish American, Table A, p. ix; U.S. Bureau of the Census, U.S. Census of Population: 1960, Subject Reports, Nonwhite Population by Race, Final Report PC (2)–1C, Population Estimates for Negroes, Indians, Japanese, Chinese, and Filipinos, Tables 1–7, pp. 1–7; U.S. Bureau of the Census, U.S. Census of Population, Detailed Characteristics, U.S. Summary, Final Report PC (1)–1D, Balkan Nations, Table 163, p. 367, whites from Central and South America and West Indies, Mexicans, Table 162, p. 366, Population Estimate, Table 155, p. 349.

tion and merge into the general American life. Prejudice against them on the part of the American majority seems to have so relaxed over the last generation that this is now quite possible. There seems to be little discrimination against Indians in any aspect of life in the larger cities, although the newcomers from reservations experience the difficulties faced by most immigrants from other countries. The ban against intermarriage, usually the last barrier to fall between groups, has become so weak that many a "white man" is proud to acknowledge a small amount of Indian ancestry. Such popular American figures as Will Rogers and former Vice-President Charles Curtis were part Indian. The reservations continue as a source of conflict, mostly with the government rather than with white people as individuals. Reservation life cannot provide the standard of living which is available elsewhere in the United States, and since reservation Indians have some claim to the economic protection and support of the government, they have become organized to demand more, rather than fewer, privileges from government. The government resists this pressure and is now trying to abandon its treaty obligations to the Indians.

The hatreds against immigrants from Europe have also declined. These people had no biological differences from the majority, and when their cultural distinctions were gradually lost, the people themselves tended to merge into the general population. Especially is this true for the American-born second and third generations. The laws limiting immigration, especially those of 1921, 1924, and 1952, which are directed against immigrants from southern and eastern Europe, have restricted new influxes of people. Immigrants still come in significant numbers from other countries in the Western Hemisphere, which American law leaves relatively unrestricted, and there are the recent refugees from Fascist and Communist Europe. These are sometimes still the objects of considerable prejudice, discrimination, and conflict.

There seems to have been relatively little discrimination against Jews in the United States until about 1905. The medieval heritage left a certain suspiciousness regarding Jews, but it was apparently not considered proper to manifest this openly before 1905 and there was a compensatory feeling that Jews were once (in biblical times) favored by God and were destined to become convinced of the righteousness of Christianity. The Jews were one of the many targets in the general antipathy toward immigrant foreigners, especially after 1880. There was a slowly mounting exclusion of Jews from clubs, areas of residence, etc., after 1905, and there were a few incidents involving violence against Jews. After World War I, perhaps because of the infiltration of ideas brought by the refugee White Russians, to a culminating fear of "foreigners" in general, and to a developing "Red scare," anti-Semitism developed rapidly in the United States. The Ku Klux Klan, moribund since the 1880's when it had been a main repressive force against the newly liberated slaves in the South, suddenly revived and attracted membership in the North as well as in the South. Its targets were not only Negroes, but Jews and Catholics as well. Another major development was that Henry Ford, the well-known automobile manufacturer, became convinced of the authenticity of the Czarist Russian forgery called

"The Protocols of the Elders of Zion"—which purported to prove that Jews were engaged in an international plot to seize control of the world. He established a newspaper, the *Dearborn Independent,* and for six years did all he could to slander the Jews. In 1927 Ford publicly repudiated his campaign and said he had been misled. The Klan, prosecuted by the federal government for various illegal practices, also declined. But by this time anti-Semitism had become somewhat popular.

In 1933 Hitler came to power in Germany and began to foster anti-Semitic campaigns all over the world. A study by Strong[23] reveals that anti-Semitic organizations grew in number and strength after 1933, which indicates that Hitler's campaign was effective and fell on fertile ground in the United States. Some of these organizations were fly-by-night affairs, but those led by Father Coughlin, Gerald L. K. Smith, and William Dudley Pelley had a great deal of influence. The United States became much more anti-Semitic, even though the alleged reason—the different culture and appearance of Jews—was declining. The United States Government broke up the anti-Semitic organizations that were receiving German funds during the war, but some were able to continue through support from within the United States. Since 1946 these organizations have declined and it is generally considered "not respectable" to precipitate incidents against the Jews. Nevertheless there are widely held anti-Semitic attitudes just below the surface of appearances.

Formerly there was a good deal of prejudice and violence against the Chinese in this country, but around 1900 the Chinese accepted segregation in residential areas and in occupations so that they became "accommodated" second-class citizens without much display of prejudice against them. A good deal of sympathy for them was engendered by the Sino-Japanese War of the 1930's and 1940's, and they have been able to emerge gradually from behind their wall of segregation.[24]

Feeling against the Japanese was stimulated by a handful of propagandists, working mainly on the West Coast, beginning around 1900. Since the Japanese in the United States were hard-working, non-protesting, and self-segregating, this campaign had only minor effect on the nation as a whole until the late 1930's. As it became apparent that Japan was an imperialist nation, and that it would likely go to war against the United States, hatred and fear mounted, even against those Japanese who were American-born, had American citizenship, and were American in their loyalties. The climax came with the Japanese attack on Pearl Harbor. There were all sorts of false rumors of treason and sabotage, and there

---

[23] Donald Strong, *Organized Anti-Semitism in America, the Rise of Group Prejudice During the Decade 1930–1940* (Washington, D.C.: American Council on Public Affairs, 1941).

[24] S. W. Kung, *Chinese in American Life* (Seattle: University of Washington Press, 1962).

were demands for internment of all persons of Japanese origin and descent. The Army took matters into its own hands and ordered the removal of all Japanese and Japanese-Americans from the West Coast into evacuation camps inland. Later in the war, those declaring loyalty were released, but the feeling against them was so strong on the West Coast that many took up permanent residence in other parts of the country. The postwar alliance with Japan and the relaxation of racial conflict generally rapidly reduced the discrimination and prejudice against Japanese Americans, so that conflict involving them as a group has all but disappeared today.

There are significant majority prejudices, discriminations, and conflicts involving Mexicans, Filipinos, Puerto Ricans, Hindus, and other Americans of non-Nordic appearance. These frictions have been much less studied than the others discussed. There are many organizations engaged in trying to reduce intergroup friction, prejudice, and discrimination, and they have had considerable success in certain fields and in certain sections of the country.

D   *The Types of Conflict*

While various scholars have sought to claim that intergroup conflict has a single source—such as in a struggle for control over the means of production (Marx) or in an inevitable opposition because of racial differences (Gumplowicz)—a survey of actual cases in history reveals that there are several distinct types of intergroup conflict with correspondingly distinct causes. To insist that there is but one source of motivation for group conflict is to distort the facts and to misdirect the search for cures. A survey of historical and contemporary group conflicts suggests the following working classifications: (1) political, or conflict over scarce values; (2) ideological, or conflict over ways of life; and (3) racist, or conflict over biological dominance. Further investigation might suggest the need for further classes of group conflict, so that this classification should by no means be considered exhaustive. In a given conflict situation more than one of the motivations may be present, although historical data would seem to indicate that only one is a dominant motivation in a given conflict situation. A secondary factor in a given conflict situation should not be overlooked when it comes to formulating a practical plan of mediation, however, as it will often be a stumbling block when the basic issue seems to be resolvable.

Let us start with a brief exposition of the threefold classification of types of intergroup conflict. Political conflict has been defined as struggle for control of scarce values. If the scarce values are economic, they could refer either to the means of production, the channels of distribution, or the economic product. Class conflict, such as Marx envisioned, referred solely to the control over the means of production, which might be either natural resources and capital equipment as in our society, or slaves as in a less advanced economy. Much of modern economic conflict, however, both between nations and between classes, is not on the direct level of competition for means of production but is on the indirect level of seeking control over channels of distribution. This kind of conflict calls for more indirect, more sophisticated techniques and hence is less overt. Also we must recognize that there has always been conflict simply over the economic product itself, as in the case of organized crime, racketeering, and piracy. Piracy, which historically has sometimes taken the form of national warfare,[25] seems never to involve the means of production or channels of trade but merely the wealth carried by the vehicles of transportation. Organized crime and racketeering have thus far been studied in a criminological context, but it might also be valuable to analyze them in terms of conflict between highly organized, powerful small groups and poorly organized, dispersed, but ultimately more powerful large groupings.[26]

Scarce values need not be solely economic, although these are probably the most important ones. Power and prestige are values in their own right, and a struggle for these values can be found in groups ranging in size from whole nations down to the smallest clubs or boys' gangs. Most of the struggles we see in university faculties and professional societies are not struggles over economic values but over influence and prestige. There are other kinds of political conflict over other scarce values that may merely be mentioned to illustrate their diversity. At the present time there is conflict between the Catholic Church, the state of Israel, and the Moslem world over possession of the city of Jerusalem. This is not so much for the economic or military value of that city, but rather, primarily, for its symbolic value as the birthplace of several religions. The so-called "conflict of generations" emphasized by many child psychologists, to take an entirely different example, is not over economics or power but primarily over the value of independence (although here we border on our second major category).

Ideological conflicts have been defined as struggles for the maintenance or supremacy of different ways of life. Perhaps the term "cultural" would be more adequate than "ideological" except that that term has

---

[25] For example, the English-Spanish "war" of Elizabethan times and the Tripolitan-American war of the last years of the eighteenth century.

[26] In a sense, such an approach has been utilized by Steffens, Landesco, and Kefauver, who were not sociologists. See Lincoln Steffens, *Autobiography* (New York: Harcourt, 1931); John Landesco, *Organized Crime in Chicago* (Chicago: Illinois Association for Criminal Justice, 1929); Estes Kefauver, *Crime in America* (New York: Doubleday, 1951).

been used in so many diverse ways that it would not aid communication. In ideological conflict groups oppose two distinct sets of values, each of which are believed to be the only right and good and even necessary ones. Historically, most ideological group conflicts have been between organized religions. In recent centuries the ideological conflicts have been less religious and metaphysical than political and economic in the specific content of the values contested.

Conflict over political and economic ideologies is to be sharply distinguished from conflict for the possession of scarce political and economic values. (The distinction exists in many areas of life: someone has remarked, "Worse than an unprincipled crook is a crook with principles.") Whereas the aim of the political group type of conflict is to assume possession of the scarce values, the aim of ideological conflict is to annihilate or convert those who do not accept what the group considers to be true necessary values; or, if victory is out of the question, the aim is to avoid annihilation or conversion. Whereas the former is selfishly motivated the latter is selfless and even self-sacrificing. In religious conflict the true values are supposed to emanate from a supernatural source, and the motivation to impose these values on non-believers is considered to be service for this supernatural power. A group that denies the true God is insulting to this highest good, and therefore must be destroyed or converted.

Groups engaged in ideological conflict that is not religious in nature have substituted such forces as history or the true happiness of mankind for God. If history is believed to decree that the bourgeoisie must disappear then the bourgeoisie must be annihilated or converted to a proletarian way of life; or if the perfect utopia does not have a class of employers, then present employers must be convinced that they should not continue to perform their current role. Ideologies that are the source of ideological conflict invariably are absolutistic. The values and forces of God, history, or utopia are in some way transcendent over all others.

The third major type of motivation for intergroup conflict that we have noted is the racist one. It rests on the desire to maintain what is believed to be biological purity and caste separation. While the goal of political conflict is the seizure of scarce values and the goal of ideological conflict is annihilation or conversion of non-believers, so the goal of racist conflict is complete separation, and the strongest demands are for the avoidance of personal contact. One group, members of which consider themselves to be a biological unit or race, takes positive steps to segregate all other groups in the society from all spheres of life where they may come in contact with the active group. The segregation is on the basis of physical distance wherever possible without interfering with economic exploitation; otherwise it is on the basis of symbolic separation. Since such segregation inevitably involves material deprivations of some groups, conflict usually is the result. The terminology usually employed refers to the active group as the "dominant" one and the segregated groups as "minorities" although it must be clearly recognized that these terms refer not at all to numerical proportions within the society but to the control over power to segregate in a certain fashion.

In its efforts to segregate the minorities, the dominant group—since it does not wish to reduce its own power or restrict its control over scarce values which it currently holds in the society—is obliged to subordinate the minorities in a great variety of ways. While discrimination may not be the intention behind segregation, it is its inevitable result.[27] Some members of the dominant group may sincerely hold to a doctrine of "separate but equal," but since any movement on the part of minority persons toward the achievement of equal values necessarily involves strains on the barriers of segregation, efforts to reinforce segregation also serve as efforts to maintain the existing distribution of scarce values.[28] The motives of minorities in this situation might very well be political rather than racist—that is, in becoming the opposing group in a conflict situation the minorities' motives may not be the desire to maintain racial purity but rather to gain some control over scarce values. On the other hand, it is also possible for non-dominant numerical minorities to have racist motives and to initiate conflict. In such cases the non-dominant numerical minorities generally segregate themselves to keep their biological condition uncontaminated, and conflicts set in when out-groups find the self-segregating activities of the minority a nuisance obstructing the maintenance of the functions of the society. Groups with racist beliefs regard themselves as biologically superior, and any publicity given to that belief encourages bad relations.

Since concern over the biological composition of a population is primarily a modern phenomenon, the racist motivation to conflict is also primarily modern. However, the "chosen people" conception of the Hebrews since ancient times, the ancient Greeks' conception of their distinctiveness from barbarians (which included all non-Greeks), and a tendency found among members of many primitive societies to consider themselves as the only true "people" to be distinguished from other semi-animals suggest that the racist basis of conflict is not exclusively a phenomenon of modern Western culture.

[27] Marxist writers, in their efforts to explain all conflict in economic terms, insist that there is always *intention* to discriminate behind all efforts to segregate. See, for example, Carey McWilliams, *A Mask for Privilege* (Boston: Little, Brown, 1948); Oliver C. Cox, *Caste, Class and Race: A Study in Social Dynamics* (New York: Doubleday 1948).

[28] "The Effects of Segregation and the Consequences of Desegregation: A Social Science Statement," Appendix to Appellants' Briefs, in School Segregation Cases, Nos. 8, 101, 191 in the Supreme Court of the United States, October term, 1952, by thirty-two social scientists.

The classification of conflict into political, ideological and racist types is in terms of basic causes or motives. There are other classifications. Coser[29] makes a distinction between realistic and non-realistic conflict, in which the former is characterized by the opposition of means or ends between the two parties, while the latter arises from the need for tension release, from deflected hostility, from historical tradition, and from ignorance or error (that is, people fight when there is no "rational reason" for fighting). Kerr[30] makes a distinction between real and induced conflict, the latter constituted of cases where representatives of conflicting groups have ends to be gained apart from the ends in dispute. This would be the situation if labor leaders precipitated a conflict with management in order to strengthen their hold over the union membership. Simpson[31] distinguishes between non-communal conflict—over the very nature of a consensual framework within which individuals and groups have hitherto operated—and communal conflict—over means and subordinate ends within a consensual framework. Conflicts have also been classified according to their longevity, the amount of violence which occurs in connection with them, whether they involve primary or secondary contacts, and almost every other characteristic by which they may be distinguished.

E *The Accommodation of Conflict*

1 GENERAL CONSIDERATIONS CONCERNING CONFLICT REDUCTION

In formulating suggestions as to the techniques most likely to be effective in reducing conflict, it is important to keep these categories of conflict distinct. This is not to say that the techniques for reducing conflict must always be directed at its causes, but merely that constructive efforts to reduce conflict must take cognizance of the goals of the groups engaged in conflict. It is an oversimplification to say that eradication or control of a phenomenon requires an attack on its sources; it might just as well be successfully directed at its symptoms or its carriers. To use analogies from the control of physical disease, we may observe that the practical eradication of malaria does not involve any attack on the protozoon that "causes" it but simply on the mosquito that carries the protozoon to humans, and that control of diabetes does not involve remedying the defec-

---

[29] *Op. cit.*, p. 49.

[30] Clark Kerr, "Industrial Conflict and Its Mediation," *American Journal of Sociology*, 60 (1954), p. 234.

[31] George Simpson, *Conflict and Community: A Study in Social Theory* (New York: T. S. Simpson, 1937), p. 17.

tive pancreas but simply requires periodic injections of insulin. "Symptom treatment" is not universally ineffective.

Coming back to group conflict, we may observe that it may never be possible to reduce motivation to seize scarce values; still it may be quite feasible to prevent that motivation from inspiring group conflict. Nevertheless, it is important to know which motivation is causing the conflict, since then a more appropriate deflecting technique can be fashioned. Medical scientists do not grope for cures at random, even when they cannot control the causes of a disease, but seek some technique that will satisfactorily "adjust" or "compensate" the patient for the cause of his disease. We would thus take a position opposed to the pessimist who states that it is impossible to stop group conflict because the human motivations leading to it are ineradicable, and to the optimist who blithely treats symptoms without considering the causes.

Before turning to the specific techniques let us recognize that there are certain limits to our discussion, outside of which our suggestions would be irrelevant. The first is that a superpower which can impose itself on conflicting groups can stop conflicts even without mediation, and that no technique can stop the deliberate bullying by a superpower which no other power can successfully oppose. Only rarely, however, are powers that strong without some other power, or combination of powers, being almost as strong.

A second limitation is something of an antithesis to the first. Mediation cannot occur in a condition of absolute anarchy, when the conflicting groups communicate neither with each other nor with third parties. This is known to have occurred temporarily, but is usually not a permanent condition of group conflict.

Third, certain psychological assumptions must be made even if all the available evidence cannot be brought in at this point to support them. For example, it must be assumed that man does not have an ever-present and uncontrollable instinct of pugnacity. If man had such an instinct, conflict—by definition—could not be eliminated or even reduced. Few informed persons today hold that the instinct of pugnacity is the root of intergroup conflicts, although frequently we do hear such a cause assigned by uninformed persons. An allied assumption is, however, still made by certain social scientists, and its implication is that conflict is uncontrollable. This assumption is that man has an inherent dislike of differences, and that conflict generally follows upon recognition of differences.[32] Since differ-

[32] Earlier writers making this assumption included Nathaniel Shaler, *The Neighbor: the Natural History of Human Contact* (Boston: Houghton Mifflin, 1904); Bernard Lazare, *Anti-Semitism. Its History and Causes* (New York: International Library, 1903). A more recent acceptance of the assumption has been stated by George A. Lundberg in an un-

ences in physical appearance, behavior patterns, dress, or beliefs are constantly found among strangers, and since strangers are always present in our society, antagonism and conflict are inevitable and frequent. It is unquestionably true that there must be some differences between two groups for them to define each other as antagonists, and it is probably true that two groups in conflict seize upon and emphasize their differences. Since no two groups are alike, the dislike of differences must come after the fact of conflict, and probably serves as a rationalization, justification, and morale builder for conflict. We can thus consider dislike of differences in appearance and belief as a "necessary cause" of conflict—because it is invariably present—but not as a "sufficient cause" in the sense that it is an effective stimulator of conflict. Differences in values and interests, on the other hand, can be "sufficient causes" of conflict.

2   SOME GENERAL PROCEDURES IN CONFLICT REDUCTION

Highly integrated societies have standard techniques for stopping at least overt conflict when it is regarded as a menace to the group as a whole. This can even extend to the means of stopping war with other societies, as the following account of the Murngin suggests:

> Peace-making was also often a matter of elaborate ritual. In Australia an injured Murngin group invites the enemy to assemble with them. Both companies appear in ceremonial paint and stand at a safe distance from each other, then the hosts dance over to their guests and informally walk back. The opposite side responds in the same way. The men accused of instigating the murder that caused the late unpleasantness then run in a zigzag across the middle of the field. Every member of the aggrieved clan hurls a headless spear at the miscreants, and those feeling most intensely throw several spears while their fellows roundly curse the enemy. To this there must be no reply lest peace be again jeopardized. Next the actual murderers must run the gauntlet in the same way, except that they are exposed to spears with stone heads. However, the old men of both groups walk about as moderators, cautioning the throwers against actually hurting their targets and the other side against answering their revilers. Finally, one of the hosts thrusts his spear through the thighs of the murderers. This signifies the atonement for the injury, removes fear of further trouble, and is followed by a joint dance to express the harmonious relationship of the former combatants. But a *slight* wound suggests a mental reservation, hence only a truce, while a mere scratch serves as a direct notice of vengeance to come. Even apart from this contingency the peace nego-

published paper, "The Survival of the Moralistic-Legalistic Orientation in Sociology" (1952).

tiations may easily merge into another battle if one of the participants gets excited. In any case, however, there is a standard technique for closing hostilities.[33]

In complex cultures such as our own, the means of putting an end to overt conflict are seldom so formalized and ritualized. As might be expected, formalized methods of putting an end to conflict are more likely to be found in those central institutions of our society that are more universally accepted and where conflict itself takes something of the form of a cere-mony. Conflict between political parties, for example, is kept rather care-fully within certain bounds and the techniques of accommodation through conferences leading to compromises and the vote. Private lawsuits may be considered as a ritualized conflict in which the judge's decision is the formalized means of achieving a settlement.

The Quakers and the Group Dynamicists[34] have advocated a means of settling disagreements among groups of individuals by aiming at what is called "the sense of the meeting" or "consensus." If the participants of the meeting are not too far from each other to begin with, they can often reach a compromise by discussion, which is then accepted and enforced by means of group pressure on the individual. There is an assumption in this process that there is a fundamental harmony among men, that if men of different opinions are presented with all the relevant facts, they will come out with a common opinion. This is probably true in a Quaker meeting, or its equivalent, where all the participants hold the same social values and have very similar interests. But where individuals have different values and/or interests, one of four outcomes seems likely if agreement is the required outcome of the meeting: (1) Some individuals willingly give up their per-sonal values or act contrary to their interests in return for the psychological satisfaction of following a dominant group leader or of gaining group ap-proval. (2) Some individuals unwillingly conform but retain their private opinions and express them in action when the group is no longer around to put pressure on them; in this case the consensus is rather a fiction which has little relation to behavior. (3) Some individuals, perceiving that their point of view is being submerged by that of the majority or that of the more aggressive members of the group, simply leave and detach them-

---

[33] Robert H. Lowie, *An Introduction to Cultural Anthropology*, rev. ed. (New York: Farrar and Rinehart, 1940), p. 229. Permission granted by Rinehart and Company, Inc., copyright holders.

[34] The Quakers are a religious denomination, more correctly known as the Society of Friends, which was founded in the seventeenth century. Group Dynamics is a school of social psychology founded by Kurt Lewin in the 1930's which promotes both scientific research and a philosophy of social life. It is in the latter respect, especially as indicated by its National Training Laboratory at Bethel, Maine, that we are concerned with the Group Dynamicists here. For approving descriptions of the "consensus" method, see Morris L. Cooke, "The Quaker Way Wins New Adherents," *New York Times Magazine*,

selves completely from the group. (4) Some individuals do not see, and therefore deny, the existence of differences.[35]

This mode of conducting a meeting is put forward as an alternative to the formal discussion, utilizing Roberts's "rules of order" or the equivalent, which culminates in a vote. The minority in such a formal meeting, while no happier with the outcome than the minority in a "consensus" meeting (and perhaps even less so), have at least had the opportunity to express their dissent and are free to try to convince some members of the majority to change their minds. Modern society, with its heterogeneity and complexity, requires the formal type of meeting if it is to be democratic, since accommodation rather than agreement is all that is possible if the individual is not to be submerged. Those who would impose the consensus type of meeting on people with different values and interests, and use group pressure to enforce this consensus, are practicing a form of tyranny.

Both "consensus" and the vote are simply the end products of the accommodation process. We shall now turn to a consideration of what can take place in the process itself, and consider how conflict can most effectively be deliberately turned from violent to non-violent forms or into a tentative accommodation. The latter activity we shall call *mediation*. Mediation implies the existence of a "third party," the mediator who is neutral between the conflicting parties, but it is quite conceivable that the mediation process can occur without a formal mediator.

3   MEDIATION AND THE TYPE OF CONFLICT

Certain suggestions about mediation can be formulated by considering the different goals of conflicting groups outlined above. Political conflict over scarce values tends to be both the most frequent kind of group conflict and also the type most amenable to mediation, since it is based on rational motives. The mediation process, which gets the conflicting groups to communicate with each other and to bring the best available information to bear on the values under conflict, may be able to get the conflicting parties to compromise—that is, to share the scarce values in certain proportions. Shares might be divided according to several principles, such as the relative power of the group, the need of the group, the abstract justice involved in the claims of the group. Mediation is especially successful in getting conflicting groups to compromise when it can be demonstrated to them that they are sacrificing other values in order to continue the conflict

---

June 17, 1951, pp. 21 ff.; Kenneth D. Benne, Leland P. Bradford, and Ronald Lippitt, *Group Dynamics and Social Action* (New York: Anti-Defamation League of B'nai B'rith, 1950).

[35] This last position is substantiated by Sheldon Stryker, "Attitude Ascription in Adult Married Offspring-Parent Relationships," unpublished Ph.D. thesis, University of Minnesota, 1955.

over certain values. A systematic study needs to be engaged in by the mediator to determine what those other values are that are being sacrificed. Certainly the conflict itself involves a certain sacrifice of values: conflict is always costly in some way. Even nations at war have been induced to call an armistice when it has been demonstrated to both sides that they have more to lose by continuation of the war than by its cessation.[36]

When the conflict involves a violation of law, sometimes the mere agreement to cease further conflict and ignore prosecution for the illegal quality of the conflict activity will serve to stop the conflict. There have been times in history when pirates and racketeers have been only too happy to stop their predatory activities upon the promise of immunity from punishment by government, and the government has been willing to accede as it is too weak to devise any effective means of stopping the conflict by physical or legal force. On the other hand, such a procedure is sometimes regarded as destructive of the prestige of the law.

Clarification of the aims of the conflicting parties will often aid in the resolution of conflict. Even though the conflict may basically be carried on for rational and selfish purposes, groups often add a whole series of secondary claims to justify and rationalize their conflict activity in order to maintain group solidarity and morale. These aid the group in carrying on the conflict but are impediments to mediation of the conflict. If the mediator can determine what the basic goals of the conflict groups are, he can, by adroit maneuvers to which we shall refer in greater detail later, readily get the group to slough off its secondary demands.

For example, some trade unions in France, Germany, Italy, and perhaps other countries claim to desire nothing less than the complete expropriation of the means of production from the employer class and sometimes make even more extreme demands, such as the complete physical elimination of the employer class. Actually it is quite possible that these trade unions, or at least the workers who form their membership and strength, would be willing to accept an equitable distribution of an increased economic product instead of the more drastic demands, especially if it could be shown that a less destructive and more institutionalized conflict process can permit an increase of the total economic product for the workers as well as for the employers. Such a compromise has actually been achieved in Sweden, and to a lesser extent in the other Scandinavian countries, and it seems to be on its way in Great Britain and even the United States. While the threat of strike remains as an ultimate possibility, in effect strikes become eliminated and the conflict takes place over a bargaining table at which a resolution is always achieved by compromise.

[36] Most wars after the religious wars of the sixteenth century until World War II were stopped by such compromise; "unconditional surrender" was never their goal or their achievement.

These observations suggest a further one. Some political conflict—especially that between labor and management—may arise basically out of a desire to satisfy a rational need. It has been suggested by many sociologists, at least as far back as Durkheim[37] that modern industrialized society disrupts satisfying social relations and creates an alienation from cultural values. Subjectively this is felt as a deep sense of personal insecurity. Studies of suicide,[38] mental disorder,[39] family disruption,[40] and industrial relations[41] give empirical support to this thesis. Other writers have suggested that the modern development of formal and informal associations, especially those intended to take some action in the society, are correctives for this.[42] A specific and important example would be the case of workers, with a sense of personal insecurity, banding together into a trade union to set some limits on the impersonal social forces that control them and to regain personal security through power conflicts with those who are perceived to create the insecurity (i.e., the employers).[43] Conflict of this type thus rests ultimately on certain socially created needs, according to this theory. If the theory is correct, conflict could be avoided by satisfying the needs as completely and expeditiously as possible. The solution would have to be worked out by further research and by trial and error, but in general it would take the form of increasing personal security and social participation. In industrial relations this would involve concessions, mostly by employers to workers, but some by unions to individual employers at the expense of free competition. The theory and the suggested solution for conflict have relevance for ethnic conflicts as well as for industrial conflicts.[44]

Still another kind of compromise can occur, although rarely, where it is possible to demonstrate that both parties stand to gain their full goals if they cease the conflict. This actually occurred in the cessation of conflict between Britain and India when Britain got fuller economic cooperation

[37] Émile Durkheim, *The Division of Labor in Society* (1st French edition, Paris: Felix Alcan, 1893; latest American edition, Glencoe, Ill.: Free Press, 1947).

[38] For example, Emile Durkheim, *Suicide* (1st French edition, Paris: Felix Alcan, 1897; American edition, Glencoe, Ill.: Free Press, 1951).

[39] For example, R. E. L. Faris and H. W. Dunham, *Mental Disorders in Urban Areas* (Chicago: University of Chicago Press, 1939).

[40] For example, R. C. Angell, *The Family Encounters the Depression* (New York: Scribner's, 1936).

[41] For example, Elton Mayo, *The Social Problems of an Industrial Civilization* (Camridge, 1945); Karl Polanyi, *The Great Transformation* (New York: Farrar and Rinehart, 1944); W. L. Warner and J. O. Low, *The Social System of the Modern Factory. The Strike: A Social Analysis* (New Haven: Yale University Press, 1947).

[42] See Chapter 9, Section C, and Chapter 10.

[43] Frank Tannenbaum, *A Philosophy of Labor* (New York: Alfred A. Knopf, 1951); Arnold M. Rose, *Union Solidarity* (Minneapolis: University of Minnesota Press, 1952).

[44] Arnold M. Rose, "Intergroup Anxieties in a Mass Society," *Phylon,* 12 (fourth quarter, 1951), pp. 305–18.

from a free India than it did from a controlled India and the Indians got their independent government. Such might be the basis of resolution in the conflict now pending between the three great Western religions over the use of the city of Jerusalem. A free Jerusalem—open to members of all three religious faiths alike and under the control of no one government—might serve the interests of all the faiths better than the exclusive control by one of them over the Holy City.

Whatever means are employed to accommodate conflicts of the power type, the mediator must use great skill to overcome the non-rational psychological barriers to accommodation. The "face" of each party must be saved, and the hostile emotions generated must, like steam, be allowed to vent themselves harmlessly (perhaps against third parties, such as the mediator himself).

Before turning from the power type of conflict we should give brief attention to an issue that has divided experts in international relations for a long time[45] and that is relevant to conflict in other spheres as well. The issue is whether consensus is needed between potential contenders as a precondition to the cessation of conflict between them. One aspect of the matter can be dealt with summarily, even though it still divides specialists in international relations. This involves the question as to whether an essential prerequisite to peace is consensus on the value of not resorting to violence to settle differences of interests. Such a value is not found among all subgroups in *any* society, since crime with violence is found in all societies. Even though it is possible to instill this value in many of the subgroups, there is no certainty that new subgroups will not arise that will be willing to resort to violence to gain their ends. Thus other groups can hold a value of non-violence only if there is a superior authority which can forcibly suppress violence and isolate its perpetrators for at least a while. The practice of non-violence in the absence of such authority leads to death; Gandhian non-violence is no exception, since the British Government was a legal authority suppressing violence at the same time that it used violence on occasion against the Indians.

Much the same case can be made against the prerequisite of a general consensus (outside of the specific value of non-violence) for the maintenance of international peace. There is no great amount of consensus within large and culturally heterogeneous nations; it is the presence of a powerful legal authority in them that keeps conflict within bounds. What is probably true in the consensus theory is that there must be enough common culture between contenders for them to communicate with and understand each other. While this is probably true within most nations—thus

[45] Richard W. Van Wagenen, *Research in the International Organization Field,* Publication No. 1 of the Center for Research on World Political Institutions (Princeton, N.J.: Princeton University, 1952).

permitting conversations that lead to compromise—a serious question can be raised as to whether it is true between nations at present. Perhaps this degree of consensus must be reached before effective international compromises can be attained. This is the only element of validity a sociologist can find in the theory that consensus must be developed before wars can be abolished. This is not to say that wars are inevitable; the development of legal forces superior in power to any single potential contender and of conflict-preventive machinery could greatly reduce the possibility of war. In fact, we may have already reached such a point with the invention of hydrogen and atomic bombs, controlled not only by the United States and the Soviet Union but also partly by a large international public opinion to which both nations for different reasons are sensitive. International public opinion is a new force that seems to be more powerful than any single nation. While mutual understanding may be a prerequisite for mediation, it is not a sure cure for conflict. The fact that understanding the real motives of an opponent may increase, rather than decrease, tensions should not be lost sight of.

Ideological conflict is the most difficult type to resolve, since both groups have the goal of either annihilating or converting the other, and since to compromise is to betray one's highest ideals. Policing by a powerful third force has been the only historical way in which satisfactory control has been established to prevent the victory of one side over another. This was the basis, of course, of the *Pax Romana* and to a lesser extent of the *Pax Britannica* and is, of course, now the goal to those who seek a strong United Nations as a force superior to any single nation that might wish to eliminate, on the most ferocious of ideological grounds, any other nation. But this goal has not yet been achieved in the contemporary world, and even if it were it would involve the use of force to prevent other kinds of force, especially when one of the contending parties is so fanatic as to prefer death to compromise of any of its principles.

Direct argument against an idealistic contender or suggestions for compromise only serve to irritate him further. The means of change must come from fairly indirect procedures. Sometimes it can be shown that the ideologies of the contending groups themselves are opposed to force. This has always been a partially effective technique in dissuading religious Christians from annihilating Jews. It is conceivable, although I would not be too sanguine about the method, that zealous Communists could be persuaded that their ideology encourages them to wait until the capitalist enemy is ripe for self-destruction rather than to take up the sword to force his demise. Sometimes diversion of the contenders is also a means of at least delaying or postponing conflict on an ideological basis.

Ideological contenders usually have many enemies, including internal ones, against which they may direct their antagonism. Thus the specific serious conflict in which ideological contenders are engaged is, in one sense, a matter of mere historical accident. A wise mediator might be able to encourage the deflection of the antagonism from a serious channel into a relatively harmless one. The advantage of this is that, like all other social institutions and behaviors, ideological fervor does change and sometimes even disappears through forces inherent in it—although we would not want to consider this an inevitable law of history.

Racist motivations to conflict have something of the ideological quality of resistance to mediation, but certain techniques developed out of understanding of the psychological basis of racist conflict have alleviated, moderated, and reduced motivations behind this kind of conflict. Whereas ideological conflict is based upon a positive desire to serve the highest good, racist conflict is ultimately based upon fear. Those promoting racist conflict are afraid that their progeny will degenerate if there is amalgamation, and hence that their civilization will decline. (Of course in ideological conflict, too, non-dominant groups may also have fear—fear of forced conversion rather than of amalgamation.) Activities that alleviate the fear will tend to alleviate the motivation for racist conflict. Scientific information that racism is based upon a biological fallacy will have its effects on a significant number—although not on all types—of racists. Demonstration to the dominant group that the minority group is not interested in biological penetration—i.e., intermarriage—but rather in equal civil rights, will have its effect on still others. From my own experience I have seen how the mere demonstration that "racial" minorities were present in only small numbers and that they were not growing in numbers served to alleviate substantially the fears of some hostile racists.[46] Still other techniques to reduce the motivation to racist conflict have been suggested by an understanding of the psychological basis of this motivation, to which we may now turn.

F   *Psychological and Sociological Factors in the Reduction of Conflict*

Various psychological theories seek to explain the motivation for aggressive behavior. At least two difficulties present themselves in translating these

[46] A few investigators have demonstrated the relationship between prejudice and exaggeration of the numbers of minority persons. In South Africa, for example, a group of public service examination candidates were asked to "underline the percentage that you think Jews constitute of the whole population of South Africa: 1 per cent, 5 . . . , 10 . . . , 15 . . . , 20 . . . , 25 . . . , 30 per cent." The mode of their estimates was 20 per cent, whereas the true figure was slightly over 1 per cent. E. G. Malherbe, *Race Attitudes and Education* (Johannesburg, South Africa: Institute of Race Relations, 1946).

theories so that they have a practical value for the mediator. One is that the theories have been developed in an effort to explain individual behavior, whereas the conflicts we are concerned with are group conflicts. In so far as a psychological theory claims to explain all of individual aggressiveness, however, it must be relevant to a consideration of group conflict since a group cannot engage in conflict unless a sufficient proporation of its members, or at least its leaders, are individually motivated to engage in that conflict. To apply a psychological theory of individual aggression to the explanation of group conflict we must assume and seek a social situation common to the members of the group which activates the psychological mechanisms. A caution must be observed, however. It is possible to have conflict without hostility (as in certain labor-management disputes), and it is possible to have hostility without conflict (as when a worker hates his employer but can do nothing but resign his job or bear with it, because there is no union in his shop). Conflict is a sociological phenomenon, whereas hostility (or aggressiveness) is a psychological phenomenon, and while there is a correlation in their manifestations, there is not necessarily a perfect relation or equivalence between them.

A second drawback in applying psychological theories to the formulation of hypotheses concerning the possibilities of mediation of group conflict arises from the fact that while there have been numerous excellent researches supporting the psychological theories, each of the theories is independent of the others and fails to indicate the social circumstances under which the psychological mechanism posited would be activated. None of the evidence supporting one theory limits its applicability nor does it disprove any of the other theories. We are thus faced with a number of unintegrated theories concerning the psychological motivation of aggressiveness, each well supported by the evidence and each purporting to explain all of individual aggressiveness, and in that sense to be mutually exclusive. As a result, one who is concerned with concrete conflicts is as yet obliged to use his imagination to determine when each of the mechanisms might be operating, thus limiting their usefulness from the scientific standpoint. The next state of research in the social psychology of aggressiveness and conflict needs to be a delimitation of the social situations under which the psychological mechanisms come into operation.[47]

1   AGGRESSION AS A PERSONALITY TRAIT

One theory, first formulated by certain psychiatrists and later supported and partially verified in research by psychologists, is that tendencies to

[47] I have suggested some hypotheses for this delimitation in an essay, "Inter-group Anxieties in a Mass Society," op. cit.

conflict are a manifestation of a troubled and insecure personality.[48] The insecurity is held to have its roots in improper care and training of the person during his infancy. Ernst Simmel, for example, developed the theory that the person with tendencies toward strong racial antagonism is one who has never learned to love, and that hatred must therefore govern all his environmental relationships.[49] Other psychiatrists have looked to more specific, buried traumatic experiences. Direct mediation cannot, of course, eliminate these deep-seated tendencies to aggression. Only psychiatric therapy would suffice, and if the tendency is so widespread as to be a source of a major group conflict, such a procedure obviously demands too much time to be practical. *Preventive* psychiatry is in order, however, as a means of avoiding the development of hostility drives in the younger generation, and short therapy sessions may be used with the leaders of group conflict even without the active compliance or awareness of the individuals involved. Experienced mediators have actually employed this approach, often without being aware of the psychiatric nature of the technique. By offering unceasing affection and personal generosity to the leaders of the contending groups, mediators are sometimes able to build up a sense of personal confidence and to satisfy a "need for love" that retards individual motivation toward aggression.

Another suggestion for the reduction of intergroup conflicts offered indirectly by the theory that tendencies toward aggression have their motivation in individual personality malformations is that the object of aggression can be transferred from one group to another. This is a procedure involving a change in social definition, a technique that is rapidly being developed by public-relations experts. In the United States, for example, organized campaigns have changed the social definitions of such politically significant terms as "isolationism" and "price control." Even in the group-conflict area we may note how the social definition of "Japanese" changed partly from that describing a weak and foolish little people before Pearl Harbor to a sly, clever, and fanatic race during World War II and to an easily led and friendly people under General MacArthur's guidance after the war. The purpose of the public-relations campaign is not to eliminate the motivation to group antagonism but to deflect its expression from one object to another.

This practice may seem like eliminating one problem at the expense

[48] T. W. Adorno *et al., The Authoritarian Personality* (New York: Harper, 1950); Nathan W. Ackerman and Marie Jahoda, *Anti-Semitism and Emotional Disorder* (New York: Harper, 1950); B. Bettleheim and M. Janowitz, *Dynamics of Prejudice* (New York: Harper, 1950); Richard Christie and Marie Jahoda, *Studies in the Scope and Method of "The Authoritarian Personality"* (Glencoe, Ill.: Free Press, 1954).

[49] Ernst Simmel, *Anti-Semitism: A Social Disease* (New York: International Universities Press, 1946), pp. 37–78.

of creating another, much in the pattern of psychiatrists who eliminate one psychopathic symptom by repressing its motivation so that the motivation seeks outlet in the formation of another symptom. Such a situation may be the unfortunate outcome of a public-relations program that merely redefines the object of aggression, when the antagonism has its root in personality malformation. On the other hand, the antagonistic tendencies may be made to express themselves toward harmless objects or may even be directed to real sources of social difficulties for the antagonistic persons. The mediator has a large enough job, to say the least, in helping to prevent the outbreak of, or in helping to bring an end to, a specific war, a specific race conflict, or a specific strike. He cannot be expected to solve all the problems of a nation, of a racial group, or of organized labor, even though he has a general moral obligation to avoid creating new problems for the groups with whom he is dealing in his efforts to stop an immediate conflict problem.

The process of socially redefining a group that is the object of antagonism of another group may also have some effect on what has already been referred to as one of the "necessary causes" of group conflict—namely, a sense of antipathy toward certain differences. The actual observable differences between dominant and minority groups, for example, are not nearly so great as the differences between the stereotypes which each group has of the other. Propaganda could both bring people's stereotypes closer to reality and make what differences do exist appear less significant. Much of the propaganda put out by organizations seeking to improve race relations is now exactly of this sort. It seeks to minimize people's distortions of racial and cultural differences and to interpret what differences there are in such a way that they will not be regarded as dangerous or distasteful.

2   AGGRESSION AGAINST A SYMBOLIC SUBSTITUTE

A second type of psychological theory offering a possible explanation of the individual motivation to aggression holds that a group against which there is apparent hatred is not really hated for itself but because it serves as a symbolic substitute for another object that is *really* hated but against which hate cannot be admitted. One cannot express antagonism against certain objects because it is socially taboo to do so, because it would seem foolish to do so, or because one has ambivalent attitudes and really likes as well as hates the object. Under such circumstances, according to the theory, one seeks a symbolic substitute object, which is psychologically identified with the real hated object, toward which to exhibit overt and conscious antagonism. Variations of this theory have been advanced by psychoanalysts, historians, and sociologists, but it cannot yet be said that the theory has had any but presumptive evidence supporting it.[50]

[50] Sigmund Freud, *Moses and Monotheism* (New York: Alfred A. Knopf, 1939); Maurice Samuel, *The Great Hatred* (New York: Alfred A. Knopf, 1940); Carl J. Friedrich, in I.

In so far as symbolic substitution is a psychological motivation for group conflict, the motivation could be reduced if the symbolic identification could be revealed to the antagonistic persons. People who repress one hatred and substitute another for it resist having the unconscious identification made conscious for them. They then have to face the facts of their basic hatred or seek a new symbolic identification, but the old prejudice would have to disappear. Another technique open to the mediator faced with symbolic antagonisms is to show the antagonistic persons how the substitute symbolism—that is, the group against which there is antagonism—is really an unsatisfactory substitute for the real underlying hatred. Objective facts can make a psychological identification seem unsatisfactory. For example, members of the hatred group can be shown in settings and engaged in behaviors that are completely out of accord with the hated object with which they are identified.

3   AGGRESSION AS LEARNED BEHAVIOR

The third theory of psychological motivations behind aggression is based upon classic theory and research in psychology. It holds that group antagonisms are learned by a process similar to the learning of any other behavior. The motivation to group conflict can thus be transmitted from parent to child, generation after generation. In so far as psychologists have learned the mechanisms underlying learning,[51] they are also familiar with the process of unlearning or relearning. These theories and processes have been but infrequently applied to group antagonisms.

The final theory of psychological motivation to individual aggression to be mentioned here is the much-publicized frustration-aggression or displacement theory.[52] The theory states, in simplified terms, that when people do not, or cannot, hit back directly at the frustrations of daily life, they are inclined to be generally aggressive. The persons toward whom they are aggressive are those who are weak and cannot retaliate or those who have been traditionally defined as safe objects of aggression. The theory does not require that these "scapegoats" be the objects of aggression. In fact,

Graeber and S. Britt (eds.), *Jews in a Gentile World* (New York: Macmillan, 1942), pp. 8, 18; Jacques Maritain, *A Christian Looks at the Jewish Question* (New York: Longmans, 1939), p. 41; Joshua Trachtenberg, *The Devil and the Jews* (New Haven: Yale University Press, 1943); Lewis Browne, *How Odd of God: An Introduction to the Jews* (New York: Macmillan, 1934), esp. pp. 225–38; Arnold M. Rose, "Anti-Semitism's Root in City Hatred," *Commentary,* 6 (October, 1948), pp. 374–78; Margaret Halsey, *Color Blind* (New York: Simon and Schuster, 1946); Helen V. McLean, "Psychodynamic Factors in Racial Relations," *Annals of the American Academy,* 244 (March, 1946), pp. 159–66.

[51] E. R. Hilgard, *Theories of Learning* (New York: Appleton-Century-Crofts, 1948).

[52] This theory is best expounded in John Dollard *et al., Frustration and Aggression* (New Haven: Yale University Press, 1939), especially p. 31. In terms of displacement, the theory is well expressed by David W. Petegorsky, "The Strategy of Hatred," *Antioch Review,* 1 (September, 1941), p. 377.

the theory holds that if the original frustrating conditions are clarified and if the frustrated persons can engage in action directed against these conditions, displacement can be avoided completely. If the original frustrating circumstances are such that no direct action can be taken in relation to them, some other insignificant thing that aggression cannot hurt can be substituted as the object of displaced antagonism. There may even be displacement of aggression onto oneself. In labor-management conflict, mediators, even without specific knowledge of the frustration-aggression theory, occasionally seek to displace aggression directed toward the opposing parties onto third parties, such as the government, competing businessmen or labor groups, a church organization, or even the mediator himself.

G   *Hypotheses Concerning Successful Mediation*

Turning now to the social role of conflict and mediation, we note the paucity of information concerning the historical circumstances under which conflict has developed and become intensified and under which mediation has been successful in being called into operation and in resolving the conflict. In addition to a historical study, a comparative cross-cultural study needs to be conducted, to specify the social conditions under which conflict has been most prevalent and mediation has been most successful. We know, in a vague way, that intergroup conflicts are not equally frequent under all forms of social structure, and that within a given society conflicts have periods of increase and periods of decrease, but we have no systematic knowledge as to the social conditions accompanying these variations. To have the greatest value, this historical and comparative research should be guided by carefully framed hypotheses. To illustrate the character of the hypotheses a few examples with respect to mediation will be mentioned.

Perhaps the most important hypothesis is that if social structures are set up in anticipation of group conflict, and techniques developed to reduce friction, mediate opposed interests, and otherwise seek to prevent the rise and spread of conflict, they can often make a greater contribution than can efforts made *ad hoc* after a conflict situation is fully developed. This is at least true if the contenders are not both overwhelmingly powerful. Levi has made this point, with a great deal of support from history, in regard to international conflict.[53] In race and ethnic conflict, the point was widely made after it was discovered that a government survey anticipated the 1943 race riot in Detroit but that there was no agency, private or public, that could take action to prevent the outbreak of the riot. Since 1943 hundreds of local public organizations, and more than a thousand private ones,

[53] Werner Levi, *Fundamentals of World Organization* (Minneapolis: University of Minnesota Press, 1950).

> The policeman uses violence illegally because such usage is seen as just, acceptable, and, at times, expected by his colleague group and because it constitutes an effective means for solving problems in obtaining status and self-esteem which policemen as policemen have in common. Since the ends for which violence is illegally used are conceived to be both just and important, they function to justify, to the policeman, the illegal use of violence as a general means. Since "brutality" is strongly criticized by the larger community, the policeman must devise a defense of his brutality to himself and the community, and the defense in turn gives a deeper and more lasting justification to the "misuse of violence." This process then results in a transfer in property from the state to the colleague group. The means of violence which were originally a property of the state, in loan to its law-enforcement agent, the police, are in a psychological sense confiscated by the police, to be conceived of as a personal property to be used at their discretion. This, then, is the explanation of the illegal use of violence by the police which results from viewing it in terms of the police as an occupational group.
>
> William A. Westley, "Violence and the Police," *American Journal of Sociology*, 59 (July, 1953), pp. 34–41. From Conclusions on p. 41.

have been set up in the United States, and have as one of their functions the foreseeing and avoidance of overt race conflict. While several cities have had incipient riots—Chicago alone has had a dozen incipient riots in the years following World War II—these agencies, with the cooperation of a great variety of other community organizations whose aid they enlisted, have prevented the outbreak of full-scale race riots such as occurred fairly frequently before the war. The 1964 federal Civil Rights Act set up a federal agency to reduce community tension and, hopefully, to avoid race riots.

The possibilities for success in mediation do not depend solely on understanding and doing something about the causes of conflict.[54] There are conditions relative to the mediation itself which affect the likelihood of its success or failure. Hypotheses concerning the conditions under which conflict-prevention machinery is likely to be formed and utilized can be formulated from common experience. If mediation is a voluntary matter, a party that considers itself the stronger in the dispute will request or permit mediation only if it has good public relations or a more permanent reconciliation as one of its aims.

Another hypothesis is that mediation is avoided when one side to a dispute believes that there are advantages—either intrinsic or in terms of maintaining the current favorable distribution of power between the two

[54] The following hypotheses emerged during the author's study of mediation of labor disputes: "Needed Research on the Mediation of Labor Disputes," *Personnel Psychology*, 5 (Autumn, 1952), pp. 187–200.

sides—to maintaining the conflict situation. For example, leaders of a labor union may avoid mediation of a strike if they believe that the strike is "educating" the membership of the union in some desired way, or if they have reason to believe that the balance of power is turning in the direction of the union's ultimate victory in the dispute.

A third hypothesis is that mediation will be sought and have possible success only when the parties to the dispute have a common framework of definitions and values so that they can communicate with each other, and when there is a belief on the part of each party that the other will abide by the terms of any agreement reached in the mediation. This hypothesis gains support from the observation of the failure of "third-force" countries such as India in their efforts to mediate between the United States and Russia in current international disputes.

Logically, it would seem that the likelihood of a mediation's being successful after it is under way is a function of (1) the attitudes with which the parties enter the mediation; (2) the intrinsic difficulty of solving the conflict—that is, the number and the complexity of the changes in the objective situation that have to occur before a resolution can be reached; (3) the perception during the mediation process of a compromise, adoption of which will give both parties greater advantages—material or psychological—than a continuation of overt conflict; and (4) the ability of the mediator to discern such compromises, to help the parties to perceive the merit of such compromises, to transform conflicts on the unconscious level into conflict on the communicable level, and to communicate viewpoints of one party so that they are understandable to the other party.

The role of the mediator as a "third person" needs to be investigated. He may be regarded as a "stranger"[55] who has wisdom and objectivity. He may be regarded as a friend who is trying to help out, or as a benevolent father figure who is to show the quarreling boys how to make peace, or as a stern father figure who has no business entering a private quarrel. He may be regarded as an expert who may be relied on to give relevant and reliable advice, as a representative of a third interest who is in opposition to both of the contending parties, and so on. Some of these perceived roles may provide the mediator with certain assets in an effort to resolve the conflict, whereas others may hinder his efforts. The possibilities for him to manipulate and change his role during the different stages of the mediation need to be studied. The specific powers of a mediator are usually very limited, but the powers that he has—to hold the parties in conversation, to speak to them privately, to determine the order in which they present their points of view—need to be investigated for their potentialities in reducing conflict.

Finally, we may list a few of the controllable conditions of the media-

[55] Georg Simmel, *Soziologie* (Leipzig: Duncker and Humbolt, 1908), pp. 685-91.

tion situation itself that have some influence on the success or failure of the mediation. Since next to nothing is known about their effects, we shall pose them as questions: the relative effectiveness of presentation of facts over against value arguments, the psychological consequences of taking a hypothetical position "for the sake of discussion," the effectiveness of presentation of false statements as facts, the psychological effects of digression and other tension-relieving devices, the reference to outside threats and outside interests, the possibility of substituting purely symbolic or "psychological" satisfactions for material ones, the usefulness of bringing all matters into the open as over against the suppression of certain sources of conflict either temporarily or permanently, the relative value of the creation of a primary-group atmosphere during mediation as over against the value of formality, the technique of getting the greatest psychological value out of minor concessions, the mentioning of values not under conflict in the original dispute but as possibilities for future dispute, the uses of drama, emotional outbursts, delay, created "crises," and reference to comparable cases. Our consideration of all these possibilities in mediation suggests that mediation is at least as complicated a process as conflict itself.

FOR ADDITIONAL READING

COSER, LEWIS A., *The Functions of Social Conflict* (Glencoe, Ill.: Free Press, 1956). A test of Georg Simmel's hypotheses about conflict that provides one of the most thoroughgoing statements of conflict theory.

DAHRENDORF, RALF, *Class and Class Conflict in Industrial Society* (Stanford: Stanford University Press, 1959). A study of class consciousness and class conflict.

GOULDER, ALVIN W., *Wildcat Strike* (Yellow Springs, Ohio: Antioch Press, 1954). A study of an industrial strike not authorized by the union.

ROSE, A. M., and C. B. ROSE, *America Divided: Minority Group Relations in the United States* (New York: Alfred A. Knopf, 1948). A text on race, nationality, and religious group antagonisms.

WILLIAMS, ROBIN M., JR., with the collaboration of John P. Dean and Edward A. Suchman, *Strangers Next Door: Ethnic Relations in American Communities* (Englewood Cliffs, N.J.: Prentice Hall, 1964). A monograph based on a wide range of theory and methods, bringing together a large amount of data, and arriving at both theoretical and practical conclusions.

17 * Morale and Group Solidarity

A The Nature and Characteristics of Group Morale

1 DEFINITION OF MORALE

All integrated groups have purposes, even if sometimes these are not stated explicitly and even if group activity does not always work to achieve group purposes. The effectiveness of a group in achieving its purposes seems to be primarily a function of three things: (1) the social setting in which the group operates, which can be either hostile or conducive to the group's purposes; (2) the internal structure and resources of the group—that is, the extent to which it has realistic means of operating in relation to its purposes; (3) what is sometimes called the "morale" or "solidarity" or "cohesiveness" of the group. The first two of these variables have been given some consideration in earlier chapters;[1] the third one is the subject of the present chapter.

Men have probably always been aware of group morale ever since they could observe that some tribes had a strong internal organization—perhaps even though the tribe was small—whereas others were weak and disorganized, and ever since they could observe that in some families the members were bound by strong internal bonds whereas in others there was so little sense of mutual obligation that the family fell apart. Social philosophers and historians, such as Ibn Khaldun (fourteenth century), have made many wise observations about group morale, and military leaders, such as Napoleon, have proclaimed its crucial importance for military effectiveness. But social scientists did not begin systematically to study morale until the late 1930's, and even today much is left to be

[1] See Chapters 5 and 9.

learned. Among the important studies on the subject are those on how the American family weathered the Great Depression and World War II,[2] how ethnic minority groups fought the prejudice directed against them,[3] how soldiers and civilians carried on the war effort,[4] and how occupational and industrial groups efficiently achieve their purposes.[5]

It soon became apparent to the students of morale that the word "morale" was being used in many different ways. While it cannot be said that one definition is better than any other, sociologists have tended to limit their interest to what they call *group* morale, which they usually define as a tendency for members of a group to hold together, to oppose the group's enemies, to be proud of their affiliation with the group, and to be willing to sacrifice their personal interests to the group's goals. Since the word "morale" has been used in so many different ways, it might be desirable to use the term "solidarity" to refer to what the sociologist means. Psychologists tend to use the word "cohesiveness" with roughly the same meaning, but since most psychologists think of a cohesive group as one in which the members know one another and like or admire one another, this sets a further limitation on the definition which the sociologists do not imply. Members of a group with high solidarity or group morale need not know one another personally and many of them may even dislike each other personally. It is enough that they have an awareness of the existence of a group to which they feel they "belong" and that they have at least a

[2] Robert C. Angell, *The Family Encounters the Depression* (New York: Scribner's, 1936); Ruth S. Cavan and K. Ranck, *The Family and the Depression* (Chicago: University of Chicago Press, 1938); Earl L. Koos, *Families in Trouble* (New York: King's Crown Press, 1946); Reuben Hill and Elise Boulding, *Families under Stress* (New York: Harper, 1949). While not dealing with families, the following volume was an important study of the effect of the depression on morale: E. A. Rundquist and R. F. Sletto, *Personality in the Depression* (Minneapolis: University of Minnesota Press, 1936). For a comprehensive survey of the literature on how the family reacts to disaster, as well as hypotheses for future research, see Reuben Hill and Donald A. Hansen, "Families in Disaster," in G. W. Baker and D. W. Chapman (eds.), *Man and Society in Disaster* (New York: Basic Books, 1963), pp. 185–221.

[3] S. Frank Miyamoto, *Social Solidarity among the Japanese in Seattle* (Seattle: University of Washington, 1939); Kurt Lewin, "Self-Hatred among Jews," *Contemporary Jewish Record*, 4 (June, 1941), pp. 219–32; Arnold M. Rose, *The Negro's Morale* (Minneapolis: University of Minnesota Press, 1949).

[4] E. L. Munson, *The Management of Men* (New York: Holt, 1921); G. G. Bruntz, "Allied Propaganda and the Collapse of German Morale in 1918," *Public Opinion Quarterly*, 2 (Winter, 1938), pp. 61–76; Goodwin Watson (ed.), *Civilian Morale* (New York: Houghton, Mifflin, 1942); Samuel A. Stouffer *et al.*, *The American Soldier* (Princeton, N. J.: Princeton University Press, 1949), 2 volumes; I. L. Janis, *Air War and Emotional Stress* (New York: McGraw-Hill, 1951).

[5] Arnold M. Rose, *Union Solidarity* (Minneapolis: University of Minnesota Press, 1952); Morris S. Viteles, *Motivation and Morale in Industry* (New York: Norton, 1953); George M. Beal, "Member Identification with Farmer Cooperatives," unpublished paper presented at Midwest Sociological Society, April, 1955.

minimum positive attitude toward the group (not necessarily toward its individual members as persons) and toward the group's goals. Another term that has sometimes been used as equivalent to morale is "group identification," in which the emphasis is on the individual's tendency to emphasize his unity with the group.

Group morale is always defined in positive terms, but it should be recognized that the attitudes that make it up can sometimes have a neutral, or even a negative, content. Under certain special circumstances morale can consist solely of hatred of the enemy. Then there is the phenomenon of "group self-hatred" in which an individual for some reason hates or despises a group to which he belongs, and he even hates himself for having some of the group's characteristics. Under some circumstances improving morale might be considered as a decrease in group self-hatred.

Morale is not the same thing for an individual as for a group. An individual belongs to several groups and therefore has different morale in the different groups. Even within a single group, his morale would vary with the different tasks that the group engages in. The morale of a group changes over time and is a highly fluctuating thing. When a group is first formed one kind of morale prevails, while at a later stage another kind of morale would be expected to predominate. Morale is a function of the group in relationship to other groups. There may even be a certain conflict between the groups in so far as they relate to the morale of an individual who belongs to several groups. The morale of one group may lower the individual's morale in another group. An example would be the case of an army draftee who comes from a happy family with a high morale. The fact that he was such a good member of his family and the family had such high morale may be detrimental to his army morale.

Morale can be related to each of the defining elements of a group. Both members and non-members of a given group tend to be aware of these elements, although their definitions and evaluations of them are seldom identical. In the first place, there are the group goals, which are more or less the common purposes of the individual members. Second, there is the history or tradition of the group, which provides its members with a subculture so that they are able mutually to adjust and coordinate their behavior to each other better than to the behavior of non-members. Third, there are usually group symbols—such as trophies, songs, rituals, writings, uniforms, or some other readily observable object or behavior—which serve as reminders of the unity of the group. Fourth, there is generally an ideology that serves to justify the group goals and to explain the need for the continued existence of the group—that is, to give reasons for evaluating highly the group and its goals. Fifth, there must be special channels of communication; either the members have the possibility of speaking to each other directly or they have a common source of communication such as a newspaper or travelers who go to and fro among them. Sixth, a group has a structure for achieving its goals; this includes, at the minimum, specialization of roles of members—mainly a hierarchy of leaders and followers—and means of achieving a group judgment as to how it is going to act more or less as a unit in a given situation.

The above are elements of all groups; otherwise they could not be considered as groups. Morale operates on each of these, so that a group with high morale is distinguishable in many respects from a group with low morale. First, in regard to group goals, the group with high morale vigorously tries to achieve them and the members are strongly agreed on the great value that is placed on the group goals. Second, the tradition of a group with high morale is clear to all members (even if the tradition is partly mythical) and they are able to predict each other's behavior in group-relevant settings fairly accurately and so coordinate well with each other. Third, a group with high morale has pride in its symbols and uses them very often and/or with great solemnity. Fourth, the ideology of a group with high morale is highly adequate to its function of justifying the existence of the group and its goals. Fifth, the channels of communication of a group with high morale are open and clear, so that consensus readily develops among the members. Sixth, members in a group with high morale carry off their roles in the division of labor appropriately (for example, the leaders are authoritative and inspire confidence) and—in our society at least—the members feel that they have a voice in setting group policy (that is, the structure has at least the appearance of being democratic). Thus we see how the morale level of a group is intimately related to all aspects of the structure of that group.

By way of summary, we cite the definition of morale given by Herbert Blumer:

> Group morale exists as a disposition to act together. Morale has two fundamental factors: The relation of the group toward its goal and the relation of the members of the group to one another. The ability of a group to realize an objective or goal depends on the intensity of its inclination toward that goal and on its capacity of sticking together as a group. Morale centers around these two features. Where morale is high, there is a persistence in carrying out the task of the group and a willingness to stick together on behalf of the group cause. Morale is poor when there is little attachment to the goal and where there is no effective willingness toward joint undertaking. Morale is undermined when adherence to the goal is lessened, as through disheartenment, and where there is a break in the spirit of cooperation, as through dissension.[6]

[6] Herbert Blumer, "Morale," in W. F. Ogburn (ed.), *American Society in Wartime* (Chicago: University of Chicago Press, 1943), pp. 207–32.

2   HYPOTHESES CONCERNING THE CAUSES
OF HIGH GROUP MORALE

The above considerations provide some clues as to what outside causes, or "independent variables" as they are usually called, contribute to the morale of a group. The following hypotheses about factors contributory to high group morale are sometimes applicable only when individual members have the possibility of leaving the group.

1 If the members of a group have the possibility of direct and frequent contact with each other, they are more likely to have higher morale than if they are scattered over a wide area and there are many barriers to communication among them.

2 If the members of a group evaluate their common goal highly relative to their other particular goals, they are likely to have higher morale than if their particular values seem more important than the common value. Individual interests reduce attention to the goals of the given group, especially when the former are seemingly in logical opposition to the latter. A corollary of this is that anything which raises the value of the common goal, or contributes to agreement in the members' perception of the common goal, enhances group morale.

3 If a group has a fair proportion of successes in the pursuit of its goals, it will have higher morale than if it experiences an unbroken series of failures. The history of labor unions has pointed up the fact that morale deteriorates unless there is at least an occasional success in working toward group goals. There is evidence of truth in the old adage, "Nothing succeeds like success," at least on its negative side. A corollary of this proposition is that if members of a group come to believe that their goal is not ultimately attainable, the group will have low morale.

4 If a group successfully demands personal sacrifices from its members, it is more likely to have high morale than if nothing is expected from the members for the benefit of the group.[7] What appears to happen psychologically when a personal sacrifice is made is that the member seems to feel that he has made an investment in the group and hence he feels that he has more at stake in its success. But this proposition has limitations, which is suggested by the second proposition, since if the group demands too many sacrifices of an individual it will begin to conflict with his personal and outside interest. It is also true that if a group places too many constraints on its members, it will lose its members. Finally, if the deprivations involve prolonged physical debilitation, the deprived individuals will no longer be able to internalize the meanings

[7] This observation seems to have first been made by Kurt Lewin, *Resolving Social Conflicts* (New York: Harper, 1948), p. 199.

and values of the group and their morale will thereby deteriorate.[8]

5 Carrying this "sacrifice" idea another step, it seems that if a group punishes (not too strongly) its members for infraction of its central rules having to do with the group's purposes or relations among members, it will have higher morale than if it allows members to do what they wish at the expense of the group. The group gains authority and respect if it can maintain its rules, and other members feel some compensation for their hurt if the offender is punished.[9]

6 If the rest of society, or significant segments of society outside the given group, accord high prestige to membership in the group, it will have higher morale than if the outside society despises membership in the group. This proposition contradicts, to a certain extent, the third proposition, which pointed up the need for opposition from the outside. It is possible, of course, for a group to get both opposition and prestige from the outside, either if these two things come from different segments of the outside society or (more rarely) if the opposing groups respect the given group while combating it. The latter seems to occur in labor-management relations, where respect on the part of union members and managers for each other seems to be greater if one opposes the other in a firm, gentlemanly fashion than if one is completely subservient to the other. The best example of high group morale stimulated by approval from one highly evaluated part of the outside world and by conflict with another, low-evaluated part of the outside world is an army. A nation that evaluates its army highly and effectively expresses this high evaluation is likely to have an army with high morale. A United States Army officer phrased the need for civilian support behind the army in terms of an analogy:

"When you are playing a football game, you like to feel that all the students are behind you. You want them to come out to watch the game, cheer their heads off and give you something to make you want to play like you never played before. But when you are playing to empty grandstands it isn't so easy."[10]

Another example of the same sort of thing applying to a different kind of group occurs when an ethnic minority group is supported by its nation of origin in its conflict with a prejudiced majority in the country of residence; its morale is then higher than if the group feels unsupported.

[8] Arnold M. Rose, "Social Psychological Effects of Physical Deprivation," *Journal of Health and Human Behavior*, 1 (Winter, 1961), pp. 285–89.

[9] This observation seems to have first been made by Durkheim in the form that the collective punishment of crime reintegrates a society whose bonds have been loosening. See Émile Durkheim, *The Rules of Sociological Method*, trans. S. A. Solovay and J. H. Mueller (Chicago: University of Chicago Press, 1938).

[10] *New York Times*, June 9, 1943, p. 8.

7 If any external event occurs that enhances the clarity or the value of the group's goals in the eyes of the members of the group, their morale will be increased. There is much evidence that workers' morale and productivity are enhanced when they are presented with a clear picture of the total work process or when their products are dramatically shown to have great social value.

8 If outside groups set barriers to the exit of members from their given group, the group will have higher morale than if members can "escape" the group whenever they wish. This negative pressure to remain in a group is not especially morale enhancing, but the opposite situation—in which members can "escape" at will—is detrimental to morale. Caste groups that do not have the other sources of morale we have considered sometimes exist as functioning groups on the basis of this factor alone. A military group faced with exposure to death is helped to remain a unified and functioning group by preventing its members from leaving (through physical force coupled with group pressure).

9 If the members of the group have "stable" and "adequate" personalities, the group will have higher morale than if members have personality deficiencies, especially if those deficiencies are connected with the ability of the members to relate themselves to each other and to their purposes. Thus the purely psychological variables influence the social phenomenon of morale as an "outside" force, conceptually speaking.

10 If individuals are removed from family and friends and deprived of the opportunity to engage in familiar, satisfying habits—as recruits are when they are inducted into the armed services or as "casuals" are when they are attached to a new military unit—their morale will be low until new friends are made and new habits are established. In other words, a new group that is erected by forces outside the members themselves will start out with low morale. Factors tending to raise the morale of such a new unit include: (a) ease of interaction; (b) facilities for the establishment of regular habits; (c) clear specification of the goals of the group; (d) an outside danger that demonstrates that all members of the group are "in the same boat" and dependent on one another.

11 If the members of a given group belong to other groups, and if these other groups have values and activities not in opposition to those of the given group, the morale of the members of the given group will be higher than in the case where the values and activities of the other groups are in opposition. That is, role conflict is detrimental to morale.[11]

[11] There have been several studies of what happens to the individual when he is a member of two groups whose values happen to conflict in certain respects. The phenomenon is usually termed "role conflict." See, for example, Samuel A. Stouffer, "An Analysis

12 If the group is divided into subgroups that have some conflicting purposes and values, the morale of the group will be lower than if there are no such internal conflicts.

13 Collective experiences—that is, events occurring to members of a group in a group setting so that they remember the events as common to the group—enhance group morale, especially if the experience involved deep emotions. The collective experience is often commemorated in a symbol, which is accidentally or purposely associated with it.

14 Conditions that produce leaders having abilities and other traits which enhance the confidence of the rank-and-file members in them tend to raise the morale of the group. For example, if there are ways in which potential leaders can get realistic training in effective leadership, the greater number of effective leaders produced ought to raise the morale of the group.

In addition to the above propositions about factors that affect the morale of a group as a whole we may note a few additional propositions about the morale of specific individuals within the group.

1 If the individual does not believe his own contribution toward the group's activity in pursuit of its goal is worth while, or if he does not understand how his personal contribution helps the group's activity, his morale will be low.

2 If he is treated by the group or its leaders as of no consequence— for example, by being "bossed around" without reason, by displayed lack of concern for his personal problems and interests—his morale will be low.

3 If an individual believes he does not know the best available techniques for making his contribution to the group goal, or is not on his way to learning them, his morale will be low.

3   SOME EFFECTS OF HIGH GROUP MORALE
ON INDIVIDUAL BEHAVIOR

Whereas the above hypotheses deal with outside influences on morale, certain other illustrative propositions can be advanced concerning the influences of morale on other aspects of behavior.

1 The higher the morale in a group, the more likely are individuals to conform to the expectations which others in the group have for their behavior.

2 The higher the morale in a group, the more can accepted leaders influence the behavior and attitudes of the members of the group.

---

of Conflicting Social Norms," *American Sociological Review*, 14 (December, 1949), pp. 707–17; Bernard C. Rosen, "Conflicting Group Membership," *American Sociological Review*, 20 (April, 1955), pp. 155–61.

3 The higher the morale in a group, the greater efforts are made by
members of the group to make the group structure more efficient.

4 The higher the morale in a group, the greater the possibility for
group members to "gripe" about specific matters of organization
within the group without hurting the group's effectiveness in working toward its purposes.[12]

This list of general propositions—or hypotheses relating to the morale of
almost any kind of human group—could no doubt be greatly extended, but
what has been advanced already will provide an adequate conception of
the nature and role of morale.

4   IDEOLOGY

We have mentioned that every group has an ideology—a generally accepted
verbal justification of the existence of the group and of the desirability
of group goals.[13] Probably every ideology has some effect in promoting
group morale, but ideologies range tremendously in the strength of this
effect. At the upper extreme, for example, there is the Soviet Communist
ideology, which is fairly complex but at its center is the notion that history
is inevitably moving in the direction of wiping out all classes but industrial
workers and farmers, and that the Communist Party is the midwife of
this change which is both inevitable and eminently desirable. It is in the
service of this ideology that millions of people today—all over the world
and of every class and educational level—devote their lives and are even
willing to be subjected to torture and death by the Communist Party itself.[14]
At a lower level of effect in promoting group solidarity would be an
ideology which once served the function of promoting group morale but
which now seems largely mythical and preposterous to the members of a
group who maintain their group identification on other bases. Such an

[12] Several independent studies have provided evidence that repression of criticisms
makes for low morale, while open expression of criticism on specific matters is consistent
with high morale. For industry: Fritz Roethlisberger and W. J. Dickson, *Management and
the Worker* (Cambridge: Harvard University Press, 1939); for unions: Arnold M. Rose,
Union Solidarity (Minneapolis: University of Minnesota Press, 1952); for military combat
units: Arnold M. Rose, "Conscious Reactions Associated with Neuropsychiatric Breakdown
in Combat," *Psychiatry*, 19 (February, 1956), pp. 87–95.

[13] For an excellent summary of thought and research on ideology, see Norman Birn-
baum, *The Sociological Study of Ideology, 1940–1960; A Trend Report and Bibliography*
(Prepared for the ISA with the support of UNESCO; Oxford, England: Blackwell, 1962).

[14] The willingness of Communists to denounce themselves for the slightest deviation
from the party line, even if it means their execution at the hands of the Party, has been
analyzed in many kinds of publications, but few have excelled in clarity the semifactual
novels of the ex-Communist Arthur Koestler. See especially his *Darkness at Noon* (New
York: Macmillan, 1941) and *Age of Longing* (New York: Macmillan, 1951). For a non-
fictional, historical account, see W. G. Krivitsky, *I Was Stalin's Agent* (London: Hamish
Hamilton, 1939). Nathan Leites and Elsa Bernant have provided extensive documentary
support for Koestler's interpretation: *Ritual of Liquidation: The Case of the Moscow
Trials* (Glencoe, Ill.: Free Press, 1954).

ideology would be the original one of the Jews—recorded in the Bible—
that they are God's chosen people, designed to prove God's supremacy and
omnipotence, and that they made a covenant with God to this effect at
the time of Abraham. Ideologies are usually accepted by the members of
the group to a differential extent.

Ideologies often claim inspiration from some supernatural power,
although what might seem supernatural to one person would not necessarily seem so to another. The effect of this is to put "God on our side," as
the German Kaiser phrased it during World War I. Ideologies tend to be
stable and even static, although the leadership of the group is often able
to change its ideology by slow stages through its power to "interpret" the
ideology in the new situations that arise. For example, during World
War II President Roosevelt was able to extend the American Creed, which
dates back at least to the Bill of Rights (1790), to the Four Freedoms.
The ideology that the United States was the land of freedom, originally
with reference solely to political freedom and civil liberties (including
Roosevelt's first two freedoms—of speech and religion), could be extended
to include freedom from "want" and freedom from "fear." The change
also internationalized the ideology, shifting it from an exclusively American possession to a set of ideals that were increasingly believed by Americans to be ideals for most of the world. Roosevelt was probably able to
get away with this change toward internationalization only by making use
of the missionary and altruistic elements already in the ideology of the
American Creed. Because of the supernatural force usually associated with
an ideology, a charismatic leader—such as President Roosevelt was—is
usually the only kind who can gain acceptance for changes in ideology.
And even so, the additions to the ideology probably have never secured
the degree of acceptance among the American people that the original
ideology has had. Changes in ideology tend to enhance group morale if
they are commonly accepted, since the changes constitute a revitalization
and a more meaningful specification of the ideology.

Thus far we have been considering morale, and its causes and effects,
as common to all groups in all settings. Actually the conditions making
for high morale in one group are seldom precisely identical with those
making for high morale in another group, especially when the groups
under consideration have different cultures.[15] There are some influences—
for example, hatred of the out-group, or rigid, externally imposed discipline—which enhance a group's morale in one culture but hurt a group's
morale in another culture. It is thus advisable for us to turn to an examination of morale in some concrete groups. The groups chosen for analysis
are the Negroes in American society and the United States Army during
World War II. Conditions affecting the morale of these two groups are

[15] Herbert Blumer, *op. cit.*

both of the general sort we have outlined above and of a specific sort that are fairly unique to these groups because of their particular histories of development.

B   *Minority Group Identification and Morale*

1   THE SIGNIFICANCE OF GROUP IDENTIFICATION

In terms of biological race or social characteristics most of the minority groups of the United States are far from being homogeneous groups. There is nothing in their biological make-up or their intrinsic social structure that holds the members together or leads them to feel a sense of kinship for one another. What mainly makes minorities into social groups is pressure from the outside and the consequences of that pressure. These create "group identification," which is defined as all the ways in which members of a group feel a sense of unity with each other and the ways by which they manifest that unity. We use the term "group identification" in a positive sense. It involves not only a recognition that one is a member of a racial or religious group because of one's ancestry, nor only a recognition that the majority group defines one as belonging to the racial or religious group. It involves a positive desire to identify oneself as a member of the group, and a feeling of satisfaction when one does so identify oneself. So defined, "group identification" is obviously equivalent to "morale," as that term was used in the previous section.

Some members of the minority groups object to the statement that group identification is a consequence of prejudice and discrimination from the majority. Obviously there are other factors, since groups that are equally discriminated against have different degrees of group identification. But the proposition is nevertheless advanced that in the United States minority groups develop group identification as an adjustment to, and a way of opposing, majority prejudice. The main reason why this is so is that American minorities have no intrinsic group purposes, while the similar individual purposes of their members are to integrate into general American society in their own way; thus opposition from the outside to their integration provides them with a common group purpose that becomes the basis upon which group morale can develop. At first a common tradition may keep the members of an ethnic group united. But this is not a group purpose, and without majority prejudice minority groups would gradually merge with the majority in all ways and disappear as separate entities, especially in the United States because of the mobility, the diversified contacts, and the pluralistic social structure characteristic of contemporary American culture. Usually the process takes longer with the lower class members of the ethnic group than with its upper and middle class members, because the former experience deprivations which they may attribute to discrimination because of their ethnic group rather than their class. This has happened with Germans and Scandinavians, against whom there was formerly much prejudice, and is now happening with the Irish. In Brazil, with the decline of prejudice, Negroes have been absorbed, and in China the Jews have completely merged into the dominant population. One of the necessary early stages in the amalgamation of groups is the disappearance of group identification. The loyalty to one's group and the desire to see it remain independent and strong must decline. Some individuals may resist the decline of group identification and participate in movements to "save our unique culture," but unless the group succeeds in separating itself, the absence of barriers to communication and contact will gradually eliminate all differences, biological and cultural, between the groups. Group morale then declines, but the individual members of the group then form new groups—on bases other than those of racial or nationality background—and new group identifications are formed.

While the decline of majority prejudice tends to decrease group identification, the mere presence of strong prejudice against a group will not guarantee that it will have strong group identification. Within the United States there is far from being a perfect correlation between the degree of prejudice against a group and the amount of group identification that that group has. Some minority groups have increased their group identification markedly in recent years without there being any corresponding increase in majority prejudice against them. These variations, their causes, and their effects, are the main focus of interest in this chapter.

When a minority group is the object of prejudice from the majority group, and yet has low group identification, it is in a sad state. The members of the minority are so ashamed of their subordinate status that the only thing they think of is to escape being identified as a member of the minority. They change their names, they disavow their ancestors, they avoid associating with other members of the group. They can develop no effective organization to protest the discrimination against them, or to fight for an improvement of group status. When one of their number is made the object of violence or other unusual deprivation, they sympathize, but do nothing to retaliate or to prevent a recurrence. In such a situation the only thing the members of the minority have in common is the characteristic of being picked on by the majority group for certain alleged reasons. This is the very definition of low group identification.

Group identification grows up as a defensive device; after developing, it becomes one of the major offensive devices. When the majority group is engaged in activities designed to harm members of a minority group and to make them feel inferior, the latter have certain reactions and seek certain compensations. They look back into their history for evidence

against the majority group's charge that they are culturally inferior. Sometimes they go so far as to find that their group has produced the world's
greatest statesmen and artists. They examine the current uniqueness in
their culture and label them manifestations of folk genius. Their apologists
produce evidence that most cultures, especially the culture of the majority
group, borrowed something from their culture, but little attention is given
to their own borrowings. They organize to protest, in strategic instances,
against manifestations of prejudice. They put pressure on those members
of their own group who act out the role demanded of them by the majority
group. All these things cement the group into a fighting force. They give
the group self-confidence, pride, bonds of loyalty, basic understandings
that allow for extensive communication without many words. In other
terms, they give it morale and solidarity. The individual member of the
minority group is not only able to withstand the majority's attacks on his
body and mind, but he is also transformed into a disciplined soldier to
fight the enemy. There are, of course, great differences of opinion, of personality, and of experience between members of a minority group, but
when group identification is high, they act as if cast in the same mold
when confronting the majority group. The character of this group identification will now be examined for the Negro minority, because changes in
its group identification have been so rapid that we can examine that phenomenon more easily.

2   EARLY HISTORY OF NEGRO GROUP IDENTIFICATION

Under slavery there was little opportunity for Negroes to identify with
their group. Most of them were repressed and in a low-status position; they
were not allowed to communicate with each other; few of them were
allowed to read or learn what was going on in the world; divisions among
them were encouraged by the masters.[16] Yet, although history is far from
complete on the subject, there are some evidences of group identification
in the slave period. The records show fifty-five mutinies on the slave ships
bound for America;[17] there were at least 250 slave revolts in the continental United States;[18] stories have come down from ex-slaves of secret
religious meetings;[19] there were an effective "underground railroad" and
abolitionist movement, in both of which some Negroes were active;[20] there

[16] This has been brilliantly described by Stanley Elkin, *Slavery* (New York: Grosset,
1963).
[17] Harvey Wish, "American Slave Insurrection Before 1861," *Journal of Negro History*,
22 (July, 1937), pp. 303–06.
[18] Herbert Aptheker, *American Negro Slave Revolts* (New York: Columbia University
Press, 1943), p. 162.
[19] Social Science Institute, Fisk University, "Unwritten History of Slavery: Autobiograph-
ical Account of Negro Ex-Slaves" (Nashville, Tenn., 1945), mimeographed.
[20] Henrietta Buckmaster, *Let My People Go* (New York: Harper, 1941).

were white patrollers on all southern roads to watch for runaway slaves and evidence of mutiny. The songs, both sacred and secular, express a spirit of protest: "Let My People Go," "Walk Jawbone, Come Jine de Re [railroad]." There were petty ways of outwitting and thwarting the whites, as by slowing down on a job, stealing a little, telling falsehoods or protective jokes. These had other motivations, such as laziness, greed, and humor, but they were also a form of protest and a way of manifesting to other Negroes that the race was not actually so stupid as the whites made out. Although all these influences helped to promote Negro group identification, it should not be thought that the group feeling was strong. The existence was too animal-like for group pride to develop; it was too repressed for effective protest.

Freedom gave a great lift to Negroes, and they gained a new awareness of their potentialities. Education was their biggest aim; both old and young went to school or took home lessons in reading. There was a good deal of interest in politics; few ran for political office, but most wanted to vote and to learn what the political issues were. There was some struggle during the Restoration of white supremacy, and the struggle lasted all the way into the 1890's, despite the severe repression in the South and the loss of interest by the North. But all through the Reconstruction and Restoration Negro group identification was not high in absolute terms, except among a few intellectuals. The prevailing ignorance and poverty effectively inhibited communication at first, and then the terror of Restoration forcibly repressed it. High morale, except for work, was the last thing the white South wanted of its Negroes. It was all right to encourage the Negroes to be happy, but everything smacking of group identification had to be wiped out. The main effort of the whites was to kill or terrorize Negro protest leaders and to encourage the compromise leaders. They, therefore, acclaimed Booker T. Washington's rise to leadership as a sign of victory.

Washington's philosophy was to make the best of a bad situation—to "cast down your buckets where you are." Instead of striving for equality all along the line, he felt that the Negroes should restrict themselves to striving for a better occupational position and for the education that would give it to them. While this may have been the only practical philosophy for Negroes living under the terror in the South, it was not conducive to high group identification. The best that a Negro could look forward to was a decent job, but no legal protection, no vote, no opportunity to use cultural or recreational facilities built for "the public." Clearly, Negroes could have little pride in themselves when their aims were so low, their leaders so humble. There was no Negro protest worthy of the name between 1890 and 1900. This was effected by Washington himself, as well as by the whites, since he had to keep the Negroes quiet in order to get anything for them. By virtue of the power granted him by the whites from President Theodore Roosevelt on down, Washington could control the appointments and promotions of most Negroes to academic, governmental, and business posts. No Negro institution could secure funds without his consent. Perhaps because he was forced to be weak in the presence of the whites, Washington was arrogant toward other Negroes and did all he could to stifle their protest.

Negroes were now in communication with each other, and were not legally divided into freedmen and slaves. Thus there was a basis for stronger group identification, and the fact that it was not strong made Negroes feel all the more hopeless. The situation was that there were Negro *advocates* of Negro subservience during a period in which Negroes were acquiring education, and after a period in which they had experienced freedom and a rapid rise. In this situation it was to be expected that some of the college-trained Negroes would rebel against the Booker T. Washington philosophy. In 1903 a most brilliant and courageous Negro scholar, Dr. W. E. B. Du Bois, attacked Washington in some of his writings, and was forced out of his post as professor at Atlanta University. He then organized a group of Negro intellectuals whose aim was to rebuild the Negro protest (although they were not interested in "race pride"). The Niagara Movement, as it was called from its first meeting place, accomplished very little, since it had no funds and it did have the powerful opposition of Booker T. Washington. It did, however, succeed in reviving interest in academic education, as over against Washington's type of vocation education, and it forced all informed Negroes to take their individual stands in favor of accommodation or protest. In 1909 a group of whites formed an organization to stop the terror against Negroes, and the following year it merged with the Niagara Movement to form the National Association for the Advancement of Colored People (N.A.A.C.P.). This event was the beginning of a new protest spirit among Negroes, which has steadily promoted group identification up to the present day.

Negroes now had an organization, supported by able and courageous whites, that would fight for their rights as citizens. Its initial successes in the federal courts, its exposure of the excesses of the southern terror, its ringing appeals to courage and faith, quickly caught the attention of a large part of the brooding, fearful population. Other organizations— notably the National Urban League and the Southern Interracial Commission—came into existence to improve the Negro's position in other respects. Beginning in 1901 with the *Boston Guardian,* and in 1905 with the *Chicago Defender,* the Negro press took its modern form of hammering home to its Negro readers that they should be proud of their race and that they should protest against discrimination. All these influences began to raise Negro group identification and morale.

The first major manifestation of the change, and a factor that itself helped to promote the change, was the great migration from South to North that began in 1915. Although the Emancipation allowed Negroes to migrate where they wanted to, there was no significant migration out of the South until 1915. Among the reasons for this must be included the low morale of the Negroes. They were held by the terror; they tended to believe the myth that the only occupations they would ever be fitted for were those of farm hand and servant; they were afraid to find out how to travel and how to find a place to live when they arrived.

The new protest movement beginning around 1910 helped to raise morale, the demands of war-boom industry in 1915 provided the economic opportunities, and Negroes migrated northward in great numbers. Although there were tremendous difficulties in finding a place to live, in becoming adjusted to the drastically different culture in the North, in learning the new type of jobs in which they were engaged, the migrant Negro population was greatly stimulated in morale, which promoted new protest activity. It is suggestive that, once the migration began, it continued even through the early 1920's and the 1930's, when job opportunities were sharply curtailed and even many northern Negroes lost their jobs. The North's chief contribution to the Negro was the regular security, the absence of violence and of the threat of violence that the southern Negro had constantly to be aware of. In general the northern white ignored the Negro, except in a purely economic relationship, and did little deliberately to improve his economic or cultural status. But there was no effort to restrict the vote, there was fairly equal treatment by the police and courts, and there was no restriction on the Negroes' efforts to improve themselves. For the young Negro there were good schools leading all the way to the top of the educational ladder. Almost immediately Negroes felt the urge to build their group defense, as well as to taste their new-found personal freedom. The circulation of the northern Negro newspapers received a tremendous boost. Membership in the N.A.A.C.P. rose so rapidly that by 1917 Du Bois was generally acknowledged as the outstanding Negro leader in the United States. The migration was a protest against the South which took the form of an escape from the South, and the escape allowed an increase in protest. The Negroes who migrated did not proceed to forget about the South—rather they used the new freedom of the North to articulate their grievances, to contribute to protest organizations, and to urge the remaining southern Negroes to migrate.

The years immediately following World War I were deeply disillusioning for all Americans. For Negro Americans this was especially true. Not only did they witness the display of selfish national and international politics, but they also experienced some of the bloodiest race riots in the history of the country, and they lost many of the good jobs they had gained during the war. White Americans reacted with cynicism and isolationism; Negro Americans reacted with radicalism and nationalism, both of which further contributed to group identification and morale. Nationalism was expressed in several ways: a revival of interest in Negro history and in African life, the development of new interest in problems of colored minorities throughout the world, and—most important of all—a mass movement, led by Marcus Garvey, looking forward to the establishment of a new government in Africa and the emigration of American Negroes to Africa. Garvey's primary appeal was a glorification of blackness: he condemned amalgamation with whites and told Negroes to keep their blood pure. He stimulated race pride by pointing out that Africa had civilization long before Europe had. Garvey created an organization of probably more than two million Negroes, and started a newspaper to reach his widely dispersed audience. His organization was in the nature of an American fraternal order, except that he also built commercial enterprises and had as his ultimate goal the creation of a new Negro state in Africa. Garvey became entangled in long-drawn-out legal suits as a consequence of the failure of some of his commercial enterprises. He was imprisoned for a short time, and then deported, since he was not an American citizen but had come from the West Indies. His movement was split between rival claimants and lost membership rapidly, although a few small splinter groups remain to this day. Its permanent effect on the bulk of the Negro masses was to instill race pride and interest in independence for Africa into their group identification.

Negro intellectuals did not participate in the Garvey movement, but sought, unsuccessfully, to appeal to the Negro masses in another way. Some of them were Socialists, and tried to get Negro workers interested in joining with white workers in a common front against capitalists. At least four Negro newspapers were organized to spread this message in the early 1920's. Among the editors was A. Philip Randolph, who was later to become the outstanding labor leader of Negroes. The appeal had little effect, partly because the only chance the Negroes had to get jobs in industry was by pleasing the employers, and because white workers were not at all friendly to Negroes. During the 1930's the same appeal was made by two other widely different groups with somewhat greater success. One group was the Communists, who attracted not only a number of Negro intellectuals, but also secured the sympathy of a significant minority of Negro workers, especially the unemployed ones. The second group was the C.I.O. (Congress of Industrial Organizations), which actually gave Negroes equality in its industrial unions and discouraged race discrimination among both white employers and white workers. Consequently Negroes joined the C.I.O. in great numbers. By the end of the 1930's Randolph was partisan to neither of these groups; he was one of the first outstanding

Negro leaders publicly to repudiate the Communists, and his strategy of remaining in the A.F. of L. (American Federation of Labor) prevented him from expressing any sympathy with the C.I.O.

Another expression of protest of the period following World War I was the outpouring of creative activity in literature, the fine arts, music (both serious and popular), and the other arts, all of which was known as the "New Negro" movement. While the movement was financially sponsored by individual whites, among whom the taste for "Negro" art was mainly a fad, the specific forms the art took were expressions of protest. The poetry, for example, ranged from the cynical-comic to the dignified battle call:

> *She even thinks that up in heaven*
> *Her class lies late and snores,*
> *While poor black cherubs rise at seven*
> *To do celestial chores.*
>   (Countee Cullen: "For a Lady I Know")[21]

> *Oh, kinsmen! We must meet the common foe;*
> *Though far outnumbered, let us still be brave,*
> *And for their thousand blows deal one death-blow!*
> *What though before us lies the open grave?*
> *Like men we'll face the murderous, cowardly pack,*
> *Pressed to the wall, dying, but—fighting back!*
>   (Claude McKay: "If We Must Die")[22]

The major effect of the New Negro movement on the Negro masses was to give them the realization that they had certain abilities that could impress even whites. While the New Negro movement declined during the early 1930's, owing to the waning interest and flattening pocketbooks of whites, a few Negroes were now established in certain fields of creative endeavor, and they continued to produce, and thus to give more ordinary Negroes a sense of group pride.

3   RECENT HISTORY OF NEGRO GROUP IDENTIFICATION

The great depression of the 1930's was a very demoralizing period for Negroes as individuals. More than half of the Negro labor force was unemployed in northern cities, and the only reason why the proportion was not quite so high in the South was that government relief was not nearly so adequate, thus forcing Negroes to take nominal jobs at greatly substandard wages. However, group identification and morale had developed to such a high point that they were not materially hurt by the depression. Southern Negroes continued to migrate, although in somewhat smaller

[21] From *Color* (New York: Harper, 1925), p. 50.
[22] From *Harlem Shadows* (New York: Harcourt, 1922).

numbers; the Negro poet, musician, and artist continued to produce, although more frequently for non-paying audiences or under the auspices of the WPA (the government's work-relief program). Radicalism became a more popular form of the Negro protest.

An event that occurred during the 1930's reveals the great extent to which group identification had grown among Negroes. Previously Negroes had always voted for the Republican Party, whenever they had a chance to vote, because that party had given them Emancipation and Reconstruction and a small but continuing amount of political patronage. However, the Republicans had officially renounced attempts to secure political equality for Negroes in 1876, and succeeding Republican presidents did less and less for their Negro voters. Negroes continued to vote Republican, partly as a matter of tradition and partly because the Democratic Party, with its strong support from southern whites, offered no alternative. President Hoover snubbed the Negroes in many ways, and there was some protest voting against him in 1932. When the new president—Franklin Roosevelt—came into office with a general program to aid the underdog and with relatively equalitarian policies for the Negro, a large number of Negroes switched their party affiliation to vote for him in 1936, again in 1940, and again in 1944. Voting had become a manifestation of the Negro protest. White politicians have become aware of this, and the Negroes' knowledge of their awareness enhanced the group's self-esteem.

Few Negroes voted radically during the depression. However, many more Negroes were then sympathetic to the Communist Party, for it offered them a political, economic, and social system opposed to that prevailing in the United States. Showing sympathy toward the Communist Party was another way of expressing the Negro protest. In 1935 a "Popular Front" organization—called the National Negro Congress—was created, which included the Communists along with many other groups working for the improvement of Negro status. Local councils were established in many cities, and they, as well as the national organization, were very active in expressing the Negro protest. It seemed like the beginning of a real mass movement, and Negroes were much heartened by its formation. However, a struggle for leadership soon developed, and by 1940 the Communists won, and most of the members dropped out. The organization remained largely a paper "front" for the Communist Party during the war. It revived temporarily in 1945, when Negroes joined it as a protest against the reaction following the war.[23]

Another type of extreme protest developed among Negroes during the

[23] For the complicated history of the relationship of the Communist Party to the Negroes, see Wilson Record, *The Negro and the Communist Party* (Chapel Hill: University of North Carolina Press, 1951); Wilson Record, *Race and Radicalism: The NAACP and the Communist Party in Conflict* (Ithaca: Cornell University Press, 1964).

1930's; this took on a fascist character. It began innocently and spontaneously as a "Jobs for Negroes" campaign against white-owned stores in Negro neighborhoods in large northern cities. Negro merchants also took advantage of the spirit of the campaign to urge Negroes to buy from them rather than from their white competitors. The movement took on a more sinister character in New York, Chicago, and a few other cities when racketeers put themselves in the leadership and began to harangue the Negro mobs against Jewish storekeepers. Some of them made a tie-up with the white-led fascist groups. To gain funds for the movement the usual racketeering method of destroying property unless the owner paid for "protection" was used. There is no doubt that this movement enhanced Negro nationalism, race protest, and group identification in at least the northern cities, even though it resorted to thuggery and anti-Semitism. Some of the riots, such as the one in Harlem in 1935, manifested the new nationalistic feeling.

Race pride was built on a much healthier base in the late 1930's as a consequence of the successes of Negro athletes, especially Joe Louis. Joe Louis in the public eye typified clean-cut Americanism as well as great physical strength. Not only did American whites have to acknowledge his physical supremacy, but they were proud of him when he beat Max Schmeling, the German boxer who was unpopular with many Americans because he was identified with the Nazis and because he boasted of his racial superiority. In the Negroes' pride there was also the element of competitive rivalry, of demonstrating that a Negro could beat a white man. (Negro boxers—like Jack Johnson—had earlier beaten white boxers, but they had not been as personally attractive as Joe Louis.) Subsequent outstanding Negro athletes—from Jackie Robinson through Cassius Clay—provided sources of individual identification and group solidarity. Great Negro achievers in other fields—Marian Anderson as a singer, Ralph Bunche as an international diplomat, Robert Weaver as a top government official—served the same functions for other Negroes.

By the 1940's Negroes had achieved a remarkable group identification. There were great divisions among them, and important divisive forces affected them, which we have largely neglected thus far in our history. Despite the divisions most Negroes are aware when anything happens in the country that drastically violates the rights of one of their number. A significant proportion can be counted on to protest whenever some important injustice befalls the group. For example, when the economic boom accompanying the outbreak of World War II created a demand for workers, and Negroes were not hired, A. Philip Randolph was able in a few months to organize the March-on-Washington Movement, with local affiliates. The mass meetings they held were impressive. Millions of Negroes were involved. By threatening to have Negroes all over the country march to Washington to protest the economic discrimination, Randolph finally forced reluctant President Roosevelt to order that no war contracts would be given to industries that refused to stop discriminating, and to create a Fair Employment Practice Committee (FEPC) to enforce the order.

Negroes also have had a great growth of race pride. In fact, some of them now have it in a pathological form—they have too much pride for the number of actual achievements on which pride can be healthily built. Consequently, the manifestations of pride have often taken the form of racialism and nationalism. This is understandable in view of the history we have considered and in view of the caste situation, but nevertheless deplorable from the standpoint of American democracy and from the standpoint of the Negro's own welfare. Some illustrations may be given of the extremes to which race pride has risen. A prominent Negro newspaper columnist, and one of the most widely read pamphleteers, obtains his huge audiences with such news as that Beethoven, Haydn, and the King of Sweden were Negroes. The Negro press, in addition to providing an excellent sounding board for the Negro protest, appeals to its readers with stories about the first Negro quartermaster company that happens to land on a completely safe island in the Pacific Ocean. In starting movements to get jobs for Negroes, demagogues tell their Negro audiences that they are a race much superior to the Jews. Great prominence is given to the story from Ethiopia that that country does not want a loan from the United States. This appeal to mediocrity and to race prejudice, this pride in the cultural achievements of people with whom they have no cultural connection, this claiming as race members persons who could be Negroes only in the narrowest racial terms (even if the facts are true)—all these appeals are just the sorts of thing that Negroes have been protesting against when done by white men. In thus accepting the racist premises of prejudiced whites, many Negroes are unconsciously accepting the conclusions of that kind of thinking. To believe that cultural products are outgrowths of biological race must unconsciously confirm their feelings of inferiority and their group self-hatred.

Since the end of the Second World War, Negro group identification has grown apace. The continuing migration out of the South and from rural areas to cities, the increasing general attention being paid to various aspects of the Negro problem, the growing list of outstanding achievements by Negroes, the rise of a number of independent Negro states in Africa and the participation of their leaders in activities on the world scene, the spread of a perspective on their common lot as a subordinated element in a prosperous and democratic country—all intensified Negro group awareness, race pride, and collective determination to end their second class citizenship.

The older protest and improvement organizations—which had relied

mainly on educated experts, lawyers and social workers, to raise the
Negro's status—were augmented by direct mass-participation organizations:
the Congress on Racial Equality (CORE), the Southern Christian Leadership Conference (SCLC) led by the Rev. Martin Luther King, and the
Student Non-Violent Coordinating Committee (SNCC) adopted techniques
of non-violent demonstrations, sit-ins, boycotts—techniques which had been
developed by Gandhi in India—to protest discrimination. The Temple of
Islam (more popularly known as the Black Muslims), its New York offshoot
formerly headed by Malcolm X, the Monroe Crusaders headed by the self-
exiled Robert F. Williams, the African Nationalist Movement were smaller
organizations that favored extreme (in one degree or another) tactics to
reject white America and its civilization. The former organizations, along
with the older interracial NAACP, Urban League, and Southern Regional
Council, and along with many non-Negro religious and labor groups,
broke down segregation in hundreds of Southern restaurants, hotels, and
recreational and transportation facilities; organized a peaceful March on
Washington in 1963; led a successful political fight for a strong federal
civil rights bill in 1964; pressured northern city governments for efforts
to end de facto school and housing segregation and to improve job opportunities for Negroes. Some of the extremist, nationalist Negro groups,
along with unorganized and unemployed Negro young men, started violent
race riots in several northern cities in 1964.

Negro group identification had grown so strong by 1964 that anyone
who spoke publicly against any of its manifestations received strong con-
demnation from Negroes generally (even to the point of excluding Negroes
who did this from social contacts with other Negroes). Even outstanding
successes in reducing or eliminating discrimination and segregation did
not halt the growth of Negro group identification, protest and manifestations of rejection of white America. By 1964 it became evident that the
strengthening group morale would outlast the achievement of most of the
goals for which it began to develop in the first instance.

4   EFFECTS OF NEGRO GROUP IDENTIFICATION

We have seen how, over a period of about sixty years, Negro group identification has been built up until it is now a powerful force in Negro life
in America. Despite class and other differences between Negroes, despite
the personal disorganization arising out of extreme poverty, despite the
migration to a culturally different, urban North, despite the selfishness
that inheres in any group, despite the group self-hatred engendered by
the majority's attitudes—despite all these blocks to group identification,
Negroes have built up a high degree of pride and attachment to their
group. Although many individual Negroes are personally demoralized,
group morale—in the sense of individuals seeking to further the interest

of the group and to resist attacks on it—is quite high. This is evidenced in the strong adherence to the leading defense organizations (such as the N.A.A.C.P.); the large audience of the Negro press; the high flexibility of the Negro vote; the general awareness of all events that affect the Negro group; the high sensitivity to insults and the readiness to react against insult; the willingness to participate in mass organizations when Negro leaders present a good and rational case for so doing (as when A. Philip Randolph, Roy Wilkins, Martin Luther King, and others exhorted Negroes to plan for a march on Washington in 1963); and in many other ways. As Negroes become more educated, as they continue to migrate northward and westward, as more and more of them vote, as they secure better jobs, as they achieve more success in their protest, as color differences within the group become less significant, as the protest and nationalistic organizations continue with their propaganda, as the Negro newspapers reach more people more of the time—and if all these trends persist— Negro group identification will continue to grow. On the other hand, if the contemporary trend toward increased acceptance of Negroes by whites continues, Negroes will have less and less basis for a separate group identification and it will ultimately decline.

The growth of group identification has increased the self-confidence of Negroes: it has made them less ashamed of being Negroes, and prouder of the fact that they are the group more sinned against than sinning. The growth of group identification has also materially affected Negroes' relations with whites. In the first place, it has given them more ease and poise in their personal relationships, partly because of increased education and the migration out of the South, but also because of heightened group morale. There is a much greater tendency for Negroes today to stand up straight when talking to a white man, look him in the eye, and speak clearly. The shifting, mumbling Negro with his eyes on the ground is found now only in the more backward areas of the South. Second, the growth of group identification, through the increased support of the protest organizations, has forced whites who are engaged in illegal activities against Negroes to retreat. It has been largely through the efforts of the N.A.A.C.P. and the Southern Regional Council that lynching has declined so remarkably in the South, and that so many southern whites are now in favor of *federal* intervention to stop lynching (in violation of the old southern sentiment for "states' rights"). Third, through increased and more intelligent use of the ballot, Negroes have made white politicians in many places aware that they have some political power and cannot be quite so mistreated by the police and courts, or so ignored when political appointments are made, as they have been in the past. Fourth, through their relatively high attention to national and international events that affect them Negroes understand something of the strategy of international relations, and are now beginning deliberately to promote world interest and sympathy toward themselves—and are thereby affecting America's position in the relations between nations.

In these and probably other ways the growing group morale and group identification among Negroes are having an influence on race relations in the United States. The "races" are constantly in conflict, even when physical violence is relatively suppressed and although there are many persons who individually refuse to participate in the conflict. The Negroes' aims are full achievement of democracy and its concomitants—liberty, equality, and fraternity—or, in negative terms, the elimination of the terror and of segregation and discrimination. One of the Negroes' chief supports in this battle is their feeling of strength and pride in their group and its cause.

c   *Bases of American Army Morale in World War II*

A survey of the not-too-reliable literature on the armies of other nations during World War II suggests that each army had a somewhat different major basis of morale. The German Army, for example, appears to have relied on a paternalism which made the officer responsible for the welfare and spirit of his men and which gave the enlisted man a feeling that his superior was really concerned about him, as a father is for his son. The American officer, on the other hand, usually had the "callous" attitude that his men could look out for themselves, and he tended to give them personal responsibility for their own welfare, even when they did not have the means or authority to take care of their personal needs and problems. Paternalism could thus not be said to be a source of morale in the United States Army. The Russian soldier during the war seems to have been motivated largely because his country was being invaded and his family was in personal danger. This also did not apply to the American soldier. The Japanese soldier seems to have fought primarily out of a sense of duty to his country and to his religion. Americans have some sense of duty, but that has not been the keystone of their morale. What weakened the American soldier's sense of duty was the American attitude of "looking out for number one." Not only was the enlisted man's sense of public duty initially weak, but also when nearly every officer and civilian seemed to be looking out for his own individual welfare, and the average enlisted man did not have the freedom or the power to compete against them for the necessities or luxuries of life, the enlisted man's sense of duty weakened. He suffered deprivations, but not willingly and gladly out of a sense of duty for something bigger than himself. Certainly he had none of the fanaticism of the Japanese soldier.

While it could not be maintained that there was only one root of mo-

rale in the United States Army during World War II, the proposition can
be advanced that the main thing which kept the American soldier at his
job was the habit of mind of getting a job done and the belief that the
means were available for winning the war. When the average American
soldier was given a task, he usually plugged away at it with efficiency and
even pride. This was especially true when there was the reward of ending
the war and going back home. This certainly does not mean that this trait
was not present among soldiers of other armies. But it does mean that the
American soldier was especially influenced by the drive to do a good job
and get it over with. Moreover, since he was not strongly influenced by
the other sources of morale, this one takes on an increased importance.

Because of the central role of his job for the American soldier, it was
very important that the job be not too greatly to his distaste and also that
it appear to be worth while. The satisfied soldier had to have a job that he
liked, although other things counted, too. In a mechanized war, and with
the average American having an interest in mechanical things, it was not
too hard to satisfy, at least to a large extent, a major proportion of the
soldiers. The worthwhileness of the job was defined by most soldiers in
terms of whether something tangible was being accomplished. The desire
to do a worthwhile job made many soldiers grieve when they saw the
Army wasting man power recklessly, and when they were forced to do
things in an inefficient manner. There were countless bitter "jokes" that
circulated among soldiers as to the "Army way" of doing things instead of
the right way.

The desire to do a worthwhile job brings up the often-argued question as to whether the American soldier knew what he was fighting for.
Did he know he was fighting for at least the promise of democracy and
freedom and against fascism and tyranny? Unfortunately, it cannot be said
that the average soldier knew much about fascism until the evidence of the
concentration camps was before his eyes, and even then, for example, the
efficiency of the Germans appealed to him more than did the independence
of the French. Hatred of the enemy played an important role in the morale
of the Russians and other armies, according to practically all observers.
But few American soldiers actively hated the Germans, and not many
more hated the Japanese. In a survey of combat infantrymen fighting in
Italy in April 1945, only 25 per cent said that they hated the German
soldiers. The proportion was the same for those who had been in combat
the longest. There were too few personal contacts with the enemy to cause
widespread hatred among the American soldiers. Most of those who really
hated the enemy had seen buddies killed or had been personally maltreated
by the enemy. But all along the American soldier possessed the basic ingredient of knowledge as to why he was fighting: he had the conviction
that his side was right and the other side was wrong. The "why we fight"

motive certainly did play a role in the soldier's morale, if only to increase the conviction that his job was worth doing and to banish any doubts about the goal of his efforts.

The Army's primary deliberate means of maintaining morale is through discipline. But the Army is not consistent as to what it means by discipline. Army Regulations state that discipline is manifested by prompt and complete obedience to orders. In practice, however, the "customs of the service" often overrule the regulations. Prompt obedience to orders is only a small, and sometimes even forgotten, part of discipline as it is actually practiced in the Army. As in any bureaucracy, most orders are transmitted through a clumsy, time-consuming, inflexible set of channels, and each man in the chain operates in terms of traditional routine unless a direct order from a high-ranking officer disturbs the placid inefficiency of the complicated system. What discipline has actually come to mean to the average junior officer and enlisted man is an adherence to certain traditions regimenting all aspects of life. Included in these is "military courtesy," which many enlisted men recognize as the opposite of civilian courtesy because it specifies the politenesses which the enlisted man has to extend to the officer while not providing for equivalent politenesses in return. Thus discipline is an obnoxious word to most soldiers, and it is used in a serious manner only when an officer is about to punish his men.

In practice, therefore, discipline in the way it was usually used in World War II helped to break morale rather than to build it up. In so far as discipline inculcated fear—and the Army did train enlisted men to fear their officers and the Army as a concept—it did succeed in getting men to accomplish their tasks. But that perhaps did not make for efficiency or for ability to keep on in the face of adversity (or of enemy blandishments), and it certainly did not make for high morale. The Army theory of discipline, as it was in practice rather than in the books, is best summed up in the often-used phrase, "Remember you're in the Army, soldier." When spoken by an officer, this ominous phrase brought to the mind of the average enlisted man all the unpleasant things the Army had done to him, or could do to him. His resulting sweat led him to action, but the mental cost was high.

Occasionally the Army uses the word "discipline" in another sense, as in the phrases "gas discipline" or "camouflage discipline." In this context the word means that the individual is to do those things that will protect the safety of the group under gas attack or air attack. If this meaning could be extended to the accomplishment of all the things that would increase the safety, health, well-being, and happiness of the group, the Army would have a concept of discipline that would increase, rather than decrease, morale. During World War II the average American soldier exhibited a high degree of loyalty to his group, although the group was seldom conceived to be larger than the company. There were innumerable cases of individual heroism in the war in which one man sacrificed himself for his buddies. Even when there was no heroism, the American soldier manifested admirable loyalty to his group. "Pride in outfit," to use the Army phrase, was certainly a central element in the morale of the American soldier in World War II, and counteracted the tendency to be primarily concerned with oneself. If the Army inculcated more of this, by showing the soldier its ramifications in areas other than safety and its extensions to soldiers outside of the immediate outfit, it would greatly increase morale and efficiency. The Army's needs for discipline could be obtained, not by fear, but by an appeal to loyalty to one's fellow soldiers.

All armies stress the importance of leadership, but in only some cultures is the role of the leader unequivocal. The German company commander is set up as a father to his men. The Japanese officer is a representative of the Emperor. The United States Army not only does not have these particular devices, but it is also hampered by the American tradition that leaders be acceptable to the majority of their followers. Instead of seeking to compensate for its handicaps in the field of leadership the United States Army engaged in practices that aggravated the bad situation. The junior officers were set to enforcing minor rules that were regarded as obnoxious by most enlisted men, while major regulations often went unheeded. Enlisted men were constantly subjected to needless and trivial deprivations. To use examples drawn from various camps or theaters, no extra shelves could be procured for a garrison barracks; no more than two blankets could be used; beds had to be made in such a way that they had to be remade before they could be slept in; at times no passes were given out even though the troops were not in operation, etc. On the other hand, officers were constantly given new privileges—for example, they were often taken out of barracks and given hotel rooms; they were given a liquor ration; they got first choice on tours; and many had a considerable amount of free time. The situation was summarized by enlisted men in the saying, "This is an officers' Army." When asked to express their attitudes toward twenty-six aspects of Army life, a representative cross-section of enlisted men in Italy in World War II were much more critical of the advantages that officers took than they were of any other item (for example, 27 per cent were critical of Army food, 10 per cent of Army clothing, as compared to 53 per cent who were critical of officers). There is no doubt that there is strain in the relations between officers and men in the United States Army. The deprivations of Army life overseas seemed worse to the ordinary soldier when seen in the perspective of officers' privileges, and "discipline" appeared as punishment when officers could frequently be observed violating some Army rule or another.

Part of this strain is unavoidable. The necessary regimentation of army life causes reactions among soldiers which lead them wrongly to blame their immediate officers. Also the fact that some officers are incompetent is not completely the Army's fault—it has to work with the material it gets, and not all the best men want to make a career of military life. It is generally recognized that the United States Army's standards of selection for lower-rank officers were less rigid than those of several other major armies. Finally, the top Army command put out a series of directives and regulations designed to narrow the gap between officers and men— specifying that the officer should see to it that his men are adequately housed and fed, and that he should make himself available to his men for discussion of such problems as he might be able to correct. But it was only occasionally that these new, ameliorative rules were put into immediate practice. When they were followed, it was not so much that the officer was obeying orders as that he was a generous man or had a keen sense of responsibility. Even where there are good relations between officers and men, there may be a certain arbitrariness.

In sum, officer–enlisted man relations must be counted as a somewhat negative element in the balance sheet of morale in the United States Army. American soldiers have often felt that they were trying to do their job in spite of their officers. This bitterness is well portrayed in the soldiers' popular literature. In combat, the platoon sergeant and squad leaders often got more respect than the lieutenants. Studies conducted wherever American soldiers are stationed around the world show that only about half the soldiers have a high degree of confidence in their officers and a considerably larger proportion have generally unfavorable attitudes toward their officers.[24]

The most important conclusion to be made about American soldier morale in World War II is that it was based on a fundamental American cultural trait from civilian life, rather than on any practice used, or doctrine inculcated, by the Army. Soldiers carried on the war with the conviction that they had a task to perform, and that they could enjoy what they felt most worth while only by completing the immediate task.

D   *Variations in Morale*

Morale, as we have considered it in this chapter, is a special quality a group may have in addition to the meanings and values which the members have in common and which make them a group. High morale thus adds to that "social glue" which permits the members of a group to hold together, to act together, and to overcome obstacles and disappointments

[24] Samuel A. Stouffer *et al.*, *Measurement and Prediction* (Princeton, N.J.: Princeton University Press, 1950), p. 274.

together. As was pointed out at the very beginning of this book, it is by
means of common meanings and values that individuals are able to predict
each other's behavior approximately and so adjust their behavior to the
behavior of others. This alone permits people to act together in the sense
that (1) they do not get in each other's way constantly, as would be the
case if each individual were operating on purely private motives unknown
to anyone else; (2) each individual can rely on others to do certain things
and so he can accomplish his private purposes if he has the other means
available. But having common meanings and values alone does not
permit collective or cooperative action. The latter requires that the group
translate its common values into common purposes, and that the group
develop some morale.

Morale is thus not to be reduced to the meanings and values that constitute the culture or subculture of a group but to certain common attitudes
and emotions. A person can have individual attitudes and emotions that
aid in the pursuit of his purely private goals. He can also have individual
attitudes and emotions that aid in the pursuit of group goals. But he has
group morale only when he has attitudes and emotions that aid in the pursuit of group goals in common with other members of the group. Thus
morale is shared, and there is generally at least some awareness that it is
shared. The individual knows, if only vaguely, that other members of the
group have the same sort of attitudes and emotions that he does with regard to the group and its goals. This awareness helps to sustain morale.
Because morale consists of attitudes and emotions it has an aspect which
is within the province of psychology and which is best left for study by
that discipline. Because morale is shared, has most of its sources in social
conditions, and has a decided influence on many social processes, it has
an aspect within the province of sociology.

Because of these characteristics of morale, it is a function of the
dominant mode of relationship prevailing in a society. Morale has a different quality as it occurs in integrated groups, crowds, audiences, and publics. Morale is inevitably low and ephemeral in audiences. It is usually
intensely high but short-lived in crowds, except when the crowd takes the
form of a panic (then morale is very low). Morale can be high or low in
integrated groups and publics, depending on the conditions we considered in the first section of this chapter. Morale tends to have a fairly stable
level in the integrated group, but is changeable in the public. As broad
historical trends shift the dominant mode of relationship,[25] the characteristic level of morale in the society as a whole also changes. In so far as
segments of our society have taken the form of an audience, morale has
practically disappeared from them, and the possibility of their taking collective action is very low. As functioning, active segments of the society

[25] See Chapter 9.

have shifted from the integrated group to the public mode of relationship, morale has generally remained high, or has even become higher. But it is now more flexible, more variable, more subject to change. One implication of this is that morale is now more subject to control than it was in pre-industrial days when society consisted predominantly of integrated groups.

A group whose morale is steadily reduced until it reaches a very low point is said to be *demoralized*. Demoralization involves loss of mutual confidence, respect, and understanding among the members of a group. As the attitudes and emotions constituting morale sink to a neutral zero point, the members usually leave the group as they no longer have reason to stay in it. But there may be external pressures that keep an individual in a group even after he has no internal motivation to remain in it. The external pressures can be physical force, prejudice against a racial group whose members cannot avoid being identified as members of the group, moral beliefs common in the society that the individual ought to remain in the group (such as the belief that a man should not leave his family), and so on. Under such circumstances the individual may develop negative attitudes and emotions with regard to the group of which he is still per-force a member. Such negative morale is called *group self-hatred,* and it has been best studied in minority groups. Group self-hatred has been found in Negro children as young as four years of age.[26] One major cause is that the Negro child perceives that, because of the direct and indirect influences of caste and the slave tradition, Negroes appear inferior to whites. The Negro child learns the general American culture, often in-cluding the tendency to be prejudiced against Negroes. Another cause of Negro self-hatred arises out of the frustrations that the Negro con-stantly experiences in the caste system. When one is abused or insulted and forces oneself to react passively, the hatred that would normally be directed toward the abusing or insulting person may instead be turned inward. One despises oneself for being "less than a man." There is evi-dence[27] that Negro group self-hatred causes intensified aggressiveness to-ward other members of the group, loss of self-confidence, and generally other consequences that would be expected to follow from a condition which is the antithesis of morale.

Earlier, we distinguished between membership groups—or groups to which the individual whose point of view we are taking belongs—and reference groups—or groups whose values he adopts as his own.[28] Thus far, our discussion of group morale has been concerned with membership groups which are also reference groups—that is, the individual has a

---

[26] Kenneth B. Clark, statement made at Race Relations Institute, Fisk University, July 3, 1947.

[27] Cited in Rose, *The Negro's Morale, op. cit.,* pp. 89–95.

[28] See Chapter 2, Section E.

positive attitude (conscious or unconscious) toward the groups to which he belongs and hence accepts most of their traditional meanings and values. There is also the phenomenon of a membership group which is not a reference group. This occurs only when some external force prevents the individual from leaving groups with whose other members he is identified and forced to interact, for if he has negative attitudes toward this group (toward its other members and its culture) he would presumably leave it if he could. Constraint keeping an individual in a group occurs in a family (especially for a child but not infrequently also for an adult), in a state, in an army, in an occupational association (when leaving the association would necessitate leaving the occupation), in an ethnic group (when there are "marks" of ethnic identification and outside prejudice prevents an individual from leaving the group). In such situations, the individual *may* develop negative attitudes toward his group and cease to use its unique meanings and values as his own. If such situations become general—that is, common to many of the members—the group may be said to have "negative morale" and the individual members to have "group self-hatred."

While it is generally recognized that a small group, and even units as large as armies, can fall so low in morale that they break up if some external force is not used to hold the members together, the question can be raised if this is not also true of whole societies. In a certain degree such a demoralization occurs when the dominant mode of relationship in a society shifts from that of the integrated group to that of the audience. When this occurs, the interacting members of the society are atomized into isolated individuals, and group morale disappears. The subgroups of the society break up—even marriage may be treated as a temporary relationship—and new groups are not formed except for short periods. The indices of social disorganization go up—suicide, mental disorder, individual crime, family desertion, inefficiency of institutional performance. Something like this may have happened in history when societies declined and their cultures all but disappeared—for example, in Italy during the decline of the Roman empire. There is nothing inevitable about the process of demoralization once it gets under way; it may be reversed just as any audience may be transformed into a public by re-establishing effective intercommunication among the participants and just as morale may be raised in a group by the processes mentioned in the first section of this chapter.

It is difficult to assess the level of morale in American society at this moment in history. Some groups have very high morale while others have low morale and even group self-hatred. In keeping with the fact that the dominant mode of relationship in our society is that of the public, morale fluctuates considerably within groups. The morale of significant numbers of individual members deviates from that of the group average. In so far as we can speak of a national morale, which we can when considering the national purposes and issues that attract the attention of the great majority of the citizenry, morale is generally fairly high. There is a tendency to face up to a national problem and to work to a solution that will be satisfactory to the largest possible number. There have been notable exceptions, of course, in such internal problems as race relations and crime, and in trying to escape international problems over which the country obviously does not have complete control. But generally the belief is held that the nation has good purposes, a strong organization, and adequate resources, and the individual citizen is willing to participate in aiding the collective purpose. In some respects morale in the United States is higher than that of many countries that have not been so successful recently in achieving their immediate national goals, and—if the comparison can be made—the morale of the United States is higher than the degree of agreement about what the national goals and values are.

E   The "Small Group"

One popular development among sociologists and social psychologists, especially in recent years, is the study of small groups. While not all of this research is pertinent to morale in these groups, enough of it is to justify our considering it in the context of group morale and solidarity. The small group is defined merely in terms of the number of its members, ranging from two to perhaps twenty or twenty-five persons.

1   THE THREE TRADITIONS OF RESEARCH
ON SMALL GROUPS

Careful examination of the kinds of studies which are lumped together and labeled "small group studies" will reveal that there is little consensus about the nature of the small group or the reasons for its being a proper object of study. Golembiewski has identified three distinct approaches to the study of the small group. The first approach, which he identifies with early studies in the field, has its own definition of the small group.

A small group (according to Designation I):

1 Consists of a small number of individuals in more or less interdependent status and role relations, who
2 Have an indigenous set of values or norms which regulates the behavior of members at least in matters of concern to the group.[29]

---

[29] Robert T. Golembiewski, *The Small Group* (Chicago: University of Chicago Press, 1962), p. 34 *et passim*.

Designation II, which is common in laboratory studies, defines a small group as "any number of persons engaged in a single face-to-face meeting or a series of meetings in which each member receives some impression of the others as a distinct person even though it was only to recall that the other was present."[30]

Designation III defines the term group simply as an aggregate. Golembiewski concludes, "Studies in the small group area are scattered over the full range of the three designations."[31]

These various definitions and approaches, at least three of which have been identified by Golembiewski, are derived from the diverse sources of small group analysis. Small group research derives from both sociological and psychological theories of human behavior. Sociologists have long considered the group to be a significant unit of society. William Graham Sumner viewed society as a group of groups. Charles Horton Cooley identified certain membership groups as primary groups. Georg Simmel was interested in the small group as a microcosm which could be observed and from which general propositions about human association could be derived.[32] This approach to the study of the small group, which seeks to make generalizations about the generic category "group," for example, in terms of role differentiation or equilibrium, has been perpetuated to the present and has prominent representatives on the current scene. George Homans, author of *The Human Group*,[33] represents this approach to the study of the small group. According to another set of current researchers in small group studies, "The study of small groups is thus a method for the study of social systems, of culture, and of personality."[34] "Small group research is more than the study of one concrete 'compartment' of social phenomena among many others. It is the study of generic social process on the microscopic level."[35]

The sociological sources of small group study include: (1) interest in groups as the significant social units of society; (2) interest in groups as the source of man's social nature, that is, the sociogenic component of behavior; and (3) interest in the small group as a prototype of society or a similar perspective which seeks universal generalizations about the genus "group."

Small group study also has direct ties with psychological theories of human behavior. Groups were conceived as being worthy objects of study

[30] *Ibid.*, p. 36.

[31] *Ibid.*

[32] Georg Simmel, "The Significance of Numbers for Social Life," in Kurt H. Wolff, *The Sociology of Georg Simmel* (Glencoe, Ill.: Free Press, 1950).

[33] George Homans, *The Human Group* (New York: Harcourt, 1950).

[34] A. Paul Hare, Edward F. Borgatta, and Robert F. Bales, *Small Groups: Studies in Social Interaction* (New York: Alfred A. Knopf, 1962), p. v.

[35] *Ibid.*, pp. v–vi.

by psychologically oriented students of behavior in that groups provide
a significant component of the environment in which individuals act. It
was a psychological theory which gave rise most directly to the tradition of
small group research. Kurt Lewin (1890–1947), a German Gestalt psychologist, along with his associates Ronald Lippitt and R. K. White, extended Gestalt theory to the study of the small group. Gestalt theory
originated as a theory of perception as an act in which the whole of something is perceived or conceptualized rather than being built up by a
pattern of stimulus-response. Lewin extended the Gestalt theory from
learning to the conceptualization of the personality as a dynamic energy
system. From this point, it was only a logical extension to take account of
the social and cultural context of behavior.[36]

Lewin takes acount of the affective as well as cognitive elements of
behavior in the theory of personality he developed. States of tension and
needs of the personality are explained in terms of the forces in the environment. His thought was an attempt to take account of the social milieu
(field) of the person, which led first to the study of the effect of types
of leaders on "group atmosphere." The general cultural atmosphere or
life space to be properly studied, according to Lewin, depends upon
manipulation and control. Therefore, rather than studying work groups,
friendship groups or other small groups in the natural setting of society,
Lewin set up experimental controls for his study which established a precedent for modern "laboratory" studies.

One such investigation by Lewin and Lippitt was the study of three
experimental groups of ten and eleven year old boys who were engaged in
making masks.[37] The study was an attempt to create distinct group atmosphere by controlling the leadership. The authoritarian atmosphere was
created by a leader who made all the decisions. In the "laissez faire" group
the leader did nothing. In the "democratic" group, decisions were arrived
at by the children through the guidance of the adult leader. In spite
of the obvious criticism that "indirect manipulation" by the leader in the
third group is hardly a model of democracy, the research design is logically
sound and led the researchers to the following conclusions: (1) a higher
state of tension was maintained in the authoritarian group, leading to
unstable group structure and the development of scapegoating; (2) the
direction and motivation were so low in the laissez-faire group that little
was accomplished; (3) the cooperative behavior in the democratic group
led to more objectivity and constructive suggestions and a stronger com-

[36] Kurt Lewin, *A Dynamic Theory of Personality: Selected Papers*, trans. Donald K.
Adams and Karl F. Zener (New York: McGraw-Hill, 1935).

[37] Kurt Lewin and Ronald Lippitt, "An Experimental Approach to the Study of Autocracy and Democracy: A Preliminary Note," *Sociometry*, 1 (January–April, 1938), pp.
292–98.

mitment to the group and its goals. While the influence of Kurt Lewin has been felt throughout the field of small group research, his thought has been perpetuated directly by his students.[38]

A continuing interest in small groups has been with motivation of the individual, and the conditions under which motivations are changed, maintained, or developed. This particular interest in groups is a development of the behaviorist and neo-behaviorist theories of psychology. As far back as 1898, Triplett reported that the presence of other people had a facilitating or "dynamogenic" effect on the level of performance of an individual.[39] Floyd Allport investigated this phenomenon and made the term "social facilitation" popular.[40] Allport found that the excitability and hyperactivity of the individual as a response to the presence of others resulted in an increase in speed and quantity of work produced but also resulted in a greater number of inhibiting effects. In the presence of others, subjects performing verbal association tests were sometimes distracted or inhibited. Allport's conclusion about the possible beneficial effect of the group situation was that such benefit depends upon the nature of the task being performed. Work requiring more imagination and concentrated and original thought, he concluded, is best performed in private, while the presence of others will facilitate the performance of simple routine tasks. Olmsted draws the following conclusion:

> . . . perhaps the most significant generalization which can be made from this tradition of research on individuals, alone and with others, is that behavior depends on the nature of the task and on the individual's perception of his relation to the group.[41]

Gestalt-field theory and Behaviorist theory, both emerging from the field of psychology, stimulated study of the small groups which fit Designation II and III, according to Golembiewski's classification. Designation I, which identifies a group in terms of patterns of interaction, or shared meanings and values, is the only truly sociological model of the group. There exist within the sociological literature several case studies of "natural groups" which have sometimes been conceived of as a part of the small group tradition. These studies are to be distinguished as representing a distinct approach both theoretically and in method, although they are

[38] See, *e.g.*, Dorwin Cartwright and Alvin Zander (eds.), *Group Dynamics: Research and Theory* (Evanston, Ill.: Row, Peterson, 1953).

[39] Borgatta, Hare and Bales, *op. cit.*, p. 3. See also G. B. Watson, "Do Groups Think More Efficiently than Individuals?" *Journal of Abnormal and Social Psychology*, 23 (1928), pp. 328–36; and J. F. Dashiell, "An Experimental Analysis of Some Group Effects," *Journal of Abnormal and Social Psychology*, 25 (1930), pp. 190–99.

[40] Floyd H. Allport, "The Influence of the Group Upon Association and Thought," *Journal of Experimental Psychology*, 15 (1920), pp. 159–82.

[41] Michael S. Olmsted, *The Small Group* (New York: Random House, 1959), p. 68.

quite appropriately considered within this context. Incorporation of the case studies of groups has been attempted especially by those students of the small group interested in generalizing the propositions derived from laboratory experimental situations to groups in general.

Case studies of groups in the natural setting are drawn from a variety of contexts. Their sources range from interest in delinquency to attempts to analyze the motivation of workers in industrial plants. The industrial work group became the focus of study largely through a pioneering study of Roethlisberger and Dixon, which has come to be known simply as the Hawthorne study.[42] The Hawthorne study is actually a series of studies which were conducted at the Hawthorne plant of the Western Electric Company in Chicago. These studies, conducted during the 1920's, were initiated by management and focused on the problem of motivating the worker to increase his production. Efficiency studies had come into their own by this time, and affected the direction which the Hawthorne studies took. The researchers sought to manipulate the working conditions of assembly line workers in order to maximize production, but in addition they introduced a new variable. They introduced wage incentive plans. They outlined every conceivable way of combining varied working conditions with varied incentive plans. The experimental conditions were put into effect with six girls, whose job it was to assemble electrical relays, as the subjects. The rather amazing result of the research in the Relay Assembly Room was that no matter how the investigators varied the experimental conditions, productivity was increased. Changes in the lighting, heating, and seating arrangements, regardless of the nature of the change, were associated with increased production. At first it was the researcher's belief that knowledge of participation in an experiment had been the factor responsible for the increase in productivity. The lasting effect of this source of stimulation was hard to account for; there had to be some other explanation. One of the significant conclusions reached by Roethlisberger and Dixon was that the girls had become integrated into their own little social world, they had become members of a small group which had its own norms and rules of conduct, group structure, and leadership. The morale and common purpose of the group were found to be significant factors in attempting to account for increased production. These, in turn, were largely a function of the interest expressed by management in the girls' welfare, as evidenced by the experiments. The girls interpreted each act of the management as an expression of interest in their well-being, and then responded by increasing their productivity as well as deriving greater personal satisfaction from their work.

An additional inquiry involving the work group at the Hawthorne

[42] F. J. Roethlisberger and William J. Dixon, *Management and the Worker* (Cambridge: Harvard University Press, 1947).

plant was the study of a small group of male workers in the Bank Wiring Room. Management assumed that the worker was rationally motivated to maximize his earnings. Manipulation of incentive plans in order to achieve this end provided the focus of this investigation. The major discovery of significance to emerge from this study was that of "restriction of production." This was not anticipated, in that it appeared non-rational from the perspective of management. Such a phenomenon could only be interpreted in terms of the workers' perspectives. The reward or satisfactions gained from work, it was discovered, are not all financial. The workers in the Bank Wiring Room, like those in the Relay Assembly Room, were members of an informal work group. Through constant contact, informal social organization developed, one of the most significant aspects of which was a feeling of belongingness expressed in a group code which demanded loyalty and involved a set of shared perspectives. Restriction of production came to be understood as an expression of group loyalty and concern for status within the work group. A definite structure emerged in the group, with a differentiation of roles into leaders and followers. In addition an array of social types or distinct roles could be identified, such as the clown of the group. Much of the significance of the Hawthorne research is that it deals with "real" social groups rather than with mere aggregates or pluralities of people assembled for an experiment.

Another such case study is that of William F. Whyte's *Street Corner Society,* a study of the Italian community in Boston, conducted during the late 1930's.[43] Whyte collected his data while a participant observer within the Italian community, in close association with members of the "Cornerville" gangs. His concern was with the internal structure of the latter as well as their place in the comunity. He gave a detailed account of a particular small group, known as *The Nortons* or Doc's gang, describing very carefully patterns of decision making and influence within the group. Doc, the leader of the group, was at the top of a status hierarchy or power structure, while positions of those under him were clearly ordered hierarchically, according to some unspoken but mutually understood rule. The behavior of group members tended to reflect their positions in the status hierarchy of the group. In bowling, for example, Whyte reports that scores tended to reflect group status position more closely than actual skill in bowling. This contention is documented by evidence that, apart from the group situation, bowling scores tended to follow different patterns of performance, as well as by observations of how the pressure of the group tended to insure performance in accordance with rank in the group. Self-confidence of a bowler or expectation of his own performance was visibly affected by the response of other group members in the bowling situation, particularly by members who enjoyed higher status in the group.

[43] William F. Whyte, *Street Corner Society* (Chicago: University of Chicago Press, 1943).

The leader, according to Whyte, is the focal point for the organization. When the leader is not present to perform his integrative function, the members split into a number of smaller groups. The leader holds his position by virtue of his independence of judgment, ability to act when the situation calls for it, his "fair-mindedness," and commitment to the norms of the group.

Thrasher's study of the juvenile gang in Chicago was another early field study of the small group and presents findings similar to those of Whyte in the matter of group differentiation and structure.[44]

During World War II, a multi-volumed work, *The American Soldier*,[45] was produced, which deals in part with the primary group in the military setting. Membership in the primary group, it was determined, is a significant factor in motivating behavior and strengthening morale for soldiers. The question of the relationship of the small primary group to the formal organization in which it exists is a theoretical problem raised by the study. Edward Shils[46] concludes that the primary group served to sustain the individual under conditions of severe stress, and that it provided for the individual norms and standards of behavior. The primary group has imposed on it certain limiting conditions by the organization in which it exists. The formal bureaucratic structure of the military provided the focus of motivation and morale for the members of the small primary group.

2   CONTEMPORARY RESEARCH ON SMALL GROUPS

We have seen in the above discussion that small group research has diverse sources, continues to have several foci, and that the order imposed on this diversity is somewhat arbitrary. In the case of recent studies, there is some justification for lumping them together into a single category, speaking of "small group research" as a unity. Theoretical concerns with small groups include motivation of the individual, performance of groups and their members, the perception of group members, communications networks, characteristics of group "personality" (syntality),[47] the process of interaction, the functions of small groups for society and for the group's

[44] Frederick M. Thrasher, *The Gang* (Chicago: University of Chicago Press, 1927).

[45] Samuel A. Stouffer *et al.*, *The American Soldier, Studies in Social Psychology in World War II* (Princeton, N.J.: Princeton University Press, 1949–50).

[46] Edward A. Shils, "Primary Groups in the American Army," in Robert K. Merton and Paul Lazarsfeld (eds.), *Continuities in Social Research: Studies in the Scope and Method of the American Soldier* (Glencoe, Ill.: Free Press, 1950). See also Edward A. Shils and Morris Janowitz, "Cohesion and Disintegration in the Wehrmacht in World War II," *Public Opinion Quarterly*, 12 (1948).

[47] Raymond B. Cattell uses the term "syntality," meaning an abstraction describing the group, as the term "personality" describes the individual. See Cattell, "Concepts and Methods in the Measurement of Group Syntality," *Psychological Review*, 55 (1948), pp. 48–63.

members. Further, the small group has been analyzed as a social system (usually in terms of equilibrium), and in terms of specialization or differentiation of structure.

The sheer number of recent research reports on small groups makes it impossible to summarize even a representative sample; however, several extensive summaries of recent research are available.[48] The following is intended merely as a topical sampling.

a   Effects of the Group on the Individual

Studies dealing with the effect of the presence of other persons on the individual's productivity, perception, and judgments are often quoted in the sociological literature, in an apparent effort to document the importance of sociological or social psychological study of human behavior. Actually, those who understand the rudiments of sociology—as presented, for example, in Chapters 2 and 3 of this book—will find such studies superfluous, and actually misleading since they neglect the force of tradition behind social norms. The best known of these studies are those of Muzafer Sherif and Solomon Asch. Sherif was interested in individual and group reaction to the "autokinetic effect."[49] The "autokinetic effect" refers to the fact that without visible perceptual standards—for example, in a darkened room—a fixed point of light appears to move. Because of the absence of perceptual standards by which to orient himself, the individual in such a position will perceive the light as moving back and forth slightly. Sherif asked his subject to report the extent to which the light moved. Each individual was permitted a series of observations and was asked to make a report on each observation. Sherif discovered that each individual established a norm around which his observations tended to cluster. One subject's norm would be three inches, while another subject's observations would cluster around a norm of one inch. Sherif then compared what individuals do when alone with what happened when subjects made their observations in groups of two or three. Each group developed its own group norm around which its observations tended to cluster. Although subjects did not consult with each other, just hearing the judgments of

[48] See Cartwright and Zander, op. cit.; John W. Thibaut and Harold H. Kelley, The Social Psychology of Groups (New York: Wiley, 1959); Borgatta, Hare, and Bales, op. cit.; Robert E. L. Faris, "The Development of the Small-Group Research Movement," in Muzafer Sherif and M. O. Wilson (eds.), Group Relations at the Cross Roads (New York: Harper, 1953); Logan Wilson, "The Sociography of Groups," in Georges Gurvitch and Wilbert Moore (eds.), Twentieth Century Sociology (New York: Philosophical Library, 1945); J. L. Moreno, The Sociometry Reader (Glencoe, Ill.: Free Press, 1960); Edward A. Shils, "The Study of Primary Groups," in Daniel Lerner and Harold Lasswell (eds.), The Policy Sciences (Stanford: Stanford University Press, 1951); and Golembiewski, op. cit.

[49] Muzafer Sherif and Carolyn W. Sherif, An Outline of Social Psychology (New York: Harper, 1956).

the others brought about a convergence of opinion. These were the same individuals who previously made judgments independently and whose judgments differed upon initial introduction into the group situation. According to the reports of the subjects, the changes in opinions were usually made unconsciously. When the groups were broken up, the individual subjects were asked again to make judgments privately, and it was found that the effect of the group-formed norms continued to affect their judgments.

In Asch's study,[50] groups of subjects (seven or eight at a time) were asked to make judgments about the lengths of lines displayed before the group. All but one of Asch's subjects were "stooges," that is, they were purposely instructed to make false judgments in accord with the experimenter's plan. This left a single subject in each group with conflict betwen his own perception and the pressure of the group. In a series of 18 trial estimates, a third of the subjects went with the majority against their own judgments over half of the time. A fourth of the subjects refused to go along with the majority at all, while the others fell between the extremes. Asch classified the yielding subjects into three categories: (1) those who actually begin to perceive as the stooges report they see the line; (2) those who believe their perceiving ability must be wrong; and (3) those who neither waiver in perception nor judgment but yield consciously to the "need" to go along with the majority opinion. In subsequent experiments, Asch varied the situation by using two naive subjects rather than one and by planting a stooge who would agree with the naive subject for a while and then reverse his opinion. The pattern of support followed by withdrawal apparently was more disturbing for the naive subject than when he received no support at all. Asch reports that the group need not be as large as seven or eight to produce the "majority effect" but that three of four persons giving wrong answers will produce almost the same effect on the fourth member.

While the effect of norms on the individual group members are somewhat like what was discovered in the Hawthorne studies, it would be a mistake to attempt to generalize from these experiments to groups in general or to norms of society. Interest in the effect of the group on the individual has been a continuing interest within the field. More recent studies than those cited above, while they have made new distinctions and attempted refinement of theory, have come to basically the same naive conclusion: The group affects the individual. A study by Perlmutter and Montmollin, while it cannot be considered representative, is at least

[50] Solomon Asch, "Effects of Group Pressure Upon the Modification and Distortion of Judgments," in Guy Swanson, Theodore Newcomb, and Eugene Hartley (eds.), *Readings in Social Psychology* (New York: Holt, 1952).

typical in its conclusions.[51] Twenty three-person groups of French-speaking students at the Sorbonne were given the task of learning two-syllable nonsense words. The experimenters varied the order: the first experiment worked with the group first and then the same persons individually (but in the presence of others), while in the other group this order was reversed. It was found that the persons who worked first with the group had significantly higher scores in learning. One result of this experiment, typical of such recent experiments, is the qualification of the findings.

> Groups were found to be superior to individuals working separately
> but in the presence of others under special conditions. The group is
> superior to the average individual in total score but is not significantly
> different from the average of the best individual in the group, if the
> best individuals have previously worked in a group on a similar task.
> In seven groups of the 20 instances, there were individuals who sur-
> passed or equalled the performance of the groups. . . . Groups require
> more time to recall during early trials but have a higher over-all recall
> rate than the individual. . . . Under some conditions a group makes
> more errors by repeating more words during a partial trial than in-
> dividuals do, but individuals on the average deform more words than
> groups.[52]

b   Group Structure

The early studies of group atmosphere stimulated by Field Theory in psychology have led in several directions. One of these has been the focus on leadership, which in turn, led to an interest in the general problem of group structure. One method for the study of group structure that has gained wider acceptance than any other is that of "sociometry." Sociometry is associated with J. L. Moreno, a psychiatrist, who views social structure as a network of affective bonds.[53] Although theoretically Moreno has extended himself far beyond the realm of small group research, replacing scientific investigation with a philosophy of cosmic proportion, the technique of sociometry has continued to be a popular technique, particularly in the study of the natural group. The sociometric method is essentially a procedure by which members of a group are asked to rate each other in terms of some criterion of desirability, for example, the person one would most like to sit next to. This technique is sometimes extended to include questions about "How do you think the person responds to you?"[54] The

---

[51] Howard V. Perlmutter and Germaine De Montmollin, "Group Learning of Nonsense Syllables," in Borgatta, Hare and Bales, *op. cit.*, pp. 194–207.

[52] *Ibid.*, pp. 206–07.

[53] See J. L. Moreno, *The Sociometry Reader* (Glencoe, Ill.: Free Press, 1960).

[54] Taguiri has given this the name of "relational analysis." See Renato Taguiri, "Relational Analysis," *Sociometry*, 15 (1952).

technique of sociometry is used to make graphic representations of group structure either in the form of circles (representing each individual) with lines and arrows denoting the directions of choice or in the form of a two dimensional matrix. Sociometry only represents "the structure of the group" for those who accept the theory it represents. It neither takes account of the disparity between behavior and verbal pronouncements nor does it take into consideration that opinions expressed to outsiders are different from those expressed to members of the "in-group."

Studies which recognize leadership as a correlate of morale and group effectiveness have taken many diverse forms. Cartwright and Zander summarize them:[55] (a) Supervisors of more effective work groups are better able to play a differentiated role, spend more time in planning, and are more active initiators than are supervisors of less effective groups. (b) The better supervisors delegate authority to others more often than do poor supervisors. (c) More effective supervisors checked up on subordinates less often. (d) Effective supervisors were those who developed "cohesiveness" among their associates. Another conclusion from such studies is that it makes more sense to talk about "leadership" than to discuss "the characteristics of leaders." In general, remarkably little theory has emerged from the numerous studies of leadership. Sub-areas of the study of leadership include functions of leadership, power and group power structure, distribution of functions among group members, and decision making.

The social structure of groups, in addition to being conceived of as differentiation of a power and prestige hierarchy with the leader at the top or as patterns of affective bonds, can be viewed as patterns of communication. Alex Bavelas attempted to produce groups experimentally with distinct patterns of communication in an effort to determine which communications structure is the most efficient.[56] Bavelas accomplished his ends, although sacrificing something in his definition of group, by creating three or four distinct kinds of seating arrangements separated by partitions within the experimental laboratory. By various means—for example, passing written notes through slots in the partitions—communication was carried on by the subjects. Bavelas found that activity was greatest in the circular arrangement. His other patterns include the chain, in which the subjects are seated in a linear pattern, the Y arrangement, and the wheel (which had five participants, four of whom could communicate with each other only through the fifth subject who was at the center of the wheel pattern). Bavelas concluded that morale is higher for those in central positions than for those at the periphery of the group. This research is obviously subject to several limitations. It is doubtful whether seating arrangements can be considered in any way a measure of group structure.

[55] Cartwright and Zander, *op. cit.*, pp. 489–508.
[56] *Idem.*

Communication was neither face-to-face nor spontaneous, unlike that which occurs in a natural group situation.

George Homans, who is also interested in group structure, has attempted to develop a theoretical framework for the analysis of groups which will encompass the activities of any group regardless of time or place. He is interested in incorporating all relevant data about groups into a comprehensive theoretical framework. His theory, or conceptual scheme, has four basic components: activity, sentiment, interaction, and norms. These he applies to groups in the natural setting, in his book, *The Human Group*. He analyzes the work group, the family in Tikopia, the small community and the gang. Homans indicates that problems of survival in the environment are met by a strategy of the group which he calls the "external system." The total social system, which includes the interaction of members, he calls the "internal system." While Homans expressed the hope of arriving at a general theory of groups, the question must be raised whether he actually does so. Olmsted summarizes the criticism:

> In short, the criticism that can be made of Homans' approach is not that it is untrue or even that it is limited in its applicability, but that it does not take us very far. It does not carry us much beyond the notion that human behavior (in its broadest sense) somehow hangs together, that its parts do relate to one another, that what men do affects who they know and how they feel (though no priority is attached to the doing or feeling, or any of the other major components).[57]

Homans makes some advances in his later book, *Social Behavior*.[58]

A major strategy of analyzing group structure in small group research is that of "interaction process analysis" as conducted by Robert Bales.[59] This approach to the study of small groups is not only similar to that of Cartwright and Zander, but is also derived from Gestalt-Field theory. Whereas the key research concepts of the Group Dynamics branch of this theory focus on locomotion, vector, valence, and cohesiveness, the theory developed by Bales does not attempt to specify a dynamic field. A key element of Bales' theory is the concept of "flow," which indicates more of a concern with process than with spatial relations. Communication is seen as a dynamic flow in the interaction process. Bales makes the assumption that all interaction is problem-solving behavior, involving motivation and direction toward a goal. He also assumes, following Talcott Parsons, that groups are in "equilibrium." Any change, according to Bales, will disturb the equilibrium of the group, which has developed as a result of the individuals' adjustment to the group. Because they have a need for predicta-

[57] Olmsted, *op. cit.*, p. 108.
[58] New York: Harcourt, Brace & World, 1961.
[59] Robert F. Bales, *Interaction Process Analysis* (Cambridge: Addison-Wesley, 1950).

bility, group members will react to the disequilibrium by trying to restore predictability. As a result the group becomes restructured, and equilibrium is again established.

Rivalry and tension within the group are given attention by Bales because they represent potential threats to equilibrium. He assumes that in the normal process of interaction within the small group, there is inevitably wear and tear as a result of rivalry and tension. This must be handled if the group is to maintain its adjustment to the external system effectively. Even the adjustment to the external system itself creates tensions which must be handled. Because group needs for stability are felt by the individual members—that is, each member requires stability if personal goals are to be attained—group structure forms, not by some mysterious process, but out of the felt needs of the members.

> A basic assumption here is that what we call the "social structure" of groups can be understood primarily as a system of solutions to the functional problems of interaction which become institutionalized in order to reduce the tensions growing out of uncertainty and unpredictability in the actions of others.[60]

Group structures develop along four primary dimensions according to Bales; these are: (a) access to resources, (b) control over persons, (c) status in a stratified scale of importance or prestige, and (d) solidarity or identification with the group as a whole.[61] These theoretical categories form an abstract conceptualization of group structure. The processes or categories of group interaction, which he studied within the small group in the laboratory, are believed by Bales to be the same as those which occur in the larger society. Originally Bales developed a large number of such categories, and later reduced them to only twelve.

Questions about Bales' method of analysis relate not only to the reliability and validity of his techniques and categories, but also as to whether it is possible to capture the essential features of all human interaction in twelve or any limited number of categories. The kinds of data produced by the process of research advocated by Bales include "profiles" indicating the quantity of communication, the number of requests for information, and so on. In addition, Bales indicates that groups pass through phases of orientation, evaluation, and control. In the course of group process, there is a swing between two extremes, optimum adaptation to the outer situation at the cost of internal integration, or optimum integration at the cost of adaptation to the outer situation.[62]

[60] *Ibid.*, p. 16.
[61] *Ibid.*, p. 73.
[62] *Ibid.*, p. 157.

Muzafer and Carolyn Sherif have extended the problem of group structure to the problem of inter-group relations. "Relations between social groups, expressed in states of conflict and tension," the Sherifs assert, "have always been significant matters in human affairs."[63] The Sherifs experimentally created groups in order to test hypotheses about the process of the formation of inter-group attitudes and behavior. The research conducted by the Sherifs was not done in the laboratory with *ad hoc* groups, but in a summer camp for boys, with eleven and twelve year old boys as their subjects.[64] The design of their 1949 study is described by the Sherifs in terms of several stages. The first stage consisted of the boys forming friendship clusters spontaneously the first couple of days at camp. The camp was then divided into two groups, matched for intelligence and social class background, and sent to participate separately in camping activities for two or three more days. Following this separation, the groups were brought together and placed in competitive situations.

The Sherifs conclude that, as a result of this competition, real conflict and antagonisms developed, which involved the formation of stereotypes to describe the other group. The greater the conflict the more intense did ingroup loyalty and morale become. A similar experiment was conducted in 1963, in which several means of controlling group antagonism and conflicts were tried. The Sherifs were considerably less successful in controlling conflict than they were in initiating it.

The studies reviewed above are meant to give some indication of the variety of problems and theoretical frameworks in the study of small groups. In tracing the development of small group research, it becomes evident that there has been some measure of convergence among those following Behavioristic and Gestaltist theories. But efforts made to incorporate the findings of small group research into the main stream of sociology have scarcely been successful. Nevertheless, the many specific findings of this research have augmented the knowledge about factors affecting morale.

[63] Sherif and Sherif, *op. cit.*, p. 280.
[64] *Ibid.*, pp. 191–208.

FOR ADDITIONAL READING

ANGELL, ROBERT C., *The Family Encounters the Depression* (New York: Scribner's, 1936). An important study of family morale under the impact of the depression.

GOLEMBIEWSKI, ROBERT T., *The Small Group* (Chicago: University of Chicago Press, 1962). One of the best brief summaries of research on "small groups."

ROETHLISBERGER, F. J., and W. J. DIXON, *Management and the Worker* (Cambridge: Harvard University Press, 1947). Pioneering researches on morale of workers in industry.

ROSE, ARNOLD M., *Union Solidarity: The Internal Cohesion of a Trade Union* (Minneapolis: University of Minnesota Press, 1952). A study of factors affecting morale in a local trade union.

STOUFFER, SAMUEL A., *et al.*, *The American Soldier* (Princeton, N.J..: Princeton University Press, 1949–50), 2 vols. A study of soldiers' morale during wartime.

Appendix A

Definitions of Selected Sociological Terms

NOTE: These are specialized "meanings" found in the subculture known as Sociology. To communicate effectively in this subculture, students will have to understand and use these meanings. It is quite possible that they refer to phenomena or objects that the student may not have perceived previously. It is also likely that other subcultures in our society give these terms other meanings. Not all the terms used in this book have been included in this glossary, and the student may wish to use the Index to locate these other definitions. For lengthier lists of definitions see Henry P. Fairchild (ed.), *Dictionary of Sociology* (New York: Philosophical Library, 1944); Constantine Panunzio, *Major Social Institutions* (New York: Macmillan, 1939), pp. 523–68; E. B. Reuter, *Handbook of Sociology* (New York: Dryden, 1941), pp. 76–172.

Accommodation: the effecting of changes in the behavior and/or attitudes of a person or group in order to reduce friction or conflict with an existing situation. *Or,* the changes themselves.

Acculturation: the adoption by a person or group of the culture of another social group. *Or,* the process leading to this adoption. (Sometimes the term "enculturation" is used to refer to *individual* adoption of culture, leaving the term "acculturation" for *group* adoption of another culture.)

Act, the: a connected series of behaviors that takes into account the expected reaction of others.

Adjustment: the fitting in of one's behavior to the expected behavior of others as a result of taking the roles of others.

Amalgamation: the combining of two or more racial stocks.

Anomie: (Durkheim's usage) a condition of a group, or of a whole society, in which older common values, and sometimes even common meanings, are no longer understood or accepted, and new common meanings and values have not been developed. A single individual who is alienated from the society is often said to be anomic, but Durkheim did not use the term to apply to individuals.

Assimilation: the adoption by a person or group of the culture of another social group to such a complete extent that the person or group no longer has any characteristics identifying him with his former culture and no longer has any particular loyalties to his former culture. *Or,* the process leading to this adoption.

Attitude: a state of mind with respect to a given object or activity.

Audience: a group of people attentive to or subjected to given communications, not in intercommunication with each other. As a mode of interaction characteristic of a whole society, the audience has the further characteristic that its coordinated actions are based on similar responses to these common stimuli, not on common understandings arrived at through intercommunication.

Authority: influence (q.v.) based on belief in expertness, special knowledge, or tradition.

Average: any statistical measure of the central tendency of any range of homogeneous objects. Often used as synonymous with *mean,* or *arithmetic mean,* which more properly is a kind of average arrived at by summing the individual items and dividing the sum by the number of items.

Behavior, collective: the similar and coordinated actions of a number of people who act in response to common stimuli, not primarily as a consequence of individual desires or traditional norms, but primarily as a consequence of the common stimuli and the group situation.

Behavior, individual: any action of an individual regardless of motivation.

Behavior, pattern of: a characteristic organization of human actions.

Caste: a group of people distinguished by enforced different patterns of behavior from other groups, with enforced endogamy and usually enforced different occupations and different appearance (either biological or in clothing, etc.), without opportunity to move into another group. A society that has castes usually has them organized into a hierarchy—each caste having different status, prestige, and power. However, it is possible for two or more castes to have the same status. The word is sometimes used to stand for the common meanings and values governing the groups defined above.

Civilization: the sum total of cultural patterns of behavior prevailing in a society provided there is included among them a written language and the existence of a set of norms for behavior based on some conception of truth and goodness.

Clan: an extended family group, part of a larger society, based on matrilineal descent.

Class: an arbitrary status group in which membership is conferred by characteristic status-conferring factors in the society (such as wealth, education, family background) and for which there is conscious recognition of affiliation. An individual must be able to change his class upon getting an increment or decrement of the status-conferring factors, otherwise the group is a caste rather than a class. A class is arbitrary in that, because of the possibility of changing class (often a gradual process), the cutting points between one class and another on the status scale are partly a matter of individual definition. It is somewhat questionable, therefore, whether a class should be considered to be a group, or rather a category. The word "class" is sometimes used to refer to common meanings and values governing status categories.

Commercial Revolution: that radical series of changes in the economic organization of society in which trade replaced the practice of a family or village consuming only that which it produced itself. Occurred in ancient times, but was lost in the Middle Ages, after which it began again, first in Italy and Flanders and then gradually spread to the rest of Europe and America, and now to the whole world.

Communication: the transfer of meanings or feeling tones from one person or group to another. Sometimes restricted to deliberate transfer of meanings from one person or group to another. (See text discussion in Chapter 2.)

Community: (1) (common usage) a spatially limited group in a society with its physical setting and institutions, having a common and unique set of culture patterns. (2) (Ecological usage) an area over which there is competition and other impersonal relations between people. (3) (Töennies' usage) an intimate, informal, closely knit group. (4) (MacIver's usage) people living in a given area among whom there is communication.

Competition: impersonal striving for identical goals without the existence, or at least the effect, of social communication. The progress of one impedes the progress of another but there is no personal antagonism toward, or possibly even identification of, the competitor.

Concept: a term that selects out the important and general characteristics of a large number of concrete cases.

Conduct: behavior in accord with the meanings and values of the group.

Conflict, culture: the rivalry of two distinct cultures or subcultures in the minds of an individual or group for their acceptance and loyalty, and the tension created by this mental conflict.

Conflict, mental: the rivalry of two opposing values or sets of values within the mind of an individual and the effects of this rivalry.

Conflict, social: activities among human beings intended to hurt others physically or mentally or to deprive others of life, liberty, or property, or activities intended to prevent one from being so hurt or deprived. Conflict, unlike competition, is personal and antagonistic.

Consciousness, social or group: (1) awareness on the part of members of a group of their existence as a group. (2) Awareness by a group of the problems facing the group, and of the assumed causes of these problems.

Consensus: A combined opinion of an integrated group or a public in which the opinions of the individual members have been considered by all and weighed into the general opinion. Need not be (and generally is not) a unanimous opinion, but one on the basis of which all members agree to act at least temporarily.

Contact: the simplest unit of relationship between two or more people in which communication is involved. Often used with qualifying adjectives: (1) *categoric contacts* are those in which the two persons or groups assume the outstanding group characteristics of the other are the sole basis on which they are acting, as distinguished from *sympathetic contacts* in which it is assumed that all the individual characteristics of the other are involved in the other's reaction; (2) *primary contacts* are intimate personal ones, as distinguished from *secondary contacts* which are formal and involve only a segment of the contacting persons' personalities.

Conversion: a change of opinion or value, usually rapid and complete.

Correlation: a statistical measure of relationship between two variables. The *coefficient of correlation* is a statistical measure of such relationship that has a numerical range from −1.00 to +1.00, where 0.00 indicates absence of relationship.

Crisis: a situation in which there is a block to individual or group action of sufficient importance so that the individual or group must find ways of getting around it.

Crowd: an ephemeral gathering of people brought into collective behavior by identical excitatory stimuli, acting spontaneously without reference to individual reason or group standards on the basis of common emotions. *Or,* the mode of interaction characteristic of this form of collective behavior.

Culture: (1) (our usage) a complete set of meanings and values held by all socialized members of a society, influencing their patterns of behavior, with the material artifacts to implement these patterns, devised by men in communication with each other and passed along by them in the process of socialization, to govern their relations with each other or with nature. Can be used in the generic sense to refer to all such complete sets of meanings and values. (2) (Anthropologists' usage—Tylor) "that complex whole which includes knowledge, belief, art, morals, law, custom, and any other capabilities required by man as a member of society." (3) (Popular usage—sometimes called "higher culture") music, literature, the fine arts, and the etiquette of interpersonal relations used by the traditional elite.

Culture area: a geographic area throughout which a certain selected group of culture traits is found.

Culture complex: a sub-set of common meanings and values that hang together and function as a unit. A culture can be conceived of as composed of a number of culture complexes as well as of individual cultural elements.

Culture element: a single meaning or value in a culture. Also called "culture trait."

Culture lag: a temporal disparity in the changes going on in two or more culture complexes so that one is out of adjustment to the other and causes hardship for the members of the group acting on the basis of these culture complexes. Usually refers to the slow adjustment of social structure and non-material culture to technological change.

Culture pattern: a set of cultural complexes that tend to be found together and seldom apart.

Demoralization: a sharp reduction in the morale of a group, at least to a neutral zero point if not to the negative level of group self-hatred.

Denomination: an accommodated religious group.

Diffusion: the process of dissemination of the traits of one culture to those who hold a different culture.

Disorganization: the loss of common meanings and/or values on the part of an individual or subgroup; anomie (q.v.).

Drive: a motivation toward some positive goal.

Economy: that part of a culture that relates to the production and distribution of scarce goods for physical and cultural sustenance.

Education: the dissemination of specialized knowledge and sometimes cultural values, usually to the young.

Environment: the sum total of the physical and social world or that part of it which influences a given individual or group (as distinguished from individuals' genetic heredity).

Environment, social: that part of the environment which consists of people and culture.

Esprit de corps: a positive group consciousness that promotes solidarity, usually for only a short while.

Ethnocentrism: the belief that one's own group and culture are superior to all others; the characteristic of judging other groups in terms of the values of one's own culture.

Fad: a temporary change in a cultural element, in the nature of an aberration.

Family: a group of people bound together by ties of blood, marriage, or adoption. Can refer either to the "immediate" or "nuclear" family—consisting of parents and children—or the "extended" family—which also includes grandparents and collateral relatives. Can refer to the "family of orientation"—in which the individual grows up—or to the "family of procreation"—in which the individual is an adult.

Fashion: a distinctive expression of a cultural element that often leads to a permanent modification of that cultural element.

Feral men: human individuals lost or abandoned at a very young age, nurtured (usually by animals) so as to be kept alive, but never socialized. There have been very few authentic cases of feral men nurtured by animals, despite the numerous legends about them, but the equivalent sometimes occurs when a child is kept completely isolated for years except for contact with one nurturing individual who does little to socialize him.

Folk society: a more or less isolated society operating largely through primary contacts.

Folkway: a characteristic behavior pattern in a society positively sanctioned to some degree; the behavioral equivalent of a group value.

Group: (1) (our usage) a number of people having some meanings and/or values in common which other persons do not share, and who therefore have a special set of perceived expectations in relation to one another as a result of previous interactions. (2) (Popular usage) A category of persons; any number of persons who sometimes come together.

Group, ethnic: a category of persons having common and distinct ancestry, usually with a unique language and nationality. Sometimes used as a generic term to refer to any minority group, whether based on nationality, language, religion, or race.

Group, expressive: a group that engages in activity which satisfies some need of its members but which does not change the external environment in any way (e.g., an artistic or hobby group; has similarity to a dancing crowd except that a crowd is not a group in our usage).

Group, primary: a group with intimate and frequent communication among its members, in which the members know several facets of each other's social personality.

Group, reference: a group whose particular values an individual uses to guide his own behavior. Found only in a pluralistic society in which an individual is a member of, or perceives the values of, several groups, and in which he can hierarchize these groups and voluntarily choose the values of the top groups as models for his own behavior.

Group, secondary: a group of people with impersonal, segmentalized relations among its members, who usually come together for some specific purpose and are not aware of each other's behavior outside this group's setting.

Group action: a group that engages in behavior which is intended to change the external environment in some way.

Group identification: morale (q.v.); conscious recognition that one is a member of a group plus a positive evaluation placed on such membership.

Group self-hatred: negative morale, or attitudes and emotions unfavorable to the group to which one belongs, to its culture, its members, and even to oneself because one is a member of the group.

Human nature: a universal character of human beings that arises neither out of innate biological traits nor out of diverse cultures but out of universal experience with other persons had by practically all persons during infancy. Consists of a number of sentiments that grow up in this fashion. The sentiments themselves are universal and cannot be changed, but people may have them in differing amounts and they express themselves in different ways.

Ideal type: an abstract concept of a class of phenomena arrived at by specifying what are thought to be the key characteristics common to these phenomena and exaggerating these characteristics to the extreme. Thus an ideal type indicates clearly the main characteristics of a class of objects, but such ideal types as unities are too exaggerated to be found in real life.

Identification: the process or practice in which an individual considers himself to be the same as someone or something else. In *group identification* the individual considers his interests to be the same as those of a group to which he belongs; since this makes for loyalty to the group the term can be considered as equivalent to morale (q.v.).

Individualization: the process by which a person becomes differentiated from the social group and identified by a unique combination of social traits.

Industrial Revolution: that radical series of changes in the economic and technological organization of society by which machines are largely substituted for hand labor and division of labor replaces the individual or family as a production and distribution unit. Began in England in the late eighteenth century and then spread to America and other countries of western Europe, reached eastern Europe in the twentieth century and is now going on in Asia.

Influence: the extent to which a person or group can deliberately affect the behavior of another person or group, without necessarily having the power (q.v.) to enforce this effect. "Rests upon the arts of persuasion" (Lord Beveridge).

In-group: a group that feels itself to be possessed of certain unique traits, as distinguished from *out-groups,* which do not have these traits and are therefore considered inferior.

Insight: thorough understanding of the relationships prevailing among all the relevant variables in a given situation.

Institution: (1) an organized group of persons having different but coordinated functions with respect to each other and the material things necessary for the cooperation of the group, in which the organization and the material things outlast the individual members and new members can take their places. (2) A number of culturally defined and evaluated behavior patterns, closely related to each other logically and culturally, which are transmitted continuously to individuals who come into an expected social role for which the institution is relevant.

Integrated group: a group or society whose members interact on the basis of traditional meanings and values.

Interaction: mutual relations between persons, usually involving communication unless they are of the sort found in the crowd.

Interest: (1) attention with a purpose, (2) something which satisfies a personal need or value, (3) formerly used to refer to a universal human need, such as an instinct.

Invention: a newly created or discovered mechanical or cultural device that satisfies a human need or desire.

Isolation: a condition or situation in which there is absence of social contact over a significantly long period of time.

Legitimacy: the approval given by a society to behavior or to persons acting in accord with traditional values.

Maladjustment: a condition of an individual or group which is so out of harmony with the demands of its physical or social environment that important needs are not being satisfied.

Marginal man: (Park's and Stonequist's usage) an individual who has been partially socialized in two or more distinct sets of cultural meanings and values, and who does not consistently follow either one of them but wavers back and forth between them.

Mass: a concept equivalent to audience (q.v.). When used in plural form, masses, refers to the bulk of the population outside of the leadership, or elite.

Mass society: (1) (our usage) a society having its dominant mode of relationship in the form of an audience. (2) (Ortega's usage) a political condition of society in which power is held by the bulk of the people as distinguished from one in which power is held by an elite group. (3) A condition of culture in a large society in which most people follow the same cultural practices (this usage is derogatory). (4) The general society, as distinguished from the local community. (5) A kind of society in which there is a high degree of division of labor and segmentalized impersonal relations between most of its members, as distinguished from folk society (q.v.).

Meaning: a definition such as is found in dictionaries except that it is in people's heads, and people act on the assumption of its reality (that is, its correspondence to some perceivable phenomenon) even if it does not always quite match what is in the dictionary. A meaning indicates how its referent is to be used, how it reacts if sensed or stimulated in various ways, and all the other kinds of information about which a good dictionary provides. Common meanings are the non-valuational elements of culture. An individual may invent a private meaning, and a subgroup may have meanings understood only by its members.

Median: a statistical measure of central tendency in a range of objects in which 50 per cent of the cases have a higher value and 50 per cent have a lower; a kind of average.

Migration: physical movement from one community to another.

Milling: a stage in crowd formation in which individuals move around almost at random, usually rapidly and in close physical proximity to each other.

Mob: an acting crowd, i.e., a crowd with a purpose.

Mobility: (1) the frequency of social contact with diverse people and cultures whether by physical movement or by heterogeneous contacts from a fixed physical position. (2) The condition of having such frequent social contacts. (3) The condition or frequency of moving upward or downward in social status.

Mode: a statistical measure of central tendency in a range of objects which is the value of the midpoint of the class interval with the highest frequency; a kind of average.

Morale: a more or less stable feeling on the part of an individual or group that keeps up the spirit and activity to achieve a goal even in the face of adversity; group morale requires that all members have at least their important meanings and values in common.

Mores: a condition of group practice that is not only expected of the individual but which is enforced on him and the violation of which is followed by emotional revulsion and violence on the part of the group; folkways with very strong sanctions; the behavioral equivalent of strong group values.

Movement, social: an informal organization (including, perhaps, formally organized subunits) of a large number of persons to gain a social goal; the combined effort of many persons to modify or replace the dominant culture complexes, institutions, or elites in a society.

Myth: a "vital lie"; an explanation devised by a group for a significant event that helps the group continue its unified existence (the event may have occurred in the past, or may be expected to occur in the future, and it may be real or imagined).

Nation: a political grouping of people with an independent government and a common territory.

Nationality: a group of people with common ancestry, sufficiently different in ancestry and culture from other groups to be distinguishable.

Natural area: a section of land in which the economic or other cultural traits of the inhabitants are sufficiently different from those of adjacent sections so as to make them distinctive and so as to reduce their contacts with the inhabitants of the adjacent sections.

Neighborhood: a section of a city or other area in which people are marked off by virtue of their common area of residence, and which has a range of institutions devised to satisfy many of the social and economic needs of the residents.

Opinion: an overtly expressed attitude.

Out-group: See *in-group.*

Participation: behavior consisting of joining and conforming to the expected behavior in formal and informal groups, especially voluntary associations.

Person: a human individual in social interaction.

Personality: the sum of an individual's interrelated drives, temperament, and social roles; the unique concatenation of characteristics which the individual manifests in his behavior. The personality has biogenic, psychogenic, and sociogenic (or social) components or aspects.

Personality, basic: that part of the psychogenic personality common to all members of a society because the distinctive culture of that society prescribes a certain pattern of child rearing.

Power: the extent to which a person or group can control the behavior of another person or group, along with the possession of means to enforce this control.

Prejudice: an attitude that considers selected categories of people in terms of stereotypes, usually for some purpose (conscious or unconscious) believed to be of advantage to the person who has the prejudice. Usually used to refer to a negative attitude toward a racial, religious, or nationality group.

Preliterate: referring to a state of society before a written language has been discovered or borrowed.

Pressure group: an organized subgroup that tries to influence the larger group of which it is a part in the direction of the subgroup's goals.

Prestige: the respect accorded to an individual by others; that aspect of an individual's status that allows him to influence other individuals.

Primitive: referring to a state of society in which the technology and economic organization is simple, and the people relatively culturally homogeneous and isolated (sometimes used as equivalent to "preliterate," q.v.).

Privacy: a condition of partial isolation (q.v.) in which the person has access to social contact and takes advantage of the opportunity to have social contact regularly.

Process, social: a characteristic series of social changes occurring to a person or group in which one step develops out of the previous one.

Propaganda: material consisting of verbal or other symbols deliberately used to change the attitudes or overt behavior of a large number of people.

Pseudo-mores: values which were formerly in the mores but at present are considered as mores by only a minority of the population, who seek to enforce them as mores. The prohibition of public discussion carries over, however, so that people generally believe that almost everyone but themselves regards these values as mores, but they will occasionally discuss them with close friends and perhaps even deviate from them if they believe they will not be observed.

Public: a large number of persons attentive to a given type of public communications, who are discussing the communications and their reactions to it; a mode of interaction in which each person participates and each person influences the resultant opinion.

Public opinion: the end product of the public's discussion, rational in that it has been thought and talked over. It may not involve agreement, but it takes into account all of the diverse opinions found among members of the public.

Race: a biological grouping of people with a distinct ancestry and region of origin and physical traits, sufficiently different from other people to make them obviously distinct but not so different as to make them a separate species.

Rapport: the condition of being able to have free and uninhibited communication with someone else. Assumed to be useful in gaining insight (q.v.) into the motives, attitudes, and behaviors of the other.

Rationalization: the tendency to give socially acceptable reasons for one's behavior rather than the real reasons.

Reform: a change in a society deliberately brought about in order to bring it into closer harmony with a particular set of social values. Distinguished from revolution in that it involves less change and less rapid change.

Region: a geographical area that has uniformity in at least one important respect, such as that a given type of culture predominates in it. What is a region in one respect may not be a region in another respect.

Religion: a popular set of beliefs designed to explain the origin and purpose of the world, a set of values related to these beliefs, and a set of behavior patterns to reaffirm the beliefs and values in various aspects of life.

Revolution: a radical and far-reaching series of changes in a society, usually occurring rapidly but not necessarily with violence.

Rivalry: competition or conflict for an identical goal, which takes place under a framework of rules.

Role: a set of behaviors appropriate to an individual in a given group and expected of him in a given situation.

Rural: pertaining to a type of social life generally found in less densely populated areas, characterized by extractive (often agricultural) occupations and by less numerous but often more intimate social contacts than those prevailing in urban areas.

Sanction, social: the enforcement power given by the society to gain conformity to its values.

Sect: a non-accommodated religious group.

Segregation: social and sometimes physical separation, usually enforced but occasionally voluntary, between two groups of persons in various areas of life.

Social: that factor in human behavior by which one individual takes into account his perceived expectations concerning the thoughts and behavior of other individuals and which in itself implies expectations for certain kinds of behavior on the part of others.

Social control: any means, or the sum total of means, by which a group influences or directs its individual members.

Social distance: a feeling of separation among persons or groups, usually as a consequence of status or caste distinctions; failure or refusal to accept other persons or groups into certain relationships.

Social organization: (1) the structure of common meanings and values of a society. (Since meanings and values are often structured into institutions, the social organization is the totality of institutions.) (2) A condition of society in which the members have most of their meanings and values in common. (3) (Popular usage) an institution or voluntary association seeking to affect some condition in a society.

Social participation: contacts with other persons and institutions in which the individual joins the activities of the others.

Social structure: social organization (q.v.); the forms and modes of social relationships as distinguished from their content or function.

Socialization: (1) (our usage) the process of communicating the culture to the biological human infant so that he understands it and uses it in his behavior. *Or,* the process of communicating a subculture to those not already familiar with it. (2) (Popular usage) the taking over of production of economic service by the government when it was formerly provided by a private source (better called "nationalization").

Society: the sum total of people who have fairly consistent communication (direct or indirect) with each other and who have significant sections of a culture in common. Consists of all the groups that have their subcultures complemented by the common culture.

Solidarity: morale (q.v.).

Status: the relative rank of a person in terms of the degree of his possession of the characteristics highly valued by the culture.

Stereotype: a false or exaggerated conception of a group of people which puts all members of that group, regardless of individual differences, under that conception.

Stranger: (Simmel's usage) an individual who understands a culture and physically lives (perhaps temporarily) in the society that bears it but accepts only a portion of the culture even though he may outwardly conform to all of it (because he identifies another society and its culture as his own).

Stratification: the process or condition whereby society is conceptually divided into several classes forming a status hierarchy.

Structure: the pattern of role relationships characteristic of an institution or society.

Subculture: the distinctive meanings and values held by a subgroup in a society and not by all members of a society. See *culture.*

Suggestion: indirect influencing of attitudes and behaviors through the communication of ideas to the unconscious mind.

Symbol: an object, material or non-material, which stands for something else. For example, a flag is a symbol of a nation, and a word is a symbol of the object to which it refers. Sometimes the equivalency is unconscious or covert.

Taboo: the prohibition by society of some act considered dangerous to it; negative mores.

Temperament: deep-seated and relatively unchangeable aspects of the biogenic personality, which guides—in a very general way—the affective and emotional side of behavior.

Tradition: meanings or values, or behaviors based on them, which have been used commonly in the past and which are passed along as part of the content of socialization.

Trend: a change in a given direction over a period of time, with a presumption that the change will continue in the same direction in the future.

Universe of discourse: a theoretical framework of terms and assumptions used for communicating or understanding something.

Unrest, social: a condition of society in which there is dissatisfaction with the meanings and values of the culture or with the availability of valued objects.

Urban: referring to a type of social life generally found in densely populated areas, characterized by numerous, segmentalized, and secondary social contacts.

Value: an attitude held by an individual or group toward an object—material or non-material, "real" or "imaginary"—such that the object is esteemed, as something worthy of choice, so that in relation to the behavior of those who hold it the value has a "should" or "ought" quality. (There are also negative values, for which the above definition holds when a "not" is inserted at the key points.)

Voluntary association: a group that individuals deliberately join and which they may deliberately leave, whose purpose is to express themselves or to accomplish something specific either for themselves or for some other segment of society.

Wish: formerly used to refer to a basic need of all human beings; now used to refer to any desire or need.

Appendix B
Vocational Opportunities in Sociology

Although sociology is still young, it is developing a large amount of knowledge that is capable of being used to aid the more effective functioning of people in many spheres of life. The public use of that knowledge has lagged behind its availability. This is partly due to the fact that there are not enough qualified students being trained to meet the demands for sociologists. As the 1947 Report of the Social Science Research Council put it: "The social sciences are failing to meet their opportunities and their obligations, primarily because they have not developed a sufficient supply of well-trained research personnel." Thus there exist a number of varied opportunities for which qualified workers, adequately trained in the social sciences, are lacking.

In describing the opportunities open to a trained sociologist we must, of course, make distinctions between those who have a bachelor's degree, a master's degree, or a doctor's degree. A bachelor's degree cannot qualify a person for professional work in sociology, just as it cannot qualify a physicist or a zoologist. However, undergraduate sociology provides a useful background for anyone going into a profession where he must deal with people. Sociology has helped undergraduates who are planning to become doctors, lawyers, teachers, journalists, social workers, and even businessmen and engineers. Some successful men in these fields have given testimony to the excellent background that sociology afforded for their respective practices. Students who have interests in politics and international relations also have found appropriate training at the undergraduate level in sociology.

Teaching provides a major source of jobs for sociologists. High-school administrators and boards are becoming increasingly aware of the necessity of teaching social studies at the secondary-school level in order to prepare youth, most of whom will never go on to college, for living in a complex and changing society. High schools have been forced to resort to the hiring of historians to teach social science courses of every type, because there were no sociologists available. In some states a bachelor's degree in sociology, if the student has taken a certain number of credits in education, makes one eligible for a teaching position in the public high schools. Some other states require a master's degree. Practically every college offers courses in sociology and therefore needs one or more sociologists. Some of the smaller colleges seek teachers whose training in sociology is combined with training in anthropology or economics. College teaching generally requires a Ph.D. degree. Teaching at the college level is usually combined in some degree with research.

While 59 per cent of the members of the American Sociological Association in 1959 were teaching in liberal arts programs, a growing proportion were joining the faculties of professional schools—architecture, business administration, engineering, education, journalism, medicine and law.[1] Even where there is no sociologist on the professional school's faculty, it is increasingly common for the school to encourage or require its students to take courses in the sociology department. Sociologists on professional school faculties are usually also engaged in research on the problems of the respective professions. Medical sociologists, for example, are studying matters of concern to medical educators, hospital administrators, and even some practicing physicians. The subjects studied are either substantive to the field (such as how to get patients better to cooperate with physicians) or are pertinent to the profession itself (such as how best to get young physicians to understand their ethical obligations).

Another kind of teaching, which holds much promise for the future, is adult education. Many adults feel their high-school and college programs were deficient in the social sciences, and seek to make up for that by joining special groups or schools that provide education during leisure hours. Certain occupational groups find it necessary to make up for certain deficiencies in their social-science education, and their employers provide this education during working hours. Sociologists give such adult courses in race relations to policemen, in social psychology and methods of research to various kinds of counselors. Some trade unions provide for certain specialized courses for their members, and sometimes sociologists are hired to teach some of these courses.

Government, especially the federal government, has made wide use of sociologists for some time. Specialists in the study of communities are found in the departments of Agriculture and the Interior. Specialists in the study of population and population problems have been welcomed by the Bureau of the Census. Those who have specialized interests in labor organization, labor problems, the labor force, the cost of living, and consumer practices find positions in the departments of Labor and Commerce. Others who have been specially concerned with problems of group morale and group effectiveness are located in the Defense Department. The Department of Health, Education and Welfare has sociologists engaged in a wide variety of capacities, including research on the causes of mental and physical illness, on means of raising the educational level of rural children, on problems of delinquency, aging, and so on. The State Department and other agencies concerned with aid to "underdeveloped" nations hire sociologists to advise on problems of community organization and social change in those nations. Many of the smaller agencies throughout the federal government also have at least a few sociologists. Penal and welfare institutions operated by state governments have some openings for sociologists.

Private business has also begun to employ sociologists in recent years. They are used to study and advise on relations between labor and management, the

[1] Matilda W. Riley, "Membership of the American Sociological Association 1950–1959," *American Sociological Review*, 25 (December, 1959), pp. 915–26, at p. 921.

morale of the working force, the structure of interpersonal relations within the plant, the public's attitudes toward industry. In addition to making reports and giving recommendations, sociologists are employed in public-relations work and personnel counseling. One large mail-order company hires sociologists to help determine who is a good credit risk.

There are commercial organizations that hire investigators of public opinion, ranging all the way from the Gallup Poll to the market-research businesses that try to find out what makes certain advertisements attractive. There are also several dozen private research organizations, which are neither governmental nor profit seeking, that hire sociologists. Research fields covered by these organizations include race and ethnic relations, problems of health and disease, propaganda analysis, housing needs, city planning, consumers' problems, industrial relations, and public opinion.

There are sociologists with special training in statistics in various organizations, such as life-insurance companies and penal institutions. Family and marriage counseling secures a number of sociologists, as does counseling for delinquent children. Some of the successful journalists and editorial writers on newspapers and magazines have a background in sociology.

This perhaps is an unusual range of opportunities, but it is not surprising in view of the long-awaited need for a science of social relations. In the period following World War II not enough qualified sociologists have been trained to meet the vocational demand.

The question is sometimes raised as to the traits and skills a good sociologist should have in addition to specialized training in sociology itself. Most sociologists would probably agree that these include: (1) an interest in human behavior and social relationships; (2) a willingness to go into a frontier science where the methods of research are not always yet what they should be; (3) sensitiveness to what is going on in a social situation; (4) ability to detect what is important among the multitude of factors that determine any given social situation; (5) a broad background in the study of culture variation and culture change (that is, the study of history and ethnology); (6) training in scientific methods of research, including statistics.

A word should be said for the benefit of those who are getting their undergraduate education not primarily to learn a vocation. Sociology offers a broad cultural background. It aids in understanding contemporary social problems and in determining what are significant social trends. It provides some of the fundamentals of an understanding of social adjustment and maladjustment. It promotes understanding of how to engage in more effective organizational and committee work. While other traits of character and personality have a major influence in making a good citizen, the information and understanding essential to good citizenship can be provided by a rounded program of education which includes sociology. Successful parenthood and personal adjustment within a family, a neighborhood, or a club are frequently aided by the study of social psychology, which is one of the fields included in sociology.

Those who would like to read more about the vocational aspects of sociology are referred to the following sources:

EMORY S. BOGARDUS, "Obtaining a Position in Sociology," *Sociology and Social Research*, 38 (1954), pp. 38–45.

————, "Teaching Problems of Young Sociologists," *ibid.*, pp. 174–82.

————, "Special Problems of Young Sociologists," *ibid.*, pp. 242–52.

BRUCE A. WATSON, "Sociology in the High School," *Sociology and Social Research*, 39 (1955), pp. 177–78.

Bureau of Labor Statistics, U.S. Department of Labor, *Employment Outlook in the Social Sciences*, Bulletin No. 1167 (Washington, D.C.: Government Printing Office, 1954). Price 30 cents.

ROBERT K. MERTON *et al.* (eds.), *Sociology Today: Problems and Prospects* (New York: Basic Books, 1959), especially chapters by Neal Gross, Everett C. Hughes, and Charles H. Page.

CHARLES H. PAGE (ed.), *Sociology and Contemporary Education* (New York: Random House, 1963), especially chapter by Charles H. Page.

NAHUM Z. MEDALIA and WARD S. MASON, "Position and Prospects of Sociologists in Federal Employment," *American Sociological Review*, 28 (April, 1963), pp. 280–87.

Index

A NOTE ON THE TYPE

The text of this book was set in BASKERVILLE, a facsimile cutting from type cast from the original matrices of a face designed by John Baskerville. The original face was the forerunner of the "modern" group of type faces.

John Baskerville (1706–75), of Birmingham, England, a writing-master, with a special renown for cutting inscriptions in stone, began experimenting about 1750 with punch-cutting and making typographical material. It was not until 1757 that he published his first work, a Virgil in royal quarto, with great-primer letters. This was followed by his famous editions of Milton, the Bible, the Book of Common Prayer, and several Latin classic authors. His types, at first criticized as unnecessarily slender, delicate, and feminine, in time were recognized as both distinct and elegant, and his types as well as his printing were greatly admired. Four years after his death Baskerville's widow sold all his punches and matrices to the Société Littéraire-typographique, which used some of the types for the sumptuous Kehl edition of Voltaire's works in seventy volumes.

The book was designed by Betty Anderson and was composed, printed, and bound by The Haddon Craftsmen, Inc., Scranton, Pennsylvania.